D1470968

Dictionary of Literary Biography

Dictionary of Literary Biography Documentary Series

Dictionary of Literary Biography Yearbooks

1980 edited by Karen L. Rood, Jean W. Ross, and Richard Ziegfeld (1981)

1981 edited by Karen L. Rood, Jean W. Ross, and Richard Ziegfeld (1982)

1982 edited by Richard Ziegfeld; associate editors: Jean W. Ross and Lynne C. Zeigler (1983)

1983 edited by Mary Bruccoli and Jean W. Ross; associate editor Richard Ziegfeld (1984)

1984 edited by Jean W. Ross (1985)

1985 edited by Jean W. Ross (1986)

1986 edited by J. M. Brook (1987)

1987 edited by J. M. Brook (1988)

1988 edited by J. M. Brook (1989)

1989 edited by J. M. Brook (1990)

1990 edited by James W. Hipp (1991)

1991 edited by James W. Hipp (1992)

1992 edited by James W. Hipp (1993)

1993 edited by James W. Hipp, contributing editor George Garrett (1994)

1994 edited by James W. Hipp, contributing editor George Garrett (1995)

1995 edited by James W. Hipp, contributing editor George Garrett (1996)

1996 edited by Samuel W. Bruce and L. Kay Webster, contributing editor George Garrett (1997)

1997 edited by Matthew J. Bruccoli and George Garrett, with the assistance of L. Kay Webster (1998)

1998 edited by Matthew J. Bruccoli, contributing editor George Garrett, with the assistance of D. W. Thomas (1999)

1999 edited by Matthew J. Bruccoli, contributing editor George Garrett, with the assistance of D. W. Thomas (2000)

2000 edited by Matthew J. Bruccoli, contributing editor George Garrett, with the assistance of George Parker Anderson (2001)

2001 edited by Matthew J. Bruccoli, contributing editor George Garrett, with the assistance of George Parker Anderson (2002)

2002 edited by Matthew J. Bruccoli and George Garrett; George Parker Anderson, Assistant Editor (2003)

Concise Series

Concise Dictionary of American Literary Biography, 7 volumes (1988–1999): *The New Consciousness, 1941–1968; Colonization to the American Renaissance, 1640–1865; Realism, Naturalism, and Local Color, 1865–1917; The Twenties, 1917–1929; The Age of Maturity, 1929–1941; Broadening Views, 1968–1988; Supplement: Modern Writers, 1900–1998.*

Concise Dictionary of British Literary Biography, 8 volumes (1991–1992): *Writers of the Middle Ages and Renaissance Before 1660; Writers of the Restoration and Eighteenth Century, 1660–1789; Writers of the Romantic Period, 1789–1832; Victorian Writers, 1832–1890; Late-Victorian and Edwardian Writers, 1890–1914; Modern Writers, 1914–1945; Writers After World War II, 1945–1960; Contemporary Writers, 1960 to Present.*

Concise Dictionary of World Literary Biography, 4 volumes (1999–2000): *Ancient Greek and Roman Writers; German Writers; African, Caribbean, and Latin American Writers; South Slavic and Eastern European Writers.*

Modern Spanish American Poets
First Series

Modern Spanish American Poets
First Series

Edited by
María A. Salgado
University of North Carolina at Chapel Hill

A Bruccoli Clark Layman Book

GALE®

THOMSON
★
™
GALE

Detroit • New York • San Diego • San Francisco • Cleveland • New Haven, Conn. • Waterville, Maine • London • Munich

Dictionary of Literary Biography
Volume 283: Modern Spanish American Poets, First Series
María A. Salgado

Advisory Board
John Baker
William Cagle
Patrick O'Connor
George Garrett
Trudier Harris
Alvin Kernan
Kenny J. Williams

Editorial Directors
Matthew J. Bruccoli and Richard Layman

LIBRARY OF CONGRESS CATALOGING-IN-PUBLICATION DATA

Modern Spanish American poets. First series / edited by María A. Salgado.
     p. cm. — (Dictionary of literary biography ; v. 283)
"A Bruccoli Clark Layman book."
Includes bibliographical references and index.
     ISBN 0-7876-6820-6
     1. Spanish American poetry—20th century—Bio-bibliography.
     2. Spanish American poetry—20th century—History and criticism.
     3. Poets, Spanish American—20th century—Biography.
     I. Salgado, María Antonia. II. Series.

PQ7082.P7M53 2003
861'.60998—dc21   2003012071

Printed in the United States of America
10 9 8 7 6 5 4 3 2 1

Para Daniel,
cincuenta años más tarde . . .

Contents

Plan of the Series

. . . Almost the most prodigious asset of a country, and perhaps its most precious possession, is its native literary product—when that product is fine and noble and enduring.

Mark Twain*

The advisory board, the editors, and the publisher of the *Dictionary of Literary Biography* are joined in endorsing Mark Twain's declaration. The literature of a nation provides an inexhaustible resource of permanent worth. Our purpose is to make literature and its creators better understood and more accessible to students and the reading public, while satisfying the needs of teachers and researchers.

To meet these requirements, *literary biography* has been construed in terms of the author's achievement. The most important thing about a writer is his writing. Accordingly, the entries in *DLB* are career biographies, tracing the development of the author's canon and the evolution of his reputation.

The purpose of *DLB* is not only to provide reliable information in a usable format but also to place the figures in the larger perspective of literary history and to offer appraisals of their accomplishments by qualified scholars.

The publication plan for *DLB* resulted from two years of preparation. The project was proposed to Bruccoli Clark by Frederick G. Ruffner, president of the Gale Research Company, in November 1975. After specimen entries were prepared and typeset, an advisory board was formed to refine the entry format and develop the series rationale. In meetings held during 1976, the publisher, series editors, and advisory board approved the scheme for a comprehensive biographical dictionary of persons who contributed to literature. Editorial work on the first volume began in January 1977, and it was published in 1978. In order to make *DLB* more than a dictionary and to compile volumes that individually have claim to status as literary history, it was decided to organize volumes by topic, period, or

*From an unpublished section of Mark Twain's autobiography, copyright by the Mark Twain Company

genre. Each of these freestanding volumes provides a biographical-bibliographical guide and overview for a particular area of literature. We are convinced that this organization—as opposed to a single alphabet method—constitutes a valuable innovation in the presentation of reference material. The volume plan necessarily requires many decisions for the placement and treatment of authors. Certain figures will be included in separate volumes, but with different entries emphasizing the aspect of his career appropriate to each volume. Ernest Hemingway, for example, is represented in *American Writers in Paris, 1920–1939* by an entry focusing on his expatriate apprenticeship; he is also in *American Novelists, 1910–1945* with an entry surveying his entire career, as well as in *American Short-Story Writers, 1910–1945, Second Series* with an entry concentrating on his short fiction. Each volume includes a cumulative index of the subject authors and articles.

Since 1981 the series has been further augmented by the *DLB Yearbooks,* which update published entries, add new entries to keep the *DLB* current with contemporary activity, and provide articles on literary history. There have also been nineteen *DLB Documentary Series* volumes, which provide illustrations, facsimiles, and biographical and critical source materials for figures, works, or groups judged to have particular interest for students. In 1999 the *Documentary Series* was incorporated into the *DLB* volume numbering system beginning with *DLB 210: Ernest Hemingway.*

We define literature as the *intellectual commerce of a nation:* not merely as belles lettres but as that ample and complex process by which ideas are generated, shaped, and transmitted. *DLB* entries are not limited to "creative writers" but extend to other figures who in their time and in their way influenced the mind of a people. Thus the series encompasses historians, journalists, publishers, book collectors, and screenwriters. By this means readers of *DLB* may be aided to perceive literature not as cult scripture in the keeping of intellectual high priests but firmly positioned at the center of a nation's life.

DLB includes the major writers appropriate to each volume and those standing in the ranks behind them. Scholarly and critical counsel has been sought in deciding which minor figures to include and how full their entries should be. Wherever possible, useful references are made to figures who do not warrant separate entries.

Each *DLB* volume has an expert volume editor responsible for planning the volume, selecting the figures for inclusion, and assigning the entries. Volume editors are also responsible for preparing, where appropriate, appendices surveying the major periodicals and literary and intellectual movements for their volumes, as well as lists of further readings. Work on the series as a whole is coordinated at the Bruccoli Clark Layman editorial center in Columbia, South Carolina, where the editorial staff is responsible for accuracy and utility of the published volumes.

One feature that distinguishes *DLB* is the illustration policy–its concern with the iconography of literature. Just as an author is influenced by his surroundings, so is the reader's understanding of the author enhanced by a knowledge of his environment. Therefore *DLB* volumes include not only drawings, paintings, and photographs of authors, often depicting them at various stages in their careers, but also illustrations of their families and places where they lived. Title pages are regularly reproduced in facsimile along with dust jackets for modern authors. The dust jackets are a special feature of *DLB* because they often document better than anything else the way in which an author's work was perceived in its own time. Specimens of the writers' manuscripts and letters are included when feasible.

Samuel Johnson rightly decreed that "The chief glory of every people arises from its authors." The purpose of the *Dictionary of Literary Biography* is to compile literary history in the surest way available to us–by accurate and comprehensive treatment of the lives and work of those who contributed to it.

The *DLB* Advisory Board

Introduction

The authors included in this two-volume set of *Modern Spanish American Poets* have been selected from among the most representative writers of each of the eighteen Spanish-speaking American countries, including the commonwealth of Puerto Rico. Within this context, "modern" refers to those poets writing from the 1880s to the present. I have chosen to start with this fin de siècle generation because the 1880s mark an important division between the literature of the Colonial/Independence periods and that of modern Spanish America. The writers of the last quarter of the nineteenth century are credited with heralding the revolutionary movement known in Hispanic letters as *Modernismo*. Literary critics are in agreement that the new worldview introduced by these poets succeeded in freeing Spanish America from its intellectual dependence on European models. The radical difference created by the works written by *Modernista* poets is suggested by Gordon Brotherston in his *Latin American Poetry: Origins and Presence* (1975): "As far as Spanish American poetry is concerned the fact stands that before the Modernists there was little worth reading (besides the limited 'Independent' successes of Bello, Olmedo, Heredia, and others, and besides the efforts in doomed local idioms like the gauchesque), and that it was partially thanks to them that the great poets of this century, Vallejo, Neruda, and Paz, were able to find their voice."

Brotherston's statement is accurate but glides over the important contributions of Colonial and nineteenth-century poets such as the Mexican nun Sor Juana Inés de la Cruz (1651–1695) and the Cuban Gertrudis Gómez de Avellaneda (1814–1873); it additionally slights the modernists' own contributions. His statement reduces the *Modernistas* to the status of mere predecessors of three important poets of the Vanguard. The excellence of Peruvian César Vallejo (1892–1938), Chilean Pablo Neruda (1904–1973), and Mexican Octavio Paz's (1914–1998) poetry is indeed undeniable, but it should in no way detract from the equally excellent contributions of other *Modernista* and Vanguard poets who, like the Cuban José Martí (1853–1895), the Nicaraguan Rubén Darío (1867–1916), and the Chileans Gabriela Mistral (1889–1957) and Vicente Huido-bro (1893–1948), first placed Spanish American poetry on the world stage.

Notwithstanding the relative subjectivity of most critical evaluations of this movement, it is important to add that in this case Brotherston's slighting of *Modernismo* corresponds to the reductionist opinions held by most critics during the first decades of the twentieth century. This reductionism is equally evident in Merlin H. Forster's *Historia de la poesía hispanoamericana* (History of Spanish American Poetry, 1981). Forster quotes Luis Leal in asserting that *Modernismo* took place between 1880 and 1910 and was restricted to poetry; according to Leal, other genres did not follow the new style of *Modernismo* but chose to write within the parameters of the realistic-naturalistic trends of the time. The year he assigns as the end of *Modernismo,* 1910, is the date of "Tuércele el cuello al cisne" (Wring the Swan's Neck), a poem in which the Mexican Enrique González Martínez (1871–1952) calls for an end to the extreme artificiality cultivated by some uninspired *Modernista* poets; he proposed instead a return to the more genuine and transcendental path of *Modernismo*. By choosing 1910 as the end of the movement, however, Forster, Leal, and many other critics are forced to differentiate the poetic production of the 1910s from that of the poets who wrote in the decades that immediately preceded and followed this decade. They do so by classifying the works published during the 1910s as *Posmodernistas* and by describing their authors as an intermediate generation, a brief period of transition. One obvious problem with this division, however, is that most of the poets writing in this decade were already writing before and would continue to write long after the 1910s were over.

In contrast with these limiting opinions, most critics today espouse a wider definition of *Modernismo*. Ivan Schulman is representative of this revisionist trend. In his essay "Poesía modernista: Modernismo/Modernidad: Teoría y poiesis" (Modernist Poetry: Modernismo/Modernity: Theory and Poiesis), published in volume 2 of Íñigo Madrigal's *Historia de la literatura hispanoamericana* (History of Hispanic American Literature, 1987), he refers to the previous reductionism as a deformation of values that resulted from a superficial reading of these fin de siècle texts by some of the contemporaries of the *Modernistas*–that is to say, by some late-nineteenth- and early-twentieth-century critics and poets. Schulman points out that these early critics succeeded in reducing the significance of the movement by carrying out a narrow codification of its most obvious external traits, by restricting it to poetry, and by emphasizing solely its decadent, artificial *(preciosista),* and exotic elements. This narrowing down of *Modernismo* resulted from the unilateral emphasis on what these critics perceived as the movement's concentration on such concerns as formal elaboration, the search for new meters and rhythms, the love of elegance and exotic backgrounds, the rejection of the prosaic in content and expression, the use of fantasy, and the delight of the sensory and the sensual. Schulman points out that what was perceived as the *Modernistas'* escapism is nothing more than a way of reacting against the spiritual crisis of the times. Escapism, however, is but one of the many postures adopted by these artists, since, as it is recognized today, Hispanic *Modernismo* is characterized by its pluralistic and contradictory aesthetics. Isolated in a bourgeois society whose traditions and values had been weakened by positivism and the experimental sciences, most fin de siècle *Modernista* artists reacted by taking refuge in their imagination to live in a world of make-believe.

In his defense of a more inclusive significance of *Modernismo* Schulman quotes the definition given by the Spanish critic Federico de Onís in 1934, whose evaluation he considers more accurate and more attuned to today's critical consensus. Onís defines *Modernismo* as the Hispanic expression of the universal crisis of humanistic and spiritual values that marked the dissolution of the nineteenth century around 1885 and that manifested itself in the arts, science, religion, and politics, eventually affecting all aspects of life, signaling, therefore, a profound and still-ongoing, as of 1934, historical change. Schulman also points out that Matei Calinescu's 1977 study of modernity, *Avant-garde, Decadence, Kitsch,* more accurately defines the "crisis" mentioned by Onís as a "major cultural shift." For Calinescu, modernity made its presence felt through "an increasingly sharp sense of historical relativism. This relativism is in itself a form of criticism of tradition. From the point of view of Modernity, an artist . . . is cut off from the normative past with its fixed criteria. . . . At best he invents a private and essentially modifiable past . . . a major cultural shift from a time-honored aesthetics of permanence, based on a belief in an unchanging and transcendent ideal of beauty to an aesthetics of transitoriness and immanence, whose central values are change and novelty."

In Spanish America, both the crisis discussed by Onís and the cultural shift noted by Calinescu are prod-

ucts of sociopolitical events. Ángel Rama, in *Rubén Darío y el Modernismo* (1970), was one of the first to point out the importance of these historical circumstances in determining the direction of *Modernismo*. Rama criticized the unfairness of defining the movement by its escapist aesthetics when in fact *Modernismo* was the concerned answer given by the fin de siècle artists to the socio-economic capitalist pressures that had subverted the values of traditional society. Discomfort at the threat posed by modernity first became obvious during the mid 1870s in the prose writings of Martí and Manuel Gutiérrez Nájera (1859–1895) of Mexico. Aníbal González also prioritizes *Modernista* prose in the chapter he dedicates to this subject in volume two of *The Cambridge History of Latin American Literature* (1996). For González, the contributions of prose are second to none: "The most cursory glance at the collected works of the major Spanish American *Modernistas* [Modernists] shows that the majority of these writings were in prose. An unprejudiced reading of that prose soon reveals that most of it is of a quality equal to the Modernists' best verse works, or to the prose works being written in Europe and the United States at about the same time." In the next pages González develops his argument in favor of the broad multiplicity of contradictory tendencies identified by Onís and Schulman and points out that most critics remained blind to the significance of the movement until it was spearheaded by Octavio Paz in *Los hijos del limo* (Children of the Mire, 1974) and mentioned explicitly in the works of the writers of the Spanish American "Boom," from *El recurso del método* (Reasons of State, 1974) by Cuban Alejo Carpentier (1904–1980), to *El amor en los tiempos del cólera* (Love in the Time of Cholera, 1985) by Colombian Gabriel García Marquéz (1928–   ).

The multiplicity of contradictory tendencies that resulted in this dynamic period of experimentation and artistic freedom is already evident in Darío's "Palabras liminares" (Preliminary Words) to his 1896 book of poems, *Prosas profanas* (Secular Prose). Darío spoke of his reluctance to write a manifesto, given what he called the "naturaleza acrática," that is to say, the total lack of rules of the *Modernista* art he practiced. The individual artistic freedom he championed allowed each artist to move in his or her own direction in order to experiment with expanding the expressive limits of the language. The variety of approaches these writers implemented accounts for the dynamic and far-reaching nature of the movement, as well as for the difficulty of providing a single definition to fit its many complexities and contradictions. In spite of its discordant, unharmonious nature, however, or perhaps and precisely because of it, *Modernismo* marked the entrance of literary modernity in Spanish America and provided the region with its multifaceted and continually metamorphosing twentieth-century aesthetics. The many styles of Hispanic *Modernismo* and modernity have thus allowed for the dynamic evolution of the various threads that connect the early experiments of Martí and Manuel Gutiérrez Nájera to those of Darío, Ricardo Jaimes Freyre (1866?–1933) of Bolivia, and Uruguayan Julio Herrera y Reissig (1875–1910), and that continue and evolve in the poetic *Vanguardia* as well as in the more recent contributions of Vallejo, Neruda, Paz, and the Nicaraguan Ernesto Cardenal (1925–   ), and even the more modern manifestations of Alejandra Pizarnik (1936–1972) of Argentina and the Peruvian Antonio Cisneros (1942–   ).

Another anomaly that has been produced by the narrow definitions of *Modernismo* established by the early critics, deals with their sexist reluctance to break down the male literary canon. Although most histories of literature unfailingly mention the overwhelming presence of women poets and the high quality of their verses during the first decades of the twentieth century, the critics glide over their own statements in order to either omit these women poets from their studies and anthologies or relegate them to a separate section designated "women's poetry." Because of this critical neglect, only four or five names, those of the Chilean Gabriela Mistral, first Spanish American writer, man or woman, to win the Nobel Prize (1945), the Argentine feminist and *Vanguardista* (Avant-Garde) poet Alfonsina Storni (1892–1938), the Uruguayans Delmira Agustini (1886–1914) and Juana de Ibarbourou (1895–1979), and sometimes the Cuban Dulce María Loynaz (1902–1997), tend to be mentioned. These women are collectively studied under the general rubric of *Posmodernistas,* but they are never included as part of the movements and generational tendencies protagonized in thier respective countries by their male counterparts. It was not, in fact, until the last quarter of the twentieth century that women began to figure in histories of literature and to be studied within the same trends of the male poets next to whom they wrote.

Hugo J. Verani's study "The Vanguadia and Its Implications," an essay also published in volume two of *The Cambridge History of Latin American Literature,* further elaborates the differences and continuities between *Modernismo* and the Vanguard. He begins by defining and setting the temporal limits of his essay: "The term *Vanguardia* (Avant-Garde) is collectively applied to a diverse range of literary movements—such as *Creacionismo, Ultraísmo* (Ultraism), *Estridentismo* (Stridentism), and numerous other *-ismos*—which appeared in Latin America between approximately 1916 and 1935." Verani points out that these dates are also important markers of literary history: "Prior to the publication of *El espejo del agua* [The Water Mirror] (1916), there were only

influential precursors and isolated anticipations within the dying rumbles of *Modernismo;* and by the time Pablo Neruda published his second *Residencia en la tierra* (1935), [Residence on Earth], the Avant-Garde had fulfilled its historic purpose. Afterwards, there was a displacement of sensibility, a notable decrease in the experimental mood and a sharp increase in the social role of the author; particularly, there was a consolidation of the literary achievements of the period."

In his *Antología de la poesía hispanoamericana actual* (Anthology of Contemporary Spanish American Poetry, 1987), Julio Ortega looks at this same group of poets and arrives at the conclusion that just as the search for transcendence gave unity to the *Modernista* poets born at the end of the nineteenth century, the rejection of these poetics of transcendence is what unites the Vanguard and Post-Vanguard poets under a poetics of difference. Opposed to transcendence, these writers were united by a historical consciousness that Verani describes as their "critical stand toward the dominant values of the time." This stand, he continues, moved them to feel "the urgent need to formulate combative, irreverent, and iconoclastic documents to develop new means of harnessing the attention of the public"; eventually literary critics defined their works as manifestations of the "aesthetics of opposition" or of a "tradition of the new." Contrary to Darío's reluctance to write a manifesto and thus reduce the limitless multiplicity of *Modernismo,* these artists eagerly functioned around a proliferation of manifestos and proclamations intended to disrupt traditional concepts of literature. They were written as public events with the intent of opening critical debate and challenging the dominant sensibility. Not surprisingly, given the public nature of the events, these breakaway movements were promoted by periodicals that foregrounded novelty and aesthetic activity.

The Spanish American *Vanguardia* includes a remarkable array of poets; among the best known and most admired are Huidobro, the founder of *Creacionismo;* Argentinian Jorge Luis Borges (1899–1986), promoter of *Ultraísmo* in the early phase of his poetry; and Vallejo and Neruda, both also known for their political commitment, as are the Cuban Nicolás Guillén (1902–1989) and the Puerto Rican Luis Palés Matos (1898–1959), both seminal in the establishment of Afro-Antillean poetry, another avant-garde accomplishment. The different emphasis in what may be perceived as an oppositional confrontation in regard to aesthetic versus political concerns is evident in the works of the poets listed and eventually contributes to the dissolution of *Vanguardismo* around the dates of the Spanish Civil War. In fact, in another essay included in the same volume of *The Cambridge History of Latin American*

Literature, "Spanish American Poetry from 1922 to 1975," José Quiroga argues that most histories of poetry divide the period covered by his study in three parts, and that these periods are directly connected to historical events: "a period of radical and violent experimentation from 1922 to about 1940, one concerned with the search for American or national identity that spans the years from 1940 to 1960, followed by a second experimental period that starts from 1960 and lasts until around 1975. The historical markers fall more or less into place if we consider two pivotal events: the Spanish Civil War from 1936 to 1939, and the triumph of the Cuban Revolution in 1960." Quiroga further argues that all aesthetic and political positions between 1920 and 1975 can be read as "competing versions of a central, yet elusive, narrative that is framed within the encounter of Spanish America with the modern age. The responses to modernity imply questions as to whether poetry serves the social or the personal order, whether it uses colloquial or erudite language, or whether it privileges metaphor or communication. Poetry frames all issues relating to the relationship between poetry, language, and history."

According to Quiroga, the consolidation of the Spanish American *Vanguardia* during the 1920s occurred while other writers continued practicing the previous trends. In order to prove his point Quiroga cites some titles: three are eminently *Vanguardista* books, Borges's *Fervor de Buenos Aires* (1923), Vallejo's *Trilce* (1922), and Girondo's *Veinte poemas para ser leídos en el tranvía* (1922); one, Palés Matos's poem "Pueblo Negro" (Black People, 1925), represents the beginnings of the new Afro-Antillean modality; and two exemplify more-traditional trends, Mistral's *Desolación* (Desolation, 1922) and Neruda's *Crepusculario* (Twilights, 1923).

Undoubtedly, the two most important movements associated with the Spanish American avant-garde are *Creacionismo* and *Ultraísmo,* but other contributions are equally significant; among them Afro-Antillean poetry stands out as a socially conscious aspect of *Vanguardismo.* Afro motifs are evident in the early verses of Palés Matos and the Cubans Mariano Brull (1891–1956) and José Zacarías Tallet (1893–1989); this movement, however, did not make its entry into literary history officially until the publication of Guillén's eight poems of *Motivos de Son* (Son Motifs) in the Cuban *Diario de la Marina* (Marine Daily) on 30 April 1930. It is said that Guillén was inspired to write these poems after meeting Langston Hughes in Havana and reading his poetry. Another contribution is made in Mexico, where a series of Vanguard poets interested in serious aesthetic pursuits, among them Carlos Pellicer (1897?–1977), José Gorostiza (1901–1973), Jaimes Torres Bodet (1902–1974), and Xavier Villaurrutia

(1903–1950), published their verses in the journal *Contemporáneos* (Contemporaries), published from 1928 until 1931. Surrealism is another movement that heavily influenced the ideology of the Spanish American Vanguard during the 1940s due to its emphasis on endorsing participation in the political arena as part of an aesthetic of liberation. Although, paradoxically, Surrealism failed to produce any major poetical voices in Spanish America, the retrenchment from the extreme experimentation of the avant-garde is closely tied to this movement's leftist ideology. It is also, however, the result of some key socio-political events that are associated with the growing importance of the Communist Party–it was formalized in Argentina in 1918, in Mexico in 1919, in Cuba in 1925, and in Peru in 1928, with the sympathies of the Spanish American intellectuals engaged in advancing Communism against the forces of Fascism during the Spanish Civil War. This ideological struggle resulted in a series of political books of poems, among them Neruda's *España en el corazón* (Spain in my Heart, 1937), Vallejo's *España, aparta de mi este cáliz* (Spain, Take Away This Chalice from Me, 1937), Guillén's *España: Poema en cuantro angustias y una esperanza* (Spain: A Poem in Four Anguishes and One Hope, 1937), and Paz's *¡No pasarán!* (They Won't Go Through!, 1936).

Not surprisingly, given this political climate, as Quiroga notes, the poetical debate of the 1930s and early 1940s centered on the question of the opposition between "politically committed art" and "art for art's sake." Even some of the most prominent *Vanguardistas,* such as Neruda and Vallejo, changed from the experimentation and existential anguish of books of poems as well-received as Neruda's first two *Residencias* (Residences, 1933, 1935) and Vallejo's *Trilce* toward the political commitment of Neruda's *Canto general* (General Song, 1950) and Vallejo's posthumous *Poemas humanos* (Human Poems, 1949).

According to Quiroga, the poets who mark the sensibility of the 1940s were born between 1910 and 1923. He names Cuban José Lezama Lima (1910–1976), Pablo Antonio Cuadra (1912–2001) of Nicaragua, Paz, Chilean Nicanor Parra (1914–), and Cuban Cintio Vitier (1921–) and points out that because of their different ages their writings overlap with those of some *Modernista* and *Vanguardia* poets. Accordingly, their aesthetics "range from the hermeticism of Lezama Lima to the colloquialism of Nicanor Parra, from the Nicaraguan scenes of Pablo Antonio Cuadra to the metaphysical and 'simple' language of Vitier." Quiroga further asserts that this lack of common traits has prompted the critics to underscore their heterogeneity. Forced to reassess the contributions of *Modernismo* and the Vanguard in order to establish their own poetic space, these poets reconstructed their own literary tradition. In many cases they did so by tracing their roots to Juan Ramón Jiménez and many of the other Spanish poets who left Spain at the end of the civil war.

Julio Ortega's study concurs with Quiroga's assessment. For Ortega, the rejection of previous aesthetics is in fact what marks the poems of Paz, Argentinians Enrique Molina (1910–) and Alberto Girri (1919–1991), and Cuban Lezama Lima as decodifiers of poetic tradition. The same can be said, Ortega adds, of the poems of other contemporaries, such as Peruvian César Moro (1903–1956), who rejected tradition by taking refuge in his verses from the infringements of modern daily life, or Parra, who employed popular humor to parody the devalued system of a modern capitalist society, or Argentinian César Fernández Moreno (1919–1985), who desacralized the loftiness of *Modernista* language through the introduction of popular speech patterns. Taking this evolution a step further, he explains that the poets born in the 1920s spoke from the immediacy of experience in the conversational tones of daily speech. Carlos Germán Belli (1927–) of Peru uses a fractured discourse to expose the betrayal of modernity while representing the violence of the poverty of the urban environment; Colombian Álvaro Mutis (1923–) reacted against the rhetorical discourses of completion associated with *Modernismo* by introducing colloquial forms and daily speech to portray a world of partial beauty and truncated memories; Argentinian Roberto Juarroz (1925–) demystified poetry through similar methods, and Uruguayan Idea Vilariño (1920–) assaulted it by alluding to the unrelenting solitude and nonsense of the modern world; the Mexican feminist Rosario Castellanos (1925–1974) and her compatriot Jaime Sabines (1925–1999) deconstruct political, patriarchal, and religious motifs; and Cardenal rewrote traditional forms and contradictory discourses from classical and biblical sources and from North American and Hispanic culture to underline human suffering in modern societies.

Following his chronological overview, Ortega next explains that those poets born in the 1930s go back to writing in a more opaque and more dramatic language, one that translates their uneasiness with the fragmentary nature of communication. He exemplifies this tendency with the poetry of, among others, Chilean Enrique Lihn (1929–1988), who reflected his shifting identity in a world without logic; Pizarnik, whose verses betrayed her ultimate discomfort with the poetic word; Cuban Roberto Fernández Retamar's (1930–) elegant exploration of his surroundings; Cuban Heberto Padilla's (1932–2000) return to a more direct expression; and Mexican Marco Antonio Montes de

Oca's (1932–) sublimation of the generation's feelings of dissatisfaction.

Despite these personal incursions into more-arcane poetic concerns, however, the oppositional struggle between aesthetics and political commitment that is evident in the poetic production of the 1940s remained strong during the following decades and came to a head in 1959 with the triumph of the Cuban Revolution and the subsequent insurgence of revolutionary movements that promised social change in countries such as Argentina, Bolivia, Chile, El Salvador, and Nicaragua. This localized political turmoil, aggravated by the tensions between East and West created by the Cold War, eventually resulted in a definitive tilt toward political commitment in the 1960s and 1970s. In the genre of poetry, this tilt changed the emphasis from the traditional rhetoric of opaque, hermetic language, characteristic of a strictly literary discourse, toward communication and everyday speech, an expression constructed around colloquial, popular language, engaged in discussing socio-political, nonliterary problems.

This streamlining of language and the move toward sociopolitical concerns were not strictly new, however. They were, in fact, integral parts of *Modernismo,* as is evident in the poetic discourse of the politically committed Martí and even in Darío's anti-imperialist warnings and optimistic vision of Hispanic culture in *Cantos de vida y esperanza* (Songs of Life and Hope, 1905); and the political stance was definitely taken by some important poets of the Vanguard, such as Vallejo, Neruda, and Guillén, who systematically began to move poetry toward themes and language that engaged the social and political problems at hand. Their poetic success notwithstanding, the deconstruction of poetic language itself was not truly successful until the irruption into the literary scene of Parra's "anti-poetry." Parra's iconoclastic antilyricism and his move toward popular speech succeeded in renovating poetic language and developed an enthusiastic response in younger poets who took hold of his everyday aesthetics and used them in their own personal involvement with history. Among the many who followed the Chilean's irreverent stance are poets whose concerns range from religion to revolution to feminism and who are as diverse as Cardenal, Castellanos, Padilla, Claribel Alegría (1924–) and Roque Dalton (1935–1975) of El Salvador, and Mexican José Emilio Pacheco (1939–).

Ortega concludes his overview of twentieth-century poetry by commenting on the works of just three poets born during the 1940s and 1950s. He excuses this scarcity of names by problematizing the difficulty of identifying the most-contemporary trends and poets due to the recentness of their production. The poets he anthologizes are Pacheco, chosen because he exemplifies a new way of writing poetry, based on an imaginative reading of the poetic tradition; Cisneros, because of his ability to manipulate colloquial language; and Chilean Raúl Zurita (1951–   ), because of the originality with which he mixes traditional poetic languages and conventions. Since 1987, when Ortega published this anthology, several other names have come to the attention of literary critics, but, again, the newness of their production continues to make it difficult to evaluate their significance. By and large, critics have not yet identified the most significant of contemporary poets, even though some have entered the pages of anthologies and critical discourse. Among these poets are the Colombians Darío Jaramillo (1947–   ) and Anabel Torres (1948–   ); the Nicaraguan Gioconda Belli (1948–   ); the Costa Rican Ana Istarú (1960–   ); the Argentine Arturo Carrera (1948–   ); the Peruvians Jorge Eduardo Eielson (1924–   ), Enrique Verastegui (1950–   ), and Carmen Ollé (1947–   ); the Mexicans Coral Bracho (1951–   ) and Alberto Blando (1951–   ); the Dominican Aléxis Gómez (1950–   ); and the Uruguayan Cristina Carneiro. The poems of these authors exemplify the varied and most representative ongoing poetic trends in Spanish America. For some of these writers, poetry continues to be a means to engage their immediate circumstances, questioning the abuses, violence, and general injustice of their sociopolitical reality; for others, poetry is the tool that provides answers to the questions that have preoccupied poets since time immemorial: the plight of human beings and the enigma of existence; for yet others, the recuperation through poetry of a mythical and legendary past seems to be aimed at attaining a collective reconstruction of lost Native American identities. Regardless of their ideology and aesthetics, or of their country of origin, however, all these poets are engaged in a common task: theirs is a daily struggle with their particular historical circumstances and the poetic conventions of the Spanish language in an effort to make poetry name the changing realities that confront the people of the twenty-first century everywhere, but which are particularly inflicted with urgency within the conflicting arena of Latin America's precarious linguistic and sociopolitical circumstances.

Argentina

Buenos Aires is one of the first cities in Spanish America to assert and celebrate its cosmopolitan modernity. There is no surprise, therefore, when one learns that it became one of the premier centers for the diffusion of literary *Modernismo* to the rest of the Spanish-speaking world. The key role Buenos Aires played in the spread of this movement is due in part to the fact that during the closing years of the nineteenth century it had become a bustling metropolis with a flourishing cultural life. This intellectual activity was instrumental when the young and revolutionary Rubén Darío decided to settle in the Argentine capital in 1888. His presence and his innovative ideas added an even more cosmopolitan bent to an intellectual community that quickly placed itself at the forefront of the *Modernista* renewal of Hispanic letters. In collaboration with poets such as the Argentine Leopoldo Lugones (1874–1938), Ricardo Jaimes Freyre, and the Colombian Guillermo Valencia (1873–1943), they initiated a dynamic renovation of Spanish letters through the pages of their journal, *Revista de América* (America Review). By the time Darío permanently left Buenos Aires in 1898 to resettle first in Madrid, Spain, and later in Paris, France, Argentina had become the leading center of literary production in Spanish America.

The vitality of this city's intellectual life during the fin de siècle continued unabated during the first decades of the twentieth century, prodding many talented younger writers to attain new heights. Buenos Aires became one of the first centers to welcome and foment the experimentation of the *Vanguardia* writers. Two outstanding members of this group, Vicente Huidobro and Jorge Luis Borges, are credited with first experimenting with their new ideas in Argentina. Huidobro claims credit for presenting his revolutionary *Creacionista* aesthetics at a talk he delivered in Buenos Aires's literary Ateneo in 1916; Borges returned to Buenos Aires in 1921 after his long European sojourn, bringing with him the *Ultraísta* tenets he had learned while collaborating in Madrid on the Spanish journal *Ultra* and with the poet-critic Rafael Cansinos Ansséns (1883–1964). The Argentine brand of *Ultraísmo* Borges introduced found expression in three seminal magazines, *Prism* (Prism), *Proa* (Prow), and *Martín Fierro*. He collaborated in all three publications and wrote an *Ultraísta* manifesto to expound on the tenets of the movement: the view that the metaphor was the ultimate synthesis of poetry; the emphasis on enjambment and fusion of images to expand the lyrical suggestions of poetry; and the rejection of the anecdotal, reflexive, ornamental, and confessional elements of poetry. Many younger Argentine poets found these tenets irresistible and soon were writing after Borges's lead; among the most outstanding practitioners of Argentine *Ultraísmo* are Oliverio Girondo (1891–1967), Leopoldo Marechal (1900–1970), and Ricardo Molinari (1898–1966).

According to María Eugenia Eroghano, Surrealism was important between 1930 and 1935, coinciding with the publication of Neruda's *Residencia en la tierra,* even though, as Giuseppe Bellini notes in his *Historia de la literatura hispanoamericana* (1985), the Generación de

1930 (Generation of 1930) was made up of poets such as Eduardo González Lanuza (1900–1984) and Romualdo Brughetti, who began to reject experimentation and Surrealism in favor of social concerns. These concerns became even more acute with the disconcertment produced by the Spanish Civil War, World War II, and the entrance of the dictator Juan Domingo Perón into the Argentine political arena.

A subsequent and important movement in Argentine poetry, combining neo-Romantic characteristics adapted from English and German Romanticism and Surrealist tendencies, was introduced by the Generation of 1940. Argentine Surrealism first appeared in the pages of the journal *Que* (That) and found its home in *A Partir de Cero* (From Zero, 1952), edited by Molina. Other poets associated with this magazine and Surrealism in general were Carlos Latorre (1916–), Alberto Girri (1919–1991), Olga Orozco (1920–1999), and César Fernández Moreno (1919–1985). Argentina's increasing sociopolitical conflicts during the mid twentieth century promoted an unabated interest in political poetry beginning with the 1950s. These poets, among them Juan Gelman (1930–) and Francisco Urondo (1930–), published in three important journals: *El Grillo de Papel* (Paper Cricket, 1959), *Agua Viva* (Live Water, 1960), and *Eco Contemporáneo* (Contemporary Echo, 1961). Although political poetry was important in the 1960s, some poets who began to write in this decade, such as the well-known critic and experimental writer Saúl Yurkievich (1931–), Alejandra Pizarnik, and Alberto Spunzberg (1940–), did it outside political influences.

The poetry introduced in the 1970s and 1980s was less well defined, being characterized by a new concentration on poetic concerns and a movement away from sociopolitical themes. Other tendencies were represented by the appearance of a militant feminism led by Diana Bellesi (1946–); the iconoclastic frivolity of poets such as Arturo Carrera (1948–) and Emeterio Cerro (1952–), who published in the journal *Último Reino* (Last Kingdom) in 1979; the objectivism of those gathered around the *Diario de Poesía* (Poetic Daily, 1986); and the neo-Baroque enthusiasm of Néstor Perlongher (1949–1992) and Eduardo Romano (1938–).

Bolivia

Modern Bolivian poetry is characterized by the late presence of Romanticism, the persistent influence of *Modernismo,* and the overriding presence of *nativista* (indigenous) and social themes. The influence of *Modernismo* may be unsurprising due in part to the fact that one of the major Spanish American *Modernistas,* Ricardo Jaimes Freyre, was a Bolivian poet who, together with Leopoldo Lugones and Rubén Darío, dominated the literary scene in Buenos Aires and the Hispanic world at large at the turn of the twentieth century. Other important Bolivian *Modernista* poets are Gregorio Reynolds (1882–1948) and José Eduardo Guerra (1893–1943), as well as Adela Zamudio (1854–1928), an ardent defender of women's rights and a controversial writer of note, but difficult to pigeonhole into a specific movement.

In the years following World War II, Bolivia began to take notice of the complexities of modernity and called for a change in the sociopolitical as well as in the artistic scene. At this time the activities of the Ateneo de la Juventud (Youth Literary Association) became crucial in awakening the country to the need for a national dialogue on modernizing. The most important poetic concerns of the time were expressed by the members of the group Eclécticos (Eclectics), some of whom were José Antonio de Sainz, Nicolás Ortiz Pacheco, Guillermo Viscarre Fabre (1901–1980), Juan Capriles (1900–1953), and Lucio Felipe Lira.

The Vanguard irrupted in Bolivia, led by Óscar Cerruto (1912–1981), well known for the beauty of his metaphorical language and the formal perfection of his verses. Important also are poets such as Viscarre Fabre and Octavio Campero Echazú (1900?–1970), elegant poets immersed in the works of the Spanish American Vanguard as well as in those of the Spaniard Juan Ramón Jiménez (1881–1958) and the Spanish Generation of '27. Of note also are Carlos Medinacelli (1899–1949); Oscar Alfaro (1921–1963), who leaned toward a simple, more direct expression; and Yolanda Bedregal (1913–1999), a more complex poet and a prolific author.

Following the great national crisis produced by the loss of the Chaco War (1932–1935), poets began to favor sociopolitical themes. Reformers called for replacing the anachronistic colonial structures with a more democratic and just social system. Some of the poets gathered around the *escuela vernácula* (vernacular school) to elaborate telluric, *indigenista* (indigenous), and social revolutionary topics, emphasizing regional and folkloric themes as a way of affirming national identity. A transcendent love of the land is evident in the poems of Cerruto and Campero Echazú, while Jesús Lara (1898–1980) represents an *indigenista* vision of the Quechua world, and Julio de la Vega (1924–) writes passionate verses of social protest.

Among contemporary writers there are three poet-critics of note, Pedro Shimose (1940–), Óscar Rivera-Rodas (1944–), and Blanca Wiethüchter (1947–). Shimose, also a critic and fiction writer, is without doubt Bolivia's most representative contemporary poetic voice. Aside from the artistic value of his well-wrought verses, there is his political commitment that has resulted in his self-imposed exile to Spain, where he continues to express his anguish on behalf of suffering man in verses that echo the compassion and bitterness of the works of César Vallejo.

Several of the poets born after 1950 gathered around "Luz Ácida" (Acid Light), an artistic group interested in pursuing beauty as a cure to counter man's spiritual anguish. These poets are well represented by Diego Torres, Guillermo Bedregal (1954–1974), and Alicia (1951–) and Susana Kavlín (1955–), two sisters who publish together without identifying their individual contributions.

Chile

In Hispanic culture, Chile has the reputation of being a country of poets, and it, in fact, has one of the premier poetic traditions in twentieth-century Spanish America. This tradition was inaugurated early in the century by some late *Modernistas* who were as respected and well known as Pedro Prado (1886–1957) and the Nobel laureate Gabriela Mistral; it continued to be sustained by the verses of Vicente Huidobro and of Pablo Neruda, who was awarded both the Nobel Prize in literature and Russia's Lenin Peace Prize; the inheritance was picked up and continued with honor by the iconoclastic antipoet Nicanor Parra and the innovative Enrique Lihn; and more recently by Jorge Teillier (1935–1988) and Raúl Zurita. Despite this brilliant array of contemporary poets, Chile's poetic history did not start auspiciously.

In the first volume of his *Antología crítica de la poesía chilena* (Critical Anthology of Chilean Poetry, 1996), Naín Nómez defines Chilean poetry of the late nineteenth century as being characterized by "lo residual y lo emergente" (the residual and the emergent). This critic uses this paradoxical opposition as a way to emphasize the failure of Chilean poets to develop an original expression after attaining political independence. In his opinion, the nation's poets at that time wavered between an anachronistic attachment to worn-out European poetic trends, particularly those of the French, and the emerging native forms of the still-unformed culture of the recently independent country. The catalyst that broke the impasse was the visit to Chile in 1886 by Rubén Darío, who remained in the country for the next few years, sharing his vision and his enthusiasm with the local poets and even publishing in Valparaíso his revolutionary book *Azul* (Blue, 1888). The friendship he established with Pedro Antonio González (1863–1903) was decisive in González's success in renewing his country's poetic tradition. In fact, his book *Ritmos* (Rhythms), published in 1895, marks the beginning of such renewal and the introduction of *Modernismo* in Chile. For Nómez, *Modernismo* lasted in Chile from 1888 until 1916, and its main characteristics are exemplified by González's works, which represent the emergence, plenitude, and eventual substitution of this poetic movement in the country.

González and his contemporaries wrote verses that expressed their poetic concerns while searching for answers to the mysteries of existence. Other well-known *Modernista* practitioners were Pablo de Rohka (1894–1968), who tackled with equal impetus poetic and political themes, and two other poets, Juan Guzmán Cruchaga (1885–1979) and Romualdo del Valle (1900–1965), whose hermetic verses eventually turned toward a more pure and intimate mode. Soon after 1916, however, younger poets began to reject metaphysical inquiries of transcendence. In this new path they followed the lead of Huidobro, who in 1914 published his essay "Non Serviam" (I Will Not Serve), starting a quest for a poetic expression outside the literary canon that ended in his discovery of *Creacionismo*.

In the 1930s, French Surrealism entered the mainstream of Chilean poetry through the pages of the journal *Mandrágora* (Mandrake), founded by poets Braulio Arenas (1913–1987), Teófilo Cid (1914–1964), and Enrique Gómez Correa (1920–1995), and after 1942 by *Leitmotiv,* where Benjamin Pèret (1899–1959) and Aime Césaire (1913–) published regularly. A more American form of Surrealism was practiced by Neruda, whose groundbreaking two volumes of *Residencia en la tierra* mark a high point for this literary trend. Neruda soon turned away from the poetic concerns and anguished existential themes of these earlier books, moved by his quest for social justice, a result of his involvement with the Spanish poets of the Generation of '27 and his participation in the Spanish Civil War.

After 1950, veering away from Neruda's political themes, some poets, such as Lihn, Óscar Hahn (1938–), and Jorge Teillier, began a move to reawaken concerns for formal perfection. The triumph of the Cuban Revolution in 1959 and the military coup against the government of Salvador Allende in Chile in 1973 changed the aloofness of the poetic tenor during the 1960s and 1970s. Revolutionary fervor and social poetry came back to the forefront and popular culture dominated poetic trends. Folk singers such as Violeta Parra (1917–1967; a sister of Nicanor) and Víctor Jara (1932–1973; killed by the Pinochet regime) became national icons, and their verses and sociopolitical themes deeply influenced the direction of poetry. Many writers fled into exile; a group in Spain became known as the "generación emergente" (emergent generation), and several of its members opted for remaining there even after the fall of the military junta in Chile.

As the 1970s came to an end Omar Lara (1941–) and Juan Armando Epple gathered the poems of the younger writers in the anthology *Chile: Poesía de la resistencia y del exilio* (Chile: Poetry of Resistance and Exile, 1978). Epple dedicated another anthology to the journal *Trilce* and included many verses written in the clandestine workshops during the Pinochet dictatorship. In the 1980s and 1990s older poets added new and important books to their repertoire—Parra published *Chistes para desorientar a la poesía* (Jokes to Disorient Poetry, 1989); Hahn published *Imágenes nucleares* (Nuclear Images, 1983) and *Tratado de sortilegios* (Treatise on Sorcery, 1992); Gonzalo Rojas (1917–) published *Las hermosas: Poesías de amor* (The Beautiful Ones: Love Poetry, 1991); and Zurita published *Antiparaíso* (Anti-Paradise, 1991)—at the same time new poets have continued to make themselves known carving out the poetic spaces they need to express their more contemporary concerns.

Yet, regardless of the abundance of good poets in Chile, the figures of Neruda and Parra loomed larger than life in the poetic scene during the largest part of the twentieth century. Neruda's first book, *Crepusculario*, was published in 1923, and he continued a steady writing pace, publishing more than forty books over the next fifty years. In fact, his death in 1973 did not stop the flow, since several posthumous volumes of poems and memoirs were added to his complete works in the late 1970s. Despite his more subdued personal and literary style, Parra has not been less overwhelming for younger Chilean poets. In his case, his struggle with the poetic language and the sociopolitical concerns of his time extend for more than six decades. They appeared in his first book, *Cancionero sin nombre* (Songs Without Name, 1937), and they were still present in the 1990s in books such as *Poemas para combatir la calvicie* (Poems to Combat Boldness, 1993) and *Discursos de sobremesa* (After-Dinner Speeches, 1997).

Colombia

Modernismo was powerfully rich in Colombia, and it maintained its sway through the first decades of the twentieth century. Some of the major Colombian *Modernistas* are poets as respected and well known as José Asunción Silva (1865–1896), Guillermo Valencia, and Porfirio Barba-Jacob (1883–1942). The youngest members of this group, among them Barba-Jacob and León de Greiff (1895–1975), also belonged to the Centenarista generation (Generation of the Centennial). A good example of the lasting effects of *Modernismo* in Colombia is the iconoclastic work of León de Greiff, a powerful poet polemically opposed to the limits imposed on poetry by any sort of school or manifesto.

The Colombian Vanguard, heavily influenced by the aesthetics of *Modernismo,* came together under the

banner of the *piedracielistas* (stone-and-sky), a group that took its name and its aesthetics from the pure poetry of Juan Ramón Jiménez, and more specifically yet from his book *Piedra y cielo* (Stone and Sky, 1919), but who also exhibited additional influences from the Spanish Generation of '27 and T. S. Eliot. One important member of this group was Eduardo Carranza (1913–1985), who began his poetic career with *Canciones para iniciar una fiesta* (Songs for Beginning a Party, 1936); other noteworthy members are Jorge Rojas (1911–1995) and Tomás Vargas Osorio (1908–1941). Pure poetry was also the main aesthetic component of another group, the Cuadrículas, who wrote cerebral classical verses. Fernando Charry Lara (1920–) and Rogelio Echevarría (1926–) are two of the best-known poets of this group.

In the 1950s another group of poets gathered around the journal *Mito* (Myth, 1955–1962), starting a movement under the sway of existentialism. The journal was founded and edited by Jorge Gaitán Durán (1924–1962) and Eduardo Cote Lamus (1928–1964), and its most outstanding member was Alvaro Mutis, a well-rounded writer with personal themes and characters that reappear through his many books of poems as well as his novels.

Coinciding with the sociopolitical turmoil known as La Violencia (Violence, 1947–1957), the *Nadaísta* (Nothingness) movement was born and held its sway through the 1960s. Writers such as Gonzalo Arango (1931–1976), Jaime Jaramillo Escobar (1932–), Mario Rivero (1935–), and Eduardo Escobar (1943–) published their reticent verses in the journal *Nadaísmo 70* (Nothingness 70). They proclaimed their discontent with language and society, exalting eroticism, the hippie movement, and the Cuban Revolution. Although they refused to take an organized stance to confront the continuous political violence and repression, they did protest specific governmental abuses. Their poetics aimed at creating vital, dynamic, innovative, and spontaneous verses.

The poets who in 1970 were included in the *Antología de una generación sin nombre* (Anthology of a Generation Without Name) appropriately reacted to the disillusionment of their *Nadaísta* predecessors. This group, headed by Giovanni Quessep (1939–), Elkin Restrepo (1942–), Jaime García Maffla (1944–), and Annabel Torres (1948–), published in the literary journals *Golpe de Dados* (A Throw of Dice) and in *Acuarimántima*. Their poems betray the influence of Constantin Cavafis (1863–1933), Parra, Lezama Lima, Borges, and Paz because of the privileged position they accorded to political themes, antipoetry, narrative, and centering the poetic image. The *Antología de la generación desencantada* (Anthology of the Disenchanted Generation, 1985) gathered together seven poets born between 1935 and 1950, among them María Mercedes Carranza (1945–), Darío Jaramillo (1948–), and Juan Gustavo Cobo Borda (1948–), who seem to break away from social topics, in order to replace them with a search for the problems of being and identity, the sensuous and magical elements of language, and the obsession with time and its cyclical nature. These poets are characterized by their individuality; rather than gathering in groups, they preferred to write in solitude an intimate poetry reflective of their active internal life. For them poetry was "fidelidad y conciencia" (fidelity and consciousness).

According to Cobo Borda, poetry of the late 1980s and early 1990s returned to the poetic tradition of the great *Modernista* writers of Colombia. He perceives this return as part of a larger social phenomenon that resulted in the "institutionalization" of poetry. Poetry became an institution in Colombia through a series of coincidences, among them, the foundation of two Houses of Poetry, residences where poets could meet, discuss, and write poetry: Casa de la Poesía Silva in 1986 and Casa de la Poesía Fernando Mejía Manizales in 1990; the publication of the journal *Golpe de Dados;* the award of a yearly poetry prize by the University of Antioquia; and the weekly poetry pages that appeared every Sunday in the newspaper *El Espectador* (The Spectator). The simultaneous spaces provided by these different institutions and events had a definitive role in fostering an appreciation for the excellent poetic tradition of Colombia and an interest in continuing to develop this potential.

Among Colombia's most recent poets, several stand out for the excellent quality of their verses. Worthy of mention are William Ospina (1954–), who wrote *Hilo de arena* (The Thread of Sand, 1986), and Rafael Castillo (1962–), author of *Canción desnuda* (Naked Song) and *El ojo del silencio* (The Eye of Silence), both of 1985, and *Entre la oscuridad y la palabra* (Between Darkness and the Word, 1992).

Costa Rica

Most Latin American literary critics would agree that although Costa Rica can boast of isolated poets, by and large, there are no consistent poetic groups and movements until the second part of the twentieth century. *Modernismo* arrived late, with the publication in 1907 of *En el silencio* (In the Silence) by Roberto Brenes Menén (1874–1947), and it extended itself, mixed with some *posmodernista* and Vanguard characteristics, for an unduly long time. In fact, according to Carlos Rafael Duverrán in *Poesía contemporánea de Costa Rica: Antología* (Contemporary Poetry of Costa Rica, 1973), all poets born prior to 1900 may be defined as *Modernistas,* while

those born between 1900 and 1917 can be defined as having been formed in *Modernista* aesthetics and having evolved toward a more personal poetic creed only after the late arrival of the Vanguard. In addition to their slow poetic evolution, this generation is also known for publishing shortly before dying at a young age; their poetic careers began with the poems of Max Jiménez (1900–1947) and Rafael Estrada (1901–1934) and ended with those of Alfredo Cardona Peña (1900–1947), who characteristically did not publish his first book, *El mundo que tú eres* (The World That You Are), until 1944.

The generation born between 1917 and 1927 and the following one are indistinctly known as "la generación perdida" (the lost generation) due to the fact that they either stopped writing early or published little. One of the best-known poets of this group is Eunice Odio (1922–1974), though her influence was minimal in her own country due to the fact that she mostly lived and published away from Costa Rica. The second of these generations, that is to say, those born between 1927 and 1937, were the first to become conscious of their poetic art and to seek out new ways of incorporating Costa Rican poetry into the modern trends prevailing in the rest of the continent. Among these poets are Mario Picado (1928–), Ana Antillón (1934–), Jorge Charpentier (1933–), and, especially, Duverrán (1935–); they all published together with poets belonging to different generations, such as Isaacs Felipe Azofeifa (1912–1997) and Jorge Debravo (1938–1967).

Debravo published important books such as *Poemas terrestres* (Earthly Poems, 1964) and *Nosotros los hombres* (We the Men, 1966), but many more appeared posthumously, including his *Antología mayor* (Main Anthology, 1974). He was a distinctive poet and influential among his counterparts, who were known as "poetas de Turrialba" after the town in which Debravo was born. These poets eventually evolved in the 1960s into the Círculo de poetas costarricenses (Circle of Costa Rican Poets), a foundational group who seriously began to challenge and question the tools and aims of their poetic art as well as their political circumstances. They took their inspiration from the Generation of '27 and Spanish American poets such as Vallejo and Neruda. Other outstanding poets from this group are Laureano Albán (1942–), an author who initiated his poetic career with *Poemas en cruz* (Poems in a Cross, 1961) and *Este hombre* (This Man, 1967) and moved on to his more fanciful *Enciclopedia de las maravillas* (Encyclopedia of Marvelous Things), published in 1995; and Julieta Dobles Yzaguirre (1943–), whose verses have steadily evolved from early books such as *Reloj de siempre* (The Clock of Always, 1972) toward the complexities of *Una viajera demasiado azul* (A Too Blue Traveler,

1990) and *Amar en Jerusalén* (To Love in Jerusalem, 1992). In general, the aesthetics of this group slowly evolved toward a "realismo poético" (poetic realism) grounded in historical poetry and politically committed trends, influenced by the *exteriorista* poetry of other Central American poets like Ernesto Cardenal, the Guatemalan Otto René Castillo (1936–1967), and Roque Dalton. Their verses sought a colloquial, everyday language, politically anti-poetic and antibourgeois.

In 1974 a "trascendentalista" group was founded by some poets of the Círculo costarricense, such as Albán and Dobles, in addition to Ronald Bonilla (1951–) and Carlos Francisco Monge (1951–). They reacted against sociopolitical poetry in order to return to transcendental poetic values, particularly in their concern with form and language. During the last quarter of the twentieth century, Costa Rican poets, like poets everywhere, questioned traditional historical and literary conventions and their own existential being by using three means: criticizing established social, political, religious, and literary systems; asking pertinent questions in reference to the validity of words and spiritual practices; and recuperating myths and dreams through memory. Some contemporary poets that stand out for their questioning are Nidia Barboza (1954–) and Mía Gallegos (1953–), author of *Los días y los sueños* (Days and Dreams, 1995), as well as Ana Istarú (1960–), whose verses (and dramatic pieces) range from the more direct *Palabra nueva* (New Word, 1975) and *Poemas para un día cualquiera* (Poems for Any Day, 1976) to the poetic quest written twenty years later in *Verbo Madre* (Mother Verb, 1995). Important also in the late twentieth century were Carlos Cortés's (1962–) books of poems *Salomé descalza* (Barefooted Salome, 1989) and *El amor es esa bestia platónica* (Love Is That Platonic Beast, 1991).

Cuba

Modern Cuban poetry–the most important and influential in the Antillean world–cannot be studied outside the intense political climate of the island since the middle of the nineteenth century. Revolutionary independence movements culminated in the 1880s with the Guerra de Cuba, or Spanish American War, which ended with the defeat of Spain in 1898. The subsequent occupation of the island by U.S. troops officially lasted until 1902, but economically and politically Cuba remained under American power until the triumph of Fidel Castro's Cuban Revolution in 1959. The onset of the revolutionary period drastically changed the direction of poetry on the island, influencing it formally and thematically and splitting the different generations between those who fled into exile and those who remained there.

Attaining independence from both Spain and the United States was only the first step in the long road to cultural recovery of the nation. Regino E. Boti (1878–1958), Agustín Acosta (1886–), and José Manuel Poveda (1888–1926) accomplished the poetic renewal between 1913 and 1922 with the help of the influential journal *Cuba Contemporánea* (Contemporary Cuba). Many of these writers, known as the Primera Generacion Republicana (First Republican Generation), published in its pages under the leadership of its premier poet, Mariano Brull (1891–1956).

The Segunda Generación Republicana (Second Republican Generation) marked one of the highlights of Cuban poetry in the twentieth century. Important members were José Zacarías Tallet (1893–1989), Juan Marinello (1898–1977), Dulce María Loynaz (1903–1999), Rubén Martínez Villena (1899–1934), and others who, like Manuel Navarro Luna (1894–1966) and Regino Pedroso (1896–1983), served as a transition to the next generation. All of them published in the journal *Revista de Avance* (Advance Review, 1927–1930) and *Diario de la Marina* (Marine Daily). *Revista de Avance* closely reported the new trends of *Ultraísmo, Futurismo,* Surrealism, and other Vanguard innovations, but few Cuban poets totally adhered to any of these modalities, even though most collaborated closely with this journal. Writers associated with this journal were Brull, the essayist Jorge Mañac (1898–1961), and the novelist Alejo Carpentier (1904–1980).

Even more successful and long-lasting was the transcendentalist tendency favored more than a decade later by the poets publishing in the journal *Orígenes* (Origins, 1944–1956). This group wrote an abstract, symbolist, and allegorical poetry heavily influenced by a variety of poets, among them Juan Ramón Jiménez; members of the Generation of '27; Neruda and Vallejo; the Italian Filippo Tommaso Marinetti (1876–1944); and T. S. Eliot and Walt Whitman. Among the many Cuban poets who stand in this transcendentalist line are Loynaz, Emilio Ballagas (1908–1954), José Lezama Lima, Gastón Baquero (1918–), Virgilio Piñera (1914–1979), Eliseo Diego (1920–1994), Cintio Vitier (1921–), and Fina García Marruz (1923–).

A poetic trend initiated by the Cuban Vanguard, but that Cuba shares with the other two Spanish-speaking Antillean islands, Puerto Rico and the Dominican Republic, is that of *Poesía Negra* (Afro Poetry). This movement has its roots in the European intellectuals' fascination with African and primitive art. Artists as diverse as Pablo Picasso, Gillaume Apollinaire, and André Gide incorporated African motifs in their works, while North American jazz music and performers such as Josephine Baker triumphed in Paris. García Lorca's visit to Havana in 1930, where he came in contact with Afro-Cuban poetry, is also credited with contributing to the spread and success of this movement. Ramón Guirao's (1908–1949) "La bailadora de rumba" (The Rumba Dancer) and José Zacarías Tallet's "La rumba" (Rumba), both of 1928, were the first poems of this modality. In 1930 Nicolás Guillén, the great Afro-Cuban poet, published his first book on this theme, *Motivos de son,* with his second book, *Sóngoro cosongo: Poemas mulatos* (Sóngoro Cosongo: Mulatto Poems), appearing the following year. With time Afro-Cuban poetry spoke of vindication, of social justice, and racial pride, but at its inception its repertoire consisted of *pregones callejeros* (street vendors' cries), lullabies, dances, satires, elegies, and protest songs. Rhythm rather than traditional Hispanic syllabic count became the poetic principle. Emphasis was on onomatopoeic sounds to reproduce drums and percussion instruments, characteristic of Afro-Cuban dances, while *jitanjáforas,* words with sonorous effects, introduced terms used to designate objects and places significant to black culture.

Authors born between 1925 and 1940 belong to La Primera Promoción de la Revolución (The First Promotion of the Revolution). In the decade of the 1950s they became involved in the fight against the dictator Fulgencio Batista while simultaneously writing their first poems. The events and the triumph of the Cuban Revolution shaped the themes and the form of their poems. The foundation of the cultural center Casa de las Américas (House of the Americas) also contributed to establishing guidelines designed to encourage intellectual and artistic endeavors inside and outside the island, while foregrounding social realism and Marxist ideology at home and abroad. Many poets of the Primera Promoción became associated with two important publications, the journal *Lunes de Revolución* (Mondays of Revolution), edited by the prestigious novelist Guillermo Cabrera Infante (1922–), and *El Puente* (The Bridge, 1960–1965). These poets can loosely be divided into two groups. One was composed of Roberto Fernández Retamar (1930–), Fayad Jamís (1930–1988), Miguel Barnet (1940–), Antón Arrufat (1935–), Heberto Padilla, and Nancy Morejón (1944–); while the second one included Isel Rivero (1941–), Belkis Cuza Malé (1942–), and Reinaldo García Ramos (1944–).

In 1962, Editorial El Puente published *Novísima poesía cubana* (Newest Cuban Poetry), creating a controversy due to the fact that its ideology opposed the official government line. When El Puente attempted to publish a second anthology, the government reacted violently, closing both *Lunes de Revolución* as well as the editorial house. Having lost their intellectual centers of power, some of these poets gathered around the journal *El Caimán Barbudo* (The Bearded Alligator), directed by

Jesús Díaz (1941–), while many others began to publish in a myriad of journals in Cuba and abroad. In general, the early poetry of this decade still maintained its ties to the transcendental poetry of *Orígenes;* younger poets, however, began to move toward a distinct colloquial tone and a deep involvement with the historical situation at hand. Some of those writing at this time were Cleva Solís (1926–1997), Carilda Oliver Labra (1924–), Luís Suardíaz (1936–), and Georgina Herrera (1936–).

The intellectual discontent that resulted in the government closing of *Lunes de Revolución* and El Puente became an international scandal in 1968 with the "caso Padilla" (the Padilla case). This scandal came about when the Casa de las Américas Poetry Prize for that year was awarded to Padilla's *Fuera del juego* (Outside the Game), only to find that the book was a scathing attack on the Castro regime. Padilla was incarcerated and released in 1971 after several international interventions in his behalf. The poetry of the 1970s was definitely tinged by this incident and the deep political fervor and censorship that followed. The poetics of this decade are clearly evident in two anthologies, *Punto de partida* (Starting Point, 1974) and *Nuevos poetas* (New Poets, 1974), which reflect the ideals of "revolutionary poetry," made up of political ideology written in a pamphlet-like expression. The new poets of the 1980s, increasingly disillusioned with the deteriorating economic and social situation, are infinitely more detached from political concerns. As a result they return to more poetical matters, thus discovering the poetry of *Orígenes* as well as the most valuable poetry of the 1960s. The best of this group and of those to follow in the 1990s appear in the anthology *Retrato de grupo* (Portrait of a Group, 1991).

The sociopolitical instability of the island contributed to the increased number of poets opting for exile. Dissatisfaction with the lack of intellectual freedom ran high among some poets, in contrast to the deep political commitment to the revolution evident in the verses of most—at least during the early years. As time passed, however, the poetry of dissidence began to gain ground. Before long many of these writers abandoned the island to join the many others who had preceded them since the onset of Castro's Revolution. The main characteristic of this Cuban poetry in exile is its lack of cohesion, a problem resulting from the fact that there is no geographic center for the group of exiles. Many came to the United States, settling mostly in Florida and New Jersey, but many others went to other states as well as to Mexico, Puerto Rico, and Spain. Perhaps Spain and Miami are the centers more closely associated with Cuban exiles and where they have found the best conditions to survive as a group. In Spain, one of the pillars of the community has been Baquero, a member of the original *Orígenes* group, and José Mario (1940–), founder of Editorial El Puente, which he continued in Spain as Resumen Literario El Puente. Other prestigious poets of the community in Spain are two well-known political prisoners and defenders of human rights, Miguel Sales (1951–) and Armando Valladares (1937–). In Miami the activities of the Editorial Universal and the literary prize Letras de Oro (Gold Letters) have contributed to fomenting intellectual pursuits. Among the many poets of note who live in the United States, one may mention Ana Rosa Núñez (1926–1999), Amelia del Castillo (1924–), Isel Rivero, Padilla, and Cuza Malé, editors of *Linden Lane Magazine,* Arrufat, José Triana (1933–), Magali Alabau (1945–), and Gustavo Pérez Firmat (1949–).

Dominican Republic

Modern currents arrived late in Dominican letters, which have no other international claim to poetry during the early part of the century than the single figure of Salomé Ureña de Henríquez (1850–1897). In fact there were few new ideas and no new poetic trends until the appearance of *Vedrinismo,* a pre-Vanguard concept of Otilio Vigil Díaz (1880–1961), who introduced free verse in the national literature in 1917 and sought to start a native poetic trend independent from all European influences. He found no sympathy for his cause, however, because of his lack of understanding of the main themes and problems that preoccupied the country at that time. In contrast, the next movement, *Postumismo,* founded in 1921, succeeded in the efforts to recuperate the native and to reject foreign influences, by discovering the Dominican landscape and the racial essence of the land. The poet Domingo Moreno Jiménez (1894–1986) was the sponsor and most prominent representative of this trend. Its success was assured when the journal *Cuna de América* (Cradle of America) dedicated a whole number to the poetry of the group, winning many adepts for their cause.

Los Nuevos (The New Ones), founded in 1935, was the name of the journal used by Rubén Suro (1916–) to continue the line initiated by Moreno Jiménez and to expand it beyond literature to cover the interest of other artists. Moreno Jiménez did in fact become the spiritual guiding light of this new group, spearheading their interest in sociopolitical and racial concerns. They were particularly interested in creating ties with their neighbor country of Haiti. Suro was also a pioneer of Afro-Antillan poetry, publishing several poems before Manuel del Cabral (1907–1999) published *Trópico Negro* (Black Tropic) in 1941 and Tomás Hernández Franco (1904–1952) published *Yélida* (1942).

During the decades of the 1930s and 1940s the dictator Rafael Leonidas Trujillo consolidated his power without really affecting the course of poetry, which at the time was mostly concerned with artistic themes rather than with criticism of the regime. As the 1940s advanced, however, political repression became harsher, and poets began to introduce symbolism and allegory to condemn indirectly the civil-rights abuses. As the situation progressively worsened, many poets marched into self-imposed exile. These poets became known as the *Independentists* of the 1940s; some of them are Cabral, who lived and published in Colombia; Manuel Rueda (1921–), who moved to Chile; Pedro Mir (1912–), who published in Cuba; and Tomás Hernández Franco (1904–1952) in El Salvador. The most distinguished Dominican poet of the twentieth century is Cabral, an outstanding practitioner of *negrismo* (black poetry) as well as of philosophical and social concerns. He was a member of this generation and more specifically of the *Independentists,* as also were Franklin Mieses Burgos (1907–1976), Héctor Incháustequi Cabral (1912–1979), and Hernández Franco.

Among those who remained at home under the dictatorship, a group published in *Cuadernos Dominicanos de Cultura* (Dominican Notebooks of Culture), a journal devised by the dictator as a way to pacify the intellectuals of the country. Max Henríquez Ureña published in this journal. Opposing this group were other poets who also remained on the island and who took their name from the journal in which they published, *La poesía sorprendida* (Surprised Poetry). They showed the influence of the Spanish Nobel laureate Juan Ramón Jiménez and of the poets of the Generation of '27, the Spanish Vanguard. These poets are Alberto Baeza Flores, Moreno Jiménez (1894–1966), and Mieses Burgos (1907–1976).

The next group to enter the Dominican literary scene took the name Grupo del 1948 (Group of 1948). Its main representatives, Máximo Avilés Blonda (1931–1988) and Lupo Hernández Rueda (1930–), published in the periodical *El Caribe* (The Caribbean) while continuing the same tenets as the preceding generation, tenets which they even reaffirmed in 1954.

The Generación del 1960 (Generation of 1960) and the Generación de la Post-Guerra (Post-War Generation) cover most of the 1960s and 1970s, two difficult decades in the history of the Dominican Republic. The first one covers the years from 1960 to 1965 and the second one from 1965 to 1978. The assassination of Trujillo in 1961 brought quick and drastic changes to the country. Upon the death of the dictator, Juan Bosch assumed constitutional power, but he was quickly overthrown by a military coup, provoking the second military occupation of the country by the United States Marine Corps. Poetry written between 1960 and 1965 addressed the many themes and types of expression not allowed by the dictatorship and incorporated into Dominican poetry the urban landscape; it was a time of Vanguard experimentation, carried out mostly by Cayo Claudio Espinal (1955–) and Alexis Gómez Rosa (1950–). Poets writing after the 1965 war became politicized, incorporating themes of social justice, political vindication, and historical commitment. These poets are divided between the *incluidos* (included) and the *excluidos* (excluded), a terminology that refers to whether or not they were able to publish in the newspaper *La Noticia* (The News). Among the former group are Norberto James (1945–), Enriquillo Sánchez (1947–), and Soledad Alvarez (1950–); among the *excluidos* are Josefina de la Cruz and René Rodríguez Soriano (1950–). Critics have observed that the poetry of these two decades suffers from lack of leadership, as no outstanding poet came to the fore to lend his or her individuality to these groups. It also witnessed the establishment of poetry workshops after 1965, a revolutionary step contributing to the poetic training of the new generations.

New vitality was interjected into Dominican poetry in 1974 when Manuel Rueda (1921–) read a manifesto on *El pluralismo* (Pluralism). It consisted of a call to return to the high poetic standards of traditional lyric poetry, motivated by what he perceived as the flood of antipoetic political and revolutionary poetry produced in the Dominican Republic and Spanish America at large. For this state of affairs he blamed the socio-political and historicist poets that came forth to answer the call of the Cuban Revolution and the tensions of the Cold War. The aim of the *pluralistas* was to create a new type of poem that would offer a multitude of readings.

The poets of the Generación de los 1980 (The Eighties Generation) and after have their roots in the poetry workshops founded in the 1960s. Among these poets are Tomás Castro (1959–) and José Mármol (1960–). One of the characteristics of this most-recent poetry is the large number of women whose verses question the passive role traditionally assigned to the female gender. Some of these writers, such as Marta Rivera (1960–), Sabina Román, and Ylonka Nacidit Perdomo (1965–), have attracted international recognition.

Ecuador

Modern poetry entered Ecuador with the generation born between 1890 and 1915, described by Hernán Rodríguez Castelo in volume one of his *Lírica ecuatoriana contemporánea* (Contemporary Ecuadorian Lyrics, 1979) as powerfully lyrical. These characteristically elitist poets were mostly concerned with the search for poetic transcendence that at that time engaged *Mod-*

ernista writers all over the Hispanic world. Among the several *Modernista* poets produced by Ecuador, critics name Humberto Fierro (1890–1929), Arturo Borja (1892–1912) and Rosa Borja (1889–1964), Ernesto Nova y Camacho (1889–1927), and Medardo Ángel Silva (1898–1919), pointing out that they were influenced by the elegant verses of Juan Ramón Jiménez and Rubén Darío.

In Ecuador, *Modernismo* progressed smoothly into *posmodernismo,* loosely defined by Rodrigo Pesántez Rodas, in his *Modernismo y posmodernismo en la poesía ecuatoriana* (Modernism and Postmodernism in Ecuadorian Poetry, 1995), as a simple "vertiente de salida" (sliding exit) for *Modernista* writers. This poetic trend was practiced by those poets who were born after 1898 and who, like Miguel Ángel Zambrano (1898–1969), Hugo Mayo (1895–1988), and Augusto Arias (1903–1974), exhibited a new artistic consciousness that made them react against the excessive ornamentation of *Modernismo* and to seek out simpler forms to express the sentimental irony characteristic of the period. This group boasts two of Ecuador's most important poets. One is Aurora Estrada Ayala (1902–1967), the most well-rounded feminine voice of any literary period. The second one is Jorge Carrera Andrade (1903–1978), without doubt the most important poet of this group and perhaps of twentieth-century Ecuadorian poetry. Carrera Andrade's consistent and successful evolution allowed him to keep ahead of literary trends and become the classical poet par excellence. He is the most influential poet at home and the best-known internationally.

Writers of African descent from the province of Esmeraldas founded *negrismo* (Afro literature and art), an important movement of the 1940s. This trend has been amply promoted and backed up by the Ecuadorian Casa de la Cultura, which has published much of these writers' important works; in fact, twenty-eight literary works, mostly poetry, written by *negrismo* writers were published between 1960 and 1981. Perhaps the two best-known authors of this movement are the novelist-poets Adalberto Ortiz (1914–) and Nelson Estupiñán Bass (1915–2002). Ortiz is internationally known for his novel *Juyungo* (1942), but he published also the first Ecuadorian *negrista* book, *Tierra, son y tambor* (Land, Son, and Drum), in Mexico in 1945; Estupiñán Bass is the author of a long list of works in poetry and fiction—a well-received book of poems written in the early 1990s is *Esta goleta llamada poesía* (This Sailing Ship Called Poetry, 1991)—but he is also known because of his editorship of the prestigious journal *Meridiano Negro* (Black Meridian).

Ecuadorian poetry of the mid twentieth century offered a varied panorama of journals and groups in quest of new poetic paths and innovative expression.

Among the first groups to establish a reputation stands out Madrugada (Dawn), which met at the Ecuadorian Casa de la Cultura in the mid 1940s under the leadership of César Dávila Andrade (1918–1967) and Jorge Enrique Adoum (1926–   ). They published in the journal by the same name, and their aim was to reject the transcendentalist efforts of the previous generations. Adoum wrote his first book, *Ecuador amargo* (Bitter Ecuador, 1944), under Neruda's influence, although he quickly moved to establish his own rich voice in the service of protest and denunciation. Another important member of Madrugada was Rafael Díaz Icaza (1925–   ). The group Presencia (Presence) was established in Quito in 1950 under Francisco Tobar García (1928–   ); later that decade several other groups were born, among them *Club 7 de Poesía* (Club 7 of Poetry), in the city of Guayaquil, headed by David Ledesma (1934–1961) and Ileana Espinel (1933–   ), and, in Quito, *Elan, Caminos* (Paths, 1958) and *Nosotros* (Us).

These groups were superseded by the Generación del 60 (Generation of '60), more unified in its iconoclastic pursuit of originality. An exception to these poetic concerns appears in the *Tzatza* group, born in the aftermath of the Cuban Revolution under the leadership of Ulises Estrella (1940–   ) and which continued writing until 1970. Other members of the Generación del 60 were the Afro writer Antonio Preciados Bedoya (1940–   ), Ignacio Carvalho Castillo (1937–   ), Francisco Araujos (1937–   ), and Ana María Tza (1941–   ).

The activities of these groups that proliferated from the 1940s through the 1970s were eventually replaced in the last decades of the twentieth century by a series of *talleres de poesía* (poetry workshops) that, in the style of those started in Cuba and Nicaragua during their respective revolutions, attempted to guide and offer opportunities to the younger generations of writers. As it has happened in so many other Spanish American countries, most poets writing at the turn of the twenty-first century are the product of these workshops.

El Salvador

The foundational aspects of the poetry of Francisco Gavidia (1863–1955) cannot be overlooked in the literary history of El Salvador. His presence is so central that many critics divide literary production in the country by his figure, speaking of pre- and post-Gavidia. Gavidia, a good friend of the Nicaraguan founder of Hispanic *Modernismo,* Rubén Darío, was the first Salvadoran writer to assume a national consciousness and to attempt to create a native tradition. The many essays and books of poetry he wrote on this

theme became a dominant influence in the works of the younger Salvadoran generations.

In El Salvador the new poetic tendencies associated with the Vanguard began to emerge in the 1920s. The first poet of notice after Gavidia was Alberto Guerra Trigueros (1898–1950). Guerra Trigueros is known for the extreme formal perfection of his verses as well as for the maturity and lyrical quality of his themes. Another early and most original voice of the Salvadoran Vanguard is that of Claudia Lars (1899–1974), often compared to the small group of outstanding women poets who triumphed in the early part of the twentieth century, namely Gabriela Mistral, the Argentine Alfonsina Storni (1892–1938), and the Uruguayans Delmira Agustini (1886–1914) and Juana de Ibarbourou (1892–1979). Lars's intimate poetry slowly moved toward a dramatic and darker vision of life. Religious themes and existential anguish rule the texts of another excellent poet, Hugo Lindo (1917–1985), a disciplined writer who valued rigor and coherence.

The poets writing at this time, many of whom were members of the Generation of 1930, were marked by the tragic happenings of 1932, when thirty thousand *campesinos* (peasants) were executed, and the incident was made to disappear through the destruction of all historical records. One of the members of the Generation of 1930 was the Vanguard poet Pedro Geoffroy Rivas (1908–1979), who tried to keep alive the memory of the events through his writing. Years later the poet and novelist Claribel Alegría and her husband, Darwin J. Flakoll, as well as the militant poet Roque Dalton, picked up this cause, writing narratives and testimonials based on this incident.

The poetry of the 1940s, heavily influenced by Pablo Neruda, is represented by the work of the Grupo Seis (Group Six). Of importance at this time also are several new voices that came forth in the 1950s. The opening year of the decade is associated with the Grupo Octubre (October Group) and the works of Italo López Vallecillo (1932–   ) and Álvaro Menéndez Leal (1931–   )–or Menén Desleal, as he sarcastically altered his name. Another important group at this time was the Comité de Artistas y Escritores Antifascistas (Committee of Antifascist Artists and Writers), started after World War II. Both groups were made up of young and aggressive poets who sought sociopolitical change following the proclamation of a new national constitution.

The year 1956 is identified with the poets of the Círculo Literario Universitario Salvadoreño (University Literary Salvadoran Circle), among them Manlio Argueta (1935–   ), Dalton, Roberto Armijo (1937–   ), and José Roberto Cea (1939–   ). As a politically committed group, these poets seriously challenged the complacency of the status quo and the official government's economic, political, and social policies. From these poets, perhaps Dalton, known as a *poeta guerrillero* (guerrilla poet) for his involvement in the Salvadoran Civil War, has attained the most international attention due to his brutal murder by his own Marxist comrades short of his fortieth birthday. As a sensitive and politically committed poet his verses resonate with the bitterness and anguish of César Vallejo. Many of these poets appeared in the anthology *De aquí en adelante* (From Henceforth), published in 1967 as a manifesto against academic poetry and the sociopolitical oppression and a vital affirmation of their lack of satisfaction with the status quo.

Another highly visible and actively political poet is Claribel Alegría. She began her poetic career as a writer of uncomplicated, highly sensitive verses but quickly evolved into a political writer, highly committed to the revolutionary cause. Alegría and Dalton are known as poets in quest of justice and solidarity. Most of those poets who experienced the horrors of political oppression and civil war became firmly committed to social and historical poetry, among them Cea, Argueta, and David Escobar Galindo (1944–   ), all of whom favor a testimonial, politically committed poetry. These writers have become particularly involved in political causes related to the Salvadoran Civil War and the continued abuses of social and political power that still go on, forcing many of them to go into exile even beyond the 1970s and 1980s.

–María A. Salgado

Acknowledgments

This book was produced by Bruccoli Clark Layman, Inc. Charles Brower was the in-house editor.

Production manager is Philip B. Dematteis.

Administrative support was provided by Ann M. Cheschi and Carol A. Cheschi.

Accountant is Ann-Marie Holland.

Copyediting supervisor is Sally R. Evans. The copyediting staff includes Phyllis A. Avant, Caryl Brown, Leah M. Cutsinger, Melissa D. Hinton, Philip I. Jones, Rebecca Mayo, and Nancy E. Smith.

Editorial associates are Amelia B. Lacey, Michael S. Martin, Catherine M. Polit, and William Mathes Straney.

In-house prevetting is by Nicole A. La Rocque.

Permissions editor and database manager is Amber L. Coker.

Layout and graphics supervisor is Janet E. Hill. The graphics staff includes Zoe R. Cook and Sydney E. Hammock.

Office manager is Kathy Lawler Merlette.

Photography supervisor is Paul Talbot. Photography editor is Scott Nemzek.

Digital photographic copy work was performed by Joseph M. Bruccoli.

Systems manager is Donald Kevin Starling.

Typesetting supervisor is Kathleen M. Flanagan. The typesetting staff includes Patricia Marie Flanagan, Mark J. McEwan, and Pamela D. Norton. Freelance typesetters are Wanda Adams and Rebecca Mayo.

Walter W. Ross did library research. He was assisted by Jo Cottingham and the following other librarians at the Thomas Cooper Library of the University of South Carolina: circulation department head Tucker Taylor; reference department head Virginia W. Weathers; reference department staff Brette Barron, Marilee Birchfield, Paul Cammarata, Gary Geer, Michael Macan, Tom Marcil, Rose Marshall, and Sharon Verba; interlibrary loan department head John Brunswick; and interlibrary loan staff Robert Arndt, Hayden Battle, Alex Byrne, Bill Fetty, Marna Hostetler, and Nelson Rivera.

Modern Spanish American Poets
First Series

Dictionary of Literary Biography

Jorge Enrique Adoum
(1926 –)

Barbara Clark
Averett University

BOOKS: *Poderes; o, El libro que diviniza* (Quito: Fernández, 1940);

Rasgando velos o la develación del Apocalipsis de San Juan (Buenos Aires: "Yo soy," 1949);

Ecuador amargo (Quito: Casa de la Cultura Ecuatoriana, 1949);

Carta para Alejandra (Quito: La Andariega, 1952);

Los cuadernos de la tierra: I. Los orígenes, II. El enemigo y la mañana (Quito: Casa de la Cultura Ecuatoriana, 1952);

Antología del río Guayas (Quito: Casa de la Cultura Ecuatoriana, 1953);

Notas del hijo prodigo (Quito: Rumiñahui, 1953);

Relato del extranjero (Quito: Ateneo Ecuatoriano, 1953);

Poesía del Siglo XX: Valery, Rilke, Claudel, Lubicz-Milosz, Hughes, Eliot, Nicolás Guillén, Maiacovski, García Lorca, Vallejo, Hikmet, Neruda (Quito: Casa de la Cultura Ecuatoriana, 1957);

Los cuadernos de la tierra: III. Dios trajo la sombra (Quito: Casa de la Cultura Ecuatoriana, 1959; Havana: Casa de la Américas, 1960);

Los cuadernos de la tierra: IV. Eldorado y Las ocupaciones nocturnas (Quito: Casa de la Cultura Ecuatoriana, 1961);

Yo me fui con tu nombre por la tierra (Quito, 1964);

Curriculum mortis (1968);

Panorama de la actual literatura latinoamericana (1969);

Informe personal sobre la situación (Madrid: Aguaribay, 1973);

Prepoemas en postespañol (1975);

Entre Marx y una mujer desnuda (Mexico City: Siglo Vientiuno, 1976);

No son todos los que están: Poemas, 1949–1979 (Barcelona: Seix Barral, 1979);

Jorge Enrique Adoum (photograph by Carlos Calderón Chico)

Teatro, La subida a los infiernos, 1976 (Quito: Casa de la Cultura Ecuatoriana, 1981)–includes *El sol bajo los patas de los caballos;*

Ecuador, imagenes de un preterio presente (Quito: El Conejo, 1981);

La gran literatura ecuatoriana del 30 (Quito: El Conejo, 1984);

Sin ambages: Textos y contextos (Quito: Planeta-Letraviva, 1989);

Guayasamín: una vida dedicada por entero a la creatividad, by Adoum, Luis María Anson, and Rodrigo Villacís Molina (Quito: Revista SITSA, 1991);

El tiempo y las palabras, introduction and notes by Vladimiro Rivas Iturralde (Quito: Libresa, 1992);

El amor desenterrado y otros poemas (Quito: El Conejo, 1993);

Ciudad sin ángel (Mexico City: Siglo Veintiuno, 1995);

Los amores fugaces: Memorias imaginarias (Quito: Planeta-Letraviva, 1997);

Postales del trópico con mujeres, prologue by Angela Vallvey (Valencia, Spain: Episteme, 1997);

Ecuador: Señas particulares (Quito: Eskeletra, 1998);

Antología poética: 1949–1998 (Madrid: Visor, 1998);

Guayasamín: El hombre, la obra, la crítica (Nuremberg, Germany, 1998);

Mirando a todas partes (Quito: Planeta del Ecuador, 1999);

. . . ni están todos los que son (Quito: Eskeletra, 1999);

El amor y la palabra, by Adoum and others (Bogotá: Fundación Casa de Poesía Silva, 2000).

Editions and Collections: *Los cuadernos de la tierra* (Quito: Casa de la Cultura Ecuatoriana, 1963);

Los cuadernos de la tierra I–IV, includes prologue by Adoum (Guayaquil, Ecuador: Ediciones de la Universidad de Guayaquil, 1988).

OTHER: José de la Cuadra, *Obras completas,* compiled, with notes, by Adoum (Quito: Casa de la Cultura Ecuatoriana, 1958);

Cuadra, *Cuentos,* compiled, with a prologue, by Adoum (Havana: Casa de las Américas, 1970);

Los 37 poemas de Mao Tse Tung, translated by Adoum (Buenos Aires: Schapire Editor, 1974);

Poesía viva del Ecuador: Siglo XX, compiled by Adoum (Quito: Grijalbo, 1990);

Tomás Borge, *El arte como herejía,* prologue by Adoum (Quito: Abrapalabra, 1991);

Cronología del siglo XX: Cultura y política en Ecuador y el mundo, compiled by Adoum (Quito: Eskeletra, 2001).

SELECTED PERIODICAL PUBLICATION-UNCOLLECTED: *The Sun Trampled Beneath the Horses' Hooves,* translated by A. McMurray and R. Márquez from Adoum's *El sol bajo los patas de los caballos, Massachusetts Review,* 15 (Winter–Spring 1974).

Jorge Enrique Adoum is one of the esteemed poets of Ecuador as well as an important voice and presence in twentieth-century Latin American literature and culture. Although his work spans six decades and many themes, the predominant concern of his poetry is the social and political reality of Latin America. The tel-luric thread that connects his many volumes of poems is not only an evocation of the land and its resources but also a denunciation of centuries of exploitation, from without and within, and a testament to many resisters and victims, the unknown as well as the famous. Critics of his work agree that this political stance is as basic and constant in his life as it is in his literature; his integrity is well established. So, too, is his reputation as a dedicated and innovative crafter of words and a scholar of world literature. He was awarded the Premio Nacional de Poesía (National Poetry Prize) in Ecuador in 1952 and later received literary awards that are among the most prestigious in Latin America: the Cuban Premio Casa de las Américas in 1960 and the Mexican Premio Xavier Villaurrutia in 1976. In addition to poetry, he has written and published novels, plays, and anthologies and critical studies of the work of other authors.

Adoum was born in Ambato, Ecuador, in 1926. According to Leonardo Barriga López in *Crítica y antología de la poesía ecuatoriana* (Critical Anthology of Ecuadorian Poetry, 1981), the Adoum family is of Lebanese descent. Though biographical information on Adoum is difficult to ascertain, it is presumed that his father was the medical writer Jorge Adoum, who was born in Beirut in 1897, earned a medical degree in France, and lived much of his life in Ecuador, where he raised his family. Rosangela Trombetti, one of the co-authors of the elder Adoum books, is thought to be Adoum's mother. Adoum attended secondary school at the Colegio de San Gabriel (St. Gabriel School), a Jesuit school in Quito, and he began his literary career at an early age with the journal *Oasis,* where some of his poetry was published. In the late 1940s Adoum traveled to Chile, where he received his degree in philosophy and law from the University of Santiago and where he served for almost two years as personal secretary to the poet Pablo Neruda. When the government of Chilean president Gabriel González Videla made life difficult for the leftists with whom he had previously been allied, Neruda was forced to flee the country, and Adoum went into hiding. After three months of living underground he received a passport that Neruda had managed to secure for him; with that and the money Neruda sent with it, he was able to return to Ecuador in January 1948.

Adoum's first collection of poetry, *Ecuador amargo* (Bitter Ecuador), was published in 1949. As the title indicates, this tribute to his homeland is not romantic or sentimental; rather, his concern with issues of justice and injustice is prevalent. These early poems are evocative of Neruda's great American canto, *Canto general* (1950; translated as *Poems from the Canto General,* 1968), in their depiction of the imposing physical reality of the

Paperback cover for the 1960 Cuban edition of the third volume in Adoum's Los cuadernos de la tierra
cycle. It was originally published in Quito, Ecuador, in 1959 (Bruccoli Clark Layman Archives).

land and Adoum's endeavor to give voice to the stories
of everyday people. The volume thus reflects his intimate working relationship with Neruda during his
years in Chile. Those poems that deal specifically with
the land have strong overtones of sadness, but the grief
expressed in these verses is most obvious in overtly
political poems such as "El desvelo y las noticias"
(Nightwatch and the News), in which the poetic voice
relates waking and waiting in the night for his lover,
who has disappeared. He expresses his fear that the official word will come that she has been wounded, murdered, or exiled, or simply that she is gone: "No está tu
compañera" (Your friend is not here). The poem captures the painful nostalgia of those left behind to worry
and wonder when they catch sight of some reminder of
their disappeared loved one: "Y no está, como Joaquín
(sólo sus botas / debajo de su cama, sólo su saco / espe-
rándolo cuatro meses en la puerta)." (And she is not
here, like Joaquín / [only his boots under his bed, only
his jacket / waiting for him at the door for four
months]). Evident in these verses is the poet's skill, par-

ticularly his ability to distill grand themes in metaphors
and his concern with the oral quality of his words.

In May 1948 Adoum was appointed secretary at
the Casa de la Cultura Ecuatoriana (House of Ecuadoran Culture), where he subsequently served as director of the publishing house. He was also secretary of
the board of the National Symphony Orchestra, secretary of the Institute of Theater and Folklore, and professor at the Central University of Quito. As these
positions were unpaid, Adoum supported himself by
writing medical articles for a pharmaceutical laboratory.
In 1952 he traveled to China, where he spent three
months, afterward returning to Ecuador to continue
working in his various professional positions and writing his most ambitious collection of poetry.

Adoum's celebration/lamentation for Latin Amer-
ica, evident in *Ecuador amargo,* reaches its full fruition in
the epic *Los cuadernos de la tierra* (Notebooks of the
Land), actually four collections of poems published in
three separate volumes over a period of nine years,
from 1952 to 1961. In 1988 they were collected in a sin-

gle volume, which includes an informative prologue by the author. These poems detail the prodigious and often hostile geography of Latin America and chronicle the difficult history of the region, but they do so in verse that is more impressionistic and suggestive than linear. In their scope, their tribute to the indigenous civilizations, and their retelling of the collective story of the Spanish Conquest and its aftermath, these poems are reminiscent of Neruda's *Canto general*. They also refer to the early epics of the region, notably Alonso de Ercilla's *La Araucana* (The Araucanian, 1569–1589), as Angela Vallvey notes in the prologue to her edition of Adoum's later poems, *Postales del trópico con mujeres* (Postcards from the Tropics with Women, 1997).

The first volume of *Los cuadernos de la tierra* comprises *Los orígenes* (Origins), and *El enemigo y la mañana* (The Enemy and Morning); it was published in 1952 and was awarded Ecuador's Premio Nacional de Poesía (National Poetry Prize) the following year. As in *Ecuador amargo,* the poems of *Los orígenes* offer descriptions of the land as majestic and beautiful but, more often, hostile and forbidding. Yet, these poems also take the form of love poems; the poetic voice addresses the land in a conversational tone, using the familiar second-person pronoun, and names it "amor" (my love). The first poem establishes this relationship: "Qué difícil, amor, tu territorio" (How difficult, my love, your land). The speaking voice in these poems is that of the original inhabitants, the indigenous peoples who learned to live with the land without attempting to dominate it; rather, they respected and, indeed, revered their physical environment, converting flora and fauna into deities. Thus, the "I" of these poems is in fact a collective voice.

El enemigo y la mañana tells of the arrival of the conquerors and the resultant clash of cultures. The Spanish Conquest is clearly established as not only the end of the way of life of native civilizations but also the beginning of a new race conceived in violence. Here, the poem becomes something of a dialogue, as the voices of the conquerors alternate with those of the natives. This multivocal quality establishes the originality and power of the text. In addition to the conflicting voices of the participants, Adoum juxtaposes quotes from Inca prayers and poems with excerpts from official Spanish documents, the *crónicas,* or exaggerated chronicles of early conquistadors and historians, and later histories of the Conquest and of pre-Columbian societies.

The third part of *Los cuadernos de la tierra* appeared some seven years after the first volume. *Dios trajo la sombra* (God Brought the Darkness, 1959) was published in Havana by Casa de las Américas in 1960 and was awarded the poetry prize by that publishing house in the same year. In this volume the style and the theme of *El enemigo y la mañana* continue. The focus is the vora-

ciousness of the conquerors for gold and for native women, as well as their cruelty. The constant movement between the voices of the indigenous peoples and those of the conquerors and historians highlights the clashing beliefs of the two groups, emphasizing the religious, linguistic, and cultural dimensions of the Conquest. In the endnotes to the text the author cites the various historical and literary references he has used, which is a helpful addition for the reader given that some of the sources are arcane.

The fourth part of *Los cuadernos de la tierra,* published in 1961, comprises two sections, *Eldorado* (The Golden One) and *Las ocupaciones nocturnas* (Nocturnal Occupations). *Eldorado,* as the title indicates, confronts the great Latin American myth of incredible riches. Again the speaking voice is in the first person, that of the explorer who relates his long journey through the various regions of Ecuador, "el País de la Canela" (Cinnamon Country). This reference establishes the explorer as Gonzalo Pizarro, one of Francisco's half brothers, who was the governor of Quito. The significant elements of the myth are included in the poem, as are the historical details of the expedition: the departure from Quito in March 1541; the cold of the mountains; the humidity of the cloud forests and the lowland jungles; and, finally, the incredible Amazon river system, "inacabable y anormal" (unending and abnormal). Also clear is the human toll; the poetic voice describes the troops and the many native servants as "cadáveres caminantes" (walking cadavers), who must build a boat as best they can, only to have to turn back eventually and cross the mountains again. The poem, however, ends with a reference to romantic love, presented as possible salvation. The poetic voice of the explorer calls to his love, Ana, who provides the inspiration he needs to continue the journey. He is determined to return and, perhaps with her, begin healing: "Tal vez contigo / un día le perdonaré a la selva" (Perhaps with you / one day I will forgive the jungle).

Las ocupaciones nocturnas consists of a prologue, which tells of the founding of the capital city of the new empire on the ruins of the destroyed city of the previous empire, and twenty-five poems that detail the way of life in the colonial "New World." These verses are both a celebration of adaptability and endurance and a critique of the imposition of alien ways of thinking and living. In the prologue to the 1988 edition of *Los cuadernos de la tierra* Adoum notes that he never finished the other volumes he had intended, which would have brought the chronicle up to the final decades of the twentieth century, partly because his plan was too ambitious or too presumptuous and partly because he

Paperback cover for Adoum's 1973 collection of political poems
(Bruccoli Clark Layman Archives)

believes that Latin America has, in fact, been unable to move past its colonial condition.

In 1963 Adoum won a UNESCO grant that enabled him to spend a year abroad, visiting Egypt, India, Japan, and Israel as a member of an East/West cultural exchange. As that trip was nearing completion, he learned that a military coup had overthrown the constitutional government of Ecuador. Though the country was really ruled by a military junta, the new president, Arosemena Monroy, a former friend of his, informed him that it would be best that he not return to his homeland. Since his UNESCO grant provided return travel as far as Paris, he went there and took a one-year position as a Spanish teacher in a school near Le Havre. During that time he established friendships with other Latin American exiles, especially the Chilean folk singer Violeta Parra and the Guatemalan writer Miguel Angel Asturias.

During that year of forced exile in France, Adoum published *Yo me fui con tu nombre por la tierra* (I Went Through the World with Your Name, 1964) clandestinely. The pattern of Adoum's earlier works is continued in these poems, as they are love poems to his homeland bristling with criticism of the oppressive social, economic, and political conditions. The title poem captures these conflicting emotions; it begins: "Nadie sabe en dónde queda mi país" (No one knows where my country is). Can it be true, the poetic voice asks, that a nation so small can have so exaggerated a reality: "¿y es tanta su desgarradura, / tanto su terremoto, tanta su tortura / militar, más trópico que el trópico?" (and is there so much heartbreak, / so much earthquake, so much military / torture, more tropical than the tropics?). As the military government in Ecuador had already warned Adoum that his safety was tenuous, the underground publication of these poems put him at greater risk.

When he returned to Ecuador in 1965 at the end of his teaching contract in Paris, Adoum found that the dictatorship had been harassing his wife and two young daughters. The family decided to sell their few possessions and attempt to establish a new life in Europe. Instead, Adoum learned of a position for an English translator in Beijing that offered a good salary and, of particular importance given his precarious economic situation, round-trip travel from Quito. He took the position, and the family spent the next two years living in China. They then moved to Paris, where they lived for two years as Adoum worked as a reporter and announcer for French radio and television and as a reader for the publishing house Gallimard.

During this time Adoum published the poems of *Curriculum mortis* (1968), which reflect his travels and residences in faraway lands. As always, there are poems about Ecuador, but others deal with Paris, Japan, and India. The prevalent concerns remain politics, injustice, and resistance, as in the poems "Mayo de 1968 (Siglo XXI)" (May 1968, Twenty-first Century) and "Hiroshima mon amour," but others deal with individual everyday preoccupations and the little details of love relationships. These poems abound with neologisms, mostly unique combinations of common words, as well as unusual syntax, alliteration and assonance, and emphasis on the aural quality of the verses. They suggest, as does the title, the need for change not only in political and social structures but also in language itself.

In 1969 Adoum and his family moved to Geneva for a two-year period, during which he worked at the United Nations. He was transferred to UNESCO in Paris in 1971 and remained there for sixteen years, working, writing, and forming friendships with many of the Latin American writers and artists who were also living there. During this time he wrote his first play, *El sol bajo los patas de los caballos* (translated as *The Sun Trampled Beneath the Horses' Hooves* in the *Massachusetts Review*, 1974), which was first performed in Geneva and was published in 1981 in *Teatro, La subida a los infiernos, 1976* (Theater, The Ascent, and the Infernos, 1976); and his first novel, *Entre Marx y una mujer desnuda* (Between Marx and a Naked Woman), which is subtitled "Texto con personajes" (A text with characters), was published in 1978. He also published two collections of poetry, *Prepoemas en postespañol* (Pre-Poems in Post-Spanish) in 1975 and *Informe personal sobre la situación* (Personal Report on the Situation) in 1973.

In *Prepoemas en postespañol* the linguistic emphasis is central, as the title of the collection indicates. There are still the same concerns as in the previous works—politics, love, death—but the priority is the word itself. Again there are unusual combinations of ordinary words with an emphasis on the way they sound when spoken. All of these features are evident in the poem "Pasadología" (Pastology). The title suggests a critique of outmoded ways of thinking and demonstrates, as do the verses of the poem, that a new language—an appropriation of the Castillian Spanish imposed centuries earlier—is fundamental to new ways of thinking and, thus, of living. The poem accents the character of the words when spoken, with repetition of *contra* (against or counter) in the litany of ideologies, traditions, and systems that are criticized as illogical and counterproductive. The poems of this collection are reminiscent of the work of the Peruvian poet César Vallejo in their emphasis on the power of words and the importance of reclaiming an autochthonous voice within the confines of an imposed or an inherited linguistic system. The poems of *Informe personal sobre la situación* are equally political in theme but more traditional in form as they were mostly written some years earlier.

Adoum finally returned to Ecuador in 1987 and has resided in his native land since then. Although he spent almost twenty-five years of his life in exile, either forced or voluntary, the vast majority of his work concerns Ecuador and Latin America. Since his return home he has published only one collection of new poems, *Ecuador: Señas particulares* (Ecuador: Special Signs), in 1998. He has, however, published several anthologies of his poetry as well as two novels, *Ciudad sin ángel* (City without an Angel) in 1995 and *Los amores fugaces: Memorias imaginarias* (Fleeting Loves: Imaginary Memories) in 1997, and various literary and critical studies, including his tribute to the Ecuadoran *Indigenista* painter Oswaldo Guayasamín, *Guayasamín: El hombre, la obra, la crítica* (Guayasamín: The Man, the Work, the Criticism), published in 1998.

In 1979 Adoum published the anthology *No son todos los que están: Poemas, 1949–1979* (Not All Those Who Are Here Are [Crazy]: Poems, 1949–1979). Twenty years later, he published the most complete collection of his poetry, *. . . ni están todos los que son* (. . . Not All Those Who Are [Crazy] Are Here). Each of the titles is half of a well-known Spanish proverb. Another anthology, *Postales del trópico con mujeres,* edited and introduced by Vallvey, is divided into four sections: "Postales del trópico con mujeres"; "Sobre la inutilidad de la semiología" (On the Uselessness of Semiology); "Tras la pólvora, Manuela" (After the Gunpowder, Manuela), in which Adoum invents poems that Simón Bolívar, the leader of the independence movement in Latin America, might have written to his mistress, Manuela; and "El amor desenterrado" (Unearthed Love). All of these works are faithful to the tradition that Adoum has established, focusing on the loves and fears of individuals and of civilizations and on the power of words and of poetry. These poems, however, are sparer than his earlier works, indicative of the poet's effort to shed description and to hone his words in order to get to the core of his concerns. Thus, they reflect Adoum's years of personal contact with Asian cultures. Although he admits that the rigors of Zen practice never appealed to him, he respects Eastern religions and appreciates the cultures, as well as the literature and art, that are informed by them. Adoum has also acknowledged that it was difficult to free himself from the influence of Neruda, and that he sought inspiration in the works of other poets in the effort to do so. These later poems are evidence that he found his poetic voice; it is both angry and awed, as in the earlier works, but more ironic, more colloquial, and more humorous.

. . . ni están todos los que son includes a prologue by Jorge Enrique Adoum that summarizes his commitment to his craft and acknowledges the heritage that he endeavors to maintain. Noting that it is not, in his opinion, mere coincidence that four of the five Nobel laureates from Latin America are poets, he concludes: "toda la poesía de nuestro continente era telúrica, en su doble vertiente de tierra y poblador: sello imborrable, marca ineludible, seña de identidad sin la cual, al parecer, el poeta no encontraba justificación para su canto o no era latinoamericano" (all the poetry of our continent has been telluric, in its double flow of land and inhabitant: an indelible stamp, an inevitable mark, a sign of identity without which, it seems, the poet found no justification for his or her song, or was not Latin American). Adoum continues to speak, to write, and to "sing" of Latin America, and of the power of love and of words.

Interview:

Carlos Calderón Chico, *Jorge Enrique Adoum: Entrevista en dos tiempos* (Quito: Editorial Universitaria, 1988).

References:

Angel Flores, *Spanish American Authors: The Twentieth Century* (New York: Wilson, 1992), pp. 3–11;

Aldo Pellegrini, *Antología de la poesía viva latino-americana* (Barcelona: Seix Barral, 1966), pp. 165–170.

Claribel Alegría

(12 May 1924 –   )

Ana Patricia Rodríguez
University of Maryland, College Park

See also the Alegría entry in *DLB 145: Modern Latin-American Fiction Writers, Second Series.*

BOOKS: *Anillo de silencio* (Mexico City: Botas, 1948);

Suite de amor, angustia y soledad (Mendoza, Argentina: Brigadas Líricas, 1950);

Vigilias (Mexico City: Poesía de América, 1953);

Acuario (Santiago, Chile: Editorial Universitaria, 1955);

Tres cuentos (San Salvador: Ministerio de Cultura, 1958);

Huésped de mi tiempo (Buenos Aires: Américalee, 1961);

Vía única (Montevideo: Alfa, 1965);

Cenizas de Izalco, by Alegría and Darwin J. Flakoll (Barcelona: Seix Barral, 1966; San José, Costa Rica: Editorial Universitaria Centroamericana, 1982); translated by Flakoll as *Ashes of Izalco* (Willimantic, Conn.: Curbstone, 1989);

Aprendizaje (San Salvador: Universitaria de El Salvador, 1970);

Pagaré a cobrar y otros poemas (Barcelona: Ocnos, 1973);

El detén (Barcelona: Lumen, 1977); translated by Amanda Hopkinson as *The Talisman* in *Family Album* (Willimantic, Conn.: Curbstone, 1991);

Sobrevivo (Havana: Casa de las Américas, 1978);

La encrucijada salvadoreña, by Alegría and Flakoll (Barcelona: CIDOB, 1980);

Suma y sigue (Madrid: Visor, 1981);

Album familiar (San José, Costa Rica: Editorial Universitaria Centroamericana, 1982); translated by Hopkinson as *Family Album* in *Family Album;*

Flores del volcán/Flowers from the Volcano, bilingual edition, English translation by Carolyn Forché (Pittsburgh: University of Pittsburgh Press, 1982);

Nicaragua: La revolución sandinista–Una crónica política, 1855–1979, by Alegría and Flakoll (Mexico City: Era, 1982);

No me agarran viva: La mujer salvadoreña en la lucha, by Alegría and Flakoll (Mexico City: Era, 1983; San Salvador: Universidad Centroamericana Editores, 1987); translated by Hopkinson as *They Won't Take Me Alive: Salvadorean Women in Struggle*

Claribel Alegría

for National Liberation (London: Women's Press, 1987);

Poesía viva (London: Blackrose, 1983);

Para romper el silencio: Resistencia y lucha en las cárceles salvadoreñas, by Alegría and Flakoll (Mexico City: Era, 1984);

Pueblo de Dios y de Mandinga (Mexico City: Era, 1985); translated by Hopkinson as *Village of God and the Devil* in *Family Album;*

Petit pays (Paris: Editions des Femmes, 1985);

Despierta, mi bien, despierta (San Salvador: Universidad Centroamericana Editores, 1986);

Luisa en el país de la realidad (Mexico City: Universidad Autónoma de Zacatecas, 1987); translated by Flakoll as *Luisa in Realityland* (Willimantic, Conn.: Curbstone, 1987);

Mujer del río (Colombia: Museo Rayo, 1987); translated by Flakoll as *Woman of the River* (Pittsburgh: University of Pittsburgh Press, 1989);

Y este poema río (Managua: Nueva Nicaragua, 1988);

Fuga de canto grande (San Salvador: Universidad Centroamericana Editores, 1992); translated by Flakoll as *Tunnel to Canto Grande* (Willimantic, Conn.: Curbstone, 1996);

Fugues, bilingual edition, translated by Flakoll (Willimantic, Conn.: Curbstone, 1993);

Somoza: Expediente cerrado: La historia de un ajusticiamiento, by Alegría and Flakoll (Managua: El Gato Negro, 1993); translated by Flakoll as *Death of Somoza* (Willimantic, Conn.: Curbstone, 1996);

Variaciones en clave de mi (Madrid: Libertarias/Prodhufi, 1993);

Umbrales/Thresholds: Poems, bilingual edition, English translation by Flakoll (Willimantic, Conn.: Curbstone, 1996);

El niño que buscaba a Ayer/The Boy Who Searched for Yesterday, bilingual edition, illustrations by Ricardo Radosh (New York: Lectorum, 1997);

Saudade/Sorrow, bilingual edition, English translation by Forché (Willimantic, Conn.: Curbstone, 1999);

Soltando Amarras/Casting Off, translated by Margaret Sayers Peden (Willimantic, Conn.: Curbstone, 2003).

OTHER: *New Voices of Hispanic America,* edited and translated by Alegría and Darwin J. Flakoll (Boston: Beacon, 1962);

Unstill Life: An Introduction to the Spanish Poetry of Latin America, edited by Mario Benedetti, translated by Alegría and Flakoll (New York: Harcourt, Brace & World, 1970);

Robert Graves, *Cien poemas de Robert Graves,* translated by Alegría and Flakoll (Barcelona: Lumen, 1981);

Nuevas voces de Norteamérica, edited and translated by Alegría and Flakoll (Barcelona: Plaza & Janés, 1981);

Alberto Corazón, ed., *Homenaje a El Salvador,* introduction by Alegría (Madrid: Visor, 1981);

"The Writer's Commitment," in *Lives on the Line: The Testimony of Contemporary Latin American Authors,* edited by Doris Meyer (Berkeley, Los Angeles & London: University of California Press, 1988), pp. 308–311;

On the Front Line: Guerrilla Poetry of El Salvador, edited and translated by Alegría and Flakoll (Willimantic, Conn.: Curbstone, 1989);

"Our Little Region," in *Being América: Essays on Art, Literature, and Identity from Latin America,* edited by Rachel Weiss and Alan West (Fredonia, N.Y.: White Pine, 1991), pp. 41–50.

SELECTED PERIODICAL PUBLICATION–
UNCOLLECTED: "Clash of Cultures," *Index on Censorship,* 15, no. 8 (September 1986): 28–30.

Claribel Alegría is one of the most respected and prolific writers of Central America. Since the late 1940s she has written more than forty books across many literary genres, including novels, novellas, stories, essays, *testimonios* (testimonials), children's stories, and poetry. Her works have been published in more than fourteen languages throughout Europe, Latin America, and the United States. With Darwin J. "Bud" Flakoll, her husband and partner in writing, Alegría has translated and edited other writers' work, produced anthologies, and cowritten novels, *testimonios,* and journalistic exposés. She has lectured and read widely from her work in diverse international media and academic forums, especially during the 1980s, when she was recognized unofficially as cultural ambassador of El Salvador in exile. In "The Writer's Commitment" (which first appeared in the journal *Fiction International* in 1984) Alegría identified herself as a profoundly "committed writer," one who envisions social change, struggles for human rights, and produces a transformational "literature of emergency." Tracing her own political and literary transformations, she explains that, early in her life, she wrote poetry without knowing "what was happening in my country–El Salvador–or my region–Central America." The Cuban Revolution in 1959, the Sandinista Revolutionary Period in Nicaragua from 1979 to 1989, the Salvadoran Civil War from 1979 to 1991, and her own personal relationship to these historical events transformed her writing. These social movements and historical moments indelibly marked both her prose and poetry.

Born in Estelí, Nicaragua, on 12 May 1924, Clara Isabel Alegría Vides was taken to live in El Salvador by her parents at the age of six months. A binational citizen and international traveler, she has claimed Nicaragua as her *matria* (motherland) and El Salvador as her *patria* (fatherland). Her father, Daniel Alegría, was a Nicaraguan citizen and medical doctor who was exiled from Nicaragua after expressing his discontent with the United States Marine occupation of Nicaragua, critiquing the Somocista repression of peasants and dissidents in his country, and voicing support for the revolution-

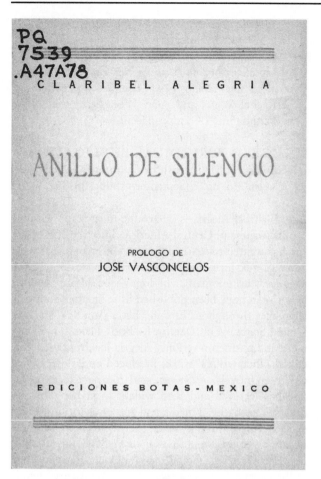

Paperback cover for Alegría's first book (1948). The Mexican philosopher José Vasconcelos had suggested Claribel Alegría as the pen name for Clara Isabel Alegría Vides (Richter Library, University of Miami).

ary forces of Augusto César Sandino. Although he never returned to Nicaragua, Alegría's father remained a fervent supporter of Sandino's ideals in Central America. Upon being terrorized by the Nicaraguan National Guard, the Alegría family fled to the northwestern department of Santa Ana in El Salvador, the home of Alegría's mother, Ana María Vides. There, Alegría grew up as a member of the landed coffee oligarchy, to which her mother's family belonged.

Alegría was reared amid the privilege of her socio-economic class, although from an early age she demonstrated a sense of autonomy and free thought, electing to attend public schools rather than the private parochial schools preferred by her siblings. In a 2000 interview with Antonio Velásquez, Alegría explains that in Santa Ana she had access to good libraries, wherein she began to read at an early age. Her parents introduced her to the poetry of the Spanish Golden Age, including that of San Juan de la Cruz and Santa Teresa,

and many Latin American writers, among them Rubén Darío, Gabriela Mistral, and Rómulo Gallegos. She learned at an early age that she wanted to be a poet, thereby challenging prescribed gender roles and traditions of Salvadoran elite society.

In 1943, perhaps seeking other directions for herself and her artistic production, Alegría moved to the United States to attend George Washington University in Washington, D.C., where she earned a bachelor's degree in philosophy and letters. In 1948 Alegría published her first book of poetry, *Anillo de silencio* (Ring of Silence), for which the Mexican philosopher and writer José Vasconcelos wrote the prologue. In his travels through Central America, Vasconcelos met the young Clara Isabel Alegría Vides. Vasconcelos, according to sources, suggested to her the pen name of Claribel Alegría. During her residence in Washington, D.C., in the late 1940s and early 1950s, Alegría met the Spanish poet Juan Ramón Jiménez, whom she called her mentor. In her interview with Velásquez, Alegría affirms that "Juan Ramón Jiménez fue, en ese sentido, muy estricto conmigo y me decía que había que tener oficio para ser poeta, para ser novelista, y yo nunca había tenido un oficio de narradora, solamente de poeta" (Juan Ramón Jiménez was, in a sense, very strict with me and he would tell me that one has to have vocation to be a poet, a novelist, and I only wanted to be a poet, not a prose writer). Despite her initiation in poetry, Alegría has been recognized both for her poetry and prose. In 1978 her book *Sobrevivo* (I Survive) received Cuba's Casa de las Américas prize for poetry, while her novel *Cenizas de Izalco* (1966; translated as *Ashes of Izalco*, 1989), cowritten with her husband, was the first Central American novel published by the prestigious Seix Barral of Barcelona.

While studying at George Washington University, Alegría met Flakoll, a student studying journalism and diplomacy, whom she married in 1947. Together they formed a deep partnership that lasted a lifetime of family commitments, worldwide travels, and writing projects. They lived in the United States, Mexico, Argentina, Chile, France, Spain, and Nicaragua, meeting many writers with whom they collaborated on various projects. During that period of living as expatriates, Alegría and Flakoll produced poetry anthologies, in which they compiled and translated the work of international writers. These anthologies include *New Voices of Hispanic America* (1962), *Unstill Life: An Introduction to the Spanish Poetry of Latin America* (1970), *Cien poemas de Robert Graves* (One Hundred Poems of Robert Graves, 1981), *Nuevas voces de Norteamérica* (New Voices of North America, 1981), and *On the Front Line: Guerrilla Poetry of El Salvador* (1989). While living in Paris from 1962 to 1966, Alegría and Flakoll met the writers of the Spanish

American "Boom" who resided in that city. The couple became lifelong friends of the Argentine Julio Cortázar, who participated in their enthusiasm and support of the Sandinista Revolution until his death. Flakoll and Alegría lived for years in Deyá, on the island of Majorca in Spain, which serves as the setting for the novella *Pueblo de Dios y de Mandinga* (1985; translated as *Village of God and the Devil,* 1991).

In 1979 Alegría and Flakoll relocated to Nicaragua to join the Sandinista reconstruction efforts. They cowrote an historical text, *Nicaragua: La revolución sandinista–Una crónica política, 1855–1979* (Nicaragua: The Sandinista Revolution–A Political Chronicle, 1855–1979, 1982), and produced several anthologies of poetry and prose, published in solidarity with the revolutionary movement in El Salvador. During this period Alegría and Flakoll were prolific, publishing *La encrucijada salvadoreña* (The Salvadoran Crossroads, 1980), *Homenaje a El Salvador,* and *On the Front Line.* They also collaborated in the writing of testimonial and resistance texts such as *No me agarran viva: La mujer salvadoreña en la lucha* (1983; translated as *They Won't Take Me Alive: Salvadorean Women in Struggle for National Liberation,* 1987), *Fuga de Canto Grande* (1992; translated as *Tunnel to Canto Grande,* 1996), and *Somoza: Expediente cerrado: La historia de un ajusticiamiento* (1993; translated as *Death of Somoza,* 1996). Alegría explained to Velásquez that, in this testimonial production, it was Flakoll who took charge: "En los testimonios los dos escribimos todo, pero él sabía estructurarlos mejor porque era periodista" (We wrote everything in the testimonies, but he knew how to structure them better than I since he was a journalist).

Many critics have marveled at Alegría and Flakoll's personal and professional relationship, often asking them to explain the secret of their success. In a 1990 interview with David Volpendesta, Alegría explained that Flakoll "at the beginning of our marriage, was my critic in poetry." In his *Gestos ceremoniales: Narrativa centroamericana, 1960–1990* (Ceremonial Gestures: Central American Narrative, 1998), the critic Arturo Arias suggests that Alegría and Flakoll's collaboration manifests a new north-south sensibility in Alegría's work, which transgresses the stereotypes ascribed to both North Americans and Central Americans and facilitates a better understanding between both peoples. Married to a progressive North American man, Alegría, according to Arias, was forced to "confrontar esa otreadad que era constitutiva de su ser" (confront an otherness that was part of her being) and to adopt a "transformativa" (transformative) and transnational perspective.

Equally known for her poetry and prose innovations, Alegría describes her work as sui generis. Her first novel, *Cenizas de Izalco,* and her novellas—*Luisa en el país de la realidad* (1987; translated as *Luisa in Realityland*), *Despierta, mi bien, despierta* (Awaken, My Love, Awaken, 1986), *El detén* (1977; translated as *The Talisman,* 1991), *Album familiar* (1982; translated as *Family Album,* 1991), and *Pueblo de Dios y de Mandinga,* the last three of which are collected in an English translation titled *Family Album* (1991)—combine various literary genres in single texts. Alegría's novels and novellas incorporate literary forms such as poetry, diaries, and letters to produce the effect of a literary montage or collage. This interpolation and mixing of literary forms articulates, at times, multiple voices and perspectives. Alegría populates her texts with members of the aristocracy and exploited groups, foreign travelers, and subjects of all classes, genders, ages, and political positions. Converging in single texts, these voices represent the constructed nature of literature and the complex mosaic of Salvadoran society. Although appearing sometimes deceptively simple and written in girls' voices, Alegria's prose texts, especially *Cenizas de Izalco* and the novellas, question the foundations of Salvadoran traditional values, social hierarchies, and power structures, which are embedded in the ideals of family, home, nation, and reality. Sometimes possessing a poetic quality, as in the case of *Luisa en el país de la realidad,* Alegría's prose narratives are also highly lyrical and enigmatic. Her poetry and prose narrative, hence, cannot be separated, although in her interview with Velásquez, Alegría claimed, "En realidad creo que mi pasión es la poesía" (In reality, I think my passion is for poetry).

Alegría began her literary career writing poetry, which has remained a constant endeavor throughout her life. She has written many books of poetry, including *Anillo de silencio, Suite de amor, angustia y soledad* (The Suite of Love, Anxiety, and Solitude, 1950), *Vigilias* (Vigils, 1953), *Acuario* (Aquarius or Aquarium, 1955), *Huésped de mi tiempo* (Guest of My Time, 1961), *Vía única* (One Way, 1965), *Aprendizaje* (Learning, 1970), *Pagaré a cobrar y otros poemas* (Paid on Delivery and Other Poems, 1973), *Sobrevivo, Suma y sigue* (Sum Up and Continue, 1981), *Flores del volcán/Flowers from the Volcano* (1982), *Poesía viva* (Living Poetry, 1983), *Mujer del río* (1987; translated as *Woman of the River,* 1989), *Y este poema río* (And This River Poem, 1988), *Fugues* (1993), *Variaciones en clave de mi* (Variations in the Key of Me, 1993), *Umbrales/Thresholds: Poems* (1996), and *Saudade/Sorrow* (1999). Flakoll and Carolyn Forché have faithfully translated many of Alegría's poems, although some of these books of poetry have not been translated into English, especially her earliest works. Throughout these works Alegría has produced poems that are lyrical, self-reflective, and intimate and that speak to the universal themes of joy, love, desire, anger, angst, sadness, loss, melancholy, and mourning. At the same time, her poetry has responded to the sociopolitical

Alegría with her husband and frequent collaborator, Darwin J. Flakoll (photograph by José María Berenguer; from the cover for Cenizas de Izalco, *1966; Jane and Alexander Heard Library, Vanderbilt University)*

struggles in Central America, increasingly becoming self-referential and critical of power structures in the region. Poetry has remained a constant in Alegría's life, and with the passing of her husband in 1995 she has returned to poetry in her later projects.

According to Alegría, her poetry is not political but rather a "mis poemas son poemas de amor a mis pueblos" (love poetry for her people), an ideal that is most apparent in her poems such as "Tamalitos de Cambray" (Little Cambray Tamales), "Mujer del río" (Woman of the River), "Documental" (Documentary), all published in *Mujer del Río,* and other poems dedicated to the memory of fallen Central American writers and revolutionaries such as Roque Dalton. Along with the Salvadoran poet Dalton, who claimed in his 1977 poem "Como tú" (Like You) that "la poesía es como el pan, de todos" (poetry, like bread, is for everyone), Alegría produces literature that is accessible to a wide range of readers. In the field of contemporary poetry, she draws from the poetic traditions of Central American *exteriorismo* (exterior poetry), Latin American conversational political poetry, and the international decolonizing militancy of engaged poets of the mid to late twentieth century. Alegría's poems abound with concrete images, historical allusions, colloquialisms, and revolutionary themes. Her "Ars poética," from *Fugues,* celebrates the literary craft that brings her closer to political awakening and understanding of the transformational power of commonplace objects and experiences. In the images of the crow, sun,

valleys, volcanoes, and debris of war the poet is able to "catch sight of the promised land."

Her book of poetry *Mujer del río* overflows with images of water, trees, and leaves, all intermingling in the poet's memory. In "Desde el puente" (From the Bridge) the poet recounts the passing of her life as "the water flows below," and she rushes to remember "la masacre / que dejó sin hombres" (the massacre / that left Izalco without men) that she witnessed at the age of seven. The adult poet asks herself, "cómo podré explicarte / que no cambiado nada / y que siguen matando diariamente?" (How can I explain to you / nothing has changed / they keep on killing people daily?). By the end of "Desde el puente" the committed poet questions an intellectualism masked in philosophy and a poetry detached from life, one that "cuidadsomente omitían / la inmundicia que nos rodea / desde siempre" (carefully omitted / the filth / that has always / surrounded all). With resolve, Alegría's committed poet grows claws and beaks in order to survive the "tufo a carroña" (stench of carrion) left behind by the destruction of El Salvador. In 2000, when interviewed by Velásquez, Alegría reconfirmed her lifelong endeavor to produce literature committed to universal themes, local struggles, and common people. She states that "Para mí el oficio de escribir es un oficio como tantos otros, y así como el zapatero tiene que hacer buenos zapatos, el escritor está llamado a comunicar, a comunicar ideas, sentimientos" (For me the craft of writing is a craft like

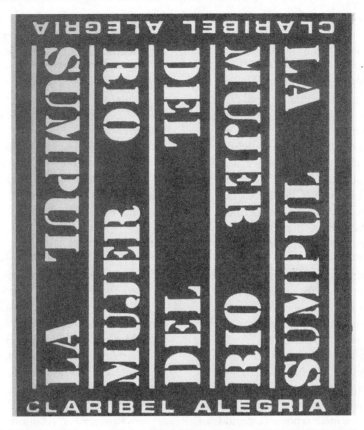

Title page for Alegría's 1987 poetry collection. It includes "Desde el puente," in which she remembers a massacre
of Salvadoran villagers she witnessed as a child (Walter Royal Davis Library,
University of North Carolina at Chapel Hill).

many others. Like the shoemaker has to make good shoes, the writer is called to communicate, communicate ideas, feelings).

In "The Writer's Commitment" Alegría recognizes that with the wars in Central America, especially in El Salvador, her "poems took on an edge of protest." She also began to write more narrative texts that assumed marginal testimonial perspectives. She dedicated herself to developing parallel yet intertwined projects: the "literary-poetic" and "crisis journalism"—in other words, poetry and prose narrative. Many critics analyze Alegría's multifaceted literary production, paying particular attention to her representation of women, social movements, revolution, and history. They examine Alegría's early use of fantastic literature, feminist discourse, and *testimonios.* In 1994 Sandra M. Boschetto-Sandoval and Marcia Phillips McGowan published *Claribel Alegría and Central American Literature,* an anthology of critical essays on Alegría's work, in which critics such as Arias, Jorge Rufinelli, Ileana Rodríguez, Margaret Crosby, Boschetto-Sandoval, and Phillips McGowan discuss Alegría's lifelong commitment to producing socially, politically, and artistically engaged literature. Along these lines, the critic George Yúdice, in "Letras

de emergencia: Claribel Alegría" (Literature of Emergency: Claribel Alegría, 1985), examines Alegría's production of "letras de emergencia," an emergent and urgent literature. Whether in poetic or prose form, Alegría's texts respond to particular historical conditions and represent distinct literary discourses and perspectives such as the testimonial voices of female revolutionary fighters and marginalized people.

According to Arias, Alegría is the initiator of a new wave of Central American poetic and prose narrative in the 1960s. Although living most of her adult life outside of Central America, Alegría is associated with a generation of committed writers in El Salvador such as Dalton, Manlio Argueta, and Matilde Elena López. Like these writers, Alegría addresses political, historical, and cultural issues and challenges power structures and hierarchies in El Salvador. She has pushed the limits of social realism and linear narrative, fusing poetry and prose in her experimental texts and crossing the lines between history and literature. Her poetry reconstructs historical events such as the conquest of El Salvador and "La Matanza" (The Massacre) in 1932, in which more than thirty thousand peasant and indigenous people were killed almost overnight in El Salvador by the military government of General Maximiliano Hernández Martínez. The dictator Martínez virtually erased this event from the public record by having all related documentation destroyed. Rectifying this act of "lobotomía cultural" (cultural lobotomy), as Alegría calls it in "Clash of Cultures," an essay for the September 1986 issue of *Index on Censorship,* Alegría's work preserves and retells the history of the massacre for generations of Salvadorans, who read her poetry and prose in school. In lieu of proper documentation, Alegría's personal memories and poetry restore the lost memory of the Salvadoran people. As she explains in "Clash of Cultures," she and Flakoll "had to reconstruct from my childhood memories when I was seven years old and what grownups had told me in hushed tones as I grew older."

Alegría and Flakoll's life of partnership and collaboration ended with his death on 15 April 1995, a loss so great that Alegría was moved to write a farewell book of poetry, *Saudade/Sorrow.* According to her, the Portuguese word *saudade* refers to the deep sense of loss and sadness experienced with the death of a loved one. Alegría has continued to live in Managua, Nicaragua, where her neighbors include the Nicaraguan writers Ernesto Cardenal and Sergio Ramírez.

Claribel Alegría's prose narrative and narrative poetry withstood one of the most repressive periods in Central American history. Writers such as Alegría sought a revolution in form and content, but always with the idea that literature belongs to people and might speak with them, not for them. Hence, *testimonio* and testimonial poetry has been a strong discursive current in Central America. Alegría's command of multiple literary genres, including prose and poetry, undoubtedly has placed her at the vanguard of political, solidarity, feminist, and third-world literary movements. During her lifetime she has worked tirelessly to put Central America on the literary map and to make literature, especially poetry, "a basic human right" within reach of all people.

Interviews:

David Volpendesta, "Enjoy the Kingdom of Heaven: A Conversation with Claribel Alegría and Bud Flakoll," *Poetry Flash,* 206 (May 1990): 1, 11, 23;

Antonio Velásquez, "Claribel Alegría," *Hispamérica,* 29, no. 86 (2000): 83–92.

References:

Arturo Arias, "Claribel Alegría: Los recuerdos del porvenir," in *Gestos ceremoniales: Narrativa centroamericana, 1960–1990* (Guatemala City: Artemis & Edinter, 1998), pp. 57–80;

Sandra M. Boschetto-Sandoval and Marcia Phillips McGowan, eds., *Claribel Alegría and Central American Literature* (Athens: Ohio University Center for International Studies, 1994);

Linda J. Craft, "Claribel Alegría: Family Ties/Political Lies," in her *Novels of Testimony and Resistance from Central America* (Gainesville: University of Florida Press, 1997), pp. 72–105;

Eugenio Martínez Orantes, *32 escritores salvadoreños: De Francisco Gavidia a David Escobar Galindo* (San Salvador: Martínez Orantes, 1993), pp. 199–206;

George Yúdice, "Letras de emergencia: Claribel Alegría," *Revista Iberoamericana,* 51, nos. 132–133 (July–December 1985): 953–964.

Jorge Artel

(27 April 1909 – 19 August 1994)

Delmarie Martínez
Nova University

BOOKS: *Tambores en la noche, 1931–1934* (Cartagena, Colombia: Bolívar, 1940; revised and enlarged edition, Guanajuato, Mexico: Universidad de Guanajuato, 1955);

Luz verde a Jorge Turner (Panama: Republica de Panama, 1960);

Poemas con botas y banderas (Barranquilla, Colombia: Universidad del Atlántico, 1972);

Sinú, riberas de asombro jubiloso (Barranquilla, Colombia: Universidad del Atlántico, 1972);

Antología poética (Bogotá: Ecoe, 1979);

No es la muerte es el morir (Bogotá: Ecoe, 1979);

Cantos y poemas (Bogotá: Presidencia de la República, 1983).

Editions: *Antología poética* (Medellín, Colombia: Universidad de Antioquia, 1986);

Cantos y poemas (Medellín, Colombia: Universidad de Antioquia, 1986);

Tambores en la noche, prologue by José Consuegra Higgins (Bogotá: Plaza & Janés, 1986).

PLAY PRODUCTION: *De Rigurasa Etiqueta,* Panama, 1964.

RECORDINGS: *La voz de Jorge Artel antologia,* read by Artel, Bogotá, HJCK LP-129, 1960–1969;

Tambores en la noche, read by Artel and song versions by Leonor González Mina, Sonolux LP 12-523.

SELECTED PERIODICAL PUBLICATIONS– UNCOLLECTED:

POETRY

"Al oído de Reagan," *Revista Mefisto de la Literatura Latinoamericana,* 2 (December 1986/January–February 1987): 26.

NONFICTION

"La literatura negra en la Costa: Carta de Jorge Artel a Gregorio Espinosa," *Tiempo,* 15 July 1932, p. 6;

"Modalidades artísticas de la raza negra," *Muros,* 1 (June 1940): 16–20;

Jorge Artel (Collection of Zoila Esquivia Vásquez de Artel)

"Presentación de Nicolás Guillén," *Voces de América,* 21 (June 1946): 385–390;

"Leyenda y realidad de la Costa Atlántica," *Cromos,* 20 November 1948, pp. 4–5, 37–38;

"Artel visto por Artel," *País,* 15 September 1959, p. 5.

Jorge Artel wrote in genres as diverse as poetry, novels, essays, and short stories. Although a lawyer by profession, he became a prolific journalist who published articles on a variety of topics such as politics, folklore, music, art, literature, and cinema. He is also the author of the novel *No es la muerte es el morir* (It Is Not Death, It Is Dying, 1979). Despite his contributions in these genres, Artel is known primarily for his poetry; his poems have gained him the reputation of being "the preeminent poet of black expression in contemporary Colombia," as Laurence E. Prescott noted in *Without Hatreds or Fears: Jorge Artel and the Struggle for Black Literary Expression in Colombia* (2000).

Artel is the pseudonym of Agapito de Arco Coneo. He was born on 27 April 1909 in the city of Cartagena, a former Spanish colonial trading port for black slaves, on the northern Atlantic coast of Colombia. His parents, Miguel de Arco Orozco and Aura Coneo González, died when the poet was still young, and he was raised under the tutelage of two of his aunts. At the age of thirteen, Artel founded the newspaper *Nuevo Horizonte* (New Horizon), which was later named *Aspiraciones* (Aspirations) and finally became a serial called *Ariel*.

Artel's poetic production started at the age of twenty-one when he began publishing poems and writing articles for various newspapers from the coastal region. The beginning of his literary career coincided with the Jazz Age of the 1920s, when African art and folklore were in vogue in Paris and the United States. This American and European interest in black culture also made its way into South America and the Antilles, where its artistic manifestations in Spanish acquired the name of *negrismo*. The *negrista* movement reflects the artistic, musical, social, and spiritual values of a black culture that struggled to define its identity amid the oppression of the prevailing system. Artel's *negrismo* is reflected in the forty-six poems he wrote between 1931 and 1934, which he collected in *Tambores en la noche* (Drums in the Night, 1940), his first and best-known book of poems. This collection was printed in an edition of 1,500 copies published at the poet's expense. Prescott, one of Artel's most important critics, wrote in "*El tambor:* Symbol and Substance in the Poetry of Jorge Artel" (1984) that *Tambores en la noche* "celebrates the music, ambience, and people of the Negroid coast while evoking the omnipresent spirit of the African ancestors." The *tambor* (drum), an ever-present image in these poems, stands as a tangible symbol for the voices and sounds of black culture, as in the titular poem of the collection:

Trémulos de música les he oído gemir,
cuando esos hombres que llevan
la emoción en las manos
les arrancan la angustia de una oscura saudade
de una íntima añoranza,

donde vigila el alma dulcemente salvaje
de mi vibrante raza,
con sus siglos mojados en quejumbres de gaitas

(Trembling with music I have heard them cry
when those men who carry
their feelings in their hands
wrench the agony of a dark sadness
of a deep nostalgia
where the sweetly savage soul
of my vibrant race watches
with centuries buried in the lament of the bagpipes).

In an essay about Artel included in *30 Latinoamericanos en el recuerdo* (Remembrance of 30 Latin Americans, 1998), Jorge Turner highlights three fundamental characteristics of *Tambores en la noche*. First, Artel incorporates the poetic style of the coastal regions to that of Colombia's high plain, bringing notoriety to the folklore of the coast. This achievement is evidenced by the profound impact of his poetry in the capital city of Bogotá. Artel's poetic message is "heard" in the geographically secluded Bogotá, thus, bringing to the somber city the sentiment of the black coast. Second, Turner recognizes the merit of the lyricism that characterizes Artel's poetry; a fact that is also underlined by Prescott in "Spirit-Voices: Jorge Artel's Poetic Odyssey of the Afro-American Soul" (1982). Prescott affirms that the poet does not employ onomatopoeic and alliterative devices like other *negrista* poets; instead, Artel aims to uncover a deeper significance, as reflected in poems written between 1931 and 1933, such as "La cumbia" (The Cumbia). This poem shows the sensual nature of the *cumbia,* a notorious dance of African origin that has become part of Colombian tradition:

la cumbia frenética,
la diabólica cumbia,
pone a cabalgar su ritmo oscuro
sobre las caderas ágiles
de las sensuales hembras

(the frenetic cumbia
the diabolic cumbia
a dark rhythm that gallops
over the swift hips
of sensual women).

The third contribution of Artel's poetry, according to Turner, stems from the poet's decisive approach for a radical ideological change in Colombian politics, where traditionally the liberal and conservative parties barely differ in tone. In Artel's view it is possible to find a conservative who is more progressive than a liberal. He indicates the need for a third sociopolitical solution, one that is different from those already provided by the two Colombian traditional parties. His poetry reflects the

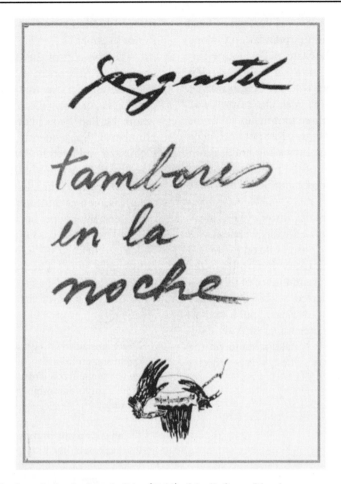

Paperback cover for the revised and enlarged edition (1955) of Artel's first and best-known poetry collection, originally published in 1940 (from Laurence E. Prescott, Without Hatreds or Fears: Jorge Artel and the Struggle for Black Literary Expression in Colombia, *2000)*

desire for a philosophical context that reflects man as a universal figure outside the realm of imposed categories that deter him in his quest for freedom.

These three points outlined by Turner underline Artel's awareness of the political role of the poet. Indeed, Artel views himself as a poet of the people and a representative of the sociopolitical causes that affect them. In "Modalidades artísticas de la raza negra" (Artistic Modalities of the Black Race, June 1940), based on a public address Artel gave at the Feria del Libro (Book Fair) in Cartagena that year, he stated that "La raza negra no trajo del África solamente ruidos, danzas sensuales y sensualizantes, sino también un profundo dolor humano, del que debe hacer trasunto el poeta que hoy quiera servir de puente emocional e histórico entre nuestros abuelos esclavos desaparecidos y la humanidad presente. Y debemos hacer una paréntesis para decir que ésta es la misión social del poeta Negro" (The black race did not only bring from Africa noises, sensual and seductive dances, but also a deep sense of human pain, a pain that the poet must

acknowledge in order to serve today as an emotional and historical bridge between our disappeared slave forefathers and present-day humanity. And we must make a parenthesis to state that this is the social mission of the black poet). In "Spirit-Voices: Jorge Artel's Poetic Odyssey of the Afro-American Soul," Prescott adds that "Bridging the gulf between past and present, mulatto and black, Ibero- and Anglo-American, Artel's poems reveal the timeless universality of a people's experience. They unveil the fraternal bonds linking Americans of African descent; reaffirm the ageless dignity, strength and beauty of Afro-American identity; and, finally, show the poet to be an authentic and integral voice of black America."

Politics and social awareness continued to be two important forces in Artel's life, especially during the late 1930s and the 1940s. He had been actively involved in the Communist Party of Colombia since 1924 and served as secretary general of the First People's Party of Cartagena in 1937. In 1945 Artel obtained a law degree from the University of Cartagena, with a thesis on

"Defensa preventiva del Estado o el Derecho Penal frente a los problemas de la cultura popular en Colombia" (Preventive Defense of the State or Penal Law Facing the Problems of Popular Culture in Colombia). His continued political involvement with the Left, however, created difficult situations for the poet. On 9 April 1948 Artel was arrested and spent three months in jail at the naval base in Cartagena due to his leftist political ideology. This event, along with the increasing political turbulence after the assassination of the popular leader of the Liberal Party, Jorge Eliécer Gaitán, led him to flee Colombia in 1948.

Artel spent the next twenty-three years away from his homeland in self-imposed exile. Panama was the first stop on an extended journey through several countries, including Venezuela, Cuba, Puerto Rico, the United States, and Mexico. The turbulence of this era is represented by the poems collected in *Poemas con botas y banderas* (Poems with Boots and Flags), published in 1972. In this collection of seventeen poems, Artel deviates from the theme of *negrismo* to take a stand on the political upheaval of his country. These verses reflect a strong sociopolitical message:

> Brigadas de obreros,
> estudiantes y campesinos
> recogerán sus ecos
> sobre el curso indetenible que nos lleva
> a un mundo ileso,
> sin explotadores,
> oligarquías ni miseria
> y es esta la consigna:
> marchad, poemas!

> (Brigades of workers,
> students and farmers
> will gather their echoes
> over the unstoppable course that moves us
> to an unharmed world
> without exploiters
> oligarchies or misery
> and this is the order:
> march, poems!).

In the early 1950s Artel decided to move to the United States, and he lived in New York for six years. He worked as a translator for *Reader's Digest* and as a scriptwriter for the Latin American Division of United Nations Radio. In 1955 a second edition of *Tambores en la noche,* revised and expanded with twenty-one additional poems, was published in Guanajuato, Mexico, where Artel resided for a while. These poems, notes Prescott in "*El tambor:* Symbol and Substance in the Poetry of Jorge Artel," "are a lyrical record of the poet's real and imagined journey in search of the spiritual val-

ues and hidden meanings inherent in the African experience in America."

By the end of the decade Artel returned to Panama, where he worked as an editorialist for some of the main newspapers in that country. There he also met poet Ligia Alcázar, whom he married in 1959 and with whom he had two children, Jorge Nazim and Miguel Humberto. Subsequently, the family moved back to Colombia and lived in Barranquilla for several years.

In 1972 Artel published the collection *Sinú, riberas de asombro jubiloso* (Sinú, Riverbanks of Jubilant Wonderment), written as a tribute to the town of Montería and other nearby towns he remembered from his childhood. The book consists of twelve poems, seven of which are defined as "cantos" while the other five are individually titled. The collection has strong biographical tones, reflected in the way in which the poet intertwines the images of the river with those of his own identity:

> Desde mis arterias vegetales,
> que resumen calor de los zenúes,
> yo te exalto. Y con lenguas de fuego,
> junto al tuyo—inmortal—grabo mi nombre
> Montería

> (From within my arteries
> that reappraise the heat from the zenues
> I exalt you. And with tongues of fire
> next to you—immortal—I engrave my name
> Montería).

In 1974 the Artel family moved to Medellín, where the poet held a teaching position at the Universidad de Antioquia. In 1975 Artel began to write a column, "Señales de humo" (Smoke Signals), for the newspaper *El Colombiano* (The Colombian).

An aspect that in some ways distinguishes Artel's entire poetic production from that of other *negrista* poets is the fact that his verses do not focus solely on the sounds, rhythms, and images provided by the black world. Instead, he intertwines the Afro-Colombian culture and language with elements from other Colombian geographical areas and non-*negrista* cultural elements to create a poetry that, while deeply rooted in its African origins, is also a personal statement and a manifestation of his social awareness. In an interview titled "Jorge Artel, un poeta que toma aliento en la savia de su pueblo" (Jorge Artel, A Poet That Finds Strength in the Vitality of His People), which appeared in the July–September 1978 issue of the journal *Revista Aleph,* the poet stated that he does not necessarily consider himself exclusively as a black poet: "me considero como un poeta marino, un poeta con mucha nostalgia de la costa. En primer lugar no se podría decir que sea inte-

Paperback cover for Poemas con botas y banderas, *Artel's 1972 collection of poems written during his self-imposed twenty-three-year exile from Colombia (Jean and Alexander Heard Library, Vanderbilt University)*

gralmente negro, porque en mí habitan las tres razas: la negra, la blanca y la india" (I consider myself a poet of the sea, a poet with a nostalgic feel for the coast. In first place, it cannot be said that I am only black for I am a product of three races: black, white and Indian).

Prescott notes in *Without Hatreds or Fears* another aspect that differentiates Artel from other well-known twentieth-century Afro-Hispanic Antillean poets such as the Cubans Nicolás Guillén and Emilio Ballagas and the Puerto Rican writer Luis Palés Matos, three poets who are the acclaimed canonical models of Spanish American poetic *negrismo*. In contrast, however, South American authors of African descent such as Artel have found themselves "doubly marginalized." This marginalization contributes to the fact that their literary significance is often overlooked. In *"El tambor:* Symbol and Substance in the Poetry of Jorge Artel" Prescott adds that the Caribbean is generally recognized as the birthplace of Spanish American *negrismo,* and thus most critical studies center on the writers of the Caribbean islands, omitting other Spanish American authors who,

like Artel, come from other areas of the continent. In "Spirit-Voices: Jorge Artel's Poetic Odyssey of the Afro-American Soul" he suggests that Artel has not received the same attention given to other Afro-Antillean poets because of "Colombia's inveterate regionalism, the subtlety of its racial discrimination, and the problems that beset its publishing business."

Artel's work did begin to receive wide acknowledgment in the late 1970s, however. In 1977 the First Congress of Black Culture of the Americas met in Cali, Colombia, and openly paid homage to the work of Artel and fellow Colombian poet Helcías Martán Góngora for their contributions to black culture. In 1983 President Belisario Betancourt invited Artel to Casa Nariño, the presidential palace in Bogotá, to give a recital of his poems; and two years later, in 1985, the Universidad de Antioquia awarded him the National Prize for Poetry.

In 1983, after residing in Panama for a year, Artel returned to Colombia, where he spent the final eleven years of his life. He established his permanent residence in Barranquilla, where he held the post of librarian of the Universidad Simón Bolívar (Simon Bolivar University) and, on occasion, served as rector (acting president). Artel died at the age of eighty-five, on 19 August 1994. According to Prescott in a 1996 tribute in the *Afro-Hispanic Review,* he left behind a legacy as "one of the last voices of original black poetic expression that emerged in the 1930's and 1940's."

Extensive study of Artel's poetry is impeded by the lack of his books in print and the fact that most texts by and about Artel remain uncollected, dispersed throughout newspapers and journals in the Americas. An added difficulty is created by Artel's bohemian lifestyle and the twenty years he spent in self-imposed exile in various cities of North America, Central America, and South America.

These difficulties notwithstanding, Jorge Artel's groundbreaking work laid the foundation that many other Colombian poets have followed. Prescott credits Artel with becoming a leader of the younger generations of coastal artists. One may also summarize Artel's importance using the definition of a poet expressed by Artel himself in "La literatura negra en la Costa: Carta de Jorge Artel a Gregorio Espinosa" (15 July 1932), to which he held true throughout his life: "Para ser un poeta, un escritor o un artista negro, se necesita llevar dentro del alma, y saberles imprimir una elocuencia, todas aquellas 'emociones ancestrales,' el juego de los dolores, de las esperanzas, de los sueños suscitados en un pueblo, que hacen su aparición condensados en determinados espíritus" (To become a poet, a writer or a Black artist, one must carry within the soul, and be able to put into words, all those "ancestral emotions," the anguish, the hopes, the dreams of a people, that appear embodied in certain spirits).

Interviews:

Enrique Santos Molano, "Habla Jorge Artel: 'Hay Divorcio Notorio entre Artista y Público,'" *Tiempo,* 22 May 1966, p. 12;

Jesús María Ossa and Farid Numa, "Jorge Artel, un poeta que toma aliento en la savia de su pueblo," *Revista Aleph,* 26 (July–September 1978): 22–24, 29–30;

Edgardo Olier M. and Jorge García U., "Artel habla de su sangre en una terraza de Malambo," *Universal,* 18 May 1986, "Dominical," p. 12.

References:

Laurence E. Prescott, "Jorge Artel frente a Nicolás Guillén: Dos poetas mulatos ante la poesía negra hispanoamericana," in *Ensayos de literatura colombiana,* compiled by Raymond L. Williams (Bogotá: Plaza & Janés, 1984), pp. 129–136;

Prescott, "Remembering Jorge Artel," *Afro-Hispanic Review,* 15, no. 1 (1996): 1–3;

Prescott, "Spirit-Voices: Jorge Artel's Poetic Odyssey of the Afro-American Soul," *Perspectives on Contemporary Literature,* 8 (1982): 67–76;

Prescott, "*El tambor:* Symbol and Substance in the Poetry of Jorge Artel," *Afro-Hispanic Review,* 3, no. 2 (1984): 11–14;

Prescott, *Without Hatreds or Fears: Jorge Artel and the Struggle for Black Literary Expression in Colombia* (Detroit: Wayne State University Press, 2000);

Jorge Turner, *30 Latinoamericanos en el recuerdo* (Mexico City: La Jornada, 1998), pp. 147–152.

Antonio Ávila Jiménez

(3 June 1898 – 16 December 1965)

Álvaro A. Ayo
University of Tennessee, Knoxville

BOOKS: *cronos* (La Paz: Ilustraciones de Fuente Lira, 1939);

signo (La Paz: Minerva, 1942);

las almas (La Paz: Renacimiento, 1950);

poemas, introduction by Jacobo Liberman (La Paz: Biblioteca Paceña, 1957);

Obras completas (La Paz: Empresa Editora Urquizo, 1988).

Antonio Ávila Jiménez is the author of only three books of poems, but his name is often mentioned among the most important Bolivian poets of the first half of the twentieth century. The quality of his work has never been questioned, and yet there is no critical consensus on either how to categorize his poetry or where to place it within the history of Bolivian literature. Many experts underline the intimate tone of his poetry and the brevity of his compositions, while those who knew him personally mention his sensitive and captivating personality, his vast culture, and his elegant demeanor. He titled his three books of poems *cronos* (chronos, 1939), *signo* (sign, 1942), and *las almas* (the souls, 1950). The international, the national, and the personal are the three main sources of inspiration for the poet. The music and the landscape of Europe, where he lived for many years, are present in his oeuvre. He is also aware of the poetic developments in the European continent and in Latin America. For instance, his refusal to use capital letters, evident in the titles of his books, has been linked, among other tendencies, to the avant-garde movement. Another important element in his works is the sociopolitical situation of his country. All of his books were published during a chaotic time in Bolivian history: the years between the Chaco War (1933–1936) and the Revolution of 1952. The sense of loss and hopelessness that ensued from the war set the tone of many of his poems. Also present in his poems are those close to him, especially his children. The disparate combination of these three elements renders his poetry both intriguing and hard to define.

Antonio Ávila Jiménez was born in La Paz, Bolivia, on 3 June 1898. He belonged to a family with deep roots in the city. They lived in downtown La Paz, in a seigniorial stone house that no longer exists. At a young age he started playing the violin at the National Conservatory of Music. Classical music played an important role in his life and poetry. Julio de la Vega, in *Poesía boliviana: Siglo XIX y XX* (1982), calls him a "poeta músico" (musician poet). Ávila published his first poems in the magazine *Inti* in 1925. One of them is a two-part poem, titled "Dos romanzas melancólicas" (Two melancholic romanzas), that shows a formal rigidity not found in his later compositions, which are characterized by loose versification and the absence of both rhyme and capital letters. Also noticeable is his early attempt to bring together music and poetry, a recurring motif throughout his literary career. In 1926 he traveled to Paris to continue his musical education. For the next thirteen years his artistic endeavors focused not on poetry but on classical music.

Ávila's first child, Genevieve, was born of a French mother while he lived in France. In 1929 he married Hendrika Vermeer, a Dutch violinist, in Haarlem, the Netherlands. He returned to Bolivia in 1932 with his wife and their three children: Leonardo, Jacobo (Jack), and Rolando. The year of his return, Ávila volunteered in the Bolivian army to fight in the Chaco War. He was placed in the auxiliary services.

In 1933 Ávila and Hendrika Vermeer started playing the violin in the National Symphonic Orchestra. She died suddenly in 1935 and, in that same year, the widowed Ávila returned to Europe as the honorary consul in France, where he remained for two years. This appointment was his last trip to the European continent. In 1937, back in his home country, he started working for the Ministry of Foreign Relations, where he had a long administrative career, using his knowledge of French and his skills as a translator. According to Augusto Guzmán, Ávila wrote some poems in French and did a translation of Pablo Neruda's poetry into this language. Ávila married the Bolivian writer

Antonio Ávila Jiménez seated next to his wife, Hendrika Vermeer, on their wedding day in Haarlem, the Netherlands, in November 1929. The others are members of her family (Collection of Jack Ávila Vermeer).

Hilda Mundy (born Laura Villanueva Rocabado) in 1938. Silvia Mercedes, his fifth child, was born two years later. She became a poet herself and the author of one of the most complete studies of her father's works.

After a long hiatus Ávila resumed his poetic activity with the publication of *cronos* in 1939. Although some poems, such as "puna" (Andean highland) and "los mendigos" (the beggars), were inspired by Bolivia, classical music and the European landscape are the predominant themes. Titles such as "volendam," "preludio en la mayor de chopin" (Chopin's prelude in A major), and "en los alpes" (in the Alps) attest to these European influences. Guzmán writes that for Ávila Europe was "su continente perdido y nunca recuperado" (his lost and never recovered continent). For Silvia Mercedes Ávila, her father's relationship with Europe is less melancholic than serenely evocative of "las aldeas apacibles, los viejos campanarios, el paisaje marino que describe simple, diáfano y apenas enumerativo" (the peaceful villages, the old bell towers, the maritime land-

scape that he describes in a simple, clear and barely enumerative manner).

Music, Europe, Bolivia, and Ávila's family are intertwined with the description of the simple things of life in *cronos,* a feature also found in his subsequent works. Some of the titles show this last feature: "el esquilón" (the bell) and "la tinaja" (the jar). Silvia Mercedes Ávila concludes that Ávila observes the world around him and tries to capture the fleeting moments and the ordinary objects of daily life. Juan Quirós links the attention the poet paid to the simple things in life to Neruda's poetry. Guzmán relates Ávila's act of contemplating the world around him to his alleged contemplative temperament.

The use of ellipses is also noteworthy in *cronos.* Instead of utilizing words, in many poems Ávila utilizes periods. For instance, in "retrato" (portrait), a seven-verse poem, the first four lines are made up of a series of periods. Óscar Rivera-Rodas attributes this feature to the avant-garde influence on the poet. According to him, a poet such as Ávila sought new ways of expression through "un vaciamiento de contenido, para aprender a ver las cosas de otra manera e intentar redescribirlas sin prejuicios ni presuposiciones, al margen de principios y órdenes presupuestos" (an emptying of content in order to learn to see things differently and try to redescribe them without prejudices and presuppositions, beyond preset principles and orders). Moreover, José Ortega, Adolfo Cáceres Romero, and Édgar Ávila Echazú characterize Ávila's poetic expression as direct and lacking rhetorical artificiality and ornament. This observation is corroborated by the brevity of most of Ávila's poems, not only in *cronos* but also in the rest of his production. Brief poems such as "retrato" are common in his work. This particular poem simply reads: "tus pupilas absortas / y tu frente trigueña / que tiene olor a campo" (your meditative pupils / and your brunet face / that has the scent of meadows).

Avila's *cronos* came out three years after the Chaco War was over. Jorge Siles Salinas defines this conflict between Bolivia and Paraguay as "una guerra insensata, una guerra sin parangón posible" (a senseless war, a war like no other war). The reality of the battlefield and the effects of the national tragedy were captured by Raúl Otero Reiche in *Poemas de sangre y lejanía* (Poems of Blood and Forlornness), published in 1934, while the war was still on. Although by 1939 the intense suffering of the conflict had lessened, Bolivians were still trying to come to terms with the consequences of war. Rivera-Rodas finds that Bolivian poetry "ha descubierto el sin-sentido después de la experiencia político-social de la guerra del Chaco" (discovered senselessness after the sociopolitical experience of the Chaco War). While Ávila's use of ellipses reflects the feeling of emptiness and loss in postwar Bolivia, his descriptions of daily occurrences and simple objects are an attempt to recover the lost sense of normalcy.

Ávila published *signo* in 1942. He dedicated the book to Riek Vermeer, his Dutch brother-in-law. Music and poetry come together in "signo," the first poem of the book: "el día nublado; / la luz en el visillo / es un poema de verlaine" (the cloudy day; / the light on the curtains / is a poem by Verlaine). The musicality of the poetry of Paul Verlaine, the French symbolist admired and followed by many Latin American poets, influenced Ávila, as well. His immediate family is present in poems such as "el primer paso de mercedes" (Mercedes's first step). He shows his paternal pride in "si ayer te vi simiente / ahora te veo tallo" (Yesterday I saw you were a seed / today I see you are a sprout).

His love for Europe did not diminish Ávila's love for Bolivia. On the contrary, the connection to his homeland is seen in the poem "mi país" (my country):

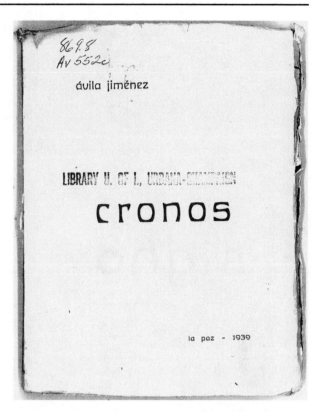

Paper cover for Ávila's first book, a collection of poems mainly inspired by classical music and the European landscape (Library of the University of Illinois at Urbana-Champaign)

"es mi esencia la conciencia / telúrica de sus campos" (it is my essence / the telluric consciousness of its fields). The landscape of his country is a constant presence in many of his poems. Jaime Sáenz points out that he loved the Andean highlands, and sometimes in conversations he used the Aymara language to describe them. The critic, who knew the poet personally, affirmed that Ávila was a notable Aymarist and a great admirer of the Aymara people and their culture but felt sorrow for the state of dejection in which the Bolivian indigenous peoples found themselves. Despite his interest in social issues, this theme appears only in a few poems. Jacobo Liberman, in his introduction to Ávila's *poemas* (1957), has explained this anomaly: "En cuanto a la inquietud social, está tan inmersa en él, la vive y apenas necesita insinuarla en su verbo" (As for his social preoccupation, it is so embedded in him that he does not need to suggest it in his works).

Published in 1950, *las almas* was Ávila's last book of original poetry. His favorite themes are still present but are expressed in a more somber fashion than before. This quality can be observed in "la marcha al cadalso (berlioz)" (marching to the gallows [Berlioz]), a poem inspired by Hector Berlioz's music. The last

ávila jiménez

signo

la paz - 1942

Paperback cover for Ávila's second book, a collection of poems about his Bolivian homeland and his family (Zimmerman Library, University of New Mexico)

stanza of this composition conveys an ominous tone: "ya bajan las palomas del consuelo / sobre el postrer momento de los ajusticiados / y se corta la arteria de todos los senderos" (descending are the doves of consolation / onto the hindmost moment of the executed / and the artery of all paths is severed). There was no major event in his personal life that might help explain this change to a darker and more fatalistic mood. This book, however, came out during a conflictive period in the history of Bolivia that led to the Revolution of 1952. It was a worrisome time for all Bolivians who focused their attention on the sociopolitical transformations that their country was undergoing. Tragedy hit Ávila's life directly in 1955 with the death of his son Leonardo. Five years later he published "leonardo" in the November 1960 issue of *Grupo Fuego*. The personal tone of this poem can be observed in its last strophe: "alguna vez suspiras / y una pequeña y contenida pena / me anuda la garganta" (sometimes you sigh / and a

small and restrained sorrow / puts a knot in my throat). This intimate poem about his family is not an exception in Ávila's production. In fact, all his children are mentioned consistently in his works, sometimes by name, other times as a group in descriptions of domestic life.

It is not clear why Ávila did not produce much poetry after *las almas*. Sáenz writes: "En realidad, Antonio Ávila Jiménez no necesitaba escribir poemas para ser poeta. Así nos lo demuestra la calidad de su espíritu" (Actually, Antonio Ávila Jiménez did not need to write poems to be a poet. The quality of his spirit is enough). Even though his poetry may have lived in his soul, as Sáenz asserts, the poetic evolution observed in his last book failed to develop. Perhaps one of the last poems he ever wrote, "y un saúz . . ." (and a willow . . .), first published in *poemas* (1957), stresses the same somberness found in *las almas*. The closing verse of the poem reveals this mood: "mi vida es una herida celeste en la fontana" (my life is a celestial wound in the mountain spring). In 1957 the Municipality of La Paz published a selection of his works titled *poemas,* which comprises the three major books and a few poems published before and after them. Rivera-Rodas states that the edition of *poemas* "no es digna de crédito debido a las alteraciones que registra, voluntarias o involuntarias de las personas a cargo de la edición" (is not reliable due to the willing or unwilling alterations made by the editors). Thus, the validity of including this book among Ávila's works, which some critics have done, is put into question.

While music and poetry were the two artistic media in which Ávila chose to express himself, professionally he worked for many years at the Ministry of Foreign Relations. In 1958 the Municipality of La Paz acknowledged both his public service and his artistic accomplishments by giving him a house, which came to be known as "La Casa del Poeta" (the House of the Poet). In this house, as in his family's old home before, he held regular, well-known *tertulias* (gatherings). Sáenz, Guzmán, and Liberman point out that Ávila was a private, even reclusive man who did not have many friends; therefore the attendees to the *tertulias* formed a select group of poets, intellectuals, and musicians. In these *tertulias* his reputation as a respected intellectual, artist, and passionate musician was reinforced. His giving and understanding nature was celebrated also.

Antonio Ávila Jiménez died on 16 December 1965. According to Silvia Mercedes Ávila, he died in his Casa del Poeta. Most of what has been written about him and his poetry came out after his death. Critics are divided not on the importance of his work but rather on its main characteristics and its place in the history of Bolivian literature. In truth, there is no consensus on the periodization of Bolivian literature in

Paperback cover for the selection of Ávila's poems published by the city of La Paz, Bolivia, in 1957 (University of Virginia Library)

general. This characteristic of the national literature seems more acute when classifying Ávila's poetry. Critical opinions illustrate the difficulty of placing his contributions within the strict limits of periods and movements. For Quirós, Ávila's poetry escapes definitions. In spite of the difficulty, he maintains that Ávila was part of the Generation of the Centenary, that is, the Generation of 1925, the year in which his first poems were published. Liberman, however, asserts that Ávila does not share the main poetic traits of the poetry of this generation. His distinctiveness is especially evident in his treatment of the landscape, less concrete and more spiritual in Ávila's case. Ávila Echazú includes him in the "simbolismo modernista" (modernist symbolism). Rivera-Rodas emphasizes the influence of the avant-garde in his poems, placing him in what he calls the third stage of modernity in Bolivian poetry, deeply marked by the Chaco War. He argues that "Modernismo" is left behind during the first stage of the process. Armando Soriano Badani and de la Vega, too, characterize Ávila's poetry as avant-garde and not "modernista." These two critics include him in an exclusive list of authors, namely, his contemporaries Óscar Cerruto, Otero Reiche, and Fernando Díez de Medina. Be it as it may, the lasting importance of Ávila's legacy was proven in 1988 when the Municipality of La Paz issued an edition of his complete works, which includes all three major books, plus a few early poems and some of his latter compositions. This 1988 edition of Ávila's works, unlike the one released in 1957, is true to the original publications.

The brevity of most of Antonio Ávila Jiménez's poems can be misleading. Behind their apparent simplicity lies a complex web of themes, influences, images, and feelings. His family, the landscapes of Bolivia and Europe, his love for classical music, and the objects and occurrences of daily life are some of the elements of his poetry. These elements render his poems direct and personal without becoming anecdotal. Ávila was a private man, which did not prevent him from being in tune with the world around him. He tapped into the renovating and international impetus of the avant-garde. The historical specificity of Bolivia, with the national disaster of the Chaco War and the strong impact of the Revolution of 1952, marked both his life and oeuvre. The respect, admiration, and love he inspired in people were confirmed by the house given to him by the Municipality in his city of birth. It is significant that this house came to be popularly known as La Casa del Poeta; no name was needed to know it belonged to Antonio Ávila Jiménez.

References:

Silvia Mercedes Ávila, "Aproximación a la obra de Antonio Ávila Jiménez," in Ávila's *Obras completas* (La Paz: Empresa Editora Urquizo, 1988), pp. 19–32;

Édgar Ávila Echazú, *Resumen y antología de la literatura boliviana* (La Paz: Gisbert, 1973), p. 148;

Augusto Guzmán, *Biografías de la literatura boliviana: Biografía, evaluación, bibliografía* (La Paz: Los Amigos del Libro, 1982), pp. 204–205;

José Ortega and Adolfo Cáceres Romero, *Diccionario de la literatura boliviana* (La Paz: Los Amigos del Libro, 1977), pp. 32–33;

Juan Quirós, *Fronteras movedizas: Crítica y estimación* (La Paz: Signo-GH, 1992), pp. 407–410;

Quirós, *Índice de la poesía boliviana contemporánea,* second edition (La Paz: Gisbert, 1983), pp. 24, 149;

Óscar Rivera-Rodas, *La modernidad y sus hermenéuticas poéticas: Poesía boliviana del siglo XX* (La Paz: Signo, 1991), pp. 85–117;

Jaime Sáenz, "Antonio Ávila Jiménez," in Ávila's *Obras completas* (La Paz: Empresa Editora Urquizo, 1988), pp. 13–18;

Jorge Siles Salinas, *La literatura boliviana de la Guerra del Chaco* (La Paz: Ediciones de la Universidad Católica Boliviana, 1969), p. 25;

Armando Soriano Badani and Julio de la Vega, *Poesía boliviana: Siglo XIX y XX* (La Paz: Biblioteca Popular Boliviana de Última Hora, 1982), pp. 202–203.

Porfirio Barba-Jacob
(Miguel Ángel Osorio Benítez)
(29 July 1883 – 14 January 1942)

Juan Carlos González Espitia
University of North Carolina, Chapel Hill

BOOKS: *Campaña florida* (Barranquilla: Imp. del siglo, 1907);

El combate de la Ciudadela, narrado por un extranjero (Mexico City: Tip. Artísticos, 1913);

En loor de los niños (San José, Costa Rica: Imp. Greñas, 1915);

El terremoto de San Salvador: Narración de un sobreviviente (San Salvador: Imp. Del Diario del Salvador, 1917); revised as *El terremoto de San Salvador: Corpus-Christi, junio 7 de 1917* (San Salvador: Ministerio de Educación, Departamento Editorial, 1961); revised as *El terremoto de San Salvador* (Medellín: Secretaría de Educación y Cultura de Antioquia; revised edition, San Salvador: C.A. Concultura, 1997; revised, 1999); revised and enlarged as *El terremoto de San Salvador: Narración de un superviviente* (Bogotá: Villegas, 2001);

El verdadero Bulnes (por el honor de México) (San Antonio: El Imparcial de Texas, 1921);

Canciones y elegías (Alcancía, 1932);

Rosas negras, edited by Rafael Arévalo Martínez (Guatemala City: G. M. Staebler, 1933; revised edition, Guatemala: Electra, 1933);

La canción de la vida profunda, y otros poemas (Manizales: Imprenta Departamental, 1937);

Seis canciones de Porfirio Barba-Jacob, edited by Jorge Zalamea (Bogotá: Hojas de Poesía, 1942);

15 poemas, edited by Carlos García-Prada (Mexico City: Colección literaria de la Revista Iberoamericana, 1942);

En la muerte de Porfirio Barba-Jacob, edited by Gabriel Henao Mejía, Cuadernillos de poesía colombiana (Medellín: Universidad católica bolivariana, 1942);

El corazón iluminado (Bogotá: Biblioteca Popular de Cultura Colombiana, 1942); republished as *Antorchas contra el viento* (Bogotá: Minerva, 1944; revised edition, Bogotá: Ministerio de Educación de Colombia, 1944; revised edition, Guadalajara:

Porfirio Barba-Jacob (from Beatriz Cuberos de Valencia, Porfirio Barba Jacob, *1989; Howard-Tilton Memorial Library, Tulane University)*

Colegio Internacional, 1980); revised and enlarged as *Antorchas contra el viento: Poesía completa y prosa selecta,* compiled by Eduardo Santo (Medellín: Gobernación de Antioquia, Secretaría de Educación y Cultura, 1983; revised edition, Antioquia: Seduca, 1983); revised as *Florilegio de antorchas contra el viento,* selected, with a prologue, by Angel José Fernández (Chiapas, Mexico: Universidad Autónoma de Chiapas, 1984); revised and enlarged as *El corazón iluminado, antología poética* (Medellín: Bedout, 1968);

Poemas intemporales (Mexico City: Compañía General de Ediciones, 1943; revised edition, Mexico City: Acuarimántima, 1944; revised edition, Mexico City: Botas, 1944; revised edition, Mexico City: Compañía General de Ediciones, 1957; revised edition, Guadalajara, Mexico: Ágata, 1992);

Sus mejores versos (Bogotá: La Gran Colombia, 1944); revised as *Los mejores versos de Porfirio Barba-Jacob* (Bogotá: La Gran Colombia, 1953);

Poesías completas (Bogotá: Organización Continental de los Festivales de Libro, 1944; revised, 1960; revised edition, Bogotá: Arango Editores: El Áncora Editores, 1988; revised, 1994; revised edition, Mexico City: Consejo Nacional para la Cultura y las Artes, Direccion General de Publicaciones, 1998; revised edition, Bogotá: Planeta, 1999);

Los mejores versos de Porfirio Barba-Jacob (Buenos Aires, 1954; revised edition, Buenos Aires: Nuestra América, 1956);

Poemas de Porfirio Barba-Jacob (Medellín: Horizonte, 1960; revised, 1963);

Obras completas (Medellín: Montoya, 1962);

Porfirio Barba Jacob: Homenaje antológico (Mexico City: Sociedad de Amigos del Libro Mexicano, 1964);

La vida profunda (Bogotá: Andes, 1973; revised, 1974); revised as *La vida profunda: Edición especial de la poesía de Porfirio Barba-Jacob [i.e. M. A. Osorio] en el trigésimo primer aniversario del deceso del maestro (enero 12 [i.e. 14], 1973) y nonagésimo de su nacimiento (julio 29, 1973), primera completa y primera ceñida a los textos auténticos* (Bogotá: Andes, 1973);

Porfirio Barba-Jacob: Sus mejores poesías, by Barba-Jacob and others (Medellín: Salesiana, 1973; revised edition, Medellín: Bedout, 1983; revised edition, Bogotá: Procultura, 1989);

Poemas, selected, with an introduction, by Carlos García Prada (Bogotá: El Dorado, 1976; revised, 1976); revised edition, edited, with annotations, by Fernando Vallejo (Bogotá: Procultura, Presidencia de la República, 1985);

Canción de la vida profunda y otros poemas (Bogotá: Oveja Negra, 1980?; revised, 1985);

18 poemas (Bogotá: Instituto Colombiano de Cultura, 1981);

Obra poética (Medellín: Bedout, 1982);

Poemas selectos, by Barba-Jacob and Alberto Bernal Ramírez (Bogotá: Banco Central Hipotecario, Compañía Central de Seguros, 1983);

La tristeza del camino; Campaña Florida (Bogotá: Grupo Grancolombiano, 1983);

Obra poética (Medellín: Bedout, 1983; revised edition, Mexico City: Domés, 1985);

Poesías (Bogotá: Círculo de Lectores, 1984);

Poemas completos (Medellín: Autores Antioqueños, 1992);

Antología (Bogotá: Panamericana, 1994; revised, 1996);

El resplandor de la aurora (Tegucigalpa: Editorial Cultura, Secretaría de Cultura y las Artes, 1997);

Selección (Bogotá: Panamericana, 2001).

Although recent studies point toward the importance of his pioneering journalistic production in Central and South America, Porfirio Barba-Jacob is especially known for his poetry. His works are considered both a late example of romanticism and a development of Rubén Darío's *modernismo*. They are mainly regarded as an isolated poetic search, however, characterized by profound despair, combined with peaks of exultation. Barba-Jacob considered himself a vanguardist. In his autobiographical essay "La divina tragedia: El poeta habla de sí mismo" (The Divine Tragedy: The Poet Talks About Himself), which served as the prologue of his poetry collection *Rosas Negras* (Black Roses, 1933), he asserts that "Mi poesía es para hechizados. Aunque se manifiesta generalmente con una apariencia de tranquilidad, está llena de temblores, de relámpagos, de aullidos" (My poetry is for the bewitched. Although it generally displays itself under the appearance of tranquility, it is full of tremors, lightning, howls). In this sense it is important to stress that his poetry is clearly self-reflective, written in the first person, with no social or universal pretensions. He is eager to express inner concerns through the use of a symbolism that divides death and life, the first as striking wind or profound abyss, the second as a burning torch, oceans, or flowing rivers; in the words of critic Eduardo Santa, he is "esencialmente un poeta vitalista. Un poeta de la vida profunda" (fundamentally a vitalist poet. A poet of the deep life) which is a reference to the title of one of Barba-Jacob's poems. Formally, his poetry is populated by Alexandrine verses, occasional production of sonnets, and some examples of irregular versification.

Barba-Jacob never published of his own will a volume compiling his poems. The only three books issued during his lifetime were the result of friends' efforts to collect funds to take care of his ailing health and low income. He was not pleased with any of the books, since he conceived that his aesthetic quest called for the continuous revision of the verses he had already written and a slow process of production, an ideal proved by the scarcity of his poems, which number about one hundred.

Barba-Jacob was born Miguel Ángel Osorio Benítez to Antonio María Osorio and Pastora Benítez on 29 July 1883, in Hoyo Rico, a mining hamlet in the town of Santa Rosa de Osos in the region of Antioquia, Colombia. At the age of three months he was left in Angostura under the care of Emigdio Osorio and Benedicta Parra, his paternal grandparents. Benedicta was the person he always remembered as his mother, the one who showed him the tenderness and care he never experienced from his own parents. At the age of six he attended a public elementary school to learn the rudiments of math and writing, until 1895, when he departed for Bogotá to meet his parents. He was not well received, however. The dry temperament of his mother, always critical of Benedicta's education of her son, and the apathy of his father, inclined to the abuse of alcohol, compelled Miguel Ángel to return to the grandparents' home in Antioquia.

Upon embarking on training as a teacher at the Esculea Normal in Medellín, his lack of application and rebellious character pushed him once again to Bogotá, where he intended to study law, with no success. Again in Angostura, he was hired as a schoolteacher, but in 1901 he was drafted by one of the factions involved in the conflict known as the *Guerra de los Mil Días* (War of a Thousand Days). He reached the rank of captain, not for his martial qualities but mainly for his personal and literary gifts, namely, the composition of campaign chronicles. Two years later, at the end of the war, Miguel Ángel went back to Angostura, where he continued teaching and published three manuscript newspapers under his first pseudonym, Maín Ximénez. This name is the same one he uses in his *Cancionero Antioqueño* (Songbook of Antioquia), a small journal he wrote in order to obtain some money in Bogotá, where he went in 1904, probably seeking a literary career, to no avail.

After his misfortune in Bogotá, Ximénez went back to Angostura to establish a series of failing pedagogical enterprises, and in 1905 he wrote "Virginia," his only novel, censored and confiscated by the town's mayor because its contents were "un atentado contra las sanas costumbres" (an attempt against healthy customs). The same year Ximénez visited Yarumal and met the love of his youth, Teresita Jaramillo, the sister of his friend, the poet Francisco Jaramillo Medina. This relationship did not prosper since Teresita's family considered Ximénez a youngster with no future—he was twenty-two years old and had no productive profession, only verses, the desire to travel, and too lively a personality. The romantic failure was followed by the death of his grandmother

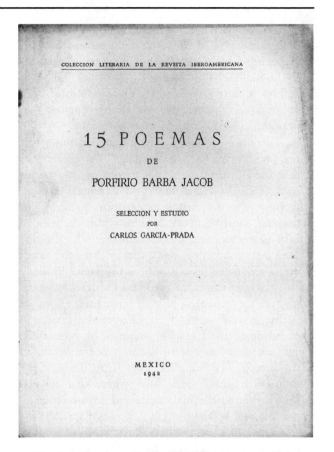

COLECCION LITERARIA DE LA REVISTA IBEROAMERICANA

15 POEMAS

DE

PORFIRIO BARBA JACOB

SELECCION Y ESTUDIO
POR
CARLOS GARCIA-PRADA

MEXICO
1942

Paperback cover for a collection of Barba-Jacob's poems published the year of his death (Bruccoli Clark Layman Archives)

Benedicta, in December 1906, an event that pushed Ximénez to head out toward the Colombian coast.

After a long and difficult journey he arrived in the coastal city of Barranquilla and stayed with the poet Lino Torregroza. During this period he studied and frequented long literary gatherings with other writers and poets such as Leopoldo de la Rosa, Miguel Rasch Isla, and Hermes Zepeda. Ximénez was exposed then to the world classics and the works of poets such as Rubén Darío, Guillermo Valencia, and Ralph Waldo Emerson. The intellectual impulse resulted in the production of some of his first well-known poems, all of which were published in 1907: "Campaña florida" (Flowery War), "Mi vecina Carmen" (Carmen, My Neighbor), "La tristeza del camino" (The Sadness of the Road), and the popular "Parábola del retorno" (The Return Parable), a nostalgic work dealing with ideas of time and places lost after exile from the land of the forefathers in Antioquia, and of hope embodied in memory. Several of these poems were published in different journals in Barranquilla under his new pen name, Ricardo Arenales. The intellectual circles of the Colombian port opened possibilities for Arenales. His appearances in the pages of *El Siglo* (The Century), *Rigoletto,* and *El Promotor* (The Promoter) inaugurated his recognition in several Central American countries, especially in San Salvador, where *La Quincena* (The Semi-Monthly), a journal directed by Vicente Acosta, a relative of Darío, published one of his poems, "La tristeza del camino," with positive comments.

There are several theories explaining the origin of the pseudonym Ricardo Arenales. To some critics it is a hidden homage to the names of two of his friends, Ricardo Hernández and Mariana Arenas; others give a more poetical explanation, pointing out that *arenal,* sandy ground, communicates the idea of infinite movement and arid contemplation by the side of the open sea; there is also a theory that "Arenales" is the evocation of a neighborhood in Santa Rosa de Osos, the town where he lived part of his early years. Whatever the explanation, with this name, which he used for several years of travel over the continent after his departure from Barranquilla, he was recognized years later as one of the first poetic voices in Latin America. He went to Costa Rica, Jamaica, the Dominican Republic, and Cuba, where he socialized in the Havana intellectual circles and devoted himself to reading and writing. In 1909 he established *Revista Contemporánea* (Contemporary Magazine), a significant Mexican literary magazine that published articles by such figures as his friend Alfonso Reyes and Pedro Henríquez Ureña.

After Cuba, Arenales moved to Monterrey, Mexico, where he wrote for the *Monterey News* and *El Espectador* (The Spectator), which he edited until his incarceration in 1910 for the political opinions he expressed against the government. In Monterrey he initiated one of his most prolific periods with the publication of poems such as "Espíritu errante" (Wandering Spirit, 1909), "Virtud interior" (Internal Virtue, 1909), "Domador, triunfador" (Tamer, Conqueror, 1909), and "Parábola de los viajeros" (The Parable of the Travelers, 1909). Arenales considered these poems to be minor works, lacking, as described by Fernando Vallejo in *Poemas* (1985), the "melodía interior" (internal musicality), less valued than "La estrella de la tarde" (The Afternoon Star, 1909), a poem about the failure to grasp reality and about astonishment when confronting nature. The poems of Areneles were always in constant flux and revision. He declined, in his own words, to "asesinarlas dentro de un libro, asesinarlas y sepultarlas dentro de un libro" (assassinate them in a book, assassinate them and bury them in a book). For this reason he did not publish by his own will any compilation of his works.

Arenales's involvement in politics, exemplified by his support of Porfirio Díaz, brought radical conse-

quences for him. He abandoned Mexico in 1911 and went to Guatemala, Honduras, El Salvador, Nicaragua, Cuba, and the United States. In 1912 he returned to Mexico City and worked as journalist for *El Imparcial,* where he also published several poems that year such as "El corazón rebosante" (The Plethoric Heart), "La hora cobarde" (The Cowardly Hour), and "El poema de las dádivas" (The Poem of Bounties). Two years later, in 1914, he founded *Churubusco,* an auspicious newspaper that lasted only for one month. In *Churubusco* Arenales expressed his contempt for the Mexican revolutionaries, and such bitter opinions forced him to flee to Guatemala once the troops of Venustiano Carranza and Pancho Villa approached the city; his apprehension about the retaliation from the insurgency proved well founded when the *Churubusco* offices were burned.

In Guatemala he developed a friendship with Rafael Arévalo Martínez, the author of a short story, "El hombre que parecía un caballo" (The Man Who Looked Like a Horse, 1915), which was based on Arenales's physiognomy and on his literary production. Arenales did not agree with many of the ideas of Arévalo Martínez's text, especially because he considered himself less candid and less innocent than the "señor de Aretal" character portrayed by Arévalo Martínez.

Around this time he also worked on a book about Guatemala that he offered to Manuel Estrada Cabrera, but the dictator was expecting a eulogy of his glories, not a book about the beauty of the landscape and its people. After the violent reaction of the despot, Arenales departed from Guatemala and arrived in Havana in 1915. His stay in Cuba was highly productive; he gathered again with the island's intellectuals and wrote what is probably his best-known poem, "Canción de la vida profunda" (The Song of Profound Life, 1915). Originally of nine stanzas but reduced by the author to seven, this work is a reflection on Michel Eyquem de Montaigne's account of humans as changeable beings. It is enticingly written in words with the accent on the antepenultimate syllable: *móviles* (movable), *sórdidos* (sordid), *lúbricos* (lubricous); a repetition of the theme on the first line of each passage: "hay días en que somos tan . . ." (There are days when we are so . . .); and a conjunction of nouns and adjectives that weld direct expressions: "obscuro pedernal" (obscure flint), "rútilas monedas" (resplendent coins), "leves briznas" (tenuous fragments). From his devoted work in Havana, which was reportedly a period of voluntary confinement for the purpose of writing, come other characteristic poems, such as "Soberbia" (Arrogance, 1915), "Sapiencia" (Wisdom, 1915), "La vieja canción" (The

Old Song, 1923), and "Canción innominada" (The Song With No Name, 1923), filled with the construction of a complete poetic universe that encompasses love, death, age, sadness, and happiness.

From Cuba, Arenales traveled to New York for a brief period, a trip not completely documented by the critics but which shows his enthusiasm for research. There he wrote for some Spanish-language publications and frequented the public library on Forty-second Street, trying to find books and information that he wished to use in the projected essays titled "Filosofía del lujo" (Philosophy of Luxury). Escaping from the harsh winter in New York, he moved to Honduras. In the small town of La Ceiba he expended long periods of time and founded *Ideas y Noticias,* a short-lived newspaper. In La Ceiba the poet also finished his "La dama de cabellos ardientes" (The Fire-haired Lady, 1925), a poem of agile interpretations of lust and voluptuousness and one of his most popular works. In *Poemas* (1985), a collection of Barba-Jacob's poems annotated by Colombian writer Vallejo, the critic connects the image of the fire-haired lady with Barba-Jacob's experiences with marijuana. His interpretation is based on Barba-Jacob's articles about drugs published in *El Heraldo* of Mexico in 1919 with another pseudonym, Califax. The first article of the series, "La dama de los cabellos ardientes se bebe la vida de sus amantes" (The Firehaired Lady Swallows the Life of Her Lovers), deals with marijuana. Marijuana is present in several of Barba-Jacob's poems, among them "El són del viento" (The Song of the Wind, 1928) written in 1920, where he describes the hallucinogen as a lady that inspires a fatal love.

From Honduras he went to El Salvador, where he experienced the earthquake of 7 June 1917, a calamity he describes in writing in his *El terremoto de San Salvador: Narración de un sobreviviente* (The San Salvador Earthquake: Chronicle of a Survivor), which was published twenty-four hours after the first quake on the salvaged presses of the *Diario del Salvador*. In his constant flux of founding newspapers, writing essays and chronicles to survive, attacking ruling governments, and living a life of economical distress, the poet was back in Monterrey in 1919, where he began a new journalistic enterprise, *El Porvenir*. He left the newspaper before the end of one year and, after wandering by the border towns of San Antonio, El Paso, and Ciudad Juárez, went back to Mexico City, where he wrote various articles for *El Heraldo,* including entries in his series on narcotics. During this stay in the Mexican capital city he wrote the celebrated sensationalist articles titled "Los fenómenos espíritas en el Palacio de la Nunciatura" (The Spiritist Phenom-

Paperback cover for the first revised edition of Barba-Jacob's posthumous 1943 collection (Bruccoli Clark Layman Archives)

ena at the Nunciature Palace), which he published in *El Demócrata*. The "Nunciature Palace" was in reality an apartment building located at Bucareli Street; it had been adapted to lodge the papal nuncio but was never inhabited by his company. Instead, Arenales lived there from July to September 1920 and wrote about supposed ghostly, mysterious events, including objects levitating; the articles feature scatological passages parallel to the ones in the fifth chapter of *El buscón* (circa 1604), Francisco de Quevedo's picaresque work.

In 1921 Arenales was appointed director of the public library in the state of Jalisco, where he received the visit of Spanish author Ramón del Valle Inclán. He used his library position to push educational reforms and ideas for a public, easily accessible, university system, but because of his personal behavior, prone to sexual scandals, he was expelled. The theme of homosexuality in the poet's works is a controversial one, and his unconventional lifestyle has been reported through several anecdotes, many of which are related to his sexual inclinations. He openly talked about his sexuality in a provocative, self-aggrandizing tone, which can be traced in the rich, evocative language of well-known compositions such as "Balada de la loca alegría" (The Ballad of Mad Happiness), first published in the Guatemalan newspaper *El Imperial* (1924): "mozuelos de la grata Cuscatlán–¡oh ambrosía!–" (Youngsters from pleasant Cuscatlán–oh, ambrosia!–); "Elegía del marino ilusorio" (Elegy of the Illusory Sailor): "¡Dáme tu miel, oh niño de boca perfumada!" (Give me your honey, oh boy of the fragrant mouth!); and "Los desposados de la muerte" (The Death's Betrothed), where, in this 1920 poem from *México Moderno,* he describes the beloved peculiarities of young men he probably knew.

Arenales was expelled from Mexico for his virulent editorials published in the journal *Cronos* against President Álvaro Obregón and his minister, General Plutarco Elías Calle. Guatemala was again the country that received him, even though in his last visit his comments had made him enemies, and there he successfully managed *El Imparcial.* In September 1922 *El Imparcial* published one of his poems under a peculiar new pseudonym: Porfirio Barba-Jacob. Barba-Jacob explained that a terrible mistake by the Guatemalan police persuaded him of the need for a change. The journalist Alejandro Arenales, editor of *Diario Nuevo,* had criticized the government, and a warrant of arrest and execution had been issued for him. The police confused the two men because of their last name; Barba-Jacob was apprehended and would have been put to death if not for the description of the poet as a horse in Arévalo Martínez's "El hombre que parecía un caballo," which one of the policemen remembered from years before.

The change of name has brought a plurality of interpretational theses. Vallejo, in *El mensajero: La novela del hombre que se suicidó tres veces* (The Messenger: The Novel of the Man That Killed Himself Thrice, 1991), an unorthodox yet rigorous biography of the poet, indicates that Barba-Jacob was the last name of two brothers, Carmen and Emiliano, who appear in some of his early poems. Vallejo claims that both of them were his lovers, and the poet might have added the name of Porfirio, similar to Pórfiro, because he considered it odd enough not to be confused. Another interpretation, one of several created by Vallejo, states that Porfirio is related to Porphyrius, the Neoplatonic philosopher from Alexandria; *barba* (beard) is a word that expresses virility; and Jacob is related to the biblical character who tried to make a ladder toward heaven. Vallejo also indicates that Barba Jacobo was the name of the true god as seen by the Florentine heretic Mossén Urbano; the story is

part of *Historia de los Heterodoxos Españoles* (History of Spanish Heterodoxes, 1911) by Marcelino Menéndez y Pelayo, which Barba-Jacob read in Havana in 1915.

In 1924 Barba-Jacob was cast out of Guatemala, and shortly after he was also exiled from San Salvador. In Honduras he worked as a banana porter and pretended to be a preacher in order to earn something to eat. In 1925 he was in Nicaragua, then in Cuba, and in 1926 was invited to head the Peruvian progovernment newspaper *La Prensa.* The dictator Augusto Bernardino Leguía stopped his financial support of Barba-Jacob when the poet refused to write his biography as if the despot were comparable with Simón Bolívar. The Colombian embassy in Lima arranged his repatriation, and after twenty years the poet went back to his country of origin.

In Colombia, Barba-Jacob offered several acclaimed poetry recitals, visited the places of his youth, and worked as journalist for *El Espectador,* but, once again, he was dismissed after publishing a series of sensationalist chronicles on a phantom that haunted a house in Bogotá. At this time, while he was in Bogotá, the first serious symptoms of tuberculosis appeared, and he was hospitalized for two months. The original welcoming gestures of his friends and admirers changed into rejection when they were confronted with his taste for alcohol and his constant requests for money. After three years in Colombia, resenting his country, Barba-Jacob traveled to Cuba. In Havana, apart from conversing with young intellectuals, he socialized with Federico García Lorca, who was on the island on his way to Spain.

The Mexican embassy in Cuba arranged the return of Barba-Jacob. He lived briefly in Mexico City and then moved to Monterrey, where he founded *Atalaya,* a failed enterprise. The deterioration of his health brought him again to México City; his finances and living conditions also worsened. During this period, however, he polished his journalistic language in his "Perifonemas" (Radio-Transmitted Discourses)–a well-known column combining cultural commentary, political critique, and literary production, considered by many as an example of journalistic clarity–which appeared in *Últimas Noticias,* an afternoon newspaper.

Poverty and sickness continued to affect Barba-Jacob's life. He constantly changed from motels to rented rooms or hospitals, still always visited by those who wanted to hear the poetry from his voice and to see the movement of his hands accompanying his tone. His consumption developed rapidly from 1940, and he was again weary of his lack of economical resources. By October 1941 his country approved monetary assistance and planned to bring him back by plane, but the rules of the Pan American Air Company did not allow tuberculosis sufferers to travel. The money destined for his trip never reached him.

In the last weeks of that year his religious beliefs were rekindled; after many years cultivating a satanic, iconoclastic image that led him to compare himself with the Wandering Jew of the medieval legend, Barba-Jacob felt the need to return to the religious environment of his childhood, to the beliefs of his beloved grandparents. Some days before his death on 14 January 1942 Barba-Jacob asked to confess to a Catholic priest. Administering the sacrament of extreme unction, the priest asked for a name under which to pray for him. The response was, "Miguel Ángel." The poet who had been Maín Ximénez, Ricardo Arenales, and Porfirio Barba-Jacob thus returned to the name he was called by his grandmother. He is buried in Santa Rosa de Osos, the town where he was born.

Letters:

Cartas de Barba-Jacob, edited by Fernando Vallejo (Bogotá: Revista Literaria Gradiva, 1992).

Biographies:

Victor Amaya González, *Barba Jacob, hombre de sed y de ternura* (Bogotá: Minerva, 1957);

Carlos Mejía Gutíerrez, *Porfirio Barba Jacob: ensayo biográfico* (Medellín: Impr. Municipal, 1982);

Alvaro Legretti, *Rasgando la niebla: en el primer centenario natalicio del poeta Porfirio Barba-Jacob* (Medellín: Sandino, 1983);

Raúl Gilberto Tróchez, *Porfirio Barba Jacob: el judío errante de la vida profunda* (Honduras, 1983);

Fernando Vallejo, *El mensajero: La novela del hombre que se suicidó tres veces* (Bogotá: Planeta, 1991);

Fedro Guillén, *Barba Jacob, el hechizado* (Villahermosa, Mexico: Gobierno del Estado de Tabasco, Instituto de Cultura de Tabasco, 1992);

Roberto Meisel Lanner, *Tres titanes de la literatura colombiana: Porfirio Barba Jacob, Rafael Pombo, Guillermo Valencia* (Barranquilla, Colombia: Ediciones Gobernación del Atlántico, 1996).

Reference:

Eduardo Santa, *Porfirio Barba-Jacob y su lamento poético* (Bogotá: Instituto Caro y Cuervo, 1991).

Yolanda Bedregal

(21 September 1913 – 21 May 1999)

Maria Elva Echenique
University of Portland

BOOKS: *Naufragio* (La Paz: Unidas, 1936);

Poemar (La Paz, 1937);

Ecos, by Bedregal and Gert Conitzer (La Paz: Unidas, 1940);

Almadía (La Paz: Amauta, 1942);

Nadir (La Paz: Universo, 1950);

Calendario Folclórico del Departamento de La Paz, by Bedregal and Antonio González Bravo (La Paz: Dirección General de Cultura, 1956);

Del mar y la ceniza: Alegatos, Antología (La Paz: Biblioteca Paceña, 1957); revised and enlarged as *Del mar y la ceniza: Alegatos, La Danza* (La Paz: Talleres Gráficos de la Universidad de San Andrés, n.d.);

Antología poética, Lírica Hispana, no. 224 (Caracas: Diciembre, 1961);

Antologia minima (La Paz: Siglo, 1968);

Bajo el oscuro sol (La Paz: Los Amigos del Libro, 1971);

El cántaro del angelito (La Paz: Talleres–Escuela de Artes Gráficas del Colegio Don Bosco, 1979);

Ayllu: El altiplano boliviano, text by Bedregal, photographs by Peter McFarren (La Paz: Museo Nacional de Etnografía y Folclore/Los Amigos del Libro, 1984);

Convocatorias (Quito: Artes Gráficas Señal Impreseñal, 1994);

Escrito (Quito: Printer Graphic, 1994).

OTHER: *Poesía de Bolivia, de la época precolombina al modernismo,* edited by Bedregal (Buenos Aires: Universitaria, 1964);

Antología de la Poesía Boliviana, edited by Bedregal (La Paz: Los Amigos del Libro, 1977);

"Good Evening, Agatha," in *Landscapes of a New Land: Short Fiction by Latin American Women,* edited by Marjorie Agosín (Fredonia, N.Y.: White Pine, 1989), pp. 27–30;

"The Morgue" and "How Milinco Escaped from School," in *Cruel Fictions, Cruel Realities: Short Stories by Latin American Women* (Pittsburgh: Latin American Literary Review Press, 1997), pp. 9–12, 13–16;

Yolanda Bedregal (from Kathy S. Leonard and Susan E. Benner,
Fire from the Andes: Short Fiction by Women from
Bolivia, Ecuador, and Peru, *1998; Thomas Cooper*
Library, University of South Carolina)

"The Traveler," in *Fire from the Andes: Short Fiction by Women from Bolivia, Ecuador, and Peru,* edited by Kathy S. Leonard and Susan E. Benner (Albuquerque: University of New Mexico Press, 1998), pp. 8–13.

SELECTED PERIODICAL PUBLICATION–
UNCOLLECTED: "Martyrdom," "Night, I Know All About You," "Nocturne of Hope," and "Pointless Journey," translated by Carolyne Wright from

Bedregal's "Viaje Inútil," *Mid-American Review,* 15, nos. 1 & 2 (1995), pp. 147–148.

Yolanda Bedregal is regarded as one of the most important women authors of twentieth-century Bolivia. In the literary circles of the country she was known as a poet, novelist, and short-story writer, as well as a scholar of Bolivian indigenous cultures, particularly the Aymara. A woman of multifaceted interests, she was also a sculptor, whose works were awarded prizes, and a ballet dancer of folk music. During her extensive career she received many awards for her writing and her contribution to the dissemination of literature in Bolivia. Some of these prizes include the Premio Nacional de Poesía (National Poetry Prize); the Premio Nacional del Ministerio de Cultura, Honor al Mérito (Ministry of Culture Award); the Premio Nacional de Novela "Erich Guttentag" ("Erich Guttentag" National Novel Prize) for her novel *Bajo el oscuro sol* (Under the Dark Sun, 1971); the Medalla a la Cultura de la Fundación Vicente Ballivián (Cultural Medal from the Vicente Ballivian Foundation) and the Condecoración Franz Tamayo en el grado de Gran Cruz (Great Cross, Franz Tamayo Decoration) in 1995; and the Bandera de Oro (Golden Flag), awarded by the Bolivian Congress, in 1997. Bedregal's work has been recognized also beyond Bolivia. In 1948 she was proclaimed "Yolanda de Bolivia" by the literary movement "Gesta Bárbara," and in 1982 "Yolanda de América" by the Argentine Society of Writers. In 1996 the Chilean government awarded her the Gabriela Mistral prize, offered every year to outstanding figures of Latin American literature.

Carmen María Yolanda Bedregal Iturri was born in La Paz on 21 September 1913. The daughter of an upper-middle-class family of intellectuals, she received a rigorous education. She was the second of six children; their names, from the oldest to the youngest, were Gonzalo, Yolanda, Jaime, Alvaro, Carmen Cecilia, and Ramiro. Her father, Juan Francisco Bedregal, a prominent writer himself, and her mother, Carmen Iturri, greatly influenced the development of her artistic career. In an interview for the Internet journal *Sincronía* (Summer 1998) with Kathy S. Leonard, a translator of her works to English, Bedregal remembered the intellectual atmosphere she breathed as a child in her home, where the masters of what she calls the "Golden Age of Bolivian culture," all of them close friends of her parents, would gather to talk about literature: "Los tíos Alcides, Greco (Gregorio), Juan, Armando, no eran otros que Arguedas, Reynolds, Capriles, Chirveches. No puede pues decirse que empecé a interesarme por la literatura como algo que estuviera fuera de mí, sino que era parte de la vida cotidiana" (My uncles, Alcides, Greco [Gregorio], Juan, Armando, were none other than Arguedas, Reynolds, Capriles, Chirveches. It cannot be said then, that I

developed my interest in literature as something that was external to me; it was part of my everyday life).

After completing a degree in fine arts at the University of San Andrés in La Paz in 1936, Bedregal received a scholarship to attend Barnard College at Columbia University in New York, where she studied aesthetics and art history. Returning to Bolivia in 1938, she became a professor at the School of Fine Arts, at the University of San Andrés, and at the Music Conservatory in La Paz; later she taught at the Benavides Academy in Sucre. On 22 February 1941 Bedregal married Gert Conitzer, a German-Jewish exiled poet and intellectual who was her lifetime companion. She regarded him as a source of inspiration and translated his poems from German to Spanish. They had two children: Rosangela, born on 25 July 1945, a philosophy major who now works as a teacher, and Juan Gert Conitzer, born in 1949, a painter and writer. Both children live in Bolivia.

Bedregal's first writings go back to her adolescent years when she wrote poems and short stories in her school notebooks. In a biography that appears in the anthology *Fire from the Andes: Short Fiction by Women from Bolivia, Ecuador and Peru* (1997), edited by Leonard and Susan E. Benner, Bedregal recounts an anecdote in relation to her first book, *Naufragio* (Shipwreck), published by her father in 1936 without her knowledge: "When I was studying in New York, I received the book already edited and in print; it was a very moving experience for me. I never would have confessed to my father that I wrote, because once, in a conversation with his friends, the most important intellectuals of the time, I heard him say that he didn't care if his sons were writers, but a woman writer in the family, never!" This personal anecdote illustrates the solitary path Bedregal followed as a woman author in a society in which writing was not considered an acceptable activity for women. Despite these discouraging circumstances, however, Bedregal continued to write, and, a decade later, she became one of the most important poets of her country.

Known mainly as a poet, Bedregal's fame parallels that of another Bolivian poet from the turn of the twentieth century, Adela Zamudio, and, as in the case of her predecessor, her name has been highly praised while her work has not yet received the encompassing critical attention it deserves. Nevertheless, some studies of her poetic work shed light upon the rich production of this author. In a 1986 article titled "Para un retrato de Yolanda Bedregal" (Toward a Portrait of Yolanda Bedregal), Marjorie Agosín briefly traces Bedregal's poetic trajectory, starting with *Naufragio* and ending with *Del mar y la ceniza: Alegatos, Antología* (Of the Sea and the Ashes: Pleas, Anthology, 1957). Agosín's analysis concludes that in Bedregal's work there is "una coherencia orgánica que empieza con la búsqueda y exaltación de la niñez y se asume finalmente en la búsqueda místico-religiosa de su ser" (an organic coherence that starts with the search and exaltation of childhood and culminates in the mystic-religious search for her own self). Agosín describes *Naufragio* as "una prosa poética cuidadosamente labrada, en la cual la descripción pictórica de los estados de ánimo es la nota central" (a carefully elaborated poetic prose where the pictorial description of states of mind is the central motif) and "la nostalgia del pasado, en la apreciación del mundo del niño" (childhood nostalgia, the main theme). The following quote from *Naufrigio* is representative of her poetic imagination: "Hace tiempo, la luna en creciente me parecía una barca y nos encargábamos de llenarla de una neblina amorosa, donde una niña muerta se cubría de jazmines" (Some time ago, the waxing moon seemed to me a small boat which we would fill with a loving mist where a dead girl was covered by jasmines).

Bedregal's second book is *Poemar* (1937), a neologism that can be a shorter form of *poemario* (book of poems) or a synthesis of *poema* (poem) and *mar* (sea). For Agosín, "En su segundo libro *Poemar,* continúa con algunos de los temas de *Naufragio,* que enriquece con una preocupación por su ciudad, los alrededores y la cultura indígena que la rodea." (In her second book, *Poemar,* Bedregal explores some of the same themes of *Naufragio,* but she also incorporates her concern for her city and the indigenous cultures that surround her; this concern is present in all of her subsequent works.) Agosín also asserts that "Con *Ecos,* Bedregal inicia una nueva fase lírica basada en la tradición mística hispánica" (with *Ecos* [Echoes, 1940], Bedregal initiates a new lyric phase based on the Hispanic mystic tradition), a phase that culminates with *Nadir* (1950), which many critics, including Agosín, regard as one of her best books. *Almadía* (1942), Bedregal's third book of poems—titled with another neologism joining the words *alma* (soul) and *día* (day)—and *Del mar y la ceniza* are, according to Agosín, mature works in which the poet returns to concrete reality but also creates highly elaborated metaphorical abstractions to describe her intimate self.

From a different perspective, that is, focusing on the emotions that the poems evoke, the Bolivian philosopher and writer Guillermo Francovich, in an essay that appears in the 1994 collection of Bedregal's works, *Escrito,* finds three different stages that develop successively in Bedregal's poetry. About the first one, he asserts: "En sus libros *Naufragio* y *Poemar* su conciencia se abre a las emociones familiares, a las realidades siempre dramáticas del país, Yolando Bedregal hacía en ellos sus confidencias trascendentes, traducía sus experiencias del mundo. . . ." (In *Naufragio* and *Poemar* her conscience was opened to the emotions related to the family and to the always dramatic reality of the country. In them, Yolanda Bedregal would make her transcendent confidences and translate her experience

about the world. . . .) In "Rebelión," a poem of this first stage, published in *Ecos,* for example, suffering acquires a cosmic dimension:

> De pronto un niño llora
> con su ponchito viejo
> entre la paja brava.
> Llora un niño, ¿Por qué?
> Quién sabe.
> Un niño. Un llanto humano es una herida abierta
> que ensangrienta este mundo
>
> (Suddenly, a child cries
> with his old little poncho
> amidst the rough straw.
> A child cries, Why?
> Who knows.
> A human cry is an open wound
> that stains this world with blood).

While in the first stage Bedregal's poems are objective and evoke definite emotions, in the second stage they become somewhat obscure, almost hermetic, as the poet tries to convey the life of her inner world. Francovich comments: "los versos salen como suspiros o gritos, las palabras se esfuerzan por expresar algo que puede ser confuso pero que, sin embargo, tiene un sentido emocional" (verses come out as sighs or screams, words struggle to express something that can be confusing but that nonetheless has emotional significance). Carolyne Wright published in the *Mid-American Review* (1995) "Pointless Journey," a translation of Bedregal's "Viaje Inútil," first published in *Almadia* and one of the poems that best represents this stage of Bedregal's work:

> Ahora me sobra todo lo que tuve
> porque soy como acuario y como roca.
> Por mi sangre navegan peces ágiles,
> y en mi cuerpo se enredan las raíces
> de unas plantas violetas y amarillas.
> Tengo en la espalda herida
> cicatrices de alas inservibles
> y un poquito en mis ojos todavía
> hay humedad inutil de recuerdos
>
> (Now all that I had is excess
> because I am like an aquarium and like a rock.
> Agile fish sail through my blood,
> and in my body the roots of violet
> and yellow plants are entangled.
> I have on my wounded shoulder
> scars of useless wings,
> and in my eyes still there is
> a little pointless moisture of recollections).

According to Francovich, in her third phase Bedregal's poems explore her inner life in depth and arrive at a religious experience in which she finds God at the beginning and the end of the universe. The poem "Convocatorias" (Convocations), from the 1994 collection of the same name, is representative:

> arena arrodillada,
> te convido al ropón-mantel-sudario
> de mi papel en blanco
> donde nazco y agonizo. Ven, Padre
> principio de mi larga cadena
> mi condena a ser hombre
> en tu prado amarillo
> para volver a ti

> (Kneeled sand
> I invite you to the robe-tablecloth-shroud
> of my blank page
> where I am born and agonize. Come, Father
> beginning of my long chain
> of my sentence to be a man
> in your yellow meadow
> to go back to you).

Critics have described Bedregal's "intimist" poetry as emotionally rebellious, disturbing in its femininity, and profoundly humane, with spiritual depth and overflowing lyricism. As for her style, the subtle and delicate nature of her dazzling images has been praised unanimously, prompting one critic to assert in a recollection from *Escrito* (1994) that "Cuando recordemos a la Mistral, la Storni, la Ibarbourou, debemos agregar el nombre de la Bedregal, mujer de Bolivia, es decir: corazón de América" (If we are to remember Mistral, Storni, and Ibarbourou, we also need to add the name of Bedregal, a Bolivian woman, that is to say, the heart of América). Bedregal personifies outstanding poetic qualities not only in Bolivia but also and particularly in the context of Latin American women's poetry. A comment from her contemporary, the Uruguayan poet Juana de Ibarbourou, illustrates the connections that existed among these Latin American women, as she recalls in *Escrito:* "Extraña alma de ensueño que desciende a la vigilia lo imprescindiblemente necesario para la vida, en sus poemas nos da sus visiones que tienen a veces la vaguedad de la niebla, a veces la riqueza de los sueños suntuosos y precisos, siempre un algo–hálito o luz–muy suyo" (Fantastic and rare soul who descends to awareness only the required time to stay alive. In her poems she shares her visions that sometimes have the vagueness of mist, sometimes the wealth of sumptuous, precise dreams, always something–breath or light–uniquely hers). Bedregal's distinctive personal style makes it difficult to ascribe her work to a particular poetic movement or current. Like her contemporary, the Chilean Gabriela Mistral, she stands alone, sharing the wealth of her inner world.

Throughout Bedregal's life she held various posts as a public servant. For several years she served as culture

Paperback cover for Bedregal's third collection of poems. The title is a combination of the Spanish words for "soul" and "day" (Bruccoli Clark Layman Archives).

officer and as a member of the Culture Committee of the City Council of La Paz. In 1971, during the brief socialist-oriented government of General Juan José Torres, she was designated Bolivia's ambassador to Madrid, Spain. She traveled to Europe, taking with her an impressive representation of Bolivian works of art and literature. Before she could take office, however, a coup d'etat by General Hugo Banzer ended her mission, forcing her to return to Bolivia. In 1973 she was elected member of the Bolivian Real Academia de la Lengua (Royal Language Academy). She also held the post of PEN Club secretary and was an honorary member of the Bolivian Committee for Peace and Democracy. Bedregal represented Bolivia in various international congresses.

Bedregal's narrative works include several short stories and a novel that was awarded the Premio Nacional de Novela "Erich Guttentag." Published in 1971, *Bajo el oscuro sol* is an example of the "new Latin American narrative" of the 1960s and 1970s, characterized by experimentation with literary structures, style, and language. The novel presents a fragmentary, nonlinear narration that concentrates on the search for the identity of a young woman journalist killed by a stray bullet in the midst of a revolution in La Paz. The contemporary writer and critic

Pedro Shimose, commenting in the journal *Pasajero* (December 1999–February 2000), regards this work as realistic, introspective, and immersed in Bolivian political history. Indeed, Bedregal's concern for the social reality of Bolivia, evident in her personal advocacy for a more inclusive, democratic society, is reflected with particular emphasis in this novel, which depicts the consequences of the violent, blind forces unleashed by revolution.

During her life in La Paz, Bedregal witnessed the ongoing social and political struggles aimed at achieving change in a country in which a majority of the indigenous and mixed-race population had been subjected to domination and poverty for centuries. This struggle reached one of its peaks in 1952 when a "National Revolution" took place, endorsing important reforms such as the redistribution of land and the nationalization of mines, which would allow large sectors of the marginal population to be incorporated into national life. Although left unfinished, the revolution had a negative impact on the upper-middle-class urban sector to which Bedregal belonged. In her 1996 doctoral dissertation, Alice Weldon studied *Bajo el oscuro sol* within the context of the National Revolution. Comparing Bedregal's novel with those of two other Bolivian women authors, Gaby Vallejo de Bolivar and Giancarla Zabalaga, Weldon concludes that "Bedregal, Vallejo, and Zabalaga have clearly questioned the political, physical, sexual, ethnic, and class specifics of violence in the day-to-day lives of their characters." According to Weldon, only "the authors express the view that any solutions must be based on a concept of equality with differences that takes into account factors of both ethnicity and gender." In addition to its social perspective, the novel is also a reflection of the act of writing. If in her poetry Bedregal explores her inner world, in her novel she concentrates on a search for her identity as a female author.

The dissemination of Bolivian literature and culture is another important contribution of Bedregal. She is the editor of two anthologies of Bolivian poetry, which cover the poetic production of the country from colonial times to the twentieth century. In addition, she translated Aymara poetry and wrote articles on the religion, myth, and craftsmanship of the Aymara and Quechua cultures. Finally, she wrote the Spanish text of Peter McFarren's book of photographs of indigenous Bolivia, *Ayllu: El altiplano boliviano* (Ayllu: The Bolivian High Plateau, 1984). As for the broader dissemination of her own writings, translations of Bedregal's poems and some short stories can be found particularly in volumes devoted to Latin American literature produced by women, such as *Fire from the Andes* and *Cruel Fictions, Cruel Realities: Short Stories by Latin American Women Writers* (1997), also edited by Leonard. Yolanda Bedregal died in La Paz, on 21 May 1999. She was an eminent poet, novelist, and citizen of her beloved La Paz, who lived to know and to learn her

place in the world, or, as she humbly explains in her poem "Frenta a mi retrato," from *Escrito,* she wrote in order "to learn to spell her life":

> Estoy ahora como he sido siempre
> y como nunca más habré de ser
> Estaba escrito todo en hoja blanca
> Ahora aprendo a leer mi adolescencia;
> y sólo podré leer mi vida toda
> cuando, como hoy me miro en el retrato
> pueda, un día, mirarme desde el marco
> sereno, inmarcesible de la muerte

> (Now I am as I have always been
> and as I shall never be again.
> It was all written on the empty page.
> I have just learned to read
> to spell my youth,
> and I shall learn to read my whole life when,
> just as today I stare back at my portrait,
> shall one day look out upon myself
> from the calm and fadeless picture
> frame of death).

(Translated by Donald D. Walsh)

Interviews:

Kathy S. Leonard, interview with Bedregal, *Sincronía* (Summer 1998) <http://fuentes.csh.udg.mx/CUCSH/Sincronia/bedregal.htm>;

Leonard, *Una revelación desde la escritura: Entrevistas a poetas bolivianas* (New York: Peter Lang, 2001).

References:

Marjorie Agosín, "Para un retrato de Yolanda Bedregal," *Revista Iberoamericana,* no. 134 (1986): 267–271;

Maria Elva Echenique, *Si nos permiten Hablar: Narradoras Bolivianas del Siglo XX,* dissertation, University of Oregon, 2002;

Guillermo Francovich, "Sobre la poesía de Yolanda Bedregal," in Bedregal's *Escrito* (Quito: Printer Graphic, 1994), pp. 9–20;

Dora Gómez de Fernández and Nicolás Fernández Naranjo, "'La Danza' de Yolanda Bedregal," in *Técnica Literaria* (La Paz: Juventud, 1971), pp. 186–200;

Lucía F. M. A. Martin, *El mundo poético de Yolanda Bedregal,* Tesis de Licenciatura, San Andrés University, La Paz, 1981;

Gaby Vallejo de Bolivar, *En busca de los nuestros: Análisis y crítica sobre literatura boliviana* (La Paz: Los Amigos del Libro, 1987);

Alice Weldon, *In Reference to the National Revolution of Bolivia: Three Novels by Women,* dissertation, University of Maryland at College Park, 1996.

Jorge Luis Borges

(24 August 1899 – 14 June 1986)

Daniel Balderston
University of Iowa

See also the Borges entry in *DLB 113: Modern Latin-American Fiction Writers, First Series* and *DLB Yearbook: 1986.*

BOOKS: *Fervor de Buenos Aires* (Buenos Aires: Privately printed, 1923; revised and enlarged edition, Buenos Aires: Emecé, 1969);

Luna de enfrente (Buenos Aires: Proa, 1925);

Inquisiciones (Buenos Aires: Proa, 1925);

El tamaño de mi esperanza (Buenos Aires: Proa, 1926);

El idioma de los argentinos (Buenos Aires: Gleizer, 1928);

Cuaderno San Martín (Buenos Aires: Proa, 1929);

Evaristo Carriego (Buenos Aires: Gleizer, 1930); translated by Norman Thomas di Giovanni and Susan Ashe as *Evaristo Carriego: A Book about Old-Time Buenos Aires* (New York: Dutton, 1983);

Discusión (Buenos Aires: Gleizer, 1932; revised edition, Madrid: Alianza / Buenos Aires: Emecé, 1976);

Las kenningar (Buenos Aires: Francisco A. Colombo, 1933);

Historia universal de la infamia (Buenos Aires: Tor, 1935; revised edition, Buenos Aires: Emecé, 1954); translated by di Giovanni as *A Universal History of Infamy* (New York: Dutton, 1972; London: John Lane, 1973);

Historia de la eternidad (Buenos Aires: Viau & Zona, 1936; revised and enlarged edition, Buenos Aires: Emecé, 1953);

El jardín de senderos que se bifurcan (Buenos Aires: Sur, 1941);

Seis problemas para Don Isidro Parodi, by Borges and Adolfo Bioy Casares, as H. Busto Domecq (Buenos Aires: Sur, 1942); translated by di Giovanni as *Six Problems for Don Isidro Parodi* (New York: Dutton, 1980);

Poemas (1922–1943) (Buenos Aires: Losada, 1943); revised and enlarged as *Poemas, 1923–1953* (Buenos Aires: Emecé, 1954); revised and enlarged again as *Poemas, 1923–1958* (Buenos Aires: Emecé, 1958);

Jorge Luis Borges, circa 1972 (photograph by Jesse A. Fernandez)

Ficciones (1935–1944) (Buenos Aires: Sur, 1944); enlarged as *Ficciones* (Buenos Aires: Emecé, 1956); translated by Anthony Kerrigan and others, and edited by Kerrigan (London: Weidenfeld & Nicolson, 1962; New York: Grove, 1962);

El compadrito, su destino, sus barrios, su música, by Borges and Silvina Bullrich Palenque (Buenos Aires: Emecé, 1945; enlarged edition, Buenos Aires: General Fabril, 1968);

Dos fantasías memorables, by Borges and Bioy Casares, as Bustos Domecq (Buenos Aires: Oportet, 1946);

Un modelo para la muerte, by Borges and Bioy Casares, as B. Suárez Lynch (Buenos Aires: Oportet & Haereses, 1946);

El Aleph (Buenos Aires: Losada, 1949; enlarged, 1952); translated and edited by Borges and di Giovanni as *The Aleph and Other Stories, 1933–1969, Together with Commentaries and an Autobiographical Essay* (New York: Dutton, 1970; London: Cape, 1971);

Aspectos de la literatura gauchesca (Montevideo: Número, 1950);

Antiguas literaturas germánicas (Mexico City: Fondo de Cultura Económica, 1951);

La muerte y la brújula (Buenos Aires: Emecé, 1951);

Otras inquisiciones (1937–1952) (Buenos Aires: Sur, 1952); translated by Ruth L. C. Simms as *Other Inquisitions, 1937–1952* (Austin: University of Texas Press, 1964; London: Souvenir, 1973);

El "Martín Fierro," by Borges and Margarita Guerrero (Buenos Aires: Columba, 1953);

La hermana de Eloísa, by Borges and L. M. Levinson (Buenos Aires: Ene, 1955);

Los orilleros; El paraíso de los creyentes, by Borges and Bioy Casares (Buenos Aires: Losada, 1955);

Leopoldo Lugones, by Borges and Betina Edelberg (Buenos Aires: Troquel, 1955);

Nueve poemas (Buenos Aires: El Mangrullo, 1955);

Manual de zoología fantástica, by Borges and Guerrero (Mexico City & Buenos Aires: Fondo de Cultura Económica, 1957);

Límites (Buenos Aires: Francisco A. Colombo, 1958);

El hacedor (Buenos Aires: Emecé, 1960); translated by Mildred Boyer and Harold Morland as *Dreamtigers* (Austin: University of Texas Press, 1964; London: Souvenir, 1973);

Antología personal (Buenos Aires: Emecé, 1961); translated by Kerrigan and others as *Personal Anthology,* edited by Kerrigan (New York: Grove, 1967; London: Cape, 1968);

El lenguaje de Buenos Aires (Buenos Aires: Emecé, 1963);

El otro, el mismo (Buenos Aires: Emecé, 1964);

Obra poética 1923–1964 (Buenos Aires: Emecé, 1964); enlarged as *Obra poética 1923–1966* (Buenos Aires: Emecé, 1966); enlarged again as *Obra poética 1923–1967* (Buenos Aires: Emecé, 1967); enlarged again as *Obra poética 1923–1969* (Buenos Aires: Emecé, 1972); enlarged again as *Obra poética 1923–1976* (Buenos Aires: Emecé, 1977);

Para las seis cuerdas (Buenos Aires: Emecé, 1965);

Introducción a la literatura inglesa, by Borges and María Esther Vázquez (Buenos Aires: Columba, 1965); translated and edited by L. Clark Keating and Robert O. Evans as *An Introduction to English Literature* (Lexington: University Press of Kentucky, 1974);

Literaturas germánicas medievales, by Borges and Vázquez (Buenos Aires: Falbo, 1965);

El libro de los seres imaginarios, by Borges and Guerrero (Buenos Aires: Kier, 1967); revised, enlarged, and translated by Borges and di Giovanni as *The Book of Imaginary Beings* (New York: Dutton, 1969; Harmondsworth, U.K.: Penguin, 1974);

Introducción a la literatura norteamericana, by Borges and Esther Zemborain de Torres (Buenos Aires: Columba, 1967); translated and edited by Keating and Evans as *An Introduction to American Literature* (New York: Schocken, 1973);

Crónicas de Bustos Domecq, by Borges and Bioy Casares (Buenos Aires: Losada, 1967); translated by di Giovanni as *Chronicles of Bustos Domecq* (New York: Dutton, 1976);

Nueva antología personal (Buenos Aires: Emecé, 1968);

Elogio de la sombra (Buenos Aires: Emecé, 1969); translated by di Giovanni as *In Praise of Darkness* (New York: Dutton, 1974; London: John Lane, 1975);

El informe de Brodie (Buenos Aires: Emecé, 1970); translated by Borges and di Giovanni as *Doctor Brodie's Report* (New York: Bantam, 1973; London: John Lane, 1974);

El Congreso (Buenos Aires: Archibrazo, 1971); translated by Borges and di Giovanni as *The Congress* (London: Enitharmon, 1974);

El oro de los tigres (Buenos Aires: Emecé, 1972); translated, in part, by Alastair Reid in *The Gold of the Tigers: Selected Later Poems* (New York: Dutton, 1977);

Prólogos, con un prólogo de prólogos (Buenos Aires: Torres Agüero, 1975);

La rosa profunda (Buenos Aires: Emecé, 1975); translated, in part, by Reid in *The Gold of the Tigers: Selected Later Poems;*

El libro de arena (Buenos Aires: Emecé, 1975); translated by di Giovanni as *The Book of Sand* (New York: Dutton, 1977; London: John Lane, 1979);

Diálogos, by Borges and Ernesto Sábato (Buenos Aires: Emecé, 1976);

La moneda de hierro (Buenos Aires: Emecé, 1976);

Qué es el budismo, by Borges and Alicia Jurado (Buenos Aires: Columba, 1976);

Cosmogonías (Buenos Aires: Librería La Ciudad, 1976);

Historia de la noche (Buenos Aires: Emecé, 1977);

Nuevos cuentos de Bustos Domecq, by Borges and Bioy Casares (Buenos Aires: Librería La Ciudad, 1977);

Borges para millones (Buenos Aires: Corregidor, 1978);

Poesía juvenil de Jorge Luis Borges, edited by Carlos Meneses (Barcelona: José Olañeta, 1978);

Borges, oral (Buenos Aires: Emecé, 1979);

Siete noches (Buenos Aires & Mexico City: Fondo de Cultura Económica, 1980); translated by Eliot Weinberger as *Seven Nights* (New York: New Directions, 1984; London: Faber & Faber, 1984);

La cifra (Buenos Aires: Emecé, 1981);

Nueve ensayos dantescos, with an introduction by Marcos Ricardo Barnatán (Madrid: Espasa-Calpe, 1982);

Milongas (Buenos Aires: Dos Amigos, 1983);

Vienticinco Agosto 1983 y otros cuentos (Madrid: Siruela, 1983);

Atlas, by Borges and María Kodama (Buenos Aires: Sudamericana, 1984); translated by Kerrigan (New York: Dutton, 1985);

Los conjurados (Madrid: Alianza, 1985);

Textos Cautivos: Ensayos y reseños en "El Hogar," edited by Enrique Sacerio Garí and Emir Rodríguez Monegal (Barcelona: Tusquets, 1986);

A/Z (Madrid: Siruela, 1988);

Biblioteca personal: Prólogos (Madrid: Alianza, 1988);

Borges en la Escuela Freudiana de Buenos Aires (Buenos Aires: Agalma, 1993);

Borges en Revista multicolor: Obras, resenas y traducciones ineditas de Jorge Luis Borges diario Critica, Revista multicolor de los sabados, 1933–1934, edited by Irma Zangara (Buenos Aires: Atlantida, 1995);

Borges: Textos recobrados 1919–1929, edited by Zangara (Buenos Aires: Emecé, 1997).

Editions and Collections: *Obras completas,* 9 volumes (Buenos Aires: Emecé, 1953–1960); revised edition, 1 volume, edited by Carlos V. Frías (Buenos Aires: Emecé, 1974);

Obras completas en colaboración, by Borges and others (Buenos Aires: Emecé, 1979);

Prose completa, 2 volumes (Barcelona: Bruguera, 1980);

Antología poética (1923–1977) (Madrid: Alianza, 1981);

Obras completas 1975–1985 (Buenos Aires: Emecé, 1989).

Editions in English: *Labyrinths: Selected Stories and Other Writings,* edited by Donald A. Yates and James E. Irby (New York: New Directions, 1962);

Selected Poems, 1923–1967, translated and edited by Norman Thomas di Giovanni (London: John Lane/ Penguin, 1972; New York: Dell, 1973);

Borges: A Reader, edited by Emir Rodríguez Monegal and Alastair Reid (New York: Dutton, 1981);

Borges on Writing, edited by di Giovanni, Daniel Halpern, and Frank MacShane (Hopewell, N.J.: Ecco Press, 1994);

Collected Fictions, translated by Andrew Hurley (New York: Viking, 1998);

Selected Non-Fictions, edited by Eliot Weinberger, translated by Weinberger, Esther Allen, and Suzanne Jill Levine (New York: Viking, 1999);

Selected Poems, edited by Alexander Coleman, translated by Willis Barnstone and others (New York: Viking, 1999);

This Craft of Verse, edited by Calin-Andrei Mihailescu (Cambridge, Mass.: Harvard University Press, 2000).

OTHER: *Antología poética argentina,* edited by Borges, Adolfo Bioy Casares, and Silvina Ocampo (Buenos Aires: Sudamericana, 1941);

Francisco de Quevedo, *Prosa y verso,* edited by Borges and Bioy Casares (Buenos Aires: Emecé, 1948);

Cuentos breves y extraordinarios, edited by Borges and Bioy Casares (Buenos Aires: Raigal, 1955);

Poesía gauchesca, 2 volumes, edited by Borges and Bioy Casares (Mexico City: Fondo de Cultura Económica, 1955);

Walt Whitman, *Hojas de hierba,* translated by Borges and Else Astete (Buenos Aires: Juárez, 1969);

Breve antología anglosajona, edited by Borges (Santiago: Ediciones la Ciudad, 1978).

Jorge Luis Borges, Argentina's best-known writer, was born on 24 August 1899 in a traditional old house in central Buenos Aires (not far from today's financial district) and grew up in the neighborhood of Palermo. His father, Jorge Guillermo Borges, was the son of an Argentine military officer who had fought in the War of the Triple Alliance in Paraguay and died in an Argentine civil war, and of Frances Haslam de Borges, an English immigrant who for a time kept a boardinghouse for English-speaking schoolteachers. Jorge Guillermo Borges taught philosophy and psychology at the secondary-school level. Borges's mother, Leonor Acevedo de Borges, was descended from a line of Uruguayan military men, and military mythology was dear to her. Raised in a partly English-speaking household, Borges and his sister, Norah Borges (later a well-known painter and the wife of the Spanish literary critic Guillermo de Torre), spent a fairly uneventful early childhood in Palermo, where their father was friends with the local poet Evaristo Carriego, with the philosopher and writer Macedonio Fernández, and with the nationalist poet Leopoldo Lugones. Their lives changed dramatically when their parents decided to take a trip to Europe in 1914; the outbreak of World War I led to a prolonged residence in Geneva, where Borges studied at the College Calvin (learning French, German, and Latin), his last period of formal education. When the war ended the family moved to Mallorca, Spain; Borges then went on to spend an important year in Madrid before the family returned to Buenos Aires in 1921. By then he had clearly chosen to be a writer.

Borges with his parents and sister, Norah, in Saint Mark's Square, Venice, 1914 (from Charles Newman and Mary Kinzie, eds., Prose for Borges, *1974; Thomas Cooper Library, University of South Carolina)*

Though best known in the English-speaking world for his short stories, Borges began his career as a poet, published dozens of books of poetry, and wrote extensively about poetry (as well as collaborating in editing various anthologies of poetry). The three volumes published by Viking in honor of the Borges centenary, *Collected Fictions* (1998), *Selected Non-Fictions* (1999), and *Selected Poems* (1999), are striking in this regard—only a small portion of Borges's book reviews and literary essays are included, and a tinier proportion still of his poetry. Although he is one of the major Latin American poets of the twentieth century, the taste for Borges's poetry has not spread as widely as the fame of

his fiction (or, for that matter, of his literary essays). Yet, his poetry has had a wide impact: many verses have been used as titles for novels and other works, many poems have been set to music, and his variety of poetic voices have been important to many younger poets.

Borges published poetry over a period of more than sixty years; from his beginnings in the avant-garde he evolved later into a sort of neoclassicist. The history of his poetry is exceedingly complex, with rewritings of poems across several decades, rearrangements of his books of poetry, insertion of late poems into new editions of early books, radical changes of style and technique, and equally important changes in his ideas about poetics. Yet, there is a poetic voice, as well as a treatment of aesthetic and philosphical concerns, that continues from his early poetry to his late. Poetry dominated his production in the 1920s and again in the 1960s, 1970s, and 1980s, and even at the moments his creative energy was channeled above all into stories and essays, there is an important dialogue within his work between his poetry and his prose.

One of the serious problems that the student of Borges's poetry encounters is the complex relationship between the chronology of the poems (their composition and first publication) and their inclusion in book form, particularly after the first collections of Borges's collected works began appearing in the 1960s. The problem is twofold: poems that were published in his early career were modified or suppressed, and often much later poems were included in their places. A well-known example is "Arrabal" (Neighborhood), a poem originally published in 1921 and included in *Fervor de Buenos Aires* (Fervor of Buenos Aires) in 1923. In editions of *Fervor de Buenos Aires* after 1964 (and indeed in the edition of *Poemas* [1922–1943] published in 1943), this poem ends:

> y sentí Buenos Aires
> esta ciudad que yo creí mi pasado
> es mi porvenir, mi presente;
> los años que he vivido en Europa son ilusorios,
> yo he estado siempre (y estaré) en Buenos Aires

> (and I felt Buenos Aires
> this city that I believed was my past
> is my present, my future;
> the years that I have lived in Europe are illusory,
> I have always been [and will always be] in Buenos Aires).

Despite the date "1921" that ends the poem in the 1964 edition of the *Obra poética* (Poetic Works), the original 1921 poem, published in *Borges: Textos recobrados 1919–1929* (Borges: Recovered Texts 1919–1929, 1997), ends in quite a different way. In it, Borges expresses no such certainty about his "destiny" being Buenos Aires. Its ending is instead:

> Y sentí *Buenos Aires*
> y literaturicé en el fondo del alma
> la viacrucis inmóvil
> de la calle sufrida
> y el caserío sosegado
>
> (And I felt *Buenos Aires*
> and made literature in the depth of my soul
> from the motionless way of the cross
> of the suffering street
> and the quiet houses).

There is a world of difference, of course, between a young man expressing certainty about his future and an older man retrospectively putting such words in the young man's mouth (because by 1943—and with greater certainty in 1964—Borges did indeed know that most of his life would be lived out in Buenos Aires). In 1921 Borges had spent a third of his twenty-two years in Europe (in Geneva from 1914 to 1918 and then three years in Mallorca and Madrid), and his "rediscovery" of Buenos Aires when the family returned from Switzerland and Spain was indeed dramatic—resulting in his first book, *Fervor de Buenos Aires*. Borges often plays this sort of game with time—in his poems about the deaths of his grandfathers, in the story "La otra muerte" (The Other Death, 1949), in the 1972 story "El otro" (The Other), and in *El libro de arena* (1975; translated as *The Book of Sand,* 1977). In "Arrabal," as in that late story, the older Borges is correcting the younger one, but the reader must beware before ascribing the sentiments expressed in the later version of the poem to the Borges of 1921. This mistake is frequently made by critics who are not sufficiently immersed in the chronology of Borges's work; similar problems exist with the second editions of *Discusión* (Discussion, 1932) and *Ficciones (1935–1944)* (Fictions, 1944). Tommaso Scarano has studied the rewriting of the poetry in great detail (as Michel Lafon has studied rewriting in Borges in general), while Enrique Pezzoni's excellent article on *Fervor de Buenos Aires* addresses the rewritings among other questions; the critic is urged to consult these works, as well as Nicolás Helft's bibliography (the most complete to date), to avoid important critical problems with the chronology of the works.

Borges's first published poem, "Himno del mar" (Hymn of the Sea) from the 31 December 1919 edition of the review *Grecia,* brims with enthusiasm for the sea and for an exuberant poetic voice that Borges had found in Walt Whitman. Even Whit-man's homoeroticism influences the voice who cries: "¡Mar! / ¡Hermano, Padre, Amado . . . !" (Sea! / Brother, Father, Lover . . . !), or later:

> Oh instante de plenitud magnífica;
> Antes de conocerte, Mar hermano,
>   Largamente he vagado por errantes valles azules con
>   oriflamas de faroles
> Y en la sagrada media noche yo he tejido guirnaldas
> De besos sobre carnes y labios que se ofrendaban,
> Solemnes de silencio,
> En una floración
> Sangrienta . . .
> Pero ahora yo hago don a los vientos
> de todas esas cosas pretéritas,
> pretéritas. . . . Sólo tú existes.
> Atlético y desnudo
>
> (Oh instant of magnificent fullness;
> Before meeting you, brother Sea,
>   I have traveled far through wandering blue trees with
>   the oriflamme of street lamps
> At sacred midnight I have woven garlands
> Of kisses upon flesh and lips that offered themselves,
> Solemn in silence,
> In a bloody
> Flowering . . .
> But now I make a gift to the winds
> of all of these past things,
> past. . . . Only you exist,
> Athletic and naked).

Or later still: "Oh proteico, yo he salido de ti" (Oh Protean one, I have emerged from you). Whitman's ideal of male "adhesiveness" is oddly present in this song to the sea, which is gendered male and addressed as Whitman often addresses his lovers.

Already in "Himno del mar" there is a verse, "El camino fue largo como un beso" (The street was as long as a kiss), that prefigures the next period in Borges's production. With his discovery of German Expressionism and then of Spanish Ultraism, Borges explores audacious metaphors, while at the same time impressing them with a rather homely quality. The majority of his Ultraist poems are written between 1920 and 1923 (that is, during the last year of the Borges family's residence in Spain, back in Buenos Aires, then during the family's second European trip in 1923); many were evidently intended to be collected in a book called "Himnos rojos" or "Salmos rojos" (Red Anthems or Psalms), the ostensible theme of which was to be the Russian revolution. (Jean Pierre Bernès has reconstructed part of this book in the Pléiade edition of Borges's works in French, and *Borges: Textos recobrados 1919–1929* echoes some of his claims of what this book was to consist of; these claims must, however, be taken rather skeptically, since Borges never published this

Borges in 1924, shortly before returning to Buenos Aires from his second journey to Europe (Collection of Jorge and Marion Helft)

3. Abolition of ornamental implements, confessionalism, circumstantial evidence, preaching, and deliberate vagueness.

4. Synthesis of two or more images in one, which thus enlarges its capacity for suggestion).

The insistence on metaphor, preferably surprising or "new" metaphor, and on the combination ("síntesis") of multiple images in a single verse is the dominant one in Borges's early poetry, and an idea that he spent much of the rest of his life rethinking. A typical example of an *ultraísta* poem is "Gesta maximalista" (Maximalist Epic) on the Bolshevik revolution:

Desde los hombros curvos
se arrojaron los rifles como viaductos
Las barricadas que cicatrizan las plazas
vibran nervios desnudos
El cielo se ha crinado de gritos y disparos
Solsticios interiores han quemado los cráneos
Uncida por el largo aterrizaje
la catedral avión de multitudes quiere romper las amarras
y el ejército fresca arboladura
de surtidores-bayonetas pasa
el candelabro de los mil y un falos
Pájaro rojo vuela un estandarte
sobre la hirsuta muchedumbre extática

(From the curved shoulders
the rifles were tossed like viaducts
The barricades that scar the squares
quiver in naked nerves
The sky has been crowned with cries and shots
Inner solstices have burned brains
Yoked by its long grounding
the cathedral airplane for crowds wants to break its tether
and the army fresh shrubbery
of fountain-bayonets passes
candelabrum of a thousand and one phalluses
Red bird flies on a flag
over the disheveled ecstatic crowd).

This poem is remarkable for its excess (but in this respect is fairly typical of Borges's *ultraísta* poems): the army is a moving forest (with echoes perhaps of Macbeth's Burnham Wood), the bayonets are fountains and candelabra and phalluses, the cathedral a grounded airplane. The images are piled upon one another in ways that defy logic, except perhaps the visual logic (influenced perhaps by Sigmund Freud) that sees fountain-bayonets as a "candelabrum of a thousand and one phalluses." Again, as in "Himno del mar," there is a strong homosocial element (Whitman's "adhesiveness"), as the image of the Red Army impresses itself on the young poet's imagination as male, erect, disheveled, and even ecstatic. The poem has a degree of historical specificity ("maximalista" is the Spanish translation of "bolshevik," for example, and the image at the end is of

book or said anything precise about what it would have been.) Some of the *ultraísta* poems, sometimes shorn of their more extravagant metaphors, survived in *Fervor de Buenos Aires* in 1923, and a few (usually much rewritten) in the greatly revised editions of *Fervor de Buenos Aires* after 1964; the reader is advised, however, to consult *Borges: Textos recobrados 1919–1929* for the original versions of these poems, which are vastly different from Borges's later poetry.

In December 1921, in an essay on *ultraísmo* in the Argentine cultural periodical *Nosotros* (We), Borges defined the principles of the movement as he saw them:

1. Reducción de la lírica a su elemento primordial: la metáfora.
2. Tachadura de las frases medianeras, los nexos, y los adjetivos inútiles.
3. Abolición de los trebejos ornamentales, el confesionalismo, la circunstanciación, las prédicas y la nebulosidad rebuscada.
4. Síntesis de dos o más imágenes en una, que ensancha de ese modo su facultad de sugerencia

(1. Reduction of lyric poetry to its basic element: metaphor.
2. Elimination of links, connecting phrases, and superfluous adjectives.

the Soviet flag); yet, at the same time the poet seems to be searching for an archetypal or timeless quality (hence the final "extático").

Another important early poem is "Carnicería" (Butcher Shop), an Expressionist poem that appeared in the first edition of *Fervor de Buenos Aires* in 1923 and survived more or less intact in subsequent editions:

> Más vil que un lupanar
> la carnicería rubrica como una afrenta la calle.
> Sobre el dintel
> la escupidora de una cabeza de vaca
> de mirar ciego y cornamenta grandiosa
> preside el aquelarre
> de carne charra y mármoles finales
> con la lejana majestad de un ídolo
>
> (More vile than a brothel
> the butcher shop marks the street like an insult.
> Over the doorway
> the spittoon of a cow head
> a blind stare and grandiose horns
> presides over the witches' Sabbath
> of gaudy meat and final marbletops
> with the remote majesty of an idol).

Unlike "Catedral" or the other *ultraísta* poems that abound in metaphor (and that perhaps for this reason were not included in *Fervor de Buenos Aires* and suppressed from later editions of the poetry that were published in Borges's lifetime), the simple, monumental central image of "Carnicería"—the cow skull that presides over the butcher shop—survives the changes in aesthetics and the processes of revision that followed.

The 1974 version of this poem is shorter but retains the essential elements of the original. Though three lines shorter and a bit simplified, the marks of Borges's readings of German Expressionism are clear even in the 1974 edition: the search for naked and intense experience, a neoprimitivist quest for human essences, the reliance on a few bold images. One of the striking elements of the 1923 version, however, the final juxtaposition of "la palabra escrita junto a la palabra que se habla" (a written word beside words that are spoken), is absent. This image of "fijeza impasible" (impassive fixity), a metaphoric and metalinguistic reading of the monumental fetish of the cow head, implies a relation between Argentine oral culture—the culture of the slaughterhouses and butcher shops so important to the rise of Buenos Aires—and its literature (one of whose first important texts is the 1871 "El matadero" [The Matador], the posthumous publication of Esteban Echeverría, which is also an allegorical reading of the slaughterhouses). Like the German Expressionist poems about trench warfare (which Borges imitated in

"Trinchera" in 1920), "Carnicería" finds human intensity in the midst of death.

Borges's reading of German Expressionism is easily charted in the publications of the early 1920s that are brought together in *Borges: Textos recobrados 1919–1929,* which include reviews, essays, and translations (of such authors as Kurt Heynicke, Wilhelm Klemm, Ernst Stadler, Johannes Becher, Alfred Vagts, and August Stramm). Indeed, it could be argued that the Germans' focus on a few intense images helped cure Borges of his *ultraísta* excesses. *Fervor de Buenos Aires* already marks something of a departure from Ultraism. Borges's walks through the backstreets of Buenos Aires—unlike Charles Baudelaire's flaneur, who walks through the center—focus on images of humble everyday life, on suffering, on death. As in Expressionism, human suffering is transmuted in the pain felt by trees, by houses, by sunsets. Metaphor becomes less extravagant (and less frequent); what Borges calls (in the preface to *Luna de enfrente* [Moon across the Way, 1925]) an aesthetics of "mi pobreza" (my poverty) can be read as a reaction to the abundant metaphorizing of Ultraism—and of Surrealism, a subsequent avant-garde movement that Borges found distasteful.

The first poem of *Fervor de Buenos Aires,* "Las calles" (The Streets), memorably defines its subject as the quiet streets of the urban periphery:

> Las calles de Buenos Aires
> ya son la entraña de mi alma.
> No las calles enérgicas
> molestadas de prisas y ajetreos,
> sino la dulce calle de arrabal
> enternecida de árboles y ocasos
>
> (The streets of Buenos Aires
> are already the innards of my soul.
> Not the energetic streets
> bothered by hurry and bustle,
> but the sweet neighborhood street
> made tender by trees and sunsets).

Particularly noteworthy are the lines "Son todas ellas para el codicioso de almas / una promesa de ventura" (All of them are—for one who is greedy for souls—a promise of joy). The poetic speaker is a hungry observer, eager for vicarious experience, a variant of Baudelaire's *flâneur,* as Sylvia Molloy suggests, who looks for the remains of the older city that is disappearing, not at the modern city that is emerging.

As Pezzoni notes in his essay on *Fervor de Buenos Aires* (the most important critical article on the book), these poems function through a sort of solipsism, whereby the outskirts of the city are a "metáfora/anécdota del Yo empeñado en la empresa de afirmarse y

*Borges's maternal grandfather, Isidoro de Acevedo Laprida,
about whom he wrote the poem "Isidoro Acevedo"
(Collection of Jorge and Marion Helft)*

Luna de enfrente continues the search for Buenos Aires, with renewed focus on the backstreets and poorer neighborhoods (though it also includes poems on Nîmes, Dakar, and Montevideo, as well as a couple of poems set in rural Argentina). Such poems as "Calle con almacén rosao" (Street with a Pink Corner Store), "Al horizonte de un suburbio" (To the Horizon of the Outskirts), "Casas como ángeles" (Houses like Angels), "Ultimo sol en Villa Ortúzar" (Sunset over Villa Ortúzar), and "En Villa Alvear" continue the motif that is dominant in *Fervor de Buenos Aires,* of the poet as night visitor to out-of-the-way parts of the city, participant-observer of its poverty, and witness to the passing of its traditions. Poverty—a poverty of form, of emotion, of theme—is erected into a creed: Borges writes in the first line of the preface, "Este es cartel de mi pobreza" (This is a sign of my poverty).

The best-known poem in *Luna de enfrente* is the stirring "El general Quiroga va en coche al muere" (General Quiroga Rides to His Death in a Carriage), on the stagecoach ride to Barranca Yaco that took Juan Facundo Quiroga to his death at the hands of assassins in 1835. Here Borges is reworking one of the most famous incidents in nineteenth-century Argentine history, the climax of Domingo Faustino Sarmiento's great *Facundo* (1845), a life of the Argentine strongman:

> Pero en llegando al sitio nombrao Barranca Yaco
> Sables a filo y punta menudiaron sobre él:
> Muerte de mala muerte se lo llevó al riojano
> Y una de puñaladas lo mentó a Juan Manuel

> (But when the brightness of day shone on Barranca Yaco
> weapons without mercy swooped in a rage upon him;
> death, which is for all, rounded up the man from La Rioja
> and more than one thrust of the dagger invoked Juan Manuel de Rosas).

In this poem Borges renders homage not only to Quiroga but also to the probable paymaster of his assassins, Juan Manuel de Rosas. In the preface he states:

> En dos [poemas de este libro] figura el nombre de Carriego, siempre con un sentido de numen tutelar de Palermo, que así lo siento yo. Pero otra sombra, más ponderosa de eternidá que la suya, gravita sobre el barrio: la de don Juan Manuel

> (In two [of the poems in this book] Carriego's name figures, always in the sense of a tutelary god of Palermo, which is how I think of him. But another shade, of a deeper eternity still, weighs on the neighborhood: that of Juan Manuel).

The invocation of Evaristo Carriego, a local poet who had been a friend of Borges's father and a neighbor in

negarse" (metaphor/anecdote of the self engaged in the enterprise of affirming and negating itself). In this enterprise the avant-garde—a collective spirit of renovation—is replaced by a more lonely quest, which, though imbued with a desire for aesthetic renovation, works through the "residuo irracional de la memoria y el recuerdo" (irrational residue of memory and recollections). Pezzoni summarizes: "En el Borges grupal del ultraísmo ya estaba presente el Borges del paseo solitario por el arrabal fabricado como ámbito para la omnipotencia del Yo soberano en su errancia entre los extremos del sí y del no" (In the collective-minded Borges of *ultraísmo* the Borges of the solitary walks in neighborhoods already exists, neighborhoods constructed as the scene for the omnipotent sovereign self in its wanderings in the extremes of affirmation and negation). The poetic self of *Fervor de Buenos Aires* is a lonely witness to empty streets, to long-suffering houses, to inscriptions on graves, to sunsets and dawns. At no other point in Borges's career is the social dimension so absent from his writing. This emptying out of social spaces is yet another way of responding to the collective spirit of the avant-garde, so full of movement and a shared enthusiasm for modernity.

Palermo during Borges's early years, is suggestive, since a few years later Borges published a biographical study, *Evaristo Carriego* (1930; translated as *Evaristo Carriego: A Book about Old-Time Buenos Aires,* 1983), a clear attempt to ally himself aesthetically with Carriego's cult of neighborhood characters: seamstresses who became pregnant, local thugs, tango dancers, organ players with their monkeys.

Luna de enfrente is also important for marking the high point of Borges's infatuation with Argentine popular speech. Here—as in the book of essays *El tamaño de mi esperanza* (The Extent of My Hope, 1926)—he adopts a spelling that echoes Argentine speech patterns (suppressing the intervocalic and final *d,* for example, or changing from *e* to *i* in certain verb endings), as well as elements of the nineteenth-century spelling reform advocated by Andrés Bello and Sarmiento. If *Fervor de Buenos Aires* marks a return to the native city, *Luna de enfrente* and *El tamaño de mi esperanza* show Borges at his most extreme moment of Argentine cultural nationalism.

In this light, then, there is a surprising inclusion in *Luna de enfrente:* the most unusual poem, and one that Borges promptly suppressed and excluded from future editions of his poems, is "Soleares" (named after an Andalusian folk song and dance). Strongly reminiscent of the work of the Spanish poet Federico García Lorca, it is a series of brief three-line poems set in Andalucía, with guitars and olive trees and winds from the Mediterranean:

> Igual que una herida abierta
> es la guitarra y la copla
> derrama su sangre negra
>
> (Like an open wound
> the guitar and its song
> spill their black blood).

García Lorca made a prolonged visit to Buenos Aires a few years later, and Borges took an intense dislike to him, which probably explains the suppression of the poem. It appeared for the last time in *Laurel,* an anthology of Spanish and Spanish American poetry published in Mexico in 1941, and then disappeared forever from Borges's collected poetry and anthologies of his work.

The third book of poems that Borges published in the 1920s (and his last book of new poetry until 1960) is *Cuaderno San Martín* (San Martín Copybook, 1929), named for the brand of notebook in which Borges wrote the poems. The original manuscript is now in the collection of the Fundación San Telmo; the cover bears a conventional likeness of José de San Martín, the liberator of the southern part of South America and Argentina's iconic national hero. The book opens on an appropriate nationalistic note with "La fundación mitológica de Buenos Aires" (Mythological Founding of Buenos Aires), later retitled "Fundación mítica de Buenos Aires" (The Mythical Founding of Buenos Aires), one of Borges's most celebrated poems. "La fundación mitológica de Buenos Aires" takes as its alleged subject the first Spanish voyage to the River Plate, that of Juan Díaz de Solís in 1516. Borges rewrites history, however, rejecting the traditional site of the founding of the city (Parque Lezama, near La Boca neighborhood) and relocating the founding of the city in the block where he grew up in Palermo (a house the Borges family left when it went to Europe from 1914 to 1921, which is evoked also in *Cuaderno San Martín* in the poem "Fluencia natural del recuerdo" [Natural Flow of Memory]). In "La fundación mitológica de Buenos Aires" the founding of the city is located precisely there:

> Una manzana entera pero en mitá del campo
> Presenciada de auroras y lluvias y suestadas.
> La manzana pareja que persiste en mi barrio:
> Guatemala, Serrano, Paraguay, Gurruchaga
>
> (A whole square block, but set down in open country,
> attended by dawns and rains and hard southeasters.
> The very block which still stands in my neighborhood:
> Guatemala–Serrano–Paraguay–Gurruchaga).

Even more radical, though, he foreshortens history, claiming that this original city block of Buenos Aires already was inhabited by organ-grinders, local thugs, tangos, and Yrigoyen posters:

> Una cigarrería sahumó como una rosa
> La nochecita nueva, zalamera y agreste.
> No faltaron zaguanes y novias besadoras.
> Sólo faltó una cosa: la vereda de enfrente.
>
> (A cigar store perfumed like a rose
> the new evening, flattering and rough.
> There were hallways and kissing girlfriends.
> Only one thing was missing—the other side of the street).

The "eternity" he feels as he evokes the founding of the city ("A mí se me hace cuento que empezó Buenos Aires: / La juzgo tan eterna como el agua y el aire" (Hard to believe Buenos Aires had any beginning: / I feel it to be as eternal as air and water) became a hallmark of various evocative texts on the foreshortening of history in Buenos Aires: "Sentirse en muerte" (Feeling in Death) in *El idioma de los argentinos* (The Language of the Argentines, 1928), an essay (included in *Borges: Textos recobrados 1919–1929*) on the Uruguayan painter Pedro Figari, and the preface to *Evaristo Carriego.*

Borges and Adolfo Bioy Casares in Mar del Lata, Argentina,
1942 (Collection of Jorge and Marion Helft)

Another interesting poem is "Isidoro Acevedo," about Borges's maternal grandfather, who
had fought in the mid-nineteenth-century civil wars.
Like the later stories "La otra muerte" and "El Sur"
(The South), this poem concerns a hero dreaming of
the death in battle that he would have preferred to
have had:

> Entró a saco en sus días
> para esa visionaria patriada que necesitaba su fé, no que
>   una flaqueza le impuso;
> juntó un ejército de sombras porteñas
> para que lo mataran.
>
> Así en el dormitorio anochecido que miraba a un jardín
> murió en milicia de su convicción por la patria
>
> (In the visionary defense of his country that his faith
> hungered for [and not that his fever imposed],

> he plundered his days
> and rounded up an army of Buenos Aires ghosts
> so as to get himself killed in the fighting.
> That was how, in a bedroom that looked onto the garden,
> he died out of devotion for his city).

The imaginative death impresses itself upon the real one:
the grandson remembers the grandfather as a warrior, not
as a tranquil old man looking out the window onto a
garden.

Cuaderno San Martín is the first of Borges's books
to include endnotes, here explaining the references in
some of the poems: particularly important is the note
on "La Chacarita" on Borges's militant support of
Hipólito Yrigoyen, the former president of Argentina
who was elected to a second term, took power in 1928,
and then was overthrown in 1930 by a military coup.
Borges later cultivated the genre of the footnote in his

stories and essays; it is noteworthy that his exploration of the note should begin in this book of poems and not in the three books of essays he published around the same time: *Inquisiciones* (Inquisitions, 1925), *El tamaño de mi esperanza,* and *El idioma de los argentinos.*

After *Cuaderno San Martín,* Borges did not publish a volume of new poetry until *El hacedor* (The Maker, 1960; translated as *Dreamtigers,* 1964), which mixed poems and short prose pieces, though the diverse editions of his poetic works constantly included new poems. There were few poems published in periodicals from 1930 to 1957: "Atardecer" (Dusk) in 1933; "Insomnio" (Insomnia) in 1936; "La noche cíclica" (The Cyclical Night) and "Para la noche del 24 de Diciembre de 1940, en Inglaterra" (On 24 December 1940, in England) in 1940; "Poema conjetural" (Conjectural Poem) in 1943; "Poema del tercer elemento" (Poem of the Third Element) in 1944; "A un poeta menor de la antología" (To a Minor Poet of the Greek Anthology) and "Mateo XXV, 30" (Matthew 25:30) in 1953; and "Página para recordar al Coronel Suárez, vencedor en Junín" (A Page to Commemorate Colonel Suárez, Victor at Junín) in 1954. After years of such modest poetic production, suddenly in 1958 Borges published ten poems in periodicals as well as the plaquette *Límites* (Limits) and *Poemas 1923–1958,* and from then to the end of his life his publications of poetry were constant. It is true enough, then, to speak (as does Zunilda Gertel in the title of her 1967 book) of a "retorno" (return) to poetry in the late 1950s and throughout the 1960s, to the extent that *El hacedor* was Borges's first book to include a large number of new poems since the three books of poetry of the 1920s.

Of these poems, the best-known are "La noche cíclica" and "Poema conjetural." The first is a meditation on the myth of eternal return that begins with the line "Lo supieron los arduos alumnos de Pitágoras" (They knew it, the fervent pupils of Pythagoras). The final stanza reads:

> Vuelve la noche cóncava que descifró Anaxágoras;
> Vuelve a mi carne humana la eternidad constante
> Y el recuerdo ¿el proyecto? de un poema incesante:
> "Lo supieron los arduos alumnos de Pitágoras . . ."

> (It returns, the hollow dark of Anaxagoras;
> In my human flesh, eternity keeps recurring
> And the memory, or plan, of an endless poem beginning:
> "They knew it, the fervent pupils of Pythagoras . . .").

The poem, then, not only speaks of an eternal return but circles back on itself, a sort of poetic Möbius strip. Like the stories later collected in *Ficciones,* this poem is a brilliant game, one that reveals the literary artifice of which it is made.

"Poema conjetural" is perhaps Borges's greatest poem. A dramatic monologue inspired at least in part by Robert Browning, as Julie Jones has shown in an essay in Carlos Cortínez's *Borges the Poet* (1986), this poem focuses on Francisco Narciso de Laprida, an Argentine lawyer who presided over the Congress of 1816 in Tucumán, which led to the Argentine Confederation. The poem purports to give the last thoughts of Laprida, surrounded by the irregular fighters who follow the strongman and former priest Félix Aldao, on the day of his death, 22 September 1829. The beginning reads:

> Zumban las balas en la tarde última.
> Hay viento y hay cenizas en el viento,
> se dispersan el día y la batalla
> deforme, y la victoria es de los otros.
> Vencen los bárbaros, los gauchos vencen

> (Bullets whine on that last afternoon.
> There is wind; and there is ash on the wind.
> Now they subside, the day and the disorder
> Of battle, victory goes to the others,
> to the barbarians. The gauchos win).

A brilliant meditation on the dialectic of civilization and savagery (the topic of Sarmiento's *Facundo* of 1845, it also figures in his 1845 biography of Aldao), "Poema conjetural" is the story of a man of letters who finds himself unexpectedly dying on a battlefield. There is more than an echo of Don Quixote's "discourse on arms and letters" in Laprida's last thoughts, but with an interesting inversion: whereas Don Quixote argued that the career of arms was superior to that of letters, Laprida still believes in the career of letters, the choice he made years before, even if his destiny has proven his choice wrong. "Al fin me encuentro / con mi destino sudamericano" (At last I come face to face / with my destiny as a South American), he says, and goes on:

> A esta ruinosa tarde me llevaba
> el laberinto múltiple de pasos
> que mis días tejieron desde un día
> de la niñez. Al fin he descubierto
> la recóndita clave de mis años,
> la suerte de Francisco de Laprida,
> la letra que faltaba, la perfecta
> forma que supo Dios desde el principio.
> En el espejo de esta noche alcanzo
> mi insospechado rostro eterno . . .

> (The complicated labyrinth of steps
> that I have traced since one day in my childhood
> led me to this disastrous afternoon.
> At last I have discovered
> the long-hidden secret of my life,
> the destiny of Francisco de Laprida,
> the missing letter, the key, the perfect form

Borges and his mother, Leonor Acevedo de Borges, on the balcony of his apartment on calle Maipu in Buenos Aires, December 1962 (Collection of Jorge and Marion Helft)

known only to God from the beginning.
In the mirror of this night I come across
my eternal face, unknown to me . . .).

The poem tells of a painful discovery, which is at the same time the discovery of a destiny. Around 1943 Borges had begun reading Dante in a serious way (his essays on Dante, collected in 1982 as *Nueve ensayos dantescos* [Nine Essays on Dante], were all published in the 1940s), and Dante's notion that a life is crystallized in its final moments, and that salvation and damnation depend on last thoughts, is as important as Browning to "Poema conjetural."

The poem ends with breakneck speed, the endecasyllabic verse infused with urgency by alliteration:

Pisan mis pies la sombra de las lanzas
que me buscan. Las befas de mi muerte,
los jinetes, las crines, los caballos,
se ciernen sobre mí . . . Ya el primer golpe,
ya el duro hierro que me raja el pecho,
el íntimo cuchillo en la garganta

(My feet tread on the shadows of the lances
that point me out. The jeering at my death,
the riders, the tossing manes, the horses
loom over me . . . Now comes the first thrust,
now the harsh iron, ravaging my chest,
the knife, so intimate, opening my throat).

The swirl of lances, of horses and horsemen, the manes, the final (and "intimate") knife: there is another poetic influence here, though its importance did not reveal itself explicitly in Borges's work until sometime later. Already in *Las kenningar* (Kennings, 1933) he had begun to show an interest in the hermetic poetry of the Icelandic skalds, but his serious study of Old English and Old Norse did not begin for another twenty years. The Old Norse image of war as a "storm of swords," cited in "Las kenningar," is present in "Poema conjetural" not only in the furious movement of the scene but also in the harsh alliteration, particularly that of the *r* sounds in the next to last line, the climax of the poem.

The epigraph to *Cuaderno San Martín* years before had been drawn from a letter of Edward FitzGerald:

As to an occasional copy of verses, there are few men who have leisure to read, and are possessed of any music in their souls, who are not capable of versifying on some ten or twelve occasions during their natural lives: at a proper conjunction of the stars. There is no harm in taking advantage of such occasions.

Borges would certainly be considered a major poet of the Spanish language even if he had only published "Poema conjetural" and a handful of other poems. A monument of historical imagination, "Poema conjetural" is a nuanced treatment of the poetic problem of how to narrate a life (and a death) and makes brilliant use of lessons learned from Dante, Browning, and the Old English and Old Norse poets.

The 1940s were also a period of intense exploration of short prose pieces, some of which could be considered prose poems. Many of these pieces ended up collected in the "Museo" (Museum) section of the second edition of *Historia universal de la infamia* (1935; revised edition, 1954; translated as *A Universal History of Infamy,* 1972), in *El hacedor,* and in various anthologies: *Cuentos breves y extraordinarios* (Brief and Extraordinary Stories, 1955), *Manual de zoología fantástica* (Manual of Fantastic Zoology, 1957), and *El libro de los seres imaginarios* (1967; translated as *The Book of Imaginary Beings,* 1969). At the same time that Borges was publishing the stories of *Ficciones* and *El Aleph* (1949; translated as *The Aleph and Other Stories, 1933–1969, Together with Commentaries and an Autobiographical Essay,* 1970) and the essays of *Otras inquisiciones (1937–1952)* (1952; translated as *Other Inquisitions, 1937–1952,* 1964), then, he was experimenting with poetic and short prose forms.

Borges never stopped publishing poetry, however, and he collected his verse written after *Cuaderno San Martín* and prior to *El hacedor* in *El otro, el mismo* (The Other, the Self) in 1964, including "Poema conjetural" and "La noche cíclica." What is notable about the 1960 and 1964 books is the fact that in them Borges returns to traditional forms such as the sonnet and to rhyme and regular rhythmical forms. His explanation at the time was that his increasing blindness (which prevented him from reading or writing after the mid 1950s) forced him to work with meter and forms that were easy to memorize and then to dictate. The change in his poetics, however, mirrors the return to traditional forms: in "Arte poética" (Ars Poetica, 1958), which closes the main section of *El hacedor,* and a host of essays, talks, and interviews in the 1960s and 1970s he argues that there are few essential metaphors, and this aesthetic conservatism (accompanying his growing political conservatism in the same period) implied a radical break with his avant-garde production of the 1920s and with essays celebrating audacity in the poetic metaphor (such as the essays on metaphor of the *ultraísta* period and "Las kenningar").

The most interesting of these texts on metaphor is one of the Norton lectures, presented at Harvard in 1967–1968 and not published until 2000 as *This Craft of Verse* (when they were also issued in CD format, moving because of the antique flavor of Borges's English, his gentleness and self-deprecating humor with the audience, and his prodigious feats of memory with poetic quotations). In this talk he argues that there are few essential metaphors, and gives his usual examples from the period (for example, rivers = life, sea = death,

flowers = women), but adds that the stock of metaphors is not exhausted (or exhaustible). Instead, he asserts that there are radically different approaches that can be taken to these essential metaphors and gives a wealth of examples to prove his point. He says at the end of the lecture:

> . . . though there are hundreds and indeed thousands of metaphors to be found, they may all be traced back to a few simple patterns. But this need not trouble us, since each metaphor is different: every time the pattern is used, the variations are different. And the second conclusion is that there are metaphors—for example, "web of men" or "whale road"—that may not be traced back to definite patterns.

Borges's point is fairly subtle: he rejects the more far-fetched metaphors that were typical of Ultraism and the other avant-garde movements, the purpose of which was to surprise the reader, but does not hold strictly to the idea that the number of essential metaphors is limited. In addition, in celebrating "new variations of the major trends" he makes explicit an important element of his ideas about literature in general, that repetition often implies divergence. This idea, which is at the heart of the 1939 story "Pierre Menard, autor del Quijote" (Pierre Menard, Author of *Don Quixote*) and of the 1940 story "Tlön, Uqbar, Orbis Tertius," opens up rich veins for poetic exploration.

"Arte poética," after rehearsing some of the important metaphors (river = time, dreams = death, day = life), argues that poetry "es inmortal y pobre" (is immortal and poor) and then concludes:

> Cuentan que Ulises, harto de prodigios
> Lloró de amor al divisar su Itaca
> Verde y humilde. El arte es esa Itaca
> De verde eternidad, no de prodigios.
>
> También es como el río interminable
> Que pasa y queda y es cristal de un mismo
> Heráclito inconstante, que es el mismo
> Y es otro, como el río interminable
>
> (They say that Ulysses, sated with marvels,
> Wept tears of love at the sight of his Ithaca,
> Green and humble. Art is that Ithaca
> Of green eternity, not of marvels.
>
> It is also like the river with no end
> That flows and remains and is the mirror of one same
> Inconstant Heraclitus, who is the same
> And is another, like the river with no end).

The point here seems to be the same as in the Norton lecture of a few years later, that the variations are as important as the themes. "Prodigios" is

Borges at the University of Oklahoma, 1969 (from Lowell Dunham and Ivar Ivask, eds., The Cardinal Points of Borges, *1971)*

in the same register as "asombro" (astonishment) and "sorpresa" (surprise), literary values that Borges had discarded in the 1920s. Borges celebrates here, as at Harvard, the "interminable" possibilities of poetry, and central to that endless quality are the always new possibilities for metaphor.

Another important poem in *El hacedor* is "El otro tigre" (The Other Tiger), a 1959 poem that reflects on the complex relationship between reality and representation. The "real" tiger in the poem, "El verdadero, el de caliente sangre" (the real one, the hot-blooded one), is a retreating mirage, impossible to imagine without the intervention of prior images of it, impossible to evoke in language without that fact turning it into a creature of artifice:

> . . . ya el hecho de nombrarlo
> Y de conjeturar su circunstancia
> Lo hace ficción del arte y no criatura
> Viviente de las que andan por la tierra

> (. . . but yet, the act of naming it, of guessing
> What is its nature and its circumstance
> Creates a fiction, not a living creature,
> Not one of those that prowl on the earth).

The poem ends with a renewed (but impossible) quest for "El otro tigre, el que no está en el verso" (the other tiger, the one not in this poem). Reality is in constant flight, out of the reach of language.

El hacedor consists largely of sonnets, rhymed quatrains, and verse in regular syllabic forms such as the endecasyllable. This change is less abrupt than it may seem, since *Cuaderno San Martín* and some poems in the later period (including "La noche cíclica" and "Poema conjetural") also use traditional poetic forms. Within the reshaping of Borges's poetics, however, the lesser use of free verse and the greater use of regular forms is significant, since it represents part of a larger quest for new possibilities within conventional forms. This shift is true not only of the poetry but also of Borges's explorations of the detective story, for instance. The tight bounds of the sonnet form, as an illustration, proved rife with new possibilities for a philosophical poetry, for example, "Ajedrez" (Chess), and for portrait poems, such as "Susana Soca," which abound in Borges's subsequent books.

"Poema de los dones" (Poem of the Gifts), written after the fall of Juan Domingo Perón in 1955, commemorates two simultaneous events: the naming of

Borges as director of the National Library (a post he held for fifteen years) and his blindness (which was not absolute but prevented him from reading or writing after this date). The irony Borges found in this coincidence is celebrated in the first stanza:

> Nadie rebaje a lágrima o reproche
> Esta declaración de la maestría
> De Dios, que con magnífica ironía
> Me dio a la vez los libros y la noche

> (No one should read self-pity or reproach
> Into this statement of the majesty
> Of God, who with such splendid irony
> Granted me books and blindness at one touch).

Blindness is one of the principal subjects also of *Elogio de la sombra* (1969; translated as *In Praise of Darkness,* 1974), which, like *El hacedor,* combines poems and short prose. Besides the title poem of this book, blindness haunts several poems, including those on James Joyce (as well as "On His Blindness," on John Milton, in *El oro de los tigres* [1972; translated as *The Gold of the Tigers: Selected Later Poems,* 1977]). "Elogio de la sombra" declares:

> Siempre en mi vida fueron demasiadas cosas;
> Demócrito de Abdera se arrancó los ojos para pensar;
> el tiempo ha sido mi Demócrito.
> Esta penumbra es lenta y no duele;
> fluye por un manso declive
> y se parece a la eternidad

> (In my life there were always too many things.
> Democritus of Abdera plucked out his eyes in order to
> think:
> Time has been my Democritus.
> This penumbra is slow and does not pain me;
> it flows down a gentle slope,
> resembling eternity).

Literature itself is reduced to those texts that are reread and reshaped in memory:

> De las generaciones de los textos que hay en la tierra
> sólo habré leído unos pocos,
> los que sigo leyendo en la memoria,
> leyendo y transformando

> (Of the generations of texts on earth
> I will have read only a few—
> the ones that I keep reading in my memory,
> reading and transforming).

And, like Laprida in "Poema conjetural," this encounter with destiny promises important insight about these "many things":

> Ahora puedo olvidarlas. Llego a mi centro,
> a mi álgebra y mi clave,
> a mi espejo.
> Pronto sabré quien soy

> (Now I can forget them. I reach my center,
> my algebra and my key,
> my mirror.
> Soon I will know who I am).

Besides the theme of blindness, *Elogio de la sombra* takes on the themes of old age and ethics, as Borges states in the preface. It is also typical of the last phase of his poetry—the books *El oro de los tigres, La rosa profunda* (The Unending Rose, 1975; translated in part in *The Gold of the Tigers: Selected Later Poems*), *La moneda de hierro* (The Iron Coin, 1976), *Historia de la noche* (The History of the Night, 1977), *La cifra* (The Limit, 1981), and *Los conjurados* (The Conspirators, 1985)—in mixing free verse and regular poetic forms (and sometimes short prose forms also) and in a preference for an accumulation of simple images (a process that is more dependent on metonymy than on metaphor). "Las cosas" (Things), from *Elogio de la sombra,* is a good example:

> Notas que no leerán los pocos días
> Que me quedan, los naipes y el tablero,
> Un libro y en sus páginas la ajada
> Violeta, monumento de una tarde
> Sin duda inolvidable y ya olvidada,
> El rojo espejo occidental en que arde
> Una ilusoria aurora. ¡Cuántas cosas,
> Limas, umbrales, atlas, copas, clavos,
> Nos sirven como tácitos esclavos,
> Ciegas y extrañamente sigilosas!
> Durarán más allá de nuestro olvido;
> No sabrán nunca que nos hemos ido

> (The few days left to me will not find time
> To read, the deck of cards, the tabletop,
> A book and crushed in its pages the withered
> Violet, monument to an afternoon
> Undoubtedly unforgettable, now forgotten,
> The mirror in the west where a red sunrise
> Blazed its illusion. How many things,
> Files, doorsills, atlases, wine glasses, nails,
> Serve us like slaves who never say a word,
> Blind and so mysteriously reserved.
> They will endure beyond our vanishing;
> And they will never know that we have gone).

Already in 1969 Borges took as his poetic task a summing up of his life. In the seventeen years that remained, he often made lists like the one in "Las cosas," lists of things, of emotions, of experiences, of friends, of books. The pathos of these lists is that they evoke a whole that is irremediably lost, experiences never fully lived or mostly forgotten. The key poem

Borges in Paris for his induction into the Legion d'honneur, January 1983 (Frank Spooner Pictures)

in this new poetics of abundance and loss is "Límites" (Limits, 1958) in *El hacedor,* ascribed to the apocryphal Uruguayan poet Julio Platero Haedo and his imaginary book from 1923 (the same year as *Fervor de Buenos Aires*):

> Hay una línea de Verlaine que no volveré a recordar.
> Hay una calle próxima que está vedada a mis pasos.
> Hay un espejo que me ha visto por última vez,
> Hay una puerta que he cerrado hasta el fin del mundo
> Entre los libros de mi biblioteca (estoy viéndolos)
> Hay alguno que ya nunca abriré.
> Este verano cumpliré cincuenta años;
> La muerte me desgasta, incesante

> (There is a line by Verlaine that I will not remember again.
> There is a street nearby that is off limits to my feet.
> There is a mirror that has seen me for the last time.
> There is a door I have closed until the end of the world.
> Among the books in my library [I'm looking at them now]
> Are some I will never open.
> This summer I will be fifty years old.
> Death is using me up, relentlessly).

In this 1958 poem Borges (who was fifty-eight or fifty-nine at the time) masquerades as an imaginary poet writing a poem of middle age and a sense of limits in the year that his younger self published the enthusiastic poems of discovery of *Fervor de Buenos Aires.* The accumulation of things and sensations, dominant in the poems of his old age, is prefigured in the poem by the imaginary Haedo.

A later poem of a similar kind is "Things That Might Have Been" (title originally in English) in *Historia de la noche:*

> Pienso en las cosas que pudieron ser y no fueron.
> El tratado de mitología sajona que Beda no escribió.
> La obra inconcebible que a Dante le fue dada acaso entrever,
> Ya corregido el último verso de la Comedia.
> La historia sin la tarde de la Cruz y la tarde de la cicuta.
> La historia sin el rostro de Helena.
> El hombre sin los ojos, que nos han deparado la luna.
> En las tres jornadas de Gettysburg la victoria del Sur.
> El amor que no compartimos.
> El dilatado imperio que los Vikings no quisieron fundar.
> El orbe sin la rueda o sin la rosa.
> . . . .

El ave fabulosa de Irlanda, que está en dos lugares a un
    tiempo.
El hijo que no tuve

(I think about things that might have been and never were.
The treatise on Saxon myths that Bede omitted to write.
The inconceivable work that Dante may have glimpsed
As soon as he corrected the Comedy's last verse.
History without two afternoons: that of the hemlock, that
    of the Cross.
History without Helen's face.
Man without the eyes that have granted us the moon.
Over three Gettysburg days, the victory of the South.
The love we never shared.
The vast empire the Vikings declined to found.
The globe without the wheel, or without the rose.
. . . .
The fabled Irish bird which alights in two places at once.
The child I never had).

This sense of loss, of pathos, is at the same time
an expression of gratitude for the things that the poet
had or has. A backhanded celebration of human experience, this poem is a complex meditation not only on
the world that might have been but also on the one
that is.

One of the great themes of Borges's poetry is the
discovery of a world. The important early poem "Barrio
reconquistado" (Neighborhood Reconquered) in *Fervor
de Buenos Aires,* for instance, tells of the rediscovery of a
familiar neighborhood after a thunderstorm. It ends:

nos echamos a caminar por las calles
como quien recorre una recuperada heredad,
y en los cristales hubo generosidades de sol
y en las hojas lucientes que ilustran la arboleda
dijo su temblorosa inmortalidad el estío

(we streamed out to walk through the streets
like someone who finds his way through a property he has
    recovered
and in the windows there were generosities of sun
and on the glowing leaves that illustrate the trees
summer spoke its trembling immortality).

In Borges's Norton lectures one of the finest passages
concerns John Keats's "On First Looking into Chap-
man's Homer" (1816), where he comments at length on
the word *first* in the title. The thirst for fresh experience
animates many of the poems, even those on blindness
("Poema de los dones" and the poems on Milton) and
on death ("El general Quiroga va en coche al muere,"
"Isidoro Acevedo," and many later poems). The Whit-
manian tone of his early "Himno del mar" is recaptured
in the selections from *Leaves of Grass* (1855) that he
translated as *Hojas de hierba* with his wife, Elsa Astete, in
1969 (they were married in 1967 and separated in

1970). Whitman's bold poetry of a New World has
unexpected echoes even in the later Borges.

Amusingly, one of Borges's best-known poems is
not by him at all. As shown in great detail by Iván
Almeida, the apocryphal poem "Instantes" (Moments),
often attributed to Borges in television commercials and
other popular media, is derived from a spiritual New
Age text that seems to have been written by one Nadine
Stair. In "Límites" and "Things That Might Have
Been" Borges uses some of the same tropes as
"Instantes," but those poems are about the things that
he did not do in his life–father a son, for example, or be
happy–rather than the things that he did. "Instantes,"
though familiar drivel, is a fascinating piece of apocrypha, amusing because it is attributed to the author of
"Pierre Menard, autor del Quijote," "Tlön, Uqbar,
Orbis Tertius," and other texts that are intimately concerned with apocrypha. Lines such as "Pero si pudiera
volver atrás trataría de tener / solamente buenos
momentos" (If I could do it over again I would try to
have / only good times) or "No intentaría ser tan perfecto, me relajaría más" (I wouldn't try to be so perfect,
I would relax more) take familiar ideas from the human
potential movement and attribute them to Borges at age
eighty-five. The apocryphal poem infuriated Borges's
executor, María Kodama (whom he married by proxy
a few weeks before his death of liver cancer in Geneva
on 14 June 1986), and has given Almeida an occasion
for a rigorous parody of philological procedures. In that
sense "Instantes" deserves attention as the most ridiculous piece of Borges apocrypha.

Some of the editions of Jorge Luis Borges's *Obra
poética* (that of 1964, for instance) include the following
epigraph taken from a letter by Robert Louis Stevenson: "I do not set up to be a poet. Only an all-round literary man: a man who talks, not one who sings. . . .
Excuse this apology; but I don't like to come before
people who have a note of song, and let it be supposed I
do not know the difference." In Borges's use of this epigraph there is a trace of false modesty. Clearly he did
set up to be a poet, and poetry is a dominant part of his
literary production in the 1920s and from 1960 to the
end of his life in 1986. At the same time, the poetry,
essays, reviews, and stories are bound together by
strong thematic links. Borges's poetics (of prose as well
as of poetry) evolves in parallel form across the decades
of his work, with bold explorations in a variety of
genres, one or two of which were dominant at a time
but never at the expense of the others.

Bibliography:

Nicolás Helft, *Jorge Luis Borges: Bibliografía completa* (Bue-
    nos Aires: Fondo de Cultura Económica, 1997).

References:

Iván Almeida, "Jorge Luis Borges, autor del poema 'Instantes,'" *Variaciones Borges,* 10 (2000): 227–246;

Daniel Balderston, *Borges: Realidades y simulacros* (Buenos Aires: Biblos, 2000);

Balderston, *The Literary Universe of Jorge Luis Borges: An Index to References and Allusions to Persons, Titles, and Places in His Writings* (Westport, Conn.: Greenwood Press, 1986);

Balderston, *Out of Context: Historical Reference and the Representation of Reality in Borges* (Durham, N.C.: Duke University Press, 1993);

Paul Cheselka, *The Poetry and Poetics of Jorge Luis Borges* (New York: Peter Lang, 1987);

Carlos Cortínez, ed., *Borges the Poet* (Fayetteville: University of Arkansas Press, 1986);

Angel Flores, ed., *Expliquémonos a Borges como poeta* (Mexico City: Siglo XXI, 1984);

Carlos García, *El joven Borges, poeta, 1919–1930* (Buenos Aires: Corregidor, 2000);

Zunilda Gertel, *Borges y su retorno a la poesía* (Iowa City: University of Iowa / New York: Las Americas, 1967);

Michel Lafon, *Borges ou la réécriture* (Paris: Seuil, 1990);

Linda Maier, *Borges and the European Avant-Garde* (New York: Peter Lang, 1996);

Sylvia Molloy, *Las letras de Borges y otros ensayos* (Rosario, Argentina: Beatriz Viterbo, 1999);

Emir Rodríguez Monegal, *Jorge Luis Borges: A Literary Biography* (New York: Dutton, 1978);

Enrique Pezzoni, "*Fervor de Buenos Aires:* Autobiografía y autorretrato," in his *El texto y sus voces* (Buenos Aires: Sudamericana, 1986);

Thorpe Running, *Borges' Ultraist Movement and Its Poets* (Lathrup Village, Mich.: International Book, 1981);

Tommaso Scarano, *Varianti a stampa nella poesia del primo Borges* (Pisa: Giardini, 1987);

Guillermo Sucre, *Borges, el poeta,* second edition (Caracas: Monte Avila, 1974).

Papers:

Though many of Jorge Luis Borges's manuscripts seem not to have survived, some papers are collected at the Fundación San Telmo, Buenos Aires.

Manuel del Cabral
(7 March 1907 – 14 May 1999)

Michele Morland Shaul
Queens College

BOOKS: *Pilón: Cantos al terruño y otros poemas* (Santiago: H. L. Cruz, 1931);

Color de agua (Santiago: H. L. Cruz, 1932);

Doce poemas negros (Santiago: Femina, 1935);

Ocho gritos (Santo Domingo: La Nación, 1937);

Biografía de un silencio (Buenos Aires: Tor, 1940);

Trópico negro (Buenos Aires: Sopena, 1941);

Compadre Mon: 1941–1942 (Buenos Aires: Los Editores del Autor, 1942);

Chinchina busca el tiempo (Buenos Aires: Perlado, 1945);

Sangre Mayor (Santiago: El Diario, 1945);

De este lado del mar (Santo Domingo: Imprenta Dominicana, 1949);

Antología tierra 1930–1949 (Madrid: Ediciones del Instituto de Cultura Hispánica, 1949);

Los huéspedes secretos (Buenos Aires: Lohlé, 1950);

Carta a Rubén (Madrid: Losada, 1951);

Segunda antología tierra: 1930–1951 (Madrid: Gráficas García, 1951);

Veinte cuentos (Buenos Aires: Lucania, 1951);

Sexo y alma (Buenos Aires, 1956);

Treinta parábolas (Buenos Aires: Lucania, 1956); revised and enlarged as *Los relámpagos lentos* (Buenos Aires: Sudamericana, 1966);

Dos cantos continentales y unos temas eternos (Buenos Aires, 1956);

Antología Clave (Buenos Aires: Losada, 1957);

Pedrada planetaria (Buenos Aires: Ediciones Alfa, 1958);

14 mudos de amor (Santo Domingo: Colección Baluarte, 1962; enlarged and corrected edition, Buenos Aires: Losada, 1963);

Historia de mi voz (Santiago: Andes, 1964);

La isla ofendida! (Santiago: Horizonte, 1965);

Los anti-tiempo (Buenos Aires: Centro Editor de América Latina, 1967);

El escupido (Buenos Aires: Quintaria, 1970);

Egloga 2000 (Buenos Aires, 1970);

Sexo no solitario (Buenos Aires, 1970);

El presidente negro (Buenos Aires: Lohlé, 1973);

Obra poética completa (Santo Domingo: Alfa y Omega, 1976);

Manuel del Cabral (photograph © by Fundación Manuel del Cabral)

La carabina piensa (Santo Domingo: Taller, 1976);

Palabra (Santo Domingo: Alfa y Omega, 1977);

El jefe y otros cuentos (Santo Domingo: Publicaciones Américas, 1979);

Cuentos cortos con pantalones largos (Santo Domingo: Publicaciones América, 1981);

Cédula del mar (Santo Domingo: Letra Grande, 1981);

Antología tres (Santo Domingo: Editora de la Universidad Autónoma de Santo Domingo, 1987);

La espada metafísica (Buenos Aires: Cuarto Mundo, 1989);

Antología poética (Buenos Aires: Biblioteca Nacional, 1998);

Antología de cuentos (Buenos Aires: Biblioteca Nacional, 1998).

Collection: *La magia de lo permanente: Antología poética de Manuel del Cabral,* compiled by Tomás Castro Burdiez (Santo Domingo: Ciguapa, 2001).

Manuel del Cabral is known not only in Latin America but also throughout the world as a poet of exceptional quality who addresses the concerns of his compatriots and the social inequities of the world. As Cabral states at the beginning of his autobiography, *Historia de mi voz* (History of My Voice, 1964), "El hombre se debate entre dos abismos: el micro y el macro. No conoce ni la profundidad del espacio infinito ni la inmensidad del interior del átomo. Pero entre esos dos abismos puede el hombre escribir su historia, su terrestre testimonio como huésped de esta gota cósmica, que aún da vueltas como otros mundos, movidos sin duda por un supremo pensamiento" (Man balances between two abysses: the micro and the macro. He knows neither the depth of infinite space nor the immensity of the interior of the atom. But between these two abysses man can write his story, his earthly testimony as a guest on this cosmic drop, that still twirls like other worlds, moved without a doubt by a supreme thought). The trajectory of Cabral's poetry follows this struggle between outer and inner concerns. His poetry can be divided into two categories: that dealing with the outward concerns of social justice and man's place in the universe, and that dealing with the interior examination of metaphysical concerns. Although the situation of black people as a theme can be seen in the works of other writers of the Caribbean, Cabral was the first Dominican poet to treat the Caribbean black population with seriousness, compassion, and respect. With maturity, he progressed toward concerns with more esoteric subjects; he never stopped being a voice for the disenfranchised, however, nor did he abandon his concern for man as an individual.

Born in Santiago de los Caballeros, Dominican Republic, on 7 March 1907, Cabral was the third child of Mario Fermín Cabral and Amalia Tavaros. Cabral's father was self-taught and worked as a barber in his youth but later became president of the Senate, a position that helped his son enter a diplomatic career. Cabral's mother died when he was young, and his unmarried maternal aunt, of whom he was fond, raised him. Cabral describes himself in his autobiography as having been an unhappy child filled with exceptional sadness. He used laughter to cope with pain and felt the loss of his mother intensely even though he had not known her.

Cabral completed secondary school at the Escuela Normal de Santiago (Normal School of Santiago). He did not study much in this institution and disliked the restrictions and regulations that were imposed on him. Upon completion of his studies at the Escuela Normal, his father pressured him to study law. In order to persuade his father to allow him to pursue his literary interests, he wrote the poem "A mi padre" (To My Father), later published in his collection *Pilón: Cantos al terruño y otros poemas* (Fountain: Songs to the Homeland and Other Poems, 1931). This poem makes evident his passion for poetry and writing in general.

With his father's blessing, Cabral left for the Dominican capital to become part of the literary world. In Santo Domingo he became acquainted with the leading intellectuals of his country. He joined "La cueva" (The Cave), an elite literary group principally concerned with poetry, whose other members included well-known writers and critics such as Pedro and Max Henríquez Ureña, Fabio Fiallo, Ricardo Pérez Alfonseca, Domingo Moreno Jiménez, Hector Inchaustegui Cabral, and Juan Bosch. The group exposed Cabral to new and innovative ideas and provided him with an audience that allowed him to develop and fine-tune his poetry.

Cabral believed that poetry should be inspired by national values and concerns. Accordingly, he and other writers rejected traditional Dominican values, including reverence for the colonial past, hatred of Haitians, and identification with everything European. *Modernismo* influenced these writers, pushing them toward innovation, free verse, and the use of color and musicality in their poetic expression. Cabral was particularly influenced by Pérez Alfonseca's meditative interior monologue, a technique he frequently used in his intimate poetry, as well as by Moreno Jiménez's ideas as postulated in the poet's *postumismo* movement, which imposed no limits of expression and no social or intellectual exclusivity, and encouraged poetic innovation to experiment both metrically and with imagery. Although Cabral was particularly enthusiastic about the poetry of writer and critic Pedro Henríquez Ureña and its universality of scope, he was never able to get the influential Henríquez Ureña to bring him to the attention of the Dominican literary community. There was no comment on his poetry from Henríquez Ureña for years.

During this period in the capital, Cabral discovered the existence of another minor poet with the same name as his (Manuel Cabral). His solution to avoid

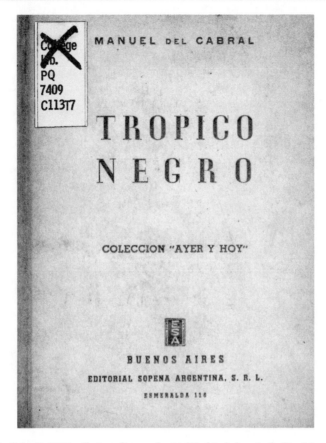

MANUEL DEL CABRAL

TROPICO NEGRO

COLECCION "AYER Y HOY"

BUENOS AIRES
EDITORIAL SOPENA ARGENTINA, S. R. L.
ESMERALDA 116

Paperback cover for Cabral's 1941 collection of poems about political turbulence in the Dominican Republic under the dictatorship of President Rafael Leónidas Trujillo (Bruccoli Clark Layman Archives)

confusion between him and this author was to add the "del" to his own name. His first book, *Pilón,* was published in the capital during this time. Many of the characteristics found in this work (national pride, musicality of language, and a concern for social justice and man as an individual) are also present in his later works.

Cabral moved to New York in 1938, where he worked as a window washer in a Manhattan skyscraper. Three months later, he moved to Washington, D.C., where he began his long career in diplomatic service. During this period of his life he began to paint, a skill for which he became known in later years in Europe. Soon after his arrival in Washington he was transferred to Bogotá, Colombia. Thinking about these experiences, Cabral wrote in *Historia de mi voz* that he found diplomatic life in Washington to be claustrophobic and much preferred his post in Colombia. There he enjoyed the availability of poets and other men of letters with whom he could share ideas in his own language. After serving for six months in Bogotá, Cabral visited Panama, Peru, and Chile, succeeding in all three places in meeting the leading literary figures that influenced his later writings.

In 1940, while assigned to the embassy in Buenos Aires, he met and married an Argentine woman named Alba, with whom he had four children (Amanda, Peggy, Amelia, and Alejandro). Although Buenos Aires became his permanent place of residence, Cabral continued to travel extensively and to publish throughout South America and Europe.

Critics consider the 1940s Cabral's most productive period. He, along with Inchaustegui Cabral, Pedro Mir, and Tomás Hernández Franco, became known in the Dominican Republic as "Los Cuatro poetas independientes" (The Four Independent Poets) of the 1940s. During this time he published *Chinchina busca el tiempo* (Chinchina Seeks Time, 1945), his first prose work, which is frequently compared to the Spanish poet Juan Ramón Jiménez's *Platero y yo* (Platero and I, 1914).

Cabral's most noted poetic works also appeared in the 1940s. These collections include *Trópico negro* (Black Tropics, 1941), *Compadre Mon* (My Pal Mon: 1942), and *De este lado del mar* (From This Side of the Sea, 1949). All three of these works reflect the turbulence of Rafael Leónidas Trujillo's dictatorship, which lasted from 1930 to 1961, in the Dominican Republic.

*Paperback cover for the 1957 edition of Cabral's 1942 collection of
political poetry (Bruccoli Clark Layman Archives)*

They include political and economic motifs and showcase the origins of Cabral's political attitudes. Predominant themes include social justice, love, and human solidarity. Also represented in these books are day-to-day Caribbean life, Dominican folklore, race, politics, and economics. Cabral attempts to combine social objectivity with personal experience and his individual vision of the world. Expressed in his social poems is his view of the negative effects of the Trujillo dictatorship on society as well as his bitterness toward the United States, not only for its occupation of the island between 1916 and 1924 but also for meddling in Dominican affairs during the 1940s. An unusual element in his works is compassion for and appreciation of the Haitian people, with whom the Dominican Republic shares the island. His inclusive attitude gains him a place of importance within the development of *poesía negra* (black poetry). Cabral's support and positive presentation of the Haitian people is surprising given the Dominicans' traditional distrust of Haitians resulting from the previous historical domination of the Dominican Republic by Haiti.

Trópico negro was written when Trujillo was actively promoting the whitening of Dominican society and discouraging interest in the African elements of the national culture. In this collection Cabral appeals for more humane treatment of Haitians and defends racial justice and the rights of the weaker nations against the strong. These poems use the black man as a means of probing human consciousness in an effort to better understand the human race. Cabral stated that *Trópico negro* is perhaps the only one of his poetry collections that is truly *poesía negra*. His poems convey a universal message through the themes of hunger, anguish, and pain, as evidenced in his poem "Trópico picapedrero" (The Stonemason Tropics): "Hombres negros pican sobre piedras blancas, / tienen en sus picos enredado el sol. / Y como si a ratos se exprimieran algo . . . / lloran sus espaldas gotas de charol" (Black men strike white stones, / they have the sun intertwined with their pickaxes. / And as if from time to time they extract something . . . / their backs cry drops of varnish). Incorporated in this collection is his earlier collection, *Doce poemas negros* (Twelve Black Poems, 1935), which

Paperback cover for Cabral's 1965 collection of poems, in which he reacts to the 1963 overthrow of Dominican president Juan Bosch (Bruccoli Clark Layman Archives)

together with the rest of the poems depict the black population as dignified human beings.

Compadre Mon deals with a time of political crimes, secret violence, injustice, and abuses of power. Other themes include the struggle for existence, the defense of the right to liberty and freedom from oppression as well as the continual struggle for self-preservation and self-assertion. The principal character of the collection is Don Mon, based on the legendary folk hero of Santo Domingo, Don Ramón. Through him the reader gains an appreciation of the hero's primitive world. Mon makes evident to the reader that discrimination against the black man is not merely a question of race but rather of class. For Cabral, Mon is the key to understanding the psychology of the Caribbean man as well as the rest of the continent, as he writes in the second poem of the collection: "Es que, Compadre Mon, cuando yo quiero / saber el mapa de la tierra, miro / la carta de tu piel" (It's just that, Compadre Mon, when I want / to know the map of the land, I look at / the chart of your skin). *Compadre Mon* has been compared to the Argentine José Hernández's epic work *Martín Fierro* (1872) because of their parallel themes, actions, and local mythical heroes.

De este lado del mar is a further indictment of the United States. Cabral speaks out against the economic exploitation of Latin America by United States companies, treating social themes that reach beyond the Caribbean. For example, in his poem "Oda al hombre que viene" (Ode to the Coming Man) Cabral criticizes the United States for meddling in the affairs of other nations: "Tú que vienes ahora, / con tu cuello planchado, con el mechón / escandoloso de tu corbata; / pero a pesar de todo, a pesar de tu plata, / tu levita, tu hygiene, tu perro, tu bastón, / aunque no vengas navegando en ron / metes 'aquí' la pata" (You who come now, / with your ironed collar, / with the scandalous tuft of your tie; / but in spite of it all, in spite of your money, / your frock coat, your hygiene, your dog, your cane, / although you don't come sailing along in rum / you stick your nose in "here"). For the poet, there is a far-reaching pattern of human degradation across the Western Hemisphere that keeps the region from achieving true democracy and meeting the needs of its impoverished population. Cabral seeks an end to social inequities and exploitation by foreign business and expresses the need for the development of a politics of goodwill.

In *Sexo y alma* (Sex and Soul, 1956), Cabral makes use of obscure symbols and metaphors to present the spiritual and biological aspects of love as being inseparable. He uses erotic detail to represent philosophical views of life because he believes that sexual imagery allows for the most profound expression of a human being's inner life. This book serves as a transition to the poetry that he wrote after the 1940s. In this later period Cabral moved away from overtly social and political themes to become more focused on psychological, spiritual, and abstract themes. His change of focus was a result of his diplomatic postings to Europe in 1948 and subsequent years on that continent. In Madrid, he met such writers and thinkers as Dámaso Alonzo, Eugenio d'Ors, Gerardo Diego, Vicente Aleixandre, Carmen Laforet, Camilo José Cela, Luis Felipe Vivanco, Luis Panero, José Luis Cano, José Hierro, Pío Baroja, José Ortega y Gasset, Gregorio Marannon, and Salvador Dalí. In Madrid he once again became interested in painting, and in 1951 and 1952 he had two exhibitions of his oil paintings in the Galería Xagra. His pictures have a dream-like, surreal, and nightmarish quality, and Spanish newspapers gave him mixed reviews. Shortly afterward, he published his short-story collection *Treinta parábolas* (Thirty Parabolas, 1956), which also reflects his preoccupation with dreams, visions, the occult, and the supernatural. From Spain, Cabral traveled to France, where he met André Gide, Paul Claudel, and Paul Valéry and developed a strong friendship with Paul Eluard. He became especially connected to the Surrealists, and his poetry began to explore the inner world of experience that was only a foreshadowing in *Pilón*. This new interest in metaphysical issues is reflected in the collections that were published in the 1950s and beyond. *Los huéspedes secretos* (The Secret Guests, 1950) and *Pedrada planetaria* (Planetary Stone's Throw, 1958) are examples of Cabral's new focus.

Los huéspedes secretos uses direct language and Surrealist elements to represent metaphysical concepts seen in other works. Themes include the smallness of man relative to the greatness of the universe, the ability to think as being the most outstanding characteristic of humans, time as an earthly concept, matter and spirit as a foundation for being, and the search for the essence of the eternal. Cabral believed that critics had difficulty understanding the concepts he presented in this collection and speculated that the reading public would better understand his message in the future.

Pedrada planetaria mainly focuses on time. Cabral associates time with the material facet of life, time as a form of death and as an obstacle to self-knowledge. Through these poems, he seeks a better understanding of himself and his relation to the universe. Additionally, he tries to instill in man a sense of social responsibility.

He deals with metaphysical anguish and makes reference to space travel, antimatter, nuclear energy, and other new scientific accomplishments that affect human life and interactions.

In 1958, while Cabral served at the Dominican embassy and lived once again in Buenos Aires, Trujillo broke off relations with Argentina. Prior to this event the poet had not been vocally opposed to the Trujillo regime. This silence was not atypical of intellectuals in the Dominican Republic. As Alejandro Paulino R. points out in his article for *El Siglo,* "Trujillo contra Manuel del Cabral" (Trujillo versus Manuel del Cabral), the intellectual community in the Dominican Republic did not speak out against Trujillo either because of fear or because they agreed with him and benefited from his policies. Intellectuals only dared to speak out against the dictator once they were outside of the country, and then only a few did so because of fear of reprisal by Trujillo's agents overseas. With the rupture of Dominican/Argentine diplomatic relations, Cabral broke his connections with Trujillo and remained in Argentina in self-imposed exile. He spoke out against the dictator at a meeting of the Asociación Argentina (Argentine Association) resulting in persecution by the *trujillistas* (those favoring Trujillo) of the chancellery, who took a dim view of Cabral's declarations, especially since he had benefited from his father's senatorial post and favor with Trujillo. The *trujillistas* circulated a paper, "Radiografía de una sanguijuela literaria" (X-ray of a Literary Leech), in which they accused Cabral of treason and plagiarism as a poet. This defamation campaign by the Dominican dictator's collaborators was not an unusual occurrence for anti-Trujillo intellectuals.

After Juan Bosch was elected president in 1963–in what Cabral believed to be the only free elections ever held in the country up to that point–Cabral reentered government service and served at the embassy in Santiago, Chile. Bosch's presidency brought an attempt at social justice and, as a result, there is a resurgence of political themes in Cabral's poetry. Bosch was overthrown on 9 September 1963 by those who fought Trujillo in exile, however, causing Cabral to question whether Latin America was ready for a pure democracy. *La isla ofendida!* (Offended Island, 1965), a collection of thirty poems, addresses his reaction to these events.

Cabral resigned his post as minister of Dominican affairs in Chile to protest the deposition of Bosch and remained in exile in Chile for a while. After publishing *Historia de mi voz* in 1964, he returned to Argentina. Two more books were published in the next three years. *Los relámpagos lentos* (Slow Lightning, 1966) is a retitled, enlarged edition of *Treinta parábolas. Los anti-*

tiempo (Anti-times, 1967) sums up his latest poetic efforts: it includes all the poems from *14 mudos de amor* (14 Mutes of Love, 1962) under the heading "Zona de amor" (Zone of Love) as well as those from *La isla ofendida!*. In these verses, the love poetry is carnal even though it appears conceptualized. His poem "Besos como monedas" (Kisses like Currency) is an excellent example of this poetry: "Panaderos de amor, besos trabajan / en mi cuerpo su pan. / Y besos van pasando por mi cuerpo / como el puente que deja agua pasar. / Besos tiro en la piel como los dados / y suben a los senos a pensar" (Bakers of love, kisses work / their bread on my body / And kisses go all over my body / like the bridge that lets water go by. / I throw kisses on your skin like dice / and they ascend to your breasts to think). A later book, *Sexo no solitario* (Unsolitary Sex, 1970), is similar in style.

In 1980, Cabral returned home to the Dominican Republic and received the Premio Nacional de Teatro (National Prize for Theater) for his play *La carabina piensa* (The Carbine Thinks, 1976). He began painting once again and soon gave an exhibition at the Biblioteca Nacional (National Library). In 1992 he was awarded the Premio Nacional de Literatura (National Prize for Literature) by the Fundación Corripio y la Secretaria de Estado de Educación (the Corripio Foundation and the Secretariat of Education) for his extensive literary work.

Manuel del Cabral died in Santo Domingo on 14 May 1999. To celebrate his literary excellence, the Comisión Permanente de la Feria del Libro (the Permanent Commission of the Book Fair) dedicated the IV Feria Internacional del Libro 2001 (the Fourth International Book Fair 2001) to his memory. His daughter Peggy Cabral, directora de procomunidad (director of public welfare), was present at the event, along with the presidents of Chile and the Dominican Republic and other local officials. At the Feria, the secretary of culture, Tony Raful, summed up Cabral's literary contribution, stating that he left "una obra que se ha extendido por toda la lengua española, trascendiendo otros idiomas y colocándose como una de las figuras fundamentales de la literatura del siglo pasado" (a body of work that has extended throughout the Spanish-speaking world, transcending other languages and situating himself among the fundamental figures of the literature of the past century).

References:

José Alcántara Almánzar, *Estudios de poesía dominicana* (Santo Domingo: Alfa y Omega, 1979), pp. 153–181;

Elmore Joseph Degrange, *The Poetry of Manuel del Cabral*, dissertation, Tulane University, 1969;

Degrange, "Political Ideology in the Poetry of Manuel del Cabral," *Xavier University Studies*, 4 (December 1965): 193–209.

Papers:

Manuel del Cabral's manuscripts are at the Fundación Manuel del Cabral, Santo Domingo.

Jorge Carrera Andrade

(18 September 1903 – 7 November 1978)

Sarah Mead Wyman
University of North Carolina at Chapel Hill

BOOKS: *El estanque inefable* (Quito: Universidad Central, 1922);

La guirnalda del silencio (Quito: Imprenta Nacional, 1926);

Boletines de mar y tierra, with a prologue by Gabriela Mistral (Barcelona: Editorial Cervantes, 1930);

Cartas de un emigrado (Quito: Editorial Elan, 1933);

Latitudes: Viajes, hombres, lecturas (Quito: Editorial Américas, 1934; corrected edition, Buenos Aires: Perseo, 1940);

Rol de la manzana: Poesías (1926–1929) (Madrid: Espasa-Calpe, 1935);

El tiempo manual, Pen Collección, no. 12 (Madrid: Ediciones Literatura, 1935);

Biografía para uso de los pájaros (Paris: Cuadernos del Hombre Nuevo, 1937);

La hora de las ventanas iluminadas (Santiago, Chile: Ediciones Ercilla, 1937);

Guía de la joven poesía ecuatoriana (Tokyo: Ediciones Asia-América, 1939);

Microgramas, precedidos de un ensayo y seguidos de una selección de Haikus japoneses (Tokyo: Ediciones Asia-América, 1940);

País secreto (Tokyo: Talleres Bunsh-Sha, 1940); translated by Muna Lee as *Secret Country* (New York: Macmillan, 1946);

Registro del mundo: Antología Poética 1922–39 (Quito: Ediciones del Grupo "América," Imprenta de la Universidad, 1940);

Canto al puente de Oakland. To the Bay Bridge, English translation by Eleanor L. Turnbull (Palo Alto, Cal.: Stanford University Press, 1941);

Mirador terrestre: La República del Ecuador, encrucijada cultural de América (New York: Las Américas, 1943);

Canto a las fortalezas volantes. Cuaderno del paracaidista: Dos poemas. Seguidos de un homenaje de los escritores y poetas venezolanos (Caracas: Ediciones Destino, 1945);

Lugar de origen (Caracas: Ediciones al Servicio de la Cultura, 1945; augmented edition, Quito: Casa de la Cultura Ecuatoriana, 1951);

Jorge Carrera Andrade (photograph by La Industrial)

Poesías escogidas, preface by Pedro Salinas (Caracas: Ediciones Suma, 1945);

El visitante de niebla y otros poemas (Quito: Casa de la Cultura Ecuatoriana, 1947; second edition, Quito: Cuadernos de Poesía Madrugada, 1947); translated from G. R. Coulthard as *Visitor of Mist* (London: Williams & Norgate, 1950);

Rostros y climas: Crónica de viajes, hombres y sucesos de nuestro tiempo (Paris: Ediciones de la Maison de l'Amérique Latine, 1948);

Aquí yace la espuma (Paris: Editorial Presencias Americanas, 1950);

Familia de la noche (Paris: Librería Española de Edi-
    ciones, 1953; second edition, Paris: Colección
    Hispanoamericana, 1954);

*La Tierra siempre verde: El Ecuador visto por los Cronistas de
    Indias, los corsarios y los viajeros ilustres* (Paris: Edi-
    ciones Internacionales, 1955);

El Camino del Sol: Historia de un reino desaparecido (Quito:
    Casa de la Cultura Ecuatoriana, 1958);

Edades poéticas (1922-1956) (Quito: Casa de la Cultura
    Ecuatoriana, 1958);

Moneda del forastero. Monnaie de l'étranger, French transla-
    tion by Jean Mazoyer (Dijon: Collection Terres
    Fortunées, 1958);

*Galería de místicos y de insurgentes: La vida intelectual del
    Ecuador durante cuatro siglos, 1555-1955* (Quito:
    Casa de la Cultura Ecuatoriana, 1959);

Hombre planetario (Bogotá: Ediciones de la revista Mito,
    1959; augmented edition, Quito: Casa de la Cul-
    tura Ecuatoriana, 1963)–includes *La Vista del
    amor, Boletines de la línea equinoccial,* and *Taller del
    tiempo;*

Viaje por países y libros (Quito: Casa de la Cultura Ecuato-
    riana, 1961);

*Mi vida en poemas: Ensayo autocrítico seguido de una selección
    poética* (Caracas: Casa del Escritor, 1962);

Antología poética, selected, with an introduction, by
    Giuseppe Bellini (Milan: La Goliardica, 1963);

*El Fabuloso Reino de Quito: Historia del Ecuador desde los tiem-
    pos más remotos hasta la conquista española* (Quito:
    Casa de la Cultura Ecuatoriana, 1963);

*Presencia del Ecuador en Venezuela: Entrevistas, artículos, dis-
    cursos* (Caracas: Editorial Colón, 1963);

Floresta de los guacamayos (Managua: Editorial Nica-
    ragüense, 1964);

Interpretación de Rubén Darío (Managua: Ediciones Cua-
    dernos Darianos, 1964);

Radiografía de la cultura Ecuatoriana (Managua: Ediciones
    del Ministerio de Educación Pública, 1964);

Crónica de las Indias (Paris: Centre de Recherches de
    l'Institut d'Etudes Hispaniques, 1965);

Retrato cultural del Ecuador (Paris: L'Institut d'Etudes His-
    paniques de la Universidad de Paris, 1965);

El alba llama a la puerta (Paris, 1966);

Interpretaciones hispanoamericanas (Quito: Casa de la Cul-
    tura Ecuatoriana, 1967);

Las relaciones culturales entre el Ecuador y Francia (Quito:
    Ministerio de Educación Pública, 1967);

Poesía última (New York: Las Américas, 1968);

Libro del desierto (Dakar, Senegal: University of Dakar,
    1970);

El volcán y el colibrí (Autobiografía) (Puebla, Mexico:
    Cajica, 1970);

Misterios naturales (Paris: Centre de Recherches de l'Insti-
    tut d'Etudes Hispaniques, 1972);

Vocación terrena, Árbol de fuego, no. 51 (Caracas, 1972);

Reflections on Spanish-American Poetry, translated by Don
    C. Bliss and Gabriela de C. Bliss (Albany: State
    University of New York, 1973)–includes "Poetry
    of Reality and Utopia"; translated as *Reflexiones
    sobre la poesía hispanoamericana* (Quito: Casa de la
    Cultura Ecuatoriana, 1987);

Selected Poems of Jorge Carrera Andrade, edited and trans-
    lated, with an introduction, by Hoffman R. Hays
    (Albany: State University of New York Press,
    1972);

Obra poética completa (Quito: Casa de la Cultura Ecuato-
    riana, 1976).

Edition: *Antología Poética: Jorge Carrera Andrade,* edited,
    with introduction and notes, by Oswaldo Enca-
    lada Vásquez (Quito: Libresa, 1990).

TRANSLATIONS: Boris Andreevich Lavreniov, *El
    séptimo camarada: Novela de la Rusia bolchevique* (Bar-
    celona: Cervantes, 1930);

Pierre Reverdy, *Antología poética* (Tokyo: Ediciones
    Asia-América, 1940);

Indice de poetas Franceses modernos (Santiago, Chile, 1940);

Paul Valéry, *Cementerio Marino. Cántico de las Columnas.
    Otros poemas,* includes notes by Carrera Andrade
    (Caracas: Ediciones Destino, 1945);

Poesía Francesa contemporánea, edited, with biographical
    notes, by Carrera Andrade (Quito: Casa de la
    Cultura Ecuatoriana, 1951).

SELECTED PERIODICAL PUBLICATIONS–
UNCOLLECTED: "Jorge Carrera Andrade: Sus
    Primeros poemas," *Lírica Hispana,* 20, no. 234
    (1962);

"José Asunción Silva, el novio de la muerte," *Cuadernos,*
    no. 98 (1965);

"Prosa y poesía de J. C. A.," *Norte,* 9, nos. 3 & 4 (1968).

Jorge Carrera Andrade is one of Ecuador's most
celebrated poets, a man who in many ways introduced
his homeland and its history to the world at large. In
the tradition of other Latin American poet-diplomats,
such as Chilean Pablo Neruda and Mexican Octavio
Paz, he served his country as ambassador in Latin
America, North America, Europe, and Asia, living
abroad the vast majority of his life. The poet explains in
*Mi vida en poemas: Ensayo autocrítico seguido de una selección
poética* (My Life in Poems: An Auto-Critical Essay Followed by Selected Poems, 1962), "Soy un hombre. . . .
que ha tratado de conocer el mundo para desenvolver
en él su vida como un viaje. . . . He vivido para ver. . . .
he intentado de formar un registro de las realidades del
munda, vistas desde la ventana de mi conciencia" (I am
a man. . . . who has endeavored to know the world by

Dust jacket for the 1946 translation of Carrera Andrade's collection País secreto *(1940). The Spanish version was published while he was serving as Ecuadoran general consul in Japan (Bruccoli Clark Layman Archives).*

living my life as a voyage. . . . I have lived in order to see the world. . . . to register its realities through the window of my consciousness). His writings include historical expositions, highly charged political articles, literary criticism, travel memoirs, autobiography, impressionistic studies of people, and issues of personal interest to him. The massive and imaginatively reconstructed history of Ecuador, *El Camino del Sol: Historia de un reino desaparecido* (The Way of the Sun: The History of a Vanished Kingdom, 1958) is Carrera Andrade's major work in prose. He is best known for his prolific poetry, however, a lyric effort spanning over sixty years. His quest to define the Latin American identity and his constant longing for social justice factor fundamentally in his poetry and in his priorities as a diplomat. Although he decries the dehumanization of mechanized modern society and mourns the plight of the underprivileged and working classes, he finds hope in the concepts of presence and solidarity. His poetic credo, "Las cosas o sea la vida" (Things: that is to say,

life)–expressed in "El objeto y su sombra" (The Object and Its Shadow) from his collection *El tiempo manual* (Manual Time, 1935)–puts trust in the present moment, as he looks with an artist's eye at the objects around him. He finds relief from his solitude by identifying himself with the universal man, as delineated in his long poem "Hombre planetario" (Planetary Man, 1959).

Carrera Andrade was born 18 September 1903 to Carmen Amelia Vaca and Abelardo Carrera Andrade on the edge of a Quito neighborhood, 2,850 meters above sea level, between the whites and mestizos of the city and the native people living on Panecillo Hill. In "Biografía para uso de los pájaros" (Biography for the Use of Birds), the title poem of his 1937 collection, he situates his birth at the crux of the defeat of idealism by a machine-oriented civilization: "Nací en el siglo de la defunción de la rosa / cuando el motor ya había ahuyentado a los ángeles" (I was born when the rose was dying / and machines had driven the angels from the earth). He grew up trying to reconcile not only the differences between the people of his city but also the contrasting philosophical outlooks of his parents. The deeply religious and conservative orientation of his well-cultured mother guided his early years. Although he soon rejected her conservatism, he felt he owed her his literary vocation. Philosophically, he followed his father, a liberal lawyer and later judge on the supreme court, renowned for his interaction with the native people and his record for defending their rights against the landowners. The large and wealthy Carrera Andrade family, with eleven children, spent considerable time at their own large country estate in El Batán, which included a working farm. He considers the time spent on the family farm to be his first contact with the realities of life, for he could see the misery of the Indians. He therefore decided that the mission of an Ecuadoran poet was to raise the national consciousness and improve the lives of the native people.

Although Carrera Andrade often idealizes rural life and childhood innocence, his early memories include direct observation of human need and political violence. At the age of eight he witnessed the bloody revolution leading to the overthrow of the liberal president General Eloy Alfaro, whom he later saw assassinated as the captive leader was paraded through the streets. As a youth he was already politically engaged, reacting on a personal level to frequent coups and other disruptions that disordered daily life and, later, his career as a diplomat. His father insisted his son be transferred from the Catholic Colegio Padres Mercedarios to the secular, liberal Mejía National Institute. There, he won a book of Rubén Darío's poetry as a prize, which instilled in him the desire to write. His first efforts were prose poems, by his definition bucolic, sometimes melancholy, and already concerned with an animist's desire to speak with things.

By the age of fifteen, Carrera Andrade was not only actively writing poetry but also editing a literary review, El Crepúsculo (Twilight), that he founded with Gonzalo Escudero and Augusto Arias in 1917. He also became editor of the school magazine, Vida Intelectual (Intellectual Life). Soon, César Ariosto Orellana and Luis Aníbal Sánchez joined him in editing the journal La Idea, and his youthful promise was recognized at home and abroad, in Quito and Guayaquil, Cuba, Argentina, and México. His enthusiastic reading at this time included works by Juan Montalvo and Paul Verlaine and various Spanish classics. He claims the French symbolists taught him sweetness, lightness, and transparency. Later favorites were André Gide's Les Nourritures terrestres (1897; translated as The Fruits of the Earth, 1949), Guillaume Apollinaire, Georges Rodembach, and Francis Jammes.

As a law student at the Central University of Quito he became increasingly politicized. He was active in student groups, including Renovación (Renovation), whose slogan was "Tierra, pan y alfabeto" (Bread, Land, and Literacy). The rise of Marxism following World War I and the Russian and Mexican revolutions greatly interested the poet and his colleagues. He helped found Ecuador's Socialist Party and acted as its general secretary. He edited and printed an underground sheet, Humanidad (Humanity), and, with Ricardo Paredes and Gonzalo Pozo, founded Antorcha (The Torch). He wrote prolifically for both humanitarian publications, attempting to educate the mostly illiterate Indians and sway them against the corrupt president, José Luis Tamayo. He also worked as a combat journalist in Guayaquil, where he moved, some have said, to enjoy his increasingly bohemian lifestyle. He participated in the uprising leading to the popular massacre of 15 November 1922 but managed to avoid arrest. That same year he was arrested by the police for participating in a left-wing uprising and was imprisoned alone in a tiny cell known as the "infiernillo" (little hell) or the "ataúd de pié" (standing coffin). Far from inhibited by this experience, in 1923 he held a conference in Quito to commemorate the National Festival of Chile, during which he gave a speech on the value of democracy.

Carrera Andrade published his first book of poetry, El estanque inefable (Inexpressible Pool), and an anthology of Ecuadoran writers in 1922. El estanque inefable demonstrates that after his first adolescent symbolist-derived poems (up to 1922) he becomes less sentimental and romantic, the tone more virile. In light of this volume and of La guirnalda del silencio (Wreath of Silence, 1926), Peter Beardsell, in his Winds of Exile: The Poetry of Jorge Carrera Andrade (1977), asserts that he is a key figure in Ecuador's movement away from Modernismo that arrived late, in 1910, and still lingered on in Ecuador into the 1930s. Essential characteristics of his mature style were already burgeoning: an emphasis on direct observation, an intense focus on small details, a disenchantment with intellectual institutions, and a reliance on the subjective imagination, metaphor, and social protest.

Carrera Andrade left Ecuador for the first time in 1928, ostensibly to represent his Socialist Party at the Fifth International Congress in Moscow. The radical poet's exile may have been necessary when Isidro Ayora came to power. Some critics contend that Carrera Andrade's decadent lifestyle, inflamed perhaps by his fascination with Charles Baudelaire's Les Fleurs du mal (Flowers of Evil, 1857), made his departure imperative. The unsanctioned publication of an improper poem he had written and an off-color love affair had disgraced his family. Instead of traveling directly to Moscow, the underfunded delegate spent his first three months working in Panama and Trinidad and living in relative poverty. To his surprise, his Socialist Party published an obituary declaring his death at sea. His feelings of abandonment fostered the recurring theme of *soledad* (solitude or loneliness) that powers the majority of his lyric work. Carrera Andrade's preferred antidote to solitude was solidarity with the working class and mankind in general. Traveling to Hamburg and Berlin, he sold hearing aids, living and working with the transitory manual laborers. His concern for the working class and grief over the progress of industrial society figures in the gradual loss of his idealistic notion of the perfect individual.

Carrera Andrade's first poems abroad, written between 1928 and 1933, grapple mainly with modern man's condition. His lyric expressions of humanist social protest figure most prominently in *El tiempo manual*. In "Historia contemporánea" (Contemporary History) from that collection, typewriters, sewing machines, and other instruments of modern technology beat out a threatening message to the established order. "Poemas de pasado mañana" (Poems from the Day after Tomorrow) is a moral tale, an allegory of the progress of industrial societies, warning that workers who rise up in revolution will be put to death. Enrique Ojeda argues that these poems testify to the advent of existentialist anxiety and a loss of the poet's initial security. While Carrera Andrade's persistent feeling of solitude comes mostly from his physical isolation and estrangement from home, the poetry of his mature years expresses the interior abandonment or spiritual impoverishment that afflicts contemporary man. His expression is different from the contemporary European poetry of the time, however, because of his forms, the novelty of his metaphoric language, and his concentration on the physical world rather than on abstractions.

After missing the conference in Moscow, he traveled to Barcelona, where he worked as French and English translator and served as general secretary of the Ibero-American University Association while attending classes at the University of Barcelona. He wrote for magazines and newspapers, especially for *Gaceta Literaria* (Literary Gazette) and *El Liberal* (The Liberal), and helped found *Hoja Literaria* (Literary Leaf). After moving to Aix-en-Provence, France, the now serene poet graduated with a bachelor's degree and a licentiate in social sciences. He made new contacts, including Peruvian political leader Haya de la Torre, and met poets César Arrayo, César Vallejo, Benjamín Carrión, and Gabriela Mistral.

Mistral invited Carrera Andrade to Avignon, where she encouraged his continuing studies of French literature and what she termed the *indianismo* (Indian-ism) of his poetry. In her "Explicación de Jorge Carrera Andrade" (Explication of Jorge Carrera Andrade) that introduces his *Boletines de mar y tierra* (Bulletins from Sea and Earth, 1930), she wrote, "Perhaps the definitive core of his poetry is this Indianism." "Cuaderno de poemas indios" (Notebook of Indian Poems), written between 1927 and 1928 and published in *Obra poética completa* (Complete Poetic Work, 1976), is generally considered his main collection on this theme. Although the poet stresses the social-protest content of this collection, many critics argue that only "Levantamiento" (Uprising) qualifies as a social-protest poem. Oswaldo Encalada Vásquez and other critics have called attention to the mainly decorative use of Indian themes, principally valued for their artful rendition of Ecuador and its history. The lush and vivid poems perpetuate the notion of the pre-Columbian Americas as an idyllic realm of simple, uncorrupted living.

The poet made his first voyage home humbly, with third-class passage, in 1933. He knew not what to expect from his former Socialist Party associates. He enjoyed a magnificent welcome, for *Boletines de mar y tierra* had been well received by Spanish critics and he now had an international reputation. He joined the opposition to the government of Martínez Mera and was named prosecretary of the Senate. His impatience with the passivity of the people and his frustration with the continuing lack of social justice in his country only worsened. Positioning himself as a moderate, opposed to both fascism and communism, he called for a United Socialist Party to serve both the working and middle classes. He taught literature at his former Mejía National Institute. When José Velasco Ibarra came to power for the first of five presidential terms, the poet-politician was suspicious of his clearly fascist tendencies and wrote the manifesto for the new Social-Agrarian Party. Upon Ibarra's election, he was appointed consul in Paita, Peru.

During this time he published *Cartas de un emigrado* (Letters from an Emigrant, 1933), a prose work intended especially for politicians and other educated audiences. It includes his most fully developed commentary on the exploitation of Ecuador's Indians. He also brought to press the impressionistic travel essays *Latitudes: Viajes, hombres, lecturas* (Latitudes: Travels, People, Readings, 1934), documenting his first impressions of Europe in the grip of industry and of the sadness of its people, cut off from nature. He blames the machine for the spiritual wasting of Depression-era Europe, once the center of justice, love of truth, and moderation. He also writes with irony of the masses speaking out against the decadence of the West and then turning toward such Fascist messiahs as Adolf Hitler and Benito Mussolini.

The same year, the poet held a conference in Quito on his poetic invention, the *microgramma*. Writing in *Microgramas, precedidos de un ensayo y seguidos de una selección de Haikus japoneses* (Micrograms, Preceded by an Essay, and Followed by Selected Japanese Haikus, 1940), Carrera Andrade defines "el micrograma no es sino el epigrama español, despejado de su matiz subjectivo" (the microgram as a Spanish epigram unencumbered by subjective nuances). It is essentially a graphic or pictorial expression that, he says, reveals the profound reality of the object. Beardsell clarifies that the "secret reality" of objects can be read as the poet's subjective interpretation of them. He further specifies two stages in the poet's development of the form. In stage one, the subject of the microgram—a "caracol" (snail)—is followed with a colon and clearly linked to a second subject to show comparison:

mínima cinta métrica
con que mide el campo Dios

(smallest measuring tape
with which God measures the countryside).

In the second, more developed stage, the subject is not as explicitly introduced but is imagined in action performing like the compared object, and the two (here, poplar and paintbrush) are fused in a single image and a single utterance:

Moja el chopo su pincel
en la dulzura del cielo
y hace un paisaje de miel

(The poplar moistens its brush
in the sweetness of sky
and paints a landscape of honey).

Such use of metaphor is the poet's most celebrated contribution to the development of poetry in Ecuador. In his metaphors, two "realities" are put together face-to-face through a system of analogies. The poet emphasizes the pictorial and biographical nature of his images, as he writes in *Mi vida en poemas*: "Mis poemas son visuales como una colección de estampas o pinturas que integran una autobiografía apasionada y nostálgica. En cada uno de mis poemas hay múltiples elementos biográficos y se despliega la geografía real de nuestro planeta." (My poems are visual like a stamp collection or pictures that integrate a passionate and nostalgic autobiography. In each of my poems, there are multiple biographical elements and our planet's actual geography is displayed). Drawing attention to the intrinsic complexity of his art, the poet describes the *microgama* as his most difficult exercise: "Debo confesar que jamás había experimentado mayor embriaguez

JORGE CARRERA ANDRADE
POESIA ULTIMA

Paperback cover for Carrera Andrade's acclaimed 1968 poetry collection (Bruccoli Clark Layman Archives)

intelectual que en este trabajo de reducción de lo creado en pequeñas fórmulas poéticas, exactas mediante la concentración de elementos característicos del objeto entrevisto o iluminado súbitamente por el reflector de la conciencia." (I must confess that I've never found a greater intoxication of the intellect than in this work of reducing creation into small, perfect poetic formulas: mediating the concentration of the object's characteristic elements with regard to or suddenly illuminated by the reflection of consciousness).

The chief criticism against Carrera Andrade has been that his poetry is too clear, overexplained, or lacking in subtlety. The poet defends his lucid style in the essay "Poetry of Reality and Utopia" in his *Reflections on Spanish-American Poetry* (1973):

Cierta crítica aduce que en la poesía debe existir una zona oscura que obligue al lector a buscar el misterio encerrado en ella. Considero que el lenguaje en sí mismo posee la dosis suficiente de enigma, el eco metafísico o la resonancia de sombras que hacen innecesaria la utilización deliberada de la oscuridad. Por añadidura, uno de los fines esenciales de lo poético es la comunión con los demás hombres. Si la poesía no puede transmitir su contenido emotivo o sensorial, deja de cumplir su misión que es la interpretación del mundo, haciéndolo tangible. No lamento que la lógica, lámpara indiscreta, haya alumbrado mi mundo poético. Todo lo contrario: su luz simboliza la vigilia sin fin, la permanente vigilancia de la conciencia sobre mi poesía

(Some criticism adduces that an obscure zone should exist in poetry that obliges the reader to search for the mystery it contains. I deem that the language itself has in it a sufficient dose of enigma, the metaphysical echo or the repercussions of darkness, which make the deliberate use of obscurity unnecessary. In addition, one of the essential aims of what is poetical is communion with other men. If poetry cannot transmit its emotional or sensory content, it no longer accomplishes its mission, which is to interpret the world, to make it tangible. I do not regret that logic, an indiscreet lamp, has lighted my poetic world. On the contrary, its light symbolizes the endless vigil, the permanent watchfulness of consciousness over my poetry).

As Carrera Andrade matured as a poet, this notion of intellectual control offered solace as he contended with ontological questions.

As a young writer, Carrera Andrade had admired the seventeenth-century Spanish poet Luis de Argote y Góngora's images, used to express concepts in a precise, condensed manner. An urge to follow this model found expression in his *microgramas*. Carrera Andrade missed the human element in Góngora's work, however; he felt it was insufficiently concerned with mankind. His move away from Góngora coincides with the way he kept the "pure poetry" of the symbolists and the avant-garde schools (including the *Ultraísmo* movement) at a distance. While he admires Vicente Huidobro and feels an affinity with the *Creacionistas,* he consistently stresses the humanist and engagé nature of his poetry over what he would consider strict aesthetics or dehumanized pure poetry. Nevertheless, his own metaphors developed in a rich climate of poetic experimentation.

From 1934 to 1938 the poet served as general consul in Le Havre, France, where he was successful in increasing Ecuadoran coffee imports. By this point his reputation as a writer and as a dandy of sorts was well established. He met his first wife, Paulette Colin Lebas, and married in 1935; the couple had one child, Juan Cristóbal. During this time he wrote prolifically and published three collections of poems: *Rol de la manzana: Poesías (1926–1929)* (The Apple's Role: Poems [1926–1929], 1935), especially noted for its twenty-four *microgramas; El tiempo manual;* and *Biografía para uso de los*

pájaros. A review in *Petit Havre* (28 November 1936) decried an absence of the "rigor of French prosody" in *El tiempo manual* but applauded the "luminosity of thought, impregnated with harmony." While in Paris the poet met José Bergamín, Louis Aragon, Pablo Neruda, Benjamin Péret, and Alejo Carpentier.

Carrera Andrade next moved to Yokohama, Japan, where he lived in relative splendor, overlooking the city of Tokyo and serving as general consul from 1938 to 1940. Here he wrote *Islas sin nombre* (Nameless Islands) and *Viento nordeste* (Northeast Wind). He traveled widely through the country and to China. Although he celebrates the physical beauty and the customs of Japan in two essays in *Viaje por países y libros* (Travel through Countries and Books, 1961) and speaks fondly of the country in his autobiography, few poems treat the subject of Japan. The experience enriched his understanding of the complexities of modern man and the relativity of human attitudes and conceptions. He also credits his Asian tenure with an increased appreciation of the transitoriness of all things and the importance of *presencia* (presence). In Tokyo he finally published *Microgramas,* written for the most part in 1926, and a new work, *País secreto* (Secret Country, 1940). The poet describes this "secret country" as a place visited in solitude, one that is everywhere, yet has no map because it lies within the self. This place, he writes in *Edades poéticas (1922–1956)* (Poetic Ages [1922–1956], 1958), contains "islas sin nombre." He also translated into Spanish an anthology of Pierre Reverdy's poetry.

La cosa (the thing) is the central element of Carrera Andrade's poetic world. His credo, "Las cosas o sea la vida," equates the reality of things with life itself. The notion of life existing in the present moment of concrete objects rather than vague speculations and philosophies is specified in a variety of poems, but most clearly in "El objeto y su sombra" (The Object and Its Shadow) from *El tiempo manual.*

> Las cosas. O sea la vida.
> Todo el universo es presencia.
> La sombra al objeto adherida
> ¿acaso transforma su esencia?
>
> (Things: that is to say, life.
> The whole universe is presence.
> Does the shadow of an object seized
> transform its essence?).

The poem promotes the supremacy of reality and presence over dream and other abstractions of thought. Physical, observable reality, as the authentic substance of life, is to be trusted as truth. Carrera Andrade traces his "habit of talking with things," as he puts it in

"Poetry of Reality and Utopia," to traditional Indian animism.

As the poet's style evolves, this preoccupation with things persists, but his poems become more philosophical, less dependent on impressionistic and pictorial elements. Carrera Andrade's "Cada objeto es un mundo: Arte poético" (Every Object Is a World: Poetic Art), from *Taller del tiempo* (Time's Workshop, written in 1958; published in the second edition of *Hombre planetario,* 1963), further develops his "cult of the object." "Invocación final a la palabra" (Final Invocation of the Word, 1963) also figures in the poet's remarkably consistent credo. Critics have occasionally conflated the poet's faith in the thing with his more problematic relationship with words themselves.

In 1940 Carrera Andrade made a brief sojourn home, where he published the first anthology of his poetry, *Registro del mundo: Antología Poética 1922–39* (Registry of the World: Poetic Anthology 1922–39). One of the best-known and most intelligent commentaries on Carrera Andrade's work (before the mature years) is Pedro Salinas's review, "Registro de Jorge Carrera Andrade," from *Revista Iberoamericana* (1942). The Spanish poet refutes Carrera Andrade's claim of "heroic visual ardor," arguing, "Carrera Andrade no sabe ver, porque sabe visionar" (Carrera Andrade does not know how to see, because he knows how to envision). In other words, he transforms what he sees into poetry. Salinas also traces the development of the window theme in Carrera Andrade's oeuvre, linking this personal symbol to two basic ideas in his poetry: *viaje* (travel) and *registro* (discovery and its documentation). In *Edades poéticas (1922–1956)* Carrera Andrade himself equates the quiet action of a window with his own act of writing: "La ventana no hacía más que registrar la presencia de las cosas." (The window did no more than register the presence of things).

The poet next traveled to San Francisco to act as general consul, just four months before the United States entered World War II. President Franklin D. Roosevelt instigated a policy of rapprochement with Latin America, fomenting new interest in Hispanic poetry. Carrera Andrade taught at Mills College and oversaw the translation of much of his poetry into English by Eleanor L. Turnbull, Muna Lee, and Hoffman R. Hays. Remigio Ugo Pane created a bibliography of his poems in English translation, including those from the journals *Fantasy, Poetry, Tomorrow, Books Abroad,* and *Old Line.* Thus, he became one of the most celebrated Latin American poets in the United States.

In 1944 President Ibarra was back in power, and Carrera Andrade was transferred to Venezuela, where he worked to improve relations between that country, Ecuador, and Colombia. He also tried to gain support

Dust jacket for the 1973 collection of essays that includes "Poetry of Reality and Utopia," in which Carrera Andrade defends his style (Bruccoli Clark Layman Archives)

in Latin America for the return of a disputed Ecuadoran province lost to Peru in 1942. Having been criticized in the past for representing governments to which he was opposed, Carrera Andrade resigned his post in protest against Ibarra's tyranny but remained in Venezuela. In 1945 he published *Poesías escogidas* (Selected Poetry), with an insightful introduction by Salinas, as well as the collection *Lugar de origen.*

Carrera Andrade happened to be in Quito in 1947 when Ibarra was removed by the army. The new liberal government appointed him envoy extraordinary and plenipotentiary minister in London, where he negotiated for rice exports to pay off his country's debt. He represented Ecuador at the Third General Assembly of the United Nations in Paris in 1948 and was one of five people charged with revising the Declaration of the Universal Rights of Man. He helped write clauses on the prohibition of exile and the workers' right to a decent standard of living. Again, his work was interrupted by a sudden change of leadership in Quito, and the poet was summoned home.

Carrera Andrade was named head of the Ministry of Foreign Affairs in Quito, but he disagreed with the chancellor in charge and resigned. Turning from public life, he focused anew on his literary interests. The period was a difficult time for personal reasons as well: his father died, and his wife divorced him. He served as vice president of the Casa de la Cultura, working especially on its periodical, but soon returned to Paris, where he edited Spanish publications for UNESCO. His volume of essays *Rostros y climas: Crónica de viajes, hombres y sucesos de nuestro tiempo* (Faces and Climates: Chronicle of Travels, Men and Events of Our Times, 1948) was published in Paris, and in 1949, the journal *Adam International Review* dedicated an entire issue to his work.

During this time, he created the popular character "Juan sin Cielo" (John without Heaven), whom he describes as a pitiful skeptic, a man dispossessed of his spiritual treasures and abandoned in a hostile universe. He explains in *Mi vide en poemas* that Juan sin Cielo has lost his tangible possessions and, more important, has lost his faith, the heavenly kingdom of happiness. He suffers physically the wounds inflicted on other people, because he is an Everyman figure.

Aquí yace la espuma (Here Lies the Sea Foam, 1950) was published to enthusiastic reviews. Carrera Andrade had written the title poem, an extended metaphor on the color white, while sitting on a beach. His fellow writers wrote to him with congratulations: Amado Alonso (11 August 1950) called it the most splendid realization of the theme of whiteness; Juana de Ibarbourou (June 1950) wrote from Montevideo that Carrera Andrade had raised the standard for poetry in the Americas; the Mexican Alfonso Reyes (17 April 1950) declared that the poet had sounded one of his clearest notes; and the Spaniard Américo Castro (17 May 1950) applauded his hand in increasing the universe of metaphors.

The French appreciation for Carrera Andrade's work was registered in a flurry of new translations in 1948–1949, with positive reviews from Robert Ganzo in *Les Clefs du feu* (Keys of Fire) and in the journal *Volonté* (Desire). Francis Miomandre commented on the sense of humor in the poet's work. Responses in England and the United States were equally warm: Carl Sandburg, in an undated letter to Carrera Andrade's translator Lee, called him more his brother than any other poet in the hemisphere; and William Carlos Williams wrote to Lee (6 July 1945) that he found relief from the spiritual torment of the day in the clear and somehow primitive vision allowed by Carrera Andrade's images.

Carrera Andrade had achieved an international reputation on a grand scale. Yet, in 1950 the self-described "poeta peregrino" (pilgrim poet), discouraged by the materialism of Europe and his own sense of alienation, felt obliged to return to Quito from Paris. Once home, he wrote the poems for the augmented second edition of *Lugar de origen*. While his earliest poems on Ecuador had often pictured a claustrophobic feeling of restrictions and suffering, as in "Boletín de viaje"— "Era un anillo de dolor / la línea ecautorial / en el dedo del corazón" (It was a ring of sorrow / the ecuatorial line / on the finger of the heart)—these later, nostalgic poems idealize the country as a land of light and childhood joy. His highly acclaimed *Familia de la noche* (Family of Night, 1953; revised, 1954) is a volume of longer, nobler poems that are often clearly autobiographical.

In 1951 he published a highly praised anthology of fifty-five French and Belgian poets, *Poesía Francesa contemporánea* (Contemporary French Poetry), and the long poem "Hombre planetario" in the journal *Mito* (Myth). In this poem Carrera Andrade synthesizes the two themes that preoccupied him throughout his life: things as the essence of life, and man's identity. "Hombre planetario" marks a new, optimistic attitude in the poet, as he endeavors to identify himself as both Latin American and man of the world, celebrates love, and calls for social justice. The poetic voice expresses uncertainty about the future and the enigma of the universe, concluding affirmatively that the destiny of man is to be "planetary" or universal.

His stay in Ecuador was relatively brief, for in 1951 he found himself back in Paris, as the permanent Ecuadoran delegate at UNESCO. That same year he married Jeannine Ruffier des Aimes; the couple had a daughter, Patricia, born in 1952. Meanwhile, he began writing his three-volume history of Ecuador: *La Tierra siempre verde: El Ecuador visto por los Cronistas de Indias, los corsarios y los viajeros ilustres* (The Evergreen Land: Ecuador as Seen by Indian Chroniclers, Corsairs, and Distinguished Travelers, 1955), *El Camino del Sol,* and *Galería de místicos y de insurgentes* (Gallery of Insurgents and Mystics, 1959). Critics consider these volumes robust in imagination but not terribly scholarly, because of their paucity of dates and hasty treatment of lengthy historical periods.

Carrera Andrade lived in Paris until 1957, again separated from diplomatic life. His writings indicate a new period of solitude and melancholy, burdened by unanswered questions of being. In 1958 he spent two months in Ecuador, where he savored tributes from intellectual circles, including the Tobar Prize, the highest distinction in Ecuador for historical research. The same year he published *Moneda del forastero* (Foreigner's Coins, 1958), a small book of four poems, in a bilingual edition in Paris. He traveled again in the United States and sought treatment for a nervous illness on Long Island.

In 1960 Carrera Andrade represented Ecuador as ambassador to the United Nations. President Ibarra, elected for the fourth time, sent him on a special mission to Chile and Brazil to discuss further the unjust 1942 treaty with Peru. In 1961 Carrera Andrade was named ambassador to Venezuela. He renewed old acquaintances in Caracas and transformed the embassy into a literary center. After the coup in 1963, Venezuela suspended relations with Ecuador, and the poet returned to Quito, where the junta had outlawed all communism and socialism. Both groups were splintered into ineffectual factions. Soon, Carrera Andrade, newly elected to the Ecuadoran Academy of Language, was sent by the government to Managua as ambassador to Nicaragua. There, he read his essay *Interpretación de Rubén Darío* (Interpretation of Rubén Darío, 1964) in front of the president and the diplomatic corps in a ceremony commemorating the death of Darío, the father of *Modernismo*. He renewed his old desire to exalt the beauty of the tropics, connecting his song with a longing for immortality. In 1964 he moved back to Paris as ambassador to France, and, dismayed by the modern dictators in power in Latin America, he concentrated on his *Crónica de las Indias* (Chronicles of the Indies, 1965), a tragic history of tyranny in the New World. In 1966 he served again as a delegate at the UNESCO conference before being recalled by the new interim president and named minister of foreign affairs. This post did not last long, for he soon resigned in order to devote himself to his essays, tracing the problem of Spanish American identity back to the arrival of the conquistadors. In *Reflections on Spanish-American Poetry* he considers the synthesis of indigenous, Creole, mestizo, and displaced European origins, as well as his own mission as an Ecuadoran poet.

In 1967 Carrera Andrade became ambassador to the Netherlands; while he was there the Dutch journal *Norte* (North) dedicated two issues to his poetry, in 1968. His stay in Holland was cut short, however, when Ibarra was elected for the fifth time. Carrera Andrade resigned as ambassador and returned to France to begin writing a long poem of twenty-five cantos, "Libro del destierro" (The Book of Exile), and his autobiography, *El volcán y el colibrí* (The Volcano and the Hummingbird, 1970), as well as to work in the Spanish translation department of UNESCO. His achievements were further recognized when the Société des Poètes Français (Society of French Poets) awarded him the International Grand Prize in Poetry for Friends of France.

During the 1960s many critics, including Isaac J. Barrera and Raquel Verdesoto de Romo Dávila, considered Carrera Andrade to be Ecuador's most important and representative poet. He published his highly acclaimed *Poesía última* (Final Poetry) in 1968. That same year he attended the International Poetry Conference at the State University of New York at Stony Brook and was invited to teach there for two years. He returned to Quito in 1976 and spent his last year working as head of the National Library. The final honor he received was the Eugenio Espejo Prize, awarded in 1977. In May 1976 the Ecuadoran Academy of Language nominated him for the Nobel Prize in literature. He died suddenly on 7 November 1978 and is buried in the San Diego cemetery in Quito.

References:

Isaac J. Barrera, *Historia de la literatura ecuatoriana* (Quito: Casa de la Cultura Ecuatoriana, 1960), pp. 1138–1141, 1161;

Peter Beardsell, *Winds of Exile: The Poetry of Jorge Carrera Andrade* (Oxford: Dolphin, 1977);

René Durand, *Jorge Carrera Andrade* (Paris: Seghers, 1966);

Enrique Ojeda, *Jorge Carrera Andrade: Introducción al estudio de su vida y de su obra* (New York: Torres, 1971);

Pedro Salinas, *Ensayos de Literatura Hispanica: Del "Cantar de mio Cid" a García Lorca,* third edition (Madrid: Aguilar, 1967), pp. 377–387;

Raquel Verdesoto de Romo Dávila, *Lecciones de Literatura,* second edition (Quito: Universitaria, 1965), p. 507.

Papers:

Jorge Carrera Andrade's papers are housed at the library of the State University of New York at Stony Brook.

Julián del Casal

(7 November 1863 – 21 October 1893)

Oscar Montero

Lehman College and The Graduate School and University Center, The City University of New York

BOOKS: *Hojas al viento* (Havana: El Retiro, 1890);

Nieve: Bocetos antiguos—Mi museo ideal—Cromos españoles—Marfiles viejos—La gruta del ensueño (Havana: La Moderna, 1892);

Bustos y rimas (Havana: La Moderna, 1893).

Editions: *Selección de poesías,* edited by Juan J. Geada y Fernández (Havana: Cultural, 1931);

Poesías completas, edited by Mario Cabrera y Saqui (Havana: Ministerio de Educación, 1945);

Poesías, Edición del Centenario (Havana: Consejo Nacional de Cultura, 1963);

Prosas, Edición del Centenario, 3 volumes (Havana: Consejo Nacional de Cultura, 1963);

Poesías, completa y prosa selecta, edited by Alvaro Salvador (Madrid: Editorial Verbum, 2001).

Editions in English: *Selected Prose of Julián del Casal,* edited by Marshall E. Nunn (University: University of Alabama Press, 1949);

The Poetry of Julián del Casal: A Critical Edition, 3 volumes, edited by Robert Jay Glickman (Gainesville: University Presses of Florida, 1976–1978).

OTHER: "El amante de las torturas / The Torture Lover," translated by David William Foster, *The Columbia Anthology of Gay Literature: Readings from Western Antiquity to the Present Day,* edited by Byrne R. S. Fone (New York: Columbia University Press, 1998), pp. 511–514.

(From Bustos y rimas, *1893)*

Julián del Casal holds a prominent place among the Spanish American writers who laid the foundation for the cultural and literary changes that came to be known as *modernismo*. In Spanish American literary histories, *modernismo* is the term used to describe the period from the 1880s to the early years of the twentieth century, a period of change and innovation in the literatures of the Spanish-speaking world. Casal's work has been an enduring presence in the art and literature of Cuba. Moreover, his life and work have been studied and admired by generations of readers and critics in Latin America and beyond. In Casal's work the relationship between words and image is a recurring topic. There is also a preoccupation with the frailty and mortality of the human body and with the relationship between desire and physical decay. At a time when progress and profit at all costs were becoming dominant values, Casal was a pioneer in a renewed struggle to express the intimacies of the human spirit through the craft of language.

Like other Latin American writers of his generation, Casal absorbed the literature and culture of France produced during the second half of the nineteenth century. Although Casal left colonial Havana only once in his entire life, for a brief visit to Madrid, he read avidly and corresponded frequently with other artists from Europe and Latin America. Some of Casal's poems have been included in dozens of anthologies. Contemporary critics have found it impossible to consider the scope of *modernismo,* particularly its subtly transgressive qualities, without discussing Casal and his works. Although known mainly as a poet, he also wrote articles and essays. Critics agree that these works in prose cast an unprecedented, influential gaze on the colonial capital.

José Julián del Casal y de la Lastra was born in Havana on 7 November 1863. He was the only son of Julián del Casal Ygareda, a Spaniard who had made his fortune in the island's sugar economy, and María del Carmen de la Lastra y Owens, a young Cuban woman with rather distinguished ancestors. When Casal was born, the couple already had two daughters, about whom little is known. By the time another daughter, Carmelina, was born in 1867, Casal's father was close to ruin. Not long after, in 1868, Casal's mother died, leaving her five-year-old son in the care of his ruined, desolate father. That same year, war against Spain broke out in the eastern end of the island. The Ten Years' War, as it came to be called, lasted until 1878. The Cuban economy was in ruins, and hopes for independence were lost as Spain regained full control of its prized colony.

In 1881 Casal published his first literary composition in a student paper. Until 1893, the year of his death, he published poems, short stories, articles, and essays in the most important Havana journals. After the death of his father in 1885, Casal struggled with dire economic circumstances, living out his brief life in modest rooms and small apartments, often provided by his friends. About the time of his father's death, he began to support himself by working as a clerk in one of the administrative offices of the colonial government.

In 1885 Casal received a legacy that proved to be far more significant than the meager inheritance left by his father. A friend of Casal's returned to Havana from Madrid with a trunk crammed with the latest books from France. Latin American poets of all stripes were already devoted to Victor Hugo, the giant of French literature, and they admired the Spanish poet Gustavo Adolfo Bécquer. However, Casal's friend introduced him to writers who were forging a new literature in light of the radical changes taking place in French culture and society during the second half of the nineteenth century. Most of these writers were little known, and certainly not widely read, either in Cuba or in the rest of Latin America. Among the many volumes in the

friend's trunk, there were works by Charles Baudelaire, Paul Verlaine, Jean-Nicolas-Arthur Rimbaud, Théophile Gautier, Guy de Maupassant, Stéphane Mallarmé, Gustave Flaubert, Pierre Loti, Joris-Karl Huysmans, Juliette Lambert, and José-María de Heredia, a French poet of Cuban descent. Casal was especially attracted by the chiseled rhymes of the French Parnassian poets, notably Gautier and Heredia, and by the subjective intimacy associated with Verlaine's symbolism.

In the hothouse of Parisian culture, Parnassianism and symbolism had been radically different poetic orientations. In order to combat the excesses of the Romantics, the Parnassians emphasized form over emotions. By contrast, the symbolists valued the nuanced expression of intimate feelings, the vaguely mystical over the hard facts of realism. *Modernista* writers absorbed both poetic tendencies and transformed their influence into an original voice. Many critics have traced the roots of Spanish American *modernismo* to these French sources, "discovered" by Casal in his friend's trunk. Casal's reading of the French writers was decisive in his development as an artist and in the subsequent blossoming of *modernismo* in Spanish America. The influence of Romanticism and specifically of the Spanish poet Bécquer is evident in Casal's early work. However, his reading of contemporary French writers put him in the forefront of a developing poetic idiom, proof of Latin America's cultural independence from Spain.

In 1888, inspired by French writer Lambert's book on Parisian society, Casal conceived of a book titled "La sociedad de La Habana" (Society in Havana). The book would be made up of articles that Casal planned for *La Habana Elegante* (Elegant Havana), a prestigious journal that published the latest works by Latin American and European writers and which circulated outside Cuba. *La Habana Elegante* was also Casal's creative home during his most productive years. Most of his poems first appeared in this journal, often on its front page. The first article of the planned book on Cuban society was dedicated to Captain General Sabas Marín, the chief representative of Spanish authority in colonial Cuba. In the article, published in the 25 March 1888 issue of *La Habana Elegante,* Casal criticizes the captain general's despotic manner, adding that he is "de una arbitrariedad de monarca absoluto" (as arbitrary as an absolute monarch). He goes on to ridicule the captain general's poor taste and the mediocrity of the Cuban cultural landscape under Spanish rule.

With evident disdain, Casal writes that "Los burócratas son los más asiduos concurrentes de las recepciones vulgares del general Marín. Sólo algunas familias cubanas, ya por razones de alta política, ya por

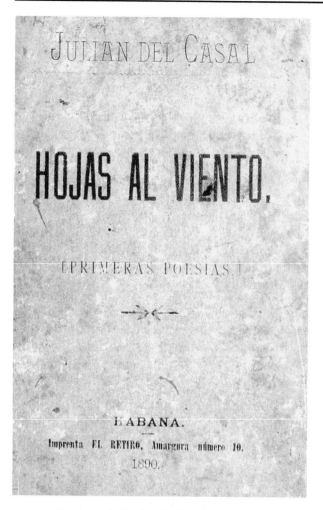

Paper cover for Casal's critically acclaimed first book
(Brenner Library, Quincy University)

hacerse merecedoras de algún favor, frecuentan todavía dichos salones." (Bureaucrats are the most assiduous visitors at the vulgar receptions hosted by General Marín. Only a few Cuban families, because of politics or because they are eager to obtain some favor, still frequent the General's salons.) In the context of colonial politics, Casal's comments on the captain general's reception proved to be more disturbing than the flippant remarks of a society journalist on the merits of a dance or a formal reception. In his chronicle Casal draws a potentially explosive distinction between fawning bureaucrats, eager to curry favor with the colonial authorities, and distinguished Cuban families who chose to keep their distance from them.

Official attempts to suppress the journal with Casal's offending article failed. In fact, the entire run disappeared from the newsstands, seized by a populace increasingly disgusted with Spanish rule. Casal was taken before a judge; although he was acquitted, he was fired from his clerical job and thus deprived of his one dependable source of income. On the other hand, Casal acquired a reputation as a daring young writer, a talented Cuban willing to stand up to Spanish despotism, if not in the battlefield at least through the power of the pen. Even though he professed a preference for poetry over prose, Casal was first known as the young journalist who unleashed a political scandal in the colonial capital. His debut as a critic of colonial society contributed to an increasing disgust with Cuba's political situation and the shortcomings of its provincial culture. Casal never completed "La Sociedad de La Habana," perhaps because he was not interested in publishing what would have certainly been a censored version of the book.

In November 1888 Casal traveled to Spain, financing the trip with the scant remains of his paternal inheritance. By January of the following year he was back in Havana, disappointed and broke. He found Madrid almost as provincial as Havana, its winters too cold and its literary groups not much interested in new work by a young poet from a distant colony. Paris, the city he admired from afar, remained beyond his reach. Casal claimed that he was not sorry about not being able to see Paris, for the ideal image he had of the great "City of Light" was preferable to the harsh realities he would surely have encountered there. The fact is that he lacked the funds to make the trip and the energy to survive in a foreign metropolis. Nonetheless, through his correspondence Casal sustained his lifelong passion for the art and literature of France.

Back in Havana, Casal managed to find work as proofreader and feature writer for *La Discusión,* while continuing his work for *La Habana Elegante* and *El Figaro.* While his income depended on his journalistic writings, he used his spare time to work on his poetry, which continued to appear regularly in the local press. The image of Casal as an isolated aesthete, dedicated to the exclusive pursuit of art, has endured, nurtured by the poet himself and evident in many of his works. Yet Casal also became the chronicler of the colonial capital, a walker in the city who takes his readers through the dusty streets, the circus, the theater, and even local department stores. As long as his health permitted it, Casal was an active participant in the cultural life of the city. His increasing reputation as a writer to be reckoned with put him in the forefront of those who were forging an independent Cuban culture in the heart of colonial oppression.

In May 1890 Casal was finally able to publish a slim volume of verse, *Hojas al viento* (Leaves in the Wind). Cuban critics, as well as critics in Mexico City and Puerto Rico, greeted Casal's book with favorable reviews. Enrique José Varona, the dean of Cuban letters, wrote the most influential contemporary review of the book. Varona's review, which appeared in *La Habana Elegante* (1 June 1890), is a thoughtful evaluation of the work of a promising young poet. It is also a paternalistic definition of what constitutes a national culture, one in which Casal was destined to occupy a marginal position, according to Varona's severe assessment. Varona's review set the tone for a critique that mistrusted the willful ambiguities and richly wrought complexities of Casal's work. Other critics followed Varona's lead and, with less subtlety and sympathy, pointed to Casal's incipient "degeneration," implying that it was both a poetic and a moral malady. The local press caricatured him as an effete bard, wearing an artist's smock and playing a tiny mandolin. In short, Casal was ridiculed as someone who wasted his time with aesthetic matters that were foreign to Cuban history and culture.

The catchall term "degeneration," applied to works of literature and art, implies exotic themes, an antibourgeois stance, and the representation of social and sexual transgressions. Although Casal certainly rejected such a facile classification, his work reveals affinities with the contemporary work of so-called decadent writers. Beginning in Casal's own lifetime, there were critics who complained of what they called his "precious" verses and penchant for extravagant locales. One critic went so far as to warn readers and admirers of Casal's supposedly dangerous influence, both moral and aesthetic, on young artists. At the same time, there were those who defended Casal's art and delighted in the innuendo and transgressive spirit of his poetry and prose. There were those who agreed that a strong, original poetic voice, regardless of its style or the subject matter it chose to treat, was an affront to Spanish political and cultural control of its island colony. After all, Casal had turned to France for ideas and inspiration, not to Spain.

By 1891, exhausted by the demands of journalism, which he said forced the writer to feed a hungry public with bits of his own body, Casal resigned from his position in *El País,* another local newspaper. Using a pseudonym, he supported himself by writing a regular column in another journal. His growing reputation as a poet paradoxically marked him as something of an eccentric. Perhaps sensing that his health was not likely to improve, Casal focused his efforts on the works that eventually made up his final literary production. Though distanced from the local limelight, he maintained an active social life with a select circle of friends. At the same time, as his health permitted, Casal continued his intense literary activities, exchanging letters with European writers, painting, and working on the poems that he hoped to include in forthcoming volumes. His ambitious plans even included the writing of

two novels, a project that, like so many others, he did not have time to begin.

Casal's second volume of verse, *Nieve* (Snow), which appeared in 1892, situated him in the vanguard of Latin America's developing *modernismo.* The year after the book appeared in Havana, a new edition was published in Mexico City. Unlike *Hojas al viento,* which gathers previously published poems, *Nieve* is meticulously crafted as a coherent volume. Divided into sections, the book includes one of Casal's most significant achievements, "Mi museo ideal" (My Ideal Museum). Casal's "museum" is based on the paintings of Gustave Moreau, the French symbolist painter he had first encountered in *A rebours* (1884; translated as *Against the Grain,* 1922), a novel by French writer Huysmans. "Mi museo ideal" includes ten sonnets based on Moreau's paintings of Salomé, Prometheus, Helen of Troy, Hercules, Venus, and others, preceded by a sonnet titled "Vestibule" and followed by a theatrical long poem "Sueño de Gloria. Apoteosis de Gustavo Moreau" (Dream of Glory. Apotheosis of Gustave Moreau). In order to complete his project, Casal corresponded with Moreau and Huysmans, who encouraged his efforts. Huysmans sent Casal reproductions of Moreau's paintings, which Casal used to compose the sonnets of his "ideal museum."

Casal's own versions of Moreau's paintings recast the classical topic on the relationship between word and image in a setting characterized by the erotically charged play between light and dark, between bare flesh and the rich, luxurious materials used to cover it. Two of the best-known sonnets in "Mi museo ideal" represent one of Moreau's many versions of the biblical story of Salomé, a recurring topic in the art and literature of the nineteenth century. In Casal's sonnets, Salomé sheds her richly embroidered gown as she recoils before the terrible image of John the Baptist's severed head. Completely naked, yet "Despójase del traje de brocado / y, quedando vestida en un momento, / de oro y perlas, zafiros y rubíes, / huye del Precursor decapitado" (dressed in gold and pearls, sapphires and rubies, she flees the decapitated Precursor). Salomé's body is both naked and encrusted with jewels; in fact, the naked body itself becomes a jewel set against the word of the prophet, whose severed head floats in midair and whose lips seem to speak even in death. As in other versions of the Salomé story the scene is a highly theatrical contrast between the erotic power of beauty, the subject of Salomé's dance, and its implicit decay, the subject of the words of the martyred prophet. "Mi museo ideal" is certainly an aesthetic achievement, but in colonial Cuba it also carried a political punch. Under Spanish rule Cuba lacked great museums; Casal attempted to create his own through a process of trans-

La Havanne, le 11 Août 1891

M.
   Gustave Moreau

      Très-adoré maître:
                              Quoique je
n'ai pas le bonheur de vous con-
naître que par des copies de vos di-
vins tableaux, j'ose vous écrire pour
vous envoyer les adjoints sonnets
que j'ai composé après des gravu-
res de ces chefs d'œuvre: Hélène,
Salomé et Galatée
            Je sais bien, très-vénéré-maî-
tre, que je n'ai pas réussi à rendre
la sublime, troublant et inexprima-
ble beauté de votres adorées figures;
mais je rêve aussi que vous vous daig-
nerez accueillir ces trois sonnets, avec
la bonté généreuse des grandes âmes,
comme un témoignage pauvre, mais
le seul possible, de ma Muse à vo-
tre genie sans egal, parce qu'il est
le plus philosophique, étant a la fois
celui de le plus pur artiste qu'a ra-
yonne sur l'humanité.
            Dans le hiver prochain, je son-
ge a publier mon second volume de
vers, dont la troisième, partie portera
ce titre: Mon Musée Idéal (Ta

Casal's first letter to the French symbolist painter Gustave Moreau, whose work inspired some of the pieces in the poet's 1892 collection Nieve *(Musée Gustave Moreau, Paris)*

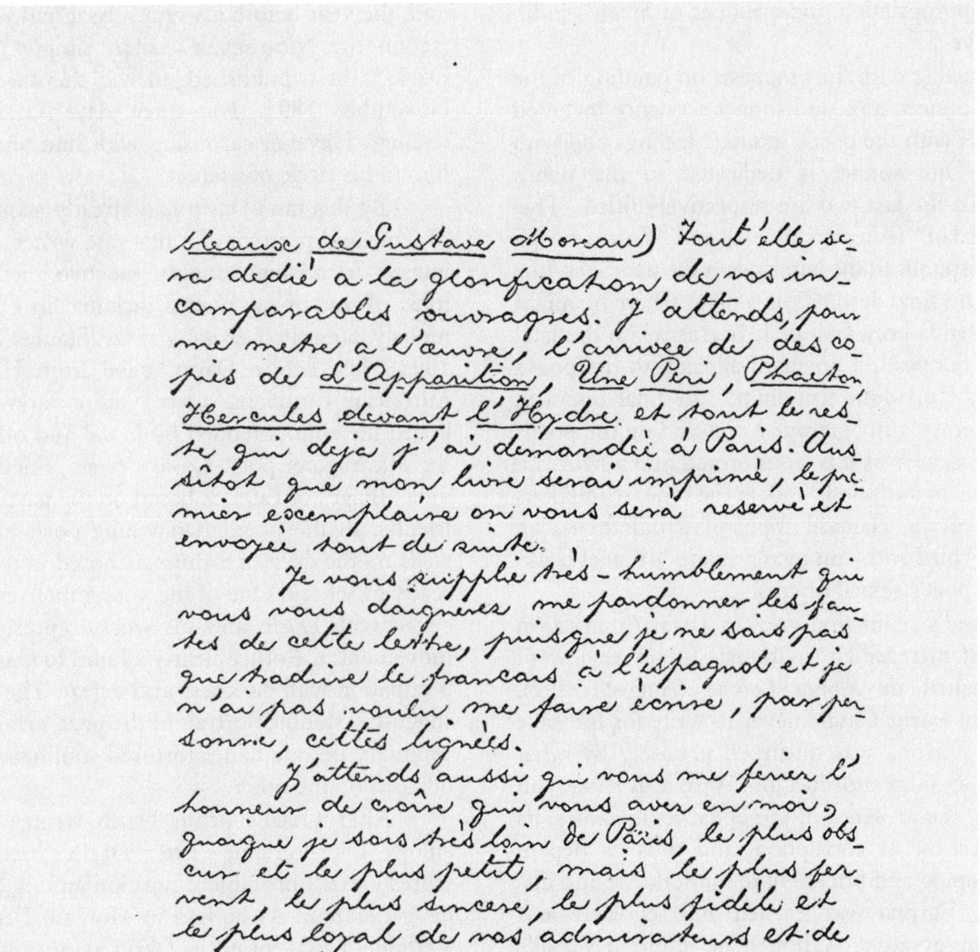

beaux de Gustave Moreau) Tout elle sera dedié a la glorification de vos in-
comparables ouvrages. J'attends, pour
me mettre a l'œuvre, l'arrivée de des copies de *L'Apparition*, *Une Péri*, *Phaéton*,
Hercules devant l'Hydre et tout le res-
te qui deja j'ai demandeé á Paris. Aus-
sitôt que mon livre serai imprimé, le premier escemplaire on vous sera reservé et
envoyée tout de suite.

    Je vous supplie très-humblement qui
vous vous daigneres me pardonner les fau-
tes de cette lettre, puisque je ne sais pas
que traduire le francais á l'espagnol et je
n'ai pas voulu me faire écrire, par per-
sonne, cettes lignées.

    J'attends aussi qui vous me feriez l'
honneur de croire qui vous avez en moi,
quoique je sois très loin de Paris, le plus obs-
cur et le plus petit, mais le plus fervent, le plus sincere, le plus fidéle et
le plus loyal de vos admirateurs et de
vos serviteurs

                Julián del Casal

    Ysla de Cuba
  Redacción de "El País"
    Teniente-Rey 39
      Habana

lation and appropriation, independent of Spain's indifferent tutelage.

Contrasting with the emphasis on painting of the "museum" sonnets, a second sonnet sequence included in *Nieve* deals with the poet's intimate feelings and with his illness. One sonnet is dedicated to the poet's mother, while the last two are respectively titled "Tras una enfermedad" (After an Illness) and "En un hospital" (In a Hospital). In the latter poem the poet sees "the hospital" as his final destination, a place where he might find refuge "en la hora fatal de la borrasca" (in the fatal hour of the tempest), a poignant allusion to the poet's own death. "Horridum Somnium," the final poem in *Nieve,* is a literary autobiography centered on the poet's body, which decays as it is transformed into a Moreau-like image. In an audacious and, at the time, scandalous misreading of the classical topic of Prometheus, an "implacable" bird with "un pico acerado" (a steel beak) devours the poet's sexual organs.

As Casal's reputation grew in Latin America, in Cuba he felt increasingly marginal. In his review of *Nieve,* published in *Revista Cubana* (August 1892), Varona again warns Casal "never to write for the sake of writing." Varona was disturbed precisely by what made Casal an innovator in Latin American letters: an insistence on the presence of the body, its maladies, its pains, its desires, its corruption, and thus its dependency on draping and ornament to mask desire and disguise death. Varona was learned and scholarly and culturally conservative. Although he admired Casal's gifts as a poet, he had little use for Casal's irony and the subtle ambiguities of his eroticism.

In 1892 even Casal's severest critics were awed when *La Habana Elegante* published a letter from Verlaine with the French poet's incisive reading of *Nieve,* a copy of which Casal had sent him. In the letter Verlaine praises the gifts of a promising talent, while gently suggesting that the poet turn to mysticism if he hoped to achieve greatness. Casal treasured the sympathy of kindred souls, evident in the letter by Verlaine. Verlaine's estrangement from his wife and his stormy relationship with Rimbaud had marked him as an outsider in his own land. Scandal only added to Verlaine's myth as a transgressive poet, however, revered for his original voice by many Latin American writers. Although Casal never alluded to his local attackers, much less replied to them, Verlaine's letter was proof that Casal was a talent to be reckoned with, regardless of what the literary establishment of Havana had to say about him.

In the summer of 1892 the peripatetic Rubén Darío, self-proclaimed leader of the emerging aesthetic of *modernismo,* stopped in Havana on his way to Spain. Darío was already well known in the Cuban capital. His poems had been published in *La Habana Elegante,* and, the year before his visit, Casal had written an article on the Nicaraguan writer, simply titled "Rubén Darío," first published in *La Habana Literaria,* 15 November 1891. For three days Casal led Darío through Havana, carousing with him and introducing him to his circle of friends.

By this time Darío had already acquired the aura of fame and prestige of a first-rate writer. The brief yet intense friendship between the two men became the topic of one of the poems included in Casal's posthumously published *Bustos y rimas* (Statues and Rhymes, 1893). Just before Darío sailed from Havana to the European continent, there was a farewell party on board the ship, attended by Casal and other friends of the Nicaraguan poet. Casal's poem, titled "Páginas de vida" (Pages of Life), is based on the parting of the two friends. In the poem two young poets say their farewells on the deck of a ship, anchored in the harbor and ready to set sail. One of the young men, evidently associated with Darío and his work, represents light and movement; the other clearly alludes to Casal's own preoccupation with darkness and defeat. The counterpoint suggests a double portrait of the poet, errant genius and visionary on one hand, tortured soul haunted by inner demons on the other.

After Casal's death Darío wrote a memorable eulogy. Like Verlaine's letter, Darío's friendship underscores Casal's prominent position among the writers of his generation. As he had in Moreau, Huysmans, and Verlaine, Casal found in Darío another kindred spirit, but there is an important difference. Darío was a Latin American, destined to revitalize Hispanic literature across all borders. In Darío, Casal perceived the power of fame and fortune, cultivated by the Nicaraguan poet as part of his poetic persona and denied to Casal, his vital energies waning in the confines of a colonial outpost.

Even before the publication of *Nieve* in 1892, Casal had been writing poems for a third volume of poetry, titled "Rimas," and a series of literary portraits written in prose. As his health continued to decline, Casal worked feverishly to complete his project. In 1893, *Bustos y rimas* was published posthumously by Casal's best friend, the editor of *La Habana Elegante,* Enrique Hernández Miyares. *Bustos y rimas* includes some of Casal's most frequently anthologized poems, notably "En el campo" (In the Country).

In "En el campo" art and nature are set in a dramatic contrast. The poem is a compact primer on the power of art. For its composition Casal revitalized an ancient, little-used poetic form, the three-verse monorhyme. The deliberate monotony of this composition is countered by dazzling images, which represent the poet's preference for the creations of art. The result is not a facile rejection of the country but a transformation of nature through the creative power of analogy. The poet affirms his "impuro amor de las ciudades" (impure love of cities), preferring the subtle shadows cast by gaslights to the glare of the sun, "ilumina las edades" (shining through the ages). Casal knew that the power of natural imagery had been spent in the sentimental landscapes of belated Romantics. Like his French counterparts, he searched for a new poetic mode, urban, cosmopolitan, and willfully artificial. In the poem he is not merely rejecting nature but is revitalizing worn poetic topics through analogies that link the phenomenal world with the creative potential of the human spirit, represented as "mi alma extraña" (my strange soul). As noted by poet and critic Octavio Paz, the Mexican Nobel laureate, analogy, rather than imitation, is the hallmark of literary modernity. Through different routes, the *modernistas,* Casal among them, came to a new understanding of an old lesson, that literary creation does not depend solely on tradition and imitation but on originality and creativity.

One of the few short stories Casal wrote has been the focus of renewed interest, in part because of its representation of erotically charged transgressions and its homoerotic drift. Casal's story provides an enlightening counterpoint to his poetry. The story, "El amante de las torturas" (translated as "The Torture Lover," 1998), was published in *La Habana Elegante* in February 1893, eight months before Casal's death. In the story the narrator visits a bookstore, where he sees a strange young man browsing through the collection of rare volumes. The young man, a book lover, is wan and frail; yet, there is something of the bird of prey in the way he picks up an exquisitely bound edition. When the strange young man leaves, the shopkeeper tells the curious narrator about his visit to the man's house to deliver a recent purchase.

The shopkeeper goes on to tell the narrator that "the torture lover" lives in sumptuous chambers, richly decorated with grotesque images of lethal plants, insects, and other creatures. This strange young man, the shopkeeper continues, finds pleasure in torturing his own body, and all his writing tools, the pen, the inkwell, are in the shape of instruments of torture. The narrator is both attracted and repelled by the shopkeeper's tale. He leaves without saying a word, meditating on the relationship between suffering and pleasure. As in the verses about the two young poets on the deck of the ship, in this story two men face each other. In the meeting of their eyes there is both rejection and identification, attraction and revulsion. Through the disturbing image of the "torture lover," the reader catches a glimpse of the narrator's own preoccupations with his own desire and its possible transgressions.

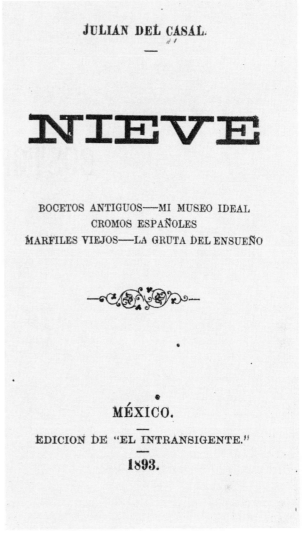

Title page for a Mexican edition of Casal's collection, which includes "Mi museo ideal"–the sonnet cycle inspired by Moreau's paintings– and "Marfiles viejos," a poetic autobiography (Jean and Alexander Heard Library, Vanderbilt University)

After one of many crises that brought him close to death, Casal recovered and continued putting the finishing touches on the work he was about to publish. The circumstances of his death, on the evening of 21 October 1893, have become part of the poet's literary persona. Although he always lived in modest lodgings, Casal was capable of dressing with the elegance of a Parisian dandy. At a dinner party given by a wealthy friend, he suffered a violent hemorrhage of his lungs, and by the time help arrived he was dead, two weeks short of his thirtieth birthday. Casal was buried with great pomp in a mausoleum belonging to the family of one of his wealthy friends, the same friend who paid for the elegant funeral.

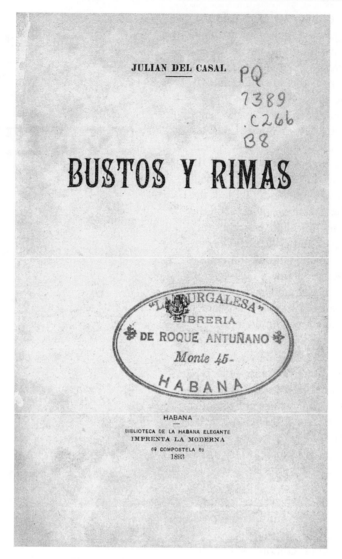

Title page for Casal's posthumously published collection. It includes "Páginas de vida" (Pages of Life),
a poem inspired by his friendship with Nicaraguan poet Rubén Darío
(University of Alabama Library).

According to posthumous reports, Casal died of a ruptured aneurysm. In this final scene there is, on the one hand, good company, luxury, and elegance; on the other, the horror of a sudden, violent death. Framed by richly wrought settings or more simply stated in the hushed tones of a confession, the contrast is also evident in many of Casal's works. In the turbulent years that followed the Spanish defeat in 1898, Casal's poems languished in old editions, while his prose was nearly forgotten in yellowing journals and newspapers. Only a small circle of loyal admirers nurtured his memory and admired his works. In a sense, Varona had been right: Casal might have been appreciated in Paris, but not in Cuba.

In 1941, however, José Lezama Lima, perhaps Cuba's greatest writer of the twentieth century, paid the ultimate tribute to Casal's enduring legacy. That year Lezama published a lengthy essay, "Julián del Casal," contrasting what he calls Casal's "aestheticism" with Baudelaire's morally richer "dandyism." Lezama's essay is the highlight in a long process of reclaiming Casal for the national pantheon. In 1963, the centennial of Casal's birth, his complete works were published in Cuba. That same year Lezama wrote another tribute to Casal, a poem titled "Ode to Julián del Casal," both a literary biography of the poet and an account of Lezama's admiration for him. In the poem Lezama writes of Casal, "Nuestro escandaloso cariño te persigue / y por eso sonríes entre los muertos" (Our scandalous love pursues you / and that is why you smile among the dead).

Letters:

Julián del Casal: Letters to Gustave Moreau, translated by Robert Jay Glickman (New York: Hispanic Institute, Columbia University, 1974).

References:

Emilio de Armas, *Casal* (Havana: Letras Cubanas, 1981);

Luisa Campuzano, ed., *El Sol en la nieve: Julián del Casal (1863–1893)* (Havana: Casa de las Americas, 1999);

Esperanza Figueroa and others, *Julián del Casal: Estudios críticos sobre su obra* (Miami: Ediciones Universal, 1974);

Lee Fontanella, "Parnassian Precept and a New Way of Seeing Casal's *Museo ideal,*" *Contemporary Literature Studies,* 7 (1970): 450–479;

José Lezama Lima, "Julián del Casal," in his *Analecta del reloj: Obras completas,* volume 2 (Mexico City: Aguilar, 1977), pp. 65–99;

José María Monner Sans, *Julián del Casal y el modernismo hispanoamericano* (Mexico City: Colegio de México, 1952);

Oscar Montero, *Erotismo y representación en Julián del Casal* (Amsterdam: Rodopi, 1993);

Montero, "Julián del Casal and the Queers of La Habana," in *¿Entiendes? Queer Readings, Hispanic Writings,* edited by Emilie L. Bergmann and Paul Julian Smith (Durham, N.C.: Duke University Press, 1995), pp. 92–112;

Montero, "Translating Decadence: Julián del Casal's Reading of Huysmans and Moreau," *Revista de Estudios Hispánicos,* 26 (1992): 369–389;

Priscilla Pearsall, "Julián del Casal: Modernity and the Art of the Urban Interior," in *An Art Alienated from Itself: Studies in Spanish American Modernism* (University, Miss.: Romance Monographs, 1984), pp. 11–39;

Ivan Schulman, "Casal's Cuban Counterpoint of Art and Reality," *Latin American Research Review,* 11, no. 2 (1976): 113–128.

Papers:

Julián del Casal's letters to Gustave Moreau are at the Musée Gustave Moreau in Paris.

Oscar Cerruto

(13 June 1912 – 10 April 1981)

Leonardo García Pabón
University of Oregon

BOOKS: *Aluvión de fuego* (Santiago: Ercilla, 1935);
Enciclopedia gramatical del idioma castellano, as Tomás Gracián (Buenos Aires: Claridad, 1942);
Cifra de las rosas y siete cantares (La Paz: Municipalidad de La Paz, 1957);
Cerco de penumbras (La Paz: Ministerio de Educación, 1958);
Patria de sal cautiva (Buenos Aires: Losada, 1958);
Estrella segregada (Buenos Aires: Losada, 1973);
Reverso de la transparencia: Elegías a cinco poetas cuya voz se extinguió entre montañas, y un texto para una cantata (Buenos Aires, 1975);
Cántico traspasado: Obra poética (La Paz: Biblioteca del Sesquicentenario, 1976);
Poesía, prologue by Juan Quirós, notes, chronology, and bibliography by Pedro Shimose (Madrid: Cultura Hispánica/Instituto de Cooperación Iberoamericana, 1985);
La muerte mágica (La Paz: Altiplano, 1988);
De las profundas barrancas suben los sueños (La Paz: Ultima Hora, 1996).
Edition in English: *Selected Stories,* translated by Phillip H. Lunceford, M.F.A. thesis, University of Arkansas, Fayetteville, 1994.

OTHER: Guy de Pourtales, *La peche miraculeuse,* translated by Cerruto as *La pesca milagrosa* (Buenos Aires: Claridad, 1940);
"La poesía paceña en el proceso de la literatura," in *La Paz en su IV Centenario 1548–1948,* 4 volumes, edited by Eloy Salmón (La Paz: Comité Pro IV Centenario de la Fundación de La Paz, 1948), III: 21–55.

SELECTED PERIODICAL PUBLICATIONS– UNCOLLECTED:

FICTION
"Relato sintético de una amor descolorido," *La Razón* (La Paz), 5 March 1927;
"El baile," *Mundo Argentino,* 1 September 1937, p. 11;
"La evasion," *Mundo Argentino,* 20 October 1937, p. 6;
"El tesoro," *Mundo Argentino,* 22 June 1938, p. 28;

Oscar Cerruto

"El testamento desaparecido," *Mundo Argentino,* 11 October 1939, p. 16;
"Conversaciones con Borges," *Presencia* (La Paz), 15 July 1979, Presencia literaria;

NONFICTION
"Oscar Cerruto polemiza sobre arte revolucionario," *La Razón* (La Paz), 25 March 1927, p. 6;
"Vibrante de entusiasmo, Oscar Cerruto defiende en estas seis columnas de ataque los altos fueros del nuevo arte," *La Razón* (La Paz), 29 March 1927, p. 5;
"En nuevo vistazo, O. Cerruto recorre el panorama del arte nuevo en América," *La Razón* (La Paz), 3 April 1927, p. 8;

"Con más puntos de vista, Oscar Cerruto reafirma su defensa de las estéticas revolucionarias de izquierda," *La Razón* (La Paz), 12 April 1927, p. 3;

"Cómo debe entenderse la metáfora en la nueva lírica, por Oscar Cerruto," *La Razón* (La Paz), 19 April 1927, p. 6;

"Panorama de la novela chilena," *Nosotros* (Buenos Aires), 21 December 1937;

"La gestión de Ezra Pound," *Presencia* (La Paz), 24 September 1963, Presencia literaria;

"Semántica de la novela," *Presencia* (La Paz), 26 April 1964, Presencia literaria;

"Poesía y lenguaje: Discurso de ingreso a la Academia Boliviana de la Lengua," *Presencia* (La Paz), 1 January 1973, Presencia literaria;

"*Los Andes no creen en Dios* y la novela del tiempo," *El Diario* (La Paz), 8 July 1973, Suplemento literario;

"El modernismo," *Presencia* (La Paz), Edición de homenaje al sesquicentenario, 6 August 1975, pp. 441–443;

"La poesía en la Biblia," *Presencia* (La Paz), 19 April 1981, Presencia literaria, p. 1;

"Respuesta de Oscar Cerruto al discurso de ingreso de Adolfo Costa du Rels en la Academia Boliviana de la Lengua," *Presencia* (La Paz), 11 April 1982, Presencia literaria.

Literary critics agree that Oscar Cerruto is among the five most important writers of Bolivian literature of the twentieth century. Cerruto produced one of the most important social novels of Bolivia, *Aluvión de fuego* (Flood of Fire, 1935), about the Chaco War between his country and Paraguay; his short stories changed the literary realism dominant in Bolivian literature; and finally, he wrote a distinctive poetry regarded as a zenith of lyrical perfection. His literary work also includes essays and literary criticism as well as a grammar of Spanish. It is fair to say that although his prose may be as significant as his poetry, he is perceived more as a poet than a prose writer. His literary activity was accompanied by a career in the foreign service and a permanent involvement with the press.

Oscar Cerruto Collier was born in La Paz, Bolivia, on 13 June 1912. His father, Andrés Cerruto Durand, was Bolivian, and his mother, Lelia Maggie Collier, British. He had two older siblings and six younger ones, two of which died at very early ages. His paternal family belonged to the upper class of Bolivian society. He was raised in a traditional Bolivian environment: a patriarchal family, where the father is the sole authority. He was sent to the country's best public schools, which Cerruto did not like because of the aggressive behavior among students. By 1918, the year he started elementary school, he already knew how to read, having been taught by his mother, a pianist and an artist. Cerruto was a precocious writer. In a 1977 interview with Alfonso Gumucio Dagrón, he recalled having written his first poem at the age of eight, about the death of a dog struck by a car. He mentions that he did not write sentimental verses but, on the contrary, somehow a cruel poem. He showed the poem to his father, who did not like it. "No volví a escribir hasta los catorce años" (I did not write again until I was fourteen years old), Cerruto recalled.

When he started high school, he was a shy student but already an avid reader. At the age of fourteen he went to live with an aunt, Lilly Collier de Conley, who had come to Bolivia as the wife of a British employee of the Bolivian Railway Company. She guided the young reader into the world of English and Spanish classical literature. Cerruto became familiar with the works of such authors as Charles Dickens, Oscar Wilde, Miguel de Cervantes, Gustavo Adolfo Bécquer, and George Gordon, Lord Byron. He started writing poetry about social inequalities and the struggles of the working class.

In 1926, at the age of fourteen, he got his first job, for the newspaper *Bandera Roja* (Red Flag), a leading publication for the dissemination of socialist ideas. He wrote articles against the government and the Catholic Church and in favor of workers. The newspaper was raided and closed by the government, and Cerruto barely escaped prison. Working for *Bandera Roja* was the beginning of his career as a newspaper journalist, columnist, and administrator. He alternated this occupation with a career in diplomacy, his main professional activity during his life.

Also in 1926, Cerruto published his first important writings, a series of articles on new trends in Bolivian poetry, in the newspaper *La Razón* (The Reason). His ideas were criticized by a well-known writer of his time, Carlos G. Cornejo. Cerruto was engaged in an intense debate over his ideas. Soon, several well-known writers of his time joined the discussion, most of them supporting the ideas of the young writer. Cerruto proved to be an informed and gifted critic, able to maintain an elevated discussion with much older and more-established intellectuals.

His political activism, influenced by the Marxist ideology popular among young intellectuals of the time, sent him to jail in 1928, accused of conspiring against the security of the state. In 1930, having finished high school, he began law school, following his father's desires. His father died the same year, and Cerruto abandoned law school. He went to work for newspapers such as *La Razón* and *El Diario* (The Daily) and continued to publish poems, short stories, and literary articles. Almost a year after his father's death, his older brother, Luis Heriberto, committed suicide. Cerruto became the head of the family and had to support his younger brothers. At this time he began to work for the Bolivian foreign service. He was appointed as secretary in the Bolivian consulate in Arica, Chile, in 1931. A few months later, he won a literary contest in Arica, which may have marked the beginning of his prestige among Chilean intellectuals. Later he became a friend of well-known Chilean poets such as Vicente Huidobro and Pablo Neruda.

In 1932 Bolivia and Paraguay were engaged in war over the remote southern region of Bolivia called "El Chaco." Cerruto was drafted to go to war, but he never made it to the front line. Because of the death of the Bolivian consul in Arica he was ordered to occupy that position. The Chaco War ended in 1935. During those years Cerruto wrote what is widely considered to be the most important Bolivian novel about the war: *Aluvión de fuego,* published in Santiago, Chile, in 1935. Rooted in Marxist and socialist ideas, *Aluvión de fuego* is the description of a nation engaged in two wars: an external one against Paraguay and an internal one against Indians, the working class, and leftist intellectuals. The novel depicts what happened not only on the battlefront but also in the highlands, where Indians were being recruited by force; in the mines, where the army was bloodily repressing the social agitation of the workers; and in the city, where authorities and conservative political leaders were promoting chauvinism to avoid political discontent. The novel ends with the hope of a social revolution forming among the workers and the veterans of the war.

Cerruto lived in Santiago until 1937, and then he moved to Buenos Aires, where he wrote for important newspapers such as *La Nación* (The Nation). In 1942 he was appointed as cultural attaché to the Bolivian Embassy in Argentina, and he remained in Buenos Aires until 1946. These years were important for the still young Cerruto because of the friendships he established with several important writers residing in Buenos Aires, including Ramón Gómez de la Serna, Eduardo Mallea, Pedro Enríquez Hureña, and Alfredo Cahn. This same time was also important because Cerruto's political beliefs radically changed, as well as the themes of his literary work. Until then both his poetry and narrative had mainly focused on social subjects, guided by his socialist ideas. The short stories he published in literary and cultural magazines in Buenos Aires, however, are centered in the daily life of the upper class in Bolivia. The plots seem to have dropped any reference to social and political struggle. It seems that Cerruto did not regard these publications as important, because he never compiled or published them again, but they show the elements of a change that was fully completed between 1957 and 1958 with the publication of the first poetry and short-story collections of his intellectual maturity.

In 1946 Cerruto went back to Bolivia, still working for the foreign service. He married Marina Luna de Orozco in 1950. The marriage lasted for the rest of his life. From 1952 to 1957 Cerruto directed the newspaper *El Diario* of La Paz. During this period he seemed to be more dedicated to the short-story genre, although he still wrote poetry. He published several short stories that later became part of his book *Cerco de penumbras* (Frame of Shadows, 1958). His only daughter, Madeleine, was born in 1954. The child motivated Cerruto to write a poetry book dedicated to her, titled *Cifra de las rosas y siete cantares* (Cipher of the Roses and Seven Songs), published in La Paz in 1957.

Cifra de las rosas y siete cantares is the first book of poems by Cerruto. It is a stylistically elaborate book. Although it does not address directly the most important subjects of his later books, it already shows his mastery of language. The poems still echo the style of Latin American modernism in their rhythms and images. Although this had been a movement of the beginning of the twentieth century, in Bolivia the style continued to be cultivated in the middle of the century by celebrated poets such as Franz Tamayo. Cerruto did not follow modernism as closely as Tamayo and other poets, but *Cifra de las rosas y siete cantares* is marked by some of the characteristics of modernist poetry, such as the emphasis on the sonority of language.

In 1958 Cerruto published two important books in Bolivian literature: his collections of short stories, *Cerco de penumbras,* and *Patria de sal cautiva* (Fatherland, Captive of Salt), a book of poetry that can be considered his first major poetic work. Critics have emphasized that with *Cerco de penumbras* Bolivian narrative abandoned traditional realistic writing and entered into the realm of purely fictional writing. Thus, *Cerco de penumbras* does not attempt to represent reality but rather to explore the unreal through fictions created in language. The themes of the short stories that form the book are dreams, death, madness, time displacement, and the magic of Indians. As the title of the book suggests, reality seems to be surrounded by shadows, the space where there is neither clarity nor darkness. It is interesting to contrast this language with the title of his novel, and to notice that the fire and violence that was predicted to change society (the revolution) has been replaced by a more ambiguous perception of the world: here the undefined sides of reality can change social interaction, but in an unpredictable manner.

Cerruto's new vision of reality is closely linked to his understanding of language. In his poetry he makes it explicit that language is not just a tool for the representation of reality but, more importantly, a tool for the investigation of reality. This distinction may be an explanation for Cerruto's obsession with the perfection of language. Cerruto told Gumucio Dagrón that for him writing was a fight for the "la palabra no intercambiable" (the nonexchangeable word). Such dedication has led critics to define his poetry as classical (in the case of Eduardo Mitre) and as the work of an artisan (in the case of Leonardo García Pabón).

Patria de sal cautiva is the first major work by Cerruto that addresses the meaning of Bolivian existence both as a country and as a community. The title of the book alludes to the fact that Bolivia had become a landlocked country through the loss of its coast to Chile in the war of 1879. Cerruto sees a country isolated not only geographically but also historically, mythically, and socially. In *Patria de sal cautiva* the landscape of the highlands and mountains of the Andes is marked by the past. Mythical times and history have left their traces in the territory, creating a permanent feeling of solitude. The destructive events of Bolivian history as well as its abandonment by the aboriginal gods have thrown the country into an almost metaphysical state of isolation. A few lines from the poem "Altiplano" (Plateau) illustrate well the tone of the book:

El altiplano es frecuente como el odio.
Ciega, de pronto, como una oleada de sangre.
. . . .
Sobre su lomo tatuado por las agujas ásperas del tiempo
los labradores aymaras, su propia tumba a cuestas,
con los fusiles y la honda le ahuyentan pájaros de luz a la
    noche.
. . . .
Altiplano sin fronteras,
desplegado y violento como el fuego.

Sus charangos acentúan el color del infortunio.
Su soledad horada, gota a gota, la piedra

(The plateau is as frequent as hatred
blinds, suddenly, as a wave of blood.
. . . .
On its back tattooed by the rough needles of time
The Aymara farmers, shouldering their own grave,
With rifles and slings scare birds of light to the night.
. . . .
Plateau with no frontiers
Unfurled and violent as fire.
Their *charangos* accent the color of misfortune.
Their loneliness erodes, drop by drop, the stone).

Seventeen years passed before Cerruto published his second major book of poetry, *Estrella segregada* (Estranged Star), published in Buenos Aires in 1975. During these years Cerruto became a recognized writer, nationally as well as internationally. In 1960 he

Paperback cover for Cerruto's first collection of poetry (1957), which he dedicated to his three-year-old daughter, Madeleine (Golden Library, Eastern New Mexico University)

traveled to Washington, D.C., to make a recording of his poetry. In 1963 the Italian government conferred on him a cultural distinction; in 1969 the Bolivian government presented him the Medalla al Mérito (Medal of Merit) for his contribution to Bolivian culture; and in 1972 the Venezuelan government awarded him the Andrés Bello Medal of Culture. All these years he continued to work as a Bolivian diplomat or in Bolivian newspapers. He occupied important positions in the Bolivian foreign service. From 1966 to 1968 he was appointed as the Bolivian ambassador to Uruguay. From 1958 to 1961 he worked as director of the newspaper *Ultima Hora* (Last Hour) in La Paz.

The publication of *Estrella segregada* is a landmark in Cerruto's poetic production. The majority of the critical reception of his work has been dedicated to this book, considering the carefully crafted language as well as the full development of the poet's vision of Bolivian reality. The title of the book refers to the Illimani, the Andean mountain that guards the city of La Paz. For Cerruto the mountain is a fallen god, a subject separated from his community. As in *Patria de sal cautiva,* he sees the loss of social and communal significance as engraved in the landscape of the city–its valley-like topography, the streets, the hills, the people. He describes this lack of social meaning as a degradation of moral values and beliefs originated by the predominance of corrupt political power in the life of the city. Even language seems to be contaminated by the sick condition of the social: the lack of certainty and truth. Cerruto writes in "El pozo verbal" (The Verbal Well):

> Las palabras te ensalzan
> te festejan
> te miman
> te enjoyan
> te besan las manos
> luego te muerden
>
> (Words exalt you
> celebrate you
> spoil you
> jewel you
> kiss your hands
> then they bite you).

Opposed to the space of "las cancerosas calles / tatuadas / por el orín y las blasfemias / donde aúlla la gente" (the cancerous streets / tattooed / by urine and blasphemy / where people howl), as the city is described in the poem "El resplandeciente" (The Shining One), the Illimani represents the world of light and meaning. Cerruto calls it "el resplandeciente," translating the word *Illimani* from the Aymara. This shining star, however, being a fallen god, only has silence and a conjectural meaning as revealed in the last poem of the book, "Sin embargo el sol brilla sobre ti" (Nonetheless the Sun Shines Upon You): "Tal vez / enigma de fulgor" (Perhaps / enigma of brightness). For Cerruto, La Paz is the symbol of a degraded social reality. Political power is not only corrupt, it has corrupted human relationships all over the social corpus. Disappointed and embittered by this perception of reality, he turns his poetry to a dialogue with the dead, the poets he admires. This dialogue is the subject of his last book of poems, *Reverso de la transparencia: Elegías a cinco poetas cuya voz se extinguió entre montañas, y un texto para una cantata* (The Backside of Transparency: Elegies to Five Poets Whose Voices Were Extinguished Between Mountains, And a Text for a Cantata), published also in 1975.

It is worth noting that as he advanced in his diplomatic and literary careers, Cerruto became more resentful about Bolivian society. Nevertheless, there are no traces of his directly criticizing the system in which he worked, nor the established literary system of which he was a consecrated figure. In 1973 he became a member of the Academia Boliviana de la Lengua (Bolivian Academy of Language), the most traditional literary and linguistic institution of the Spanish language in the country. From 1968 to 1976 he took leave of his diplomatic career and dedicated his time to reading and writing, during which years he wrote *Estrella segregada* and *Reverso de la trasparencia.* In 1976 he resumed his work with the foreign service and founded the Academy of Diplomacy of the Secretary of Foreign Affairs, an institution that he directed until 1980.

Cerruto's life exemplified the same quality of classicism as his poetry. He lived surrounded by politicians, diplomats, and traditional writers. He participated in private literary salons, and he dressed formally most of the time. He was a true *letrado* (man of letters), the name given to Latin American intellectuals who, since the colonial period, are at the service of the state. He may well be considered the last *letrado* of Bolivian society in the twentieth century. In the circles he frequented, he was already considered the most important living Bolivian writer. He seems to have achieved a position of success and happiness. Still, the acrimony of his poetry suggests the profound degree of his loneliness.

The isolation into which Bolivia had fallen according to *Patria de sal cautiva* and the degradation of society depicted in *Estrella segregada* become in *Reverso de la transparencia* the absolute loneliness of the poetic voice. A collection of songs to dead poets, the book is a dialogue with the texts of classical Bolivian poets such as Tamayo and Ricardo Jaimes Freyre. Cerruto recognizes in them his own loneliness and bitterness. He wonders where Bolivian community is and why he feels so alone. He does not know if it is he or society, however, that is to be blamed for his alienation:

> Pobre país
> o pobre yo,
> todos nosotros,
> en este inmenso
> país tan nuestro
> y tan ajeno.
> . . . .
> Fui hombre
> Y me olvidaron.
> Y luego me borraron.
> ¿O yo los ignoré
> y así los expulsé
> del mundo?

(Poor country
or poor me,
all of us,
in this immense
country so ours
and so foreign.
. . . .
I was a man
And they forgot me.
And then they erased me.
Or did I ignore them
And thus I expelled them
From the world?).

After publishing *Reverso de la trasparencia* Oscar Cerruto did not write more poetry. The last poem of the book is a dialogue with death, and it would seem that the poet felt that he had nothing else to say. Six years later he became ill, and he died during surgery on 10 April 1981. His death at the age of sixty-eight was felt as a major loss for Bolivian literature. A wide variety of homages, private and public, have followed his death over the years. There is no doubt that his poetry is a major literary work in Bolivian as well as in Latin American literature. Many of his views on Bolivia are still the best description of a society struggling with its own flaws and inadequacies. And no poet in Bolivia has expressed so absolutely the loneliness that comes of being a poet–an illuminated consciousness–in times of ethical degradation.

Interview:

Alfonso Gumucio Dagrón, "Precisión: Aluvión de poesía: Oscar Cerruto," in his *Provocaciones* (La Paz: Los Amigos del Libro, 1977), pp. 39–65.

References:

Luis H Antezana, "Prólogo: Cerruto en (el) 'Cerco de penumbras,'" in Cerruto's *Cerco de penumbras,* third edition, edited by Antezana (La Paz: Plural, 2000), pp. vii–xviii;

Antezana, "Sobre 'Estrella segregada,'" in *Ensayos y lecturas* (La Paz: Altiplano, 1986), pp. 17–45;

Leonardo García Pabón, "La soledad nacional del sujeto poético: La poesía de Oscar Cerruto," in *La patria íntima: Alegorías nacionales en la literatura y el cine de Bolivia* (La Paz: Centro de Estudios Superiores Universitarios/Plural, 1998), pp. 193–212;

Eduardo Mitre, "La soledad del poder," in *El árbol y la piedra: Poetas contemporáneos de Bolivia* (Caracas: Monte Avila, 1986), pp. 26–33;

Blanca Wiethüchter, "Poesía boliviana contemporánea: Oscar Cerruto, Jaime Saenz, Pedro Shimose y Jesús Urzagasti," in *Tendencias actuales en la literatura boliviana,* edited by Javier Sanjinés (Minneapolis: Institute for the Study of Ideologies / Valencia: Instituto de Cine y Radio-Televisíon, 1985), pp. 75–114.

Roque Dalton
(14 May 1935 – 10 May 1975)

Rafael Lara-Martínez
New Mexico Tech

BOOKS: *La ventana en el rostro* (Mexico City: Andrea, 1961);

El mar (Havana: La Tertulia, 1962);

El turno del ofendido (Havana: Casa de las Américas, 1962);

César Vallejo (Havana: Editorial Nacional de Cuba, 1963);

Los poetas (San Salvador, 1964);

El hijo pródigo (y otros poemas del retorno) (San Salvador: Torneo Cultural de la Asociación de Estudiantes de Derecho, 1964);

Los testimonios (Havana: UNEAC, 1964);

México (Havana: Casa de las Américas, 1964);

El Salvador: Monografía (Havana: Enciclopedia Popular, 1965; revised and enlarged edition, Havana: Biblioteca Popular, 1985);

Poemas (San Salvador: Universitaria de El Salvador, 1968);

Taberna y otros lugares (Havana: Casa de las Américas, 1969);

Los pequeños infiernos, edited by José Goytisolo (Barcelona: Libres de Sinera, 1970);

¿Revolución en la revolución? y la crítica de derecha (Havana: Casa de las Américas, 1970);

Miguel Mármol: Los sucesos de 1932 en El Salvador (San José: Universitaria Centroamericana, 1972); translated by Kathleen Ross and Richard Schaaf as *Miguel Mármol* (Willimantic, Conn.: Curbstone, 1987);

El amor me cae más mal que la primavera (San Salvador, 1973);

Dalton y CIA (N.p., 1973);

Las historias prohibidas del Pulgarcito (Mexico City: Siglo Veintiuno, 1974);

Pobrecito poeta que era yo . . . (San José: Universitaria Centroamericana, 1976);

Poemas clandestinos (San Salvador: Publicaciones por la Causa Proletaria, 1977); revised and enlarged as *Poemas clandestinos: Historia y poemas de una lucha de clases* (Puebla, Mexico: Universidad Autónoma de Puebla, 1980); translated by Jack Hirschman as

Roque Dalton (photograph by Chinolope)

Clandestine Poems (Willimantic, Conn.: Curbstone, 1986);

Poesía, edited by Mario Benedetti (Havana: Casa de las Américas, 1980);

Poesía militante/Militant Poetry (London: El Salvador Solidarity Campaign, 1980);

Poesía elegida (Tegucigalpa: Guaymuras, 1981);

Las enseñanzas de Vietnam: Apuntes (California, 1981);

Poesía escogida (San José: Universitaria Centroamericana, 1983);

Poems, translated by Schaaf (Willimantic, Conn.: Curbstone, 1984);

Un libro rojo para Lenin (Managua: Nueva Nicaragua, 1986);

Con manos de fantasma, edited by Vicente Muliero (Buenos Aires: Nueva América, 1987);

Un libro levemente odioso, edited by Elena Poniatowska (Mexico City: La Letra Editores, 1988);

Roque Dalton: Antología poética, edited by Juan Manuel Roca (Cali: Fundación para la Investigación y la Cultura / Bogotá: Tiempo Presente, 1990);

En la humedad del secreto: Antología poética de Roque Dalton, edited by Rafael Lara Martínez (San Salvador: Dirección de Publicaciones e Impresos, CONCULTURA, 1994);

Atado al mar y otros poemas (Buenos Aires: Espasa Calpe, 1995);

Roque Dalton: Antología, edited by Juan Carlos Berrio (Tafalla, Nafarroa, Spain: Txalaparta, 1995);

Small Hours of the Night: Selected Poems, edited by Hardie St. Martin, translated by Jonathan Cohen and others (Willimantic, Conn.: Curbstone, 1996);

Antología mínima, edited by Luis Melgar Brizuela (San José: EDUCA, 1998);

La ternura no basta: Antología, edited by Victor Casaus (Havana: Fondo Editorial Casa de las Américas, 1999);

Antología, edited by Benedetti (Madrid: Visor, 2000).

Edition in English: *Poetry and Militancy in Latin America,* translated by Arlene Scully and James Scully (Willimantic, Conn.: Curbstone, 1981);

Roque Dalton was born 14 May 1935 in San Salvador, El Salvador, and was killed by his own guerrilla group forty years later, also in the month of May. Despite the brevity of his life span, Dalton wrote more than fifteen books that transformed the political and poetic spheres of his native country. He has been recognized as one of the leading poets of El Salvador, who united artistic and political varieties of the avant-garde into a whole. He cultivated diverse genres—essay, novel, drama, movie script, journalism, and political commentary—all with sarcastic humor and irony. His works have been translated into English, German, Japanese, and several other languages.

The illegitimate son of a wealthy Salvadoran of Irish-American origin, Winnal Dalton, and a humble nurse, Marcía García, Dalton lived his childhood with his mother. His official name was Roque García; before graduating from secondary school he never used the name of his father. It is possible to trace how he identified himself with his paternal lineage by his gradually erasing the name of his mother in exchange

for the one of his father: Roque García, Roque D. García, Roque Dalton García, and, finally, Roque Dalton.

Thanks to the financial support of his father, he attended the prestigious Externado de San José, a private Jesuit secondary and preparatory school. His poetry and prose capture some of this early experience; with a tender irony he re-creates his initiation to poetry by Father Alfonso de María Landarech, S.J., in section 9 of his collection "Los Hongos" (The Mushrooms), published in *Poesía* (Poetry, 1980). In his posthumous novel, *Pobrecito poeta que era yo . . .* (Poor Little Poet that I Was . . . , 1976), he confers an autonomous voice and character on his adolescent former life and narrates it through the voice of Roberto. His high school diploma was issued in 1953 under the name of Roque D. García.

After his graduation, again thanks to the financial support of his father, he traveled to Chile via Panama. His plans to attend a Catholic institution of higher education suddenly changed, and he registered at the National University. In Santiago, according to his own narrative—at times not accurate—he met Pablo Neruda, Diego Rivera, and Nicolás Guillén. Much like his character Roberto in *Pobrecito poeta que era yo . . . ,* he transformed his previous Catholic belief into a Marxist political agenda. The influence of Neruda and Rivera was so overwhelming that he abandoned his studies and returned to El Salvador.

Upon his return he attended the law school at the Salvadoran National University. Dalton became the editor of the *Opinión Estudiantil* (Student Opinion) for several years. He met a group of young poets who were also studying law, including Roberto Armijo, Manlio Argueta, the Guatemalan Otto René Castillo, José Roberto Cea, and Alfonso Quijada Urías. They formed the Circulo Literario Universitario (CLU, University Literary Circle) and later were recognized as the "generación comprometida" (engaged generation). Besides some mimeographed underground publications, such as *La Jodarria* (The Depravity), *Gallo Gris* (Grey Rooster), *Hoja* (Leaf, 1953–1956), and *La Pájara Pinta* (The Painted Bird, 1966–1974), most of the publications of the circle were distributed through the cultural and literary supplements of the capital newspapers. A well-known critical newspaper, the afternoon *Sábados de Diario Latino* (Saturday Literary Section of *Diario Latino*), directed by the Nicaraguan-Salvadoran writer Juan Felipe Toruño, devoted a weekly page to the CLU, which allowed these poets to publish their early works while expressing opinions to a wider audience.

Paperback cover for Dalton's 1969 collection, which established him as one of the leading figures in Spanish American poetry (University of Knoxville Library)

Until recently, because of a lack of development in the field of Central American literary historiography, most of Dalton's early poems and essays were unknown. In addition to their literary and artistic value, these early writings are of special interest to cultural historians. Indeed, Dalton's poems and cultural journalism point to the early influence of Neruda, as well as to his Aristotelian and Jesuit background. Dalton and Castillo won their first literary prize in 1955 with their poem "Dos puños por la tierra" (Two Fists for the Land). A revised version of this Nerudian reconstruction of a nineteenth-century revolt was included in *La ventana en el rostro* (The Window in the Face, 1961) under the title "Cantos a Anastacio Aquino" (Songs to Anastacio Aquino). In 1956, in a public debate that lasted several months in the most important Salvadoran newspapers, Dalton justified the need for a political approach to poetry, quoting the *Politics* of Aristotle in *La Prensa Gráfica* (30 September 1956): "el hombre es un animal social" (humans are political or social animals).

His engagement with several student organizations and, later, with the Salvadoran Communist Party earned him a trip to Eastern Europe and to the Soviet Union in 1957. His impressions were recorded in a short essay, "El sexto festival mundial de la juventud" (The Sixth World Festival of Youth, 1958), and in several poems such as "Recuerdo cuando hablaba de Lisa" (I Remember When I Used to Talk About Lisa). This latter poem was included in his book *La ventana en el rostro*.

Dalton's increasing involvement in Salvadoran internal politics first led him into prison, and then into exile. In 1961—as a result of his opposition to the military regime of José María Lemus—he traveled to Mexico along with his wife, Aída Díaz de Dalton, whom he married in 1955, and their three sons: Vladimir, Juan José, and Jorge. In Mexico he published *La ventana en el rostro*. The avant-garde Nicaraguan poet Mauricio de la Selva wrote the introduction for the collection. De la Selva recognized in Dalton's poetry a "verso encendido" (a lighting verse) and in his first book "un recorrido a través de experiencias que denotan los cambios sufridos por un hombre que marcha hacia la verdad" (a journey through the experiences that denote the changes endured by a man that walks toward truth). *La ventana en el rostro* is a collection of autobiographical poems depicting his first experiences of love; his literary approach to prison, a place where he meets the classic poets; and several Nerudian re-creations of Salvadoran history. While in Mexico he also attended classes in anthropology at the Escuela Nacional de Antropología e Historia (National School of Anthropology and History) for two semesters, and then he traveled to Cuba.

Once on the island he established close connections with several cultural centers founded by the Revolution. He worked for several years as a board member of Casa de las Américas (House of the Americas), Radio Habana (Havana Radio), and the Unión de Artistas y Escritores de Cuba (Union of Artists and Writers of Cuba). His constant exchange with poets such as Pablo Antonio Fernández, Heberto Padilla, Roberto Fernández Retamar, and Fayad Jamis suggests that Dalton considered Cuba his second home, and himself a Cuban poet. Cuba represented the country in which, for the first time, he was recognized as a professional writer. His classical "Paraphrase" of José Martí—included in *Un libro levemente odioso* (A Slightly Hateful Book, 1988)—expresses his attachment to the island: "Dos patrias tengo yo: Cuba y la mía" (I have two countries: Cuba and mine).

In 1962 Dalton published his lyric poem *El mar* (The Sea), which has been considered a reflection on the French poet Saint-John Perse as well as on Surrealism. The same year, his book *El turno del ofendido* (The Turn of the Offended One) obtained a literary award at Casa de las Américas. This book granted him a wide recognition in all Cuban intellectual circles. His poems are an original mixture of intimate poetry and of ironic, sometimes bitter, political commentary. "Alta hora de la noche" (High Hour of the Night) is probably his most often-quoted poem:

Cuando sepas que he muerto no pronuncies mi nombre
porque se dentendría la muerte y el reposo
Tu voz que es la campana de los cinco sentidos,
sería el tenue faro buscando por mi niebla.

Cuando sepas que he muerto dí silabas extrañas
Pronuncia flor, abeja, lágrima, pan, tormenta

(When you will know that I have died do not pronounce
    my name
because death and rest would be stopped
Your voice that is the bell of the five senses
would be the tenuous lighthouse searching for my fog
When you will know that I have died say strange syllables
Pronounce flower, bee, tear, bread, storm).

"Yo quería" (I Wanted) has been interpreted as a premonition of his death:

Yo quería hablar de la vida de todos sus rincones
melodiosos yo quería juntar en un río de palabras
los sueños y los nombres lo que no se dice
. . . .
Y no he podido daros—puerta cerrada
de la poesía—
que mi propio cadáver decapitado en la arena

(I wanted to talk about life of all its melodious
places I wanted to join in a river of words
dreams and names what it is not said
. . . .
And I have not been able to give to you—close door
of poetry—
that my own decapitated dead body in the sand).

One year later, also in Cuba, Dalton published two essays: one on the Peruvian poet César Vallejo and the other on Salvadoran political and economic history. While *César Vallejo* is a declaration of his renewed poetic principles in which he renounces his previous dedication to Neruda, the monograph on El Salvador—*El Salvador: Monografía* (1965)—represents a political declaration on the violent and unjust history of his native country.

Upon his return to El Salvador in 1964, he was captured and put into prison in the city of Cojutepeque. The most memorable literary reconstruction of his incarceration and escape is the last chapter of *Pobrecito poeta que era yo . . . .* The narration of his breakout is an homage to the Argentine writer Jorge Luis Borges. That same year in Cuba, he published the book *Los testimonios* (The Testimonies). This work is divided into four sections. In the first two Dalton elaborates a folkloric and native poetry; he poetically re-creates the historical sources and codices that he studied during his short stay at the School of Anthropology in Mexico City. In the last two sections he develops an intimate and self-oriented poetic prose. "El tlamatini" (The Tlamatini or "The Wise One") should be contrasted with "La memoria" (Memory).

Y ahora hablaré–salven los dioses
la rectitud y la frescura de mi lengua–
del lugar de los muertos
del sitio sin salida ni calle a donde todos van
pues es casa común región de perderse
. . . .
Así he dicho en alta voz el secreto
el tlamatini es posible que yo sea
el que la melodía del secreto conoce

(And now I will talk–save the gods
the straightness and the freshness of my tongue–
of the place of the dead
of the site without exit or street where everybody goes
because it is common house region to be lost
. . . .
As such I have said aloud the secret
it is possible that I am the tlamatini
the one who knows the melody of the secret).

While "El tlamatini" is Dalton's re-creation of a pre-Hispanic source, "La memoria" recovers Dalton's early love experience.

Tu desnudez surgía en la pequeña noche de la alcoba
del fuego entre las cosas de madera
bajo la lámpara golpeada
como una flor extraña la de todos los dones
siempre para llenarme de asombro
y llamarme a nuevos descubrimientos
y tu respiración y mi respiración eran dos ríos vecinos
y tu piel y mi piel dos territorios sin frontera
y yo en ti como la tormenta tocando la raíz de los volcanes
y tú para mí como el desfiladero llovido
para la luz del amanecer

(Your nakedness emerges in the small night of the bed-
    room
of the fire among the wooden things
under a stricken lamp
as a strange flower the one of all the gifts
always to fill me with wonder
and to call me to new discoveries
and your breathing and my breathing were two neighbor-
    ing rivers
and your skin and my skin two territories without border
and I in you as the storm touching the roots of the volca-
    noes
and you for me like the rained gorge
for the light of dawn).

In 1964 the first two incomplete versions of *Pobrecito poeta que era yo . . .* circulated in literary circles of El Salvador under the title "Los poetas" (The Poets); one of those versions was signed with the pseudonym of Juan de la Lluvia. Dalton's original intention was to write a bildungsroman in which he would reconstitute the different artistic, philosophical, and political positions of his avant-garde literary group at the end of the 1950s. Various Cuban literary reviews such as *Casa de las Américas* (House of the Americas), *La Gaceta de Cuba* (The Gazette of Cuba), and *El Caimán Barbudo* (The Bearded Caiman) published other shorter fragments of the novel. These early versions are important for critics to understand the dynamic of revision in the works of the poet. "Los poetas" not only anticipates alternative versions of chapters 1, 2, and 4 in *Pobrecito poeta que era yo . . .*, but it can also be read as an independent novel. The articles published in the Cuban reviews prefigure the concluding chapter 5 of the novel. The manner in which Dalton uses the multiple autonomous voices of his colleagues to represent specific periods of his own life is of particular interest. For Dalton, several segments of his past life are as independent in character and in thought as any of the members of his literary circle.

Between 1965 and 1967 Dalton traveled to Europe. Although he lived in Prague, he visited several other continental capitals. As a correspondent for Prensa Latina (Latin Press), he was a board member of the prestigious periodical *Revista International (Problemas de la Paz y el Socialismo)* (International Review [Problems of Peace and Socialism]). His political essays appeared in English translation in the Canadian-based magazine *World Marxist Review*. Aside from his editorial responsibilities, he continued to write poetry and prose. During his stay in Prague he wrote *Los pequeños infiernos* (The Little Hells), which was published in 1983 in his *Poesía escogida* (Selected Poetry). In this book Dalton poetically re-creates his passage to adolescence. In 1968 the most important compilation of his works to date, *Poemas* (Poems), was published by the press of the Universidad de El Salvador (the University of El Salvador). *Poemas* remained the most comprehensive edition until Mario Benedetti published *Poesía* (Poetry, 1980) in Havana, five years after Dalton's death.

While in Prague, he met and interviewed Miguel Mármol. Mármol–a legendary Salvadoran shoemaker and union leader–was one of the founders of the Salvadoran Communist Party. In 1932 he participated in and organized the most important native and peasant revolt in the first half of the twentieth century, in the western region of El Salvador. The revolt–known as *La Matanza* (The Slaughter)–led to a period of ethnic cleansing. The army repression almost eliminated the most important native group of El Salvador, the Izalco Indians. For more than half a century, because it identified native tradition with communism, the official policy of the Salvadoran state suppressed any reference to the native inhabitants of the country. Even though the account of Mármol is clearly a partisan one, his testimony and life story recapture a facet of Salvadoran history erased by all official historiogra-

Paperback cover for the 1981 English translation of Dalton's essay "Poesía y militancia en América Latina," originally published in 1963. The book also includes a poem, "Old Shit," that was published as "Viejuemierda" in Dalton's 1974 collection, Las historias prohibidas del Pulgarcito *(Bruccoli Clark Layman Archives).*

phy. A first version of Dalton's dialogue with Mármol appeared in the Cuban review *Pensamiento Crítico* (Critical Thinking) in 1971. In 1972 the elaborated written version of their conversation was published in Costa Rica under the title *Miguel Mármol: Los sucesos de 1932 en El Salvador* (Miguel Mármol: The Events of 1932 in El Salvador; translated as *Miguel Mármol,* 1987). The half a decade is significant of the distance between the original oral testimony in 1967 and its narrative, complex, and final novel form, published in 1972.

Another book that Dalton started to write during his years in Czechoslovakia was "Los Hongos," although apparently he finished it five years later in Havana. "Los Hongos"–dedicated to the Nicaraguan poet Ernesto Cardenal–is a late confession, a declaration of faith, that the adult Dalton, having converted to Marxist ideology, maintains in secret with his old Jesuit professors. By rescuing heretic voices from different periods of the history of Christianity, the poet imagines a possible new heresy in the twentieth century: the fusion of Christian faith and Marxism. Nev-

ertheless, as he states in section 11, being "idiota" (an idiot), any belief of his will always be considered as a dream and a chimera.

Also during his stay in Prague, Dalton started to write the work that made him one of the main representatives of Latin American poetry at the end of the 1960s: *Taberna y otros lugares* (Tavern and Other Places, 1969). This book received the Casa de las Américas Award in Havana in 1969. The final poem, "Taberna" (Tavern), is a long conversation between anonymous voices of discontent, which Dalton collected during his bohemian nights at the U Fleku bar in Prague. Dalton transforms poetry into a dialogical and polyphonic discourse, intuitively anticipating the events of Prague in 1968. This same year he resigned from the Salvadoran Communist Party. In 1969 he collaborated in translating the works of the Korean Kim Il Sung into English and Spanish.

As early as 1969, the Cuban writer Alfonso López Morales praised Dalton's personal approach to poetry. In his article "La liberación es el turno del ofendido" (Liberation Is the Turn of the Offended One), not published in *Casa de las Américas* until 1982, López Morales proclaimed that Dalton's project is comprehensive. Dalton prefers to offer a comprehensive scrutiny of his own time rather than preparing only a political testimony on oppression and human-rights violations. Dalton himself confirms his own particular view on poetry and *testimonio* in two published works: "Poesía y militancia en América Latina" (translated in *Poetry and Militancy in Latin America,* 1981), also published in *Casa de las Américas,* and his 1964 interview with Fayad Jamis, "Un testigo corroído por la pasión" (A Witness Corroded by Passion). He maintains that his eyewitness and poetic accounts have to take into consideration all current issues, such as psychoanalysis, torture, Coca-Cola, and jazz, although not all of these themes have a direct impact on revolution or on politics.

The subject of poetry is "todo lo que cabe en la vida . . . expresar toda la vida" (everything that fits in life . . . expressing the whole life), he relates in "Un testigo corroído por la pasión." The poet is not only interested in a political tradition, but he is also responsible for teaching the most refined poetic works to the members of his party. The role of the communist writer is "hacer que el Secretario de Organización del Comité Central, por ejemplo ame a San Juan de la Cruz, a Henri Michaux o a Saint John-Perse" (to make the Secretary of the Organization of the Central Committee, for example, love Saint John of the Cross, Henri Michaux, or Saint John-Perse), he wrote in "Poesía y militancia en América Latina."

In 1970 the Spanish writer José Goytisolo edited a brief collection of Dalton's works under the title *Los pequeños infiernos* (The Little Hells) in Barcelona. Despite the similar title, this book should not be confused with the poems Dalton wrote in Prague in 1966–1968. After this date Dalton's whereabouts became less certain. In 1974 he published in Mexico one of his best-known books, the best-seller *Las historias prohibidas del Pulgarcito* (The Forbidden Histories of Little Thom). Using a collage and an avant-garde form of mixing poetry, popular proverb, irony, political commentary, and historical fact, Dalton captures multiple artistic and social voices that, until then, had been silenced by Salvadoran official history. In this work, which was immediately considered a classic, he crafted a counter-history that became required reading for the general public throughout Latin America.

In 1972–1973 Dalton traveled to Chile by invitation of the government of Salvador Allende and the Unidad Popular (Popular Unity). There are not many records of his trips and whereabouts during these years. Probably, from Chile via Havana, Dalton trav-

eled to Vietnam. Indeed, the last letter that his friend, the Argentine Julio Cortázar, received in France was dated "Hanoi, August 15, 1973." In North Vietnam, Dalton received training in guerrilla and insurgent organization, without, however, losing either his commitment to poetry or his sense of humor. For Dalton, humor was one of the most important and secret weapons against imperialism, as well as one of the essential tools for building socialism. In his letter to Cortázar, Dalton states that he is rereading Cortázar's novel *Rayuela* (1963; translated as *Hopscotch,* 1966) and laughing while the United States Air Force bombs North Vietnam. After the defeat of the democratic socialist project in Chile, it became obvious to him that only an armed struggle would be able to accomplish a more just socialist society.

Also in 1973, Dalton's Surrealist view on love– *El amor me cae más mal que la primavera* (Love Fits Me Worse than Spring)–circulated in a small edition in San Salvador. As the Chilean writer Isidora Aguirre affirms in her tender *Carta a Roque Dalton* (Letter to Roque Dalton, 1990), published in *En la humedad del secreto: Antología poética de Roque Dalton* (In the Humidity of the Secret: Poetic Anthology of Roque Dalton, 1994), flirting, love, and eroticism were subjects as important to him as politics.

> El amor es mi otra patria
> la primera
> no la de que me ufano:
> la que sufro
>
> (Love is my other country
> the first one
> not the one I am proud of:
> the one I suffer).

This same year, he wrote the novella "Dalton y CIA" (Dalton and Company), in which he fictionally traces his paternal genealogy to the outlaw Dalton brothers in the Arizona desert. He repeated the title *Dalton y CIA* (Dalton and the CIA, 1973) to reconstruct his various conflictive encounters with the American intelligence agency. In this work, in specific, he offers an account of the early support of the United States government against insurgency to the Salvadoran prison system, the army, and the military dictators.

In December 1973 Dalton entered El Salvador clandestinely. He had previously resigned from the Salvadoran Communist Party and joined a radical guerrilla group, the Ejercito Revolucionario del Pueblo (Revolutionary Army of the People). As indicated by one of his last poems, "La violencia aquí" (Violence Here), Dalton had come to the conclusion

Paperback cover for the 1986 bilingual edition of a collection that was first published in 1977–two years after Dalton was executed by Ejercito Revolucionario del Pueblo, the guerrilla group to which he belonged (Darcus Library, Winthrop University)

that "la violencia es la partera de la historia" (violence is the midwife of history). The Revolutionary Army clandestinely circulated one of the last books of poems he wrote, *Poemas clandestinos* (1977; translated as *Clandestine Poems,* 1986), which includes "La violencia aquí." Despite its partisan and sometimes orthodox views on revolution, *Poemas clandestinos* has the appeal of recovering multiple voices or points of view—feminist, Social-Democrat, Marxist, Christian—on the meaning of social change and justice in Central America. He was sentenced to death by his guerrilla group, accused of spying for a foreign nation, and killed on 10 May 1975, only four days before his fortieth birthday.

After his death, Dalton came to represent the Salvadoran struggle to put an end to the fifty-year-old military dictatorship. During the 1980s, because of the Salvadoran civil war, only his politically oriented poems received attention from the critics. Some of his poems—such as "Poema de amor" (Love

Poem, 1974), written under the influence of the Cuban Heberto Padilla and the German Hans Einsenberger—became anthems of the Salvadoran Left. After his assassination several unedited works were published, sometimes without consideration for literary posterity; politics had overruled almost all academic and literary perspectives. Books such as *Doradas cenizas del Fénix* (Golden Ashes of the Phoenix, 1983), included in *Poesía escogida; Un libro levemente odioso, Un libro rojo para Lenin* (A Red Book for Lenin, 1986), and *Pobrecito poeta que era yo . . .* were published in different countries stating dubious dates and, sometimes, spurious publication imprints. It is therefore difficult to establish a direct correspondence between the events in the life of the poet and the writing of some of his most prominent works. Even the two compilations of his poems—*Poesía* and *Poesía escogida*—that were upheld as models of his works and upon which various translations were based, present serious divergences from the original editions. Several of his contributions to poetry, narrative, cinema, theater, and politics are still unedited.

After the Salvadoran Peace Treaty in 1992, for the first time, the official printing house of El Salvador edited an exhaustive compilation of his poetry in 1994. *En la humedad del secreto: Antología poética de Roque Dalton* includes the most complete critical bibliography on the writer. His first book of poems, *La ventana en el rostro,* was thoroughly edited in the Biblioteca Básica de Literatura Salvadoreña (Basic Library of Salvadoran Literature) in 1997–1998, along with other classics by writers such as Alfredo Espino, Salarrué, and Claudia Lars. Dalton suddenly became required reading in all national secondary schools. In 1997 the National Congress declared him the national poet.

Dalton is both canonized and lionized. He is currently the most often-quoted and best-known Salvadoran writer by the general public. Some of his poems are recited by heart in the streets of San Salvador and are written along with other graffiti on the walls of public buildings. In May 1995, during the commemoration of the twentieth anniversary of his assassination, the slogan "¡Roque Dalton vive!" (Roque Dalton is alive!) was painted on the walls of several buildings in downtown San Salvador. He has also become a popular literary character. The most acclaimed novel in which Dalton appears as one of the main heroes is *Las palabras perdidas* (The Lost Words, 1992) by the Cuban Jesús Díaz.

For recent generations Roque Dalton represents the Salvadoran poet par excellence. Several of his unedited works are now available, thanks to the effort of several young Salvadoran literary historians such as Javier Alas, Luis Alvarenga, and Carlos Cañas Dinarte. His wife, Aída Díaz de Dalton, and his two living sons, Juan José and Jorge, also hold a wealth of manuscripts. His works will undoubtedly continue to have an enormous influence on the new generations of Salvadoran writers. The Jesuit University of El Salvador–Universidad Centroamericana José Simeón Cañas–has undertaken the task of publishing some of his most recognized works. Nonetheless, a complete critical edition of his works, as well as several critical evaluations from diverse current theoretical perspectives, are still lacking and would surely be a welcome contribution to the field of Dalton studies.

References:

Bárbara Harlow, *After Lives: Legacies of Revolutionary Writing* (New York: Verso, 1996);

Rafael Lara Martínez and Denis Seager, eds., *Otros Roques: La poética múltiple de Roque Dalton* (New Orleans: University Press of the South, 1999);

Alfonso López Morales, "La liberación es el turno del ofendido," *Casa de las Américas,* no. 134 (September/October 1982): 48–60;

Ileana Rodríguez, *Women, Guerrillas, and Love: Understanding War in Central America* (Minneapolis: University of Minnesota Press, 1996), pp. 77–90.

Julieta Dobles Yzaguirre

(1 March 1943 –   )

Ruth Lorraine Budd
Longwood University

BOOKS: *Reloj de siempre* (San José: Círculo de Poetas Costarricenses, 1965);

El peso vivo (San José: Editorial Costa Rica, 1968);

Los pasos terrestres (San José: Editorial Costa Rica, 1976);

Manifiesto trascendentalista y poesía de sus autores, by Dobles, Laureano Albán, Ronald Bonilla, and Carlos Francisco Monge (San José: Editorial Costa Rica, 1977);

Hora de lejanías (Madrid: Adonais, 1982);

Los delitos de Pandora (San José: Editorial Costa Rica, 1987);

Una viajera demasiado azul (Jerusalem: La Semana / San José: Liga de Amistad, 1990);

Amar en Jerusalén (San José: Editorial Universidad Estatal a Distancia, 1992);

Costa Rica poema a poema: Un recorrido por el alma secreta de la patria (San José: Editorial Universidad Estatal a Distancia, 1997).

OTHER: "De Faldas y otras prisiones," in *Voces Femeninas del Mundo Hispánico,* edited by Ramiro Lagos (Bogotá: Hispanic Poetic Studies Center, 1991), pp. 90–93.

SELECTED PERIODICAL PUBLICATION–
UNCOLLECTED: "Canto en vano para una resurrección," translated by Lisa Bradford as "Song in Vain for a Resurrection," *Mundus Artium,* 7, no. 2 (1974): 108–109.

Julieta Dobles Yzaguirre (from the cover for El peso vivo, *1968; Pollak Library, California State University)*

One of Costa Rica's most respected literary figures, Julieta Dobles Yzaguirre has been writing creatively since the age of eight. Since her first publication in 1965 she has published eight additional volumes of poetry.

Born in San José, Costa Rica, to Jorge Dobles Ortiz and Ángela Yzaguirre Moya, Julieta Teresita del Niño Jesús Dobles Yzaguirre was the first of five daughters. Jorge Dobles, the family patriarch, had the distinction of owning the first pet store in San José; his wife was a primary-school teacher and later director of the same school where she had previously taught. Julieta inherited her poetic ability from both sides of the family. Her father's relatives include several illustrious Costa Rican writers, among them Fabián Dobles, Álvaro Dobles, Gonzalo Dobles, and Luis Dobles Segreda. From her mother, a talented orator and lover of poetry, she learned to recite from memory many popular poems even before she could read.

Paperback cover for Dobles's first book (1965), a collection of poems about the many forms of love
(Charles E. Young Research Library, University of California, Los Angeles)

Because of her family background, Dobles became acquainted at an early age with the classic texts of other Spanish American poets such as Rubén Darío, José Martí, Gabriela Mistral, Alfonsina Storni, and Juana de Ibarbourou. While in secondary school she began to write love poems, but unlike the earlier ones she had so eagerly presented to her mother, she carefully hid these more intimate creations in secret notebooks. During her high school years she came to know and love the poetry of many other well-known Hispanic literary figures, including Juan Ramón Jiménez, Pablo Neruda, Federico García Lorca, and Roberto Brenes Mesén. Added to the large repertoire of poets with whom she was already familiar, these writers served as an ample source of inspiration for her own poetic creations.

Although Dobles grew up surrounded by classic poetry and loved to read and write poems, she had no serious thoughts about becoming a professional poet until the age of twenty-one, when she met her future husband, Laureano Albán. In 1961 Albán and fellow poet Jorge Debravo founded the Círculo de poetas costarricenses (Costa Rican Circle of Poets), a literary group of promising new writers who formed the basis for the so-called Generation of 1960. Subsequent members of this group, among them Dobles, participated in literary workshops in order to receive peer support and positive criticism of their work.

When Dobles entered the University of Costa Rica in 1961, she was interested in many different areas of study and had difficulty limiting herself to one specialization. She finally opted to major in biology, receiving her undergraduate degree in that discipline, although she also studied philology and linguistics while continuing to write poetry and to participate in the Circle of Poets. Following her graduation in 1965,

Dobles taught high-school biology for fifteen years at the Liceo Vargas Calvo. In addition to graduating from the University of Costa Rica, Dobles celebrated another important milestone in 1965, when her first book, *Reloj de siempre* (The Same Clock as Always), was published and received immediate critical acclaim. The book was reprinted in 1968 and 1976 and consists of ten poems with the common theme of love in its many aspects. Critic Mayra Herra notes that all these forms of love are tinged by a kind of anguish that cannot be resolved by either human vision or by God.

On 14 September 1967 Dobles and Albán married, and in 1968 the first of their five children, Jorge, was born. Also in 1968 Dobles's second book, *El peso vivo* (The Live Weight), was published, and that same year she received her country's national poetry award, the Premio Nacional de Poesía Aquileo Echeverría, the first of many awards. The poems of *El peso vivo* emphasize the fleeting nature of life and the importance of living each day to the fullest. The initial poem, "Canto en vano para una resurrección" (Song in Vain for a Resurrection), exemplifies the manner in which life and death are so intimately related: "Alguien se nos está muriendo / siempre, /con esa muerte lenta de los pulsos vacíos, / mientras tú y yo besamos, / reímos de las cosas y del viento, / comemos, nos amamos, / y sabemos / que toda nuestra luz nos pertenece, / sin ser nuestra siquiera" (Someone is always dying, / with that slow death of empty heartbeats, / while you and I kiss, / laugh at things and at the wind, / we eat, we love, / and we know / that all our light belongs to us, / without even being ours).

During the years from 1969 to 1975 Dobles concentrated on raising Jorge and his four siblings. Esteban was born in 1969, Federico in 1971, Rolando in 1972, and Ángela in 1975. In 1976 *El peso vivo* was reprinted, and Dobles also published her third book, *Los pasos terrestres* (Earthly Footsteps), which was awarded another Aquileo Echeverría award, as well as the Editorial Costa Rica Award. The poems in this book share a nostalgic view of life past, as demonstrated by their colorful verbal portraits of people and places. Children and childhood are important themes; in fact, these poems were inspired by the poet's own children. In his preface to *Los pasos terrestres* Albán describes his wife's skill at creating what he calls "la difícil sencillez" (difficult simplicity). He explains this paradoxical phrase as characteristic of a poet who, besides demonstrating her complete mastery of the formal content and technique necessary in any good poetry, is also imbued with a deep sincerity and humanism that cause her poems to make a strong emotional impact on readers. Many of the poems, such as those in this collection, speak of such deceptively simple things as furniture, clothing,

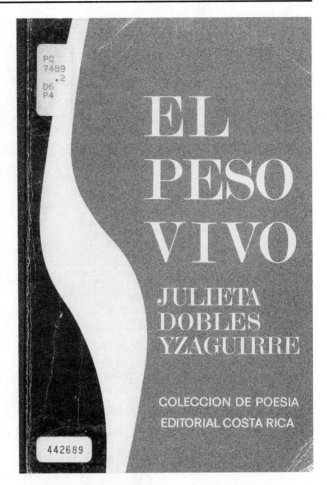

Paperback cover for Dobles's second book, which received the national poetry prize of Costa Rica, the Premio Nacional de Poesía Aquileo Echeverría, in 1968 (Pollak Library, California State University)

rain, wind, and parts of the body, but in an intricate manner that makes them transcend the classification of mere simplicity. *Los pasos terrestres* continues to be critically acclaimed, and "Retrato cotidiano" (Everyday Portrait), one of its most cited poems, was selected by the Ministry of Education to become required reading for Costa Rican public-school students.

In 1974 Albán and Dobles joined with two other Costa Rican poets, Carlos Francisco Monge and Ronald Bonilla, to collaborate on a book that became a guide for contemporary poetry and that was later cited by many aspiring writers as a source of personal inspiration. In *Manifiesto trascendentalista y poesía de sus autores* (Transcendental Manifesto and Poems by Its Authors) the authors lament the quantity of "falsos poetas" (false poets) and advocate a restoration and renovation of transcendental poetry, the only true poetry, which they believe is in serious danger of extinction. Referring to Chilean poet Mis-

Paperback cover for Dobles's third book (1976), a collection of nostalgic poems dealing mainly with childhood (Howard-Tilton Memorial Library, Tulane University)

tral's definition of poetry as a language of intuition and musicality, they state as their objective the resuscitation of that same type of poetry from the contamination it has suffered in modern society.

Although *Manifiesto trascendentalista y poesía de sus autores* was published decades ago, its influence is still evident in its authors' literary production, as well as in the poetry of several other members of the new generation of the Costa Rican Circle of Poets. This influence is visible in the number of young writers who eagerly participate in the workshops guided by Dobles and her collaborators, as well as in the many published poets who give credit to these same four authors for their inspiration and support.

Since the late 1970s Dobles and her husband have performed diplomatic duties abroad as representatives of Costa Rica. They have resided and worked in Spain, Israel, the United States, and France. While in Spain,

Dobles saw her fifth book, *Hora de lejanías* (Faraway Hour, 1982), published in both Madrid and San José. This book earned her the runner-up position for the prestigious Adonais Award of Spain. Because of its success a second edition was printed in 1983 in Costa Rica. *Hora de lejanías* was motivated by a depression Dobles suffered during her first months in Spain. Her feelings of isolation and aloneness served as the inspiration for the poems in this collection, which has been praised for its strong humanistic tone.

After their stay in Spain, Albán and Dobles moved to New York, where they studied Hispanic literature at the State University of New York at Stony Brook. Dobles obtained her master's degree in 1986 and subsequently completed all course work plus the prospectus for her doctorate. In the preface of her next book, *Los delitos de Pandora* (Pandora's Crimes, 1987), written while at Stony Brook, Dobles explains her experimentation with a new theme and style. The poems in this collection can be classified as her first openly feminist work. In them she poeticizes the history of women through the presentation of the mythical Pandora, whose desire for knowledge causes her to open the forbidden box. Dobles expresses the necessity for women to have their own voices and to write their own history, as opposed to allowing their stories to be controlled by men. In his review of *Los delitos de Pandora* for *La Prensa Libre* (28 May 1987), Alberto Cañas praised Dobles's poetic style and singled out one poem, "Cinco heridas para morir de amor" (Five Mortal Wounds of Love), as exceptional and, in his opinion, her best poem to date. He further states that it is one of the ten or twelve best poems thus far written in Costa Rica. *Los delitos de Pandora* was reprinted in 1999 by Editorial Costa Rica as part of a commemorative series of twentieth-century Costa Rican literature.

In 1987 Dobles and her husband interrupted their university studies in order to represent Costa Rica as diplomats in Israel; she never returned to complete her dissertation. Her travels in various countries, especially Israel, served as inspiration for her next two books, *Una viajera demasiado azul* (A Too Sentimental Traveler, 1990) and *Amar en Jerusalén* (To Love in Jerusalem, 1992). The first joyously sings the benefits of travel, painting vignettes of people, places, and cultures that the lyric speaker has experienced in various countries, as well as detailing her own spiritual journeys inward and the permanent changes they have produced in her. She describes herself as "Una viajera demasiado azul / que discurre parajes y caminos / y que va recogiendo voces, / afectos, músicas humanas / en su mochila de eterna caminante / que no se detendrá ni ante la puerta inmóvil de la muerte . . ." (A too sentimental traveler, / who skips along pathways and roads, / gathering up voices, / affections, human music, / in her backpack of the eternal hiker, / who will not be detained even before the unyielding door of death . . .). In an unpublished interview on 19 June 2001 Dobles admitted that she became so completely attached to each of the countries in which she lived that when the time came to leave, she always felt a great sadness and reluctance to say goodbye. *Una viajera demasiado azul* is one way of expressing her love and solidarity for the different peoples and cultures of which she has been a part, both physically and emotionally.

Unlike *Una viajera demasiado azul,* the poems of *Amar en Jerusalén* possess a noticeably sad and melancholy tone, at least until the end, during which the married couple portrayed is reunited after a stormy period of betrayal and mistrust. These poems have as their protagonist the poet herself and are the result of her

Paper cover for the 1982 Costa Rican edition of Dobles's fifth book, first published in Madrid the same year. The poems in the collection were inspired by the isolation she felt after moving to Spain as a diplomat (Yale University Library).

own personal crisis as expressed by the poem "Agonía de una noche de verano" (Agony of a Summer Night):

Sólo mi alma se escindió en dos mitades
cuando a la medianoche
levantaste el teléfono,
donde no te alcanzara
la hondura de mi sueño,
para leerle a alguien tu poema nocturno
—ese poema diario que siempre fue tan mío—
con la ternura aquella que habíamos olvidado
en algún irrecuperable recodo del camino

(Only my soul ripped in half
when at midnight
you picked up the phone,
where your voice would not reach
the depth of my sleep,
in order to read your nocturnal poem
—that poem that was always so much mine—
with that tenderness that we ourselves had forgotten
in some irretrievable twist of the road).

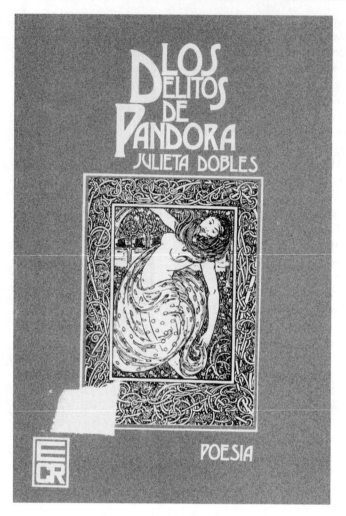

Paperback cover for Dobles's 1987 collection, her first openly feminist work
(Howard-Tilton Memorial Library, Tulane University)

Herra explains that although the poems of this collection are at times painful to read because of their intimate revelations, this honesty makes a powerful impact on those who experience them. This assertion is especially true for female readers, who, because of the poet's willingness to expose unfiltered her own emotional trauma, can feel a sense of personal identification with the betrayal and pain so evident in the relationship described in *Amar en Jerusalén*. Dobles herself has admitted that her poetic inspiration is derived from the biographical events of her own life, a statement definitely supported in this book, and she firmly believes that it is impossible to understand fully a work of literature without knowing at least something about its author.

Dobles's *Costa Rica poema a poema: Un recorrido por el alma secreta de la patria* (Costa Rica Poem by Poem: A Journey Through the Secret Soul of the Homeland),

published in 1997, marks another first in the poet's career. In her *La Nación* (San José) review (2 October 1997) critic Aurelia Dobles pointed out that this book was the first of its kind published in Costa Rica. Never before had there been a book in which, by means of good poetry, so many aspects of Costa Rican identity were reconstructed from a notably feminine perspective. As its title indicates, *Costa Rica poema a poema* takes readers on a poetic excursion through the poet's native country, paying tribute to the flowers, fruits, trees, and rivers of Costa Rica, as well as nostalgically remembering people, places, and events from an earlier time. The second section of the book, "Calendario secreto de la patria" (The Country's Secret Calendar), is an additional tribute to Costa Rica and its profusion of nature during each month of the year. For example, in "Octubre" (October) the lyric speaker describes the renovating properties of the rains so characteristic of her country during this season: "Octubre, octubre, / savia para la tierra / y la vena sedienta de los pastos, / savia para mi corazón / reseco de nostalgia y latitudes, / en donde los desiertos aumentaron / mi sed por esta lluvia bienvenida, / cuya gloria empapó mis tercas soledades . . ." (October, October, / nourishment for the land / and the thirsty vein of the pastures, / nourishment for my heart / parched from nostalgia and latitudes / where the deserts increase / my thirst for the welcomed rain, / whose glory drenched my obstinate solitude . . .).

In her prologue to *Costa Rica poema a poema*, Gabriela Chavarría emphasizes the significance of the evident feminine tone, which gives the book special significance and value. She notes that Costa Rica as a country is converted to Costa Rica as Mother Nature, the earth mother, a regenerating and constructive force for her children. The poet issues a call for readers to rediscover the national identity of Costa Rica, an identity that goes far beyond the traditional patriarchal perspective to include female and male, rich and poor, young and old, as heirs to the natural resources of their country.

This book has received much critical acclaim, including another prestigious Aquileo Echeverría award, the fourth for Dobles. Because of its patriotic themes, Enrique Vargas Soto recommended in the Costa Rican newspaper *La Nación* (10 February 1998) that the Ministry of Education add the entire book to the required reading list for all Costa Rican schoolchildren, so that they could share the pride and love poetically expressed for the customs and traditions of their native country. In an earlier article in *Viva*, Aurelia Dobles had already advocated the same thing, going a step further by suggesting that the new book would be a splendid way to teach foreign visitors about Costa Rica's many natural treasures.

In addition to her diplomatic work and her writing, teaching has always been an important factor in Dobles's life. Since 1990 she has been a member of the General Studies faculty of the University of Costa Rica and often teaches courses there. She is enthusiastic about her teaching, telling Herra that it helps to keep her young and up-to-date on current happenings. She also remains active in literary workshops, serving as a mentor for many aspiring writers, and she is frequently invited to give public readings of her poetry. Dobles has completed work on two new books, *Casas de la memoria* (Houses of Memory), to be published in 2003 by Editorial de la Universidad de Costa Rica, and *Poemas para arrepentidos* (Poems for the Repentent), accepted by Editorial Costa Rica for publication in 2003. She is hard at

Paperback cover for the 1993 edition of Dobles's 1990 poetry collection, inspired by her travels in various countries (Howard-Tilton Memorial Library, Tulane University)

work on her next project, "Fotografías fuera del album" (Photographs outside the Album).

Every one of Julieta Dobles Yzaguirre's books of poetry has been well received by critics and the public. Unlike many struggling authors who endured years of uncertainty and hardship before achieving recognition, this author has enjoyed success from the beginning of her professional writing career. During four decades she has received praise from even the severest critics, who laud her purity of expression and her poetic sensibility. Critic Carlos Cortés seems to summarize the opinions of his colleagues when commenting about this favorite daughter of Costa Rica: "Es una creadora enormemente sensible, cálida, con una gran pureza para captar los pequeños monumentos gloriosos del ser humano" (She is an enormously sensitive and warm creator, with a great purity enabling her to capture the small glorious monuments of the human essence). Popular and greatly respected in her native Costa Rica and long recognized by other countries such as Spain for her poetic talents, Dobles is now enjoying increasing recognition in the United States, where her poems are beginning to appear with some frequency in anthologies.

References:

Thais Aguilar Zuñiga, "Julieta Dobles: En nombre de la mujer," *La Nación* (San José), 6 July 1986, p. 2D;

Carlos Cortés, "Julieta Dobles: En los hilos de la insaciable vida," *La Nación* (San José), 24 June 1990, *Áncora* supplement: 3D;

Mayra Herra, "Julieta Dobles Izaguirre: Semblanza," *Identidad Centroaméricana, Órgano de Cofática,* no. 2, pp. 63–70;

Carmen Juncos, "Julieta: La mujer poeta," *Rumbo,* 393 (9 June 1992): 46–47;

Juan Carlos Peña Morales, "Una viajera demasiado azul," *Perfil,* 9 (April 1993): 16–18;

Any Pérez, "Gitana de vivencias," *La Nación* (San José), 15 September 1996, p. 2;

Margarita Rojas and Flora Ovares, *100 años de literatura costarricense* (San José: Farben Grupo Editorial Norma, 1995), pp. 214–217;

Enrique Tovar, "La siempre viva llama de la poesía," *La Nación* (San José), 13 July 1991, p. 2D;

Rima de Valbona, "Julieta Dobles: De la poesía intimista al lirismo trascendental," *La Nación* (San José), 26 February 1989, *Áncora* supplement: 1D.

Fina García Marruz

(28 April 1923 –   )

Jana F. Gutiérrez
Auburn University

BOOKS: *Poemas* (Havana: Úcar García, 1942);

Transfiguración de Jesús en el Monte (Havana: Orígenes, 1947);

Las miradas perdidas, 1944–1950 (Havana: Úcar García, 1951);

Estudios críticos, by García Marruz and Cintio Vitier (Havana: Biblioteca Nacional, 1964);

Los versos de Martí (Havana: Instituto del Libro, 1968);

Temas martianos, by García Marruz and Vitier (Havana: Biblioteca Nacional, 1969);

Visitaciones (Havana: Instituto del Libro, 1970);

Bécquer o la leve bruma (Havana: Arte y Literatura, 1971);

Poesías escogidas, selected, with an introduction, by Jorge Yglesias (Havana: Letras Cubanas, 1984);

Hablar de la poesía (Havana: Letras Cubanas, 1986);

Viaje a Nicaragua, by García Marruz and Vitier (Havana: Letras Cubanas, 1987);

Créditos de Charlol (Havana: Letras Cubanas, 1990);

Los Rembrandt de l'Hermitage (Havana: Unión de Escritores y Artistas de Cuba, 1992);

Viejas melodías (Caracas: Pequeña Venecia, 1993);

Nociones elementales y algunas elegías (Caracas: Fundarte, 1994);

Antología poética, introduction by Jorge Luis Arcos (Havana: Letras Cubanas, 1997);

La familia de Orígenes (Havana: Unión, 1997);

Habana del centro (Havana: Unión, 1997);

Poesía escogida, by García Marruz and Vitier (Bogotá: Norma, 2000);

Libro de Job (Matanzas, Cuba: Vigía, 2000);

Darío, Martí y lo germinal americano (Havana: Unión de Escritores y Artistas de Cuba, 2001).

OTHER: José Martí, *Diarios,* preface by García Marruz (Havana: Libro Cubano, 1956);

Juana Borrero, *Poesías,* edited by García Marruz (Havana: Academia de Ciencias de Cuba, 1966);

Borrero, *Poesías y cartas,* edited by García Marruz and Cintio Vitier (Havana: Arte y Literatura, 1978);

Fina García Marruz (photograph by Vasco Szinetar; from the cover for Viejas melodías, *1993; Smathers Library, University of Florida)*

Flor oculta de la poesía cubana (siglos XVIII y XIX), edited by García Marruz and Vitier (Havana: Arte y Literatura, 1978);

Juana Inés de la Cruz, *Páginas escogidas,* edited by García Marruz (Havana: Casa de las Américas, 1978);

Samuel Feijóo, *Ser,* edited by García Marruz and Vitier (Havana: Unión de Escritores y Artistas de Cuba, 1983);

Martí, *Obra literaria,* notes by García Marruz and Vitier (Buenos Aires: Ayacucho, 1986);

Martí, *Ideario,* edited by García Marruz and Vitier (Managua: Nueva Nicaragua, 1987);

La literatura en el Papel periódico de la Habana, 1790–1805, introductions by García Marruz, Vitier, and Roberto Friol (Havana: Letras Cubanas, 1990);

Martí, *Textos antimperialistas,* edited by García Marruz (Havana: Pueblo y Educación, 1990; revised, 1996);

San Juan de la Cruz, 1591–1991, edited by García Marruz and Vitier (Matanzas, Cuba: Vigía, 1993);

Martí, *Poesía completa: Edición crítica,* edited by García Marruz, Vitier, and Ramón de Armas (Havana: Letras Cubanas, 1993);

Nuevos poetas cubanos II, edited by García Marruz, Roberto Fernández Retamar, and Eliseo Diego (Havana: Letras Cubanas, 1994);

"Los versos sencillos," in *A cien años de Martí,* edited by Tony T. Murphy (Las Palmas de Gran Canaria: Cabildo Insular, 1997), pp. 17–50;

Cleva Solís, *Obra poética,* edited by García Marruz and Vitier (Havana: Letras Cubanas, 1998);

Juana Inés de la Cruz, *Dolor fiero,* edited by García Marruz (Havana: Casa de las Américas, 1999);

José Luis Moreno del Toro, *Cántigas salvadas,* preface by García Marruz (Havana: Unión de Escritores y Artistas de Cuba, 2000).

Fina García Marruz is a dedicated Cuban poet and a literary essayist. She holds a doctorate in social sciences from the Universidad de La Habana (University of Havana) and has worked as an investigative researcher at Havana's Biblioteca Nacional de José Martí (José Martí National Library) and Centro de Estudios Martianos (Martí Studies Center). She stands out as the sole original female member of the celebrated *Orígenes* (Origins) group, whose magazine lasted only twelve years but whose legacy continues to influence the Cuban literary scene. In 1994 the fiftieth anniversary of the group's inception sparked a publishing renaissance of the works of all its early members, leading readers in Cuba and abroad to rediscover García Marruz. The resurgence of interest in the *Orígenes* movement also increased publishing opportunities for its authors. In fact, García Marruz published more works in the 1990s than she had throughout her entire publishing career. Renewed attention to García Marruz's contribution to Cuban letters led to well-deserved, albeit delayed, accolades such as the 1987 Cuban Critics' Award for her essay collection *Hablar de la poesía* (Speaking of Poetry, 1986), the 1991 Cuban Critics' Award for the poetry collection *Créditos de Charlol* (Charlol's Credits, 1990), and the ultimate domestic honor for a Cuban writer, the 1990 Cuban

National Literature Prize. In addition, she was nominated in Spain for the coveted Cervantes Prize. She has yet, nonetheless, to make a significant international impact. Perhaps her own humility is to blame, for García Marruz shuns the spotlight. Most notable among the peers who tend to eclipse her is the poet's own husband, fellow Cuban intellectual and poet Cintio Vitier. In short, García Marruz has received some international acclaim, but that fame is slight in comparison to her national prestige. While international critics acknowledge her in passing, Cuban critics insist upon her role as both mentor for a new generation of writers and preserver of her nation's literary tradition.

García Marruz was born in the heart of Havana on 28 April 1923. Her father, Sergio, was a physician and voracious reader, and her mother, Josefina Badía, was an accomplished pianist. The poet had one sister, Bella, and two brothers, Sergio and Felipe. García Marruz showed an early predilection for the fine arts. The artistic environment that surrounded her childhood permeates her life's work. García Marruz recollects that she inherited a propensity for the arts from her mother and a love of the written word from her father.

She began composing verse at a young age. The 1936 visit of Spanish poet Juan Ramón Jiménez to Cuba indelibly marked her decision to become a poet. The Andalusian poet encouraged the thirteen-year-old García Marruz to proceed with her writing, giving her, according to Jorge Luis Arcos, "un juicio muy favorable sobre sus primeras composiciones poéticas" (a very favorable opinion of her first poetic compositions), as recounted in the introduction to *Antología poética* (Poetic Anthology, 1997). The nod of approval García Marruz received from someone whose work she so greatly admired propelled her to further explore her own poetic voice.

Two Cuban poets directly impacted García Marruz's life and work to an even greater extent than Jiménez. The first was Vitier, whom García Marruz met while at the University of Havana and whom she subsequently married in the early 1940s. Since their marriage, they have shared every aspect of their personal and professional life. The second influential Cuban poet in her life was José Lezama Lima, a writer whose work she admired and whom she befriended through mutual acquaintances. The friendly triumvirate formed by García Marruz, Vitier, and Lezama Lima remained steadfast. Some critics misjudge their close relationship, dismissing it as a political convenience. A review of statements made by the poets prior to the 1959 Cuban Revolution, however, discredits this argument. On the contrary, it is quite evident that García Marruz, Vitier, and Lezama Lima based their admiration on the merits of one another's work.

Together they strove for a common pursuit: stimulating in Cuba artistic creation and intellectual curiosity.

García Marruz initiated her literary career in 1938 when local journals published two of her works: "Aviones" (Airplanes) appeared in *Ayuda* (Help) and "Esquema de un cuento" (Sketch of a Story) in *Cúspide* (Pinnacle). She followed that tentative start with a more ambitious endeavor, editing the literary magazine *Clavileño* in 1942–1943, a task she shared with fellow friends and future *origenistas* (*Orígenes* members) Vitier, Eliseo Diego, Gastón Baquero, Octavio Smith, and Lorenzo García Vega. She describes in *La familia de Orígenes* (The *Orígenes* Family, 1997) the collaboration as a labor of love: "Hacíamos *Clavileño* casi sin ocuparnos de enviárselo a nadie" (We did *Clavileño* almost without bothering to send it to anyone). She also suggests that the project served as a necessary escape from the political reality of the time. The *Clavileño* editors withdrew from the inhospitable environment of the failed Cuban Republic, favoring instead a hermetic, esoteric, and, some might say, elitist retreat.

The *Clavileño* group eventually joined forces with Lezama Lima and José Rodríguez Feo to create *Orígenes,* a magazine featuring vanguard Cuban poets, essayists, musicians, painters, and sculptors, which was published from 1944 to 1956. The editors of the magazine regarded poetry as the supreme genre, and an introspective brand of lyrical mysticism influenced all of their editorial decisions. *Orígenes* was distinctive in that it combined two opposing branches of poetry: pure aesthetics and social consciousness. As García Marruz insists in "Hablar de la poesía," the final essay in the book of the same title, "Debiera cesar la envejecida polémica de arte puro y arte comprometido. Ni arte 'puro' ni arte 'para'" (The age-old debate between pure art and compromised art should cease. Neither "pure" art nor "for" art).

Orígenes was esoteric and plastic, without lapsing into frivolity. Grounded in a moral, Christian ethic, its contributors sought in their idyllic imagery transcendence from the decadent Cuban reality of their time. The magazine eventually led to the creation of a publishing house by the same name. The members hoped to remedy the scant publishing opportunities for all Cuban writers, though they always favored fellow *origenistas*. While García Marruz contributed mainly essays to the magazine, *Orígenes* publishing showcased her poetry. Her poems appeared in one fundamental *Orígenes* anthology, *Diez poetas cubanos, 1937–1947* (Ten Cuban Poets, 1937–1947), published in 1947 and edited by her husband, Vitier. In addition, *Orígenes* published for her in 1947 a small verse collection titled *Transfiguración de Jesús en el Monte* (Transfiguration of Jesus on the Mount). García Marruz revealed in each contribution

FINA GARCIA MARRUZ

LAS MIRADAS PERDIDAS

1944 - 1950

LA HABANA
1951

Title page for García Marruz's third book and first major poetry collection, comprising the verse inspired by her membership in the group of poets, essayists, musicians, painters, and sculptors associated with Orígenes *magazine (Library of the University of North Carolina at Chapel Hill)*

to the *Orígenes* project, be it essay or poetry, the same ultrarefined, mystical aesthetic of everyday transcendence that she also develops in later works.

Two components define *Orígenes,* and they are essential for understanding not only the *origenista* movement but also each of its members and their individual labors. The first crucial aspect that led to the success of the magazine was the intense friendship shared by its members. Fraternity was for them an institution, and it guided all of their editorial choices. Nonetheless, friendship also contributed to the demise of the magazine. As with even the tightest fraternities, emotions sometimes won over reason. Historians and members cannot agree on the specific details surrounding the final incident that caused the cessation of the magazine. Most concur that a petty disagreement between two of the founders

Paperback cover for García Marruz's 1970 collection, in which the realism of the poems reflects her attempt to adhere
to the standards laid down by the government of Fidel Castro (Langsam Library, University of Cincinnati)

forced a schism between the friends, causing them to abandon their project rather than resolve their differences amicably. Nostalgia and maturity have permitted the *origenistas* to reframe the whole experience in a positive light. In a 1997 interview for *La Jornada Semanal,* Vitier insisted that whatever animosity existed between the members at one point had ceased: "fue, por cierto, mucho más que una revista: ésta terminó y *Orígenes* siguió. Yo creo que *Orígenes* sigue vivo" (it was certainly much more than a magazine: that ended and *Orígenes* remained. I believe that *Orígenes* remains alive).

The *Orígenes* members tend to reference their fellow collaborators so profusely and with such high esteem that some critics accuse them of narcissism. For example, García Marruz writes an elegy to the group's mentor in the poem "A nuestro Lezama" (To Our Lezama in *Visitaciones* (Visitations, 1970). The poem, aside from encapsulating the fond memories of the *Orí-*

genes project, also serves as a sample of García Marruz's humility and eclectic lyrical style:

Temor de hacer este poema
<<Fina, escríbeme una elegía
con esos versos que usted hace a lo Claudel.>>
(La risa baritonal, la ironía paterna,
como un rocío grueso.)
<<Escríbeme nuestras memorias de Orígenes.
Usted es buena memorialista.
Recuérdeme bajo el balcón de Neptuno,
con deseos de verlos, y que ustedes me mandaran a
    pasar>>

(Fear of writing this poem
<<Fina, write me an elegy
with those verses you do like Claudel.>>
[The baritone laugh, the paternal irony,
like a stout drop of dew.]
<<Write me our memories of Orígenes.

112

You're a good memorialist.

Remember me below the Neptune balcony,

with hopes of seeing you all, and that you would send for
me to come up>>)

The second key factor to the success of *Orígenes* was its faith. Some confuse the magazine's profound spirituality with religion, specifically with Catholicism, but the *origenistas* never promoted religious propaganda. For them the quest was more related to freeing the soul and to achieving enlightenment through the contemplation of the mundane and the beautiful. Often, however, Catholic rhetoric provided a recognizable and appropriate vocabulary for communicating this ontological quest; thus, a cursory reading could mislead one to believe the *origenistas* were just fervent Catholics. In reality, *Orígenes* was much more philosophical: poetry (and to a lesser extent all art forms when perceived as lyrical expressions) for the *origenistas* was a means toward attaining enlightenment. *Orígenes,* then, nurtured García Marruz's quest for finding truth in poetry. Surrounded by her *origenista* brethren, she grew as a thinker and a poet. The group encouraged her to develop a philosophy of writing, one that reflected the friendship and ethics of the *Orígenes* project, and one that emerges in all her later work.

García Marruz published *Las miradas perdidas, 1944–1950* (Lost Looks, 1944–1950) in 1951; it marked her first major poetry publication. The book recollected some of her previously published poems in addition to debuting most of her unpublished work. Together with the *Diez poetas cubanos* anthology, *Las miradas perdidas* garnered only slight critical attention for García Marruz, perhaps owing to the critics' inability to decipher her abstract, conceptualist imagery. García Marruz, however, had both talent and influential connections in the publishing world. In 1952, therefore, her work appeared in another anthology edited by her husband, *Cincuenta años de poesía cubana, 1902–1952* (Fifty Years of Cuban Poetry, 1902–1952). In 1954 Roberto Fernández Retamar speaks of her in *La poesía contemporánea en Cuba, 1927–1953* (Contemporary Poetry in Cuba, 1927–1953). Save for the inclusion of previously published poems in Carmen Conde's 1967 *Once grandes poetisas hispanoamericanas* (Eleven Great Spanish American Poetesses), readers had to wait almost two decades to hear from García Marruz again. In the meantime, she dedicated herself to raising her sons, Sergio and José María, both of whom became distinguished composers and musicians.

The publication of *Visitaciones* launched García Marruz once more into the public arena, but this time the environment had changed drastically because of the Cuban Revolution. The book was a gamble for García

Paperback cover for García Marruz's 1986 collection of essays on poetry, which won the 1987 Cuban Critics' Award (San Diego State University Library)

Marruz, given the shifts in the Cuban political climate; the government of Fidel Castro expected artists to adhere to socialist standards. García Marruz had never really infused her work with political ideology. In *Visitaciones,* however, a concrete realism begins to permeate her imagery. She never abandoned her early aesthetic goals; her work just took on an increasing tone of historical immediacy. The Cuban government played a part in her evolution, heightening her sensitivity toward the plight of the common people. Cuban critics praised García Marruz's newfound ability to write for herself and for the masses. Bitter political quarrels between artists and government officials, however, contributed to trepidation on the part of many Cuban writers, and García Marruz chose to avoid the public battle as much as possible. She withdrew as an artist, favoring instead critical research. Until the political debates subsided, she diverted her attention to literary inves-

Title page for García Marruz's 1990 collection of poetry centering on Charlie
Chaplin (Howard-Tilton Memorial Library, Tulane University)

tigation, publishing on a wide spectrum of topics, from nineteenth-century Spanish poets such as Gustavo Adolfo Bécquer to historical studies of forgotten Cuban poetry from the eighteenth and nineteenth centuries. She also assisted the Centro de Estudios Martianos with the laborious recovery of Martí's writings for a critical edition of his complete works. She pressed on with her own poetry, but responsibilities to her country's needs supplanted her personal aspirations.

García Marruz the poet resurfaced in the 1980s, appearing in two anthologies, Margaret Randall's 1982 *Breaking the Silence* and Francesca Tenton Montallo's 1987 *Poeti ispano del novecento* (Twentieth-Century Hispanic Poetry). The poems "Ya yo también estoy entre los otros" (I Am Also Already Among the Others), "También esta página" (This Page Also), "Edipo" (Oedipus), "Con que lenguaje tan rudo me hablas" (You Speak to Me With a Language so Rude), "También tú" (You Too), and "En la muerte de Martín Lutero King" (On the Death of Martin Luther King)

appeared in the bilingual *Breaking the Silence*. She also published *Poesías escogidas* (Selected Poetry, 1984) as well as *Hablar de la poesía*. Both works include poems and essays she had accumulated during her absence from the public eye. Critical response to García Marruz was mixed at the time. Some critics lauded her, while others ignored her. Whereas Randall called her one of Cuba's "madres vivientes" (living mothers) in *Álbum de poetisas cubanas* (Album of Cuban Poetesses, 1997), Cuban critics lamented the uninspired reception of García Marruz's poetry during the decade. Some allude to the possibility that silence on the part of Cuban readers was an intentional shunning, motivated by island politics. García Marruz kept laboring, writing for herself rather than the critics.

Since the 1990s García Marruz has enjoyed a renaissance. Half of her entire corpus of lyrical and scholastic writing has appeared since the early years of the decade. The political undertones have subsided, and the poet has returned to her pre-Revolutionary topics: the arts, religion, family, acquaintances, and Cuba (not so much in the patriotic, political sense as in the notion of the island as her home and mother). She often allows popular culture to inspire her verse. For example, the innovative *Créditos de Charlot* centers around American silent-movie star Charlie Chaplin. *Los Rembrandt de L'Hermitage* (The Rembrandts of Hermitage, 1992) also addresses a visual medium, only this time the poet presents lyrical interpretations of Rembrandt's classical portraits. *Viejas melodías* (Old Melodies, 1993) represents a nostalgic return to the poet's youth; in this collection García Marruz remembers the music that filled her childhood home, and she features classic Cuban and American tunes. *Habana del centro* (In the Heart of Havana, 1997) includes previously published poems as well as new ones, most notably the poet's lyrical caricatures of her well-known poet friends in addition to sentimental remembrances of her Havana home. One special collaboration between García Marruz and Vitier, *Poesía escogida* (Selected Poetry, 1999), is distinctive in that the editors asked the couple to compile an anthology of each other's works; the end result stands as a testament to the couple's enduring love for each other and for their poetry.

The 1990s were difficult times for Cuba, but for García Marruz it was a decade of unprecedented professional success. Her audience widened as her international exposure increased. In the late 1990s, for example, Cuban editors selected one of García Marruz's poems as the title of an anthology of contemporary Cuban poetry: *Con una súbita vehemencia: Antología de poesía contemporánea en Cuba* (With a Sudden Vehemence: Anthology of Contemporary Poetry in Cuba, 1996). The editors also emphasized her important role as a mentor for a new generation. Juan Nicolás Padrón Barquín, editor of the anthology, even remarked in introducing the poet that García Marruz delights readers with her life-affirming poetry. Most importantly, the anthology circulated beyond Cuban borders, amassing a significant international readership for García Marruz. In recognition of her lifelong achievements and patriotic dedication, the Cuban government also sent García Marruz across the globe in the 1990s as an intellectual ambassador. One such trip took the poet and her husband to Spain in the late 1990s. Both García Marruz and Vitier served as visiting poets at the Residencia de Estudiantes (Student Dormitory) in Madrid.

The 1990s, then, brought García Marruz long overdue praise and publicity. She, nevertheless, maintains that the adulation in and of itself does not validate her work. The solitary and mystical writing process, rather, is what most rewards her. Her poem "Si mis poemas . . ." (If My Poems . . .), from *Visitaciones,* reflects her

Paperback cover for García Marruz's 1993 poetry collection, in which Cuban and American songs evoke memories of her childhood (Smathers Library, University of Florida)

unassuming sentiment as well as the source of her lyrical inspiration:

Si mis poemas todos se perdiesen
la pequeña verdad que en ellos brilla
permanecería igual en alguna piedra gris
junto al agua, o en una verde yerba

(If my poems were all lost
the tiny truth that in them shines
would remain the same as in a gray rock
next to the water, or in a green blade of grass).

In spite of her own humility, García Marruz is undeniably a powerful poet, for her poetry represents no less than the essence of life itself. She, as a poet, must capture this essence in the poem, and she finds inspiration in both the mundane and the profound. Her words in "Hablar de la poesía," from the collection of the same name, encapsulate her working methodology:

Es esa poesía invisible la que lo sustenta todo: la acción más pura y la más pura contemplación. Su fuente no se sabe: la bondad primera, una voz, un rostro, algo que, quizás, hemos olvidado. . . . Todo poeta sabe que los poetas son los otros, los que no escriben versos, y no sólo los servidores magnos . . . sino aún los más humildes, la hermana que cose en la habitación de al lado, la bocanada fresca que entra cada mañana cuando abrimos la puerta, el canario en el balcón . . . , y quizás sólo hemos sido verdadero poetas en los raros instantes en que no nos dimos cuenta de ello

(It is the invisible poetry that sustains everything: the purest action and the purest contemplation. Its source is unknown: the first kindness, a voice, a face, something that, maybe, we have forgotten. . . . Every poet knows that the real poets are the ones who do not write verse, and not just the great servants . . . but rather the most humble ones, the sister who sews in the next bedroom, the fresh breeze that enters each morning when we open the door, the canary on the balcony . . . , and maybe we've only been real poets in those rare instances when we didn't realize it).

Fina García Marruz is in some ways a contradictory poet. She challenges the reader to decipher her obscure, yet strangely simple, images. Her language also presents the reader with a formidable task in that she hides sophisticated concepts and complex vocabulary in familiar settings and simple forms. That unsettling, yet reassuring, ambiguity drives her work. Her life, like her art, is also a study in contrasts. She is at once a genteel lady, a keen critic, a loving wife and mother, a profound philosopher, a kind grandmother, and, most of all, an important Cuban poet.

References:

Ángel Gurria Quintana, "De Origenismos: Interview with Cintio Vitier," *Jornada Semanal* (Mexico City), 5 October 1997, p. 1;

Juan Nicolás Padrón Barquín, "Fina García Marruz," in *Con una súbita vehemencia: Antología de poesía contemporánea en Cuba,* edited by Padrón Barquín (Havana: Martí, 1996), p. 90;

Mirta Yáñez, "Poetisas, sí," in *Álbum de poetisas cubanas,* edited by Yáñez (Havana: Letras Cubanas, 1997), p. 29.

Oliverio Girondo

(17 August 1891 – 24 January 1967)

Emily E. Stern
University of North Carolina at Chapel Hill

BOOKS: *Veinte poemas para ser leídos en el tranvía* (Argenteuil, France: Coulouma, 1922);

Calcomanías (Madrid: Calpe, 1925);

Espantapájaros (Al alcance de todos) (Buenos Aires: Proa, 1932);

Interlunio; relato en prosa (Buenos Aires: Sur, 1937);

Nuestra actitud ante el desastre (Buenos Aires, 1940);

Persuasión de los días (Buenos Aires: Losada, 1942);

Campo nuestro (Buenos Aires: Sudamericana, 1946);

En la masmédula (Buenos Aires: Losada, 1954);

En la masvida (Barcelona: Libres de Sinera, 1972).

Collections: *Veinte poemas para ser leídos en el tranvía. Calcomanías. Espantapájaros* (Buenos Aires: Centro Editor de América Latina, 1966);

Obras completas (Buenos Aires: Losada, 1968);

Antología, edited by Aldo Pellegrini (Buenos Aires: Argonauta, 1986);

Obra completa: Edición crítica, coordinated by Raúl Antelo (Madrid & Paris: ALLCA XX, 1999).

Edition in English: *Scarecrow and Other Anomalies,* translated by Gilbert Alter-Gilbert (Riverside, Cal.: Xenos, 2002).

PLAY PRODUCTION: *La madrastra,* by Girondo and René Zapata Quesada, Buenos Aires, Teatro Apolo, 30 November 1915.

OTHER: *El periodico Martín Fierro, 1924–1949,* edited by Girondo (Buenos Aires: Colombo, 1949).

Oliverio Girondo

Oliverio Girondo is closely identified with the Latin American avant-garde movement, both as a poet and an intellectual. This movement represented a new spirit and energy, and a break with the Modernists. The poets who pertained to this "vanguardia artística" (artistic vanguard) rebelled against traditional subjects and style, pushing language to its limits. Girondo's poetry has been defined as an adventure in and of language, in which he experiments stylistically with strange rhythms, clever word games, the "feísmo" (ugliness) characteristic of the Hispanic baroque tradition,

and the new rhetoric of superrealism. Girondo's interest in poetic innovation lasted throughout his career. It existed from the beginning, as is made clear in the following line taken from the "Carta abierta a 'La Púa'" (Open Letter to "La Púa"), dated Paris, 1922, which serves as an introduction to *Veinte poemas para ser leídos en el tranvía* (Twenty Poems to Be Read in the Tram) when the volume was published in the literary magazine *Martín Fierro:* "Y ¿cuál sería la razón de no admitir cualquier probabilidad de rejuvenecimiento?" (And what would be the reason for not admitting any probability of rejuvenation?).

Girondo in 1920

Girondo was born on 17 August 1891 in Buenos Aires into an upper-middle-class family. Both of his parents, Juan Girondo and Josefa Uriburu de Girondo, were of Basque descent, and his mother's family had strong roots in Argentina. Her surnames, Uriburu y Arenales, are those of two of the founding fathers of Argentina. At the age of nine Girondo made his first trip to Europe, to the World's Fair of 1900 in Paris. He studied English at Epsom College in London and French at the Lyceé Albert Le Grand in Paris, from which he was expelled because one day he poured an inkwell over the geography professor's head after a lesson about nonexistent cannibals in Buenos Aires, which was incorrectly named by the professor as the capital of Brazil. Throughout his childhood Girondo returned to Europe many times, also visiting Egypt and Morocco, where he began his lifelong interest in paleography. Girondo graduated in 1908 from the Colegio Nacional de Buenos Aires, one of the most prestigious public high schools in the nation, and went on to study law.

Girondo co-authored a play with René Zapata Quesada, *La madrastra* (The Stepmother), which premiered on 30 November in 1915. In 1916 Girondo, Zapata Quesada, and Raúl Monsegur founded a short-lived theater newspaper called *Comoedia* (1916–1917). Girondo and Zapata Quesada collaborated again in 1917 to write *La comedia de todos los días* (Everyday Comedy), which was never produced because no actor wanted to participate in a play with lines that referred to the audience as "idiotas" (idiots). This setback marked the end of Girondo's brief career as a dramatist, as he began to take more interest in French Symbolist poets as well as in the Nicaraguan poet Rubén Darío. Girondo also began to read philosophy, especially Friedrich Nietzsche; he cites his brother, Eduardo, as his biggest intellectual influence during these years, however.

During an extended trip to Europe in the early 1920s, Girondo published his first collection of poetry, *Veinte poemas para ser leídos en el tranvía*, in Argenteuil, France, in 1922. The lighthearted title of the book

Page from Girondo's notebook for 1921, listing subjects for Argentine poems (from Girondo's Obra completa: *Edición crítica, 1999; University of Delaware Library)*

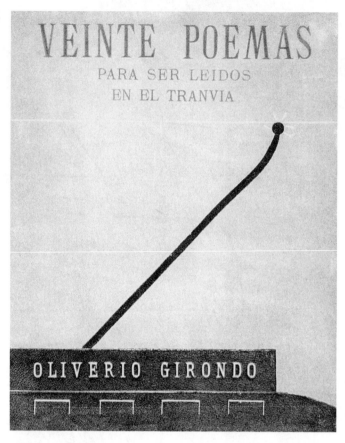

*Paperback cover for Girondo's first poetry collection, published in 1922 while he
was on an extended tour of Europe (Collection of Susana Lange de Maggi)*

pokes fun at a more serious view of poetry, with its suggestion that poetry break out of exclusively literary environments and be read in the tram. Girondo reiterated this idea with the epigraph to the collection: "Ningún prejuicio más ridículo que el prejuicio de lo sublime" (No prejudice is more ridiculous than the prejudice of the sublime). The poems form a sort of *cuaderno de viaje* (traveler's notebook), each poem capturing an image of different destinations: Buenos Aires, Seville, Venice, Dakar. As with many avant-garde poets, Girondo embraced a cosmopolitan, urban vision of the world and transmitted it through poetic snapshots of his travels.

In September 1923 the director of the Editorial Babel, Samuel Glusberg, proposed to Evar Méndez that he create a new avant-garde magazine, to be called *Martín Fierro*. Mendéz suggested inviting Girondo to participate. Throughout the rest of that year Girondo met several times with the other collaborators in the bars Richmond on Florida Street and La Cosechera (The Harvester) on Mayo Avenue to plan its publication, which began in 1924. By the third issue it became clear that the project lacked definition; thus, Girondo proposed and wrote a manifesto for the group that

appeared in issue number 4 (15 May 1924). Girondo signaled the group's affinity for modernity, writing that "todo es nuevo bajo el sol, si todo se mira con unas pupilas actuales y se expresa con un acento contemporáneo" (everything under the sun is new if it is observed with current eyes and expressed with a contemporary accent).

Girondo's manifesto also defends a specifically native or *criollo* (Creole) modernity, while recognizing the inevitable influence of Europe on Latin America. The *Martín Fierro* manifesto challenges Argentine writers and intellectuals to find a new voice that expresses the distinctive position of Latin America while incorporating elements from other parts of the world in an act of cultural cannibalism. With its new manifesto, the *Martín Fierro* group grew to include many important Argentine intellectuals of the moment, including writer Jorge Luis Borges and painter Xul Solar. During this same year Girondo traveled to various Latin American nations with the purpose of opening a dialogue between the magazines and intellectuals of that region. This trip was quite successful, inspiring an exchange among the different avant-garde groups of the continent.

Girondo with the poet Norah Lange, whom he married in 1926
(Collection of Susana Lange de Maggi)

In 1925 Girondo's second poetry collection, *Calcomanías* (Decalcomania), was published, with a cover illustration by the author. In addition, his *Veinte poemas para ser leído en el tranvía* was published for the first time in Buenos Aires. These first two books are often grouped together by critics, as chronicles of a traveler seeing the marvels of the world through fresh eyes and recording these experiences. In them Girondo explores the way in which daily experiences enter the world of poetry, recording seemingly mundane events in tones of wonder to show that the duality of what is real lies in a juxtaposition of appearances. The poem "Siesta" (Nap) in *Calcomanías* describes a sleepy Andalusian town on a warm afternoon, ending with the exclamation "¡Es tan real el paisaje que parece fingido!" (The countryside is so real that it seems fake!).

Girondo met and married poet Norah Lange the following year, 1926. In addition to their mutual interest in poetry and art, Girondo and Lange were both known among friends for their generosity and sense of humor. In 1927 Hipólito Yrigoyen began his second term as Argentine president, which provoked a division within the *Martín Fierro* group. Although the group always declared serious aesthetic commitments, their political position was not as clear. The eventual demise of the magazine that year was largely due to the breach between those contributors who were more politically committed, such as Borges, and those, including Girondo, who prioritized the project's artistic element. Without the magazine to produce, Girondo spent much of the year traveling throughout Europe to Egypt, where his interest in paleography deepened. Indeed, thanks to his inherited wealth, Girondo was able to travel and live abroad extensively throughout his life.

Girondo returned to Buenos Aires in 1931. The following year he published *Espantapájaros (Al alcance de todos)* (Scarecrow [In Everybody's Reach]). The book made quite an impression, perhaps more for the publicity campaign undertaken by Girondo than its contents. Girondo hired a coach that was normally reserved for funeral processions, along with its six horses and coachman, and attached a large scarecrow to the top, taking to the streets of Buenos Aires to announce his latest publication. The collection opens with a concrete poem in the shape of a scarecrow, which Francine Masiello—in "Oliverio Girondo: Naturaleza y artificio" (Oliverio Girondo: Nature and Artifice), an essay that appears in Girondo's *Obra completa* (Complete Works, 1999)—

Dust jacket for Girondo's 1932 poetry collection, which he publicized by riding through the streets of Buenos Aires in a horse-drawn hearse with a scarecrow on top (from Girondo's Obra completa: Edición crítica, *1999; University of Delaware Library)*

argues "demanda el reconocimiento del texto literario como cuerpo y palabras a la vez" (demands recognition of the literary text as both body and words). The remaining works in the collection are poems written in prose. With *Espantapájaros,* Girondo's poetics shifted from ironic, mocking comments on urban life to an exploration of his inner life. The ruminations in this collection show that, while he did not entirely join their groups, Girondo was keenly aware of the work and ideas of the French Surrealists. The prose poems explore the poet's vision of how false the world is and how poetry should capture inner realities. To achieve that goal, the poetic self must be constantly changing, as the opening line of the eighth poem suggests: "Yo no tengo una personalidad; yo soy un cocktail, un conglomerado, una manifestación de personalidades" (I do not have a personality; I am a cocktail, a conglomeration, a manifestation of personalities).

In 1937 Girondo published *Interlunio* (New Moon), a short work in which he deals in prose with many of the themes introduced in his poems. He also published two articles in the newspaper *La Nación* that year, becoming more politically outspoken than in the past. The first, "El mal del siglo" (The Evil of the Century), appeared on 21 February and proposed a nationalistic rhetoric that Adriana Rodríguez Pérsico sees as the journalistic parallel to *Interlunio.* On 25 April, "Nuestra actitud ante Europa" (Our Attitude Toward Europe) was published, putting what Girondo sees as European decadence in opposition with American vitality, signaling the breaks and continuities between the two continents. These articles were later published in the volume *Nuestra actitud ante el desastre* (Our Attitude in the Face of Disaster, 1940), along with the title essay, which criticizes Argentina's dependence and exhorts nationalizing the Argentine economy, defending its culture, and integrating the South American continent.

With *Persuasión de los días* (Persuasion of the Days, 1942) Girondo returns to poetic verse. In the collection the poet continues to explore ever more deeply his inner self. The theme of travel is still present in *Persuasión de los días,* but the poetic journey

Paperback cover for the 1937 prose work in which Girondo elaborates the nationalist themes of his poetry
(Collection of Susana Lange de Maggi)

moves from cosmopolitan cities to more-private worlds filled with multiple meanings. This multiplicity extends even to the poetic voice, as the final line of "Nocturno 1" indicates: "No soy yo quien escribe estas palabras huérfanas" (It is not I who write these orphaned words). Following the publication of *Persuación de los días,* Girondo and Lange spent six months traveling through Brazil.

Girondo published *Campo nuestro* (Our Countryside) in 1946, shifting his focus from urban subjects to the Argentine pampa. Most critics signal this change of landscape as a significant one in Girondo's poetry. At the same time that *Campo nuestro* explores a new environment, it returns to a favorite theme of Girondo's: travel. In this work the poet travels through all of the literary perspectives that have constructed the pampa. Delfina Muschietti, in her essay "Oliverio Girondo y su tienda nómade" (Oliverio Girondo and his Nomadic Tent, published in *Obra completa*), writes, "El de Girondo es un *viaje* alucinatorio que, en lugar de constituir identidades, trabaja por la deconstrucción" (Girondo's is a hallucinatory *trip* that, instead of constructing identities, works for

deconstruction). The poet's pampa is not the traditional pastoral one but rather a sandy desert. This new vision, together with Girondo's longtime urban focus, may explain why he received some criticism for not really knowing his subject when *Campo nuestro* was published.

In the late 1940s Girondo became increasingly involved with the younger generation of Argentinian poets, such as Olga Orozco and Enrique Molina. Girondo and Lange's home in Buenos Aires was a center of literary activity. They hosted meetings, and Girondo's unlimited enthusiasm in mentoring younger poets on matters poetic or personal became legendary. In 1948, after World War II had ended, Girondo and Lange returned to Europe for the first time in many years. At this point Girondo began to dedicate even more time to painting, a pursuit he had enjoyed throughout his life, often including illustrations in his poetry collections.

Girondo continued to write poetry, however, and published the first edition of *En la masmédula* (In the MoreMarrow) in 1954. It is considered Girondo's most experimental work; the poet shatters syntax and tries to

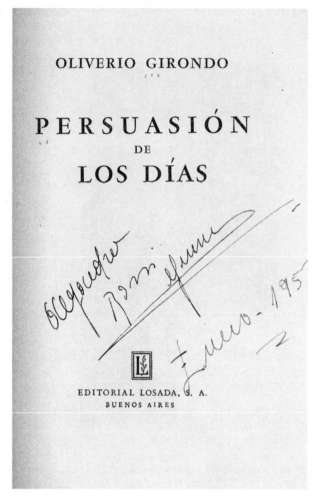

OLIVERIO GIRONDO

PERSUASIÓN

DE

LOS DÍAS

EDITORIAL LOSADA, S. A.
BUENOS AIRES

Title page for Girondo's 1942 poetry collection, which marked his return to verse after several volumes
of essays and prose poetry (Doheny Memorial Library, University of Southern California)

create a new language that goes beyond what conventional words are capable of expressing. In "Girondo o el triunfo de una ética posagónica" (Girondo or the Triumph of a Postagonic Ethic), an essay published in *Obra completa,* Adriana Rodríguez Pérsico writes that in *En la masmédula* "la violencia se ejerce sobre una lengua a la que se despoja de la función comunicativa, que se hace opaca mediante las acumulaciones, la destitución de los significados y la quiebra de la sintaxis o la semántica" (violence is exercised on a language that is stripped of the communicative function, which is made opaque through accumulations, the destitution of meanings, and the breakdown of syntax or semantics). For example, the "pure no" that the poetic voice attempts to articulate in the poem "El puro no" (The Pure No) is "el no más nada todo / el puro no / sin no" (the no more nothing everything / the pure no / without no).

After an evening at the cinema in 1965 Girondo was hit by a car in the same street where he had been born. He managed to get up and walk home but never fully recovered. On 24 January 1967 Oliverio Girondo died in Buenos Aires. Although he did not publish many books, his importance to Argentine poetry is undeniable. Girondo always searched for poetic and linguistic innovation in his work. Through his involvement with the Latin American avant-garde movement, he made an important contribution to the intellectual life of the period. Girondo recognized European influences but never lost his distinctly American voice. As José Carlos Mariátegui wrote, "En la poesía de Girondo el bordado es europeo, es urbano, es cosmopolita. Pero la trama es gaucha" (In Girondo's poetry, the embroidery is European, urban, cosmopolitan. But the plot is gaucho).

Reference:

José Carlos Mariátegui, "Oliverio Girondo," in his *Crítica literaria: Ensayo preliminar de Antonio Melis* (Buenos Aires: Álvarez, 1969), p. 101.

León de Greiff

(22 July 1895 – 11 July 1976)

Mari Pino del Rosario
Greensboro College

BOOKS: *Tergiversaciones de Leo Legris, Matías Aldecoa y Gaspar. Primer mamotreto, 1915–1922* (Bogotá: Augusta, 1925);

Libro de signos. Tergiversaciones de Leo Le Gris, Matías Aldecoa, Gaspar von der Nacht y Erik Fjordsson. Segundo mamotreto (Medellín, Colombia: Imprenta Editorial Medellín, 1930);

Variaciones alredor de nada. Cuarto mamotreto (Manizales, Colombia: A. Zapata, 1936);

Prosas de Gaspar: Primera suite, 1918–1925. Tercer mamotreto (Bogotá: Imprenta Nacional, 1937);

Antología poética, 1914–1937 (Bogotá: Editorial Cultura, 1942);

Farsa de los pingüinos peripatéticos, 1915–1926 (Bogotá: Lit. Colombia, Sección Editorial, 1942);

Poemillas de Bogislao Von Greiff (Bogotá, 1949);

Fárrago. Quinto mamotreto (Bogotá: SLB, 1954);

Relatos de oficios y menesteres de Beremundo (Bogotá: Hojas de Cultura Popular Colombiana, 1955);

Bárbara Charanga. Bajo el signo de Leo. Sexto mamotreto (Bogotá, 1957);

Velero paradójico. Séptimo mamotreto (Bogotá, 1957);

Obras completas, 2 volumes (Medellín, Colombia: Aguirre, 1960);

Nova et vetera (Bogotá: Tercer Mundo, 1974);

Obras completas, 2 volumes (Bogotá: Tercer Mundo, 1975);

Obra completa, 3 volumes, edited by Hjalmar de Greiff (Bogotá: Procultura, 1985–1986);

Obra dispersas: Prosa-Poesía, 4 volumes, edited by Hjalmar de Greiff (Bogotá: Universidad de Antioquia, 1995–1999).

TRANSLATION: *Antología Multilingüe: 50 poemas,* selected, with a prologue, by Hjalmar de Greiff (Bogotá: Instituto Colombiano de Cultura, Biblioteca Nacional de Colombia, 1995).

RECORDING: *La voz de León de Greiff,* read by de Greiff, Bogotá, HJCK, 1960.

León de Greiff (from Orlando Rodríguez Sardiñas, León de Greiff: Una poética de vanguardia, *1975)*

Poet Francisco León de Greiff Haeussler was born to Luis de Greiff Obregón and Amalia Haeussler Rincón on 22 July 1895 in Medellín, in the province of Antioquia, Colombia. De Greiff's last names betray his northern European ancestry. His Swedish paternal great-grandfather arrived in South America to explore mining, while his maternal grandfather was Prussian. In addition, de Greiff had Incan roots via his maternal grandmother. He was the second of four children raised amid Nordic legends, classical music, and an appreciation for the arts. His rebellious nature manifested itself in mischief during the early stages of his life and continued to show by his failure to complete any academic degrees. Early rebellion, however, metamorphosed into unrelenting creativity and self-expression in de Greiff as an adult; Cuban poet Nicolás Guillén, in *Valoración múltiple sobre León de Greiff* (Multiple Assessments of León de Greiff, 1995), called him a "genial" (genius) and a verbal "prestidigitador" (juggler). *Valoración múltiple sobre León de Greiff,* a collection of reminiscences, studies, opinions, and letters compiled by Arturo Alape, offers contrasting and complementary views of the Colombian poet.

With its French Symbolist and Parnassian resonances, Latin American *Modernismo,* embodied in Nicaraguan poet Rubén Darío, had already traveled to Spain and taken hold of audiences on both sides of the Atlantic by the time de Greiff was born. During his young-adult life he became acquainted with many other "isms": Creationism, Ultraism, Futurism, Surrealism, and Dadaism. Critics have failed, however, to place any particular label on the poet's work. In an essay in *Valoración múltiple sobre León de Greiff,* Alvaro Rojas de la Espriella mentions that the "Maestro" was impervious to emerging trends and that, in spite of his having loyal readers, other poets did not pursue his sense of aesthetics and particular style. Described by most as an eccentric, to the end of his life de Greiff remained a solipsistic maverick who pushed against attempts to frame his writings or define him by common standards. He chose the owl as a personal icon that stood for knowledge, solitude, self-control, introversion, aloofness, the power of observation, the love of nocturnal life, and the ability to escape the pull of earthly demands.

The exact age at which de Greiff began to write is unknown. In *León de Greiff: Una poética de vanguardia* (León de Greiff: Poetics of the Vanguard, 1975), Orlando Rodríguez Sardiñas states that he was fifteen years old; Hjalmar de Greiff, son of the poet, says that he was sixteen in "Deshilvanadas precisiones acerca de León de Greiff" (Disjointed Statements on León de Greiff), an article published in the newspaper *El Tiempo* on the one hundredth anniversary of his father's birth. De Greiff's first poem, however, did not become available to a wide audience until 1915, when he was twenty years old. That year he and twelve other intellectual men, most younger than twenty, began to gather at El Globo (The Globe), a coffeehouse, to discuss art, poetry, and politics. They are described by Eduardo Castillo in *A propósito de León de Greiff y su obra* (A Determination of León de Greiff and His Work, 1991) as "trece muchachos—músicos, pintores, poetas—dispuestos a conquistar la tierra y a forzar la entrada de ese reino de la Gloria que, como el de los cielos, padece violencia; trece nefelibatas—como hubiese dicho Darío—locos de azul, de ensueño y de armonía, paradójicos, petulantes, románticos, melenudos y aficionados, como Alcibíades, a cortarle la cola a su perro para épater les bourgeois" (thirteen young men—musicians, painters, poets—ready to conquer the planet and to force their entry into the kingdom of Glory, which like the kingdom of Heaven, suffers from violence; thirteen creatures who loved to dream, as Darío would have said, crazy with blue, dreams, and harmony, paradoxical, petulant, romantic, long-haired and fond, as Alcibíades, of cutting a dog's tail to *épater les bourgeois* [shock the bourgeois]).

On 15 February 1915 the first issue of *Panida,* the group's biweekly magazine devoted to creative writing, was published under de Greiff's editorship. The group of young intellectuals was immediately identified with the journal, and its contributors came to be known as the Panidas. In the first issue appeared one of the many pseudonyms de Greiff used during his life, Leo Legris. Legris's "La balada de los búhos estáticos" (The Ballad of Static Owls, 1915) can be considered the group's manifesto to search for new arenas and strategies in poetry. In 1920 Los Nuevos (The New Ones), another group of approximately twenty writers, came into existence. Critic Rodríguez Sardiñas explains: "un grupo de rebeldes y bohemios se reunía en el desaparecido café Windsor, de Bogotá, a discutir enardecidos sus intranquilidades liberales, nacionales, radicales, socialistas y hasta comunistas, así como a componer versos y a leerlos en el corrillo poético" (a group of rebels and bohemians would get together in what used to be the Café Windsor, in Bogotá, to discuss passionately their liberal, national, radical, socialist and even communist worries, as well as to write poetry and read it to the group). During this five-year interval, according to Castillo, de Greiff had continued to publish poems in magazines and newspapers but seemed to be in no hurry to publish a book. Critics and friends of de Greiff concur in attributing his late debut at book publishing to a lack of interest and not to difficulty in accessing publishing houses.

In 1925 de Greiff's first collection of poems, *Tergiversaciones de Leo Legris, Matías Aldecoa y Gaspar. Primer mamotreto, 1915–1922* (Distortions of Leo Legris, Matías Aldecoa, and Gaspar. First Thick Volume, 1915–1922), was published. Ten years had passed since the first issue of *Panida,* but in this book de Greiff included poems that dated as far back as 1913—a testament to his earlier start in writing. De Greiff's long wait to publish may have been the result of his striving for perfection; clear indication of this fact is the revisions made to "La balada de los búhos estáticos," first published in 1915 and republished in 1925 in *Tergiversaciones de Leo Legris, Matías Alde-coa y Gaspar.* Changes from one publication to the next are minimal but do show that revision took place.

De Greiff's first book is composed of six parts: "Tergiversaciones" (Distortions), "Libro de las baladas" (Book of Ballads), "Rondeles" (Rondels), "Arietas" (Ariettas), "Ritornelos y otros ritmos" (Ritornellos and Other Rhythms), and "Estampas" (Depictions). The first poem, a sonnet titled "Tergiversaciones I," shows traits to be found throughout his work—a first-person poetic voice, references to world literary figures, a rich lexicon, and a search for identity through various characters: "Porque me ven la barba y el pelo y la alta pipa / dicen que soy poeta . . ." (Because they see my beard and hair and my big pipe / I am called a poet . . .).

De Greiff's critics have commented on the difficulty presented by his use of neologisms, regionalisms, learned words, archaic expressions, literary and musical references, and prolixity. Germán Espinosa, in an essay from *Valoración múltiple sobre León de Greiff,* explains from an historical point of view his invention of words, stating that "puede no ser un vocablo verbal en un paisaje geográfico donde el español fue impuesto a arcabuza-zos, pero donde el español no es suficiente para expre-sar la realidad que nos rodea. Todo latinoamericano—y también de Greiff—anda en busca de su propio lenguaje, al que lo exprese satisfactoriamente" (a word may not exist in a landscape where the Spanish language was imposed by arquebuses, but where Spanish is insuffi-cient to express its surroundings. Every Latin American person—including de Greiff—is in search of his or her own language to express this reality satisfactorily). For Cecilia Hernández de Mendoza, de Greiff's choice of words comes from a search for musical meaning and sound in verbal language. In other essays in *Valoración múltiple sobre León de Greiff,* Hernando Valencia Goelkel views de Greiff's complexity as indicative of the poet's heightened sensibility, while Juan Felipe Toruño calls it "sinfonism." He also explains that de Greiff's poems are like open scores that show a full orchestra's potential being exploited; this technique is not excess, as others have called it, states Toruño, but a reflection of the poet's vantage point and hypersensitivity to his milieu.

De Greiff's writings demand vast knowledge and a desire to be suspended in a verbal universe; they require readers to embark on a galactic journey with a large number of characters and often with no point of arrival in sight. To literary historians, linguists, and crit-ics, de Greiff's literary output offers an opportunity to observe poetic development in Colombia before Gabriel García Márquez and his fictional village of Macondo captured the world's imagination, took over the literary scene, and made it possible for the novel to become the genre of the 1960s. De Greiff and García Márquez have

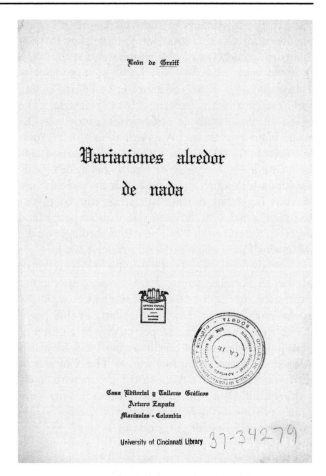

Title page for de Greiff's 1936 collection, in which he writes from the points of view of imaginary personae such as "Sergio Stepansky" and "Erik Fjordsson" (Langsam Library, University of Cincinnati)

in common a gift for character development and a quest to break boundaries in and through language. Both writers also share a predilection for humor—most frequently in the form of irony in García Márquez. De Greiff, on the other hand, infuses his language with a sense of humor that runs the gamut from irony and sar-casm to self-deprecation.

The title *Tergiversaciones de Leo Legris, Matías Aldecoa y Gaspar. Primer mamotreto* is a prime example of de Greiff's humor; its title, "Distortions of Leo Legris, Matías Aldecoa and Gaspar," and its subtitle, "First Thick Volume," purposefully confront readers with their pejorative names and connotations, since *mamotreto* is used colloquially to refer to a useless big item. The rubric is a personal assessment of the book's worth that bluntly shows the poet's indifference to pub-lic opinion. It simultaneously discourages readers by its use of negative connotations regarding its content and form while it defies them by announcing that this thick book is the first in a series.

At thirty years of age and with his first collection published, de Greiff revealed on the title page three of the many pseudonyms he utilized throughout his work to avoid being pinned down. These shifting identities are symptomatic of his reluctance to be labeled in any way, except under adjectives such as "eccentric." The origin of these multiple self-representations may be found in his diverse ancestry as well as his unwillingness to adhere to the norm. Luis Vidales, in *Valoración múltiple sobre León de Greiff,* explains de Greiff's behavior by calling him a lifelong child. He adds that the poet did not measure his responses when interacting with colleagues and maintained a Manichaean stance about people and events to the end of his life. These facts shed light on the motivating force behind de Greiff's creative work.

"Balada trivial de los 13 Panidas" (Trivial Ballad of the 13 Panidas), from *Tergiversaciones,* is another expression of de Greiff's noncompliance with the poetic establishment. De Greiff reflects in this poem the collective sentiment and personality of a group of young men who share a rebellious spirit and are called *camorristas* (quarrelsome hooligans). The Colombian poet was one of only three in the group who made writing his life and who, in spite of harsh realities, continued to show his noncompliance with the poetic and political establishment. "Aquesta es la pipa" (This Is the Pipe) is a prime example of such an attitude. In this poem de Greiff portrays his poetic persona as the "loco archilunático" (craziest lunatic) and his verse as a "canción hereje" (heretical song); he calls for "aquelarres" (witches' sabbats) and "conjuros" (spells) and longs for the darkness of the night—at times he uses adjectives and nouns relating to the Prince of Darkness. "Aquesta es la pipa" attests to the poet's commitment to live and write against the norm, even if it meant being associated with the biblical fallen angels or twentieth-century communists.

In an essay in *Valoración múltiple sobre León de Greiff,* Tomás Vargas Osorio refers to de Greiff's style as "goticismo musical" (musical gothic), while others call it baroque. In fact, the medieval origin of gothic and its use of darkness and embellishment to contrast with Romanesque openness and simplicity of form describes more accurately the Colombian poet's linguistic and thematic natures than the seventeenth-century aesthetics. In de Greiff's poems music is ubiquitous. He chooses musical forms from the Renaissance and classical periods (sonata, arietta, ritornello); composers mostly from the classical period (Ludwig van Beethoven and Wolfgang Amadeus Mozart); and a large number of instruments. Woodwind instruments become the focal point of a few poems, but, with a few exceptions, the entire orchestra, including Renaissance instruments, appears in his work. This predilection for music stemmed from his

central and northern European ancestry and his training in the bassoon. His ideology and worldview are, however, more in accordance with Richard Wagner's operas—imbued with Nordic myth and rich textures—or with Igor Stravinsky's ingenious exploration of sound.

De Greiff demands of his readers full attention and an encyclopedic background. Some of his critics perceive the poet's willfulness as violent; indeed, readers witness violence throughout his work. One must contend with multiple poetic personae and an explosion of musical references. In an essay in *Valoración múltiple sobre León de Greiff,* Espinosa comments on how the poet successfully transgresses against the poetic vanguard by embracing all connections between music and poetry. In another essay from the same collection, Hernández de Mendoza chooses a discourse of domination to characterize de Greiff's language, rhyme, and rhythm. One perceives that the poet forces language in order to verbalize his rebellion; he stretches, shapes, and reshapes it to reflect his ideology of nonconformity. Aggression is thus present in his linguistic, thematic, and stylistic choices.

In contrast to de Greiff's active resistance to the status quo and his fruitful imagination and verbal exploration, his daily life was monotonous. He failed to complete his university studies and was required throughout most of his life to hold perfunctory jobs. After having worked at the Banco Central for ten years, he began employment with the railroad in 1926. A year later he married Matilde Bernal Nicholls, with whom he fathered three children—Astrid, Hjalmar, and Axel. In 1930 he published his second collection of poems, *Libro de signos. Tergiversaciones de Leo Le Gris, Matías Aldecoa, Gaspar von der Nacht y Erik Fjordsson. Segundo mamotreto* (Book of Signs. Distortions of Leo Le Gris, Matías Aldecoa, Gaspar of the Night, and Erik Fjordsson. Second Thick Volume). Once again, de Greiff included in this second volume poems dating as far back as 1915, implicitly emphasizing his concept of writing as a long process of rewriting.

The evolution of de Greiff's poetic personae is evident in the title of this collection. Leo Legris becomes Leo Le Gris (Leo the Gray One), a color associated with northern latitudes and somberness; Gaspar is associated with nighttime, de Greiff's favorite time of the day, when he could retire to write. Erik Fjordsson foregrounds de Greiff's Scandinavian roots: the name Fjordsson means "son of the fjords" and metaphorically alludes to the poet's feeling of being caught between powerful forces. This volume is divided into six parts; the first one comprises three loose compositions—"Farsa de los pingüinos peripatéticos" (Farce of the Peripatetic Penguins), "El solitario" (The Loner), and "Amo la soledad" (I Love Solitude). The other five longer sections are "Segundo libro de las baladas: Otras canciones" (Second Book of Ballads: Other Songs), "Música de cámara y al aire libre (Primer ciclo)" (Chamber and Outdoor Music [First Cycle]), "Música de cámara y al aire libre (Segundo ciclo)" (Chamber and Outdoor Music [Second Cycle]), "Música de cámara y al aire libre (Tercer ciclo)" (Chamber and Outdoor Music [Third Cycle]), and "Fantasías de nubes al viento (Primera ronda: Esquema)" (Fantasies of Clouds at the Winds [First Round: Sketch]).

Together these six parts continue what Rafael Maya calls "un largo monólogo interior" (a long interior monologue). Paradox, travel, and music as the foremost art intensify as the poet's thematic preferences. Oxymorons are used to title parts of this book as well as several poems: "Música de cámara y al aire libre" (Outdoor Chamber Music) is an example. Chamber music, by its very nature, is not intended to be played outdoors; nevertheless, de Greiff chose this paradoxical title for three parts of *Libro de signos*. One particular poem, "Balada de asonancias consonantes o de consonancias disonantes o de simples disonancias" (Ballad of Consonantal Assonance or Dissonant Consonances or Simple Dissonances), exploits paradox as a device but also uses it as a means to demonstrate the poet's refusal to provide definitiveness. De Greiff also reflects his deviation from the norm by his inclusion of archaic syntax and morphology, for example, "trujéronme" (they brought me), and juxtaposition of learned words with colloquiallisms, as in "un maremágnum de majaderías" (a pandemonium of stupidities). Finally, in this book travel is portrayed as a foundation for the exploration of literature, music, language, and places. The poet is on an existential journey on his way to no particular place. As a matter of fact, it took de Greiff another twenty-eight years to travel for the first time to Europe, the continent he evoked, imagined, and named most in his work.

The Colombian poet chose next to express himself in prose in *Prosas de Gaspar: Primera suite, 1918–1925. Tercer mamotreto* (Gaspar's Prose Works: First Suite, 1918–1925. Third Thick Volume). Although its subtitle affirms that it is de Greiff's third work, it was not published until 1937. In *Valoración múltiple sobre León de Greiff*, Rafael Vázquez refers to *Prosas de Gaspar* as "uno de los más atrevidos ensayos poemáticos que se hayan intentado en nuestra lengua" (one of the most daring poematic essays ever written in our language). Although still dealing with multiple personae, de Greiff deviates from his previous works by choosing prose to present these many selves and by coining the word *leogrifo* (leogryph) to refer to his monster-like, hybrid nature. Unapologetic, he claims his right to solitude and shows his wisdom and power in this collection of essays.

In 1936 *Variaciones alredor de nada. Cuarto mamotreto* (Variations on Nothing. Fourth Thick Volume) was

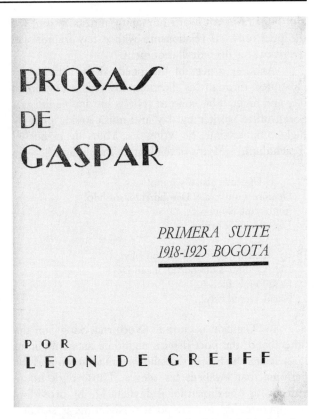

PROSAS
DE
GASPAR

PRIMERA SUITE
1918-1925 BOGOTA

POR
LEON DE GREIFF

Title page for de Greiff's 1937 collection of essays, written from the viewpoint of "Gaspar von der Nacht" (Gaspar of the Night), a persona the poet created to serve as his spokesman (Robert Manning Strozier Library, Florida State University)

published; it is structured in five sections: "Fantasías de nubes al viento" (Fantasies of Clouds at the Winds), "Segunda ronda" (Second Round), "Musurgia" (Muse as Artificer of the World), "Mitos de la noche" (Myths of the Night), and "Libro de relatos" (Book of Stories). To his previous alter egos, de Greiff now adds Sergio Stepansky and a Russian retreating to the steppes to create: "En mi rincón le insuflo a mi fagote / vientos de libre poesía" (In my corner I blow winds of free poetry / in my bassoon). Musical forms are used to title the collection, and individual poems and even musical dynamic markings appear in "Fantasía cuasi una sonata" (Fantasy Quasi Sonata)—a play on Beethoven's "Sonata quasi una fantasia," op. 27, no. 1, also known as the "Moonlight Sonata." More importantly, the musical title of the collection reflects a poetic persona aware of possessing several selves that are variations around nothingness: "Yo quiero sólo andar, errar–viandante / indiferente–, andar, errar, sin rumbo" (I just want to walk, to wander–indifferent / wayfarer–, to walk, to wander, without a direction). Vidales explains that de Greiff's worldview is saturated with nihilism and hopelessness toward humanity and its future; for the poet only his relationship with a few friends can overcome his deep disillusionment.

Another aspect of the poet's daily activities is illustrated through his dichotomous representation of day and night. This contrast reflects his double life as a bored office worker by day and music-loving poet by night. On daytime, he writes in "Mitos de la noche: 'Praeludium'" (Myths of the Night: 'Praeludium'):

> . . . el Día cuán actual y tonto!
> Siempre a mi vera el Día–hórrido, sórdido!
> Junto a mí, el bobo
> Día, plácido y bruto!

> (. . . the Day, how present and silly!
> Always at my side–horrid, mean Day!
> Next to me, foolish,
> placid, stupid Day!).

In "Canción nocturna" (Nocturnal Song), on the other hand, the poet depicts nighttime as symbolic of knowledge, the breath that allows him to go on and the perfume that awakens his senses. Those dark hours redeem his one-dimensional daylight life by providing the opportunity to write poetry. Nighttime is simultaneously painful and joyful, as another one of de Greiff's poems describes: "Clavos en ti me clavan, oh Noche deleitosa! / Noche . . . ! tibio madero de mi cruz!" (Nails nail me down, oh delightful Night! / Night . . . ! warm beam of my cross!). The poet presents himself here as a Christ-like figure crucified by the oppressive and redeeming centrifugal force of creativity.

This poem stands out also because of its religious references. René Uribe Ferrer, in an essay from *Valoración múltiple sobre León de Greiff,* points out that religious sentiment is nonexistent in de Greiff's work. The poet, according to Uribe Ferrer, does not take a position on religion; his existential angst ends in a comforting nothingness. De Greiff's lack of interest in this theme, however, indicates a neutrality that does not fit in with his otherwise clear positions on political or literary topics. Rather, one should view the poet's ubiquitous poetic and musical concerns as the true spiritual forces and sources of comfort in his life.

If religious poems are rare in de Greiff's work, erotic ones are not, and, furthermore, their frequency increases in *Variaciones alrededor de nada.* The object of desire is not a single woman but dozens of mythical, biblical, literary, and historical women. There is no attempt to follow Golden Age aesthetics that idealize feminine beauty. De Greiff's object of desire is multiple yet concrete; she is described from head to toe and her hidden parts named: "la delicia del sexo" (the delight of the sex organ).

In the following twenty years de Greiff did not publish but accomplished much in other areas. In 1940 he cofounded the Radiodifusora Nacional (National Radio) and became professor of literature and composition at the Engineering School of the Universidad Nacional. In 1944 he cofounded the Instituto Cultural Colombo-Soviético (Colombian-Soviet Cultural Institute). A year later he began work at the Ministerio de Educación Nacional as associate director for secondary education, scholarship counselor, and director of cultural and fine arts. In 1945 he traveled abroad for the first time; he went to Mexico as a member of a commission in charge of returning the poet Porfirio Barba-Jacob's ashes to Colombia. In 1946 he was appointed professor of music history at the Universidad Nacional's Conservatory. A year later he participated in the II Juegos Bolivarianos (Second Bolivar Games) held in Lima, Peru, as a representative of the Ministry of National Education. In 1949 he was detained along with Diego Montaña Cuéllar, Alejandro Vallejo, and Jorge Zalamea, allegedly for political reasons. A year later he began work at the Contraloría General de la República (State Comptroller's Office).

In 1954 de Greiff published *Fárrago. Quinto mamotreto* (Hopscotch. Fifth Thick Volume). It consists of five parts: "Secuencias (Primer tranco)" (Sequences [First Stride]), "Baladas in modo antico para me divertir" (Ballads in Antique Style to Amuse Myself), "Poemillas" (Little Poems), "Fantasías de nubes al viento" (Fantasies of Clouds at the Winds), and "Dos relatos (del segundo libro dellos)" (Two Stories [from the Second Book of Stories]). The use of medieval Spanish in the title of the first part echoes the subject matter of a jongleur and his trade. Themes of solitude, silence, tediousness, and disgust populate this volume, along with themes of the redeeming sounds of verse. In this late work de Greiff introduces popular musical instruments such as the *pandero* (tambourine) and the *bandurria* (similar to a mandolin); this folkloric element reflects his contact with alternative musical languages and instruments at the conservatory.

In *Fárrago* the fifty-nine-year-old poet expressed fiercely his antagonistic attitude toward his critics. In "Balada faceta" (Facet Ballad), for example, he bluntly dismisses them with an unusual choice of words for a poem: "A todos aquesos mandarlos a un cuerno" (Send all of them to hell). Aware of the difficulty others encountered in classifying his poetry, he attempts to provide his own definition:

> Yo soy Gaspar, ex-poeta romántico, mas sí
> con cierta huella aún de lo romántico que fui
> cuando poeta: quédanme aún trazas o señas
> del fantasista cuasi romántico ex-simbólico,

magüer hoy soy Gaspar, Gaspar bufón en prosa
—sarcástico bufón y bufón melancólico—

(I am Gaspar, former romantic poet, but I still
carry remains of the romantic I was
as a poet: I still have marks and traces
of the fantasist former symbolist, quasi-romantic,
although today I am Gaspar, Gaspar buffoon in prose
—sarcastic buffoon and buffoon full of melancholy—).

In the same poem, de Greiff refers to his prolix style
and often exhausting lexicon with his customary self-
deprecation, as "verborragia oceánica" (logorrhea of
oceanic proportions). He clearly states in "Admonición
a los impertinentes" (Admonition to Those Who Are
Impertinent), however, that he will not change.

De Greiff's defensiveness and attempts at self-
representation appear to follow his inability to achieve
recognition. In 1955, however, his contemporaries
began to shower him with attention. That year, the
Institute for Colombian and Argentinean Cultural
Exchange paid him and Ricardo Rojas homage. A year
later the Premio Hispanoamericano de Poesía León de
Greiff (León de Greiff Spanish-American Poetry Prize)
was instituted in Caracas by Carlos Celis Cepero, and
the poet was the recipient of another homage in Madrid
by poets such as Vicente Aleixandre, Dámaso Alonso,
and Dionisio Ridruejo.

In 1957 *Bárbara Charanga. Bajo el signo de Leo. Sexto
mamotreto* (Barbaric Brass Band. Under the Sign of Leo.
Sixth Thick Volume) was published. This collection of
essays is subtitled "Memorias, desventuras, venturas y
aventuras de Bogislaus y su escudero y su escribano y
su espolique" (Memoirs, Misfortunes, Fortunes, and
Adventures of Bogislaus and His Squire, and His
Scribe, and His Aide), which suggests the comic and
lavish play on words of the subtitle of the book. It bor-
rows Don Quixote's unwillingness to express a preference for one term out of many to name an object.
Language is exploited for its own sake; it becomes the
subject and object of manipulation.

Velero paradójico. Séptimo mamotreto (Paradoxical Ship.
Seventh Thick Volume) is the poet's seventh publication,
dated the same year as his sixth one. De Greiff chose to
portray himself here as a paradoxical sailing ship that
had visited many places without ever having left port.
The book opens with "Relato de los oficios y mesteres de
Beremundo" (Stories of Beremundo's Trades and Occupations), a long poem that shows the poet's continued
exploration of the lexical universe of poetry. Also
included is a set of metapoetic sonnets, which echo
Golden Age poet Francisco de Quevedo's sarcasm. This
tone of voice can be heard, for example, when de Greiff
addresses the issue of trends in writing and exhorts his

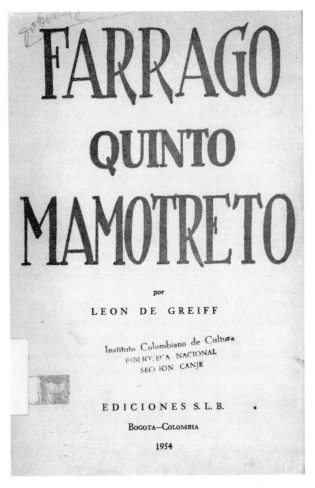

Paperback cover for de Greiff's fifth mamotreto *(thick volume),
in which he defends his prolix poetic style against disparaging
literary critics (University of Mississippi Library)*

poet reader in "Secuencia sin consecuencias VIII"
(Sequence without Consequences VIII):

No hagas versos según tu propio gusto
que es petulancia! En verso, el Sindicato
cosa es de Ley: tus versos . . . a la Moda!
De otra guisa, no pienses ni en tu Busto!
Si te sobra nariz, haz por ser chato . . . :
no ves que cada quisque se la poda?

(Do not write verse as you please
for this is petulance! In verse, the Union
is the Law: your verse . . . as the times mandate!
Otherwise, do not think of a Bust!
If your nose is too long, try to make it short . . . :
Don't you see that everyone is cutting his off?)

True to his selves, de Greiff restated in this poem and
the entire volume his need and right not to conform.

Nearly thirty years elapsed before de Greiff's
eighth and final volume was published, but during
those silent years the poet initiated a new and dynamic

stage in his life. In 1958 he traveled for the first time to Europe to participate in the World Congress for Peace in Stockholm. Subsequently he was invited to the Soviet Union and the People's Republic of China and visited Austria, Yugoslavia, and France. In 1959 he was appointed first secretary at the Colombian Embassy in Sweden and resided in that country for four years. During his appointment he met other writers and, in 1962, attended the Iberoamerican-German Colloquium. In 1964 he was knighted by the king of Sweden. The following year he participated in an international writers' conference, hosted by Anna Seghers and Arnold Zweig, on the twentieth anniversary of the victory of the Allied powers over Hitlerian Fascism. In 1966 his wife, Matilde, died. The poet forged ahead with his international work and travels and, a year later, was elected president of the Association for Colombian and Czechoslovakian Friendship. In 1968 he went to Havana to attend the Congreso de la Cultura (Cultural Congress) and to adjudicate the Casa de Américas poetry prize.

Two years later, de Greiff received the First National Prize in Literature from the Colombian Institute of Culture and visited Caracas, Venezuela, to attend the Comunidad Iberoamericana de Escritores (Iberoamerican Community of Writers) conference. In 1971 de Greiff continued to receive recognition in his country and was awarded the Jorge Zalamea Medal, the Symbolic Hatchet of Antioquia, the Star of Antioquia, and the General Civil Medal from the Education Ministry in Santander; he was also paid homage by the Colegio Nacional de Periodistas (National Association of Journalists) sponsored by García Márquez and was elected president of the House for Colombian and Cuban Friendship. Two years later he received the Antioquia Prize awarded by Coltejer.

In 1974 de Greiff published his last book, *Nova et vetera* (New and Old), and became an honorary member of the Instituto Caro y Cuervo. The collection includes poems dated as far back as 1915 and as recently as 1970. At the end of his life and in this collection, de Greiff reiterates his themes, calling night his "monomanía" (only obsession), restating his indifference to public opinion, and referring unapologetically to his self-absorption. He also revisits eroticism. Aware of his decrepit state, however, his tone is this time self-deprecatory, as witnessed in "Balad-baladina del vate caduco" (Ballad-Balladine of the Expired Poet):

> Caduco vate ya de edad provecta,
> más vecino a la fosa que a la fusa,
> persiste en galanteos con la Musa,
> y entre los tibios muslos se delecta

> de hembra real y venus inconcusa.
> Qué le vamos a hacer! Eros comanda:
> y ogaño como antaño el fin detecta,
> del vivir en la concha tibia y blanda

> (Senile prophet of old age
> closer to the grave than to the demisemiquaver,
> he persists in flirting with the Muse
> and in the warm thighs takes delight
> of a real female and an indisputable venus.
> What to do! Eros commands:
> and now like long ago the end of
> inhabiting a warm and soft shell
> he detects).

In his last work de Greiff continued to face his critics by demonstrating his mastery of the sonnet, the classical poetic form par excellence, and retaining his sense of humor; thus, he wrote several sonnets and with a tongue-in-cheek attitude titled them "sonetete" (big sonnet), "sonetín" (little sonnet), and "sonecillo" (sonette).

In the year preceding his death, the poet was conferred an honorary degree by the Universidad del Valle, he won the Order of San Carlos, and he received an homage from the National Association of Financial Institutions in Colombia. De Greiff died in Bogotá on 11 July 1976.

The one hundredth anniversary of León de Greiff's birth was commemorated in 1995, and several publications of critical studies as well as biographical recollections by his friends and literary figures were produced. In the twenty-first century there has been a renewed interest in the Colombian poet's work and life, pointing to the fact that León de Greiff's particular style and personality will continue to pique the public's curiosity.

References:

Arturo Alape, ed., *Valoración múltiple sobre León de Greiff* (Bogotá: Fundación Universidad Central, 1995);

Eduardo Castillo, "Leo Legris, el Panida," in *A propósito de León de Greiff y su obra* (Barcelona: Grupo Editorial Norma, 1991), pp. 9–14;

Hjalmar de Greiff, "Deshilvanadas precisiones acerca de León de Greiff," *El Tiempo,* 23 July 1995, Sunday Supplement;

Rafael Maya, "Como un esbelto monolito," in *A propósito de León de Greiff y su obra* (Barcelona: Grupo Editorial Norma, 1991), pp. 25–31;

Juan Luis Mejía A., foreword to *Panida,* 1–10 (1915): n.p.; reprint (Bogotá: Cocultura, 1990), n.p.;

Orlando Rodríguez Sardiñas, *León de Greiff: Una poética de vanguardia* (Madrid: Playor, 1975);

Luis Suardíaz, *El múltiple rostro de León de Greiff* (Havana: Arte y Literatura, 1995).

Nicolás Guillén
(10 July 1902 – 16 July 1989)

Keith Ellis
University of Toronto

BOOKS: *Motivos de son* (Havana: Rambla, Bouza, 1930); translated by Langston Hughes and Ben F. Carruthers as *Cuba Libre* (Los Angeles: Anderson & Ritchie, 1948);

Sóngoro cosongo: Poemas mulatos (Havana: Ucar, García, 1931);

West Indies, Ltd. (Havana: Ucar, García, 1934);

Cantos para soldados y sones para turistas (Mexico City: Masas, 1937);

España: Poema en cuatro angustias y una esperanza (Mexico City: México Nuevo, 1937);

Sóngoro consongo y otros poemas (Havana: La Verónica, 1942);

El son entero: Suma poética 1929–1946 (Buenos Aires: Pleamar, 1947);

Elegía a Jacques Roumain en el cielo de Haití (Havana: Ayón, 1948);

Elegía a Jesús Menéndez (Havana: Páginas, 1951);

Elegía cubana (Havana: MOU, 1956);

La paloma de vuelo popular (Buenos Aires: Losada, 1958);

Sus mejores poemas (Havana: Organización Continental de los Festivales del Libro, 1959);

Buenos días, Fidel (Mexico City: Gráfica Horizonte, 1959);

¿Puedes? (Havana: Ucar, García, 1960);

Balada (Havana: Movimiento por la Paz y la Soberanía de los Pueblos, 1962);

Poesías (Havana: Comisión Nacional Cubana de la UNESCO, 1962);

Tengo (Havana: Universidad Central de Las Villas, 1964); translated by Richard J. Carr as *I Have* (Detroit: Broadside, 1974);

Poemas de amor (Havana: La Tertulia, 1964);

Antología mayor: El son entero y otros poemas (Havana: Unión de Escritores y Artistas de Cuba, 1964); translated by Roberto Márquez and David Arthur McMurray as *Man-Making Words: Selected Poems* (Amherst: University of Massachusetts Press, 1972);

En algún sitio de la primavera: Elegía (Havana: Privately published, 1966); translated by Keith Ellis as *New*

Nicolás Guillén (from Keith Ellis, Cuba's Nicolás Guillén: Poetry and Ideology, *1983; Thomas Cooper Library, University of South Carolina)*

Love Poetry/Nueva Poesía de Amor (Toronto: University of Toronto Press, 1994);

El Gran Zoo (Havana: Ediciones Unión, 1967); translated by Márquez as *¡Patria o Muerte! The Great Zoo and Other Poems* (New York: Monthly Review Press, 1972);

Che Comandante (Havana: Instituto Cubano del Libro, 1967);

Cuatro canciones para el Che (Havana: Consejo Nacional de Cultura, 1969);

La rueda dentada (Havana: Unión de Escritores y Artistas de Cuba, 1972);

El diario que a diario (Havana: Unión de Escritores y Artistas de Cuba, 1972); translated by Vera M. Kutzinski as *The Daily Daily* (Berkeley: University of California Press, 1989);

Obra poética, 2 volumes (Havana: Unión de Escritores y Artistas de Cuba, 1972);

El corazón con que vivo (Havana: Unión de Escritores y Artistas de Cuba, 1975);

Poemas manuables (Havana: Unión de Escritores y Artistas de Cuba, 1975);

Prosa de prisa 1929–1972, 3 volumes, edited by Angel I. Augier (Havana: Arte y Literatura, 1975–1976);

Elegías (Havana: Unión de Escritores y Artistas de Cuba, 1977);

Por el mar de las Antillas anda un barco de papel: Poemas para niños mayores de edad (Havana: Unión de Escritores y Artistas de Cuba, 1977);

Música de cámara (Havana: Unión de Escritores y Artistas de Cuba, 1979);

Coplas de Juan Descalzo (Havana: Letras Cubanas, 1979);

Claudio José Domingo Brindis de Salas (Havana: Unión de Escritores y Artistas de Cuba, 1979);

Sputnik 57 (Havana: Ediciones Unión, 1980);

El libro de las décimas (Havana: Unión de Escritores y Artistas de Cuba, 1980);

Páginas vueltas: Memorias (Havana: Unión de Escritores y Artistas de Cuba, 1982);

Sol de domingo (Havana: Unión de Escritores y Artistas de Cuba, 1982);

Martín Morúa Delgado: Quién fue–? (Havana: Unión de Escritores y Artistas de Cuba, 1984);

Cronista en tres épocas, selected by María Julia Guerra Avila and Pedro Rodríguez Gutiérrez (Havana: Editora Política, 1984);

En la guerra de España: Crónicas y enunciados, edited by Antonio Merino (Madrid: Ediciones de la Torre, 1988);

Ay, señora, mi vecina (Buenos Aires: Colihue, 1991);

Todas las flores de abril, selected by Juan Nicolás Padrón Barquín (Havana: Letras Cubanas, 1992);

Cuba: En el ala de nuestro tiempo, edited by María Victoria Naya (Havana: Letras Cubanas, 1995);

Cuba's Nicolás Guillén: A Bilingual Anthology, edited by Keith Ellis (Havana: Editorial José Martí, 2003).

Edition in English: *Latin Soul: Poetry Anthology* (San Francisco: Society of Umbra, 1974).

RECORDINGS: *Nicolás Guillén por él mismo,* Montevideo, América Hoy EGL508, 1962;

Los poemas del Gran Zoo, read by Guillén, Montevideo, América Hoy, 1967;

A Reading in Havana, read by Guillén, Washington, D.C., Watershed Foundation C-129, 1979;

Selected Poems, read by Guillén, Guilford, Conn., Jeffrey Norton, 1980;

Nicolás Guillén: Poet Laureate of Revolutionary Cuba, read by Guillén, New York, Folkways FL9941, 1982;

Poesía, read by Guillén, Havana, Centro de Investigaciones Literarias, Casa de las Américas, 1985.

Nicolás Guillén is one of the leading twentieth-century Spanish American poets. His work as an essayist and journalist has also won him acclaim. This work complements his poetry, reinforcing its principal themes and his indisputable opposition to racial discrimination, his championing of the racial and cultural mixtures that form the Cuban nation, and his revulsion at slavery, at its intimate association with colonialism and its kinship with imperialism. He also manifests in his work pride in and loyalty to the Cuban Revolution, and he has written superb love poetry. Because he managed in his poetry over a period of some five decades to treat the salient features of Cuban life, to articulate with consistent wit and grace and in innovative and broadly attractive ways what was on the minds of his progressive compatriots and of others who shared or sympathized with aspects of their experience, he came to be regarded as Cuba's national poet. Cuba bestowed on him its highest honor, the José Martí National Order. Other countries were equally appreciative. Like Pablo Neruda, he was awarded the Lenin Peace Prize by the Soviet Union. Literary critics and fellow writers in many countries nominated him for the Nobel Prize in literature. He was elected president of the Union of Writers and Artists of Cuba upon its founding in 1961 and held that position for the rest of his life. At a national symposium on his work convened in his native Camagüey to commemorate his eighty-seventh birthday, he was awarded the Maurice Bishop Prize, the only significant regional award he had not already held, by Casa de las Américas, the Havana-based institution that promotes cultural activities in the Caribbean and Latin America. His poetry, much of which has been set to music, is sung and recited by people worldwide and has been translated into more than thirty languages.

Nicolás Cristóbal Guillén was born in Camagüey on 10 July 1902 (some seven weeks after the establishment of the Republic of Cuba), the eldest of six children of Nicolás Guillén y Urra and Argelia Batista y Arrieta. His parents, both of them descendants of Africans and Spaniards, were well established in Camagüey.

His father served as editor of a local newspaper, *Las Dos Repúblicas* (The Two Republics), and was a leader of the Partido Liberal Nacional, which vied with the Partido Republicano Conservador for what local control existed of the nation's political life. The elder Guillén's involvement with the Liberals increased during Nicolás's childhood when he represented Camagüey as a senator and subsequently became editor of the newspaper *La Libertad* (Liberty). This involvement led to his death at the hands of soldiers in 1917, as the consequence of his participation in military action between Liberals and Conservatives, when Mario García Menocal, the Conservative president of the country, refused to step down despite, in the view of the Liberals, losing the elections.

Printing, which Guillén had learned as a hobby from his father, became the means by which he provided financial support for his needy family. His secondary education had to be undertaken in evening classes. The inherited weight of responsibility extended to a role he perceived for himself in elevating the cultural life of Camagüey. His assessment of the trivial manner in which his father lost his life had a profound impact on his political outlook and on his poetry.

He began writing poems in 1916. His first publications appeared in 1919 in the journal *Camagüey Gráfico*. In 1920 he left for Havana to study in the University of Havana's School of Law. Pressing financial needs forced him to abandon his studies and to return (within weeks) to Camagüey, where he continued to earn an income as a printer. At the same time, he wrote a considerable amount of poetry and shared with Vicente Menéndez Roque responsibility for editing the literary section of *Las Dos Repúblicas*. He went back to Havana in 1921; and, though he completed his first year of law school, his lack of genuine interest in that field, which he expressed in poetry, the absence of compatibility with many of his fellow students, chronic financial need, and the feeling that his contribution to cultural life was more assured in Camagüey caused him to abandon his studies and return to that city in 1922. With his brother Francisco he founded the literary journal *Lis*. In addition, he served as an editor of the newspaper *El Camagüeyano* and was a moving force in the city's Círculo de Bellas Artes. He also compiled his early poems for a book that he intended to call "Cerebro y corazón" (Brain and Heart).

Although some of the poems appeared in journals, including *Lis,* the collection remained unpublished until 1965, when it appeared as an appendix to Angel I. Augier's *Nicolás Guillén, Estudio biográfico-crítico* (Nicolás Guillén, Biographical and Critical Study). He wrote no poetry between 1923 and 1927. He decided in 1926 to accept again the challenge of the capital city, where,

thanks to a friend of his late father, he secured a job as a typist in the Ministry of the Interior. Most of the poems he wrote between 1927 and 1931 are published in Guillén's *Obra poética* (Poetic Works, 1972) in the section "Poemas de transición" (Poems of Transition). Several of them, as an indication of his continuing estrangement from Havana, were published originally in provincial journals such as *Orto* in Manzanillo.

His introduction to Gustavo E. Urrutia was decisive for his passage from the transitional stage. Urrutia invited him to contribute to a page devoted to the cultural achievements of the black sector of the Cuban population, "Ideales de una raza" (Ideals of a Race), that Urrutia had been allowed to edit by the newspaper *Diario de la Marina* for one of its weekly supplements. On that page, the first version of the collection that marked the beginning of his principal poetic works, *Motivos de son* (Son Motifs), appeared in 1930. In the eight poems of the definitive edition, Guillén departed from his own previous Modernist-influenced poetry and from the *negrista* poetry practiced by several of his fellow poets, such as Ramón Guirao and José Zacarías Tallet, in which blacks were treated from a European perspective as an exotic presence. Instead he opened a literary window on the reality of the black presence in Cuba.

The Spanish employed in these poems is influenced by the popular musical form, the *son,* and is altered by popular phonetics, representing issues of racism and poverty that beset the society. The poem "Búcate plata" (Go Get Money) is an example:

> Búcate plata,
> búcate plata,
> poqque no doy un paso má.
> etoy a arró con galleta,
> na má.
>
> Yo bien sé cómo etá to,
> pero biejo, hay que comé:
> búcate plata,
> búcate plata,
> poqque me boy a corré
>
> (Go get money,
> go get money,
> for I can't go a step further:
> I'm down to rice and crackers, that's all.
>
> I know very well how things are,
> but man, I've got to eat:
> go get money,
> go get money,
> for I'm going to run away).

The overwhelming sense of hardship—of racial discrimination, hunger, and other ills that arise from

NICOLÁS GUILLÉN

TENGO

Prólogo de
JOSÉ ANTONIO PORTUONDO

EDITORA DEL CONSEJO NACIONAL DE UNIVERSIDADES
UNIVERSIDAD CENTRAL DE LAS VILLAS
1 9 6 4

NICOLAS GUILLÉN (Caricatura por JUAN DAVID)

Frontispiece and title page for Guillén's collection of poems contrasting Cuban society before and after the overthrow of the dictator Fulgencio Batista by rebels under the leadership of Fidel Castro in 1959 (Howard-Tilton Memorial Library, Tulane University)

economic neglect and degradation—in the experience of the characters in *Motivos de son* is made all the more poignant because a common thread among the eight poems is the desire to achieve satisfying love relationships. The contradiction between harsh socio-economic circumstances and this human aspiration is at the root of the dialectic that gives conceptual vigor to the book, especially since the contradiction is an impulse for starting the characters in *Motivos de son* on the course toward their real identity, toward the full realization of their humanity. By addressing the ramifications of this quest in poetic forms that display unsurpassed inventiveness and musicality, based on his people's cultural heritage, Guillén developed a body of works that is firmly tied to the identity of his nation and its major historical event, the Cuban Revolution.

In 1931 the *Diario de la Marina* stopped allowing the publication of "Ideales de una raza," and Guillén contributed to its successor, the page "La marcha de una raza" (The Progress of a Race), edited by Lino Dou, a leading Cuban black patriot and a distinguished veteran of the War of Independence, in the newspaper *El Mundo*. Inevitably, Guillén produced poetry that showed the depth of the passion deriving from the indignation caused by the early loss of his father, as well as his own encounters and those of black people in general with racial prejudice, and the links between all these factors and the febrile national condition, a subject that he had been explaining in prose since 1929. The indignation was heightened by his recognition of a Cuban heritage of uncompromising struggle against oppression and injustice that began with slave rebellions and continued in the arduous quest for independence. Guillén brought the black sector of the Cuban population into the national picture, with images of their real lives and by adapting the *son* for use in an innovative poetic way, as a vehicle to convey their privations and their aspirations.

That he sought to achieve this goal within the concept of patriotism manifested by predecessors such as Juan Gualberto Gómez and Antonio Maceo is made clear as well by some of the themes he developed in his poetry that immediately preceded and followed *Motivos de son*. The poems "Pequeña oda a un negro boxeador cubano" (Little Ode to a Black Cuban Boxer) and "Caña" (Sugarcane), written in 1929 and 1930 and published in his second book, *Sóngoro cosongo* (1931), place race in the context of the imperialistic relations that were sucking the lifeblood from Cuba. The combative content of *Sóngoro cosongo,* including its preface, gave a jolt to those who were reluctant to admit to Cuba's cruel racism despite the country's substantial, though often unacknowledged, mulatto population and culture. At the same time, the book cemented Guillén's friendships in the progressive sector of the country with others who were aware of the book's background of blood and misery, the bitter root from which the poems spring. The simple and powerful poem "Caña," with its charged prepositions, is an example:

El negro
junto al cañaveral.

El yanqui
sobre el cañaveral.

La tierra
bajo el cañaveral

¡Sangre
que se nos va!

(The black man
next to the cane field.

The Yankee
over the cane field.

The land
under the cane field.

Blood
that goes out from us!).

These poems are joined in the book by the assertive expression of the black presence in Cuba, found in the poem "Llegada" (Arrival); by poems that uphold the sagacity of the popular perspective, such as "La canción del bongó" (The Bongo's Song); and by poems that expose the harsh social reality that underlies what might otherwise be seen as colorful local custom, such as "Pregón" (Street Cry).

Racial stratification, social chaos, and economic devastation for the large base of an exploited workforce, all under the governance of unrelenting imperialist greed and arrogance, are intensely exposed in *West Indies, Ltd.* (1934). The focus of the collection is on Cuba, but the scope of Guillén's concern now extends to other Caribbean islands. The intensity of this poetry owes much to the vast array of expressive devices the poet has employed in this book: from the insertion of the *son* into poems with conventional verse forms, as in the poem "West Indies, Ltd.," to the intromission of

Parnassian traits into his Alexandrine sonnet "El abuelo" (The Grandfather), to the African-sounding *jitanjáforas* (nonsense words) in his richly allegorical poem "Sensemayá."

Guillén's "Cantos para soldados" (Songs for Soldiers), published together with his "Sones para turistas" (*Sons* for Tourists) in 1937, bears the dedication "A mi padre, muerto por soldados" (To my father, killed by soldiers). The poet demonstrates in the book how a firm ideological position nurtures the transformation of a personal tragedy into a revolutionary national cause. The didactic thrust of poems such as "Soldado, aprende a tirar" (Soldier, Learn to Shoot) and "No sé por qué piensas tú" (I Don't Know Why You Think)—his determination to make of the soldier a comrade—is strengthened and rendered all the more memorable by the unsurpassed musicality Guillén achieves in his poetry.

In all these works Guillén masterfully creates a protean synthesis of African motifs, working-class concerns, and traditional Spanish poetry within a new Caribbean poetic mold that is musical and revolutionary. Some critics, whom Guillén called in *Prosa de prisa* "urgentes y apresurados" (urgent and hasty), have emphasized what they call the Afro-Cuban—playful, hypnotic, or folkloric—aspects of his poetry. G. R. Coulthard, for example, has summarized Guillén's poetic world as consisting of Afro-Cuban folkloric elements such as dancing, drumming, and alcoholic frenzy (he mentions "La balada del güije" [The Ballad of the Guije] and "Sensemayá") and poems of social and racial protest. Even in the latter, Coulthard states, one finds Afro-Cuban mannerisms: rhythmic repetitions of words and racy turns of speech. This emphasis on Afro-Cuban elements is the result of a superficial reading that distorts Guillén's contribution and prevents a clear understanding of the national and universal scope of the social, political, and revolutionary focus of his work. Guillén himself has insistently rejected the concept "Afro-Cuban," pointing out that there is no corresponding usage of the term "Spanish-Cuban" and that the Cuban nation is in fact "Afro-Spanish."

The fall of the Gerardo Machado dictatorship in 1933 allowed Guillén greater scope for political expression in the following years, but not enough to enable him to keep a job he got in 1935 in the Department of Culture in the Municipality of Havana, from which he was dismissed for political activities. He served on the editorial board of the journal *Resumen,* an organ of the Cuban Communist Party. In 1936 he began to serve on the editorial board of the journal *Mediodía;* and, as the journal grew in importance and in conflict with the government, he emerged as its director. In 1937 he attended the Congress of Writers and Artists in Mexico and while there arranged for the publication of *Cantos para soldados y sones para turistas* and wrote *España: Poema en cuatro angustias y una esperanza* (Spain: A Poem in Four Anguishes and One Hope), which was also published that year. The centrality of ideology becomes evident again in this latter book. Unlike his peers, such as the Chilean Neruda and the Peruvian César Vallejo, Guillén wrote and published his book of poetry dealing with the Spanish Civil War before he went to Spain. He well understood the political context, including its relationship to the Cuban situation; and, anticipating the characteristics of the hostilities, he exhorted his allies optimistically. The lament for Cuba continues in *El son entero: Suma poética 1929–1946* (The Entire Son: Collected Poetry, 1947), in poems such as "Mi patria es dulce por fuera . . ." (My Country Is Sweet on the Outside . . .), along with a reaffirmation of authentic Cuban values, as in the coherently integrative "Son No. 6" (*Son No. 6*). *El son entero* also includes love poems, such as "Rosa, tú melancólica" (You Melancholy Rose).

In the late 1940s and early 1950s a variety of circumstances prompted Guillén to write a succession of elegies. He based six great elegies on the deaths of two of his dearest friends, Jesús Menéndez and Jacques Roumain (the former by murder, the latter from a condition brought on by his imprisonment); the lynching of Emmett Till in Mississippi in 1955; his reflections on the loss of the name he should have inherited from his African forebears; nostalgia for the Camagüey of his intimate associations during his period of exile; and a lament for the condition of Cuba.

Guillén was on a lecture tour in Latin America when, on 26 July 1953, Fidel Castro led a group of young Cuban patriots in an attack on a prime pillar of the Fulgencio Batista dictatorship's repressive structure, the Moncada military barracks in Santiago de Cuba. Having been arrested twice in 1952 for his political activities, Guillén could not return to Cuba from Brazil. Thus began for him a long and difficult period of exile that ended only with the triumph of the revolution in 1959.

As his book *La paloma de vuelo popular* (The Dove of Popular Flight, 1958) shows, Guillén's poetry benefited from the hardships of exile. In the first place, in poems such as "Epístola" (Epistle), "Exilio" (Exile), and "Tres poemas mínimos" (Three Tiny Poems), he finds various innovative and imaginative ways to speak of nostalgia, of longing, of uselessness, of desperate impatience. A characteristic of Guillén's poetry in the pre-revolutionary period is his use of the future tense to indicate a time when the servile attitude of Cuba, pictured in the poem "Un largo lagarto verde" (A Long Green Lizard) in *La paloma de vuelo popular,* will be no more. The experience of exile now makes liberation all the more urgently desired, so that the new sun mentioned in "Arte poética" (Poetic Art), the initial poem of *La paloma de vuelo popular,* will shine. He also indicates, with the technical diversity afforded by his poetic mastery, that he keenly desires that this new sun shine as well in countries such as Kenya, Puerto Rico, Paraguay, and Guatemala, even as he salutes its splendor in China.

La Paloma de vuelo popular was published in Buenos Aires in December 1958, less than a month before Batista and his henchmen fled from Cuba on 1 January 1959 in the face of the advancing rebel army. Guillén returned to Cuba on January 23 from Argentina, where he had finally found exile after his long, uncomfortable stay in France. His first public poetry reading was at the invitation of Che Guevara, to soldiers of the recently victorious rebel army at La Cabaña Fortress in Havana, where Guevara was in command and presided at the event.

The contrast between the old society and the incipient but, from the point of view of the poet, definitive new society is a major theme in *Tengo* (1964; translated as *I Have,* 1974), Guillén's first book of poetry of the new epoch. Poems such as "Allá lejos" (Back Then) and "Cualquier tiempo pasado fue peor" (All Past Times Were Worse) tell of the humiliations that touched broad sections of life in the neocolonial period. Poems such as "Se acabó" (It's Over) and "Tengo" celebrate change; the summarizing lines of each poem—"Se acabó" ends with "Vino Fidel y cumplió / lo que prometió Martí" (Fidel came and carried out / what Martí had told us about) and "Tengo" concludes: "tengo lo que tenía que tener" (I have what I had to have)—are illustrative of Alfred Melon's characterization of Guillén, in his essay for *Tres ensayos sobre Nicolás Guillén* (Three Essays on Nicolás Guillén, 1980), as "poeta de la síntesis" (poet of synthesis). All is not indignant recollection or celebration in this book, however. History continues, and a variety of vengeful measures taken by the old occupiers, ranging from the forging of a so-called alliance for progress to the invasion of the homeland, are rebuffed in poems of informed wit, of sometimes mordant sarcasm, and of deep solemnity at other times. The collection signals Guillén's welcoming of the opportunity to display the scope of his poetic powers.

In 1964, Guillén also published a small collection of love poems, *Poemas de amor.* Two years later, he wrote *En algún sitio de la primavera: Elegía* (In Some Springtime Place: Elegy), which was privately published in 1966. Intense, warm, mature, intellectual, and earnestly conversational, *En algún sitio de la primavera* elucidates the whole body of Guillén's poetry, revealing the pervasiveness in it of love poetry; the poems of *Motivos de son,* for example, are also love poems, although not dealing with the sentiments of an "I" that speaks for the author, as happens with the love poems that are dispersed throughout *El son entero*. The depth of the passion in most of his love poems alerts readers to the fact that his love for all struggling humanity is the mainspring of his poetry: love for his ancestors and their fellow beings who suffered the unspeakable atrocities of slavery and, subsequently, the deprivations caused by racial discrimination; love for the broader Cuban community that suffered the brutality of colonialism and the humiliations and strictures of neocolonialism. He extends the sympathy internationally to other similar sufferers. Besides, in the newly published love poetry, Guillén displays an overt dimension of literariness that gives immediate breadth to his poetry. Guillén frequently refers to the works of other poets as sources of reinforcement and debate, enriching his own work and enhancing his poetic stature. Surprising, for instance, because they have been overlooked for so long, are his extensive ties to Rubén Darío, to Gustavo Adolfo Bécquer, and to Dante, in addition to his Golden Age ties.

In fact, Guillén's penchant for innovation has always had as its concomitant an awareness of the state of poetry. This relationship is more visible in the period of the triumph of the revolution because of the freedom he evidently feels to infuse his work with the spirit of the new reality. In 1959, in the weekly *Lunes de Revolución,* he published "El Caribe" (The Caribbean), the first of the poems that make up *El Gran Zoo* (1967; translated in *¡Patria o Muerte! The Great Zoo and Other Poems,* 1972). Guillén, as distinct from Jean de La Fontaine, Guillaume Apollinaire, Neruda, or Jorge Luis Borges, employs a concept of the bestiary in which each poem features a social phenomenon, presented in concise allegorical form, with sharp wit.

Guillén's sensitivity to developments that have an impact on the well-being and emotions of the Cuban people led him to publish in his next book of poetry, *La rueda dentada* (The Gear Wheel, 1972), works that deal with a variety of issues of contemporary times, giving them enduring significance. The murder of Guevara in Bolivia occasioned three poems in which in different styles he presents images of the impact of his death on himself, Bolivia, and the international community. These poems can be linked to the 1959 sonnet "Che Guevara," in which Guillén salutes the Argentine for his complete devotion to the Cuban cause. Martin Luther King Jr. also receives Guillén's tribute, as does radical black activist Angela Davis. Cuban values, personified for example by the poet Nancy Morejón, are extolled, while present-day lapses in historical judgment that allow the horrors of slavery to be overlooked are excoriated in "Noche de negros junto a la Catedral"

Paperback cover for Guillén's 1967 collection of poems, in which he uses the bestiary form to examine a variety of social phenomena (Jean and Alexander Heard Library, Vanderbilt University)

(Night of Blacks Next to the Cathedral). The sense of stern disapproval is made retrospective in "Burgueses" (Bourgeois People), as he recalls the oppression and penury imposed on the large masses of his compatriots by the selfish privileged class.

In *La rueda dentada* Guillén demonstrates once more, in a variety of works revealing instances of satisfaction and vigilance, how the postrevolutionary period provided the opportunity for elevated artistic achievement, particularly in the poems that deal with art itself. Yet, in this period he never withdrew from journalism, and his three-volume *Prosa de prisa, 1929–1972* (Hurried Prose, 1929–1972), published in 1975–1976, reveals the constant interest in and incisive understanding of social and political history that have coincided with and nurtured his poetic career. His other book of 1972, *El diario que a diario* (translated as *The Daily Daily,* 1989), is in several senses a culmination and synthesis of his total expression and ideological vision. Poetry and journalism are wedded in this book, the format of which parodies the Cuban newspaper of times past. It carries representative news items, official proclamations, and a wide range of advertisements and society notes, all presented with a sharp irony and satire that expose the weaknesses of Cuban colonial and neocolonial society from the beginning of Spanish rule to the flight of Batista and the triumph of the revolution. This large historical span and the diverse social strata treated allow Guillén to display a broad expressive range, from the quaintly anachronistic to the raucously colloquial. Guillén broadens his formal procedures by combining narrative, journalistic, and poetic arts with a deftness that owes a great deal to his versatile and at the same time economical means of producing irony and satire and to his unerring judgment in selecting from his array of techniques those best suited to conveying a mature vision based on a profound and many-faceted knowledge of the history of his country.

Guillén demonstrates further the enlarged scope the revolution has afforded for creativity in his final book of poems, *Por el mar de las Antillas anda un barco de papel: Poemas para niños mayores de edad* (A Paper Boat Sails Along the Antillean Sea: Poems for Older Children, 1977). Here, with exquisite simplicity, he develops allegories about a new world, a new person, new ties and responsibilities, new courage, and new strength.

Guillén is acclaimed as the national poet of his country not only because he deals with the salient aspects of Cuban life but also–as is the case with other national poets, the Russian Aleksandr Sergeevich Pushkin, for example–he reflects the essential character of his people. The term "negative capability" is well known in literary studies to refer to a prominent tendency to passivity on the part of poets out of which they may be jolted by an event or object into producing a poem. Guillén's capacity for indignation has nothing to do with passivity. As with the long line of Cuban heroes, extending from the sixteenth-century participants in slave revolts to nineteenth-century agitators for independence such as Félix Varela and the heroes of the independence struggle such as Martí and Maceo, indignation is a pronounced and positive quality in Guillén. Indignation is at the root of the motivation to effect real change, to be uncompromising concerning the will to put an end to injustice and to prevent its recrudescence. Guillén's capacity for indignation is the twin of his capacity for love, and it underlies the strength and power of the imagery of Guillén's poetry and its connectedness with the poet's compatriots, among whom the spirit of the heroes is widely dispersed.

Communicativeness is at once another Cuban trait and a central characteristic of Guillén's poetry. His

is a dramatic, dialogic, conversational poetry in which the poetic "I" is wont to engage a "you" with imaginative propositions or to base itself on verifiable knowledge that spans the disciplines. This poetry is characterized by wit and attractive music. T. S. Eliot, in his 1942 essay "The Music of Poetry," observed that "the music of poetry . . . must be a music latent in the common speech of its time." Guillén's poetry reflects this observation and is further favored by the fact that, in his case, some of the music in the common speech had already made its way into popular song, principally the *son,* which he incorporates into his poetry. All of these qualities allow him to communicate powerfully with his people.

The atrocity that was slavery lasted in Cuba for more than 350 years, during which generation after generation of black human beings enjoyed absolutely no rights and suffered many abuses. The pain of this historical memory had a strong impact on Guillén's poetry, which displays the firm resolve that in no guise whatsoever will slavery, which for him came to entail institutional racism, national powerlessness, and absence of sovereignty, ever again afflict his country and his people.

In this context, love figures in two principal ways, revealing Guillén's powerful humanist bent. In the first place, there is his profound sympathy for those, including the characters of *Motivos de son,* who were for so long deprived of the conditions in which they could express and find contentment in the crowning emotion of romantic love. Secondly, in the love poetry in which he expresses a personal pining after an absent or lost love, a level of desperation is shown that is not surpassed in Western poetry. What is more, as is demonstrated in *En algún sitio de la primavera,* the plenitude of the enjoyment of love is associated with the triumphant revolution. For Guillén love and social justice are indispensable human necessities.

Throughout his poetry Guillén emphasizes the value of clarity, of frankness, as in his self-characterization in the poem "Crecen altas las flores" (The Flowers Are Growing Tall), from *Tengo:*

Pero que no me vengan con cuentos de camino,
pues yo no sólo pienso, sino además opino

en alta voz y soy antes que nada un hombre
a quien gusta llamar las cosas por su nombre

(But don't come to me with tall stories instead of news,
for I not only think, I also give my views

out loud and I am first of all a man,
and call a spade a spade I can).

His condemnation of North American behavior in the poem "Allá lejos" is similarly blunt:

Como y por qué
cegaron su propio pueblo y le arrancaron la lengua.
Como y por qué
no es fácil que éste nos vea y divulgue nuestra simple verdad

(How and why
they blinded their own people and plucked out their tongues.
How and why
it isn't easy for their people to see us and spread our simple truth).

In the poem "Canta el sinsonte en el Turquino" (The Mockingbird Sings in the Turquino) from 1960 he vigorously bids "adiós" to a list of United States leaders, which he calls an "animal muchedumbre" (gang of beasts), who had meddled in Cuban affairs. He concludes by saying "–Buenos días, Fidel. / Buenos días, bandera; buenos días, escudo . . ." (–Good morning, Fidel. / Good morning, flag; good morning, coat of arms . . .). The positive pole of this antithesis represents enormous fulfillment, which for Guillén continued through *Por el mar de las Antillas anda un barco de papel*. In this book his sense of fulfillment was expressed ultimately in the poem "Fidel."

Arteriosclerosis and Parkinson's disease took a heavy toll on Guillén's health during the last four years of his life. Upon his death on 16 July 1989 the Cuban people went into mourning for their national poet. Thousands of them filed past his body which lay in state at the base of the José Martí Monument in Havana's Revolution Square. The Cuban flag, wreaths sent by President Fidel Castro and Vice President Raúl Castro, and the many medals and distinctions awarded to him during his lifetime were among the objects surrounding his coffin. His body was accompanied by thousands of mourners to the Colón Cemetery in Havana where then minister of culture, Armando Hart, gave the eulogy. Guillén was accorded military honors before being buried in the Revolutionary Armed Forces pantheon. The acclaim his work continues to receive was evident in the broad international participation in the academic and popular recognition in 2002 of the centenary of his birth. Years after his death he is still regarded by Cubans as their national poet.

Bibliography:

María Luisa Antuña and Josefina García-Carranza, *Bibliografía de Nicolás Guillén* (Havana: Insituto Cubano del Libro, 1975).

References:

Angel I. Augier, *Nicolás Guillén: Estudio biográfico-crítico* (Havana: Unión de Escritores y Artistas de Cuba, 1965);

G. R. Coulthard, *Race and Colour in Caribbean Literature* (London & New York: Oxford University Press, 1962), pp. 34–35;

Roberto Márquez, Alfred Melon, and Keith Ellis, *Tres ensayos sobre Nicolás Guillén* (Havana: Ediciones Unión, 1980).

Papers:

Nicolás Guillén's papers are held by the Fundación Nicolás Guillén (the Nicolás Guillén Foundation).

Vicente Huidobro
(10 January 1893 – 2 January 1948)

Cedomil Goic
Pontificia Universidad Católica de Chile

BOOKS: *Ecos del alma* (Santiago: Imprenta y Encuadernación Chile, 1912);

La gruta del silencio (Santiago: Imprenta Universitaria, 1913);

Canciones en la noche (Santiago: Imprenta y Encuadernación Chile, 1913);

Pasando y pasando: Crónicas y comentarios (Santiago: Imprenta y Encuadernación Chile, 1914);

Las pagodas ocultas (Santiago: Imprenta Universitaria, 1914);

Adán (Santiago: Imprenta Universitaria, 1916);

El espejo de agua (Buenos Aires: Biblioteca Orión, 1916 [i.e., 1918]);

Horizon carré (Paris: Paul Birault, 1917);

Ecuatorial (Madrid: Pueyo, 1918);

Poemas árticos (Madrid: Pueyo, 1918); translated by William Witherup and Serge Echeverria as *Arctic Poems* (Santa Fe: Desert Review Press, 1974);

Tour Eiffel, illustrated by Robert Delaunay (Madrid: Pueyo, 1918);

Hallali: Poème de guerre (Madrid: Jesús López, 1918);

Saisons choisies (Paris: La Cible, 1921);

Finis Britannia: Une redoutable société secrète s'est dressée contre l'impérialisme anglais (Paris: Fiat Lux, 1923);

Automne régulier (Paris: Librairie de France, 1925);

Tout à coup (Paris: Au sans Pareil, 1925);

Manifestes (Paris: Editions de la Revue Mondiale, 1925);

Vientos contrarios (Santiago: Nascimento, 1926);

Mio Cid Campeador: Hazaña (Madrid: Compañía Ibero Americana de Publicaciones, 1929); translated as *Portrait of a Paladin* (London: Eyre & Spottiswoode, 1931; New York: Liveright, 1931; revised edition, Santiago: Ediciones Ercilla, 1942);

Mirror of a Mage, translated by Warre B. Wells (London: Eyre & Spottiswoode, 1931; Boston: Houghton Mifflin, 1931); original Spanish version published as *Cagliostro: Novela-film* (Santiago: Zig-Zag, 1934; revised, 1942);

Altazor (Madrid: Compañía Ibero Americana de Publicaciones, 1931); translated by Eliot Weinberger

Vicente Huidobro (Fundación Vicente Huidobro)

as *Altazor, or, A Voyage in a Parachute (1919): A Poem in VII Cantos* (St. Paul, Minn.: Graywolf, 1988);

Temblor de cielo (Madrid: Plutarco, 1931; revised edition, Santiago: Cruz del sur, 1942);

Gilles de Raiz (Paris: Totem, 1932);

Presentaciones (Barcelona, 1932);

Tremblement de ciel (Paris: l'As de Cœur, 1932);

La próxima: Historia que pasó en poco tiempo más (Santiago: Walton, 1934);

Papá, o, El diario de Alicia Mir (Santiago: Walton, 1934);

En la luna: Pequeño guiñol en cuatro actos y trece cuadros (Santiago: Ercilla, 1934);

Tres novelas ejemplares, by Huidobro and Hans Arp (Santiago: Zig-Zag, 1935);

Sátiro; o, El poder de las palabras (Santiago: Zig-Zag, 1938);

Ver y palpar (Santiago: Ercilla, 1941);

El ciudadano del olvido (Santiago: Ercilla, 1941);

Ultimos poemas (Santiago: Ahués, 1948);

Textos inéditos y dispersos, edited by José Alberto de la Fuente (Santiago: Dirrección de Bibliotecas Archivos y Museos, Centro de Investigaciones Diego Barros Arana, 1993);

Salle XIV: Vicente Huidobro y las artes plásticas (Madrid: Museo Nacional Centro de Arte Reina Sofía, 2001).

Editions: *Antología,* edited by Eduardo Anguita (Santiago: Zig-Zag, 1945);

Obras completas, 2 volumes (Santiago: Zig-Zag, 1964);

Obras completas, 2 volumes (Santiago: Andrés Bello, 1976);

Altazor de puño y letra, 2 volumes, edited by Andrés Morales (Santiago: Banco del Estado de Chile, 1999);

Atentado celeste: Facsimilares (Santiago: DIBAM/LOM, 2001);

En mares no nacidos: Obra selecta (1916–1931), edited by Saúl Yurkievich (Barcelona: Círculo de Lectores, 2001).

Editions in English: *Relativity of Spring: Thirteen Poems,* translated by Michael Palmer and Geoffrey Young (Berkeley, Cal.: Sand Dollar, 1976);

The Selected Poetry of Vicente Huidobro, edited by David M. Guss, translated by Guss and others (New York: New Directions, 1981);

The Poet Is a Little God: Creationist Verse, translated by Jorge García-Gómez (Riverside, Cal.: Xenos, 1990);

Manifestos manifest, translated by Gilbert Alter-Gilbert (Copenhagen & Los Angeles: Green Integer, 1999).

OTHER: *Indice de la nueva poesía americana,* edited by Huidobro, Alberto Hidalgo, and Jorge Luis Borges (Buenos Aires: El Inca, 1926);

Antología de poesía chilena nueva, edited by Eduardo Anguita and Volodia Teitelboim, includes poems by Huidobro (Santiago: Zig-Zag, 1935).

Vicente Huidobro is the founding father of the Latin American and Spanish literary avant-garde move-

ments of the twentieth century. As early as 1918 he began publishing the most strikingly innovative poetry in the Spanish language. He participated in the French avant-garde, identifying himself with the group of the literary magazine *Nord-Sud* (North-South, allusive to the Paris subway line of that name), which he helped to finance, a group composed of poets such as Guillaume Apollinaire, Pierre Reverdy, Paul Dermée, Blaise Cendrars, Max Jacob, and André Breton. He wrote in French *Horizon carré* (Square Horizon, 1917), *Tour Eiffel* (Eiffel Tower, 1918), *Hallali: Poème de guerre* (Hallali: War Poem, 1918), *Saisons choisies* (Chosen Seasons, 1921), *Automne régulier* (Regular Autumn, 1925), *Tout à coup* (Suddenly, 1925), and *Tremblement de ciel* (Heavenquake, 1932), as well as the long poem "Le passager de son destin" (The Passenger of His Destiny, 1932), and, most important, the painted poems *Salle XIV* (Room XIV, seen also as allusive to *Sâle,* which in its translation is a reference to the "Dirty Year" of 1914), which he exhibited beginning on 16 May 1922 at the Théâtre Edouard VII in Paris. Together with the members of *Nord-Sud,* Huidobro experimented with new possibilities of spatial poetry, particularly with calligrammatic and ideogrammatic forms. He gave his own original poetics the name Creationism, a mode of poetry emphasizing the autonomy of poetic expression and the systematic use of ungrammatical language, of which the building blocks are what he called "Imágenes creadas, situaciones creadas y conceptos creados (created images, created situations, and created concepts). His poetic theory had affinities with Cubism, rejected Surrealism and its emphasis on automatic writing and unconscious revelation, and developed its own line of conscious construction and creative play within a Romantic conception of the poet and poetic writing. In Spain he developed a following among young Spanish poets, especially Gerardo Diego and Juan Larrea, who became his steadfast friends, and among the Spanish American poets whose poetry was collected in the *Indice de la nueva poesía americana* (Index of the New American Poetry), published in Buenos Aires in 1926 by Huidobro, Alberto Hidalgo, and Jorge Luis Borges.

His books of poems *Ecuatorial* (Equatorial, 1918), *Poemas árticos* (1918; translated as *Arctic Poems,* 1974), *Altazor* (1931; translated as *Altazor, or, A Voyage in a Parachute,* 1988), and *Temblor de cielo* (Heavenquake, 1931) are some of the most original and influential books of poetry within the Spanish-speaking world. He is the founder of avant-garde literature in the Spanish-speaking world and the creator of an innovative poetic language consisting of modern images, poetic modes, and genres and particularly of the modern long poem. In addition to books of poetry, he wrote short and long narratives, dramatic texts, and essays and manifestos

Huidobro; his first wife, Manuela Portales Bello Huidobro; and their children, Manuela and Vicente, en route
to Europe in November 1916 (Collection of the Huidobro family)

and published and directed several literary reviews of the poetic avant-garde: *Création, Vital, Ombligo* (Belly Bottom), *Total,* and *Actual.*

More than half a century after his death Huidobro is seen as the initiator of the Spanish, Spanish American, and Chilean avant-garde movements and as an equal to Apollinaire, Reverdy, Breton, and Paul Eluard. A friend of Pablo Picasso, Juan Gris, Jacques Lipchitz, Hans Arp, and Joan Miró, he benefited from important theoretical exchanges with them, as he did with the composers Erik Satie and Edgard Varèse. Huidobro's painted poems can be counted among his most original contributions to visual poetry.

Vicente García Huidobro Fernández was born 10 January 1893 in Santiago, Chile, the son of Vicente García Huidobro and María Luisa Fernández Bascuñán, belonging to traditional Chilean aristocracy. Educated from early childhood by French and English governesses, Huidobro studied in Santiago at the Jesuit San Ignacio School. At age seventeen he published his first article, "La cuestión social" (The Social Question), in *La Estrella de Andacollo* (The Star of Andacollo, 15 October 1910). Soon after graduating from high school, he married Manuela Portales Bello, with whom he had

four children: Vicente (born 1913), Manuela (born 1914), María Louise (born 1918), and Carmen (born 1922). He studied literature for a while at the University of Chile in Santiago. In 1912 he founded the literary magazine *Musa Joven,* which ran for six issues, and in 1913 *Azul,* which ran for three issues. He published his first book of poetry, *Ecos del alma* (Echoes of the Soul), in 1912, followed by *Canciones en la noche* (Songs in the Night), and *La gruta del silencio* (The Grotto of Silence) in 1913 and *Las pagodas ocultas* (The Hidden Pagodas) in 1914.

These early books mark the first distinct period of Huidobro's poetic career. *Ecos del alma* collects his early compositions written during high school under the supervision of Father Rafael Román S.J., some of them from as early as 1909. The original manuscripts have headers and footers that read JHS and AMDG, the acronyms normally used by the Jesuits. This extensive book includes Romantic compositions, translations, and imitations of Spanish and other European literatures.

The books written by the young Huidobro in 1913–*Canciones en la noche* and *Crepúsculos del jardín*–show him involved in the Modernista and Mundonovista trends. He revived the tradition of visual poetry, or *car-*

mina figurata, which had disappeared from the Spanish-language tradition following the viceregal period of the seventeenth century. Using metrical lines of verse as building blocks, the poet designed three *carmina figurata* with Japanese motifs—"Triángulo armónico" (Harmonic Triangle), "Fresco nipón" (Nipponese Fresco), and "Nipona" (Nipponese)—and one with a Mundonovista motif, "La capilla aldeana" (The Village Chapel), all of which he collected in the section of *Canciones en la noche* titled "Japonerías de Estío" (Japanese Summer Things). He read and imitated *Modernismo* and *Mundonovismo* in its parodic strain, with a twist in the treatment of the motifs common to these literary movements. He remains close, in this respect, to the Argentinean poet Leopoldo Lugones and the Uruguayan Julio Herrera y Reissig, who introduced humor and distance in the configuration of poetic images. Already at this early modernist stage, Huidobro began using "created images," some of which he reproduced verbatim in his Creationist poems of 1917. All these books were written in metrical verses within the Spanish and particularly the *Modernista* poetic preferences of the period. This stage of Huidobro's poetry can be characterized as the appropriation of nineteenth-century poetry.

Las pagodas ocultas, written in poetic prose, was for the most part an appropriation of the new trend of poetic prose initiated by the Spanish American poets Manuel Gutiérrez Nájera and Rubén Darío, but with a new oriental bent related to the extensive influence of Rabindranath Tagore's writing on Spanish American writers. Huidobro refers to this work in Canto 2 of *Altazor,* when the speaker "again" asks "Irías a ser muda que Dios te dio esos ojos" (Were you meant to be mute that God gave you those eyes?) and "Irías a ser ciega que Dios te dio esas manos?" (Were you meant to be blind that God gave you those hands?)—both of which are direct quotations from *Las pagodas ocultas.*

In 1913 he wrote with Gabry Rivas the play *Cuando el amor se vaya* (When Love Is Gone); though unpublished, it was staged in Santiago at the Teatro Palace. In 1914 he collected all the articles he had published as well as some new ones in *Pasando y pasando* (Give and Take). In these essays Huidobro expresses his initial reaction to the Futurist and avant-garde movements as well as to the Chilean, Spanish American, and Spanish poetry of the time, with references to such literary colleagues as Amado Nervo, Rubén Darío, and Pedro Antonio González. The book includes chronicles and essays marking his break with his Jesuit education and with traditional Chilean society, which he denounced as hypocritical. The edition was withdrawn by his grandfather, who had it burned. The same year he delivered the lecture "Non serviam" at the Ateneo de Santiago. In it one finds the first theo-retical statements anticipating his Creationist poetics; he affirms a rebellious attitude against realism and postulates the autonomy of the literary work.

In 1915 he published "Vaguedad subconsciente" (Subconscious vagueness) in the Concepción literary magazine *Ideales;* the poem was announced as part of a forthcoming book, "El canto imperceptible," of which nothing else is known. In June 1916 he traveled to Buenos Aires, taking secretly with him the young poet Teresa Wilms Montt, who had been confined in a convent by her husband. The overt purpose of the trip was to deliver a lecture at the Ateneo Hispano-Americano de Buenos Aires. There, Huidobro met Argentinean writers Leopoldo Lugones and José Ingenieros, as well as the Spanish writers José Ortega y Gasset and Ramón Pérez de Ayala. The magazine *Nosotros* offered a dinner in his honor. In July 1916 his book *Adán* (Adam) was published in Santiago.

Adán represents Huidobro's radical break with the dominant poetic trend of the time and his developing interest in relating poetry to science. In this collection he privileges the immediate impressions of human senses and the individual's sensitivity as an organ of objective perception of the world, men, and women. What becomes important is the poet's unmediated contact with the world, the purity of his primal contact with the facts of experience, unprejudiced by previous knowledge or information. Throughout *Adán* he uses free verse in harmony with the meaning it conveys. Huidobro accompanied this book with a preface in which he underlines the significance of free verse but, more important, the influence of Ralph Waldo Emerson's thought on poetry.

In November 1916 Huidobro moved his family to Europe. In Madrid he met Rafael Cansinos-Asséns and visited Ramón Gómez de la Serna's Pombo's Café. From Madrid the family traveled to Paris, where for the next ten years they resided at 41 rue Victor Massé. During this initial period Huidobro's poetry, provoked and stimulated by the French avant-garde, evolved at a fast pace. Soon after arriving in Paris, he was taken by Pierre Albert-Birot to the *Lyre et Palette* homage to Reverdy, where he met a group of poets that included Apollinaire, Reverdy himself, Eluard, Cendrars, Maurice Raynal, and Jean Cocteau; the painters Picasso, Gris, Georges Braque, and Diego Rivera; the sculptors Lipchitz and Louis Marcoussis; and the composer Satie.

In 1917 Huidobro contributed to the founding and financing of the first ten issues of *Nord-Sud,* a poetry magazine directed by Reverdy. Huidobro published several poems in *Nord-Sud,* that in the same year, 1917, made up the first section of *Horizon carré* (Square Horizon) in the French version, and some of which he would shortly thereafter collect in *El espejo de agua. Poems*

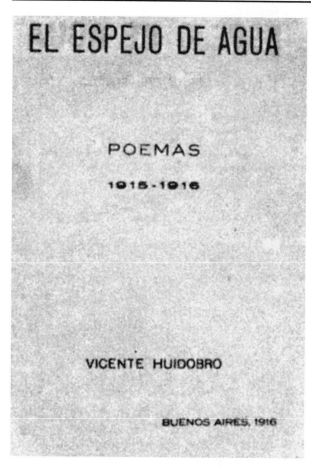

EL ESPEJO DE AGUA

POEMAS

1915-1916

VICENTE HUIDOBRO

BUENOS AIRES, 1916

Paper cover for Huidobro's collection of poems written in an experimental style associated with the French avant-garde journal Nord-Sud. *The book was actually published in 1918 (from René de Costa,* En pos de Huidobro, *1978).*

1915–1916 (Water Mirror: Poems 1915–1916) in Spanish, published in Madrid, 1918. These poems bear an obvious affinity with Reverdy's poetry of the time. Following Reverdy's ideas, punctuation is suppressed and lines of verse are spatially distributed on the page to indicate pauses; all spatial or visual design is avoided. These traits characterize the so-called *Nord-Sud* style.

The first poem Huidobro published in *Nord-Sud* was translated into French by Reverdy; soon he began translating his poems himself in collaboration with Gris. Huidobro's poems were published in issues 2 through 10 of *Nord-Sud* from March through December 1917. For Reverdy, poems in the *Nord-Sud* style were brief poems of imminence, in which closure and openness to the world are signified through the images of houses, rooms, doors, and windows. The poems Huidobro published in *Nord-Sud,* while sharing the qualities of the *Nord-Sud* style, were more strikingly original productions. Self-reflective images, the dyna-

mism of creative consciousness, the sense of the marvelous, and the encounter of two worlds are their dominant and distinguishing traits. "Arte poética," his most-quoted poem, is a metapoetical text that does not formulate poetic wisdom so much as the youthful impulse of a rebellious avant-garde poet who rejects the fixation of Futurism with energy–"muscle"–and antagonistically postulates a revolutionary poetics of "nerves."

> Estamos en el ciclo de los nervios.
> El músculo cuelga,
> Como recuerdo en los museos;
> Mas no por eso tenemos menos fuerza;
> El vigor verdadero
> Reside en la cabeza.
> . . . .
> El poeta es un pequeño Dios
>
> (We are in the cycle of nerves
> Like a memory
> The muscle hangs in the museums;
> Nevertheless, we are no less strong than before:
> True vigor
> Resides in the head.
> . . . .
> The Poet is a little God).

He postulates what can be called "inventionism": "Inventa nuevos mundos y cuida tu palabra; / El adjetivo, cuando no da vida mata" (Invent new worlds and watch your words; / The adjective, when it does not give life, kills). In "inventionism" Huidobbro clearly echoes the expressionist concept of an inner point of view that projects its own forms onto the world. He later modulates this point of view to an intermediate position that highlights the functional origin of language–it originates in the throat, at the midpoint between head and heart. He proclaims the poet to be a "pequeño Dios" (little God), a second-class Creator who makes poetry out of the elements of a preexistent world.

Another determinant of his poetics at this stage is the notion of suggestive art derived from French poet Stéphane Mallarmé, which links *El espejo de agua* to the books he had published in Chile before moving to France. In the poem "El espejo de agua," Huidobro represents the creative imagination as a glass mirror that comes alive at night as a stream of consciousness, the current of which bears along a ship on which the captain stands, a rose miraculously blooming in his breast and a nightingale fluttering its wings on his finger. These poems are often quoted verbatim from some verses in his previous books of 1913.

In another poem, "Año Nuevo" (New Year), Huidobro went into an entirely original modality of Creationism in which he ventured far beyond

Reverdy's more conventional poetics of *Nord-Sud*. The poem describes the communication of two worlds—Jacob's dream becomes a reality, time is characterized as the unrolling of movie film, real life and celluloid images intermingle inside and outside the cinema hall, all at a single point in time (the beginning of 1916):

El sueño de Jacob se ha realizado.
Un ojo se abre ante el espejo
Y las gentes que bajan a la tela
Arrojaron su carne como un abrigo viejo.

La película mil novecientos dieciséis
Sale de una caja

(Jacob's dream is fulfilled;
Before the mirror an eye opens
And the people coming onto the film
Cast away their flesh like old wraps.

The film nineteen hundred and sixteen
Comes out of a box).

Though written in 1916 and in the early months of 1917, *El espejo de agua* was not published until 1918, in three different editions. The first bore the false imprint "Buenos Aires, Colección Orión, 1916"; the second was printed in Madrid; the third was also published in Madrid that same year but used different typography. A 30 June 1920 article by Enrique Gómez Carrillo in *El Liberal* (Madrid) set off a debate on the actual date of publication. Reverdy's mention to Gómez Carillo, printed in this article, of a fraudulently predated edition led to an argument between the two poets that lasted until 1925.

Huidobro moved on to a new phase of Creationism when in 1917 he published *Horizon carré*. This book established his poetic singularity, differentiated him from the French poets of *Nord-Sud,* and in particular marked his break from Reverdy. An epigraphic note at the beginning of the book formulates the new precept: "Crear un poema tomando a la vida sus motivos o transformándolos para darles una vida nueva e independiente. Nada anecdótico ni descriptivo. La emoción debe nacer de la única virtud creadora. Hacer un poema como la naturaleza hace un árbol" (To create a poem by taking the motifs from life and transforming them so as to give them a new and independent life. Nothing anecdotal nor descriptive. Emotion must spring from the one and only creative virtue. To write a poem like Nature makes a tree).

The poems of *Horizon carré* are characterized by their visual effects. Huidobro uses diagonal, vertical, scaled, and curved lines and calligrams (shaped poems) to strikingly contradictory effect in the dialogue between verbal text and visual representation and, with all these printing resources, gave the poems structures that underline textual autonomy and visual effect. The poem "Guitare" disposes the lines of verse in such a way as to draw a guitar. "Matin" shows the sun reaching the four corners of the world. The poems of this book were written at a time when Huidobro was in daily contact with his friend Gris, who helped Huidobro with his French and, particularly, with his theoretical Cubist concepts. Properly speaking, this book represents the Cubist moment of Huidobro's Creationism. Huidobro's break with Reverdy began during this time, related to the fact that he had withdrawn his financing of *Nord-Sud* after the publication of the tenth issue in December 1917.

The Huidobro, Gris, and Lipchitz families spent the summer of 1918 at Beaulieu-près-Loches, near Tours, fleeing the war, which was approaching Paris. On 26 April Huidobro's second daughter, María Luisa, was born. Between June and November of the same year, Huidobro and his family stayed in Madrid, renting an apartment in Plaza de Oriente 6, next to the Teatro Real and across the street from the Royal Palace.

In Madrid he published four books: two in Spanish (*Ecuatorial* and *Poemas árticos*) and two in French (*Hallali* and *Tour Eiffel*). These books were received enthusiastically by the Spanish critic and writer Cansinos-Asséns, who published and translated some of the poems in *Cervantes,* a literary magazine he directed at the time. This reception was echoed in *Cosmópolis* and in several Spanish avant-garde literary magazines. At this time Huidobro became acquainted with the young generation of Spanish poets: Guillermo de Torre, Mauricio Bacarisse, Isaac del Vando Villar, Alfredo Villacián, José Rivas Paneda, Larrea, and Diego. Teresa Wilms Montt was staying in Madrid at the time, as were the French painters Robert and Sonia Delaunay. Huidobro published two poems in the third issue of the magazine *Dada* in 1918: "Cowboy" (illustrated by Arp) and the calligram "Paysage." This last poem, together with "Orage," also from *Horizon carré,* were included later in Richard Huelsenbeck's *Dada Almanach* (1920). Diego and Larrea were Huidobro's most faithful disciples, but many other young poets imitated his Creationist poetry. His personality and poetry inspired Cansinos-Asséns and Torre, who founded the literary movement Ultra. Borges learned the Ultraist poetics in Madrid and brought it to Argentina, where the movement took on a life of its own. Imaginismo (Imagism) in Chile, Simplicismo (Simplicism) in Peru, and Estridentismo (Stridentism) in Mexico were directly or indirectly inspired by Huidobro.

Poemas árticos, Ecuatorial, Tour Eiffel, and *Hallali* are books of a new poetry in which created images, concepts, and situations serve to define a created poem.

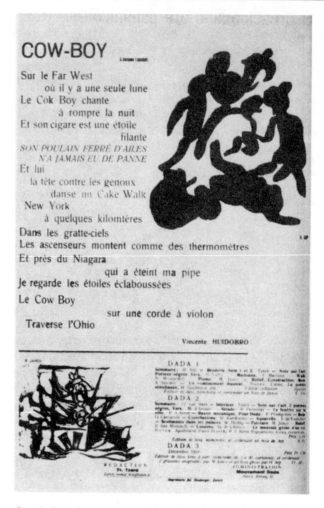

Page from the December 1918 issue of the journal Dada *with a poem by Huidobro*
(*from René de Costa,* En pos de Huidobro, *1978*)

The main aspects of this poetic language are ungrammatical constructions in which nouns and adjectives with contradictory meaning are brought together and sentences are built from contradictory subjects, verbs, and complements, juxtaposing the material and the immaterial, the human and the nonhuman, and the immediate and the distant. These resources provide the poems with an autonomous character. From the point of view of genre, *Poemas árticos* are short lyrics, *Ecuatorial* is a long poem of alienation and "metanoia," or spiritual change, *Hallali* is an elegiac poem, and *Tour Eiffel* is an ode.

Ecuatorial is written as a sequence of two anaphoric models: one of the poetic speaker (*yo, nosotros*) who is a traveler, and the other of the secular world, (*el Siglo*). The matrix of the poem is the speaker's awakening to a new vision of the world and a new poetic consciousness that prophetically envisions the apocalyptic *signa judici,* or signs of the Last Judgment. The poem enunciates the speaker's experience of leaving his homeland for Europe, only to find there the destruction of the world. The allusive content of the poem, centering around the image of Europe destroyed by World War I, points to the disastrous effects of history on the spirit of a traveler who comes from a natural setting devoid of history. *Ecuatorial* is the first example of a Creationist and avant-garde long poem in Spanish. It was imitated by Diego in his poem "Gesta" (Exploit, 1919) and by Larrea in "Cosmopolitano" (Cosmopolitan, 1919).

Poemas árticos is a book of short poems that repeats some of the visual devices found in *Horizon carré*. These elements reappear in three of the poems—"Exprés," "Niño" (Child), and "Vermouth"—but gradually Huidobro abandoned the visual effects in favor of indicating pause and rhythm by means of spacing, blanks, and emphasis (printing entire lines of verse in uppercase). Travel, urban, cosmic, and poetic motifs are systematically transformed by the new poetic consciousness of the Creationist speaker. The poems of this book can be classified according to the presence and the nature of the poetic speaker: tableau poems in which there is neither a pronominal presence nor any representation of the speaker; tableau poems that do include the pronominal presence of the speaker or the addressee; poems in which the speaker is represented as a traveler, explorer, tourist, vagabond, or globe-trotter; and poems in which the speaker is represented as a feathered bird or as a crucified or wounded poet.

Huidobro's bilingualism can be appreciated in the six books he wrote and published in French from 1917 to 1932. Besides *Horizon Carré*, he published *Hallali*, a collection of five short poems that center on the experience of World War I: imminent danger, expectation, terror, hope, and the threat of war on city dwellers. *Tour Eiffel*, a poem printed on four pages of different colors—blue, green, pink, and beige—is a panegyric to the Eiffel Tower in a series of superimposed eulogistic images that exalt its form, function, and magnitude. Illustrated by Robert Delaunay, this book is Huidobro's poetic response to Delaunay's series of paintings of the tower.

Toward the end of 1919 the poet and his family traveled to Chile to attend the wedding of Huidobro's sister, Carmen, to the Chilean poet Diego Dublé Urrutia. He traveled to the south of Chile in a ritualistic trip before returning to Paris with his family. On his return to Europe he made a stop in Madrid, where he gave the first news about the writing of his poem *Altazor*—or "Voyage en parachute," as it was initially known—as he recounted in an interview with Cansinos-Asséns in *La Correspondencia de España*.

In 1920 Huidobro returned to Paris, where he published articles and poems in *L'Esprit Nouveau* (The New Spirit), an important magazine directed by Paul Dermée, which had Amedée Ozenfant and Le Corbusier among its regular collaborators; *La Bataille Littéraire* (The Literary Battle); *L'Action; Le Coeur à Barbe* (The Bearded Heart); *La vie des Lettres* (The Life of Letters); and the Spanish literary reviews *Cervantes, Grecia, Tableros,* and *Ultra*. In 1921 he published *Saisons choisies*, the only anthology he published of his own poems in French. The book includes a portrait of the poet by Picasso. *Saisons choisies* collects poems from his previous books, as well as five poems that later appear in *Automne régulier*. Also in *Saisons choisies* is "Miroir d'eau," the French version of "El espejo de agua," a poem he had not included in *Horizon carré*, where he had replaced it with an entirely new poem on the same subject, "Glace." This anthology is particularly important because it shows the four stages through which Huidobro's Creationism had evolved.

Returning to Spain in December, Huidobro gave a lecture on modern aesthetics at the Ateneo de Madrid, where Bacarisse presented him to the audience. He met personally with Larrea and Diego and published two issues of his new magazine, *Creación,* in Madrid in April 1921 and in Paris in November. In 1922 he delivered lectures on his aesthetics in Paris, Berlin, and Stockholm. In May of that year, Varèse, an avant-garde composer and friend of Huidobro's, released in New York his "Chanson de là-haut," based on an excerpt from *Tour Eiffel*. His daughter Carmen, the fourth of his children, was born in Paris on 9 July 1922. At the time he collaborated with Sonia Delaunay on a dress-poem, "Corsage," of which the designer embroidered only the first line on a blouse: "Petite chanson pour abriter le cœur" (Small song to warm the heart).

The most important event of Huidobro's career in 1922 was the exhibition of painted poems, *Salle XIV,* at the foyer of the Théâtre Edouard VII. The exhibition provoked harsh reactions from the public on account of the singular character of the painted poems. Of the original thirteen works only ten are extant. The verbal texts of the other three are known but not their final visual form. The painted poem establishes a dialogue between verbal and visual contents in which the verbal aspect does not find a strict correspondence with the visual one. "Paysage," a painted version of the poem in *Horizon carré,* presents a mountain so large that it exceeds the limits of the earth, a tree taller than the highest mountain, the moon as a mirror in which one can see one's reflection, and a written warning not to step on the grass recently painted. Dimensionality plays a contradictory role, mixing proximity and distance, smallness and immensity, the human and the cosmic. In the case of "Marine," the visual image of waves coming to die at the seashore correlates to lines from the poem the sadness of a sea on the surface of which are no people (*matelots*) and where nothing dramatic happens (*oubliée de naufrages*). The program for the exhibit included a folded flier (which had already been published in 1921) with a reproduction of one of the poems in the exhibition, "Moulin" (Windmill).

In 1923, at age thirty, Huidobro published *Finis Britannia: Une redoutable société secrète s'est dressée contre l'impérialisme anglais* (The End of Britain: A Fearful Secret Society Has Been Established to Oppose English Imperialism) attacking the British Empire and anticipating the process of decolonization. In connection with this publication, the poet apparently staged his own kidnapping, which was extensively reported in the French press.

Juan Emar translated and published Huidobro's preface to *Altazor* in his "Notas de Arte" in the Santiago

Manuscript for Huidobro's French translation of his poem "automne," with revisions by his friend,
the Spanish painter Juan Gris (Collection of the Huidobro family)

newspaper *La Nación* (29 April 1925). It was clear then that the poet was writing the poem in two versions, one in Spanish, the other in French; because of his bilingualism Huidobro considered publishing his entire output in Spanish and French. In the poem "Anuncio" (Announcement), written in 1931 and collected in 1945, the heroes Altazor and Isolda appear together. Huidobro later devoted a separate book to each of these characters.

In 1925 Huidobro published two books of poetry, *Automne régulier* and *Tout à coup,* as well as *Manifestes* (Manifestos), which defined his own theoretical stance, in opposition to that of the recently published *Manifeste du surréalisme* (Surrealist Manifesto, 1924) by André Breton. Although he maintained his friendship with Breton and the Surrealist poets, he was strongly opposed to the significance they attributed to the roles of the unconscious and the haphazard, to gratuitous action, and to madness, and he favored the classic sense of poetic

delirium as a creative state of superconsciousness. No other Spanish American poet has a metapoetic discourse so lucid or coherent, and of the magnitude of, Huidobro's manifestos. He continued his practice of publishing brief and long manifestos until 1935.

Automne régulier and *Tout à coup* were inspired by Huidobro's search of the miraculous, the marvelous, and the unusual. In these books the poet abandons altogether the graphic visual dimension of his poetic writing. Though the book suppresses almost entirely the Mallarméan page composition, *Automne régulier* occasionally uses a line of verse or a word entirely in the uppercase. Here the poet places the lines on the left margin and writes a few indented lines and some tabulated verses. The use of duplicated words, humorous rhymes, and paronomasia anticipate the playful forms of the later books.

The poetic language of *Automne régulier* shows the use of longer and more articulated lines, images prolonged by comparisons or similes, arbitrary connections, semantic discontinuity, and humorous or arbitrary rhymes. One also finds duplication of words and paronomastic figures as well as anaphoric repetition. These resources are new to Huidobro's poetry; they become prominent in *Altazor* and *Ver y palpar* (Seeing and Touching, 1941). The divided or superimposed self appears simultaneously in these poems as a *moi* (me) and a *tu* (you). Huidobro condemned the Surrealists' belief in creative arbitrariness, though he did praise some poems of Tzara and Eluard, poets he often quoted in his essays. Irrationality pervades these poems. The travel and urban motifs, the images of the poet as sailor and as Christ, which are also found in *Poemas árticos* and *Ecuatorial,* are repeated here in modified forms.

Tout à coup is a book of thirty-two poems without titles. One finds here a new kind of poem with no direct precedents in Huidobro's previous books, although the poems bear some relation to the those of *Automne régulier.* They are shorter poems of ascending and descending flight, representing the unusual, the sudden, and the marvelous. The sudden miracle is proposed now as a playful distraction from a tired vision of infinity that dissolves commonplace coherence. An added dimension is the construction of a "sujet d'énonciation" (subject of enunciation), an ambiguous figure who becomes the poetic speaker of what Huidobro calls "divagations," a kind of playful and joyous self-proclamation of his own virtues.

On 4 March 1925 Huidobro made his way back to Chile with his family, mother, and brothers. All of them had traveled to Paris as soon as they had heard of Huidobro's intention to end his marriage. Huidobro remained in Chile until 1927. During this period he became involved in Chilean politics and directed *Acción,* a political magazine, and later, *Reforma.* He was a candidate for the presidency and then a candidate for the Chilean congress. His attitude at this time symbolized the aggressive leadership of the up-and-coming generation and the will for political change.

During his time in Chile, Huidobro published a book of essays and aphorisms, *Vientos contrarios* (Head Winds, 1926), in which he writes:

En mis primeros años toda mi vida artística se resume en una escala de ambiciones. A los diecisiete años, me dije: "Debo ser el primer poeta de América"; luego, al pasar de los años, pensé: "Debo ser el primer poeta de mi lengua". Después, a medida que corría el tiempo, mis ambiciones fueron subiendo y me dije: "Es preciso ser el primer poeta de mi siglo"; y más tarde estudiando la poesía con un amor cada vez más profundo, llegué a convencerme de que la poesía no ha existido jamás y que era necesario constituirnos unos cuantos en verdadera secta para hacerla existir. Lo que se ha llamado poesía hasta hoy es un mezquino comentario de las cosas de la vida y no una creación de nuestro espíritu. Son vanos floreos puestos en torno de las cosas, pero no es la creación de un hecho nuevo inventado por nosotros. El poeta es un pequeño dios. Se trata, pues, de condensar el caos en diminutos planetas de emoción

(My entire artistic life in my early years can be summarized as a scale of ambitions. At seventeen I said to myself: "I must become the first poet of America"; then, after a few years I thought: "I must become the first poet of my language." Later, as time passed by, my ambitions grew and I said to myself: "I need to become the first poet of the century"; much later, studying poetry with an ever deepening love, I convinced myself that poetry has never really existed and that the time had come for some of us to establish a sect in order to allow poetry to come into being. What has been called poetry until now is only a miserable commentary on life experiences and not an authentic creation of our spirit. It has been a vain ornament that we have imposed on things, but not the creation of a new fact invented by us. The poet is a little god. It's about condensing chaos in minute planets of emotion).

Among other things, this book provided information regarding the composition of Canto 5 of *Altazor.* In 1926 some anticipations of the poem can be found in the Santiago literary magazine *Panorama* and in the French *Favorables París Poema,* edited by Larrea and Cesar Vallejo, where two poems were published that later became part of Canto 4 of *Altazor.*

In 1927, after another marriage crisis, Huidobro abandoned his wife and children. He published the poem "Pasión y muerte" (Passion and Death), which makes several allusions to his passion for the eighteen-year-old Ximena Amunátegui. He traveled to New York City, where he met celebrities such as Charles Chaplin, Douglas Fairbanks, and Gloria Swanson. In Hollywood he was awarded a $10,000 prize by the League for Better Motion Pictures for his script titled *Cagliostro,* the story of the self-proclaimed count of Cagliostro, a pseudohistorical character from the eighteenth century who inspired the novel *Joseph Balsamo* (1846–1848) by Alexandre Dumas *père. Cagliostro* was written as a silent movie, however, and plans to produce it were immediately scrapped after the first "talkie," *The Jazz Singer,* was released in October 1927.

Huidobro published some articles in *Vanity Fair* and wrote a poem, "Canto to Lindbergh," that remained unpublished until René de Costa published it in *Poesía* in 1989. In 1928, as soon as Ximena obtained her passport, Huidobro returned incognito to Chile, met her at the door of her high school, and eloped with her to Buenos Aires with her relatives in pursuit. From

La Galerie G. L. Manuel Frères
47, Rue Dumont-d'Urville, 47

Présente au Théâtre Edouard VII
du 16 Mai au 2 Juin

UNE EXPOSITION DE POÈMES
DE
Vincent HUIDOBRO

Vernissage Mardi 16 Mai, de 3 h. à 5 h.
Ce Catalogue tient lieu d'Invitation.

VINCENT HUIDOBRO, par Pablo Picasso

Cover for the 1922 exhibition catalogue of Huidobro's painted poems Salle XIV *(Collection of the Huidobro family)*

there they went to Paris, where Luis Vargas Rozas, a Chilean painter friend of Huidobro's, helped them to get settled. They lived at 16 rue Boissonade.

That same year, in collaboration with Tristan Tzara, Huidobro edited "Feuilles Volantes" (Loose Leaves), the literary section of *Cahiers d'Art*. In 1929, while in Madrid, he published his first version of the novel *Mio Cid Campeador* (translated as *Portrait of a Paladin*, 1931). In Paris he attended the wedding of his friend Juan Larrea and Marguerite Aubry. He and Tzara accompanied the couple on a trip to Chartres.

Another segment of the poem *Altazor* was published in a French version in issue 19–20 of *Transition* (June 1930). While staying at Villa Oriolo, the home of his friend Roberto Suárez in the Italian Alps, he wrote his prophetic novel *La próxima: Historia que pasó en poco tiempo más* (The Next One: a Story That Took Place in the Near Future, 1934), which foretold World War II.

Huidobro went back for a few months to Madrid in 1931, where he contacted his old friends. That same year Bacarisse, who had presented him at the Ateneo de Madrid ten years earlier, died. The Chilean poet wrote some lines in remembrance of his youthful friend. The Spanish writer César González-Ruano, in an interview with Huidobro for *El Heraldo de Madrid* (6 January 1931), referred to him as "el que trajo las gallinas (de los huevos de oro)" (he who brought the hens [of the golden eggs]). Huidobro was honored at a dinner organized by the leading Spanish poets. Federico García Lorca delivered a festive verse salute to the Chilean poet. Later, Huidobro commented generously on the talent of poets such as Luis Cernuda, Vicente Aleixandre, and other members of the Generation of 1927. That year Huidobro published in Madrid *Altazor* and *Temblor de cielo*. These books were announced in the Spanish press, but upon publication they were absolutely ignored by the press and by Spanish critics. They were reviewed for the first time in Santiago in July 1931.

The sublime poetic expression of *Altazor* relates to the fifth and the most important period of Huidobro's Creationism. *Altazor o el viaje en paracaidas* is a poem of flight in seven cantos, which narrates simultaneously an ascensional flight and a fall through seven heavenly regions, an ambiguous voyage representing both death and mystical experience. It is expressed in a variety of poetic languages, beginning with the fullness of meaning and syntactical structure, moving on to the progressively reduced integrity of syntax and the syntagmatic and lexical dimensions, leading finally to the gradual destruction of language as it verges on the unutterable. All through the poem Huidobro uses the many forms introduced by the poetic avant-garde and accomplishes a distinctive imaginative feat. The preface narrates the heavenly experience of Altazor falling in a parachute through the stars and planets, meeting the Creator and the Virgin Mary, representing mixed and extremely different dimensions, and includes a reflection on the meaning of new poetry, life, and death. Altazor is born at age thirty-three, on the day Jesus died, meaning that the poet is a new or reinvented Christ, a point of intersection between time and space whose love is the passion for creativity, miracle, and the marvelous and whose unavoidable fate is to feel an unquenchable thirst for eternity and to be, at the same time, simply a mortal being condemned to die. This conception of the poet is the central Romantic motif of Huidobro's major works.

Temblor de cielo is a prose poem that Huidobro wrote at the same time as *Altazor,* and it is also divided into seven parts or segments. In a letter to César Miró Quesada, Huidobro compared the poem with Isidore Lucien Ducasse, Comte de Lautréamont's *Les Chants de*

Maldoror (1868–1869; translated as *The Lay of Maldoror*, 1924) and Arthur Rimbaud's *Une Saison en enfer* (1874; translated as *A Season in Hell*, 1932) and wrote that he considered the poem to be better constructed than *Altazor*. *Temblor de cielo* deals with the similar subject of infinite aspiration to absolute love as an impulse inscribed in man in his continuous search of perfect love. The mythic argument is that of Tristan and Isolde. The poem unfolds in seven sections out of an introductory meditation on how the individual looks for the fulfillment of absolute love in the erotic possession of the woman he loves. The theme is developed with allusions to Richard Wagner's opera but at the same time follows a strict Creationist path that makes the pursuit of the marvelous, love, and poetry infinite within the limited compass of human existence. A particular dimension of this pursuit is the way in which the poem provides a new foundation for Creationist imagism. In a manner similar to that of the paintings of Salvador Dali or René Magritte, Huidobro creates new objective forms of uncommon images or situations. These range from the image of a killer shooting at people, much like the gratuitous act suggested by the first Surrealist manifesto, to images of visual portents like a flying island or a phantom woman. Of the latter, the poet says: "Ella es el fantasma de piel transparente que no tiene rostro, sino un vacío redondo entre el pelo y el cuello" (She is a phantom of transparent skin, without a face, who has nothing but a round empty space between her hair and her neck). Beginning with the speaker's initial aspiration toward absolute love, the poem progresses toward the experience of the demise of heaven and to the speaker's consciousness of his own death, both events signifying the apocalyptic end of the world.

Also in 1931 the English-language version of *Cagliostro*, titled *Mirror of a Mage*, was published in Boston and London. *Mio Cid Campeador* was translated that year into English as *Portrait of a Paladin*, in Boston and London. In 1931, while spending the summer with Arp in Arcachon, they wrote "Trois nouvelles exemplaires" (Three Exemplary Novellas), which Huidobro included as part of his *Tres novelas ejemplares* (1935). One of his last manifestos, "Total" (1931), appeared in the only issue of the Paris literary review *Vertigral* in 1932, edited by Eugène Jolas, in which Arp and Georges Perlorson also collaborated.

Later in 1932 Huidobro published in Paris a play, *Gilles de Raiz*, and *Tremblement de ciel*, his French version of *Temblor de cielo*, with a reproduction of his portrait by Gris. He spent the summer in Cadaquès on Mallorca with Arp and his wife, Sophie Tauber-Arp. In November of that year, the international financial crisis hit the family business, and he stopped receiving financial assistance from home. As a result Huidobro moved back to Chile with Ximena. He left Barcelona after an emotional farewell from his friends Diego and Larrrea. He left them copies of his painted poems as gifts. He took with him four nightingales, hoping to acclimatize them in Chile, but they died soon after their arrival.

Back in Santiago, he settled at San Ignacio 56 and later at Cienfuegos 33-A, where he received the young poets of the time. He participated regularly in literary meetings at the Librería Julio Walton. He published another of his avant-garde literary magazines, *Ombligo*, of which only one issue was ever published.

In 1933 part of *Gilles de Raiz* was staged at the Théâtre de L'Œuvre in Paris. He published "Manifiesto a la juventud de América" (Manifesto to the American Youth) in the Barcelona journal *Europa* (September 1933), proposing the creation of a confederation of South American states to be named Andesia. That same year, his wife, Ximena, reported to Larrea that Huidobro suffered a serious concussion to the head while attempting a somersault. By May he appeared to have fully recovered. In December an exhibit of the works of a group of young painters who became known as "Decembristas" (Gabriela Rivadeneira, María Valencia, Jaime Dvor, Waldo Parraguez, and Carlos Sotomayor) included artistic transpositions of poems of Huidobro.

In 1934 Ximena gave birth in Santiago to their son, Vladimir. Huidobro collaborated in a new magazine, *Pro*, which published several issues. He also turned his attention to writing novels. In that year alone he published several novels in Spanish. The first was *Cagliostro*, which Huidobro had made into what he called a "novela-film." His next novel, *Papá, o, El diario de Alicia Mir* (Dad, or Alicia Mir's Diary), is allusive in a general way but not in the details to the crisis and separation of Huidobro from his first wife. It takes the form of the personal diary of a daughter who identifies herself intensely with her father's sensibility and whose passionate feeling of empathy for him structures her inner world. *La próxima* is an ecological and a prophetic novel. He also published that year a political farce, *En la luna: Pequeño guiñol en cuatro actos y trece cuadros* (On the Moon: Small Satirical Play in Four Acts and Thirteen Scenes). Around the same time in 1934, Manuela Portales Bello, his first wife, sued him for "por abandono de sus hijos y privación de paternidad" (abandonment of his children and deprivation of fatherhood).

The following year, 1935, Huidobro published *Tres novelas ejemplares*, comprising the three novellas he had written in collaboration with his friend Arp as well as two other stories, "Dos ejemplares de novela" (Two Examples of Novella), written by Huidobro alone. The original French versions of the novellas by Huidobro and Arp have been lost. He published two issues of *Ombligo/Vital*, a literary magazine subtitled "Revista de

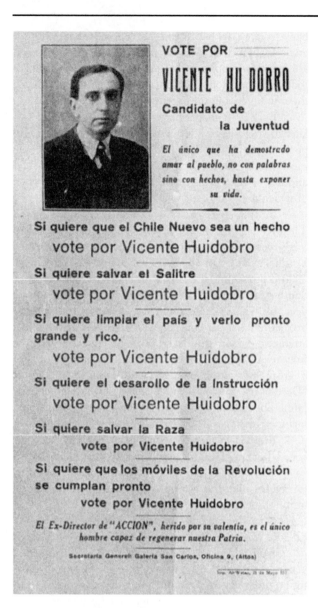

VOTE POR

VICENTE HUIDOBRO

Candidato de
la Juventud

*El único que ha demostrado
amar al pueblo, no con palabras
sino con hechos, hasta exponer
su vida.*

Si quiere que el Chile Nuevo sea un hecho
vote por Vicente Huidobro

Si quiere salvar el Salitre
vote por Vicente Huidobro

**Si quiere limpiar el país y verlo pronto
grande y rico.**
vote por Vicente Huidobro

Si quiere el desarollo de la Instrucción
vote por Vicente Huidobro

Si quiere salvar la Raza
vote por Vicente Huidobro

**Si quiere que los móviles de la Revolución
se cumplan pronto**
vote por Vicente Huidobro

*El Ex-Director de "ACCION", herido por su valentía, es el único
hombre capaz de regenerar nuestra Patria.*

Secretaría General Galería San Carlos, Oficina 9, (Altos)

*Flyer advertising Huidobro's 1925 campaign for president
of Chile as the "candidate of youth" (Collection
of the Huidobro family)*

higiene social" (Review of Social Hygiene), and at the same time he engaged in a war of insults with Pablo Neruda and Pablo de Rokha, which was waged in literary magazines, newspapers, and pamphlets. Neruda received at this time a written tribute from the Spanish poets, though Juan Ramón Jiménez and Larrea refused to sign and Diego signed only after his demand had been met that nothing be mentioned in the statement against Huidobro. That year, the *Antología de poesía chilena nueva* (Anthology of Chilean New Poetry) was published by Eduardo Anguita and Volodia Teitelboim with Huidobro's assistance. This publication represents the literary triumph of Huidobro's generation and of the Chilean and Spanish American avant-garde.

In 1936 Huidobro moved to Los Leones 234, in Providencia, Santiago. He published the poem "Gloria y Sangre" in the book *Madre España: Homenaje de los Poetas Chilenos* (Mother Spain: An Homage by Chilean Poets, 1937), and "Está sangrando España" (Spain is Bleeding) in *Escritores y Artistas Chilenos* (Chilean Writers and Artists, 1936). That year Huidobro signed the Dimensionist Manifesto with Arp, Marcel Duchamp, Wassily Kandinsky, Lázló Moholy-Nagy, Francis Picabia, and the Delaunays. In Lima, Huidobro was attacked in *El obispo embotellado* (The Bottled Bishop, an image taken from *Temblor de cielo*), a pamphlet written by César Moro and Adolfo Westphalen in response to Huidobro's mockery of Moro in *Ombligo*. That same year, he published the first issue of another avant-garde magazine, *Total* (a second issue was published in 1938).

No sooner had the civil war started in Spain than Huidobro went to Madrid, where his arguments with Neruda were resumed. The European avant-garde poets tried to reconcile the two Chileans. A 1 May 1937 letter signed by Tzara, Vallejo, Larrea, Alejo Carpentier, and José Bergamín tried to mediate in the polemics between the men. Huidobro was willing to put an end to the conflict, but Neruda was not.

On 1 May 1937 Huidobro took part in the Congress of the Association Internationale des Ecrivains pour la Défense de la Culture in Paris. Huidobro planned to go to the war front as a soldier, but General Lister indicated in a letter to him that he would be more effective to the Republican cause by supporting it at the political level. In the same year, he attended the Second Congress of the association in Valencia, where he read his essay "Hombre y escritor" (Man and Writer). Back in Chile, he wrote in the newspaper *La Opinión* a violent diatribe, "Fuera de aquí!" (Out of Here!), against Italian aviators promoting Italian warplanes in Chile.

In 1938 Huidobro was forty-five years old. He published *Sátiro; o, El poder de las palabras* (Satyr; or, The Power of Words), the last of his novels. He also published the second and last issue of *Total* in Santiago. The poets of the Surrealist group Mandrágora published *Homenaje a Vicente Huidobro* (Tribute to Vicente Huidobro), commemorating the twentieth anniversary of the publication of *Ecuatorial* and *Poemas árticos*. Mandrágora also published a poetic tribute to Ximena in 1939. On 5 September, following a National Socialist university student uprising, sixty of the students who had been detained were massacred at the Seguro Obrero (Workers' Social Security) building. The poet was detained following his visit to General Carlos Ibáñez del Campo, who in fact was not involved in the student uprising and did not wish to protest against the repressive manner in which the government dealt with the students. Huidobro published in *La Opinión* (13 September 1938) an article titled "Queremos justicia" (We Want Justice). The Chilean Popular Front won the presidential elections of that year.

Huidobro remained in Chile throughout 1939 and began to publish poems from that year on in various literary magazines–the Chilean journals *Mandrágora, Multitud,* and *Babel;* the Argentinian *Sur;* and the Mexican *Romance.* During this period he became especially close to the young generation of Chilean poets, particularly those belonging to the Mandrágora group, in whose magazine he had collaborated in the past. He also collaborated in other journals, such as *Multitud,* which was directed by his old friend and constant challenger Pablo de Rokha. He published in *La Nación* (5 November 1939) his "Cuentos diminutos" (Minute Stories): "La joven del abrigo largo" (The Girl with the Long Overcoat), "La hija del guardaaguja" (The Signalman's Daughter), and "Tragedia" (Tragedy). During this time he frequently wrote in *La Opinión.* In 1940 he left the Communist Party in protest against the German-Soviet pact. He published in *El Mercurio* and *La Nación* (21, 23, and 29 August 1941) his "Cartas al Tío Sam" (Letters to Uncle Sam), urging the United States to enter the European conflict.

In 1941 Huidobro published the last two books that appeared in his lifetime: *Ver y palpar* and *El ciudadano del olvido* (The Citizen of Oblivion). This extensive and heterogeneous production conditioned the creative vigor of his generation as well as the innovative spirit of successive generations. He was the acknowledged forerunner of the young generation of Mandrágora poets in Chile, of Nicanor Parra's antipoetry, and of the poetry of Gonzalo Rojas, Eduardo Anguita, Braulio Arenas, and Humberto Díaz Casanueva, as well as of Spanish American poets such as Octavio Paz.

Ver y palpar and *El ciudadano del olvido* comprise the sixth and last period of Huidobro's published Creationist poetry. In these books his creative ingenuity is displayed in poems rich in verbal play as well as in tragic visions of life and the world. *Ver y palpar* is connected to *Altazor* through a reflective allusion as well as in the constructivist and playful structure of the poem. In this aspect *Ver y palpar* illustrates and develops a kind of poetry that Huidobro had already explored in *Altazor,* particularly in Cantos 4 and 5. The book is divided into two sections. The first one establishes a direct link with *Altazor,* making an explicit allusion to the understanding of the poem in the first segment of "Hasta luego" (Au revoir), a poem consisting of eight numbered segments. The second section, "Poemas giratorios y otros" (Revolving Poems and Other Poems), comprises poems that use the verbal components of a previous poem in an entirely new reordering of words. The words are changed from the singular to the plural or from primi-

Paperback cover for the work in which Huidobro defines his theory of poetry in opposition to André Breton's Manifeste du surréalisme, published in 1924 (from René de Costa, En pos de Huidobro, 1978)

tive to derived forms. This relation exists between "Poemas giratorios I" (Revolving Poems I) and "Poemas giratorios II," between "Halo" and "El paladín sin esperanza" (The Paladin Without Hope), and between "La suerte echada" (The Die Is Cast) and "Colores ascendentes" (Rising Colors). A different kind of revolving poem is a poem built like an incantation or exorcism, as is the case, for example, in "Fuerzas naturales" (Natural Forces), "Los señores de la familia" (The Lords of the Family), "Ronda" (Ring-a-Ring-a-Roses), and "Contacto externo" (External Contact), in which the poem develops from an initial model into several sections progressively enriched through the gradual addition of words and increasing derivation.

These poems are scrambled texts, written with the same corpus of words that gives form to two different poems, with distinctive kinds of speech acts and

*Huidobro's third wife, Raquel Señoret Huidobro, in 1945,
the year they were married (Fundación Vicente Huidobro)*

varying content, textual order, and form. Instead of taking the Surrealist stance of haphazard composition or the "recette pour faire un poème dadaiste" (recipe for a Dadaist poem), Huidobro uses a text of his own to provide the material for another text in which the same repertory of words give form to an entirely different poem. Some poems are like magical incantation formulas or verbal rituals; others are like children's songs; while others are openly constructive and even playful. A different kind of scrambled text revolves around the same words by ordering and reordering them, line by line, increasing gradually their number and turning them playfully around once and again. One also finds here poetic texts that mix all these different kinds of poems. These poems are intended to define a new way of producing a created poem: the poem itself becomes a performance or action, something to be seen and touched, a kind of concrete poetry.

El ciudadano del olvido is framed by the first and last poems of the book in a self-reflective identification of the lyric speaker's anguish over his unconquered ambi-

tions and the mortal condition of human existence. It is also characterized by what Huidobro called "poesía parlante" (talking poetry), a kind of poetry in which the verbal dimension departs from everyday oral expression and becomes transformed through linguistic deviation or ungrammatical usage. Diego followed this mode in his *Biografía incompleta* (Unfinished Biography, 1953), which has the epigraphic note: "Hablando con Vicente Huidobro" (Talking with Vicente Huidobro). This "talking" expression, or conversational quality, comes through in the titles of many poems: "Entre dos viajes" (Layover), "Tiempo de espera" (Waiting Time), "Aquí estamos" (Here We Are), "Al oído del tiempo" (On Time's Ear), "Esa angustia que se nos pega" (That Anguish We Can't Get Rid Of), "Un día vendrá" (A Day Will Come), "Camino inútil" (Useless Road), "De alto a bajo" (Up and Down), and "Entre uno y otro" (Between the One and the Other). Less formal than those of *Ver y palpar,* the ritualistic texts of *El ciudadano del olvido* use refrains and anaphoric repetition.

The most notable poem of this book is "Tríptico a Stéphane Mallarmé" (Triptych to Stéphane Mallarmé), a eulogy of the great French poet, who is a definite precursor of Huidobro's poetry. Other notable poems are "Balada de lo que no vuelve" (Ballad of What Will Never Return), "La raíz de la voz" (The Root of the Voice), and "Tiempo de alba y vuelo" (Time of Dawn and Flying).

In 1942 Huidobro's revised versions of *Temblor de cielo, Cagliostro,* and *Mio Cid Campeador* were published in Santiago. In 1943 Ximena and Huidobro separated. In 1944 Huidobro published his last literary magazine, *Actual.* That same year he traveled to Europe as a correspondent for the Chilean newspaper *La Hora* and for the Uruguayan newspaper *Crítica* to cover the Allied advance against Germany. He made stops in Buenos Aires and Montevideo to deliver lectures on poetry. He was introduced by Esther de Cáceres at the *Amigos del Arte* center in Montevideo. He published the poem "Edad negra" (Dark Age) in the Mexican magazine *Cuadernos Americanos* and in the Santiago magazine *Babel.*

Donning the uniform of the United States Army, he joined General Delattre de Tassigny as the Allied army advanced into Germany, serving as an embedded war correspondent for the Uruguayan newspaper *Crítica* and the Chilean newspaper *La Opinión.* He entered Berlin with the Allied forces and witnessed as a reporter the freeing in Lindau of the French politicians Paul Reynaud and Edouard Daladier, and of the army generals Maurice-Gustave Gamelin and Maxime Weygand. He was wounded twice, in April and May 1945 at the war front at Elba. He was hospitalized in Magdeburg and then in Heidelberg, then discharged and sent back to Paris. In Paris he participated in radio broadcasts on the

Huidobro (second from right) as a war correspondent in France in 1945
(Collection of the Huidobro family)

Voice of America. He wrote *Deucalión,* a dramatic lecture that was staged in Paris in 1945 by Pierre Darmangeat.

Huidobro traveled to London, where he met Raquel Señoret, who worked at the Chilean Embassy. Huidobro and Señoret married in June and returned to Chile via New York, where they visited his friends Breton, Duchamp, Lipchitz, and Varèse. Huidobro suffered a stroke, from which he soon recovered. The couple left New York on 10 September 1945; made stops in Rio de Janeiro, Montevideo, and Buenos Aires to visit friends; and arrived in Chile in October. Huidobro's *Antología,* with an introduction by Eduardo Anguita, was published that year. In 1946 *Trois nouvelles exemplaires,* the French version of *Tres novelas ejemplares,* was published in Paris.

Huidobro retired to his seaside estate, "El Cardal," in Cartagena, where he built a small house and lived with Raquel and his son Vladimir. There he received his friends and the young writers Anguita and Braulio Arenas, who visited him regularly.

From this period date the interviews and correspondence referring to the last books of poetry he planned and to his personal appraisal of the historical meaning of his poetic revolution. On 5 April 1947 he published the article "Por qué soy anticomunista" (Why

I Am Anticommunist) in the Santiago newspaper *El Estanquero.* On 19 December he suffered a stroke that left him comatose for some time. He died at his home on 2 January 1948, eight days before his fifty-fifth birthday. He was buried in Cartagena, where his tombstone reads: "Aquí yace el poeta Vicente Huidobro / Abrid la tumba / Al fondo se ve el mar" (Here lies the poet Vicente Huidobro / Open the tombstone / At the bottom you will see the sea).

Shortly after Huidobro died, his daughter Manuela García Huidobro published his last poems, which she collected under the title *Ultimos poemas* (Last Poems, 1948) with the assistance of Huidobro's friend Arenas, and which includes poems he had published in magazines as well as many unpublished poems. The edition also collects poetry on political topics, particularly those alluding to the Spanish Civil War, the Popular Front, and the U.S.S.R. and to Communist figures such as Lenin, Chinese general Chu Teh, and Dolores Ibárruri (La Pasionaria). The main impetus behind this publication seems to have been the desire to make accessible the book to the Spanish public during the regime of Francisco Franco.

Although the edition includes both published and unpublished poems, textual analysis allows separating, on the one hand, published poems and published circumstantial poems and, on the other, unpublished poems with and without titles that are shorter and have more synthetic forms. In interviews that Huidobro gave in 1946, he mentioned the titles and salient characteristics of the books he had written or was writing at the time. None of the existing manuscripts correspond exactly to what he described, but some poems show a similarity in content. Among the *Ultimos poemas,* some long poems had already been published: "El pasajero de su destino" (The Passenger of His Own Destiny; the French version had also been published as "Le passager de son destin" [1931], though it has never been collected in a book), "Monumento al mar" (Monument to the Sea), "Edad negra" (Dark Age), and "El paso del retorno" (Passage of Return). The previously unpublished poems include "Coronación de la muerte" (Coronation of Death); "Madre" (Mother), elegies related to the death of Huidobro's mother; and "Hija" (Daughter), a poem in which the speaker evokes his daughter's image. The latest poems in *Ultimos poemas* appear to be the entire set of untitled works. Huidobro, in an interview with Jorge Onfray Barros for the Santiago newspaper *Nuevo Zig-Zag* (26 September 1946), seems to refer to these as his last productions: "poemitas en un tono muy diferente, quizás con algún parentesco con *Tout à coup.* Algunos que han leído esos versos inéditos los encuentran demasiado desprendidos o desencarnados. Tal vez lo sean. En todo caso, obedecen a un momento muy primordial de mi vida." (Brief poems of a different tone, somehow related to the poems of *Tout à coup.* Those who have read these unpublished poems consider them too detached and raw. At any rate, they correspond to a meaningful moment of my life).

In 1990 the Fundación Vicente Huidobro (Vicente Huidobro Foundation) was created in Santiago. The archive preserves the poet's manuscripts on microfilm as well as his published works and is open to researchers and students of his poetry. It also holds his personal library and a permanent and circulating exhibit of documents of the literary avant-garde. The foundation organized the celebration of the centennial of Huidobro's birth in 1993. In 2001 the Museo Nacional Centro de Arte Reina Sofía commemorated in Madrid, Spain, the eightieth anniversary of the exhibition (and projected album) *Salle XIV* by mounting an exhibition of the original painted poems and silkscreen printings of each of them, along with documents of the Chilean, Spanish American, Spanish, French, and European avant-garde movements. This exhibition was soon after brought to Santiago, where it was shown at the Fundación Telefónica's exhibition rooms. At the same time, the center published in Madrid a magnificent facsimile edition of ten of the thirteen painted poems of the album planned by Huidobro in 1922 as well as a complete catalogue of the exhibition.

On 24 December 1947 Vicente Huidobro formulated his last views on poetry in a letter addressed to his friend Larrea:

Los hombres aman lo maravilloso, especialmente los poetas, y lo maravilloso ha pasado a manos de la ciencia. Los poetas se sienten tan huérfanos de maravillas que ya no saben qué inventar. Esto solo prueba que la poesía murió, es decir lo que hasta ahora hemos llamado poesía. Seguramente vendrá otra clase de poesía . . . si es que el hombre necesita de ella. Nosotros somos los últimos representantes irresignados de un sublime cadáver . . . El nuevo ser nacerá, aparecerá la nueva poesía, soplará en un gran huracán y entonces se verá cuán muerto estaba el muerto. El mundo abrirá los ojos y los hombres nacerán por segunda vez – o por tercera o cuarta . . .

(Men love the marvelous, particularly the poets, but the marvelous has passed into the hands of science. Poets feel so much in need of marvels that they do not know what else to invent. This only proves that poetry is dead, that is to say, what we until now have called poetry. A new kind of poetry will certainly appear . . . if man has any need of poetry. We are the last unflinching representatives of a sublime corpse. . . . A new being will be born, the new poetry will arise, a great hurricane will blow and we will then see how dead the corpse was. The world will open its eyes and men will be born for a second time, or a third or a fourth . . .).

Letters:

Epistolario 1924–1945, selected, with a prologue and notes, by Pedro Pablo Zegers and Thomas Harris (Santiago: DIBAM/LOM, Archivo del Escritor, 1997);

Gabriele Morelli, "La correspondencia inédita Huidobro- Diego-Larrea: Primeras cartas: En busca del inevitable encuentro," *Insula,* 642 (June 2000): 5–8.

Interviews:

Rafael Cansinos-Asséns, "Vicente Huidobro," *Correspondencia de España* (Madrid), 24 November 1919;

César González-Ruano, "Vicente Huidobro: El que trajo las gallinas," *Heraldo de Madrid,* 6 January 1931, p. 1;

René de Costa, ed., *Vicente Huidobro y el creacionismo* (Madrid: Taurus, 1975), pp. 61–109;

Cecilia García-Huidobro, ed., *Vicente Huidobro a la intemperie: Entrevistas, 1915–1946* (Santiago: Sudamericana, 2000).

Bibliographies:

Cedomil Goic, "La poesía de Vicente Huidobro," *Anales de la Universidad de Chile,* 101 (1956): 61–119;

Goic, *La poesía de Vicente Huidobro* (Santiago: Ediciones de los Anales de la Universidad de Chile, 1956), pp. 299–313;

Goic, *La poesía de Vicente Huidobro* (Santiago: Ediciones Nueva Universidad, 1974), pp. 261–283;

Nicholas Hey, "Bibliografía de y sobre Vicente Huidobro," *Revista Iberoamericana,* 91 (1975): 293–353;

Hey, "Ad[d]enda a la bibliografía de y sobre Vicente Huidobro," *Revista Iberoamericana,* 106–107 (1979): 387–398;

Hey, "Bibliografía," in *Poesía,* Número monográfico dedicado a Vicente Huidobro, nos. 30–32 (1989): 397–404;

María Angeles Pérez López, "Bibliografía de y sobre la prosa narrativa de Vicente Huidobro," *Anales de Literatura Hispanoamericana,* 26, no. 2 (1997): 111–126.

References:

Eduardo Anguita, "Vicente Huidobro, el creador," *Estudios,* 124 (1943): 43–59;

Braulio Arenas, "Vicente Huidobro y el creacionismo," *Atenea,* 420 (1968): 171–201;

Pedro Aullón de Haro, "La teoría poética del creacionismo," *Cuadernos Hispanoamericanos,* 427 (1986): 49–73;

Aullón de Haro, "La trascendencia de la poesía y el pensamiento poético de Vicente Huidobro," *Revista de Occidente,* 86–87 (1988): 41–58;

Juan Jacobo Bajarlía, *La poesía de vanguardia: De Huidobro a Vallejo* (Buenos Aires, 1965);

David Bary, "*Altazor* o la divina parodia," *Revista Hispánica Moderna,* 28, no. 1 (1962): 287–294;

Bary, "El estilo *Nord-Sud,*" *Revista Iberoamericana,* 53 (1962): 87–101;

Bary, *Huidobro o la vocación poética* (Granada: Universidad de Granada, 1963);

Bary, *Nuevos estudios sobre Huidobro y Larrea* (Valencia: Pre-Textos, 1984);

Bary, "Sobre los orígenes de *Altazor,*" *Revista Iberoamericana,* 106–107 (1979): 111–116;

Nicolas Beaudoin, "La poésie nouvelle et Vincent Huidobro," *Bataille Littéraire,* 2, no. 4 (June 1920): 121–126;

Susana Benko, *Vicente Huidobro y el cubismo* (Caracas & Mexico City: Banco Provincial, Monte Avila Editores Latinoamericana, Fondo de Cultura Económica, 1993);

Alicia Borinsky, "*Altazor:* Entierros y comienzos," *Revista Iberoamericana,* 86 (1974): 125–128;

Estrella Busto Ogden, *El creacionismo de Vicente Huidobro en sus relaciones con la estética cubista* (Madrid: Playor, 1983);

Mireya Camurati, *Poesía y poética de Vicente Huidobro* (Buenos Aires: García Cambeiro, 1980);

Rafael Cansinos-Asséns, "El arte nuevo: Sus manifestaciones entre nosotros," *Cosmópolis,* 1, no. 2 (February 1919): 262–267;

Cansinos-Asséns, "La nueva lírica (*Horizon carré, Poemas árticos, Ecuatorial*)," *Cosmópolis,* 1, no. 5 (May 1919): 72–80;

Enrique Caracciolo Trejo, *La poesía de Vicente Huidobro y la vanguardia* (Madrid: Gredos, 1974);

Emilie Carner Noulet, "Etude sur Vicente Huidobro," *Synthèse,* 140–141 (1958);

Belén Castro Morales, *Altazor: La teoría liberada* (Santa Cruz de Tenerife: Pilar Rey, 1987);

Castro Morales, "Os traigo los recuerdos de Altazor" and "Creacionismo y metapoesía en *Ver y palpar* de Vicente Huidobro," *Revista Iberoamericana,* 159 (1992): 379–392;

Jaime Concha, "*Altazor,* de Vicente Huidobro," *Anales de la Universidad de Chile,* 133 (1965): 113–136;

Concha, *Vicente Huidobro,* Los Poetas, no. 27 (Madrid: Júcar, 1980);

René de Costa, *En pos de Huidobro: Siete ensayos de aproximación* (Santiago, Chile: Editorial Universitaria, 1978);

de Costa, *Vicente Huidobro: The Careers of a Poet* (Oxford: Clarendon Press, 1984);

Gerardo Diego, "Poesía y creacionismo de Vicente Huidobro," *Cuadernos Hispanoamericanos,* 222 (1968): 528–544;

Diego, "Posibilidades creacionistas," *Cervantes* (Madrid) (October 1919): 23–28;

Diego, "Vicente Huidobro," *Atenea,* 295–296 (1950): 10–20;

Lee H. Dowling, "Metalanguage in Huidobro's *Altazor,*" *Language & Style,* 15, no. 4 (1982): 253–266;

Damián Fernández Pedemonte, *La producción del sentido en el discurso poético: Análisis de* Altazor *de Vicente Huidobro* (Buenos Aires: Edicial, 1996);

Antonio Fernández Spencer, "*Ecuatorial,* obra maestra," *Cuadernos Hispanoamericanos,* 471 (1989): 59–71;

Merlin H. Forster, "*Ver y palpar* y *El ciudadano del olvido:* Fórmulas gastadas o creaciones nuevas," *Revista Iberoamericana,* 106–107 (1979): 285–290;

Magdalena García Pinto, "El bilingüismo como factor creativo en *Altazor,*" *Revista Iberoamericana,* 106–107 (1979): 117–127;

Cedomil Goic, "*Altazor* de Vicente Huidobro," in his *Los mitos degradados: Ensayos de comprensión de la literatura hispanoamericana* (Amsterdam: Rodopi, 1992), pp. 43–49;

Goic, "Cien años de Vicente Huidobro," *Revista Atlántica,* 7 (1993): 11–17;

Goic, "La comparación creacionista: El Canto III de *Altazor,*" *Revista Iberoamericana,* 106–107 (1979): 129–139;

Goic, "Fin del mundo, fin de un mundo: *Ecuatorial* de Vicente Huidobro," *Revista Chilena de Literatura,* 55 (1999): 5–29;

Goic, "Huidobro, Neruda y Arteche: Tres y un modos de decir poético," *Anales del Instituto de Chile* (1995): 69–85;

Goic, "Mares árticos, de Vicente Huidobro," *Dispositio,* 40 (1990): 151–159;

Goic, *La poesía de Vicente Huidobro,* second edition (Santiago: Ediciones Nueva Universidad, 1974);

Goic, "'Vermouth,' de Vicente Huidobro," *Página,* 38 (1999/2000): 5–11;

Goic, "Vicente Huidobro, poesía de dos tiempos: 'Perit ut vivat,'" *Revista Iberoamericana,* 168–169 (1994): 715–722;

César González Ruano, *Veintidós retratos de escritores contemporáneos hispanoamericanos* (Madrid: Ediciones Cultura Hispánica, 1952), pp. 69–73;

Oscar Hahn, *Vicente Huidobro o el atentado celeste* (Santiago: LOM, 1998);

Nicholas Hey, "Nonsense en *Altazor,*" *Revista Iberoamericana,* 106–107 (1979): 149–156;

Henry Alfred Holmes, *Vicente Huidobro and Creationism* (New York: Columbia University, 1934);

Lucía Invernizzi, "Las figuras de disyunción en el poema 'Sombra' de *Poemas árticos* de Vicente Huidobro," *Revista Chilena de Literatura,* 8 (1977): 83–107;

Orlando Jimeno-Grendi, "Ateismo y nihilismo en *Temblor de cielo* de Vicente Huidobro," *America,* 6 (1990): 123–135;

Jimeno-Grendi, "Huidobro et la destructuration du langage: Une cosmogonie verbal," in *L'Avant-garde littéraire chilienne et ses précurseurs: Poétique et réception des œuvres de Juan Emar et de Vicente Huidobro en France et au Chili,* edited by Alejandro Canseco-Jerez (Paris: Harmattan, 1994), pp. 73–86;

Jimeno-Grendi, *Vicente Huidobro: Altazor et Temblor de Cielo, la poétique du Phénix* (Paris: Caribéennes, 1989);

Juan Larrea, "Vicente Huidobro en vanguardia," *Revista Iberoamericana,* 106–107 (1979): 213–273;

Pedro López-Adorno, *Vías teóricas a Altazor de Vicente Huidobro* (New York: Peter Lang, 1986);

Berta López Morales, "*Altazor,* hacia una verticalización de la épica," *Revista Chilena de Literatura,* 14 (1979): 23–54;

Eduardo Mitre, *Huidobro, hambre de espacio y sed de cielo* (Caracas: Monte Avila, 1980);

Hugo Montes Brunet, "Nota sobre un poema de Vicente Huidobro," *Romance Notes,* 11, no. 2 (1969): 272–277;

M. E. Moscoso de Cordero, *La metáfora en Altazor de Vicente Huidobro* (Cuenca, Ecuador: Universidad de Cuenca, Facultad de Filosofía, Letras y Ciencias de la Educación, 1987);

Luis Navarrete Orta, *Poesía y poética de Vicente Huidobro (1912–1931)* (Caracas: Fondo Editorial de Humanidades y Educación, Universidad Central de Venezuela, 1988);

Adolfo de Nordenflycht, "*Ver y palpar:* Articulación en la trayectoria poética de Huidobro," *Signos,* 22 (1986): 25–34;

Jorge Onfray Barros, "La colina del desencantado," *Nuevo Zig-Zag* (Santiago), 26 September 1946, pp. 31–32;

Octavio Paz, "Decir sin decir: *Altazor* (Vicente Huidobro)," in his *Convergencias* (Barcelona: Seix Barral, 1991), pp. 49–59;

Luisa Marina Perdigó, *The Origins of Vicente Huidobro's "Creacionismo" (1911–1916) and Its Evolution (1917–1947)* (Lewiston, N.Y.: Mellen University Press, 1994);

María Angeles Pérez López, "Dramaturgia y modernidad en *Gilles de Raiz* de Vicente Huidobro," *Anales de Literatura Chilena,* 2 (2001): 163–175;

Pérez López, *Los signos infinitos: Un estudio de la obra narrativa de Vicente Huidobro* (Lérida, Spain: Edicions de la Universitat de Lleida, 1998);

Ana Pizarro, *Vicente Huidobro, un poeta ambivalente* (Concepción: Universidad de Concepción, Consejo de Difusión, 1971);

Samuel M. Porrata, *El creacionismo de Gerardo Diego y Vicente Huidobro* (Lewiston, N.Y.: Edwin Mellen Press, 2001);

Waldo Rojas, "*Altazor de puño y letra:* Aciertos y desaciertos de un desafío editorial," *Taller de Letras,* 29 (2001): 217–228;

Sergio Saldes Báez, "La novela-film: Algunas consideraciones acerca de *Cagliostro* de Vicente Huidobro," *Literatura y Lingüística,* 2 (1988): 69–80;

Rosa Sarabia, "Una aproximación a los poemas pintados como reflexión del signo artístico," in *Salle XIV: Vicente Huidobro y las artes plásticas* (Madrid: Museo Nacional Centro de Arte Reina Sofía, 2001), pp. 55–65;

Federico Schopf, "Poesía y lenguaje en *Altazor,*" *Revista Chilena de Literatura,* 58 (2001): 5–18;

Guillermo Sucre, "Huidobro: Altura y caída," in his *La máscara, la transparencia: Ensayos sobre poesía hispano-*

americana (Mexico: Fondo de Cultura Económica, 1985), pp. 90–112;

Volodia Teitelboim, *Huidobro: La marcha infinita* (Santiago: BAT, 1993);

Eduardo Thomas Dublé, "*En la luna,*" *Anales de Literatura Chilena,* 2 (2001): 177–190;

Guillermo de Torre, "La polémica del creacionismo: Huidobro y Reverdy," in *Vicente Huidobro y el creacionismo,* edited by de Costa (Madrid: Taurus, 1975), pp. 151–165;

Gilberto Triviños, "Profecía, nueva novela y utopía en *La Próxima* de Vicente Huidobro," *Atenea,* 470 (1994): 83–96;

Antonio de Undurraga, ed., "Teoría del creacionismo," in Huidobro's *Poesía y prosa, antología,* edited by de Undurraga (Madrid: Aguilar, 1957), pp. 19–186;

Adriana Valdés, "La coordinación en *Poemas árticos* de Vicente Huidobro," *Taller de Letras,* 4–5 (1974–1975): 7–60;

Gloria Videla de Rivero, "Huidobro en España," *Revista Iberoamericana,* 106–107 (1979): 37–48;

Cecil G. Wood, *The "Creacionismo" of Vicente Huidobro* (Fredericton, N.B.: York, 1978);

Ramón Xirau, "Teoría y práctica del creacionismo," in *Poesía hispanoamericana y española* (Mexico City: Imprenta Universitaria, 1961), pp. 57–75;

George Yúdice, *Vicente Huidobro y la motivación del lenguaje* (Buenos Aires: Galerna, 1978);

Saúl Yurkievich, "Altazor, la metáfora deseante," *Revista Iberoamericana,* 106–107 (1979): 141–147;

Yurkievich, *Fundadores de la nueva poesía latinoamericana: Vallejo, Huidobro, Borges, Neruda, Paz* (Madrid: Barral, 1971), pp. 55–115;

Yurkievich, "Una lengua llamando sus adentros," in *A través de la trama: Sobre vanguardias literarias y otras concomitancias* (Barcelona: Muchnik, 1984), pp. 40–45;

Gustavo Zonana, *Metáfora y simbolización literaria en la poética y la poesía de los movimientos hispanoamericanos de vanguardia:* Altazor *(1931) de Vicente Huidobro* (Mendoza: Editorial de la Facultad de Filosofía y Letras, Universidad Nacional de Cuyo, 1994).

Papers:

Vicente Huidobro's papers, including his manuscripts on microfilm, his published works, and his personal library, are held at the Fundación Vicente Huidobro in Santiago, Chile. More original manuscripts can be found at the Library of the Getty Research Center, Los Angeles, California.

Ricardo Jaimes Freyre

(12 May 1866? – 24 April 1933)

Josefa Salmón
Loyola University

BOOKS: *Castalia bárbara* (Buenos Aires: Imp. de Juan Schürer-Stolle, 1899);

La hija de Jefté (La Paz, 1899);

Tucumán en 1810: Noticia histórica y documentos inéditos (Tucumán, 1909);

Historia de la República de Tucumán (Buenos Aires: Coni Hermanos, 1911);

Leyes de la versificación castellana (Buenos Aires: Coni Hermanos, 1912);

El Tucumán del siglo XVI (bajo el gobierno de Juan Ramírez de Velasco) (Buenos Aires: Coni Hermanos, 1914);

El Tucumán Colonial: Documentos y mapas del Archivo de Indias, introduction and notes by Jaimes Freyre (Buenos Aires: Coni Hermanos, 1915);

Historia del descubrimiento de Tucumán seguida de investigaciones históricas (Buenos Aires: Coni Hermanos, 1916);

Los sueños son vida; Anadiomena; Las víctimas (Buenos Aires: Sociedad Cooperativa Editorial Limitada, 1917);

Los conquistadores: Drama histórico en tres actos y en verso (Buenos Aires: Perrotli, 1928).

Editions: *Castalia bárbara y otros poemas* (Mexico City: Tip Murguia, 1920);

Poesías Completas, introduction by Eduardo Joubin Colombres (Buenos Aires: Claridad, 1944);

Cuentos (La Paz: Instituto Boliviano de Cultura, 1975).

Ricardo Jaimes Freyre, together with Nicaraguan poet Rubén Darío, is regarded as one of the best Spanish American modernist poets. Best known for his first book of poems, *Castalia bárbara* (Savage Castalia, 1899), and his *Leyes de la versificación castellana* (Rules of Spanish Versification, 1912), he was also a journalist, historian, short-story writer, playwright, and one of Bolivia's foremost diplomats.

Though the fact is unconfirmed, Freyre was said to be born on 12 May 1866 in Tacna, Peru, in the Bolivian Consulate, where his father, Julio Lucas Jaimes, served as Bolivian consul. His mother, Carolina Freyre, a Tacna native, was recognized as a talented writer. Jaimes Freyre's family moved to Lima, where he

Ricardo Jaimes Freyre

attended primary and secondary schools, albeit without receiving his diploma because of his family's unexplained return to Tacna in 1883. After a short stay the family returned to Bolivia, where in 1886 Jaimes Freyre married Felicidad Soruco. In 1890 he began teaching philosophy at the Colegio Junín in the Bolivian department of Sucre. His tenure was cut short, however, when President Mariano Baptista called on him to serve as his personal secretary, roughly from 1892 to 1894. When his father was sent to Brazil as Bolivian ambassador, Jaimes Freyre quit his job with the president to become his father's secretary. They never reached their destination, however, because the Brazilian empire met its demise while they were still in transit.

Father and son diverted to Buenos Aires, where Jaimes Freyre and Darío launched the noted journal *Revista de América* (America's Review). Despite the fact that the Bolivian writer's first book had yet to be published at that time, it appears that the publication of his poems in newspapers and magazines had already earned him considerable recognition. As he recounts in "Jaimes Freyre: Un poema juvenil" (James Freyre: A Poem of Youth), from *Ricardo Jaimes Freyre: Estudios* (Ricardo Jaimes Freyre: Studies, 1978), poet and critic Óscar Rivera Rodas discovered one of Jaimes Freyre's earliest poems, a 612-line text titled "Una Venganza" (Act of Vengeance). This lengthy composition was published in the Bolivian newspaper *El Comercio* (Commerce) in consecutive installments from 8 June to 15 June 1883, when the poet was seventeen years old. The time frame for this poem—the medieval period—is the same the poet used in his later poetic texts. By the time *Castalia bárbara* was published in 1899, several of the poems in this first collection had already appeared. For instance, "Aeternum Vale" (Eternal Farewell), considered by critics to be representative of this book, had first been published in 1894 in the third issue of *Revista de América,* according to Emilio Carilla. In 1897 this poem was published a second time in the Venezuelan magazine *El Cojo Ilustrado* (The Illustrated—or Illustrious—Cripple). In the introduction to this second publication of the poem the poet announced his forthcoming collection, *Castalia bárbara.* This book confirmed his reputation as the leading poet of his generation, a position he shared with Darío and Leopoldo Lugones of Argentina.

Castalia bárbara is divided into three sections: "Castalia bárbara," "País de sueño" (Country of Dreams), and "País de sombra" (Country of Shadows). It brings forth moments of great individual valor in the heroes, gods, and poets that come alive in these pages. "Castalia bárbara" is a series of thirteen poems that take place in the world of Norse mythology, where heroes and gods confront one another and face death. These themes permeate such poems as "Los héroes" (The Heroes), "La muerte del héroe" (Death of the Hero), and "El Valhalla" (Valhalla).

In the second section, "País de sueño," Jaimes Freyre turns to Greek mythology for "De la Thule Lejana" (From Distant Thule) and to the medieval past in "Medioevales" (Medievals) and "Complainte." In this section the poet looks to women, nature, and love, seeking supreme values of beauty worthy of his acclaim. Thus, in the poem "Complainte I," his image of woman is intrinsically tied to the beauty of nature: "Eres la rosa ideal" (You're the ideal rose), the speaker tells a woman. The same association is made in "De la Thule Lejana"–"Flores de lis tus hombros y tu seno" (Fleur de Lis, your shoulders and your bosom)—and in the poem "País de sueño": "ya sentí florecer tu primavera / sobre mi pena, misteriosa y honda" (I've felt your springtime blossom / over my sorrow, mysterious and deep). Woman, especially the female body, is perceived through images of nature as a medium of beauty and eroticism with which women throughout history have been traditionally identified.

"País de sombra," the last section, conveys a more melancholic tone as it deals with death, night, fall, and winter. This section is also more personal; the poet becomes the subject in poems such as "El poeta celebra el goce de la vida" (The Poet Celebrates the Enjoyment of Life). The love themes also continue in this section, but now they bring pain, as in "Sombra" (Shadow) and "Siempre" (Always).

The leading modernists of the day, Darío and Lugones, hailed *Castalia bárbara* as Jaimes Freyre's greatest accomplishment. In his introduction to *Poesías completas* (Complete Poems, 1944) Lugones highlights the importance of rhythm in his Bolivian colleague's poetry:

> el ritmo, haciendo intervenir en la expresión la armonía, sugiere desde luego la idea de la unidad. . . . Sentir la belleza es percibir la unidad del Universo en la armonía de las cosas. De este postulado se desprende una consecuencia que antes que ahora tengo expresada así: el estilo es el ritmo. . . . En el poeta cuya es esta obra, predomina el ritmo

> (rhythm, bringing harmony to expression, suggests, naturally, the idea of unity. . . . To feel beauty is to perceive the unity of the Universe in the harmony of things. From this premise flows the conclusion that elsewhere I have stated as follows: The style is the rhythm. . . . In this poet's work, rhythm rules).

Lugones, a premier critic of Jaimes Freyre's work, further asserts that "Aeternum Vale," the exemplary poem from *Castalia bárbara,* is one of the most outstanding pieces of Latin American poetry.

The main theme of "Aeternum Vale" is the end of the Nordic cosmology with the arrival of Christianity. Jaimes Freyre's repeated use of Norse mythology sets him apart from other modernist poets, such as Darío, who look to the Greeks for their mythological references. His poetic framework of a mythological past has led crit-

Paperback cover for the second of Jaimes Freyre's two poetry collections, which includes verse with Greek mythological and medieval themes (from Emilio Carilla, Ricardo Jaimes Freyre, *1962)*

ics to characterize Jaimes Freyre as a poet who feels great affinity for the ideals of that heroic legendary era. According to Lugones, "Vuelve sus ojos al pasado, mejor cuanto más irrestituible. . . . siéntese apegado a esos muertos, a esa fe, a esos ideales" (He turns his eyes to the past, the less reachable the better. . . . he feels devoted to those dead beings, to that faith, to those ideals).

In addition to publishing *Castalia bárbara* in 1899, Jaimes Freyre also published his first play, *La hija de Jefté* (Jefté's Daughter). Later, however, he destroyed all the copies of the play. Thus, no scholar is certain as to the significance of this work, not even his most comprehensive critic, Carilla, who was unable to find a single copy for his study of the poet, *Ricardo Jaimes Freyre* (1962).

Jaimes Freyre's life took another turn in 1900, when he moved to the Argentine city of Tucumán. There he began a career teaching literature and philosophy at the Colegio Nacional de Tucumán (Tucuman's National School), where, according to Eduardo Joubin

Colombres, he was employed between 1901 and 1923. Among the many literary and research activities he undertook during this tenure, he founded the *Revista de Letras y Ciencias Sociales* (Journal of Letters and Social Sciences) in 1904 with the assistance of Juan B. Terán and Julio López Mañan. Subsequently, he became a professor at the Escuela Normal (Normal School) and at Tucumán University. In his capacity as journal editor he came into contact and forged a friendship with the Spanish writer and philosopher Miguel de Unamuno. Carilla indicates that Jaimes Freyre published three of his five short stories in the *Revista de Letras y Ciencias Sociales,* as well as four chapters of his unfinished novel, "Los jardines de Academo" (Academo's Gardens). Of the five short stories, "En las montañas" (In the Mountains) and "En una hermosa tarde de verano" (A Beautiful Summer Afternoon) deal with the indigenous people's daily life in a social-realist style. The other three stories are framed in a mythical past: "Zoe" is the story of a Greek courtesan in Byzantium; "Los viajeros" (The Travelers) tells of the hermit Anthropos; and "Zaghi" narrates the adventures of a beggar in ancient China.

In 1907 Jaimes Freyre was asked to organize the historical archives of the city, which led him to the publication of *Tucumán en 1810: Noticia histórica y documentos inéditos* (Tucumán in 1810: Historical Information and Unpublished Documents, 1909), the first in a series of books on Tucumán history, which commemorated the centenary of the 1809 Revolution. His second book, *Historia de la República de Tucumán* (History of the Tucumán Republic, 1911), focuses largely on General Bernabé Aráoz, the founder of the short-lived Tucumán Republic, which lasted from 1819 to 1821. A year later the poet published his widely acclaimed *Leyes de la versificación castellana.*

In this last publication Jaimes Freyre demonstrates his scholarly knowledge of rhythm, pointing out how to measure verse according to accents rather than long and short syllables, the accepted way of counting until the publication of his research. In this sense this book is revolutionary in terms of poetic rhetoric. According to Alberto Hidalgo's *Tratado de poética* (Poetic Treatise, 1944), "Lo que Jaimes Freyre hizo en este orden, no tiene precedentes en América ni España, no ha sido rebatido ni menos superado después" (What Jaimes Freyre did in this area has no precedents, neither in America nor in Spain, it has not been refuted, let alone surpassed).

In subsequent years Jaimes Freyre continued to live in Tucumán and to publish his historical series: *El Tucumán del siglo XVI (bajo el gobierno de Juan Ramírez de Velasco)* (Sixteenth-Century Tucumán [Under the Governance of Juan Ramírez de Velasco], 1914), *El Tucumán*

Colonial: Documentos y mapas del Archivo de Indias (Colonial Tucumán: Documents and Maps of the Archive of the Indies, 1915), and *Historia del descubrimiento de Tucumán seguida de investigaciones históricas* (History of Tucumán's Discovery Followed by Historical Research, 1916). The first two of these books include historical documents on Tucumán from the time of Juan Ramírez de Velasco's government until 1684, with all notations by Jaimes Freyre. The third book includes two sections, one directly concerned with historical documents and the second dealing with historical criticism on the history of Tucumán's discovery.

Many critics view Jaimes Freyre's second and last book of poetry, *Los sueños son vida* (Dreams Are Life, 1917), as continuing the same modernist currents of *Castalia bárbara*. The poems in this collection, however, are not framed spatially or temporally within the context of Norse mythology; rather, the mythology invoked in such poems as "Alma helénica" (Greek Soul) and "Dios sea loado" (May God Be Praised) is that of Greek or medieval times. "Los antepasados" (The Forebears) and "Los Charcas" take Latin America as a point of reference, within the context of past conquest. Elsewhere in *Los sueños son vida* love themes are present, and the female body is still represented through metaphors from nature.

Jaimes Freyre's days in Tucumán ended in 1921, when he was called by the newly elected Bolivian president, Bautista Saavedra, to serve as minister of education, agriculture, and war. Within months of assuming his position as minister, however, he was made Bolivian representative before the League of Nations and left for Geneva. He returned to Bolivia in 1922 to become minister of foreign affairs, only to resign a few months later. Subsequently, he became the Bolivian minister in Chile, and on 30 August 1923 he was dispatched as Bolivian ambassador to Washington, D.C., where he served until 1927, the year of his wife's death. Shortly afterward, Bolivian president Hernando Siles Reyes appointed him representative to Brazil. At this point, however, he left his diplomatic career to return to Argentina, where the following year he published in Buenos Aires an historical drama, *Los conquistadores: Drama histórico en tres actos y en verso* (The Conquerors: Historical Drama in Three Acts and Verse, 1928), closely tied to *Historia del descubrimento de Tucumán. Los conquistadores* recounts the death of the Spanish conquis-

tador Diego de Rojas through a series of historical episodes that narrate how Rojas is wounded in a confrontation with the Indians, while his generals dispute the succession of power, a plot further complicated by a love triangle.

After a long career as a writer, professor, and diplomat Jaimes Freyre died on 24 April 1933, in Buenos Aires, with his daughter, two sons, and several friends by his side. Major literary and political authorities spoke at his funeral, celebrating his life and works. On 8 November 1933 his remains and those of his father were repatriated to Potosí, Bolivia, where they have remained ever since.

The eminence of Ricardo Jaimes Freyre's literary and political contributions are unquestionable, but despite his fame, his poetry has received little critical attention and his other writings have been mostly ignored. No edition of his complete works has been published, and his extensive journalistic work, his poems outside the two aforementioned collections, short stories, unfinished novel, dramas, and historical research still wait to be compiled. A comprehensive bibliography of his works does not exist. Paradoxically, and despite this lack of critical attention, his work as a major representative of Spanish American *Modernismo* continues to be widely recognized, and his poems are consistently included in all anthologies of modern Latin American poetry.

References:

Emilio Carilla, *Ricardo Jaimes Freyre* (Buenos Aires: Ediciones Culturales Argentinas, 1962);

Carlos Castañón Barrientos, *Ricardo Jaimes Freyre: Notas sobre su vida y su obra* (La Paz: Proinsa, 1980);

Guillermo Francovich, *Tres poetas modernistas de Bolivia* (La Paz: Juventud, 1971), pp. 61–81;

Mireya Jaimes-Freyre, *Modernismo y 98 a través de Ricardo Jaimes Freyre* (Madrid: Gredos, 1969);

Raúl Jaimes Freyre, *Anecdotario de Ricardo Jaimes Freyre* (Potosí: Editorial Potosí, 1953);

Eduardo Ocampo Moscoso, *Personalidad y obra poética de don Ricardo Jaimes Freyre* (Cochabamba: Los Amigos del Libro, 1968);

Ricardo Jaimes Freyre: Estudios (La Paz: Instituto de Estudios Bolivianos, Universidad Mayor de San Andrés, 1978).

Roberto Juarroz

(1925 – 31 March 1995)

Emily E. Stern
University of North Carolina at Chapel Hill

BOOKS: *Poesía vertical* (Buenos Aires: Equis, 1958); translated by W. S. Merwin as *Vertical Poetry* (Santa Cruz, Cal.: Kayak Books, 1977);

Segunda poesía vertical (Buenos Aires: Equis, 1963);

Tercera poesía vertical (Buenos Aires: Equis, 1965);

Guatemala plan para el desarrollo de las bibliotecas públicas y escolares, 20 de enero – 6 de abril de 1968 (San Miguel de Tucumán, Argentina: Universidad Nacional de Tucumán, Biblioteca Central, 1968);

Cuarta poesía vertical (Buenos Aires: Aditor, 1969);

El curso audiovisual de bibliotecología para América Latina (San Miguel de Tucumán, Argentina: Universidad Nacional de Tucumán, Biblioteca Central, 1971);

Quinta poesía vertical (Buenos Aires: Equis, 1974);

Sexta poesía vertical (Buenos Aires, 1975);

Poesía y creación: Diálogos con Guillermo Boido, by Juarroz and Guillermo Boido (Buenos Aires: Lohlé, 1980);

Séptima poesía vertical (Caracas: Monte Avila, 1982);

Octava poesía vertical (Buenos Aires: Lohlé, 1984);

Las ciencias de la información (Buenos Aires: Centro de investigaciones bibliotecológicas de la Facultad de filosofía y letras, 1984);

Novena poesía vertical; Décima poesía vertical (Buenos Aires: Lohlé, 1986);

Poésie et réalité, translated by Jean-Claude Masson (Paris: Lettres vives, 1987); Spanish version published as *Poesía y realidad* (Valencia, Spain: Pre-Textos, 1992);

Undécima poesía vertical (Buenos Aires: Lehlé, 1988);

Duodécima poesía vertical (Buenos Aires: Lehlé, 1991);

Décimotercera poesía vertical (Valencia, Spain: Pre-Textos, 1994);

Décimocuarta poesía vertical; Fragmentos verticales (Buenos Aires: Emecé, 1997).

Collections: *Poesía vertical 1958–1975* (Caracas: Monte Avila, 1976);

Antología mayor (Buenos Aires: Lohlé, 1978);

Poesía vertical, 2 volumes (Buenos Aires: Emecé, 1993);

Roberto Juarroz (from Cuadernos Hispanoamericanos, *June 1990)*

166

Poesía vertical: Antología esencial, edited by Laura Cerrato (Buenos Aires: Emecé, 2001).

While Roberto Juarroz is perhaps not as well known as some of his Argentine contemporaries, his work is respected by poets and critics alike. Thorpe Running characterizes his work as an "experimental and intellectually disturbing contribution to the development of modern poetics." Juarroz's poetry is not known for technical innovations; its originality stems from its constant questioning of its own composition and meaning. His fourteen volumes of poetry represent a lifetime of exploring language and the act of creation in order to better understand the human experience.

Roberto Juarroz was born in 1925 in Coronel Dorrego, a small town in the province of Buenos Aires. He credits his experience growing up outside of Buenos Aires's urban environment with giving him more perspective on people and things. As a child, Juarroz was an avid reader, spending much of his time alone contemplating poetry and art. After graduation Juarroz began working at his former high school, organizing its library. He stayed in that job for several years, as it reinforced his love of books. During this time he entered the law school at the Universidad de La Plata but abandoned it after a couple of years. He also studied medicine and literature at the Universidad de Buenos Aires, although he never finished those degrees.

Finally, Juarroz found a career that suited his passion and experience and graduated with a degree in library and information science from the Universidad de Buenos Aires. Shortly thereafter he won a scholarship to continue his studies at the Sorbonne in Paris. After his return to Argentina, Juarroz was a professor in the library and information science department at the Universidad de Buenos Aires for many years. Few personal anecdotes and details are known about Juarroz. He commented in a 1977 interview with Guillermo Boido that "no me parece importante para los demás mi biografía" (to me, my biography does not seem important for other people) and goes on to say that he cannot live "pendiente de experiencias del pasado, y lo cierto es que no recuerdo demasiados detalles" (thinking about experiences from the past, and the truth is that I don't remember too many details).

In 1956 Juarroz began writing movie reviews for the magazine *Esto Es* (This Is It). In 1958 he left that magazine and began working as a literary critic for the cultural supplement of *La Gaceta* (The Gazette), a newspaper in Tucumán. That same year he founded the magazine *Poesía=Poesía* (Poetry=Poetry) with fellow poet Mario Morales in Buenos Aires. And, perhaps most important, he also published his first volume of poetry, *Poesía vertical* (translated as *Vertical Poetry,* 1977). Its opening poem immediately reveals his poetic project and creative world. The first line of the poem indicates the absolute necessity of seeing in order to understand, and even maintain, the world in which people exist: "Una red de miradas / mantiene unido al mundo, / no lo deja caerse" (A network of looks / keeps the world together, / not letting it fall). The look is an instrument used to dig beneath the surface of appearances. The poem continues: "Mis ojos buscan eso / que nos hace sacarnos los zapatos / para ver si hay algo más sosteniéndonos debajo / o inventar un pájaro / para averiguar si existe el aire / o crear un mundo / para saber si hay dios / o ponernos el sombrero / para comprobar que existimos" (My eyes search for that / which makes us take off our shoes / to see if there is something else sustaining us underneath / or invent a bird / to find out if the air exists / or create a world / to know if there is god / or put on a hat / to prove that we exist). For Juarroz, the look does not just describe, but it creates what it sees, penetrates it to find out what makes people who they are.

Juarroz published *Segunda poesía vertical* (Second Vertical Poetry) in 1963. In this volume elements of his poetry that can be linked to structuralism are already present. Critic Running highlights this connection to the structuralist critics, especially Jacques Derrida: "Although it is true that Juarroz has been following his own path as a poet, it now turns out that the concerns which underlay even his earliest poetry are the very elements which have been singled out as crucial issues by the new wave of (mostly) French critics. Before the modern critical theories of structuralism and semiotics had begun to be fashionable, Juarroz was already constructing a corpus of poetry based on a questioning of its own composition." One of those concerns is the search for a center, a theme that reappears throughout Juarroz's work. Poem 16 of *Segunda poesía vertical* expresses this preoccupation as well as the difficulty of the task: "El centro no es un punto. / Si lo fuera, resultaría fácil acertarlo" (The center is not a point. / If it were, it would be easy to find it). Juarroz also explores the concept of the word as a sign and its limitations in expressing its true meaning. In poem 33 of the same volume, he writes: "El signo no es algo que ocurre entre sus extremos / sino la anulación de esos extremos. / Lo que ocurre entre ellos / sucede en verdad afuera" (The sign is not something that occurs between its extremes / but rather the annulment of those extremes. / What happens between them / actually happens outside). Here Juarroz differs from his avant-garde contemporaries who believed

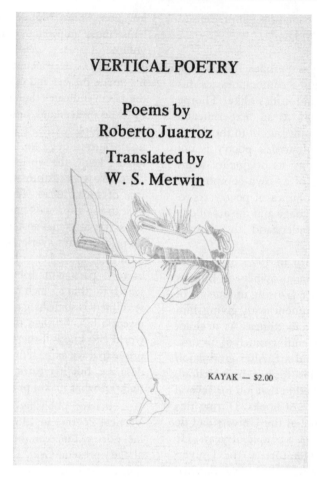

VERTICAL POETRY

Poems by
Roberto Juarroz

Translated by
W. S. Merwin

KAYAK — $2.00

Paperback cover for the English translation (1977) of Juarroz's first book, Poesía vertical, *published in 1958 (Bruccoli Clark Layman Archives)*

that words had determined and limited, albeit multiple, meanings that they were searching to discover. For Juarroz, the word was its own being, its own poetic sign.

This second volume begins what became a pattern for Juarroz; he published all successive volumes under the same title, *Poesía vertical,* numbering them successively according to date of publication. Juarroz also numbered rather than named the poems in each volume. This absence of titles contributes to the sense that each book and each poem is an almost anonymous component of a larger poetic project that lasted throughout Juarroz's entire career. The title he chose has been interpreted as the poet's aspiration to imaginative heights, as a desire for continued refinement of his project. The reference to verticality in the title also reflects the intensely personal nature of that journey, one that takes place in a solitary inner world, without any mediation between the poet and the pinnacle he seeks. Graciela de Sola characterizes Juarroz's journey

as a "búsqueda de una inteligencia que anhela la comprensión total; búsqueda de un ojo intuitivo que mira en torno suyo y se mira a sí mismo en permanente y aguda reflexión" (search for an intelligence that yearns for complete understanding; search for an intuitive eye that looks around itself and looks at itself in deep and constant reflection). Juarroz himself said to Boido, "Yo siento que a través de la poesía esa búsqueda cobra vida, calidez, que todo esto no es frío, no es inhumano, no es cálculo más o menos inteligente, sino que es la angustia esencial del ser humano, así, estremecida" (I feel that through poetry that search takes on life, warmth, that all of this is not cold, is not inhuman, is not a more or less intelligent calculation, but rather it is the essential angst of the human being, like this, shuddering).

Juarroz is known for his originality and individuality, thus, he is not usually categorized with other movements or schools of poetry. For example, in the work he published during the 1960s, he was clearly concerned with the idea of creation and was an admirer of Chilean poet Vicente Huidobro, although Juarroz was not a Creationist. Francisco José Cruz Peréz does, however, suggest that Juarroz can be seen as part of the tradition of European and Argentine metaphysical poetry, such as that of relatively unknown Argentine poet Antonio Porchia, who was active two decades earlier. Juarroz commented to Boido that "lo que me ha unido a Porchia es sentir que nos movíamos en una misma dimensión en cuanto a búsqueda de la realidad última" (what has connected me to Porchia is feeling that we were moving in a same dimension in regard to searching for the ultimate reality).

In 1965 Juarroz published *Tercera poesía vertical* (Third Vertical Poetry), and the magazine he co-directed, *Poesía=Poesía,* stopped publication. During the 1960s Juarroz worked as a consultant for such prestigious world organizations as UNESCO and the Organization of American States, producing studies of and recommendations for the library systems in different Latin American nations. In 1968 he published *Guatemala plan para el desarrollo de las bibliotecas públicas y escolares, 20 de enero – 6 de abril de 1968* (Guatemala Plan for the Development of Public and School Libraries, 20 January – 6 April 1968). The following year he published *Cuarta poesía vertical* (Fourth Vertical Poetry).

Juarroz continued to move between his two vocations, library science, and poetry. In 1971 he developed training materials for librarians throughout the region with *El curso audiovisual de bibliotecología para América Latina* (The Audiovisual Library Science Course for Latin America). *Quinta poesía vertical* (Fifth Vertical Poetry) was published in 1974, and *Sexta poesía vertical* (Sixth Vertical Poetry) the following year. Although Juarroz's publications span more than thirty years of his adult life, his poetics do not include concrete references to his biography or specific historical events. Juarroz's poetry is, however, intensely linked to his own inner world and, in that sense, his experience. His work confronts the most authentic aspects of human existence: death, language, the search for meaning. It constantly explores the relationship between poetry and creation. Cruz Pérez argues that Juarroz's poetry "no busca reflejar la realidad entendida como experiencia inmediata sino demostrar que poesía y vida interior son lo mismo, o sea que la vida interior depende, en gran medida, de nuestra capacidad de vivir la poesía" (does not try to reflect reality understood as immediate experience, but rather to demonstrate that poetry and inner life are the same, that is, that inner life depends, in large part, on our capacity to live poetry).

In 1977 Juarroz was awarded the prestigious Gran Premio de Honor (Grand Prize of Honor) given by the Fundación Argentina para la Poesía (Argentine Poetry Foundation). In 1980 he participated in a dialogue with Boido, reflecting on poetry and creation, which was published as *Poesía y creación: Diálogos con Guillermo Boido* (Poetry and Creation: Dialogues with Guillermo Boido). The 1980s were a decade of significant production by Juarroz. *Séptima poesía vertical* (Seventh Vertical Poetry) was published in 1982 and *Octava poesía vertical* (Eighth Vertical Poetry) in 1984. Two years later, the *Novena poesía vertical* (Ninth Vertical Poetry) and *Décima poesía vertical* (Tenth Vertical Poetry) were published together in one volume. In 1988 Juarroz published *Undécima poesía vertical* (Eleventh Vertical Poetry).

A common thread in these volumes is the idea that the text is never complete; the search for words and expression is eternal. One example is poem 19 of *Undécima poesía vertical:* "Si un texto alguna vez se completase / ya no leería ningún otro" (If some time a text completed itself / I would not read another one). In the same vein as the concept of the changing center, words are also constantly shifting in Juarroz's poetics. In the 1977 interview with Boido, Juarroz described his relationship with language: "cuando uno ha ido aprendiendo ese humilde, ese tremendo oficio de ir amando las palabras, de no ir conformándose a las palabras como instrumentos desgastados, ni siquiera como instrumentos, sino también sentirlas como seres vivos, entonces el manejo o la entrega a todo eso es algo muy decisivo, muy grave, porque no admite la superficialidad, el apuro" (when one has been learning this humble, this tremendous profession of loving words, of not conforming to words as spent instruments, not even as instruments, but also feeling them as living beings, then the handling or the surrender to all of that is something very decisive, very serious, because it does not permit superficiality, haste). The question of language is fundamental to the interplay between poetry and creation, and Juarroz constantly searches for the limit of language, always conscious that such a limit exists.

In 1991 Juarroz published *Duodécima poesía vertical* (Twelfth Vertical Poetry), followed by *Décimotercera poesía vertical* (Thirteenth Vertical Poetry) in 1994. He died in Buenos Aires on 31 March 1995. The final volume of his work, *Décimocuarta poesía vertical; Fragmentos verticales* (Fourteenth Vertical Poetry; Vertical Fragments), was published posthumously in 1997. These fourteen volumes of *Poesía vertical* make up a poetic project to which Juarroz dedicated himself throughout his career. While he did not experiment much with poetry techniques, he did, by questioning the limits of language, constantly strive for a poetry in which each word was irreplaceable. The nature and purpose of Juarroz's ephemeral journey are perhaps best expressed in his own words, as told to Boido:

> entre las cosas que el hombre puede hacer, y en este sentido no hacer, me parece que pocas son tan trascendentes, tan definidoras del ser humano como llevar la palabra a su extremo, a su última posibilidad de configurar, crear o expresar algo. Hay en el fondo de esto un acto de fe muy profundo en que la experiencia humana, por muy desnuda que sea, se enriquece con esa otra forma de la experiencia que es el lenguaje y la poesía

> (among the things that man can do, and in this sense not do, few seem to me as transcendent, as definitive of the human being as taking the word to its extreme, its ultimate possibility to configure, create, or express something. In the root of this, there is an act of very deep faith in which the human experience, as naked as it may be, is enriched by this other form of experience, which is language and poetry).

Interview:

Guillermo Boido, "Entrevista," *Hispamérica,* 6 (1977): 47–59.

References:

Francisco José Cruz Peréz, "Roberto Juarroz: la emoción del pensamiento," *Cuadernos Hispanoamericanos,* 501 (March 1991): 62–73;

Juan Malpartida, "La perfección indefensa," *Cuadernos Hispanoamericanos,* 480 (June 1990): 45–51;

Thorpe Running, "Roberto Juarroz: Vertical Poetry and Structuralist Perspective," *Chasqui: Revista de Literatura Latinoamericana,* 11, nos. 2–3 (February–May 1982): 15–22;

Graciela de Sola, "Roberto Juarroz y la nueva poesía argentina," *Cuadernos Hispanoamericanos,* 193 (January 1966): 85–95.

Claudia Lars

(20 December 1899 – 22 July 1974)

Rafael Lara-Martínez
New Mexico Tech

BOOKS: *Tristes mirajes* (San Salvador: Cañas, 1916);

Estrellas en el pozo (San José, Costa Rica: Convivio, 1934);

Canción redonda (San José, Costa Rica: Convivio, 1937);

La casa de vidrio (Santiago: Zig-Zag, 1942);

Romances de norte y sur (San Salvador: Galería Renacimiento, 1946);

Sonetos (San Salvador: Estrella, 1947);

Donde llegan los pasos (San Salvador: Dirección General de Bellas Artes, Ministerio de Cultura, 1953);

Escuela de pájaros (San Salvador: Departamento Editorial del Ministerio de Cultura, 1955);

Tierra de infancia (San Salvador: Departamento Editorial del Ministerio de Cultura, 1958);

Fábula de una verdad (San Salvador: Departamento Editorial del Ministerio de Cultura, 1959);

Canciones (San Salvador: Departamento Editorial del Ministerio de Cultura, 1960);

Sobre el ángel y el hombre (San Salvador: Dirección General de Publicaciones, 1961);

Del fino amanecer (San Salvador: Dirección General de Publicaciones, 1966);

Nuestro pulsante mundo: Apuntes sobre una nueva edad (San Salvador: Dirección General de Publicaciones, 1969);

Obras escogidas, 2 volumes, edited by Matilde Elena López (San Salvador: Editorial Universitaria, 1973, 1974);

Poesía última, 1970–1973, edited by David Escobar Galindo (San Salvador: Dirección General de Publicaciones, 1975);

Peregrina (Berkeley, Cal.: Canterbury, 1988);

Poesía completa, 2 volumes, edited by Carmen González Huguet (San Salvador: Dirección de Publicaciones e Impresos, 1999).

Editions and Collections: *Presencia en el tiempo: Antología* (San Salvador: Dirección General de Publicaciones, 1962);

Sus mejores poemas, edited by David Escobar Galindo (San Salvador: Dirección General de Publicaciones, 1976).

Claudia Lars

OTHER: *Girasol: Antología de poesía infantil,* selected by Lars (San Salvador: Dirección General de Publicaciones, 1962).

Margarita del Carmen Brannon Vega was born in El Salvador on 20 December 1899 to Patrick (Patricio) Brannon, an Irish engineer, and a Salvadoran,

*Paperback cover for Lars's 1937 poetry collection, inspired by her encounters with the Salvadoran writers Salarrué
and Serafín Quiteño and Alberto Guerra Trigueros and by the deaths of her father and the Spanish poet
Federico García Lorca (Howard-Tilton Memorial Library, Tulane University)*

Manuela Vega. From her father she acquired a liberal education and a taste for poetry and literature, as well as sympathy for socialism and theosophy. In her early years she was educated at home and later attended the Colegio de La Asunción, run by Catholic French nuns in the western city of Santa Ana. She was a classmate of the mother of another well-known writer, Claribel Alegría. Both Lars and Alegría have been recognized as the most prominent Salvadoran female poets.

Brannon wrote her first book, *Tristes mirajes* (Sad Mirages), in 1915–1916, when she was sixteen years old. Although there are no copies extant, in the May 1921 issue of *Repertorio Americano* (American Repertoire) the Nicaraguan avant-garde poet Salomón de la Selva mentions that Juan José Cañas–the author of the Salvadoran anthem–originally published this early book in San Salvador.

At the beginning of the 1920s Brannon traveled to Long Island and stayed with her aunts, the sisters of her father. She later chose to live in New York City. In Manhattan she met Leroy Francis Beers Kuehm, whom she married in November 1923. In 1924 Alberto Masferrer published her poem "Un canto de recuerdo" (A Song of Remembrance) in the newspaper *La Escuela Salvadoreña* (The Salvadoran School) in San Salvador.

Although when she wrote the poem she was living in Brooklyn and teaching languages in a Berlitz school, "Un canto de recuerdo" is dedicated to the western Salvadoran city of Sonsonate, a region known for its native Nahuat influence. Despite her Irish paternal background and her daily life in the United States, Lars strongly identified with the tropics and its inhabitants.

In 1928 Kuehm's husband was named general vice consul of the United States in El Salvador. Her son, Leroy Manuel, was baptized in San Salvador in March 1928. The family was transferred to Costa Rica in 1930. While in San José she contributed to *Repertorio Americano,* thereby establishing an enduring collaboration with an important group of Latin American intellectuals associated with the review. She published about ninety-eight items in different genres–poetry, essay, book review, and interview–in *Repertorio Americano* between 1921 and 1948. Before incorporating a poem in a book, she usually published it in that review.

The first appearance of her pseudonym, Claudia Lars, dates from July 1933 in the *Repertorio*. She created her poetic persona for the poem "Poeta soy" (Poet Am I), which appears at the beginning of the book *Estrellas en el pozo* (Stars in the Well), published a year later in Costa Rica by the *Repertorio*. Lars therefore forged a lit-

Paperback cover for Lars's 1942 poetry collection, which she published in Santiago, Chile, with the help of the Chilean poet
Gabriela Mistral and the Chilean diplomat Juan Guzmán Cruchaga (Charles E. Young Research Library,
University of California, Los Angeles)

erary mask by distinguishing between herself as the individual and as the poet:

Poeta soy . . . y vengo, por Dios mismo escogida,
a soltar en el viento mi canto de belleza
a vivir con más alto sentido de nobleza

(Poet am I . . . and come by God Itself chosen
to free into the wind my song of beauty
to live with the highest sense of nobility).

After separating from her husband, Lars returned to El Salvador at the end of 1934. Writers and artists such as Salarrué and Serafín Quiteño used to meet in the house of Alberto Guerra Trigueros. The poem "Romance de los tres amigos" (Ballad of the Three Friends), included in her second book, *Canción redonda* (Round Song, 1937), is dedicated to those encounters with the circle of Salvadoran writers. This book also

reflects the deaths in 1936 of her father and the Spanish poet Federico García Lorca; the poems are clearly influenced by Lorca. At the end of the 1930s she worked as a journalist for *Diario Nuevo* (New Journal) and for the critical and influential afternoon newspaper *Diario Latino* (Latino Newspaper). At this time she interviewed George Bernard Shaw, who passed briefly through the port of La Libertad.

In 1943 Lars moved to Mexico City. She established some contacts with Spanish Republicans and attended El Rancho del Artista (The Ranch of the Artist), where she became a close friend of María Asúnsolo, a patron of artists. When the military dictatorship of Maximiliano Hernández Martínez collapsed in April 1944 in San Salvador, she wrote two of her most explicitly political poems: "Romance de la sangre caída" (Ballad to the Fallen Blood) and "Romance de los héroes sin nombre" (Ballad of the Nameless Heroes). She

Yo levantaré la sangre,
¡La sangre de mis hermanos!...
La que ha corrido, desnuda,
Bajo metal y soldados.
La que subía en el aire,
—por altas nubes girando—,
y al derrumbarse quedó
hecha de sal en los párpados.
¡Sangre de los hombres libres!
¡Imán de rumbos marcados!

(I will raise the blood
The blood of my brothers!
The one that has run, naked,
Under metal and soldiers
The one that arose into the air,
—by high clouds turning—,
and upon collapsing remained
turned into salt in the eyelids
Blood of free men!
Magnet of marked routes!).

In *Romances de norte y sur* Lars develops the dual character of her two cultural and ethnic traditions: the Irish American and the Mestizo Salvadoran. She also summarizes some of her trips and includes poems about several Central American countries.

In 1947 Lars published two works: *Sonetos* (Sonnets) and *Ciudad bajo mi voz* (City under My Voice). The first book consecrated her as a master of one of the most classical and difficult forms of the Spanish poetic tradition. The second one earned her the prize in the contest in commemoration of the fourth centenary of San Salvador in 1946. Besides rescuing the history of the capital, Lars poetically represents some of the causes of the Salvadoran social conflict. The sixth poem in this book, "Ecos" (Echoes), introduces an innovative dramatic verse in which Lars transforms poetry into a dialogic and polyphonic discourse, anticipating a popular device used by young avant-garde poets in the 1970s. Officially, however, there was a total indifference to her work. The high esteem in which she holds poetic language is evident in "Ecos":

Me salva de mí misma:
huesped del alma en alma devolviendo
la palabra que abisma
lo que entiendo y no entiendo
por este viaje en que llorando aprendo

(It saves me from myself:
guest of the soul in soul returning
the word that plunges
what I understand and do not understand
by this voyage in which crying I learn).

Also in 1947 Lars traveled to San Francisco, California, with her son. She worked at a cookie factory,

Paperback cover for Lars's 1946 collection, in which she writes about her complex heritage as the daughter of an Irish American father and a Mestizo Salvadoran mother (Charles E. Young Research Library, University of California, Los Angeles)

included these poems, as she wrote in an undated letter to Ana Julia Alvarez, published in *Poesía completa* (Complete Poetry, 1999), in "mis cinco romances a la revolución . . . a nuestro pueblo" (my five ballads to the revolution . . . to our people).

Originally, the ballads were to appear in Lars's *Romances de norte y sur* (Ballads of North and South, 1946). But owing to political events in El Salvador in 1944—when the conservative Salvador Castaneda Castro was ruling the country without opposition—"Romance de la sangre caída" and "Romance de los héroes sin nombre" ultimately were not included in the book. Because of a publication of the Salvadoran National University, *Opinión Estudiantil* (Student Opinion, December 1945), scholars have fully recognized her most radical and political poems:

the National Biscuit Company (Nabisco), and also at a peach-packing company. Thanks to a friend, Lars started to sew bonnets in a Masonic lodge. Through her friendship with the Chilean Nobel laureate, Gabriela Mistral, Lars was asked to give conferences at several California colleges. She lived in Santa Barbara in the house of Mistral. This friendship was not new, as, undoubtedly, Lars had previously published her book *La casa de vidrio* (The House of Glass, 1942) in Santiago with the help of Mistral and the Chilean diplomat Juan Guzmán Cruchaga.

Lars returned to El Salvador in 1948. After the coup d'état of Oscar Osorio in December 1948, her brother Max Brannon was incarcerated. Lars protested directly to the military junta. Thanks to her reputation, Osorio named her cultural attaché at the Salvadoran Embassy in Guatemala. Osorio also helped her buy the house where she lived until her death in the Colonia Nicaragua in San Salvador.

While in Guatemala Lars established contacts with poets and was active in several cultural circles. She met Carlos Samayoa Chichilla and married him in December 1949. This second marriage ended in divorce in 1967. In 1953 she published *Donde llegan los pasos* (Where the Steps Arrive) in San Salvador. This book has been considered a pivotal work, in which Lars initiates a more complex and mature voice.

In 1955 she began working at the recently founded Departamento Editorial (Editing Department) of the Salvadoran government. The Salvadoran poet Hugo Lindo was minister of culture at the time and promoted the creation of several cultural institutions attached to the government. Lars worked in the literary section of the Departamento Editorial for several years, where she directed one of the most prestigious Salvadoran cultural magazines, *Cultura*. She concurrently collaborated on *Guión literario* (Literary Sketch), an artistic newspaper and a national cultural agenda of the same ministry, from 1956 to 1967. Because of the rising price of coffee in the international market, the ensuing economic development allowed a rebirth of the arts and culture in the Salvadoran capital. Lars was one of the main promoters of this brief renaissance.

During that long stay in El Salvador, which lasted until her death in 1974, Lars continued to publish and to develop her more mature, accomplished works. In 1958 she published her poetic memories, *Tierra de infancia* (Land of Infancy). This book is her work most celebrated by the general public and is required reading at the high-school level in El Salvador. In her early *Estrellas en el pozo* Carmen Brannon invented her poetic persona, "Claudia Lars"; twenty-five years later Lars reinvented the childhood of her alter ego and her discovery of her poetic vocation.

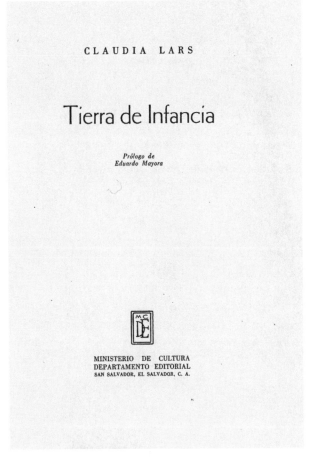

CLAUDIA LARS

Tierra de Infancia

*Prólogo de
Eduardo Mayora*

MINISTERIO DE CULTURA
DEPARTAMENTO EDITORIAL
SAN SALVADOR, EL SALVADOR, C. A.

Title page for Lars's 1958 collection of poems based on her childhood memories. The book is her most popular work and is required reading in Salvadoran high schools (University of Kentucky Library).

The following year she published *Fábula de una verdad* (Fable of a Truth). In this work Lars uses an intricate form to root poetry in the landscape of the country and in its cultural identity.

Lars also published two books on children's poetry: *Canciones* (Songs, 1960) and an anthology, *Girasol: Antología de poesía infantil* (Sunflower: Anthology of Children's Poetry, 1962). During the 1960s she developed her most hermetic, complex, and mature works. In 1962 the first compilation of her works appeared under the title *Presencia en el tiempo: Antología poética* (Presence in Time: Poetic Anthology). That same year she published the book that has been considered the summit of her poetry, *Sobre el ángel y el hombre* (About the Angel and the Man). Its formal perfection is comparable to any work of San Juan de la Cruz in the Golden Age or to the works of the Uruguayan Sara de Ibañez in the twentieth century. In 1966 Lars published *Del fino amanecer* (Of Fine Dawn). In this work she changes from the classical form of poetry to freer, avant-garde verse. It has also been

CLAUDIA LARS

Sobre el Angel y el Hombre

P O E S I A

SEGUNDO PREMIO REPUBLICA DE EL SALVADOR
CERTAMEN NACIONAL DE CULTURA
1 9 6 1

MINISTERIO DE EDUCACION
DIRECCION GENERAL
DE PUBLICACIONES
SAN SALVADOR, EL SALVADOR, C. A.

*Paperback cover for the collection that includes what critics
consider Lars's most formally perfect poetry
(John C. Hodges Library, University
of Tennessee)*

renowned because of its elaborate irrational images. One year before, this book obtained the shared prize in the Hispano-American contest in commemoration of the fifth centenary of the poetic recitals of Quetzaltenango. Her last book, *Nuestro pulsante mundo: Apuntes sobre una nueva edad* (Our Pulsating World: Notes on a New Age), was published in 1969. In this collection she celebrates modern technology and portrays the scientific world as a messianic era in which justice and the brotherhood of humans will triumph.

Despite the omissions in her poetry of references to concrete political events in El Salvador—notably the 1969 war against Honduras—several later generations consider Lars the most relevant female poet of the country. She compensated for the lack of reference to politics and feminism by her dedication to the most classical forms of poetry and by her civic ethic. The most diverse contemporary Salvadoran writers, such as Manlio Argueta, José Roberto Cea, David Escobar Galindo, and Matilde Elena López, have all regarded her poetry as one of the most prominent bodies of work in the Central American region. Even Salvadoran anthologies published during the civil war in the 1980s judge Lars by her aesthetic accomplishments and moral integrity.

One year before Lars's death López compiled her works in two volumes produced by the Salvadoran National University. This publication was one of the last honors she received. Lars declined both a nomination to the Salvadoran Academy of Language and a Doctorate Honoris Causa offered by the Jesuit University in El Salvador, Universidad Centroamerica José Simeón Cañas. She died on 22 July 1974 and was buried in San Salvador with all honors at the Cementerio de los Ilustres (Cemetery of the Illustrious). In 1999, in commemoration of the centennial of her birth, Carmen González Huguet published two volumes that compile Lars's complete poetry. This last collection has the merit of including her posthumous *Poesía última, 1970–1973* (Last Poetry, 1975), as well as forty poems that appeared originally in *Repertorio Americano*.

Although in the United States Claudia Lars's works have not motivated serious critical responses—probably due to her lack of a sharp political and feminist position—in El Salvador she is considered the most prominent female poet of the country. The discrepancy between these two perceptions of the Salvadoran canon should lead critics to question the diverse political and aesthetic motifs that serve as guidelines to the recognition of artists in Latin America, as well as in U.S. academic circles.

Reference:

Bruno Bosteels and Tina Escoja, eds., *Delmira Agustini y el modernismo: Nuevas propuestas de género* (Rosario, Argentina: Viterbo, 2000), pp. 165–172.

José Lezama Lima

(19 December 1910 – 9 August 1976)

Aída Beaupied
Pennsylvania State University

See also the Lezama Lima entry in *DLB 113: Modern Latin-American Fiction Writers,* First Series.

BOOKS: *Muerte de Narciso* (Havana: Ucar, García, 1937);

Coloquio con Juan Ramón Jiménez (Havana: Secretaría de Educación, 1938);

Arístides Fernández (Havana: Dirección de Cultura, 1938);

Enemigo rumor (Havana: Ucar, García, 1941);

Aventuras sigilosas (Havana: Orígenes, 1945);

La fijeza (Havana: Orígenes, 1949);

Analecta del reloj (Havana: Orígenes, 1953);

La expresión americana (Havana: Instituto Nacional de Cultura, Ministerio de Educación, 1957);

Tratados en La Habana: Ensayos estéticos (Havana: Universidad Central de Las Villas, 1958);

Dador (Havana: Ucar, García, 1960);

Antología de la poesía cubana, 3 volumes (Havana: Consejo Nacional de Cultura, 1965);

Paradiso (Havana: Unión Nacional de Escritores y Artistas de Cuba, 1966);

La expresión americana y otros ensayos (Montevideo: Arca, 1969);

Posible imagen de José Lezama Lima (Barcelona: Llibres de Sinera, 1969);

La cantidad hechizada (Havana: Unión Nacional de Escritores y Artistas de Cuba, 1970);

Esferaimagen: Sierpe de Don Luis de Góngora. Las imágenes posibles (Barcelona: Tusquets, 1970);

Poesía completa (Havana: Instituto del Libro, 1970);

Algunos tratados en La Habana (Barcelona: Anagrama, 1971);

Las eras imaginarias (Madrid: Fundamentos, 1971);

Introducción a los vasos órficos (Barcelona: Barral, 1971);

Obras completas, 2 volumes, introduction by Cintio Vitier (Mexico City: Aguilar, 1975, 1977);

Cangrejos y golondrinas (Buenos Aires: Calicanto, 1977);

Fragmentos a su imán (Havana: Arte y Literatura, 1977);

Oppiano Licario (México: Era, 1977);

José Lezama Lima (from the cover for Coloquio internacional sobre la obra de José Lezama Lima, *volume 1, 1984; Thomas Cooper Library, University of South Carolina)*

Imagen y posibilidad, selected, with prologue and notes, by Ciro Bianchi Ross (Havana: Letras Cubanas, 1981);

Juego de las decapitaciones, prologue by José Angel Valente (Barcelona: Montesinos, 1982);

Poesía completa (Havana: Letras Cubanas, 1985);

Relatos, prologue by Reynaldo González (Madrid: Alianza Editorial, 1987);

La Habana (Madrid: Verbum, 1991);

Fascinación de la memoria: Textos inéditos, edited by Iván González Cruz (Havana: Letras Cubanas, 1993);

Diarios: 1939–49/1956–58, edited by Bianchi Ross (Mexico City: Era, 1994);

La visualidad infinita (Havana: Letras Cubanas, 1994);
Archivo de José Lezama Lima: Miscelánea, compiled, with
  prologue and notes, by González Cruz (Madrid:
  Centro de Estudios Ramón Areces, 1998);
La posibilidad infinita: Archivo de José Lezama Lima, edited
  by González Cruz (Madrid: Verbum, 2000).

José Lezama Lima is not only one of Cuba's most important writers to date but is also recognized among the most distinctive Latin American poets and novelists of the twentieth century. Although he cultivated all genres except drama, poetry interested him the most. This interest explains why the subject of poetry predominates everywhere in his essays, fictional works, lectures, interviews, and even in the letters that he wrote to his friends. It is not an exaggeration to say that Lezama Lima's life was almost exclusively dedicated to literature and to the development of an elaborated poetic system. To this effect, Lezama Lima himself used to say that the events of his biography were so few that they could all be connected to his literary works.

Despite his untiring dedication to literature, for many years Lezama Lima was only known by a small group within Cuba's intelligentsia. His hermetic style and the obscurity with which he conveyed his metaphysical concepts prevented this avant-garde writer from gaining popularity for almost three decades. However, after the publication of his 1966 novel, *Paradiso* (Paradise), Lezama Lima gained sudden international recognition and eventually came to be known as one of the writers of the "Boom," a publicity success experienced worldwide by Latin American literature during the 1960s. One of the consequences of this recognition came in 1972 when the Spanish Maldoror Prize was given to his *Poesía completa* (Complete Poetry, 1970). Also in 1972 the Italian translation of *Paradiso* was selected as Italy's best Latin American book for the previous year.

Lezama Lima was born on 19 December 1910 and lived most of his life in Trocadero, a modest street in the heart of what is known as Old Havana. His father was José María Lezama, and his mother was Rose María Lima; Lezama Lima also had two sisters. Except for two brief trips, one to Mexico in 1949 and the other to Jamaica in 1950, he never left Cuba. The sudden death of his father when he was overseas made Lezama Lima uncomfortable with the idea of leaving Havana and dying away from it. This attachment for the city where he was born, lived, and died became an important topic throughout his writings, not only as a subject in Lezama Lima's essays, such as his 1958 *Tratados en La Habana* (Treaties in Havana), but also as a symbol in his fictional and poetic works, as in *Paradiso*. Lezama Lima's attachment to the city became a link to

the profound love that he felt for his mother and his ideas about poetry. In his poetics the city and the mother became symbols of the interactions between the poet and his muse. In other words, the relationships between the man and his city, and between the son and his mother, were used by Lezama Lima as models of the interaction between poet and poetry (poetry as expressive of spirit). Whether as city, as mother, or as poetry, the presence of these feminine entities were transformed into images of a womb-like paradise that gave birth to the poet/son. Furthermore, being a Catholic writer, poetry was for Lezama Lima an avatar of the Holy Spirit. Nevertheless, these correlations between spirit, poetry, Havana, and mother are to be understood in relation to the role of the father as another significant figure in Lezama Lima's poetic system. The relevance of these figures in Lezama Lima's works has much to do with the death of his father, a captain in the Cuban army who died while doing military training in the United States when Lezama Lima was nine years old. The death of his father in a foreign land, together with the close attachment that Lezama Lima formed with both his mother and Havana, is at the core of his poetic system. It can also be said that one of the ingredients in Lezama Lima's system emerges from his spiritual misreading of Sigmund Freud. Eloísa Lezama Lima, literary critic and sister of the Cuban poet, comments that her brother used to describe himself as an Oedipal character, which explains why the Oedipus myth plays such an important role throughout his works.

Lezama Lima's poetic system represents a continuation of the tradition initiated by the Romantic poets. His system is in accord with that effort to find answers in poetry to alleviate an existential crisis that emanated from a generalized feeling of destitution, typical among modern poets. The alienation felt by these poets was often experienced as a sentiment of orphanhood that Friedrich Nietzsche described as God's death. In his book *José Lezama Lima: Poet of the Image* (1990), Emilio Bejel traces the legacy imprinted in Lezama Lima's works by Western thinkers and writers such as Giambattista Vico, Nietzsche, Martin Heidegger, Stéphane Mallarmé, and Paul Valéry. Bejel discusses how Lezama Lima's system is indebted to Western metaphysics, and he also shows how it builds on Blaise Pascal's ideas on the subject of fallen nature. According to Bejel, Lezama Lima's answer to the idea of a fallen nature, represented in his works by the death of the father, is the freedom of the poet/son who rejects imitation in favor of invention. His distinctive and difficult style allows him constantly to invent himself and the world around him. The image is the tool used by the poet to reinvent a world that is so much his own creation that readers find it difficult to elucidate it. As Bejel has indicated, Lezama Lima's rejection of rational metaphysics allows this aspect of his poetics to be described as postmodern.

Lezama Lima's commitment to literature has left such an impact on Cuban letters that—whether following his literary ideas or strongly rejecting them—one can detect the legacy of his influence in the generations of Cuban writers that have come after him. The strength of Lezama Lima's legacy can be partly explained by considering the seminal role he played in Cuba's literary history during a period known as the Republican era, the years after Cuba's independence and just before Fidel Castro's revolution in 1959. Lezama Lima has often been credited for being a tireless promoter of culture at a time when Cuba's cultural scene was suffering the effects of a general apathy and malaise, mostly instigated by political corruption and economic instability.

In 1937, while he was enrolled as a law student at the University of Havana, Lezama Lima became the editor of *Verbum,* the journal that was to represent the law students' association at that university. It is said that the journal only produced three issues and that the students and professors of the law school complained not only about its difficult and obscure style, but also about the fact that the prose and poetry of *Verbum* had no relevance whatsoever with the issues concerning justice and law. After this first experiment as editor, Lezama Lima edited two more short-lived literary journals until his efforts culminated in *Orígenes* (1944–1956), which has been recognized, with the Argentinian journal *Sur,* as one of the two most important Latin American journals of the 1940s and 1950s.

Lezama Lima took his role as editor with utmost seriousness; he concentrated his efforts, however, on the development of his poetic system, in theory—as in the case of his essays—and in practice in his poetic and fictional works. He was already an accomplished writer when in 1937 he published his first long poem, *Muerte de Narciso* (Death of Narcissus). While some critics have detected an evolution in Lezama Lima's works, others have stated that his style and the main thrust of his message did not change over the years. One can thus always recognize his characteristic expression in everything he ever wrote. Although it is true that there are significant changes over the years in both his style and his themes, one can perceive a consistency throughout his works, which can only be explained by the fact that Lezama Lima was always faithful to his poetic system. His complete dedication to his literary works also explains why he was never a politically committed writer and why, in politicized Cuba, he remained uncommitted, except for his participation in a student

JOSE LEZAMA LIMA

ENEMIGO RUMOR

EDICIONES
ESPUELA DE PLATA
LA HABANA
1 9 4 1

Paper cover for Lezama Lima's second collection of poetry. It had a major impact on the writers associated with the Cuban literary journal Orígenes, *which Lezama Lima edited from 1944 to 1956 (Dartmouth College Library)*

demonstration against the Cuban dictator Gerardo Machado in 1930.

Although Lezama Lima's first poems are dated 1927, his first important publication was *Muerte de Narciso* in 1937. Much has been written about this poem, but the critics agree that, in spite of the fact that it was Lezama Lima's debut as a poet, one can already detect in it the poetics that he spent his entire life developing into a system. The one aspect that connects this poem with the rest of Lezama Lima's works is the importance given to the role of the image, in this case, the image of Narcissus's death and resurrection. As Guillermo Sucre wrote in an essay included in the critical anthology *Lezama Lima* (1987), the image for Lezama Lima is not a substitute for reality but is reality itself: "La imagen para Lezama, sabemos, nunca es un doble, ni siquiera una sustitución. La imagen es la realidad del mundo invisible" (The image for Lezama Lima, as we know, is never a double, nor even a substitution. The image is the reality of the invisible world).

In 1941 Lezama Lima published what for many is one of his best books of poetry, *Enemigo Rumor* (Enemy Rumor). The readers of these poems were few, but among them was the group subsequently known as the generation of Orígenes, consisting of poets, writers, and intellectuals who gathered around Lezama Lima as their central figure and who published or exhibited their artistic designs in the journal of the same name. The effect that *Enemigo rumor* had on this group was best described in the testimony offered by the Cuban poet and critic Cintio Vitier in an essay in *Lezama Lima:* "Yo me siento impotente para comunicarles a ustedes lo que ese libro significó en aquellos años. Leerlo fue algo más que leer un libro. Su originalidad era tan grande y los elementos que integraba (Garcilaso, Quevedo, San Juan, Lautréamont, el surrealismo, Valéry, Claudel, Rilke) eran tan violentamente heterogéneos que si aquello no se resolvía en un caos, tenía que engendrar un mundo" (I feel impotent to convey to you what that book signified in those years. Reading it was more than to read a book. Its originality was so vast, and the elements that constituted it [Garcilaso, Quevedo, San Juan, Lautréamont, Surrealism, Valéry, Claudel, Rilke] were so violently heterogeneous, that if that did not result in chaos, it had to give birth to a world).

When explaining the meaning of the word *enemigo* in the title of the book, Vitier reminds readers that, for Lezama Lima, poetry is so real a substance that it is more genuine than the real world. Being even more real than reality, poetry is also a sound or a rumor capable of devouring everything, particularly the poet, who—in the tradition of the Romantic poets—claims to be more aware than most people of its presence. The poem—specifically, the image it creates—is the answer given by the poet in his interactions with that ever-present and always elusive enemy. That love affair in the interaction between poet and poetry is nothing new. The Romantic poets, and the Latin American *Modernistas,* had been portraying it for many years. What Lezama Lima adds to that interaction is the idea that in a world where fallen nature is absent, the only hope for redemption is the reality of the poet's image.

In 1945 Lezama Lima published his next book of poetry, *Aventuras sigilosas* (Surreptitious Adventures). Although this title is consistent with the representation of that amorous battle between poet and Poetry depicted in his previous books, here the interactions are more sexual than before. Because of the highly sexual content present throughout the poems, and also because they are connected by a narrative thread, the "surreptitious adventures" of this collection have often been compared to some of the scenes that appear in

Paradiso. The narrative level of the poems gives sustenance to an allegorical interpretation, but the esoteric content is a reproduction of the idea of the poet's penetration into the obscure world of poetry. This penetration is depicted by a series of sexual adventures in which the theme of incest is often present. This sexuality, marked by the incest taboo, gives the adventures their highly charged covert aspect. In his essay "Lezama o las probabilidades del olvido" (Lezama or the Probabilities of Oblivion) in *Lezama Lima* Bejel writes that "la penetración en lo oculto se establece aquí con la analogía del acto sexual, y en especial en la sexualidad erótica donde la mujer se ve como madre y donde se apetecen incestuosamente las hijas de la esposa" (the penetration in that which is hidden is established here with the analogy of the sexual act, and specifically by means of an erotic sexuality where the woman is seen as mother and where the daughters of the wife are incestuously desired). The incest taboo that appears so prominently in this book is always present in Lezama Lima's works. It is important because it is consistent with Lezama Lima's choice of the Oedipus myth to portray the obstacles that a poet must encounter in his path toward redemption.

Lezama Lima's next book of poems, *La fijeza* (Fixity), was published in 1949. The notion of fixity conveyed in this book re-creates the idea of a sustained—fixed—exchange of glances between poet and poetry. For Lezama Lima this fixation does not suggest immobility; rather, it is indicative of the steady manner in which poetry secures its contemplation of the poet. At the same time, with this idea of fixity Lezama Lima wants to convey the persistent manner in which the poet returns the gaze of poetry, by fixing his own sight into the object of his obsession. The spiritual element implied in this mutual contemplation is to be understood by the fact that poetry, identified by Lezama Lima as the Holy Spirit, is a divine presence whose persistent look corresponds to a calling toward the transcendental realm. Precisely because the fixed sight of poetry comes from the invisible world, however, the gap that separates it from the poet can only be crossed by poetry itself, that is to say, by the images the poet creates.

The divine role of poetry in Lezama Lima's works is more clearly stated in the title of another of his poetry collections, *Dador* (Giver, 1960). As Fina García Marruz indicated in his essay on the collection included in *Recopilación de textos sobre José Lezama Lima* (Collection of Texts about José Lezama Lima, 1970), Dador is one of the names of the Holy Spirit. In its role as mediator between God and man, the messages conveyed by this divine entity usually appear in the form of revelation, which explains their obscure nature and also accounts

Drawing of Lezama Lima from his Enemigo rumor *(Dartmouth College Library)*

for the need for an exegesis with a demanding process of initiation on the part of the interpreter. Obscurity has always been a characteristic of Lezama Lima's baroque style; Saúl Yurkievich, in an essay that appears in *Coloquio internacional sobre la obra de José Lezama Lima* (International Colloquium on the Works of José Lezama Lima, 1984) remarks of *Dador* that its exegesis can only be done in that cabalistic manner in which interpretations are, at the same time, hidden and revealed. According to Yurkievich, "el símbolo tiende a sobre pasar la esfera de la lengua, apunta a lo inefable. Deja entrever o entreoír aquello que no puede ser dicho, que no puede tornarse explícito: lo profundo o lo elevado, inaccesibles por vía verbal" (the symbol tends to surpass the sphere of language, to signal the ineffable. It allows us to nearly see and hear what can not be said, nor become explicit: that which is profound or elevated, and also inaccessible through language).

When in 1960 Lezama Lima published the spiritual *Dador,* the Cuban Revolution of 1959 had already started. This revolution was soon defined as Marxist, destined to affirm Karl Marx's assessment of religion as "the opium of the people." It is no wonder that Lezama Lima's place within an atmosphere so incompatible with religion and spirituality was soon to be the target of much criticism. Religion was not the only reason why Lezama Lima became a target for the revolutionary writers. They represented a new generation of poets and as such, they used politics to affirm themselves against the members of the Orígenes group, with Lezama Lima as its most representative figure. For these poets and writers, associated with the literary supplement of the newspaper *Lunes de Revolución* (Mondays of Revolution), Lezama Lima incarnated the elitist, bourgeois, politically uncommitted writer, whose retreat into a literary ivory tower was synonymous with the evils of capitalism. Although he admitted to having been wounded by these attacks, Lezama Lima once stated that such rivalries were typical among writers and poets. Years later, in 1968, Lezama Lima was among the members of the jury that voted unanimously in favor of one of those young poets that had been so

JOSE LEZAMA LIMA

AVENTURAS SIGILOSAS

EDICIONES ORÍGENES
LA HABANA
1945

*Paperback cover for Lezama Lima's collection of poems in which the relationship between the poet and poetry
is portrayed allegorically as a form of incest (Biblioteca Daniel Cosio Villegas, Colegio de México)*

critical of him: Herberto Padilla, who won Cuba's most prestigious poetry prize with his controversial book *Fuera del juego* (Out of the Game).

In spite of the fact that Lezama Lima had always strayed away from politics, his participation in Padilla's jury placed him at the epicenter of what soon was a monumental political storm. Not only was Padilla's book critical of the revolution, but the attention it received was the flame that ignited conflicts between the state and many intellectuals, including international figures of the stature of Jean-Paul Sartre and Octavio Paz. The conflicts between the establishment and intellectuals had already started in 1961 in a series of meetings between Castro and Cuba's intelligentsia. These meetings culminated with what is known as Castro's "speech to the intellectuals," which ended with a warning to those who were critical of the revolutionary government. Lezama Lima acquired international fame precisely during this same decade, which marked the beginning of a repression that had not only intellectuals

but also homosexuals as its main targets. Although he never publicly acknowledged whether he was a homosexual, Lezama Lima, at a time when many homosexuals were being taken to labor camps, became the Cuban writer who achieved international fame with *Paradiso,* the eighth chapter of which offers an elaborate description of a homosexual encounter.

Paradiso models the structure of a bildungsroman (a novel of education or development), and one can see in it the legacy of writers such as Johann Wolfgang von Goethe, Marcel Proust, and James Joyce. Although in many ways *Paradiso* is an autobiographical novel, its aim is to demonstrate how the poetic image is man's vehicle for understanding the world around him and for achieving redemption from it. As in Lezama Lima's poetry, within the novel the poetic image is presented as the means to both understand and to transcend the world. Thus, critics such as Emir Rodríguez Monegal have said that traditional narrative strategies do not offer useful approaches to the novel and that, as in

Dante's *Divine Comedy, Paradiso* demands an allegorical analysis with the objective of unveiling the spiritual meaning that serves as its foundation.

Lezama Lima published the first chapter of the novel in *Orígenes* in 1949; significantly, its appearance coincided with the writing of his essay "Las imágenes posibles" (Possible Images, 1948), which later appeared as one of the essays in *Analecta del reloj* (Analect of the Clock, 1953). Because "Las imágenes posibles" is the first important essay in which Lezama Lima assumes the task of elucidating his poetic system, critics have said that its appearance at the same time that the novel was being written demonstrates how both fiction and nonfiction were Lezama Lima's vehicles for the elaboration of his poetic system. After the essays of *Analecta del reloj* Lezama Lima wrote two important collections of essays, *La expresión americana* (American Expression, 1957) and *La cantidad hechizada* (Bewitched Quantity, 1970). This last collection includes "Las eras imaginarias" (Imaginary Eras), the essay in which Lezama Lima gives a more definitive touch to his theory that poetry offers the best path toward the understanding of history.

During the 1960s, and until his death in 1976, Lezama Lima kept a low profile in Cuba's literary circles. He was still able to work, however, and he did not retire completely from the literary scene. When the Academy of Cuban Sciences founded the Institute for Literature and Linguistics in 1965, Lezama Lima began working there as investigator and consultant. Considering the menial jobs he held during the Republican era, it is no surprise that this job at the institute was to be his favorite. He once said that he liked it because it gave him the opportunity to work at the library of the Sociedad de Amigos del País (Society of the Nation's Friends). Critics are divided in their assessment of the way in which Lezama Lima, as a professional writer, was treated in revolutionary Cuba. This topic has been an important one because, given that in a Marxist state all jobs and promotions come from the establishment, Lezama Lima's professional satisfaction, or the absence of it, has been the critics' way to gauge the impact the revolution had on his professional life. Some critics argue that Lezama Lima was well treated by the revolutionary organizations until his death. They also call attention to the fact that in 1968 he was one of the delegates to a cultural congress in Havana, and that in that same year the National Library included him in its homage to Cuban writers. Moreover, in 1969 Lezama Lima was named literary consultant to Cuba's most important editorial and cultural center, La Casa de las Américas (The House of the Americas).

Critics at the opposite end of the spectrum have indicated that these jobs and nominations concealed the fact that Lezama Lima was being ignored as a literary

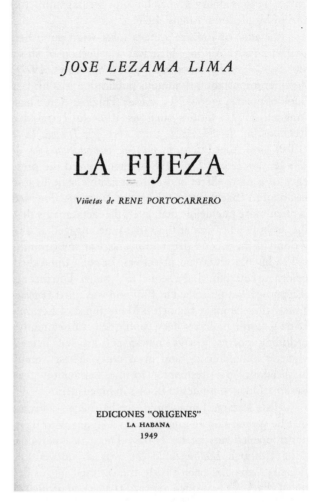

JOSE LEZAMA LIMA

LA FIJEZA

Viñetas de RENE PORTOCARRERO

EDICIONES "ORIGENES"
LA HABANA
1949

Title page for the collection in which Lezama Lima identifies poetry as a divine presence that holds the poet in a fixed gaze (University of Iowa Libraries)

figure. Many have stated that he lived in fear and that he would have been attacked and persecuted—as was the case with other intellectuals—if it had not been for his international fame, and especially for his discreet silence when it came to proclaiming, in writing, his disenchantment with the revolution. For these critics it is obvious that in the highly politicized climate that has prevailed in Cuba since the 1959 revolution, someone such as Lezama Lima, who never belonged to any of the political organizations and who from the beginning was identified as an elitist, could never be among the writers and artists who were being favored by the establishment. The one thing that remains incontestable with respect to this controversy is the fact that Lezama Lima's poetics, with its emphasis on transcendence and its complete disregard for time, runs contrary to the Marxist concept of history. Another evident truth is that, no matter how he felt as a professional writer within revolutionary Cuba, he kept writing until the end of his life, on 9 August 1976.

Several of Lezama Lima's texts were published posthumously. Among them was a collection of short stories, *Cangrejos y golondrinas* (Crabs, Sparrows, 1977). Another important posthumous publication was his last book of poems, *Fragmentos a su imán* (Fragments to Their Magnet, 1977). Critics such as Roberto Fernández Retamar, in *Recopilación de textos sobre José Lezama Lima* (1970), and Abel Prieto, in *Coloquio internacional sobre la obra de José Lezama Lima* (1984), have noticed the presence of a more direct and communicative style in this last book. While it is true the poet of *Fragmentos a su imán* is often more intelligible than ever, the fact remains that the author, who was at the same time engaged in the writing of the second part of *Paradiso,* was still committed to his old ideas and objectives. Lezama Lima died before he could finish the sequel to *Paradiso.* The incomplete novel was published in 1977 and was titled *Oppiano Licario* after its main character. Many more of Lezama Lima's writings have been published subsequently, including poems, essays, newspaper articles, letters, vignettes, conferences, and even notes. These recent publications give testimony to the fascination that Lezama Lima continues to inspire in his readers.

José Lezama Lima's influence has been so strong that he is well known among many Cubans who have never opened any of his books. There is a paradox here: although his personal life was so uneventful, Lezama Lima has been slowly transformed into a fictional character that often appears as a legendary figure in Cuban literature and film. For him, this transformation likely would be seen as proof that his image has guaranteed his transcendence.

Letters:

Cartas (1939–1976), edited by Eloísa Lezama Lima (Madrid: Orígenes, 1979);

Mi correspondencia con Lezama Lima, edited by José Rodríguez Feo (Havana: Unión Nacional de Escritores y Artistas de Cuba, 1989);

Cartas y Eloísa y otra correspondencia, edited by José Triana (Madrid: Verbum, 1998);

Como las cartas no llegan, edited by Bianchi Ross (Havana: Ediciones Unión, 2000).

Interview:

Félix Guerra, *Para leer debajo de un sicomoro: Entrevistas con José Lezama Lima* (Havana: Letras Cubanas, 1998).

References:

Emilio Bejel, *José Lezama Lima: Poet of the Image* (Gainesville: University of Florida Press, 1990);

Iván González Cruz, *Diccionario: Vida y obra de José Lezama Lima* (Valencia, Spain: Generalitat Valenciana, 2000);

Eloísa Lezama Lima, *Una familia habanera* (Miami: Ediciones Universal, 1998);

Emir Rodríguez Monegal, "Paradiso en su contexto," *Imagen,* 25 (1968): 27–33;

Pedro Simón, ed., *Recopilación de textos sobre José Lezama Lima* (Havana: Casa de las Américas, 1970);

Eugenio Suárez-Galbán, ed., *Lezama Lima* (Madrid: El Carezón, 1987);

Suárez-Galbán and Cristina Vizcaíno, eds., *Coloquio internacional sobre la obra de José Lezama Lima* (Caracas: Fundamentos, 1984).

Enrique Lihn

(3 September 1929 – 10 July 1988)

Luis Correa-Díaz
University of Georgia

BOOKS: *Nada se escurre, 1947–1949* (Santiago: Talleres Gráficos Casa Nacional del Niño, 1949);

Introducción a la poesía de Nicanor Parra: Estudio, datos biográphicos y selección (Santiago: Editorial Universitaria, 1952);

Poemas de este tiempo y de otro, 1949–1954 (Santiago: Renovación, 1955);

La pieza oscura, 1955–1962 (Santiago: Editorial Universitaria, 1963);

Agua de arroz (Santiago: Litoral, 1964);

Poesía de paso (Havana: Casa de las Américas, 1966);

Escrito en Cuba (Mexico City: Era, 1969);

La musiquilla de las pobres esferas (Santiago: Editorial Universitaria, 1969);

La cultura en la via chilena al socialismo (Santiago: Editorial Universitaria, 1971);

Algunos poemas (Barcelona: Llibres de Sinera, 1972);

Batman en Chile; o, El ocaso de un ídolo; o, Solo contra el desierto rojo (Buenos Aires: Ediciones de la Flor, 1973);

Por fuerza mayor (Barcelona: Ocnos-Editorial Llibres de Sinera, 1975);

La orquesta de cristal (Buenos Aires: Sudamericana, 1976);

París, situación irregular (Santiago: Aconcagua, 1977);

A partir de Manhattan (Valparaíso, Chile: Ganymedes, 1979);

El arte de la palabra (Barcelona: Pomaire, 1980);

Noticias del extranjero: Pedro Lastra cumple cincuenta años (Santiago: Editorial Universitaria, 1981);

Estación de los desamparados (Mexico City: Premià Editora, 1982);

Sobre el antiestructuralismo de José Miguel Ibáñez Langlois (Santiago: Camaleón, 1983);

El Paseo Ahumada (Santiago: Minga, 1983);

Al bello aparecer de este lucero (Hanover, N.H.: Ediciones del Norte, 1983);

Paradiso, lectura de conjunto (Mexico City: Universidad Nacional Autónoma de México, 1984);

Pena de extrañamiento (Santiago: Sinfronteras, 1986);

Mester de juglaría (Madrid: Hiperión, 1987);

Enrique Lihn (photograph by Paz Errazuriz)

La aparición de la Virgen: Textos y dibujos (Santiago: Cuadernos de Libre(e)lección, 1987);

Eugenio Téllez, descubridor de invenciones (Santiago: S. N., 1988);

Asedios a Oscar Hahn, edited by Lihn and Pedro Lastra (Santiago: Editorial Universitaria, 1989);

La República Independiente de Miranda (Buenos Aires: Sudamericana, 1989);

Diario de muerte, edited by Pedro Lastra and Adriana Valdés (Santiago: Editorial Universitaria, 1989);

Un cómic, by Lihn and Alejandro Jodorowsky (Santiago: P. Brodsky, 1992);

Porque escribí, selected, with a prologue and critical appendix, by Eduardo Llanos Melussa (Santiago: Fondo de Cultura Económica, 1995);

El circo en llamas: Un crítica de la vida, edited by Germán Marín (Santiago: LOM, 1997).

Editions and Collections: *Antología al azar* (Lima: Ruray/Poesía, 1981);

La pieza oscura, preface by Waldo Rojas (Madrid: Literatura Americana Reunida, 1984);

Album de toda especie de poemas (Barcelona: Lumen, 1989);

Editions in English: *This Endless Malice: Twenty-five Poems,* selected and translated by William Witherup and Serge Echeverria (Northwood Narrows, N.H.: Lillabulero, 1969);

If Poetry Is to Be Written Right, translated by Dave Oliphant (Texas City: Texas Portfolio Press, 1977);

The Dark Room and Other Poems, edited, with an introduction, by Patricio Lerzundi, translated by Jonathan Cohen, John Felstiner, and David Unger (New York: New Directions, 1978);

Figures of Speech, translated by Oliphant (Austin: Host, 1999).

OTHER: Jorge Edwards, *Temas y varaciones: Antologia de relatos,* selected, with a prologue, by Lihn (Santiago: Editorial Universitaria, 1969);

Diez cuentos de bandidos, selected, with a prologue, by Lihn (Santiago: Quimantú, 1972);

Oscar Hahn, *Asedios de Oscar Hahn,* edited by Lihn and Pedro Lastra (Santiago: Editorial Universitaria, 1989).

Enrique Lihn is a Chilean poet who appears together with Nicanor Parra, Gonzalo Rojas, and Oscar Hahn—not to mention the universally acknowledged Chilean masters: Gabriela Mistral, Vicente Huidobro, and Pablo Neruda—in all major and comprehensive anthologies of Spanish (and Spanish American) verse. Lihn's poetic work—like his other literary and artistic production in fiction, drama, essay, video, and comics—is highly independent, experimental, dynamic, and protean. These characteristics do not cancel other qualities of his work, such as pragmatism, extreme intertextuality, and ever-present criticism, as stated by Mauricio Ostria in his seminal article "Enrique Lihn o la desdicha sin respuesta" (Enrique Lihn or the unresponded unhappiness, 1992).

Lihn was born on 3 September 1929 in Santiago de Chile to Enrique Lihn Doll and Maria Carrasco and died almost sixty years later in the same city and country. Between these two dates he created a distinctive body of literary work and became one of the most original Latin American poets. During his lifetime he was greatly influential, especially among young writers, and he has remained so. This influence is due not only to his never-ending interest in what younger generations have to say, but also to the fact that his poetry constantly sought to challenge both his own achievements and modern poetic conventions. Lihn began his studies in Saint George School and continued them at the Colegio Alemán (German School). He also studied drawing and painting for a few years in the School of Fine Arts at the Universidad de Chile. Although Lihn wanted to be a painter—an artistic calling he never totally abandoned—he developed his literary career early in life, publishing his first book of poetry in 1949 at the age of twenty. In addition to his career as a writer Lihn served as a public intellectual and promoter of the arts. He contributed his writing (and occasionally his drawings) to several scholarly journals, magazines, and newspapers; coedited literary journals such as *Cormorán* and *Quebrantahuesos;* presented various radio programs; gave lectures; directed poetry workshops; organized events; and finally since 1972 served as a professor of literature in the humanities department of the Universidad de Chile. He traveled to Europe, visiting Spain, France, Italy, Belgium, and Switzerland, and to the United States, where in the late 1970s, as a Guggenheim fellow, he was invited by several universities to read and discuss his work. In 1978, while in the United States, Lihn published a bilingual edition of *The Dark Room and Other Poems* with the support of the Center for Inter-American Relations and the collaboration of writer Patricio Lerzundi and American poet David Unger. He won a series of literary awards, including the Juegos de Poesía in 1956, the Casa de las Américas (Cuba) in 1966, and Premio Municipal de Literatura in 1970. Despite these biographical landmarks, it is necessary to clarify that instead of speaking of his civil biography, the poet himself proposed a different way of understanding his life using a concept that he named "biopoética" (biopetics)—comprising the lives and writings of the *personajes* (characters) who speak in his opus. In her book *Enrique Lihn: Escritura excéntrica y modernidad* (Enrique Lihn: Eccentric Writing and Modernity, 1995), the critic Carmen Foxley has fully satisfied Lihn's request, studying his poetry from that biopoetic perspective. Foxley's aim was to offer a more global reading of Lihn's works in contrast to the more specific way in which previous critics had interpreted his opus.

Lihn was a prolific and protean writer who successfully cultivated diverse genres: poetry, novel, short story, essay, drama, comics, and video. He is best known for his poetry, however, which comes across as cruelly self-conscious and constantly critical of poetry as a genre and as a social/cultural phenomenon. An example of this critique is one of Lihn's best-known poems, "Mester de juglaría" (1966; the title refers to a medieval traveling minstrel or storyteller), in which he accuses poetry of being an "alquimia del verbo" (alchemy of the word) and calls poems "vicios de la palabra" (vices of the word) that no longer have an historical role or impact. Because of this type of critique, critics and readers alike have seen Lihn as an absolutely and irredeemably negative artist, an image that has not changed even after the poet's death. In the first chapter of his *Lengua muerta: Poesía, post-literatura & erotismo en Enrique Lihn* (Dead Tongue: Poetry, Post-literature & Eroticism in Enrique Lihn, 1996), Luis Correa-Díaz reviews and deconstructs the apparent gratuity of that negativity, and of self-directed irony and parody carried to their extremes as critical formulas, in order to show their aesthetic, literary, and social values.

Perhaps the best way of defining Lihn's poetry is to examine the poet's own attempt at a definition of his work. On several occasions, for example in poet and critic Pedro Lastra's *Conversaciones con Enrique Lihn* (Conversations with Enrique Lihn, first published in México in 1980), Lihn called his discursive strategy "poesía situada" (situated poetry) and contrasted it to what he called "poesía poética" (poetic poetry). By means of this definition he is referring to "la relación de un texto con la situación" (the relationship of a text with its situation). Lihn explains: "El pretexto de los textos es su situación: en este caso 'el discurso social implícito que ellos contradicen.' Creo que el aspecto sedmántico de un escrito no es menos importante que cualesquiera otros; es decir, el sentido específico que el autor le ha dado a su obra consciente o inconscientemente, su relación con la situación, y una obra no deja nunca de estar situada" (The pretext of texts is their situation: in this case "the implicit social discourse that they contradict." I think the semantic nuance of a writing is no less important than any other aspect; that is to say, the particular meaning that unconsciously or consciously the author has given to his work, its relationship with its situation, and all works are situated). In sum, Lihn's poetry is "el producto de un cierto enfrentamiento con la situación" (the product of a certain confrontation with the situation), within the historical-cultural context.

Lihn started writing poetry in the late 1940s, and his first published collection of poems was *Nada se escurre, 1947–1949* (Nothing Vanishes, 1947–1949), published in 1949. This collection was followed in 1955 by *Poemas de este tiempo y de otro, 1949–1954* (Poems of This Time and of Another, 1949–1954). According to Lihn, neither book deserves serious critical attention. In 1957, however, the critic and writer Jorge Elliot included Lihn in *Antología crítica de la nueva poesía chilena* (Critical Anthology of Chilean New Poetry); and in 1972 Lihn was included in the anthology edited by Saul Yurkievic, *Poesía hispanoamericana 1960–1970* (Hispano-American Poetry 1960–1970), which includes poems that had won the prestigious Casa de las Américas award throughout that decade. Lihn's work also

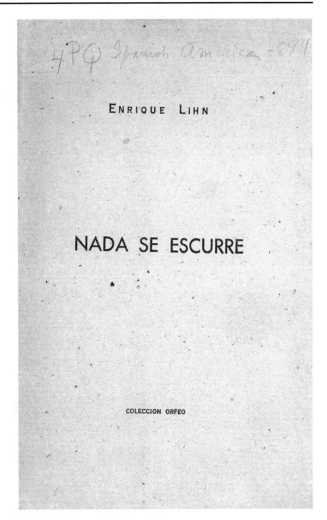

Paperback cover for Lihn's first book (1949), a collection of his poems written from 1947 to 1949 (Library of Congress)

appears in several other Latin American poetry anthologies, among them those edited by Jorge Rodríguez Padrón, *Antología de poesía hispanoamericana, 1915–1980* (Anthology of Hispano-American Poetry, 1915–1980, 1984); Lastra and Luis Eyzaguirre's *Catorce poetas hispanoamericanos de hoy* (Fourteen Hispano-American Poets of Today, 1984); Juan Gustavo Cobo Borda's *Antología de la poesía hispanoamericana* (Anthology of Hispano-American Poetry, 1985); Julio Ortega's *Antología de la poesía hispanoamericana actual* (Anthology of Current Hispano-American Poetry, 1987); and Stephen Tapscott's *Twentieth-Century Latin American Poetry: A Bilingual Anthology* (1996). In his brief introduction to the poet, Tapscott writes: "Since the publication of *La pieza oscura, 1955–1962* (*The Dark Room*, 1963), Enrique Lihn has been acknowledged as one of the foremost experimental writers of Chile." Many critics and major poets, who since then have praised each of the poet's books, have confirmed Tapscott's statement.

Paperback cover for Lihn's 1963 collection, which marks a decisive break with the aesthetics of his first three books in favor of more-experimental poetry (Vanderbilt University Library)

Lihn himself recognized the importance of *La pieza oscura* as a definitive rupture with the aesthetics of his previous books and an anticipation of his future works. In the chapter "En los alrededores de *La pieza oscura*" (In the Surroundings of *The Dark Room*) of his interviews with Lastra, Lihn provides his vision of the book: nonpoetic (that is, traditional) poems that develop a new grammar and rhetoric of the making of poetry. Talking about the central text, the poet says: "La pieza oscura, por ejemplo, es un texto cuidadoso de los efectos que puede producir, envolviendo al lector-auditor con su oleaje de ritmo fónico y semántico" ("The Dark Room," for instance, is a text that carefully considers the effects that it wants to produce, involving the reader with its phonic and semantic rhythm).

Before he began to use his poetry primarily to focus on his experience as a world traveler, Lihn published *La musiquilla de las pobres esferas* (The Little Music of the Poor Spheres) in 1969, a challenging collection that definitively consolidated his reputation. Both "Mester de juglaría" and

"Porque escribí" (Because I Write), another well-known poem, appear in this book. In his "Nota Preliminar" (Preliminary Note), Waldo Rojas defines Lihn's work as "Poesía de la contradicción, esto es, poemas que son documento de un conflicto: la destrucción de la poesía misma, pero la destrucción justamente a través de ella, serpiente alquímica que devora su cola" (Poetry of contradiction, this is to say poems that document a conflict: the destruction of poetry itself, but the destruction of it precisely through the means of poetry itself—the alchemical snake that swallows up its own tail). Rojas writes that Lihn shows in most of the poems what was one of his long-term poetic subjects—"una poesía que va a nutrirse del cuestionamiento de sí misma" (a type of poetry that nurtures a questioning of itself)—and in general makes problematic "la inanidad del lenguaje literario" (the inutility of literary language). Rojas concludes that "esta contradicción debe resultar necesariamente inquietante para el lector habitual de poesía, pero aún más para los poetas" (this contradiction might be disturbing to regular readers of poetry, but even more so to other poets).

Another of Lihn's poetic cycles is what his critics, such as Foxley, have called "poesía o notas de viaje" (poetry or notes of travel), in which the author poetizes his contrasting impressions while exploring cities and cultures. Books representative of this cycle are *Poesía de paso* (Poetry in Passing, 1966); *Escrito en Cuba* (Written in Cuba, 1969); *París, situación irregular* (Paris, Irregular Situation, 1977); *A partir de Manhattan* ([Re]Starting from Manhattan, 1979); *Estación de los desamparados* (Station of the Unsheltered), written in 1962 in Lima but not published until 1982; and *Pena de extrañamiento* (Sentence of Exile), published in 1986. Although they specifically focus on Chilean social and political life during the 1980s and have been considered as a type of urban chronicle rather than travel poetry, two other collections should be included in this group: *El Paseo Ahumada* (The Ahumada Boulevard, 1983) and *La aparición de la Virgen: Textos y dibujos* (The Apparition of the Virgin: Texts and Drawings, 1987).

In addition to these works Lihn published three anthologies during his lifetime: *Algunos poemas* (Some Poems), published in Barcelona in 1972; *Antología al azar* (Anthology at Random), published in Lima in 1981; and *Mester de juglaría*, published in Madrid in 1987. There have also been two posthumous anthologies of his verses. The first of them came out in Barcelona a year after his death: *Album de toda especie de poemas* (Album of All Kind of Poems, 1989). In the prologue of this collection, assembled by Lihn before his death, the poet reviews his own work and explains the main principles of his poetics, the spirit of which this single quotation could represent: "A la experiencia poética como solución imaginaria al problema de la realidad, subyace la infraexperiencia del fracaso, la otra cara del 'triunfo' que es, de por sí, el arte de la palabra" (Beneath the poetic experience, as an imaginary solution to the problem of reality, lies the infraexperience of failure, the other side of success, which is precisely the art of speech). The second posthumous anthology, *Porque escribí* (Because I Wrote, 1995), includes a critical appendix by Chilean poet Eduardo Llanos Melussa, in which he emphatically states: "creo que la poesía de Enrique Lihn–en especial la publicada en la década de los sesenta–es una de las más significativas del mundo contemporáneo" (I believe that Enrique Lihn's poetry–especially that published in the 1960s–is one of the most significant in the contemporary world). In order to support his opinion Llanos Melussa states that a personal and poetic coherence is what gives Lihn's work its future relevance–particularly in historical moments when poets are reluctant to look at poetry itself. As well as the aforementioned, there are three other English-language anthologies of Lihn's work: the bilingual edition *This Endless Malice: Twenty-five Poems* (1969), with poems selected and translated by William

Witherup and Serge Echeverria; and two volumes translated by the American poet Dave Oliphant, *If Poetry Is to Be Written Right* (1977) and *Figures of Speech* (1999). Despite his undisputable literary reputation–and presence in so many anthologies–Lihn's complete poetry has not yet been gathered in a single volume.

Related to and fused with the metapoetical force and art in Lihn's poetry, there are two major and permanent subjects, love and death. These subjects and every possible combination of them–love for death, the death of love, love beyond death, death overcoming love–appear in his works. Unquestionably, Enrique Lihn is an unusual love poet and an inconsolable "aprendiz del arte de morir" (apprentice of the art of dying), as he portrayed himself in one of the poems of his last book, *Diario de muerte* (Journal of Dying, 1989). As for his love poetry, the best example is his collection *Al bello aparecer de este lucero* (To the Beautiful Rise of This Bright Star, 1983), the title of which comes from a verse of the sixteenth-century Spanish poet Fernando de Herrera. Here the poet furiously delivers a self-defeated discourse in the form of a journal of a dying– or already dead–amatory experience. In these poems Lihn meditates on the forever-unsolved contradiction between experiencing love and writing about love while at the same time depicting the painful and capricious paradoxes of Eros. The poem "Sobre el amor" (On Love) ironically reads: "Escribo para quienes creen que van a morir en un momento / de ofuscación sobre el amor" (I write for those who believe that they are going to die in a moment / of exasperation with love).

Lihn's poetry about death is best represented in *Diario de muerte*, posthumously published by two of his best friends and readers, Lastra and Adriana Valdés a year after Lihn's death. This work stands as the poet's masterpiece and as his final testament to the world and to himself. Written during the last year of his life under extreme conditions–while the author was dying of cancer–this book attempts the impossible for poetic discourse: the crude documentation of this solitary and unspeakable experience, which the poet sees as the terminal state of his own writing as well. In an effort to capture and assure for future readers the literary value of *Diario de muerte,* Lastra and Valdés say in their "Nota preliminar" that they do not know of a similar work in the context of Chilean literature, an argument that could be extended to all of Spanish American writing.

Enrique Lihn died on 10 July 1988 after a long and agonizing struggle with illness. The abundance and prestige of Lihn's poetic work, as well as other writings, will last as an example of one of the highest Latin American lifelong literary achievements. In all of his intense and extensive works of poetry, fiction, and criticism Lihn concerned himself with that complex equation between man and his culture, brandishing his "espíritu de negación"

Paperback cover for Lihn's 1986 collection of poems based on his travels outside of Chile (Vanderbilt University Library)

(spirit of negation) against powers of all kind and fossilized modes of existence that offer ready-made ways of perceiving reality or life instead of freedom. He never hesitated to wield this spirit of negation even when he was aware that it was neither understood nor appreciated. Even so, Lihn's extremely critical spirit has proven through the years to be the core of an intelligence that cannot be disregarded.

Interviews:

Pedro Lastra, *Conversaciones con Enrique Lihn,* second edition (Santiago: Atelier, 1990).

References:

Luis Correa-Díaz, *Lengua muerta: Poesía, post-literatura & erotismo en Enrique Lihn* (Providence, R.I.: INTI, 1996);

María Luisa Fischer, *Historia y texto poético: La poesía de Antonio Cisneros, José Emilio Pacheco y Enrique Lihn* (Concepción: Literatura Americana Reunida, 1998): pp. 125–188;

Carmen Foxley, *Enrique Lihn: Escritura excéntrica y modernidad* (Santiago: Editorial Universitaria, 1995);

Tamara Kamensain, "Enrique Lihn: por el pico del soneto," in *El texto silencioso: Tradición y vanguardia en la poesía sudamericana* (México: Universidad Nacional Autónoma de México, 1983), pp. 37–44;

Mauricio Ostria, "Enrique Lihn o la desdicha sin respuesta," *Revista de Crítica Literaria Latinoamericana,* 35 (1992): 49–60;

Mario Rodríguez F. and María Nieves Alonso, *La ilusión de la diferencia: La poesía de Enrique Lihn y Jaime Gil de Biedma* (Santiago: La Noria, 1995);

Oscar Sarmiento, "La deconstrucción del autor: Enrique Lihn y Jorge Teillier," *Revista Chilena de Literatura,* 42 (1993): 237–244;

Karin Waisman and Juan Medrano-Pizarro, *Enrique Lihn: (des)encuentros* <http://www.dartmouth.edu/~lihn/intro.html>;

George Yúdice, "The Poetic of Breakdown," *Review: Latin American Literature and Arts,* 23 (1978): 20–24.

Papers:

Some of Enrique Lihn's papers are at the Biblioteca Nacional in Chile.

Dulce María Loynaz

(10 December 1902 – 27 April 1997)

Elizabeth Ely Tolman
University of North Carolina at Chapel Hill

BOOKS: *Canto a la mujer estéril* (Havana: Molina, 1938);
Versos, 1920–1938 (Havana: Ucar García, 1938);
Juegos de agua: Versos del agua y del amor (Madrid: Editora Nacional, 1947); translated by Judith Kerman as *Waterplay* (Matanzas, Cuba: Vigía, 1997);
Las corridas de toros en Cuba (Havana: Mariano, 1950);
Jardín: Novela lírica, foreword by Federico Carlos Sainz de Robles (Madrid: Aguilar, 1951);
Poetisas de América: Discurso pronunciado en la Academia Nacional de Artes y Letras (Havana: Empresa Editora de Publicaciones, 1951);
El día de las artes y de las letras (Havana: Sociedad de Artes y Letras Cubanas, 1952);
Poemas sin nombre, foreword by Sainz de Robles (Madrid: Aguilar, 1953); translated by Harriet de Onís as *Poems Without Name* (Havana: Editorial José Martí, 1993);
La Avellaneda: Una cubana universal (Havana, 1953);
Carta de amor al Rey Tut-Ankh-Amen (Madrid: Nueva Imprenta Radio, Col. Palma, Serie Americana, 1953); translated by Kerman as *Love Letter to King Tut-Ankh-Amen* (Montreal: Coleccíon Cotidianas de Estival, CCLEH, 2002);
Un verano en Tenerife (Madrid: Aguilar, 1958);
Ultimos días de una casa, preface by Antonio Oliver (Madrid: Soler, 1958);
Bestiarium, edited by Pedro Simón (Havana: Editorial José Martí, 1991);
La novia de Lázaro (Madrid: Betania, 1991);
Poemas náufragos (Havana: Letras Cubanas, 1991);
Ensayos literarios (Salamanca: Ediciones Universidad de Salamanca, 1993);
Yo fui (feliz) en Cuba: Los días cubanos de la Infanta Eulalia (Havana: Letras Cubanas, 1993);
Melancolía de otoño (Pinar del Río, Cuba: Hermanos Loynaz, 1997);
Diez sonetos a Cristo (Santa Clara, Cuba: Sed de Belleza, 1998);
Cartas de Egipto (Pinar del Río, Cuba: Hermanos Loynaz, 2000);
Fe de vida (Havana: Letras Cubanas, 2000);

Dulce María Loynaz (from the 1993 Madrid edition of Ultimos días de una casa; *College of Charleston Library)*

La palabra en el aire: Conferencias y discursos, edited by Vivian Milagros González González and Rosa Pablos de la Rosa (Pinar del Río, Cuba: Hermanos Loynaz, 2000);
El áspero sendero, edited by Roberto Carlos Hernández (Havana: Extramuros, 2001).

Editions and Collections: *Obra lírica: Versos (1920–1938). Juegos de agua. Poemas sin nombre,* foreword by Federico Carlos Sainz de Robles (Madrid: Aguilar, 1955);
Poesías completas, edited by Margaret Bates (Madrid: Aguilar, 1962);
Poesías escogidas, edited, with an introduction, by Jorge Yglesias (Havana: Letras Cubanas, 1984);

Dulce María Loynaz (Canto a la mujer estéril y Ultimos días de una casa), edited, with an introductory note, by Alejandro González Acosta, Serie Poesía Moderna, no. 169 (Mexico City: Coordinación de Difusión Cultural de la U.N.A.M., 1991);

Dulce María Loynaz: Ensayos, edited by Luis Raúl (Havana: Instituto Cubano del Libro, Dirección de Literatura, 1992);

Dulce María Loynaz: Premio de Literatura en Lengua Castellana Miguel de Cervantes 1992 (Madrid: Ministerio de Cultura, 1993);

Poemas escogidos, selected by Pedro Simón (Madrid: Visor Libros, 1993);

Poesía completa (Havana: Letras Cubanas, 1993);

Antología lírica, introduction by María Asuncion Mateo (Madrid: Espasa Calpe, 1993);

Ultimos días de una casa (Madrid: Colecion Torremozas, 1993).

Edition in English: *A Woman in Her Garden: Selected Poems of Dulce María Loynaz,* edited and translated by Judith Kerman (Buffalo, N.Y.: White Pines, 2001).

Although few collections of her work have been published, Dulce María Loynaz is one of the most widely read and critically acclaimed Latin American poets of the twentieth century. Born into a prominent Cuban family in the early part of the century, Loynaz met and influenced some of the most prominent Spanish-language poets of her age. Her work was widely praised by writers as diverse as Juan Ramón Jiménez, Federico García Lorca, and Gabriela Mistral. In addition to her poetry, Loynaz also published a novel, a travel book, and several essays, all of which were well received. Despite her status as one of the social elite of Cuba, Loynaz never abandoned her homeland and consistently demurred when asked for an opinion about the political situation in her country. As a result of her loyalty to her country and her international success as an author, she is revered in her native homeland. Among her many awards and honors are the Alejo Carpentier Medal in 1933; induction into the Cuban National Order of Merit Carlos Manuel de Céspedes in 1947; the Grand Cross of Alfonso X the Wise in 1947; election as president of the Cuban Academy of Language in 1952 (a position she held until the 1990s); the Cuban National Literature Prize in 1987; an honorary doctorate from the University of Havana in 1987; the Spanish journalists' prize Isabel la Católica in 1991; and the Cervantes Prize in 1992. This latter prize sparked a revival of interest in her work, which only intensified after her death in 1997.

Loynaz was born on 10 December 1902 in Havana near El Vedado for much of her life. Her parents, General Enrique Loynaz del Castillo and María de las Mercedes Muñoz Sañudo, counted themselves among the elite of Cuba. Enrique Loynaz was an officer under Antonio Maceo in his liberating army of the War for Cuban Independence, known in the United States as the Spanish American War, and earned the rank of general as a result of his efforts in the war. Despite his country's struggle against Spain and his own participation in the war, the general never lost his love of his ancestral home and inculcated this love into his four children, of which Dulce María Loynaz was the eldest. General Loynaz is best known in Cuba for having composed the music and written the lyrics to the patriotic anthem "Himno Invasor" (Invading Anthem). He also wrote a book about his wartime experiences, which his daughter arranged to have published in 1989 under the title *Memorias de la Guerra* (Memories of the War). Just as General Loynaz passed on a love of the arts to his children, so too did María de las Mercedes Muñoz Sañudo. Loynaz's mother presided over the European-style gatherings in her home, singing and playing the piano for her family and guests.

From an early age, Loynaz and her three younger siblings, Enrique, Carlos Manuel, and Flor, enjoyed playing musical instruments, composing poetry, drawing, and writing and enacting dramas. The Loynaz family never sent their children to school, instead hiring tutors to come to the house. As a result of this unconventional schooling, Loynaz developed an early love for literature and the arts, and as a young girl translated the works of Jean Racine and Pierre Corneille into Spanish. Her affection for poets and their works was not limited to the French and included Rubén Darío and the Cuban poet José Martí.

In a 1991 interview with Pedro Simón, Loynaz recounts the much-discussed story of her first publication. In 1919, as a result of a death in the family when she was sixteen years old, Loynaz and her siblings were compelled to observe the strict social rules of mourning, which forbid social excursions. She and her siblings, along with two cousins, conceived of staging a poetry contest with her grandparents as judges. Loynaz won the contest, and her father was so impressed with her poem, "Invierno de almas" (Winter of Souls), that he gave it to his friend Osvaldo Bazil, editor of the popular Cuban newspaper *La Nación* (The Nation). Bazil not only published her poem and a biographical sketch, he also personally presented Loynaz with a journalist's card.

This experience emboldened Loynaz to seek other avenues to publish her poetry, although it was not until 1938 that her first book was published. Just as she was beginning to write poetry seriously, she had the fortunate occasion to meet Spanish poets Lorca and Jiménez, who both came to stay at the

DULCE MARIA LOYNAZ

CANTO A LA MUJER

ESTERIL

Publicado en la Revista
Bimestre Cubana, número de
Julio - Octubre de 1937

1938
—
MOLINA Y CIA.
MURALLA 55 - 57
LA HABANA

*Title page for Loynaz's first book, a series of poems about a woman unable to bear children
(Albany University Library)*

Loynaz home. Lorca became friends with all the Loynaz siblings, though he was especially fond of Flor and Carlos Manuel, to whom he gave original manuscript copies of his plays *Yerma* (Barren, 1934) and *El público* (The Public, 1978), respectively. Jiménez later wrote about his visit with Loynaz in *Españoles de tres mundos* (Spaniards of Three Worlds, 1942). Although many critics have claimed the influence of these two poets on Loynaz's work, she always maintained her originality, saying that her literary voice was formed in the tutoring sessions of her childhood.

Despite her love for literature and the arts, Loynaz followed family tradition and entered law school. She graduated in 1927 from the University of Havana and practiced law for several years, though by

her own admission she rarely worked on cases outside the family's interests. Because of her family's wealth, she was able to travel widely, visiting many European countries, the Middle East, much of South America, and the United States. These travels greatly influenced her writing, inspiring many of the poems she wrote during the 1920s.

Although most of Loynaz's poetry was not published until the 1930s, she actually wrote the majority of her work in the 1920s. *Bestiarium* (Bestiary), written in 1921 when she was nineteen years old but not published as a complete collection until 1991, reflects both her interest in logic and in the exotic things she saw on her travels abroad. Begun as revenge against a college professor who gave out a rather tedious assignment for her natural history exam, *Bestiarium* soon became a fanciful description of the animal kingdom. Pedro Simón claims in his introduction to the 1991 edition, a facsimile that includes Loynaz's original manuscript with handwritten corrections, that *Bestiarium* is a whimsical "muestrario de esencias que, en su gracia y pureza, puede llevarnos a veces hasta a algún retrato irónico de la insensatez humana" (sample of essences that, in its charm and purity, can lead us at times to an ironic portrayal of human folly). From the mosquito, which carries yellow fever, to the butterfly kept inside a museum display case, Loynaz's animals resemble the fanciful creatures depicted in the medieval bestiaries and carry with them a commentary on humankind's frequently destructive relationship with the natural world.

Although *Bestiarium* is the work in which Loynaz developed her distinctive literary voice, the Cuban people first became acquainted with her upon the publication of the poem *Canto a la mujer estéril* (Song to the Sterile Woman) in 1937. This poem, thought to be autobiographical since Loynaz had no children from either of her two marriages, depicts the raw emotions of a woman unable to reproduce. The poetic voice swings between descriptions of the infertile woman's intense desire to become pregnant and adamant justifications that this woman has already given birth to many artistic creations, dreams, and poems that can enrich the world just as a living child. If the sky, wind, and sea have no need to reproduce and remain admired by all, muses the poetic voice, why should sterile women be judged on their inability to bear children? The poem ends by proclaiming that the sterile woman is Eve: "¡No saben que tú guardas la llave de una vida! / ¡No saben que tú eres la madre estremecida / de un hijo que te llama desde el Sol!" (They don't know that you hold the key to a life! / They don't know that you are the trembling mother / of a son who calls you from the Sun!).

The powerful expression of emotions found in *Canto a la mujer estéril* is likewise present in nearly all of Loynaz's work. This quality is apparent in *Versos, 1920–1938* (Verses, 1920–1938), published in 1938 in Spain, a collection that includes *Canto a la mujer estéril*. Although some critics reading *Versos* and the later works have placed Loynaz in the Cuban Vanguard movement because of the purity and introspection of her poetry, her verse differs greatly from the more political work of Cuban poets Nicolás Guillén and Juan Marinello. Even when she writes about such potentially polemical sociological subjects such as bridges and handicapped children, Loynaz avoids social statements, preferring instead to emphasize the beauty of nature, the endurance of the human condi-

tion, and the universality of emotions. Poets, according to her, are people who see both the surrounding world and the internal world of the psyche more deeply than others. Their responsibility, believed Loynaz, was to describe not how they wanted reality to be, but how it really was.

In the poem "Los puentes" (Bridges), for example, included in *Versos,* Loynaz writes that bridges unite rather than divide, but that "¡ . . . que aun sobre el abismo tan hondo de la vida, / para todas las almas no haya un puente de amor . . . !" (. . . even over the deep abyss of life, / there is no bridge of love for all those souls . . . !). Similarly, the handicapped girl of "El madrigal de la muchacha coja" (The Madrigal of the Lame Girl) is not exalted as a member of a repressed class but as a person touched with her own special beauty: "Nadie la hallara bella; / pero había en ella / como una huella / celeste . . . Era coja la niña: / Se hincó el pie con la punta de una estrella" (Nobody would find her beautiful; / but there was in her, / like a celestial footprint / . . . The girl was lame: / she sank her foot in the point of a star). In her introduction to *Antología lírica* (Lyrical Anthology, 1993), María Asunción Mateo writes about the poems in *Versos:* "Junto a una constante inquietud metafísica, hay un alma de mujer que nos transmite la sensorialidad y sensualidad, el perfume de los paisajes antillanos, pero teñido siempre de una honda añoranza y de una profunda desolación por ese tiempo ido que no le es posible recuperar ya" (Alongside a constant anxious mysticism there is the soul of a woman who transmits sensuality, the perfume of forgotten landscapes, but that is always tinged with a deep yearning and a profound grief for the past that cannot possibly be recovered). The strong voice that characterizes Loynaz's later poetry is clearly present even among her earliest work.

Shortly before the publication of *Versos,* Loynaz married her cousin Enrique de Quesada y Loynaz. The marriage was unhappy and ended in divorce six years later. In 1946, however, Loynaz married Spanish journalist Pablo Álvarez de Cañas and moved with him to the Canary Islands. Both the move and the marriage encouraged her literary endeavors, inspiring her personally and professionally. During the time Loynaz lived in Spain and the Canaries, she delivered many speeches, attended conferences, and published articles in several Spanish journals. Many of these speeches and essays deal with the theme of women and their role within society and academe. Despite the nascent feminist movement, and the female poets who protested the use of the term *poetisa* (poetess), Loynaz never objected to its use or to the treatment of her as a woman. She claimed that rather than feel discriminated against because of her sex, she felt empowered by it. Her writings about poets such as Mistral, Delmira Agustini, Alfonsina Storni, Juana de Ibarbourou, and Gertrudis de Avellaneda were well received, and she was granted some authority on the subject, perhaps because of her sex. Loynaz maintained that women's writing and men's writing were distinct and easily recognizable. In spite of her long friendship with Mistral and her acknowledged debt to other women poets, Loynaz denied claims that they influenced her work or that she could be categorized as a women's poet. In *Confesiones de Dulce María Loynaz* (Confessions of Dulce María Loynaz, 1993), an interview with long-time friend Aldo Martínez Malo, Loynaz stated that she was "en el proceloso mar de la poesía algo así como un navegante solitario" (something of a solitary navigator in the stormy sea of poetry).

Loynaz dedicated her second book, *Juegos de agua: Versos del agua y del amor* (Water Games: Verses of Water and of Love, 1947; translated as *Waterplay*, 1997), to her husband, writing, "A Pablo Álvarez Cañas, en vez del hijo que él quería" (To Pablo Álvarez Cañas, instead of the child he wanted). According to poet and critic Emilio Ballagas, the book represents Loynaz's attempt to capture the four fundamental elements that constitute the universe. The three sections of *Juegos de agua* describe water, above the other elements, as the origin of life. This theme is seen in the poet's other work as well and stems from Loynaz's interest in her island home, in the natural world, and in religion.

The title poem of the book, "Juegos de agua," portrays water as a force that both nourishes and assails the man-made world. Humankind cannot grasp water either literally or figuratively, as it remains a part of nature largely outside of control: "Hay que apretar el agua / para que suba fina y alta / . . . / Un temblor de espumas / la deshace en el aire; la vuelve a unir" (It's necessary to squeeze water / so that it will rise fine and tall / . . . / A shudder of foam / undoes it in the air; it forms anew). The "games" water plays with people, evaporating and flooding, cleansing and sullying, gushing and trickling, are present in all of the poems of the collection and represent the essential quality Loynaz sees in nature itself: something alive and intrinsically intertwined with, but apart from, humankind.

This ambiguity regarding the character of nature and humankind's relationship with it is reflected in the brief poem "Duda" (Doubt), found in the first section of *Juegos de agua,* "Agua de mar" (Water of the Sea). The one-line poem reads, "Cuando la ola viene impetuosa sobre la roca . . . ¿La acaricia o la golpea?" (When the wave comes impetuously over the rock . . .

VERSOS

DE DULCE MARIA LOYNAZ

1920 - 1938

LA HABANA

Title page for Loynaz's second book, published in 1938, which includes the poems from Canto a la mujer estéril *(Doheny Memorial Library, University of Southern California)*

does it caress it or hit it?). Another poem, "Presencia" (Presence), depicts a blind girl who wants to know what the sea is like. When led to the ocean, she dips her hand into it and trembles. The poem concludes: "La niña ciega se sonríe . . . / ¿Sabrá ya / —mejor que yo, mejor que tú . . . – / cómo es el mar?" (The blind girl smiles . . . / I wonder if she knows / —better than me, better than you . . . – / what the sea is like?). Both poems demonstrate the impossibility of truly understanding not only nature, but also the role of nature in people's lives. The collection ends with the poem "Noé" (Noah), which proclaims that words, like water, eventually disappear without a trace, never to return.

Loynaz received great praise for her strong literary voice and was awarded the Grand Cross of Alfonso X the Wise shortly after the publication of *Juegos de agua* in 1947. This prize confirmed her as one of the leading intellectuals of Spain, despite her Cuban citizenship. The Cuban government made her a grande dame of the National Order of Merit Carlos Manuel of Céspedes later that same year. The critical success that Loynaz enjoyed during this period enabled her to travel widely around South America and Europe, attending literary conferences and giving speeches. *Las corridas de toros en Cuba* (Bullfights in Cuba), published in 1950, confirmed Loynaz not only as a leading intellectual of the day but also as a social crusader. Although ultimately unsuccessful in her attempts to rid Cuba of its bullfights, Loynaz's work was widely read and discussed.

The 1951 publication of *Jardín* (Garden) established Loynaz as a novelist as well as a poet. Despite her success as a journalist, essayist, and novelist, Loynaz considered herself first and foremost a poet. She even called her novel a "poema en prosa" (prose poem), claiming that although the difference between a poem and a prose poem is difficult to define, there exist poetic ideas that do not fit within verse and that only prose will allow to flourish. As if to further blur the lines between the genres, Loynaz subtitled her book *Novela lírica* (Lyrical Novel). Many critics have noted that this blending of the novelistic and the poetic is paralleled by the thematic ambiguity of the work: it is nearly impossible to distinguish between dream and reality, between the supernatural and the concrete within the pages of the novel. In his essay "La mujer en el jardín y la luna en el mirador" (The Woman in the Garden and the Moon in the Window, 1993) Juan Remos asks, "¿es el poema o la novela así inspirados, lo que traiciona la realidad, o es la realidad impuesta lo que traiciona a la inveterada realidad?" (Is it the poem or the novel thus inspired that betrays reality, or is it the imposed reality that betrays the inveterate reality?) Loynaz, ever the poet, leaves the question unanswered, claiming that poetry that does not cause the reader to question, to change her opinion, is not poetry.

Jardín is the story of a woman, Bárbara, who lives in an isolated mansion surrounded by a large garden. In the prelude to the novel Loynaz writes:

> Esta es la historia incoherente y monótona de una mujer y un jardín. No hay tiempo ni espacio, como en las teorías de Einstein. . . . No es, gracias a Dios, una novela humana. Quizá no sea siquiera una novela. El Diccionario de la Lengua dice—y hay que creerle—que novela es una obra literaria donde se narra una acción fingida; y cabe preguntar si merece el nombre de acción este ir y venir infatigable, este hacer caminar infinitamente a una mujer por un jardín"

(This is the incoherent and monotonous story of a woman and a garden. There's no time or space, as in Einstein's theories. . . . It is not, thanks be to God, a human novel. Perhaps it is not even a novel. The Dictionary of Language says—and it must be believed—that a novel is a literary work that narrates a made-up action; and it is worth questioning if this indefatigable coming and going, this infinite walking of a woman through a garden, deserves the name of action).

Regardless of the lack of action, however, *Jardín* does capture the essence of the protagonist and her search for truth as she paces the walls of her garden.

Much in the way her later poem *Ultimos días de una casa* (Last Days of a House, 1958) tells the sad story of a family home in decline, *Jardín* chronicles Bárbara's actions over the span of one hundred years. From the day she watches the moon fall into the moist earth of her garden to the day one hundred years later when she watches ghost-like as a workman turning her garden into a hotel discovers the piece of moon she buried years before, Bárbara remains, like the Eve figure in *Canto a la mujer estéril,* isolated and separate from those around her. She is unable to participate in the outside world and sequesters herself in her home and garden, finding comfort in her great-aunt's love letters and the magical images that appear before her eyes.

Although Loynaz always rejected claims that her novel constituted one of the precursors to the magical realism that flourished in works such as Gabriel García Márquez's *Cien años de soledad* (One Hundred Years of Solitude, 1968), *Jardín* undeniably juxtaposes the real and the supernatural, the factual and the fictive. She asserted that the novel sprang from life in her native Cuba, from her study of the arts, from poetry, and from motion pictures. Spanish director Luis Buñuel, in fact, decided to adapt the novel for the screen, although the project was never realized. The Cuban National Ballet, however, did stage the work, with ballerina Alicia Alonso as Bárbara.

Loynaz's popularity as a lecturer grew after the publication of *Jardín,* and in the years immediately following she traveled widely and spoke on topics ranging from Queen Isabel of Spain to the women poets of Latin America. Loynaz's Spanish publishers, Aguilar, capitalized on the poet's growing reputation and in 1953 published her next volume of poetry, *Poemas sin nombre* (translated as *Poems Without Name,* 1993) and *Carta de amor al Rey Tut-Ankh-Amen* (translated as *Love Letter to King Tut-Ankh-Amen,* 2002), a poem written years before while Loynaz was on a visit to Egypt and the Middle East.

Loynaz dedicated *Poemas sin nombre* to her mother, who had inspired her art in many ways. Just as the poems in *Juegos de agua* center around an examination of water, so too do the poems in this collection explore a single theme. The poems in *Poemas sin nombre* deal with love–jealous love, romantic love, brotherly love, passionate love, and finally, patriotic love–demonstrating both the depth of pain that heartbreak can reach and the hope that continues to exist despite the pain. The first, untitled poem references the dove that flew out from Noah's ark in search of dry land, announcing: "Palomita que vas volando / y en el pico llevas hilo, / dámelo para coserme / este corazón herido" (As you fly, little dove, / and in your beak carry thread, / give it to me, so that I may stitch up / this wounded heart). Each poem in the collection represents an attempt to repair the damage done to that heart wounded by love.

Loynaz's interest in religion and religious imagery surfaces in these poems as well. Although all of her work is concerned with faith and religion, the emphasis is particularly strong in *Poemas sin nombre*. From the dove to Jesus' tomb, Loynaz's images remind the reader of both the terrible absence of God and the promise of redemption. Even the poems that speak most explicitly of despair include references to Christ and salvation. The poetic voice that piercingly speaks of the pain of abandonment in "Poema XXXV," for example, also echoes the words of the Lord's Prayer, suggesting that hope remains even in the midst of anguish. The poem begins, "Como una guerra civil, como una rebelión sordamente contenida, el dolor ha estallado en alguna parte de mi cuerpo sin darme tiempo a huir, cogida por sorpresa entre su furia" (Like a civil war, like a secretly contained rebellion, the pain has exploded in some part of my body without giving me time to flee, caught by surprise by its fury), but ends with the speaker's realization that the sustenance she has given her body, Christ's daily bread, is sufficient to overcome her difficulties.

The last poem in the collection, "Poema CXXIV," is a paean to Loynaz's native Cuba. All of the heartache and the longing for God's peace seem to come together in the soothing image of the island. On the shores of Cuba no pain can last, no depression can linger. Only peace and the love of the natural world exist on the island, asserts the poetic voice. "Descanso de gaviotas . . . avemaría de navegantes, antena de América: hay en ti la ternura de las cosas pequeñas y el señorío de las grandes cosas" (Resting place of gulls . . . Ave Maria of navigators, antenna of America: in you there is the tenderness of small things and the dignity of big things). The love the

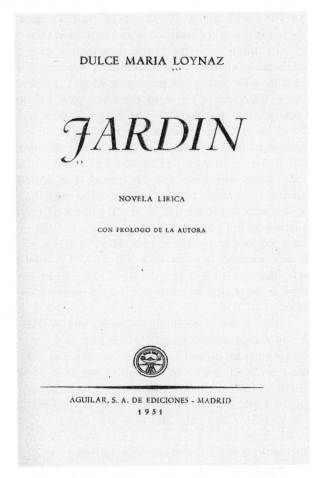

DULCE MARIA LOYNAZ

JARDIN

NOVELA LIRICA

CON PROLOGO DE LA AUTORA

AGUILAR, S. A. DE EDICIONES - MADRID
1951

Title page for Loynaz's "lyrical novel" about a woman who remains sequestered in her garden for one hundred years (Jackson Library, University of North Carolina at Greensboro)

poet feels for Cuba seems to suffice for all the pain expressed in the earlier poems.

Carta de amor al Rey Tut-Ankh-Amen, published in Spain in 1953, also exalts love. Actually written in 1929, this poem is the only remaining part of "Diario de viaje" (Travel Journal), a diary Loynaz kept while on a trip to Luxor. Loynaz made the trip seven years after the discovery of the young king's tomb in 1922, and her poem captures some of the awe felt around the world as news of the find spread. In some of the most erotic language found in Loynaz's poetry, she lovingly describes the tomb and the beautiful objects filling it, including the sarcophagus and the vial containing the remains of the king's heart. Filled with a love for the king she knows can never be returned, she yearns to possess, or even just to touch, his body. "Por esos ojos tuyos que yo no podría entreabrir con mis besos, daría a quien los quisiera, estos ojos míos ávidos de paisajes, ladrones de tu cielo, amos del sol del mundo" (For those eyes of yours that I could not half open with my kisses, I would give my greedy eyes filled with landscapes, thieves of your sky, masters of the sun of the world to whoever wanted them).

In addition to the erotic descriptions of the king's body, the poem demonstrates a yearning for times past. By loving and possessing King Tut-Ankh-Amen, the speaker wants to enter the past and to know what it was like to live so long ago. She says she would give her own eyes in order to see the king's world even for a moment. The poem ends exclaiming that if she could gain this knowledge, if she could really know the king and his world, she would remove him from his sarcophagus and rest him against her chest like a sick child: "Y como a un niño enfermo habría empezado a cantarte la más bella de mis canciones tropicales, el más dulce, el más breve de mis poemas" (And as with a sick child I would have begun to sing to you the most beautiful of my tropical songs, the sweetest and the shortest of my poems).

The years immediately following the publication of *Poemas sin nombre* and *Carta de amor al Rey Tut-Ankh-Amen* were fruitful for Loynaz: she began to publish a series of articles in the Cuban newspapers *El País* (The Country) and *Excelsior* (Excelsior); the first collected edition of her poetry, *Obra lírica* (Lyrical Work, 1955), was published in Spain; and she was named a member of the Arts and Letters Academy. During these years Loynaz and her husband traveled widely and lived for months at a time in the Canary Islands. These stays in the islands led to the creation of Loynaz's next book, *Un verano en Tenerife* (One Summer in Tenerife, 1958).

Un verano en Tenerife is a travel book, but like the novel *Jardín,* it is more of a prose poem than an essay. Through the thirty chapters of the book, Loynaz attempts to write a lyrical portrait of the Canary Islands. The book includes evocations of happy family memories alongside descriptions of the countryside, folklore, and historical interpretations. Among these varied descriptions are Loynaz's expressions of love for the islands. "¿Pedazos de qué cosa son las Islas Canarias? ¿Pedazos de un mundo desaparecido, de un jardín mitológico, del Paraíso bíblico?" (The Canary Islands are pieces of what thing? Pieces of a disappeared world, of a mythological garden, of the biblical Paradise?). *Un verano en Tenerife* became so popular in the islands that the government named a street after their adopted writer.

It is difficult to read *Ultimos días de una casa,* the long poem also published in 1958, outside of a political context. The poem tells the story of an old family home, much like El Vedado, that has seen generations of the family come and go. This fully conscious house mourns for its former residents, in particular a little girl who died of diphtheria, and reflects that it will soon pass away, and with it the memories of all the people who once lived there. Like *Carta de amor al Rey Tut-Ankh-Amen, Ultimos días de una casa* is filled with nostalgia for a bygone era. Although the poem was not published until 1958, on the eve of the Cuban revolution, Loynaz wrote it in 1928, when she was twenty-six years old. Her musings about the decline of a particular social class in Cuba presaged many societal changes that eventually culminated in Fidel Castro's revolution. These reflections are as close as Loynaz ever came to expressing an opinion about Cuban politics. Initially seen as aloof by the new government, who discouraged public recognition of her work, Loynaz eventually came to be respected by the Cuban people for her ability to stay above the fray and not involve herself in political disputes.

With the publication of *Ultimos días de una casa,* Loynaz's literary career slowed; she did not publish another book of new material until *Bestiarium* and *La novia de Lázaro* (Lazaro's Bride) in 1991. Her literary activities, however, did not cease. She continued to attend conferences, write articles, and give speeches. Gradually, however, Loynaz confined herself more and more to her home and her small circle of friends. Her husband left Cuba for Spain in 1962 and did not return until 1972. He died in 1974. After the 1970s Loynaz rarely left her home, preferring to hold her literary meetings in El Vedado. Her nomination for the Cervantes Prize in 1984 sparked a renewed interest in her work and led to the publication of *Poesías escogidas* (Selected Poems, 1984), a collection of her previously published poetry. The awarding of the Cervantes Prize eight years later caused Loynaz's friends and reviewers to convince her to release much of her unpublished material.

La novia de Lázaro is an exploration of the emotions experienced by a woman whose beloved has died. The speaker knows that Jesus raised Lazarus from the dead but chooses to concentrate on her psychological state in the days in between receiving the news of his death and his resurrection. Although everyone in the family naturally focuses on Lazarus's death, the young woman feels that it is she who died, that she has become a ghost haunting the places that once brought her such happiness. The poem ends with the young woman's declaration to the newly risen Lazarus that she has died and that she too needs Christ's healing powers. Lazarus's resurrection restored his body, but not his marriage.

Loynaz named her 1991 collection of poetry *Poemas náufragos* (Shipwrecked Poems) because of the many poems she considered adding to the volume, only to cast them away. She destroyed many of these forsaken poems so that they could not be published posthumously. Among the poems included is the "Tríptico de San Martín de Loynaz" (Triptych of Saint Martin Loynaz), a work written for Loynaz's ancestor by the same name. The poem describes the life and works of this Franciscan saint, born in Spain in the sixteenth century and martyred in Japan. In the middle of winter the saint envisions his martyrdom and knows he must say some comforting words to those who will die with him, words that he understands will burn with the truth. Similarly, in the poem "El primer milagro" (The First Miracle), Christ realizes that he cannot disappoint his mother when she announces that the wine at the wedding feast has run out. Even though he thinks her implied request wasteful, the dutiful son understands that his words and actions have power. With these largely religious poems, Loynaz affirms her belief that by exploring the actions and emotions of religious figures, poetry can enrich faith.

Yo fui (feliz) en Cuba: Los días cubanos de la Infanta Eulalia (I Was [Happy] in Cuba: The Cuban Days of the Princess Eulalia) was published in 1993, one hundred years after Princess Eulalia of Bourbon's visit to Cuba. Loynaz originally wrote the pieces in the collection some fifty years after the princess's trip and published several of them in the newspaper *El País*. In them the author expresses surprise at the princess's intelligence, writing, "La Infanta era joven y rubia; era también—nota curiosa—inteligente y llena por sí misma de una muy viva personalidad" (The Princess was young and blonde; she was also—curious note—intelligent and possessed of a very lively personality). From the descriptions of the princess's lavish ball gowns, the parties she attended, and the gentlemen attending her emerges a respectful portrait of a young woman who, like Loynaz herself, came from a class that expected women to behave in a certain way and yet rose above the restrictions placed upon her.

Dulce María Loynaz died on 27 April 1997 in her home. Among her unpublished papers were two novels and many poems. Loynaz rejected these novels, "Los caminos humildes" (Humble Roads) and "Mar muerto" (Dead Sea), because she thought they added nothing to the already voluminous works about Cuba. One collection of poetry published posthumously in 1998, *Diez sonetos a Cristo* (Ten Sonnets to Christ), was illustrated by Cuban schoolchildren as a tribute to Loynaz's life and contribution to Cuban letters. The sonnets depict Christ's birth, his agony in the garden, the betrayal by Judas, the Crucifixion, and finally, his Resurrection. "Apoteosis" (Apotheosis), the final poem, proclaims that though Christ has

died, his love and peace remain in the world, a message of hope amid troubling times.

In a time when poetry became more of a vehicle for political expression, Loynaz reminded the world of the purity of the poetic voice. While deliberately remaining on the sidelines as debates about feminism, revolution, and social experimentation raged around her, Loynaz's poetry nevertheless informed some of the very same topics she eschewed. Contemporary criticism exalts not only the beauty of her poetry but also the delicate balance she maintained between portraying the many injustices she saw while not condemning the social and political forces that led to them. Paradoxically, Loynaz is valued both as a poet who focused solely on her verse and as an artist who injected subtle political messages into her work. Whatever the approach, however, the critics all agree that Dulce María Loynaz was one of the most important poets of the twentieth century.

Letters:

Cartas a Julio Orlando, edited, with an introduction, by Aldo Martínez Malo (Havana: Gente Nueva, 1994);

Cartas a Chacón, cartas a Ballagas, edited by Virgilio López Lemus (Havana: Extramuros, 1996);

Cartas que no se extraviaron, edited by Martínez Malo (Havana: Fundación Jorge Guillén, 1997).

Interviews:

Pedro Simón, "Conversación con Dulce María Loynaz," in his *Dulce María Loynaz: Valoración múltiple,* edited by Simón (Havana: Centro de Investigaciones Literarias, 1991), p. 33–34;

Aldo Martínez Malo, ed., *Confesiones de Dulce María Loynaz* (Pinar del Río, Cuba: Hermanos Loynaz, 1993);

Vicente González Castro, *Un encuentro con Dulce María Loynaz* (Havana: Artex/Prelasa, 1994).

References:

Dulce María Loynaz: Valoración múltiple, edited by Pedro Simón (Havana: Centro de Investigaciones Literarias, 1991);

Homenaje a Dulce María Loynaz: Obra literaria, poesía y prosa, estudios y comentarios, edited by Ana Rosa Núñez (Miami: Ediciones Universal, 1993);

Verity Smith, "Dwarfed by Snow White: Feminist Revisions of Fairy Tale Discourse in the Narrative of María Luisa Bombal and Dulce María Loynaz," in *Feminist Readings on Spanish and Latin-American Literature,* edited by L. P. Condé and S. M. Hart (Lewiston, N.Y.: Edwin Mellen Press, 1991), pp. 137–149.

Leopoldo Lugones
(13 June 1874 – 18 February 1938)

Lee Skinner
University of Kansas

BOOKS: *Las montañas del oro: Poema* (Buenos Aires: Kern, 1897);

La reforma educacional: Un ministro y doce académicos (Buenos Aires, 1903);

El imperio jesuítico: Ensayo histórico (Buenos Aires: Compañía Sudamericana de Billetes de Banco, 1904);

Los crepúsculos del jardín (Buenos Aires: Moen, 1905);

La guerra gaucha (Buenos Aires: Moen, 1905);

Las fuerzas extrañas (Buenos Aires: Moen, 1906); translated by Gilbert Alter-Gilbert as *Strange Forces* (Pittsburgh: Latin American Literary Review Press, 1999);

La cacolitia: Ensayo sobre antiestetíca moderna (Buenos Aires: Coni, 1908);

Lunario sentimental (Buenos Aires: Moen, 1909);

Odas seculares (Buenos Aires: Moen, 1910);

Las limaduras de Hephaestos: I. Piedras liminares (Buenos Aires: Moen, 1910);

Las limaduras de Hephaestos: II. Prometeo (Un proscripto del sol) (Buenos Aires: Moen, 1910);

Didáctica (Buenos Aires: Otero, 1910);

Historia de Sarmiento (Buenos Aires: Otero, 1911);

El libro fiel (Paris: Piazza, 1912);

El ejército de la Ilíada (Buenos Aires: Otero, 1915);

Elogio de Ameghino (Buenos Aires: Otero, 1915);

El payador. Tomo I: Hijo de la pampa (Buenos Aires: Otero & García, 1916);

El problema feminista (San José, Costa Rica: Greñas, 1916);

Mi beligerancia (Buenos Aires: Otero & García, 1917);

El libro de los paisajes (Buenos Aires: Otero & García, 1917);

Las industrias de Atenas (Buenos Aires: Atlántida, 1919);

La torre de Casandra (Buenos Aires: Atlántida, 1919);

Rubén Darío (Buenos Aires: Glusberg, 1919);

El tamaño del espacio: Ensayo de psicología matemática (Buenos Aires: El Ateneo, 1921);

Las horas doradas (Buenos Aires: BABEL, 1922);

Acción (Buenos Aires: Círculo Tradición Argentina, 1923);

Leopoldo Lugones

La funesta Helena (Estudios helénicos) (Buenos Aires: BABEL, 1923);

Un paladín de la Ilíada: Estudio crítico sobre el personaje de Diomedes (Buenos Aires: BABEL, 1923);

200

Estudios helénicos (1923–1924) (Buenos Aires: BABEL, 1924);

Romancero (Buenos Aires: BABEL, 1924);

Cuentos fatales (Buenos Aires: BABEL, 1924);

Filosofícula (Buenos Aires: BABEL, 1924);

La organización de la paz (Buenos Aires: La Editora Argentina, 1925);

El ángel de la sombra (Buenos Aires: Gleizer, 1926);

Poemas solariegos (Buenos Aires: BABEL, 1928);

Nuevos estudios helénicos (Buenos Aires & Madrid: BABEL, 1928);

La grande Argentina (Buenos Aires: BABEL, 1930);

La patria fuerte (Buenos Aires: Círculo Militar: Taller Gráfico de Luis Bernard, 1930);

Política revolucionaria (Buenos Aires: Librería Anaconda, 1931);

El estado equitativo (Ensayo sobre la realidad argentina) (Buenos Aires: Editora Argentina, 1932);

Romances del Río Seco (Buenos Aires: Sociedad de Bibliófilos Argentinos, 1938);

Roca (Buenos Aires: Coni, 1938);

Diccionario etimológico del castellano usual (Buenos Aires: Edición de la Academia Argentina de Letras, 1944);

Cuentos desconocidos, compiled by Pedro Luis Barcia (Buenos Aires: Ediciones del 80, 1982);

Cancionero de Aglaura: Cartas y poemas inéditos, compiled by María Inés Cárdenas de Monner Sans (Buenos Aires: Tres Tiempos, 1984);

Cuando Lugones conoció el amor: Cartas y poemas inéditos a su amada, edited by Cárdenas de Monner Sans (Buenos Aires: Seix Barral, 1999).

Editions and Collections: *Antología poética,* selected, with a prologue, by Carlos Obligado (Buenos Aires & Mexico City: Espasa-Calpe Argentina, 1941);

Obras poéticas completas (Madrid: Aguilar, 1948);

Obras en prosa (Madrid: Aguilar, 1962);

El payador y antología de poesía y prosa (Caracas: Ayacucho, 1979);

La hora de la espada y otros escritos (Buenos Aires: Perfil, 1999);

Romances del Río Seco, introduction and notes by Pedro Luis Barcia (Buenos Aires: Pasco, 1999).

OTHER: *La Montaña: Periódico socialista revolucionario: 1897,* edited by Lugones and José Ingenieros (Buenos Aires: Universidad Nacional de Quilmes, 1996).

Leopoldo Lugones had a lengthy and prolific career, producing ten volumes of poetry, several collections of short stories, a novel, and many essays of literary criticism, political thought, and intellectual biographies during his more than forty years as a writer. During his lifetime and beyond he was a controversial figure for his strong stands on political issues; a socialist as a young man, later in life he professed allegiance to the ideas of fascism. His poetry, too, shifted in focus, style, and thematic content. His early works reveal the influence of *Modernismo* in their use of exotic imagery and wordplay, while the collections from 1910 and later turn increasingly toward themes of Argentine nationalism. Although some may take issue with Jorge Luis Borges's statement, made almost thirty years after Lugones's suicide, that, "Leopoldo Lugones fue y sigue siendo el máximo escritor argentino" (Leopoldo Lugones was and continues to be the greatest Argentine writer), Lugones is widely acknowledged as one of the most important Latin American poets of the twentieth century.

Lugones's poetic output, while difficult to classify, can be seen as falling into at least two, and possibly three, major periods. The first three collections, *Las montañas del oro: Poema* (The Mountains of Gold, 1897), *Los crepúsculos del jardín* (The Twilights of the Garden, 1905), and *Lunario sentimental* (Sentimental Moon Calendar, 1909), demonstrate his interest in and reactions to *Modernismo.* Beginning with *Odas seculares* (Secular Odes, 1910), Lugones moved away from the tenets of *Modernismo* and began to write consciously nationalist poetry. *Odas seculares* was followed by *El libro fiel* (The Faithful Book, 1912), *El libro de los paisajes* (The Book of Landscapes, 1917), and *Las horas doradas* (The Golden Hours, 1922). With the exception of *El libro fiel,* a decidedly intimate exploration of love and loss, the other works in this period establish the Argentine landscape as the basis for national identity. Lugones continued to address the question of nationalism in the last stage of his poetry. *Romancero* (1924), *Poemas solariegos* (Ancestral Poems, 1928), and *Romances del Río Seco* (Romances of the Río Seco, published posthumously in 1938) draw on Lugones's lifelong interest in epic forms as he pursued his interest in the construction of Argentine cultural identity.

Lugones was born on 13 June 1874 in Villa María, Córdoba, Argentina. His parents, Santiago Lugones and Custodia Argüello, were well-off members of the provincial middle class, with homes in both the town and the countryside. Lugones's childhood was spent in various towns in Córdoba and on the family's country estate, until he was sent to the city of Córdoba at age twelve to live with his maternal grandmother and to pursue his studies. His parents lost their ranch in the economic crash of 1890 and joined their son in Córdoba. In 1893 Lugones joined the National Guard, eventually reaching the rank of captain, and published his first poem, "Los mundos" (The Worlds), in the newspaper *Pensamiento Liberal, Periódico Literario Liberal.*

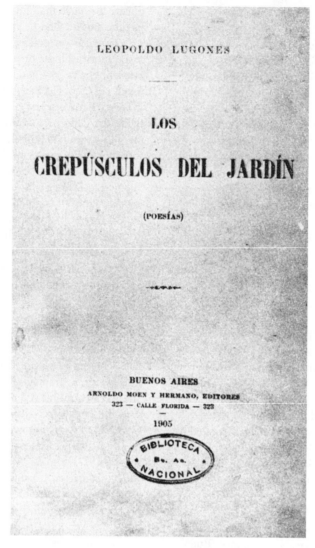

LEOPOLDO LUGONES

LOS

CREPÚSCULOS DEL JARDÍN

(POESÍAS)

BUENOS AIRES
ARNOLDO MOEN Y HERMANO, EDITORES
323 — CALLE FLORIDA — 323
—
1905

Title page for Lugones's second poetry collection, in which the poet further develops his linked themes of eroticism and technology (from Jorge Luis Borges and Betina Edelberg, Leopoldo Lugones, *1965)*

He rapidly gained fame in Córdoba for his poetry, as well as for his political activities; he organized student strikes and founded the first Socialist Center in the province.

In 1896 Lugones moved to Buenos Aires, where he took a position with the postal service. He was an instant sensation in literary and political circles, publicly welcomed by the Nicaraguan poet Rubén Darío. He married Juana González on 13 December. In April 1897 his only child, also named Leopoldo, was born, and Lugones cofounded the journal *La Montaña* (The Mountain) with José Ingenieros and R. J. Payró. His first book, *Las montañas del oro,* appeared in November of that same year.

Las montañas del oro, divided into three "cycles" as Lugones called them, combines free verse and prose poetry and reveals his debt to writers such as Edgar Allan Poe, Walt Whitman, and the *modernistas,* as well as lingering elements of Romanticism. In this first collection Lugones presents a powerful poetic persona who proclaims:

El poeta es el astro de su propio destierro.
Él tiene su cabeza junto a Dios, como todos,
pero su carne es fruto de los cósmicos lodos de la Vida

(The poet is the star of his own exile.
He has his head next to God, like everyone,
but his flesh is the fruit of the cosmic mud of Life).

The poet receives the divine message and transmits it to the people of the New World. The book also includes highly erotic imagery, frequently coupled with references to technology and science, prefiguring the poetry to follow in *Lunario sentimental.* Thus, he melds

202

the trope of the stallion with that of the locomotive in one of the prose pieces, *Tercer ciclo* (Third Cycle): "mira cómo se llena de amor el metal . . . y cómo los carros sonantes corren por la paralela de hierro, en pos del corcel de hierro" (look how the metal is full of love . . . and how the sonorous cars run on the iron track, pursuing the iron stallion). As Gwen Kirkpatrick notes, *Las montañas del oro* introduces some of Lugones's major thematic concerns, including the emphasis on the poet as near-sacred artist and the use of organic and technological imagery. Lugones's techniques include the mixture of prose and verse pieces; the use of sexual imagery associated with violence, decadence, and profanation; and the consistent employment of eleven-syllable lines, even in the prose pieces, to augment and enhance rhythm and repetition.

Lugones continued to move up in the ranks of the governmental bureaucracy; he was named director of *La Revista de Correos* (The Journal of the Postal Service) in 1899. He frequented the Ateneo (Atheneum) of Buenos Aires and was befriended by Darío. In addition, he joined the Sociedad Teosófica Argentina (the Argentine Theosophist Society) and became its secretary-general in 1900. In 1901 Lugones left the postal service and obtained a position in the National Department of Secondary and Normal Education. He also traveled to Montevideo as a delegate to the Latin American Scientific Congress and while there met with Uruguayan writers, including Horacio Quiroga. He resigned from the Department of Education in March 1903 because of ideological differences with the head of the department but was reinstated as inspector-general of education in 1904, only to resign once more in 1907. During his time away from the Department of Education in 1903 and 1904, he was sent to inspect the ruins of the Jesuit missions, with Quiroga as the official photographer. He also wrote and spoke publicly to proclaim his support of the presidential candidate Manuel Quintana. Despite these jobs and his political activities, the first decade of the twentieth century was a productive time for Lugones, as he published several major works.

Lugones further developed the twinned themes of eroticism and technology that he had begun to explore in *Las montañas del oro* in *Los crepúsculos del jardín* and *Lunario sentimental*. *Los crepúsculos del jardín* is a more overtly personal, intimate collection than Lugones's previous work; while *Las montañas del oro* frequently alludes to a mass audience, this second book posits an individual reader. Poetry is a private, not a collective or public enterprise. *Los crepúsculos del jardín* conveys an almost nostalgic, bittersweet atmosphere, often with a fragmented poetic persona. One of the best-known poems in the book, "El solterón" (The Bachelor), describes the bleak and empty life of an aging bachelor:

Y como enturbiada espuma
una idea triste va
emergiendo de su bruma:
¡Qué mohosa está la pluma!
¡La pluma no escribe ya!

(And like clouded foam
a sad idea is
emerging from his mist:
How moldy the pen is!
The pen doesn't write any more!).

Lugones uses the trope of a failed or incomplete writing to symbolize the (pro)creative failure of the title character of the poem, incapable of giving voice to love. Other poems focus on the twilight landscapes alluded to in the title of the book and on the topic of lost or vanished love, often embellished with typically *modernista* exotic details and synesthetic images, as in "Historia de Phanión" (Story of Phanión):

La música anodina del agua entre las flores
expelían las gárgolas de antiguos surtidores,
decía por nosotros las caricias inciertas
que expresar no sabían las bocas inexpertas.
Los ojos componían la glosa de ese canto,
con frecuencia invadidos por ilógico llanto.
Las tardes se portaban como buenas amigas

(The gargoyles expelled from ancient spouts
the anodyne music of the water among the flowers,
spoke for us the uncertain caresses
that inexpert mouths did not know how to express.
The eyes, frequently invaded by illogical weeping,
composed the variation of that song.
The afternoons behaved themselves like good friends).

At the same time, as Kirkpatrick has indicated, the excessive, even exaggerated use of *modernista* elements constitutes a metapoetic commentary on the movement, serving to question its status and validity.

La guerra gaucha (The Gaucho War, 1905), Lugones's next work, was his attempt to create a grandly populist and nationalist epic on the scale of *Martín Fierro* (1872, 1879), José Hernández's narrative poem about the iconic Argentine gaucho. The novel, which takes place during the Wars of Independence, which lasted from 1810 to 1824, combines scenes of intense action, vividly drawn characters, and dense descriptions of the Argentine landscape. Lugones based the work in part on the historical figure of Martín Güemes and on his own rural childhood. He combined the nationalist subject matter with his distinctive prose style, which derives much of its power from elaborate, striking images functioning on multiple levels of meaning. His repeated use of Argentine dialect and vocabulary, however, tends to render some scenes almost

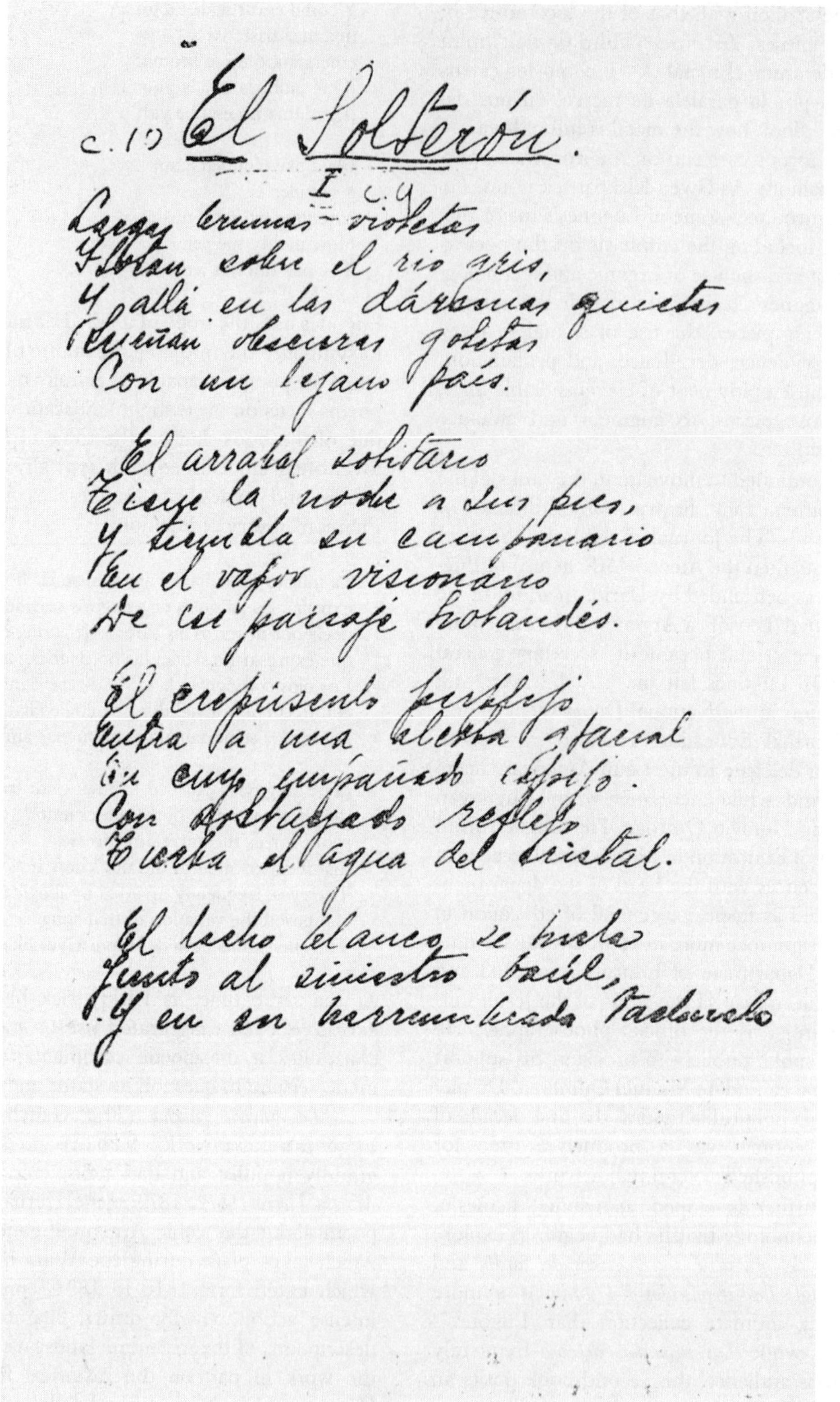

El Solterón

I

Largas brumas violetas
Flotan sobre el río gris,
Y allá en las dársenas quietas
Sueñan oscuras goletas
Con un lejano país.

El arrabal solitario
Tiene la noche a sus pies,
Y tiembla su campanario
En el vapor visionario
De ese paisaje holandés.

El crepúsculo perplejo
Entra a una alcoba glacial
En cuyo empañado espejo.
Con destartalado reflejo
Tiembla el agua del cristal.

El lecho blanco se hiela
Junto al siniestro baúl,
Y en su borrumbrada tela

First pages of the manuscript for Lugones's poem about the solitary life of a bachelor. It is included in Los crepúsculos del jardín *(Biblioteca Sarmiento de Gualeguaychu).*

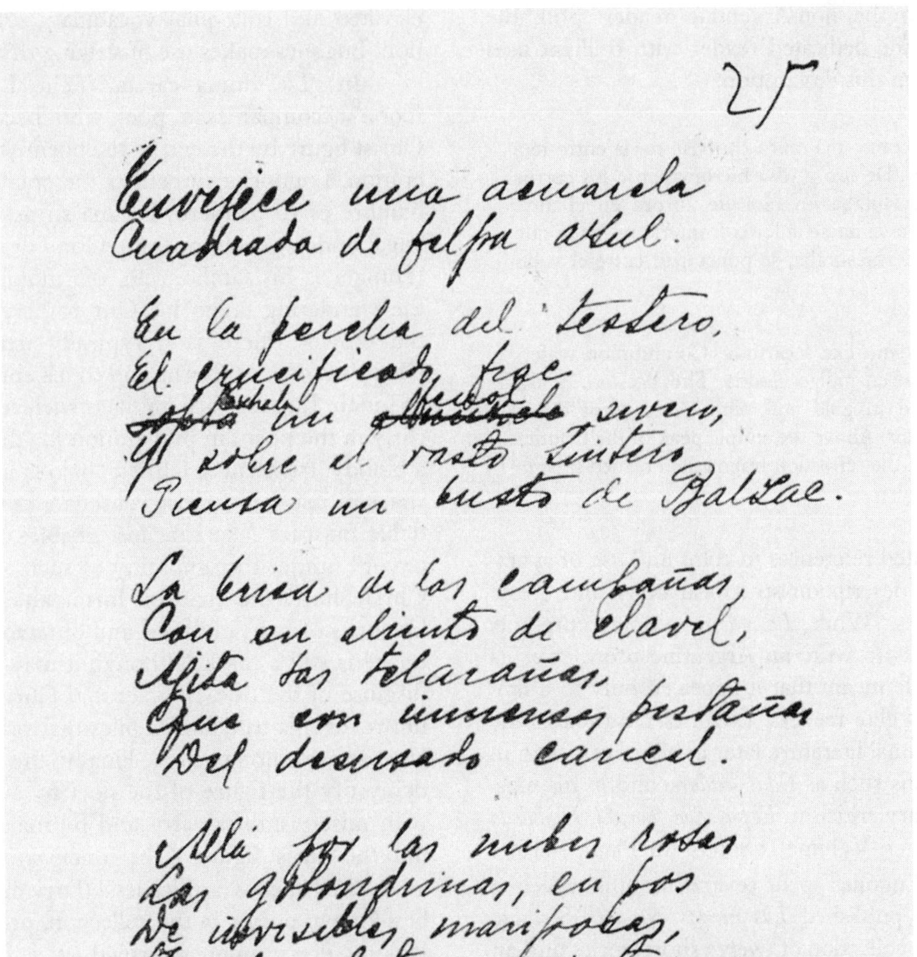

25

Envejece una acuarela
Cuadrada de felpa azul.

En la percha del testero,
El crucificado, fue
~~Ahora~~ un ~~crucifijo~~ suyo,
Y sobre el rústico tintero
Piensa un busto de Balzac.

La brisa de las campañas,
Con su aliento de clavel,
Agita las telarañas,
Que son inmensas pestañas
Del desusado cancel.

Allá por las nubes rosas
Las golondrinas, en pos
De invisibles mariposas,
Trazan letras misteriosas
Como escribiendo un adiós.

En la alcoba solitaria,
Sobre un raído sofá

unintelligible to the non-Argentine reader. Still, the novel rewards the dedicated reader with brilliant uses of language, as in this description:

> . . . ya el sol, como una oblea carmesí, nacía entre nieblas de índigo. De oro y rosa bicromábanse los cerros de occidente. Flotaba un olor de aurora en el aire. Sobre la escueta cima de la loma frontera, un buey que la refracción desmesuraba, se ponía azul entre el vaho matinal

> (. . . now the sun, like a carmine Communion wafer, was born between indigo clouds. The Western peaks were bicolored in gold and pink. A scent of dawn floated in the air. Above the simple peak of the frontier hill, an ox that the refraction fragmented turned blue in the morning mist).

Here, the repeated references to color and use of synesthesia give the description structural unity and create powerful images. While *La guerra gaucha* represents Lugones's efforts to write an Argentine prose epic, its dense prose style meant that it appealed only to a limited audience of elite readers. Lugones returned to the problem of national literature later in his career, both in poetry collections such as *Odas seculares* and in his masterwork of literary criticism, *El payador. Tomo I: Hijo de la pampa* (The Singer. Volume 1: Son of the Plain, 1916).

In 1906 Lugones spent several months traveling in Europe and published *Las fuerzas extrañas* (Strange Forces, 1999), a collection of twelve short stories and an essay on cosmogony. The stories explore the supernatural and occult without any of the fervent nationalism of *La guerra gaucha*. Lugones also questions the tendency of science to attempt to supplant God and nature; several stories feature protagonists who are destroyed by their own scientific discoveries. The stories explore the outer edges of human behavior, frequently displaying a marked interest in abnormal psychology.

Lugones returned to his poetic critique of *Modernismo* in *Lunario sentimental,* his acknowledged masterwork. He forcefully undermines the precepts and codes of *Modernismo,* again with the devices of hyperbolic description and parody, as he demonstrates implicitly that the organizing framework of *Modernismo* was collapsing under its own weight. The collection includes odes, sonnets, eclogues, short stories, and short plays, all connected by the trope of the moon. Lugones also wrote a polemical prologue calling for poetic renovation, especially with respect to imagery. Indeed, Borges commented that in *Lunario sentimental* Lugones "presenta una de las mayores colecciones de metáforas de la literatura española" (presents one of the greatest collections of metaphors in Spanish literature). The effect of the metaphors is enhanced by unexpected combinations of

elevated and colloquial vocabulary or terms. In addition, Lugones makes use of striking rhyme schemes.

In "La última careta" (The Last Mask), the moon accompanies a poet who becomes an ironic Christ figure by the end of the poem. With subtle alliteration, Lugones enumerates the poet's attributes: "El hambre es su pandero, la luna su peseta / y el tango vagabundo su padrenuestro. Crin / de león, la corona" (Hunger is his tambourine, the moon his coin / and the wandering tango his Our Father. Lion's / mane, the crown). Here is a typically dense allusion to Christ's crown of thorns and to his epithet as the Lion of Judah. Lugones accumulates such religious imagery early in the poem in preparation for the final vision of a bloody, frightening Christ: "bajo la ignominia de tan siniestra máscara / Cristo enseña a la noche su formidable máscara / de cabellos terribles, de sangre y de pavor" (under the ignominy of such a sinister mask / Christ shows the night his formidable mask / of terrible locks of hair, of blood and of terror). Yet, this last image is still a mask; although it may well be the last disguise of the title, the fact that Christ/the poet does not reveal his true face implies that reality is unknowable or even nonexistent. Finally, the poem works to demystify the figure of the poet by surrounding him with misery and poverty and by making him vanish into the Christ figure of the conclusion.

"Los fuegos artificiales" (Fireworks), one of the best-known poems in the collection, presents the moon looking down upon a crowd at a fireworks show. Lugones adopts a distant, skeptical attitude to the masses, a stance far from the heroic appeal to the people of *Las montañas del oro.* Instead, the crowd is grotesque in its attraction to the spectacle of the fireworks and in its mass mentality; Lugones likens them to insects or animals in his description of the plaza: "que hormiguea / de multitud, como un cubo de ranas" (that boils like ants / in a crowd like ants, like a box of frogs). His fascination with and aversion to technology are expressed in vivid metaphors describing the fireworks and the crowd's reaction:

> Primero despertando arrobos
> de paganismo atávico, en cursivas alertas,
> es la pura majestad de los globos
> sobre la O vocativa de las bocas abiertas

> (First awakening raptures
> of atavistic paganism, in alert italics,
> is the pure majesty of the balloons
> over the vocative O of open mouths).

Lunario sentimental is a definitive break with and attack on *Modernismo.* Lugones accumulates *modernista* images and techniques in order to confront them with the realities of the modern world, which include scientific knowledge, the impact of capitalism, and the continuing fragmentation of the once-unitary subject. This last is signaled by the increasingly degraded state of the figure of the poet and of the poetic narrator. The poet cannot bring order out of chaos; he can only describe chaos.

Having brought closure to his *modernista* period with *Lunario sentimental,* Lugones initiated a new stage in his poetry. His political ideology grew more conservative as well, and he gradually drew away from his earlier antimilitaristic stance. He counted some high-ranking military officials among his friends and gave a talk, "El ejército de la Ilíada" (The Army of the *Iliad*), to the Círculo Militar (Military Circle), a fascist organization of which Lugones was a member, in 1908. Nation, family, and home are the major themes of his next four works of poetry, beginning with the publication of *Odas seculares* in 1910. In the same year the Council on Education commissioned him to write a biography of Domingo Faustino Sarmiento, the pre-eminent political figure of nineteenth-century Argentina. Both works coincided with the centenary celebration of the independence of Argentina, in which Lugones participated actively. *Odas seculares* is one of Lugones's earliest efforts to inscribe his vision of Argentine history and identity in poetry, although he had already begun such a project with his novel *La guerra gaucha. Odas seculares* comprises a prologue and three sections, "Las cosas útiles y magníficas" (Useful and Magnificent Things), "Las ciudades" (The Cities), and "Los hombres" (The Men). The odes are neoclassical in style and echo Andrés Bello's "Oda a la agricultura de la zona tórrida" (Ode to the Agriculture of the Torrid Zone, 1826). The chief rhetorical devices used in the odes are enumeration and metonymy, in contrast with the shocking images and synesthesia of the earlier works. The odes posit an inclusive Argentina in which class differences are swept away by patriotism and by national identity. Hence, in "A la patria" (To the Nation) Lugones proclaims:

Patria, digo, y los versos de la oda
Como aclamantes brazos paralelos,
Te levantan Ilustre, Única y Toda
En unanimidad de almas y cielos

(*Nation,* I say, and the lines of the ode
like acclamatory parallel arms,
raise you up, Illustrious, One and Complete
in the unanimity of souls and skies).

This and similar statements elsewhere in the *Odas seculares* have the effect of underlining the importance of the poem itself, since the poem is the mechanism by

Lugones and his wife, Juana González Lugones, in October 1924
(from Jorge Luis Borges and Betina Edelberg,
Leopoldo Lugones, 1965)

which the nation is elevated to such greatness. As he did in *Las montañas del oro,* he frequently references the importance of the poetic project and of the figure of the author. Another point of similarity between the two texts is Lugones's desire to address his work to a collective audience, not to an individual. Hugo Achúgar, noting the repeated use of the image of a cornucopia throughout the book, points out that *Odas seculares* envisions Argentina as a material and spiritual horn of plenty, available to people of all classes and occupations, from the cities to the countryside.

"A los ganados y las mieses" (To the Cattle and Fields) stands out among the *Odas seculares* for its length and epic sweep; running 1,500 lines, the poem praises the Argentine landscape and the animals and men that inhabit it. The densely packed metaphors of the earlier works have almost disappeared here, although Lugones's love of language and rhythmic patterns is evident in such lines as the following:

En la fiel solidez del pan seguro

la vida es bella y la amistad sonora.
Suave corre la vida en las cordiales
tierras del pan, como una lenta sombra

(In the faithful solidity of the sure bread

life is beautiful and friendship resonant.
Life runs smoothly in the cordial
lands of bread, like a slow shadow).

Unexpected adjective choices *(sonora)* and judicious use of alliteration (*corre* and *cordiales; seguro, sonora, suave,* and *sombra*) remain hallmarks of Lugones's style and prevent the description from sinking to triteness. Toward the end of the poem Lugones brings in references to and descriptions of his own family history, thus inscribing himself into Argentine national identity. In particular, he recalls family celebrations of Argentine independence:

Como era fiesta el día de la patria . . .
nuestra madre salía a buena hora. . . .
Y adelante, en pandilla juguetona,
corríamos nosotros con el perro
que describía en arco pistas locas

(As Independence Day was a holiday . . .
our mother went out early. . . .
And ahead of her, in a playful bunch,
we ran with the dog,
who made arcs with wild leaps).

In this way he not only links his personal history to that of his country but also connects his poetic celebration of Argentina to past commemorations. *Odas seculares* marks Lugones's increasing engagement with specifically Argentine concerns that are explored in later works as well.

In 1911 Lugones moved to Paris with his wife and son as a correspondent for *La Nación* (The Nation). There he was able to renew his friendship with Darío, also residing in the French capital, and, at the beginning of 1914, to found and edit the *Revue Sudaméricaine* (South American Review). Despite his absence from Buenos Aires, he became an independent candidate for the Argentine Congress in 1912, but he was not elected. His journalistic writings demonstrate his increasing conservatism; he condemned the feminist movement and liberal pacifism as he observed Europe moving toward war.

Yet, Lugones's next book of poetry, *El libro fiel,* returns to the intimate, private world sketched in *Los crepúsculos del jardín,* although without the densely metaphoric phrases and exotic allusions of that work. Dedicated to his wife, the love poems that compose *El libro*

fiel are melancholy and often express themes of solitude and the absence of love, as in "La blanca soledad" (White Solitude). The poem describes a night scene that progressively becomes more and more abstract:

La luna cava un blanco abismo
de quietud, en cuya cuenca
las cosas son cadáveres
y las sombras viven como ideas

(The moon digs a white abyss
of silence, in whose cavern
things are corpses
and shadows live like ideas).

These lines signify the increasing alienation the poet experiences in the absence of the loved one. Lugones accentuates the loneliness of the poetic voice with multiple images of emptiness, caverns, and holes, as well as with vocabulary that evokes geometric precision and sterility and with references to clocks and the inevitable passing of time.

Lugones returned to Argentina in 1913 for several months and made a permanent return in the summer of 1914, when World War I was clearly imminent. Back in Buenos Aires he took the position of librarian of the National Council of Education, a job he held until his death in 1938. He continued to write articles for *La Nación* through the 1920s and 1930s. During this time his political beliefs evolved still further away from the radical socialism and anarchism of his youth to a conservative nationalism, already expressed in *Odas seculares.* He criticized the masses for their tendency to elect demagogues and despots but maintained that democracy was the ideal form of government; somewhat confusingly, he advocated a blend of nationalist individualism and collectivism, the latter, he believed, inherited from pre-Conquest indigenous cultures.

Lugones further developed his twin interests of Argentine nationalism and literary criticism in *El payador,* his most important work of literary analysis. The book grew out of a series of lectures on *Martín Fierro* that Lugones gave during his 1913 visit to Buenos Aires. Lugones's extensive work on classical Greek culture and history is evident in his view of *Martín Fierro* as the *Odyssey* of Argentina; as such, it is also linked to his own effort to create an Argentine epic in *La guerra gaucha.* At the same time he deliberately evoked the troubadours and *juglares* of the Middle Ages, singers who created and perpetuated an oral culture. *El payador* traces the debt of *Martín Fierro* to that dual heritage and simultaneously declares Hernández's work fundamentally Argentine. He also used *Martín Fierro* in order to advance his own ideas about Argentine national identity and celebrated the vanished lifestyle of the gaucho

LEOPOLDO LUGONES

ROMANCES DEL
RIO SECO

CON DIBUJOS DE
ALBERTO GÜIRALDES

SOCIEDAD DE BIBLIOFILOS ARGENTINOS
BUENOS AIRES　—　MCMXXXVIII

Title page for Lugones's posthumously published collection of gaucho poems, all of which had originally been published in 1929
(from Josefina Delgado, Alfonsina Storni: Una biografia esencial, *2001)*

as he had in "A los ganados y las mieses," claiming, "El gaucho fue el héroe y el civilizador de la Pampa" (The gaucho was the hero and civilizer of the Plain). He believed that Argentine nationalism was rooted in the pampas and in the gaucho, but that a nostalgic love of the past was not sufficient for national progress. Finally, he believed that the elites had to understand the masterwork of popular culture in order to achieve the all-encompassing nationalism he had previously advanced in *Odas seculares. El payador* was instrumental in securing the preeminent place of *Martín Fierro* in the canon of Argentine literature.

Lugones followed *El payador* with *El libro de los paisajes;* like *El libro fiel,* it is dedicated to Lugones's wife, but unlike that book, many of the poems focus on the titular landscapes, and, for the most part, those of Argentina in particular. The book is usually paired with *Las horas doradas,* which also presents the natural wonders of Argentina in a direct, expressive style. "Salmo pluvial" (Rain Psalm), in *El libro de los paisajes,* is perhaps the most absorbing poem in the collection. In describ-

ing a storm and its aftermath, Lugones deftly evokes the atmospheric tension at the instant the storm breaks:

Una fulmínea verga rompió el aire al soslayo;
sobre la tierra atónita cruzó un pavor mortal,
y el firmamento entero se derrumbó en un rayo,
como un inmenso techo de hierro y cristal

(A lightning strike broke the air sideways;
over the stricken earth crossed a mortal fear,
and the entire firmament collapsed in a bolt,
like an immense roof of iron and crystal).

Elsewhere, Lugones is less successful in maintaining the equilibrium among delicate use of imagery, straightforward description, and his desire to praise Argentina's places and people, causing some of the poems to appear mundane. Neither book is counted among his more important works.

With *Romancero* Lugones began to investigate the possibilities of applying traditional poetic and epic forms, including ballads and lieder, to contemporary poetry. Other influences include the *Arabian Nights* and the romances of the Spanish Middle Ages. The subject matter and tone in general remain more personal; love, solitude, and death figure among the topics addressed. In "Preludio" (Prelude) Lugones exhorts the gaucho balladeer, the pampas's version of the medieval troubadour, to tell of his sorrow: "Canta guitarra doliente / publica mi ceguedad; / . . . / con mi corazón herido / sabré ponerte a compás" (Sing sad guitar, / publish my blindness; / . . . / with my wounded heart, / I will know how to put you to the rhythm). In addition, in 1924 he published his second book of short stories, *Cuentos fatales* (Fatal Stories), which comprises five relatively lengthy pieces. These stories do not compare well with those of *Las fuerzas extrañas*.

More importantly, in 1924 Lugones gave his controversial speech "La hora de la espada" (The Hour of the Sword) in Lima, Peru. The speech marked a dramatic, but not unexpected, turn in his political philosophy. After World War I he became increasingly disillusioned with the shaky state of democracy in Argentina and abroad and expressed ever more conservative ideas. He believed that immigration should be controlled more strictly, that the influence of the uneducated masses should be curtailed, and that the military should play an important role in national life. At the same time he criticized organized religion, thus alienating many Catholic conservatives. These ideas were expressed in his political writings and speeches and culminated in "La hora de la espada," given at the invitation of the Peruvian government to mark the centennial anniversary of the Battle of Ayacucho. There he proclaimed, "En el conflicto de la autoridad con la ley, cada vez más frecuente, . . . el hombre de espada tiene que estar con aquélla" (In the increasingly frequent conflict of authority with law, . . . the man of the sword must side with the former). The speech permanently alienated Argentina's leftists, who felt betrayed by Lugones's shift of allegiance.

Poemas solariegos unites Lugones's interests in Argentine nationalism and in traditional and epic poetic forms. By this time he had published widely on classical Greek literature and culture, as is evident in the purposefully epic sweep of many of the poems. "Dedicatoria a los antepasados" (Dedication to the Ancestors) uses an almost Homeric style as Lugones narrates the history of his own ancestors in Argentina:

> Al maestre de campo Francisco de Lugones,
> quien combatió en los reinos del Perú y luego aquí,
> donde junto con tantos bien probados varones,
> consumaron la empresa del Valle Calchaquí

> (To the fieldmaster Francisco de Lugones,
> who fought in the kingdoms of Peru and later here,

> where together with many well-tried men,
> they brought to an end the conquest of the Calchaquí Valley).

The poems in this collection recall the *Odas seculares* as they revisit what María Teresa Gramuglio has called the mythopoeic tropes of lineage, inheritance, and the land. With the exception of "Estampas porteñas" (Scenes from the Port), which vividly evokes Buenos Aires, the poems treat the interior, its history, and its inhabitants. Once more Lugones turned to the figure of the *payador,* or gaucho singer, in "El arpista" (The Harpist), using this figure as a stand-in for his poetic self. He also incorporates childhood reminiscences, as he does in *Odas seculares* and *La guerra gaucha*.

Poemas solariegos is usually analyzed alongside Lugones's *Romances del Río Seco*. Although the latter work was not published until after his death in 1938, the poems it comprises are contemporary with those of *Poemas solariegos;* all were published in *La Nación* in 1929. In *El payador* he claims that the eight-syllable line is the purest, most aesthetic form of language; the poems of *Romances del Río Seco* are written in four-line stanzas with eight syllables in each line, lending formal unity to the works. Morever, all the poems take place near the Río Seco in Córdoba, Lugones's birthplace. *Romances del Río Seco* signals his renewed efforts to create an authentic Argentine literary work along the lines of *Martín Fierro*. While in *La guerra gaucha* this attempt was thwarted by the convoluted prose style, Lugones now explicitly rejected such *modernista* stylings:

> Acaso alguno desdeñe
> Por lo criollo mis relatos.
> Esto no es para extranjeros,

> Cajetillas ni pazguatos

> (Maybe someone will scorn my stories
> for their Creole style.
> This isn't for strangers,

> dandies or fools).

In *Romances del Río Seco* Lugones assumes the voice of the gaucho singer with which he had experimented in his earlier collections. This persona narrates events from Argentine history and describes episodes that typify the characters inhabiting the pampas.

In 1930 Lugones participated in a military coup d'état that toppled the government of Hipólito Irigoyen on 6 September and placed General José Uriburu in power; he drafted Uriburu's revolutionary proclamation and gave a funeral oration for military cadets killed in the fighting. These actions were presaged by his increasingly fascist political writings, in which he argues that man's natural state is one of war and that the nation demands total obedience and sacrifice from its citizens. These writings were published in *La Nación* and were distributed to the members of the Círculo Militar. After the coup, however, Lugones complained of liberal tendencies within the new government and began to turn toward Catholicism. Uriburu named him director of the National Library, but he refused this position. The last eight years of his life were dedicated to exploring the conjunction of religion and politics and to fighting socialism and communism. He founded "Acción republicana" (Republican Action), a political movement, but it did not attract widespread support. His publications were for the most part limited to his political writings, with a few forays in Hellenic cultural criticism.

Lugones committed suicide on 18 February 1938. He left behind an immense and diverse body of work spanning his literary career of more than forty years. Indeed, the diversity of his writings poses difficulties for critics wishing to summarize his career and assess his significance, while his dramatic shifts of political conviction have polarized others. He began as a socialist who reveled in the daring iconoclasm of *Modernismo,* then turned against his own *modernista* tendencies and worked to destabilize the discourse he had deployed in earlier works. Later he became a fervent nationalist who looked back with increasing nostalgia to an idealized Argentine past. Lugones's most important works are *Lunario sentimental,* for its forceful critique of *Modernismo,* its explosive use of imagery, and

its insistent and shocking coupling of eroticism and technology; *Odas seculares,* for its efforts to inscribe an authentic Argentine identity; and *El payador,* for its work in establishing *Martín Fierro* as one of the most important works in the Argentine canon. Leopoldo Lugones remains a controversial figure in many regards, but his contributions to Argentine and Latin American literature are undeniable.

Biography:

Julio Irazusta, *Genio y figura de Leopoldo Lugones* (Buenos Aires: Editorial Universitaria de Buenos Aires, 1968).

References:

Hugo Achúgar, "*Odas seculares:* Monumento populista del Centenario," *Revista de Estudios Hispánicos,* 19 (October 1985): 17–48;

Jorge Luis Borges and Betina Edelberg, *Leopoldo Lugones* (Buenos Aires: Pleamar, 1965);

Josefina Delgado, *Alfonsina Storni: Una biografía esencial* (Buenos Aires: Planeta, 1990; corrected and enlarged, 2001);

María Teresa Gramuglio, "Literatura y nacionalismo: Leopoldo Lugones y la construcción de imágenes de escritor," *Hispamérica,* 64–65 (April–August 1993): 5–22;

Gwen Kirkpatrick, *The Dissonant Legacy of Modernismo: Lugones, Herrera y Reissig, and the Voices of Modern Spanish American Poetry* (Berkeley: University of California Press, 1989).

Gabriela Mistral

(7 April 1889 – 10 January 1957)

Santiago Daydí-Tolson
University of Texas at San Antonio

BOOKS: *Desolación* (New York: Instituto de las Españas, 1922; enlarged edition, Santiago: Nascimento, 1923);

Ternura: Canciones de niños (Madrid: Saturnino Calleja, 1924; revised edition, Buenos Aires: Espasa-Calpe, 1945);

Tala (Buenos Aires: Sur, 1938; revised edition, Buenos Aires: Losada, 1946);

Croquis mexicano, edited by Alfonso Calderón (Mexico City: Costa-Amie, 1957);

Recados: Contando a Chile, edited by Alfonso M. Escudero (Santiago: Editorial del Pacífico, 1957);

Poesías completas, edited by Margaret Bates (Madrid: Aguilar, 1958);

Páginas en prosa, edited by José Pereira Rodríguez (Buenos Aires: Kapelusz, 1962);

Motivos de San Francisco, edited by César Díaz-Muñoz Cormatches (Santiago: Editorial del Pacífico, 1965);

Poema de Chile (Barcelona: Pomaire, 1967);

Materias: Prosa inédita, edited by Calderón (Santiago: Editorial Universitaria, 1978);

Gabriela anda por el mundo, edited by Roque Esteban Scarpa (Santiago: Andrés Bello, 1978);

Gabriela piensa en . . . , edited by Esteban Scarpa (Santiago: Andrés Bello, 1978);

Gabriela Mistral en el "Repertorio Americano," edited by Mario Céspedes (San José: Editorial Universidad de Costa Rica, 1978);

Prosa religiosa de Gabriela Mistral, edited by Luis Vargas Saavedra (Santiago: Andrés Bello, 1978);

Magisterio y niño, edited by Esteban Scarpa (Santiago: Andrés Bello, 1979);

Grandeza de los oficios, edited by Esteban Scarpa (Santiago: Andrés Bello, 1979);

Elogio de las cosas de la tierra, edited by Esteban Scarpa (Santiago: Andrés Bello, 1979);

Reino: Poesía dispersa e inédita, en verso y prosa, edited by Gastón von dem Bussche (Valparaíso: Ediciones Universitarias de Valparaíso, 1983);

Gabriela Mistral

Lagar II, edited by Ana María Cuneo and Pedro Pablo Zegers (Santiago: Dirreción de Bibliotecas, Archivos y Museos, Biblioteca Nacional, 1991);

Bendita mi lengua sea: Diario íntima de Gabriela Mistral, 1905–1956, edited by Jaime Quezada (Santiago: Planeta/Ariel, 2002);

Recopilación de la obra mistraliana, 1902–1922, edited by Zegers (Santiago: Ril, 2002).

Collections: *Antología poética de Gabriela Mistral,* selected by Alfonso Calderón (Santiago: Editorial Universitaria, 1974);

Poesía y prosa, edited by Quezada (Caracas: Biblioteca Ayacucho, 1993).

Editions in English: *Selected Poems of Gabriela Mistral,* translated by Langston Hughes (Bloomington & London: Indiana University Press, 1957);

Selected Poems of Gabriela Mistral, translated and edited by Doris Dana (Baltimore: Johns Hopkins University Press, 1971);

A Gabriela Mistral Reader, translated by Maria Giachetti, edited by Marjorie Agosín (Fredonia, N.Y.: White Pines, 1993);

Selected Prose and Prose-Poems, edited and translated by Stephen Tapscott (Austin: University of Texas Press, 2002).

OTHER: *Lecturas para mujeres,* edited by Mistral (Mexico City: Secretaría de Educación Pública, 1924).

Gabriela Mistral, literary pseudonym of Lucila Godoy Alcayaga, was the first Spanish American author to receive the Nobel Prize in literature; as such, she will always be seen as a representative figure in the cultural history of the continent. One of the best-known Latin American poets of her time, Gabriela—as she was admiringly called all over the Hispanic world—embodied in her person, as much as in her works, the cultural values and traditions of a continent that had not been recognized until then with the most prestigious international literary prize. "It is to render homage to the riches of Spanish American literature that we address ourselves today especially to its queen, the poet of *Desolación,* who has become the great singer of mercy and motherhood," concludes the Nobel Prize citation read by Hjalmar Gullberg at the Nobel ceremony. Mistral's works, both in verse and prose, deal with the basic passion of love as seen in the various relationships of mother and offspring, man and woman, individual and humankind, soul and God.

A dedicated educator and an engaged and committed intellectual, Mistral defended the rights of children, women, and the poor; the freedoms of democracy; and the need for peace in times of social, political, and ideological conflicts, not only in Latin America but in the whole world. She always took the side of those who were mistreated by society: children, women, Native Americans, Jews, war victims, workers, and the poor, and she tried to speak for them through her poetry, her many newspaper articles, her letters, and her talks and actions as Chilean representative in international organizations. Above all, she was concerned about the future of Latin America and its peoples and cultures, particularly those of the native groups. Her altruistic interests and her social concerns had a religious undertone, as they sprang from her profoundly spiritual, Franciscan understanding of the world. Her personal spiritual life was characterized by an untiring, seemingly mystical search for union with divinity and all of creation.

Mistral's writings are highly emotional and impress the reader with an original style marked by her disdain for the aesthetically pleasing elements common among modernist writers, her immediate predecessors. Rhythm, rhyme, metaphors, symbols, vocabulary, and themes, as well as other traditional poetic techniques, are all directed in her poetry toward the expression of deeply felt emotions and conflicting forces in opposition. Love and jealousy, hope and fear, pleasure and pain, life and death, dream and truth, ideal and reality, matter and spirit are always competing in her life and find expression in the intensity of her well-defined poetic voices. In her poems speak the abandoned woman and the jealous lover, the mother in a trance of joy and fear because of her delicate child, the teacher, the woman who tries to bring to others the comfort of compassion, the enthusiastic singer of hymns to America's natural richness, the storyteller, the mad poet possessed by the spirit of beauty and transcendence. All of her lyrical voices represent the different aspects of her own personality and have been understood by critics and readers alike as the autobiographical voices of a woman whose life was marked by an intense awareness of the world and of human destiny. The poetic word in its beauty and emotional intensity had for her the power to transform and transcend human spiritual weakness, bringing consolation to the soul in search of understanding. Her poetry is thus charged with a sense of ritual and prayer.

Although she mostly uses regular meter and rhyme, her verses are sometimes difficult to recite because of their harshness, resulting from intentional breaks of the prosodic rules. This apparent deficiency is purposely used by the poet to produce an intended effect—the reader's uncomfortable feeling of uncertainty and harshness that corresponds to the tormented attitude of the lyrical voice and to the passionate character of the poet's worldview. Even when Mistral's verses have the simple musicality of a cradlesong, they vibrate with controlled emotion and hidden tension. In her prose writing Mistral also twists and entangles the language in unusual expressive ways as if the common, direct style were not appropriate to her subject matter and her intensely emotive interpretation of it. Although she is mostly known for her poetry, she was an accomplished and prolific prose writer whose contributions to several major Latin American newspapers on issues of

Mistral at age eight (from Jaime Concha,
Gabriela Mistral, *1987)*

interest to her contemporaries had an ample readership. Several selections of her prose works and many editions of her poetry published over the years do not fully account for her enormous contribution to Latin American culture and her significance as an original spiritual poet and public intellectual. Her complete works are still to be published in comprehensive and complete critical editions easily available to the public.

Lucila Godoy Alcayaga was born on 7 April 1889 in the small town of Vicuña, in the Elqui Valley, a deeply cut, narrow farming land in the Chilean Andes Mountains, four hundred miles north of Santiago, the capital: "El Valle de Elqui: una tajeadura heroica en la masa montañosa, pero tan breve, que aquello no es sino un torrente con dos orillas verdes. Y esto, tan pequeño, puede llegar a amarse como lo perfecto" (Elqui Valley: a heroic slash in the mass of mountains, but so brief, that it is nothing but a rush of water with two green banks. And this little place can be loved as perfection), Mistral writes in *Recados: Contando a Chile* (Messages: Telling Chile, 1957). She grew up in Monte Grande, a humble village in the same valley, surrounded by modest fruit orchards and rugged deserted hills. She was

raised by her mother and by an older sister fifteen years her senior, who was her first teacher. Her father, a primary-school teacher with a penchant for adventure and easy living, abandoned his family when Lucila was a three-year-old girl; she saw him only on rare occasions, when he visited his wife and children before disappearing forever. This evasive father, who wrote little poems for his daughter and sang to her with his guitar, had a strong emotional influence on the poet. From him she obtained, as she used to comment, the love of poetry and the nomadic spirit of the perpetual traveler. Her mother was a central force in Mistral's sentimental attachment to family and homeland and a strong influence on her desire to succeed. Not less influential was the figure of her paternal grandmother, whose readings of the Bible marked the child forever. An exceedingly religious person, her grandmother—who Mistral liked to think had Sephardic ancestors—encouraged the young girl to learn and recite by heart passages from the Bible, in particular the Psalms of David. Mistral declared later, in her poem "Mis libros" (My Books) in *Desolación* (Despair, 1922), that the Bible was one of the books that had most influenced her:

¡Biblia, mi noble Biblia, panorama estupendo,
en donde se quedaron mis ojos largamente,
tienes sobre los Salmos las lavas más ardientes
y en su río de fuego mi corazón enciendo!

Sustentaste a mis gentes con tu robusto vino
y los erguiste recios en medio de los hombres,
y a mí me yergue de ímpetu solo el decir tu nombre;
porque yo de ti vengo, he quebrado al destino

Después de ti tan solo me traspasó los huesos
con su ancho alarido el sumo florentino

(Bible, my noble Bible, magnificent panorama,
where my eyes lingered for a long time,
you have in the Psalms the most burning of lavas
and in its river of fire I lit my heart!

You sustained my people with your strong wine
and you made them stand strong among men,
and just saying your name gives me strength;
because I come from you I have broken destiny

After you, only the scream of the great Florentine
went through my bones).

These few Alexandrine verses are a good, albeit brief, example of Mistral's style, tone, and inspiration: the poetic discourse and its appreciation in reading are both represented by extremely physical and violent images that refer to a spiritual conception of human destiny and the troubling mysteries of life: the scream of "el sumo florentino," a reference to Dante, and the pierced bones of the reader impressed by the biblical text.

The poet always remembered her childhood in Monte Grande, in Valle de Elqui, as Edenic. Under the loving care of her mother and older sister, she learned how to know and love nature, to enjoy it in solitary contemplation. There, as Mistral recalls in *Poema de Chile* (Poem of Chile, 1967), "su flor guarda el almendro / y cría los higuerales / que azulan higos extremos" (with almond trees blooming, and fig trees laden with stupendous dark blue figs), she developed her dreamy character, fascinated as she was by nature around her:

> Me tenía una familia
> de árboles, otra de matas,
> hablaba largo y tendido
> con animales hallados
>
> (I had a family
> of trees, and another of plants,
> and I talked and talked
> with the animals I found).

The mountains and the river of her infancy, the wind and the sky, the animals and plants of her secluded homeland became Mistral's cherished possessions; she always kept them in her memory as the true and only world, an almost fabulous land lost in time and space, a land of joy from which she had been exiled when she was still a child. In the quiet and beauty of that mountainous landscape the girl developed her passionate spirituality and her poetic talents. As she evoked in old age, she also learned to like the stories told by the old people in a language that kept many of its old cadences, still alive in the vocabulary and constructions of a people still attached to the land and its past. In *Poema de Chile* she affirms that the language and imagination of that world of the past and of the countryside always inspired her own choice of vocabulary, images, rhythms, and rhymes:

> Me llamaban "cuatro añitos"
> y ya tenía doce años.
> Así me mentaban, pues
> no hacía lo de mis años:
> no cosía, no zurcía,
> tenía los ojos vagos,
> cuentos pedía, romances,
> y no lavaba los platos . . .
> ¡Ay! Y, sobre todo, a causa
> de un hablar así, rimado
>
> (They called me "little four-years"
> and I was already twelve.
> They called me thus, because
> I did not act my age:
> I did not sew, I did not darn,

Mistral in 1914, the year she won first prize in a poetry contest sponsored by the city of Santiago (National Library, Santiago, Chile)

> I had a vague gaze,
> I asked for stories, narrative poems,
> and I did not wash the dishes . . .
> Alas! And, above all, because
> I spoke thus, in rhyme).

Having to go to the larger village of Vicuña to continue studies at the only school in the region was for the eleven-year-old Lucila the beginning of a life of suffering and disillusion: "Mi infancia la pasé casi toda en la aldea llamada Monte Grande. Me conozco sus cerros uno por uno. Fui dichosa hasta que salí de Monte Grande; y ya no lo fui nunca más" (I spent most of my childhood in the village called Monte Grande. I know its hills one by one. I was happy until I left Monte Grande, and then I was never happy again). This sense of having been exiled from an ideal place and time characterizes much of Mistral's worldview and helps explain her pervasive sadness and her obsessive search for love and transcendence. Her love of the material world was probably also because of her childhood years spent in direct contact with nature, and to an emotional manifestation of her desire to immerse herself in the world.

Among the several biographical anecdotes always cited in the life of the poet, the experience of having been accused of stealing school materials when she was in primary school is perhaps the most important to consider, as it explains Mistral's feelings about the injustice people inflict on others with their insensitivity. Mistral refers to this anecdote on several occasions, suggesting the profound and lasting effect the experience had on her. Throughout her life she maintained a sense of being hurt by others, in particular by people in her own country. This impression could be justified by several other circumstances in her life when the poet felt, probably justifiably, that she was being treated unjustly: for instance, in 1906 she tried to attend the Normal School in La Serena and was denied admission because of her writings, which were seen by the school authorities as the work of a troublemaker with pantheist ideas contrary to the Christian values required of an educator. She had been sending contributions to regional newspapers—*La Voz de Elqui* (The Voice of Elqui) in Vicuña and *El Coquimbo* in La Serena—since 1904, when she was still a teenager, and was already working as a teacher's aide in La Compañía, a small village near La Serena, to support herself and her mother.

Mistral was determined to succeed in spite of having been denied the right to study, however. She prepared herself, on her own, for a teaching career and for the life of a writer and intellectual. She also continued to write. Among her contributions to the local papers, one article of 1906—"La instrucción de la mujer" (The education of women)—deserves notice, as it shows how Mistral was at that early age aware and critical of the limitations affecting women's education. "Instrúyase a la mujer, no hay nada en ella que la haga ser colocada en un lugar más bajo que el hombre" (Let women be educated, nothing in them requires that they be set in a place lower than men). Some time later, in 1910, she obtained her coveted teaching certification even though she had not followed a regular course of studies. By studying on her own and passing the examination, she proved to herself and to others that she was academically well prepared and ready to fulfill professionally the responsibilities of an educator. She always commented bitterly, however, that she never had the opportunity to receive the formal education of other Latin American intellectuals.

With the professional degree in hand she began a short and successful career as a teacher and administrator. A series of different job destinations took her to distant and opposite regions within the varied territory of her country, as she quickly moved up in the national education system. These various jobs gave her the opportunity to know her country better than many who stayed in their regions of origin or settled in Santiago to be near the center of intellectual activity. This direct knowledge of her country, its geography, and its peoples became the basis for her increasing interest in national values, which coincided with the intellectual and political concerns of Latin America as a whole. Beginning in 1910 with a teaching position in the small farming town of Traiguén in the southern region of Araucanía, completely different from her native Valle de Elqui, she was promoted in the following years to schools in two relatively large and distant cities: Antofagasta, the coastal city in the mining northern region, in 1911; and Los Andes, in the bountiful Aconcagua Valley at the foothills of the Andes Mountains, about one hundred miles north of Santiago, in 1912. In this quiet farming town she enjoyed for a few years a period of quiet dedication to studying, teaching, and writing, as she was protected from distractions by the principal of her school.

Among many other submissions to different publications, she wrote to the Nicaraguan Rubén Darío in Paris, sending him a short story and some poems for his literary magazine, *Elegancias*. They appeared in March and April 1913, giving Mistral her first publication outside of Chile. Pedro Aguirre Cerda, an influential politician and educator (he served as president of Chile from 1938 to 1941), met her at that time and became her protector. In 1918, as secretary of education, Aguirre Cerda appointed her principal of the Liceo de Niñas (High School for Girls) in Punta Arenas, the southernmost Chilean port in the Strait of Magellan. This position was one of great responsibility, as Mistral was in charge of reorganizing a conflictive institution in a town with a large and dominant group of foreign immigrants practically cut off from the rest of the country. In this faraway city in a land of long winter nights and persistent winds, she wrote a series of three poems, "Paisajes de la Patagonia" (Patagonian Landscapes), inspired by her experience at the end of the world, separated from family and friends. They are the tormented expression of someone lost in despair. The stark landscape and the harsh weather of the region are mostly symbolic materializations of her spiritual outlook on human destiny.

"Desolación" (Despair), the first composition in the triptych, is written in the modernist Alexandrine verse of fourteen syllables common to several of Mistral's compositions of her early creative period. The poem captures the sense of exile and abandonment the poet felt at the time, as conveyed in its slow rhythm and in its concrete images drawn with a vocabulary suggestive of pain and stress:

La bruma espesa, eterna, para que olvide dónde
Me ha arrojado la mar en su ola de salmuera.
La tierra a la que vine no tiene primavera:
Tiene su noche larga que cual madre me esconde

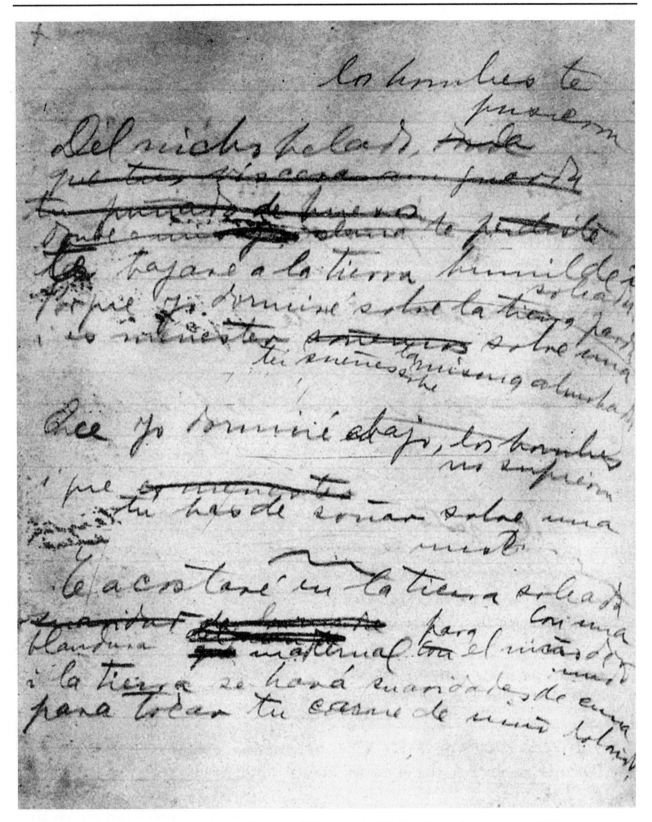

Page from the draft for "Los sonetos de la muerte," the poem with which Mistral won a Santiago contest in 1914
(Fundación Pablo Neruda, Universidad de Chile)

*Mistral in 1916, while she was teaching at the Liceo
de Los Andes in the Aconcagua Valley*

(Fog thickens, eternal, so that I may forget where
the sea has thrown me in its wave of brine.
The land I have come to knows no spring:
it has its long night that like a mother hides me).

As she had done before when working in the
poor, small schools of her northern region, she doubled
her duties by organizing evening classes for workers
who had no other means of educating themselves. She
was always concerned about the needs of the poor and
the disenfranchised, and every time she could do something about them, she acted, disregarding personal gain.
This attitude toward suffering permeates her poetry
with a deep feeling of love and compassion. "Tres árbo-
les" (Three Trees), the third composition of "Paisajes
de la Patagonia," exemplifies her devotion to the weak
in the final stanza, with its obvious symbolic image of
the fallen trees:

El leñador los olvidó. La noche
Vendrá. Estaré con ellos.
Recibiré en mi corazón sus mansas

Resinas. Me serán como de fuego.
Y mudos y ceñidos,
Nos halle el día en un montón de duelo.

(The woodsman forgot them. The night
Will come. I will be with them.
In my heart I will receive their gentle
Sap. They will be like fire to me.
And may the day find us
Quietly embraced in a heap of sorrow).

After two years in Punta Arenas, Mistral was
transferred again to serve as principal of the Liceo de
Niñas in Temuco, the main city in the heart of the Chilean Indian territory. She was there for a year. Pablo
Neruda, who at the time was a budding teenage poet
studying in the Liceo de Hombres, or high school for
boys, met her and received her advice and encourage-
ment to pursue his literary aspirations. Witnessing the
abusive treatment suffered by the humble and destitute
Indians, and in particular their women, Mistral was
moved to write "Poemas de la madre más triste"
(Poems of the Saddest Mother), a prose poem included
in *Desolación* in which she expresses "toda la solidaridad
del sexo, la infinita piedad de la mujer para la mujer"
(the complete solidarity of the sex, the infinite mercy of
woman for a woman), as she describes it in an explana-
tory note accompanying "Poemas de la madre más
triste," in the form of a monologue of a pregnant
woman who has been abandoned by her lover and
chastised by her parents:

Mi padre me dijo que me echaría, gritó a mi madre que
me arrojaría esta misma noche.
   La noche es tibia; a la claridad de las estrellas yo
podría caminar hasta la aldea próxima; pero ¿y si nace
a estas foras? Mis sollozos le han llamado tal vez; tal
vez quiera salir por ver mi cara

(My father said he would get rid of me, yelled at my
mother that he would throw me out this very night.
   The night is mild; by the light of the stars, I might
find my way to the nearest village; but suppose he is
born at such a time as this? My sobs perhaps have
aroused him; perhaps he wants to come out now to see
my face covered with tears).

In 1921 Mistral reached her highest position in the
Chilean educational system when she was made principal
of the newly created Liceo de Niñas number 6 in Santiago,
a prestigious appointment desired by many colleagues.
Now she was in the capital, in the center of the national literary and cultural activity, ready to participate fully in the
life of letters. A year later, however, she left the country to
begin her long life as a self-exiled expatriate.

During her years as an educator and administrator in Chile, Mistral was actively pursuing a literary

career, writing poetry and prose, and keeping in contact with other writers and intellectuals. She published mainly in newspapers, periodicals, anthologies, and educational publications, showing no interest in producing a book. Her name became widely familiar because several of her works were included in a primary-school reader that was used all over her country and around Latin America. At about this time her spiritual needs attracted her to the spiritualist movements inspired by oriental religions that were gaining attention in those days among Western artists and intellectuals. She was for a while an active member of the Chilean Theosophical Association and adopted Buddhism as her religion. This inclination for oriental forms of religious thinking and practices was in keeping with her intense desire to lead an inner life of meditation and became a defining characteristic of Mistral's spiritual life and religious inclinations, even though years later she returned to Catholicism. She never ceased to use the meditation techniques learned from Buddhism, and even though she declared herself Catholic, she kept some of her Buddhist beliefs and practices as part of her personal religious views and attitudes.

Another reason Mistral became known as a poet even before publishing her first book was the first prize—a flower and a gold coin—she won for "Los sonetos de la muerte" (The Sonnets of Death) in the 1914 "Juegos Florales," or poetic contest, organized by the city of Santiago. As a means to explain these three poems about a lost love, most critics tell of the suicide in 1909 of Romelio Ureta, a young man who had been Mistral's friend and first love several years before. Although the suicide of her former friend had little or nothing to do with their relationship, it added to the poems a strong biographical motivation that enhanced their emotional effect, creating in the public the image of Mistral as a tragic figure in the tradition of a romanticized conception of the poet. With "Los sonetos de la muerte" Mistral became in the public view a clearly defined poetic voice, one that was seen as belonging to a tragic, passionate woman, marked by loneliness, sadness, and relentless possessiveness and jealousy:

Del nicho helado en que los hombres te pusieron,
Te bajaré a la tierra humilde y soleada.
Que he de dormirme en ella los hombres no supieron,
Y que hemos de soñar sobre la misma almohada.
. . . .
Me alejaré cantando mis venganzas hermosas,
¡porque a ese hondor recóndito la mano de ninguna
bajará a disputarme tu puñado de huesos!

(From the cold niche where they put you
I will lower you to the humble and sunny earth.
They did not know I would fall asleep on it,

and that we would dream together on the same pillow.
. . . .
I shall leave singing my beautiful revenge,
because the hand of no other woman shall descend to this depth
to claim from me your fistful of bones!).

From then on all of her poetry was interpreted as purely autobiographical, and her poetic voices were equated with her own. Mistral was seen as the abandoned woman who had been denied the joy of motherhood and found consolation as an educator in caring for the children of other women, an image she confirmed in her writing, as in the poem "El niño solo" (The Lonely Child). The scene represents a woman who, hearing from the road the cry of a baby at a nearby hut, enters the humble house to find a boy alone in a cradle with no one to care for him; she takes him in her arms and consoles him by singing to him, becoming for a moment a succoring mother:

La madre se tardó, curvada en el barbecho;
El niño, al despertar, buscó el pezón de rosa
Y rompió en llanto . . . Yo lo estreché contra el pecho,
Y una canción de cuna me subió, temblorosa . . .

Por la ventana abierta la luna nos miraba.
El niño ya dormía, y la canción bañaba,
Como otro resplandor, mi pecho enriquecido . . .

(His mother was late coming from the fields;
The child woke up searching for the rose of the nipple
And broke into tears . . . I took him to my breast
And a cradlesong sprang in me with a tremor . . .

Through the open window the moon was watching us.
The baby was asleep, and the song bathed
Like another light, my enriched breast . . .).

It is difficult not to interpret this scene as representative of what poetry meant for Mistral, the writer who would be recognized by the reading public mostly for her cradlesongs.

To avoid using her real name, by which she was known as a well-regarded educator, Mistral signed her literary works with different pen names. By 1913 she had adopted her Mistral pseudonym, which she ultimately used as her own name. As Mistral she was recognized as the poet of a new dissonant feminine voice who expressed the previously unheard feelings of mothers and lonely women. The choice of her new first name suggests either a youthful admiration for the Italian poet Gabrielle D'Annunzio or a reference to the archangel Gabriel; the last name she chose in direct recognition of the French poet Frèderic Mistral, whose work she was reading with great interest around 1912, but mostly because it serves also to identify the power-

Mistral with pupils of the Liceo de Niñas in Punta Arenas, Chile, where she served as principal from 1918 to 1920 (National Library, Santiago, Chile)

ful wind that blows in Provence. Explaining her choice of name, she has said:

> Siento un gran amor por el viento. Lo considero como uno de los elementos más espirituales—más espiritual que el agua. Deseaba, pues, tomar un nombre de viento que no fuese "huracán" ni "brisa," y un día, enseñando geografía en mi escuela, me impresionó la descripción que hace Reclus, del viento, en su célebre obra, y en ella encontré ese nombre: Mistral. Lo adopté en seguida como seudónimo, y esa es la verdadera explicación de por qué llevo el apellido del cantor de la Proveza

> (I have great love of the wind. I take it for one of the most spiritual of the elements—more spiritual than water. I wanted, then, to adopt a name of wind, but not "hurricane" or "breeze"; one day, teaching geography in my school, I was impressed by the description of the wind made by Reclus in his famous work, and I found in it that name: Mistral. I immediately adopted it as my pseudonym, and this is the true explanation of why I use the last name of the singer of Provence).

In whichever case, Mistral was pointing with her pen name to personal ideals about her own identity as a poet. She acknowledged wanting for herself the fiery

spiritual strength of the archangel and the strong, earthly, and spiritual power of the wind.

The year 1922 brought important and decisive changes in the life of the poet and marks the end of her career in the Chilean educational system and the beginning of her life of traveling and of many changes of residence in foreign countries. It is also the year of publication of her first book, *Desolación*. Coincidentally, the same year, Universidad de Chile (The Chilean National University) granted Mistral the professional title of teacher of Spanish in recognition of her professional and literary contributions. Invited by the Mexican writer José Vasconcelos, secretary of public education in the government of Alvaro Obregón, Mistral traveled to Mexico via Havana, where she stayed several days giving lectures and readings and receiving the admiration and friendship of the Cuban writers and public. This short visit to Cuba was the first one of a long series of similar visits to many countries in the ensuing years.

Once in Mexico she helped in the planning and reorganization of rural education, a significant effort in a nation that had recently experienced a decisive social revolution and was building up its new institutions. In fulfilling her assigned task, Mistral came to know Mexico, its people, regions, customs, and culture in a profound and personal way. This knowledge gave her a new perspective about Latin America and its Indian roots, leading her into a growing interest and appreciation of all things autochthonous. From Mexico she sent to *El Mercurio* (The Mercury) in Santiago a series of newspaper articles on her observations in the country she had come to love as her own. These pieces represent her first enthusiastic reaction to her encounter with a foreign land. They are the beginning of a lifelong dedication to journalistic writing devoted to sensitizing the Latin American public to the realities of their own world. These articles were collected and published posthumously in 1957 as *Croquis mexicano* (Mexican Sketch). In Mexico, Mistral also edited *Lecturas para mujeres* (Readings for Women), an anthology of poetry and prose selections from classic and contemporary writers—including nineteen of her own texts—published in 1924 as a text to be used at the Escuela Hogar "Gabriela Mistral" (Home School "Gabriela Mistral"), named after her in recognition of her contribution to Mexican educational reform.

While she was in Mexico, *Desolación* was published in New York City by Federico de Onís at the insistence of a group of American teachers of Spanish who had attended a talk by Onís on Mistral at Columbia University and were surprised to learn that her work was not available in book form. *Desolación* was prepared based on the material sent by the author to her enthusiastic North American promoters. While the invitation by the Mexican government was indicative of Mistral's growing reputation as an educator on the continent, more than a recognition of her literary talents, the spontaneous decision of a group of teachers to publish her collected poems represented unequivocal proof of her literary preeminence. Most of the compositions in *Desolación* were written when Mistral was working in Chile and had appeared in various publications. As such, the book is an aggregate of poems rather than a collection conceived as an artistic unit. Divided into broad thematic sections, the book includes almost eighty poems grouped under five headings that represent the basic preoccupations in Mistral's poetry. Under the first section, "Vida" (Life), are grouped twenty-two compositions of varied subjects related to life's preoccupations, including death, religion, friendship, motherhood and sterility, poetic inspiration, and readings. The following section, "La escuela" (School), comprises two poems—"La maestra rural" (The Rural Teacher) and "La encina" (The Oak)—both of which portray teachers as strong, dedicated, self-effacing women akin to apostolic figures, who became in the public imagination the exact representation of Mistral herself. "La maestra era pura" (The teacher was pure), the first poem begins,

and the second and third stanzas open with similar brief, direct statements: "La maestra era pobre" (The teacher was poor), "La maestra era alegre" (The teacher was cheerful). The second stanza is a good example of the simple, direct description of the teacher as almost like a nun:

> La maestra era pobre. Su reino no es humano.
> (Así en el doloroso sembrador de Israel)
> Vestía sayas pardas, no enjoyaba su mano
> ¡y era todo su espíritu un inmenso joyel!
>
> (The teacher was poor. Her kingdom is not of this world.
> [Thus also in the painful sewer of Israel]
> She dressed in brown coarse garments, did not use a ring
> And her spirit was a magnificent jewel!).

"Dolor" (Pain) includes twenty-eight compositions of varied forms dealing with the painful experience of frustrated love. "Los sonetos de la muerte" is included in this section. Also in "Dolor" is the intensely emotional "Poema del hijo" (Poem of the Son), a cry for a son she never had because "En las noches, insomne de dicha y de visiones / la lujuria de fuego no descendió a mi lecho" (In my nights, awakened by joy and visions, / fiery lust did not descend upon my bed):

> Un hijo, un hijo, un hijo! Yo quise un hijo tuyo
> y mío, allá en los días del éxtasis ardiente,
> en los que hasta mis huesos temblaron de tu arrullo
> y un ancho resplandor creció sobre mi frente
>
> (A son, a son, a son! I wanted a son of yours
> and mine, back then in the days of burning ecstasy,
> when even my bones trembled at your whisper
> and a wide light grew in my forehead).

"Naturaleza" (Nature) includes "Paisajes de le Patagonia" and other texts about Mistral's stay in Punta Arenas. A series of compositions for children—"Canciones de cuna" (Cradlesongs), also included in her next book, *Ternura: Canciones de niños* (Tenderness: Songs for Children, 1924)—completes the poetry selections in *Desolación*. An additional group of prose compositions, among them "Poemas de la madre más triste" and several short stories under the heading "Prosa escolar" (School Prose), confirms that the book is an assorted collection of most of what Mistral had written during several years. In 1923 a second printing of the book appeared in Santiago, with the addition of a few compositions written in Mexico.

Mistral's stay in Mexico came to an end in 1924 when her services were no longer needed. Before returning to Chile, she traveled in the United States and Europe, thus beginning her life of constant movement from one place to another, a compulsion she

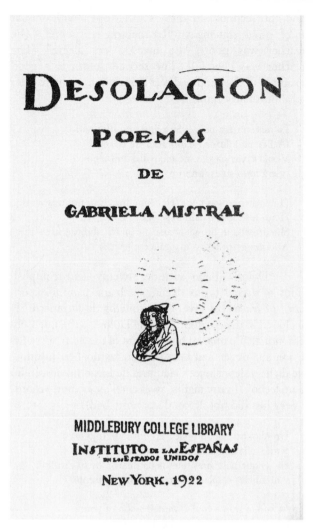

Title page for Mistral's first book
(Middlebury College Library)

attributed to her need to look for a perfect place to live in harmony with nature and society. In 1925, on her way back to Chile, she stopped in Brazil, Uruguay, and Argentina, countries that received her with public manifestations of appreciation. By then she had become a well-known and much admired poet in all of Latin America. Her second book of poems, *Ternura,* had appeared a year before in Madrid. Subtitled *Canciones de niños,* it included, together with new material, the poems for children already published in *Desolación.* Because of this focus, which underlined only one aspect of her poetry, this book was seen as significantly different from her previous collection of poems, where the same compositions were part of a larger selection of sad and disturbing poems not at all related to children.

In *Ternura* Mistral attempts to prove that poetry that deals with the subjects of childhood, maternity, and nature can be done in highly aesthetic terms, and with a depth of feeling and understanding. As she wrote in a letter, "He querido hacer una poesía escolar nueva, porque la que hay en boga no me satisface" (I wanted to write a new type of poetry for the school, because the one in fashion now does not satisfy me). She wanted to write, and did write successfully, "una poesía escolar que no por ser escolar deje de ser poesía, que lo sea, y más delicada que cualquiera otra, más honda, más impregnada de cosas del corazón: más estremecida de soplo de alma" (a poetry for school that does not cease to be poetry because it is for school, it must be poetry, and more delicate than any other poetry, deeper, more saturated of things of the heart: more affected by the breath of the soul). *Ternura* includes her "Canciones de cuna," "Rondas" (Play songs), and nonsense verses such as "La pajita" (The Little Straw), which combines fantasy with playfulness and musicality:

> Era que era una niña de cera;
> pero ne era una niña de cera,
> era una gavilla parada en la era.
> Pero no era una gavilla
> sino una flor tieza de maravilla

> (There was this girl of wax;
> but she wasn't made of wax,
> she was a sheaf of wheat standing in the threshing floor.
> But she was not a sheaf of wheat
> but a stiff sunflower).

The book also includes poems about the world and nature. They are attributed to an almost magical storyteller, "La Cuenta-mundo" (The World-Teller), the fictional lyrical voice of a woman who tells about water and air, light and rainbow, butterflies and mountains. "La piña" (The Pineapple) is indicative of the simple, sensual, and imaginative character of these poems about the world of matter:

> Allega y no tengas miedo
> De la piña con espadas . . .
> Por vivir en el plantío
> Su madre la crió armada . . .

> Suena el cuchillo cortando
> La amazona degollada
> Que pierde todo el poder
> En el manojo de dagas

> (Come near, don't be afraid
> Of the pineapple and her swords . . .
> Because they live in the field
> Her mother raised her well-armed . . .

> The knife makes a sound as it cuts
> The decapitated amazon
> Who loses all her power
> With her bundle of daggers).

There is also a group of school poems, slightly pedagogical and objective in their tone.

In *Ternura* Mistral seems to fulfill the promise she made in "Voto" (Vow) at the end of *Desolación:* "Dios me perdone este libro amargo. Lo dejo tras de mí como a la hondonada sombría y por laderas más clementes subo hacia las mesetas espirituales donde una ancha luz caerá sobre mis días. Yo cantaré desde ellas las palabras de la esperanza, cantaré como lo quiso un misericordioso, para consolar a los hombres" (I hope God will forgive me for this bitter book. I leave it behind me, as you leave the darkened valley, and I climb by more benign slopes to the spiritual plateaus where a wide light will fall over my days. From there I will sing the words of hope, I will sing as a merciful one wanted to do, for the consolation of men). *Ternura,* in effect, is a bright, hopeful book, filled with the love of children and of the many concrete things of the natural and human world.

Back in Chile after three years of absence, she returned to her region of origin and settled in La Serena in 1925, thinking about working on a small orchard. The same year she had obtained her retirement from the government as a special recognition of her years of service to education and of her exceptional contribution to culture. The rest of her life she depended mostly on this pension, since her future consular duties were served in an honorary capacity. Mistral returned to Catholicism around this time. A fervent follower of St. Francis of Assisi, she entered the Franciscan Order as a laical member. This decision says much about her religious convictions and her special devotion for the Italian saint, his views on nature, and his advice on following a simple life. As a member of the order, she chose to live in poverty, making religion a central element in her life. Religion for her was also fundamental to her understanding of her function as a poet. Her admiration of St. Francis had led her to start writing, while still in Mexico, a series of prose compositions on his life. Fragments of the never-completed biography were published in 1965 as *Motivos de San Francisco* (Motives of St. Francis). At the time she wrote them, however, they appeared as newspaper contributions in *El Mercurio* in Chile.

Mistral stayed for only a short period in Chile before leaving again for Europe, this time as secretary of the Latin American section in the League of Nations in Paris. A designated member of the Institute of Intellectual Cooperation, she took charge of the Section of Latin American Letters. In Paris she became acquainted with many writers and intellectuals, including those from Latin America who lived in Europe, and many more who visited her while traveling there. She was the center of attention and the point of contact for many of

Title page for Mistral's collection of poems on childhood, maternity, and nature (Pomona College Library)

those who felt part of a common Latin American continent and culture. She started the publication of a series of Latin American literary classics in French translation and kept a busy schedule as an international functionary fully dedicated to her work. She was gaining friends and acquaintances, and her family provided her with her most cherished of companions: a nephew she took under her care. She was living in the small village of Bedarrides, in Provence, when a half brother Mistral did not know existed, son of the father who had left her, came to her asking for help. He brought with him his four-year-old son, Juan Miguel Godoy Mendoza, whose Catalan mother had just died. The young man left the boy with Mistral and disappeared.

A few months later, in 1929, Mistral received news of the death of her own mother, whom she had not seen since her last visit to Chile four years before.

Mistral visiting Chile in 1938, between diplomatic appointments in Lisbon and Rio de Janeiro

In a series of eight poems titled "Muerte de mi madre" (Death of My Mother) she expressed her sadness and bereavement, as well as the "volteadura de mi alma en una larga crisis religiosa" (upsetting of my soul in a long religious crisis):

> Madre mía, en el sueño
> ando por paisajes cardenosos:
> un monte negro que se contornea
> siempre, para alcanzar el otro monte;
> y en el que siempre estás tú vagamente,
> pero siempre hay otro monte redondo
> que circundar, para pagar el paso
> al monte de tu gozo y de mi gozo
>
> (Mother, in my dream
> I walk purplish landscapes:
> a black mountain that sways
> trying to reach the other mountain;
> and you are always in it vaguely,
> but there is always another round mountain
> to be walked around to pay the toll
> to get to the mountain of your joy and mine).

The dream has all the material quality of most of her preferred images, transformed into a nightmarish representation of suffering along the way to the final rest. In this poem the rhymes and rhythm of her previous compositions are absent, as she moves cautiously into new, freer forms of versification that allow her a more expressive communication of her sorrow. When still using a well-defined rhythm she depends on the simpler Spanish assonant rhyme or no rhyme at all. The strongly physical and stark character of her images remains, however, as in "Nocturno de la consumación" (Nocturne of Consummation):

> Hace tanto que masco tinieblas
> Que la dicha no sé reaprender;
> Tanto tiempo que piso las lavas
> Que olvidaron vellones los pies;
> Tantos años que muerdo el desierto
> Que mi patria se llama la Sed
>
> (I have been chewing darkness for such a long time
> That I cannot learn my joy again;
> I have been walking the lavas so long
> That my feet have lost memory of softness;
> I have been biting the desert for so many years
> That Thirst is the name of my homeland).

In 1930 the government of General Carlos Ibáñez suspended Mistral's retirement benefits, leaving her without a sustained means of living. The most prestigious newspapers in the Hispanic world offered her a solution in the form of regular paid contributions. She had to do more journalistic writing, as she regularly sent her articles to such papers as *ABC* in Madrid; *La Nación* (The Nation) in Buenos Aires; *El Tiempo* (The Times) in Bogotá; *Repertorio Americano* (American Repertoire) in San José, Costa Rica; *Puerto Rico Ilustrado* (Illustrated Puerto Rico) in San Juan; and *El Mercurio,* for which she had been writing regularly since the 1920s. Also, to offset her economic difficulties, in the academic year of 1930–1931 she accepted an invitation from Onís at Columbia University and taught courses in literature and Latin American culture at Barnard College and Middlebury College. The same year she traveled in the Antilles and Central America, giving talks and meeting with writers, intellectuals, and an enthusiastic public of readers.

By 1932 the Chilean government gave her a consular position in Naples, Italy, but Benito Mussolini's government did not accept her credentials, perhaps because of her clear opposition to fascism. In 1933, always looking for a source of income, she traveled to Puerto Rico to teach at the University in Río Piedras. The Puerto Rican legislature named her an adoptive daughter of the island, and the university gave her a doctorate Honoris Causa, the first doctorate of many she received from universities in the ensuing years. Several of her writings deal with Puerto Rico, as she developed a keen appreciation of the island and its people. In June of the same year she took a consular position in Madrid. As had happened previously when she lived in Paris, in Madrid she was constantly visited by writers from Latin America and Spain who found in her a stimulating and influential intellect. Neruda was also serving as a Chilean diplomat in Spain at the time.

In spite of all her acquaintances and friendships in Spain, however, Mistral had to leave the country in a hurry, never to return. In characteristically sincere and unequivocal terms she had expressed in private some critical opinions of Spain that led to complaints by Spaniards residing in Chile and, consequently, to the order from the Chilean government in 1936 to abandon her consular position in Madrid. Mistral was asked to leave Madrid, but her position was not revoked. She left for Lisbon, angry at the malice of those who she felt wanted to hurt her and saddened for having to leave on those scandalous terms a country she had always loved and admired as the land of her ancestors. In 1935 the Chilean government had given her, at the request of Spanish intellectuals and other admirers, the specially created position of consul for life, with the prerogative to choose on her own the city of designation.

Included in Mistral's many trips was a short visit to her country in 1938, the year she left the Lisbon consulate. It coincided with the publication in Buenos Aires of *Tala* (Felling), her third book of poems. In solidarity with the Spanish Republic she donated her author's rights for the book to the Spanish children displaced and orphaned by the war. In *Tala* Mistral includes the poems inspired by the death of her mother, together with a variety of other compositions that do not linger in sadness but sing of the beauty of the world and deal with the hopes and dreams of the human heart. These poems are divided into three sections: "Materias" (Matter), comprising verse about bread, salt, water, air; "Tierra de Chile" (Land of Chile), and "America." Particularly important in this last group are two American hymns: "Sol del trópico" (Tropical Sun) and "Cordillera" (Mountain Range). These poems exemplify Mistral's interest in awakening in her contemporaries a love for the essences of their American identity.

Because of the war in Europe, and fearing for her nephew, whose friendship with right-wing students in Lisbon led her to believe that he might become involved in the fascist movement, Mistral took the general consular post in Rio de Janeiro. After living for a while in Niteroi, and wanting to be near nature, Mistral moved to Petropolis in 1941, where she often visited her neighbors, the Jewish writer Stefan Zweig and his wife. The suicide of the couple in despair for the developments in Europe caused her much pain; but the worst suffering came months later when her nephew

died of arsenic poisoning the night of 14 August 1943. For Mistral this experience was decisive, and from that date onward she lived in constant bereavement, unable to find joy in life because of her loss. Although it was established by the authorities that the eighteen-year-old Juan Miguel had committed suicide, Mistral never accepted this troubling fact. In her pain she insisted on another interpretation, that he had been killed by envious Brazilian school companions. She never brought this interpretation of the facts into her poetry, as if she were aware of the negative overtones of her saddened view on the racial and cultural tensions at work in the world, and particularly in Brazil and Latin America, in those years. In "Aniversario" (Anniversary), a poem in remembrance of Juan Miguel, she makes only a vague reference to the circumstances of his death:

Me asombra el que, en contra el logro
De Muerte y de matadores,
Sigas quedado y erguido,
Caña o junco no cascado
Y que llamado con voz
O con silencio, me acudas

(I am surprised that, contrary to the accomplishment
Of Death and the killers,
You still remain and standing,
Unbroken cane or bulrush
And that, when called by my voice
Or by silence, you come to me).

This poem reflects also the profound change in Mistral's life caused by her nephew's death. She composed a series of prayers on his behalf and found consolation in the conviction that Juan Miguel was sometimes at her side in spirit. In her sadness she only could hope for the time when she herself would die and be with him again.

Despite her loss, her active life and her writing and travels continued. She was still in Brazil when she heard in the news on the radio that the Nobel Prize in literature had been awarded to her. It was 1945, and World War II was recently over; for Mistral, however, there was no hope or consolation. She traveled to Sweden to be at the ceremony only because the prize represented recognition of Latin American literature. In the same year she published a new edition of *Ternura* that added the children's poems from *Tala,* thus becoming the title under which all of her poems devoted to children and school subjects were collected as one work. As a consequence, she also revised *Tala* and produced a new, shorter edition in 1946. Minus the poems from the four original sections of poems for children, *Tala* was transformed in this new version into a different,

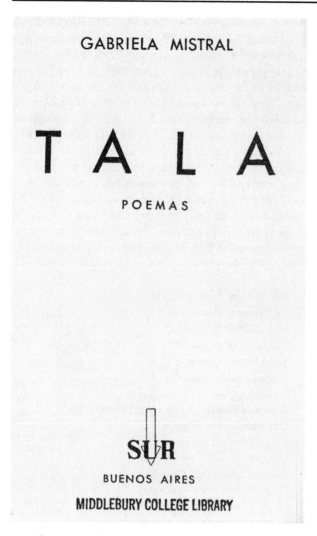

GABRIELA MISTRAL

T A L A

POEMAS

SUR

BUENOS AIRES

MIDDLEBURY COLLEGE LIBRARY

*Title page for Mistral's 1938 collection, which includes poems
inspired by the death of her mother in 1929
(Middlebury College Library)*

bara, where she established herself for a time in a house she bought with the money from the Nobel Prize. Ciro Alegría, a Peruvian writer who visited her there in 1947, remembers how she divided her time between work, visits, and caring for her garden. Mistral liked to believe that she was a woman of the soil, someone in direct and daily contact with the earth. In all her moves from country to country she chose houses that were in the countryside or surrounded by flower gardens with an abundance of plants and trees. According to Alegría, "Todo el panteísmo indio que había en el alma de Gabriela Mistral, asomaba de pronto en la conversación y de manera neta cuando se ponía en contacto con la naturaleza" (The American Indian pantheism of Mistral's spirit was visible sometimes in her conversation, and it was purest when she was in contact with nature).

Mistral's love of nature was deeply ingrained from childhood and permeated her work with unequivocal messages for the protection and care of the environment that preceded present-day ecological concerns. She had a similar concern for the rights to land use in Latin America, and for the situation of native peoples, the original owners of the continent. After two years in California she again was not happy with her place of residence and decided in 1948 to accept the invitation of the Mexican president to establish her home there, in the country she loved almost as her own. Her failing health, in particular her heart problems, made it impossible for her to travel to Mexico City or any other high-altitude cities, so she settled as consul in Veracruz. The Mexican government gave her land where she could establish herself for good, but after building a small house she returned to the United States.

The beauty and good weather of Italy, a country she particularly enjoyed, attracted her once more. War was now in the past, and Europe appeared to her again as the cradle of her own Christian traditions: the arts, literature, and spirituality. For a while in the early 1950s she established residence in Naples, where she actively fulfilled the duties of Chilean consul. These duties allowed her to travel in Italy, enjoying a country that was especially agreeable to her. In part because of her health, however, by 1953 she was back in the United States. This time she established her residence in Roslyn Harbor, Long Island, where she spent her last years. While in New York she served as Chilean representative to the United Nations and was an active member of the Subcommittee on the Status of Women.

Besides correcting and re-editing her previous work, and in addition to her regular contributions to newspapers, Mistral was occupied by two main writing projects in the years following her nephew's death and the reception of the Nobel Prize. These two projects—

more brooding book that starkly contrasts with the new edition of *Ternura*.

These changes to her previous books represent Mistral's will to distinguish her two different types of poetry as separate and distinctly opposite in inspiration and objective. While the first edition of *Ternura* was the result of a shrewd decision by an editor with expertise in children's books, Saturnino Calleja in Madrid, these new editions of both books, revised by Mistral herself, should be interpreted as a more significant manifestation of her views on her work and the need to organize it accordingly. The same creative distinction dictated the definitive organization of all her poetic work in the 1958 edition of *Poesías completas* (Complete Poems), edited by Margaret Bates under Mistral's supervision.

Not wanting to live in Brazil, a country she blamed for the death of her nephew, Mistral left for Los Angeles in 1946 and soon after moved to Santa Bar-

Mistral with schoolchildren in Petropolis, Brazil, in 1945 (National Library, Santiago, Chile)

the seemingly unending composition of *Poema de Chile,* a long narrative poem, and the completion of her last book of poems, *Lagar* (Wine Press, 1954)–responded also to the distinction she made between two kinds of poetic creation. In the first project, which was never completed, Mistral continued to explore her interest in musical poetry for children and poetry of nature. Both are used in a long narrative composition that has much of the charm of a lullaby and a magical story sung by a maternal figure to a child:

> Vamos caminando juntos
> Así, en hermanos de cuento,
> Tú echando sombra de niño,
> Yo apenas sobra de helecho
>
> (We are walking together,
> Thus, like brothers in a story,
> Yours is the shadow of a boy,
> Mine barely resembles the shadow of a fern).

The delight of a Franciscan attitude of enjoyment in the beauty of nature, with its magnificent landscapes, simple elements–air, rock, water, fruits–and animals and plants, is also present in the poem:

> En pasando el frío grande
> Las mariposas han vuelto
> Y en el aire, amigo, va
> Un dulce estremecimiento
> Y las hojas del romero
> Baten de su ángel sin peso,

> Un ángel garabateado
> Como por veras y juego
>
> (As soon as the big cold left
> The butterflies returned
> And in the air, my friend, is
> A sweet tremor
> And the rosemary leaves
> Sway under their light angel,
> An angel all painted
> As if it were for real or just for play).

The aging and ailing poet imagines herself in *Poema de Chile* as a ghost who returns to her land of origin to visit it for the last time before meeting her creator. Inspired by her nostalgic memories of the land of her youth that had become idealized in the long years of self-imposed exile, Mistral tries in this poem to conciliate her regret for having lived half of her life away from her country with her desire to transcend all human needs and find final rest and happiness in death and eternal life. In characteristic dualism the poet writes of the beauty of the world in all of its material sensuality as she hurries on her way to a transcendental life in a spiritual union with creation. *Poema de Chile* was published posthumously in 1967 in an edition prepared by Doris Dana. This edition, based on several drafts left by Mistral, is an incomplete version.

Lagar, on the contrary, was published when the author was still alive and constitutes a complete work in spite of the several unfinished poems left out by Mistral

Mistral receiving the Nobel Prize in literature from King Gustav V of Sweden in 1945

and published posthumously as *Lagar II* (1991). A book written in a period of great suffering, *Lagar* is an exemplary work of spiritual strength and poetic expressiveness. It follows the line of sad and complex poetry in the revised editions of *Desolación* and *Tala*. In *Lagar* Mistral deals with the subjects that most interested her all of her life, as if she were reviewing and revising her views and beliefs, her own interpretation of the mystery of human existence. As in previous books she groups the compositions based on their subject; thus, her poems about death form two sections—"Luto" (Mourning) and "Nocturnos" (Nocturnes)—and, together with the poems about the war ("Guerra"), constitute the darkest aspect of the collection. At the other end of the spectrum are the poems of "Naturaleza" (Nature) and "Jugarretas" (Playfulness), which continue the same subdivisions found in her previous book. Other sections address her religious concerns ("Religiosas," Nuns), her view of herself as a woman in perpetual movement from one place to another ("Vagabundaje,"

Vagabondage), and her different portraits of women—perhaps different aspects of herself—as mad creatures obsessed by a passion ("Locas mujeres," Crazy Women). Indicative of the meaning and form of these portraits of madness is, for instance, the first stanza of "La bailarina" (The Ballerina):

> La bailarina está ahora danzando
> La danza del perder cuanto tenía.
> Deja caer todo lo que ella había,
> Padres y hermanos, huertos y campiñas,
> El rumor de su río, los caminos,
> El cuento de su hogar, su propio rostro
> Y su nombre y los juegos de su infancia
> Como quien deja todo lo que tuvo
> Caer de cuello, de seno y de alma
>
> (The ballerina is now dancing
> The dance of losing all she had.
> She lets fall everything she owned,
> Parents and brothers, orchards and fields,
> The sound of her river, the roads,

The story of her home, her own face
And her name, and the games of her childhood
As if everything she had she let
Fall from neck, bosom and soul).

In 1951 Mistral had received the Chilean National Prize in literature, but she did not return to her native country until 1954, when *Lagar* was published in Santiago. She had not been back in Chile since 1938, and this last, triumphant visit was brief, since her failing health did not allow her to travel much within the country. The following years were of diminished activity, although she continued to write for periodicals, as well as producing *Poema de Chile* and other poems. Late in 1956 she was diagnosed with terminal pancreatic cancer. A few weeks later, in the early hours of 10 January 1957, Mistral died in a hospital in Hempstead, Long Island. Her last word was "triunfo" (triumph). After a funeral ceremony at St. Patrick's Cathedral in New York City, the body of this pacifist woman was flown by military plane to Santiago, where she received the funeral honors of a national hero. Following her last will, her remains were eventually put to rest in a simple tomb in Monte Grande, the village of her childhood.

Her tomb, a minimal rock amid the majestic mountains of her valley of birth, is a place of pilgrimage for many people who have discovered in her poetry the strength of a religious, spiritual life dominated by a passionate love for all of creation. Almost half a century after her death Gabriela Mistral continues to attract the attention of readers and critics alike, particularly in her country of origin. Her poetic work, more than her prose, maintains its originality and effectiveness in communicating a personal worldview in many ways admirable. The strongly spiritual character of her search for a transcendental joy unavailable in the world contrasts with her love for the materiality of everyday existence. Her poetic voice communicates these opposing forces in a style that combines musicality and harshness, spiritual inquietudes and concrete images, hope and despair, and simple, everyday language and sometimes unnaturally twisted constructions and archaic vocabulary. In her poetry dominates the emotional tension of the voice, the intensity of a monologue that might be a song or a prayer, a story or a musing.

Mistral in 1946, the year she moved to Santa Barbara, California (National Library, Santiago, Chile)

Letters:
Epistolario: Cartas a Eugenio Labarca (1915–16), edited by Raúl Silva Castro (Santiago: Anales de la Universidad de Chile, 1957);
Cartas de Gabriela Mistral a Juan Ramón Jiménez (San Juan, Puerto Rico: Ediciones de La Torre, 1961);
Cartas de Gabriela Mistral, edited by Luis Vargas Saavedra (Santiago: Biblioteca Nacional, 1970);

Cartas de amor de Gabriela Mistral, edited by Sergio Fernández Larraín (Santiago: Andrés Bello, 1978);
Eduardo Frei Montalva, *Memorias y correspondencias con Gabriela Mistral y Jacques Maritain* (Santiago: Planeta, 1989);
Gabriela Mistral y Joaquín García Monge: Una correspondencia inédita, edited by Magda Arce (Santiago: Andrés Bello, 1989);
Tan de usted: Epistelario de Gabriela Mistral con Alfonso Reyes, edited by Vargas Saavedra (Santiago: Hachette/Editorial Universitaria Católica de Chile, 1991);
En batalla de sencillez: De Lucila a Gabriela: Cartas a Pedro Prado, 1915–1939, edited by Vargas Saavedra, María Ester Martínez Sanz, and Regina Valdés Bowen (Santiago: Dolmen, 1993);
Epistolario de Gabriela Mistral e Isolina Barraza (La Serena, Chile: Rosales, 1995);

Vuestra Gabriel: cartas inéditas de Gabriela Mistral a los Errázuriz Echenique y Tomic Errázuriz, edited by Vargas Saavedra (Santiago: Zig-Zag, 1995);

Cartas de amor y desamor, edited by Jaime Quezada and Fernández Larraín (Santiago: Andrés Bello, 1999);

Castilla, tajeada de sed como mi lengua: Gabriela Mistral ante España y España ante Gabriela Mistral, 1933 a 1935, edited by Vargas Saavedra (Santiago: Ediciones Universidad Católica de Chile, 2002);

This America of Ours: The Letters of Gabriela Mistral and Victoria Ocampo, edited and translated by Elizabeth Horan and Doris Meyer (Austin: University of Texas Press, 2003).

Bibliographies:

Compendio bibliográfico de Gabriela Mistral (Vicuña, Chile: Museo de Gabriela Mistral de Vicuña, 1985);

Patricia Rubio, *Gabriela Mistral ante la crítica: Bibliografía anotada* (Santiago: Dirección de Bibliotecas, Archivos y Museos, Centro de Investigaciones Diego Barros Arana, 1995).

Biography:

Isauro Santelices E., *Mi encuentro con Gabriela Mistral, 1912–1957* (Santiago: Editorial de Pacífico, 1972).

References:

Ciro Alegría, *Gabriela Mistral íntima* (Lima: Editorial Universo, 1968?);

Fernando Alegría, *Genio y figura de Gabriela Mistral* (Buenos Aires: Editorial Universitaria de Buenos Aires, 1966);

Jaime Concha, *Gabriela Mistral* (Madrid: Júcar, 1987);

Santiago Daydí-Tolson, *El ultimo viaje de Gabriela Mistral* (Santiago: Aconcagua, 1989);

Licia Fiol-Matta, *A Queer Mother for the Nation: The State and Gabriela Mistral* (Minneapolis: University of Minnesota Press, 2002);

Grínor Rojo, *Dirán que está en la gloria (Mistral)* (Santiago: Fondo de Cultura Económica, 1997);

Isauro Santelices E., *Mi encuentro con Gabriela Mistral, 1912–1957* (Santiago: Pacífico, 1972);

Martín C. Taylor, *Gabriela Mistral's Religious Sensibility* (Berkeley: University of California Press, 1968);

Volodia Teltelboim, *Gabriela Mistral pública y secreta: Truenos y silencios en la vida del primer Nobel latinoamericano* (Santiago: BAT, 1991).

Papers:

Gabriela Mistral's papers are held in the Mistral Collection at the Barnard College Library in New York.

Nancy Morejón

(7 August 1944 –)

Ana Garcia Chíchester
Mary Washington College

BOOKS: *Mutismos* (Havana: El Puente, 1962);

Amor, ciudad atribuída (Havana: El Puente, 1964);

Richard trajo su flauta y otros argumentos (Havana: UNEAC, 1967);

Lengua de pájaro: Comentarios reales: Monografía histórica, by Morejón and Carmen Gonce (Havana: UNEAC, 1971);

Recopilación de textos sobre Nicolás Guillén (Havana: Casa de las Américas, 1974);

Parajes de una época (Havana: Letras Cubanas, 1979);

Elogio de la danza (Mexico City: UNAM, 1982);

Nación y mestizaje en Nicolás Guillén (Havana: UNEAC, 1982);

Octubre imprescindible (Havana: UNEAC, 1982);

Cuaderno de Granada (Havana: Casa de las Américas, 1984); translated by Lisa Davis as *Grenada's Notebook* (New York: Círculo de Cultura Cubana, 1984);

Piedra pulida (Havana: Letras Cubanas, 1986);

Fundación de la imagen (Havana: Letras Cubanas, 1988);

Paisaje célebre: Poemas 1987–1992 (Caracas: FUNDARTE, 1993);

El río de Martín Pérez y otros poemas (Matanzas, Cuba: Vigía, 1996);

La Quinta de los Molinos (Havana: Letras Cubanas, 2000);

Cántico de la huella (Matanzas, Cuba: Vigía, 2002).

Editions: *Poemas* (Mexico City: UNAM, 1980);

Baladas para un sueño (Havana: UNEAC, 1988);

Elogio y paisaje (Havana: UNEAC, 1996);

Botella al mar (Madrid: Olifante, 1996);

Richard trajo su flauta y otros poemas: Antología poética, edited by Mario Benedetti (Madrid: Visor, 1999);

Cuerda veloz: Antología poética, 1962–1992 (Havana: Letras Cubanas, 2002).

Editions in English: *Where the Island Sleeps like a Wing: Selected Poetry,* translated by Kathleen Weaver (San Francisco: Black Scholar Press, 1985);

Ours the Earth, translated by J. R. Pereira (Mona: University of the West Indies, 1990);

Nancy Morejón (photograph by Kathleen Weaver; from the cover for Where the Island Sleeps like a Wing: Selected Poetry, *1985; Thomas Cooper Library, University of South Carolina)*

Looking Within: Selected Poems, 1954–2000, edited, with an introduction, by Juanamaría Cordones-Cook, translated by Gabriel Abudu and others (Detroit: Wayne State University Press, 2002).

OTHER: Paul Laraque, *Poesía cotidiana; Las armas cotidianas,* translated by Morejón (Havana: Casa de las Américas, 1981);

Ernest Pépin, *Remolino de palabres libres,* translated by Morejón (Havana: Casa de las Américas, 1991).

Nancy Morejón is an Afro-Cuban poet who first became known outside of her country after the publication of her third book of poetry, *Richard trajo su flauta y otros argumentos* (Richard Brought His Flute and Other Arguments, 1967). Morejón exemplifies the kind of writer the Cuban Revolution of 1959 produced: committed to the political and social ideology of the revolution yet faithful to the idea of an aesthetic impulse in literature. Her native Havana, love, family, history, and racial and class identity find expression in her poetry. Political and social themes appear in all of her early output and continue, albeit to a lesser extent, in her later writings. Throughout her career Morejón has maintained a lyrical voice that transcends thematic shifts. Indeed, her work has remained vital because of its persistent commitment to beauty and lyricism. In her later collections Morejón seems to have traded the revolutionary fervor of her youth for a mature poetic voice that seeks to express much more of the personal than the collective.

Nancy Morejón was born in Old Havana on 7 August 1944. She lived there all of her formative years and into adulthood, thus developing her love for the city and its character. In 1959 she began her pedagogical career as a teacher of English. She finished high school at the Institute of Havana in 1961. From 1963 to 1964 she taught French at the academy "Gustavo Ameijeiras" and worked as a translator for the Ministry of the Interior. Between 1963 and 1965 Morejón entered the ranks of the Unión de Jóvenes Comunistas (Young Communists Union), serving as a member of its Base Committee. She studied French in the School of Arts of the University of Havana, where she received the degree of *licenciatura,* the equivalent of a bachelor's degree, in 1966.

Morejón is a scholar of Francophone literature of the Caribbean. She specializes in the translation of French narrative and poetry and has worked as a translator for Cuba's Instituto del Libro. The noted Martinican poet Aimé Cesaire and Haitians Jacques Roumain and René Depestre are among the authors translated into Spanish by Morejón. Poet, journalist, theater critic, and translator, Morejón has collaborated in several Cuban literary publications from the start of her career, notably in *Unión* (Union), *Cultura '64* (Culture '64), *El Caimán Barbudo* (The Bearded Caiman), *La Gaceta de Cuba* (Cuban Gazette), and the journal *Casa de las Américas* (House of the Americas). More recently she worked for the Ministry of the Interior, the UNEAC (Unión de Escritores y Artistas de Cuba, or Cuban Union of Artists and Writers), and the cultural institute Casa de las Américas. Among many awards, Morejón received the Premio de la Crítica (Cuba) for her poetry in 1986 and the Pérez Bonalde International Poetry Prize (Venezuela) for *Paisaje célebre: Poemas 1987–1992* (Celebrated Landscape: Poems, 1987–1992, 1993). In February of 2002, Morejón was awarded Cuba's highest literary honor when she won the Premio Nacional de Literatura de 2001 (the 2001 National Prize for Literature).

Two central themes in Morejón's poetry have received the greatest attention of the critics and the reading public. On the one hand, there is the exploration of her identity (cultural and historical) as a black woman, while on the other is her need to inscribe her poetry within the boundaries (geographical, historical, social, and political) of her experience as a Cuban. As Catherine Davies points out in her entry on Morejón for the *Encyclopedia of Latin American Literature* (1997), the poet "articulates in her poems the complex interplay of class, race, nation and gender." In the 1960s and 1970s her poems struggle with these issues. Moreover, critics have been careful to point out that Morejón's work never embraced the propagandistic tone of some of the literature produced in Cuba during the initial *promociones,* that is, promotions of literary writing by the revolutionary government in the 1960s and 1970s. Toward the end of the 1960s, literary criticism in Cuba (both institutionalized and not) promoted the writing of poems that were didactical in intention and ideologically compatible with the objectives of the revolution.

Several decades later, Cuban critics such as Osvaldo Sánchez recognized that the generation of writers including Morejón and others associated with the journal *El Caimán Barbudo* (published bimonthly during part of the 1960s) suffered the consequences of such promotions as these young writers reduced "su perspectiva personal a monólogo, su intransigencia a disyuntivas falsas y su productividad a la concesión formal y a la didáctica panfletaria" (their personal perspectives to monologues, their obstinacy to bogus alternatives and their productivity to formal concessions and to pamphletic didacticism). In the 1980s a renewed interest in aesthetics supplanted social and political statements in literature. This shift is not surprising, as Alan West explains, since by the mid 1980s Cuban literature "had drifted away from overtly social commentary and/or exhortation," which was "partly due to a certain stability of the Cuban Revolution" and also in part by "a rejection of a socially committed aesthetic of the 1970s which had had a deadening effect on literary culture." Morejón's work in the 1980s reflects this change as political fervor paves the way to feminist solidarity and an intense lyrical quality. Efraín Barradas speaks of Morejón's poetic voice in terms of three essential elements: "su conciencia social, su exaltación de la negritud y el cultivo de un sutil intimismo que a veces adopta oscuras capas verbales" (her social conscience, her exaltation of negritude, and the fostering of a subtle intimate voice that often adopts veiled layers of meaning). While the first two remained strong in her early

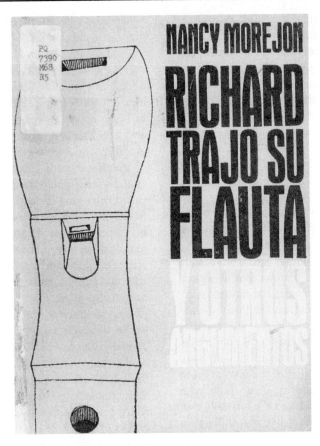

*Paperback cover for Morejón's third book (1967), the poetry collection that introduced
her to the literary world outside Cuba (Albany University Library)*

work, this last element begins to prevail after *Piedra pulida*
(Polished Stone, 1986).

A scholar of the Afro-Cuban poet Nicolás
Guillén, Morejón produced a collection of essays on
his work, *Recopilación de textos sobre Nicolás Guillén* (Collection of Texts on Nicolás Guillén), in 1974 and wrote
a critique of his poetry, *Nación y mestizaje en Nicolás
Guillén* (Nation and Mestization in Nicolás Guillén) in
1982. Morejón's poetry establishes a dialogic connection with Guillén and the *negrista* literature of the past
but with markedly different objectives. Even less so
than Guillén, Morejón does not view black Cuban life
as one that merits registering as exotic or unique. In
Morejón's postrevolutionary world, African ancestry
and its cultural legacies no longer need justification;
Cuban revolutionary ideology granted black Cubans a
sense of purpose and belonging and the possibility to
reconcile with the painful history of the past. Afro-
Cuban and Afro-Caribbean references in her poetry
express more than a personal urgency: they are images
that endeavor to reveal the collectivity and universality
of the black experience.

With her poem "Amor, ciudad atribuida" (Love,
Attributed City, 1964), written while she was a student
at the University of Havana, Morejón begins her lyrical
journeys through the streets, parks, and landmarks of
her native city. Havana, family memories, Afro-Cuban
religious deities, and the Cuban Revolution are the
themes echoed in *Richard trajo su flauta y otros argumentos*,
in poems such as "Los ojos de Eleggua" (Eleggua's
Eyes) and "Madrigal para cimarrones" (Madrigal for
Runaway Slaves).

In a 1999 interview with Gabriel A. Abudu,
Morejón speaks of her first poems as works that
express the anguish of someone who had difficulty
communicating with the world around her and with
her loved ones, of someone who was "trying to see this
world, trying to attain a horizon that seemed out of
reach." "Richard trajo su flauta" is a frequently cited
example of the way in which Morejón weaves Cuban
history and family memories in a stream of images in
which music, religion, and the city of Havana predominate. The poem juxtaposes the values of past and
present. For instance, there is a reference to the church

of St. Nicholas, followed by the image of the family at dinnertime eating bread and drinking. The gathering is in preparation for a night of storytelling and music. The image of the church and the observation that "no nos gustaban los curas" (we did not like priests) establishes a contrast to the reunion of the family on a Monday, which is the day to honor the Afro-Cuban deity Eleggua. This festive gathering denotes the observance of a sacred and revered tradition. At the end of the poem, the quiet *orishas* (deities) that haunt the house become part of a celebration viewed as mysterious and marvelous. Past history–for example, stories inspired by black Cuban patriot Juan Gualberto Gómez–contrasts to the easiness of the day, conveying the notion of an historical debt to the sacrifices of the previous generation.

This theme is echoed in other poems from *Richard trajo su flauta y otros argumentos*. In "Parque central, alguna gente" (Central Park, a Few People) the city is represented as an enormous, flowering, and brilliantly white park where those who walk across it may fail to see its sacred trees and statues unless they walk with eyes wide open, then slowly take a breath of air and sigh. The city is described as the bladder of the revolution to stress the notion of fullness and urgency; those who traverse it must do so "rabiosamente" (furiously), in fierce awareness of the price paid to live peacefully in it. To see the white light of the park, therefore, is to recognize that the sacrifices of Cuban patriot and martyr José Martí and the Cubans of the past–los viejos que anora permanecen en un banco y toman / el sol y toman el sol y toman el sol" (the old men that now remain on a bench and take / the sun and take the sun and take the sun)–have been made manifest by the accomplishments of the present: "the old men take a seat on a bench they light a cigar look at each other and talk about the Revolution and about Fidel."

In "La cena" (The Supper), the poet arrives home for the evening meal, seeking her mother's gaze and considering the benefits her father had to renounce "alli donde no estuvo" (there where he never was) but that are possible for her in the new social order. A momentary fear that such a society might end violently is brushed aside as the poet recognizes the dedication of other Cubans to the revolutionary enterprise. The partaking of bread at nightfall is the closing image of this poem in which Morejón portrays the forces that restore her: family unity, love, and a sense of purpose.

The Cuban Revolution of 1959 had a decisive influence on the early work of Morejón, who speaks of it in personal terms, as in the interview with Abudu: "The Revolution for me is like the air which I breathe; like everything around me and like writing, for me it is a totally natural activity which I need many times a day." A few poems from *Richard trajo su flauta y otros*

argumentos make references to the process of writing. In "La razón del poema" (The Reason for the Poem) Castro and the revolution form the backdrop to a questioning of the writer's task. The poet situates herself within a familiar space that seems to reject her; her bed coverings do not recognize her body. Loneliness is equated to being inside a "vejiga informe" (shapeless bladder), an image that is transformed in other poems to express gratitude and a feeling of achievement. From a moment of intense solitude, she seeks to escape the sense of anguish and isolation that envelops her: "y doy un golpe entre mis libros / y acudo presurosa al papel" (and I strike between my books / and I rush quickly to my paper). She writes about the memories and gestures found in her everyday life: a conference, a movie theater, the sugarcane harvest, Castro's hands. A similar movement from contemplation to performance is the central theme in "Amor, ciudad atribuida." From the slower rhythm of the first fifteen verses, the poem begins to accelerate as the poet allows the images that surround her to fill the page. Beginning with the image of the waves of the coast and the revolution, the poet finds her identity outside of herself, as she meanders among blacks, *orishas,* and schoolchildren reciting Martí's poems and moves along streets, parks, the port, and la Catedral de la Habana (as Havana's Gothic St. Cristóbal or St. Christopher Cathedral is simply known). In this poem Morejón has written a moving tribute to the city of her birth and to its people; she presents these images as the foundations for her identity.

In taking stock of the present, Morejón avoids easy characterizations of Cuba's old society. One poem from *Richard trajo su flauta y otros argumentos* that makes a reference to the past is "La dama de los perros" (The Lady with the Dogs). The poem is dedicated to the square in front of the cathedral and was written on New Year's Eve 1964, a date that marks the fifth anniversary of the triumph of the revolution. It is an excellent example of Morejón's skills as a poet because of the complexity of its language and images. Inserting motifs that allude to religious functions, architectural elements, and to a past that was gentle for some but not for all (as the references to slavery suggest), Morejón portrays the present confusion of a woman seeking refuge in a friendly tower. The loneliness and fear of the central figure are captured in the description of the church and the plaza, trembling under a sad moon. Of particular note in this poem is Morejón's construction of compound words such as "aguademar dientedemar" (seawater seacusp) and "caballoférreo" (steelknight) to describe the mass of columns in the plaza, a reference to the ornate Gothic architecture of the cathedral. Morejón's attention to the musicality of the verse is evident

*Paperback cover for Morejón's 1979 poetry collection, which includes the frequently
anthologized "Mujer negra" (Smathers Library, University of Florida)*

throughout this collection, where internal rhyme, alliteration, and anaphora prevail in many poems.

The 1960s brought a growing awareness in Cuba of events in the United States dealing with racial tension. Morejón and other Afro-Cuban intellectuals were suspected of "holding meetings and drafting a position paper on race and culture in Cuba to be presented before the World Cultural Congress meeting in January 1968," according to William Luis in his essay "Race, Poetry, and Revolution in the Works of Nancy Morejón" for the collection *Singular Like a Bird: The Art of Nancy Morejón* (1999). After the group was accused of promoting division along racial lines among revolutionary Cubans, Morejón retreated from racial activism.

The tightening of censorship that followed the disastrous economic enterprises of the 1970s meant diffi-

cult years for Cuban writers and artists. After a long period of silence, having only produced a monographic ethno-historical study titled *Lengua de pájaro: Comentarios reales: Monografía histórica* (Bird's Tongue: Real Commentaries: Historical Monograph, 1971) in collaboration with Carmen Gonce, Morejón published *Parajes de una época* (Places of an Epoch, 1979), which includes the frequently anthologized poem "Mujer negra" (Black Woman).

Parajes de una época reflects Morejón's renewed commitment to the ideals of the revolution. Many of her best-known poems are from *Parajes de una época,* in particular the superbly conceived "Mujer negra." The poet has not eschewed characterization of "Mujer negra" as a work that might serve the cause of feminism, although she asserted in an interview with Soledad Hernández that feminist ideology did not inspire her writing of it. Nevertheless, critics perceive a feminist sensibility in the presentation in the poem of a woman as the core figure in the struggle for emancipation from racial bondage. The poem is divided into several sections, each assessing the cost of history as seen from the female perspective. The first section of the poem recalls the slave's extrication from her native land and the struggle to preserve her cultural memory: "Acaso no he olvidado ni mi costa perdida, ni mi lengua ancestral" (Perhaps I have not forgotten my lost shoreline or my ancestral tongue).

Each section of the poem is marked by a short verse that chronicles the woman's path from bondage to rebellion. She becomes a white man's mistress: "Su Merced me compró en una plaza / Bordé la casaca de Su Merced y un hijo / macho le parí" (His Lordship bought me at the market / I embroidered His Lordship's dress coat and to a male son / I gave birth). She seems to address her master directly, since "Su Merced" could mean "your lordship" as well as "his lordship." The reader is witness to her acts of rebellion as she escapes to work in the fields and then joins the revolutionary struggle for emancipation that spanned several generations.

The section "y cabalgué entre las tropas de Maceo" (and I rode among the troops of Maceo) alludes to the black patriot Antonio Maceo, one of the leaders of the Revolution of 1895, the last struggle for Cuban independence from Spanish colonial rule. The significance of the Revolution of 1959 is underscored in the last stanza of the poem, in which the female voice speaks of herself as a participant: "Bajé de la Sierra" (I came down from the Sierra), referring to the Sierra Maestra, a Cuban mountain range in the eastern part of the country that has been the cradle of Cuban revolutions, thus emphasizing that racial emancipation was achieved a century later, "alrededor del árbol que plantamos para el / comunismo" (around the tree we planted for / communism). This poem is not only an affirmation of the role of women in Cuban history and society but of the essential contribution of Afro-Cubans to a revolutionary process that began during the colonial era. The revolutionary ideology proposed by Maceo and others included racial equality as inherent to their vision for the new independent nation. "Mujer negra" propounds the perspective that this ideological process culminated with the triumph of the Revolution of 1959. Critics have agreed that this poem represents a feminist perspective on the Cuban community at large. At the end of the poem the black woman becomes a symbol of the community as she finds her essence and purpose in the revolutionary process. Race and gender differences are thus viewed through the accomplishments of national politics. Morejón's views on the

achievement of racial and gender equality result from her understanding of Cuban history as a long and arduous struggle for emancipation and independence.

Shortly after the publication of *Parajes de una época,* an edition of poems, *Poemas* (Poems, 1980), and a new book, *Elogio de la danza* (Praise for the Dance, 1982), were published in Mexico by the UNAM (Universidad Nacional Autónoma de México, or National Autonomous University of Mexico). The 1980s proved to be a prolific decade for Morejón; in 1982 she published *Octubre imprescindible* (Indispensable October), her most important achievement since *Richard trajo su flauta.* Revolutionary ideology and politically engaged poems continue to appear in Morejón's works published in the early 1980s. Social and political awareness predominate in the poems from *Octubre imprescindible.* The most striking characteristic of this collection, however, is the tone of introspection expressed in many poems. "Obrera del tabaco" (Tobacco Laborer) is an example of Morejón's portrayal of women as vital to the history of her nation. In this poem the subject is a laborer who is also a poet, a revolutionary, and a visionary who foresees Cuba in the year 1999. In her poem the world of the future lacks darkness and need, the lure of Miami, falsehoods, and violations of labor laws. Instead, her poem offers the seeds of the future society: militant sagacity, intelligence, discipline, the seething blood of the past, a treaty of popular economy—"todos las deseos y toda la ansiedad" (all of the desires and all the zeal) of a revolutionary of her time. Her vision, however, was unknown to her brothers and sisters or to her neighbors because she kept her poem hidden inside the pages of an old book by Cuban patriot and poet José Martí. Like "Mujer negra" before it, "Obrera del tabaco" honors women's participation in the struggle to find justice for all people suffering repression. In paying tribute to this laborer, Morejón inscribes her poem in the tradition of feminist writing, the primary function of which is to rectify the anonymity of women in official accounts of history.

The title of *Octubre imprescindible* comes from the poem "En octubre y el aire" (In October and the Wind), an evocation of hurricane season and cool weather in Havana, as well as of solemn and "lógicos" (logical) uprisings in a winter palace (a reference to the Bolshevik uprising against the czar of Russia in October 1917). The silent, deathly air of October brings strange menacing sounds from the neighboring coast to the north. The poem closes with a litany of verses expressing the fear of the winds of October and of distant tears that distress Cubans. The October wind "nos despeina, urgente, con su diáspora, / como a eternos moradores del Caribe" (blows away our hair, urgently, with its diaspora, / like eternal inhabitants of the Caribbean). Unlike some of her early poems, in which the city of

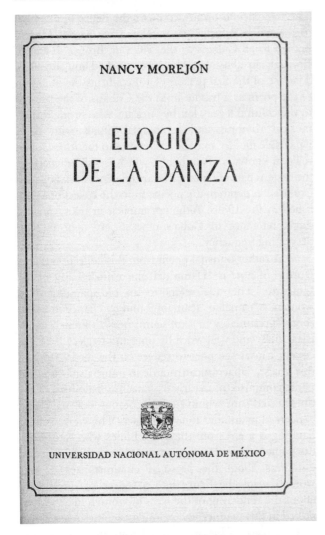

NANCY MOREJÓN

ELOGIO
DE LA DANZA

UNIVERSIDAD NACIONAL AUTÓNOMA DE MÉXICO

*Paperback cover for one of the three poetry collections
Morejón published in 1982 (Robert W. Woodruff
Library, Emory University)*

Havana appears as a place of refuge and wonder, in this poem Morejón depicts Havana in autumn as a fearful place that invites solitude and intimacy. The references to the Russian Revolution, the menaces from the north, and the diaspora frame the political context of a poem in which Morejón seems to reflect on Cuba's difficult decade of the 1970s. Although the government continued to discourage young artists and intellectuals who emphasized their distinct history as black Cubans, informal meetings called "Afro-Cuban Study Groups" lasted well into the decade of the 1970s. Like many other Cubans of African descent, Morejón continued to explore her racial identity in her work.

Octubre imprescindible includes several poems that speak to the collectivity of the black experience, notable among them "Madrigal para cimarrones," "Negro" (Black Man), "Madre" (Mother), and "Amo a mi amo" (I Love My Master). This last poem also appears in *Pie-*

dra pulida. A work that explores the dialectical slave/master relationship, it is written from the perspective of a slave woman. Many elements in the poem place it within the colonial period, as, for instance, the reference to the guitar-like medieval instrument known as the *vihuela* and to the sixteenth-century Spanish poet Jorge Manrique. The notion of passivity and submissiveness to the master appears repeatedly in the phrase "Amo a mi amo," contrasting with descriptions of him that stress his cruelty: "Mi amo muerde y subyuga" (My master bites and subdues) and "da latigazos en las calderas del ingenio" (gives whippings in the cauldrons of the sugar mill). The word *ingenio* could also mean intelligence or ingeniousness.

As the poem progresses, the woman undergoes a transformation from passive submission to awareness and resistance. She curses her abdication to male power and foreign domination, most evident in her struggle to embrace a language that is not her own. Morejón's reference to the language of the oppressor as "esta lengua abigarradamente hostil que no mastico" (this indiscriminately hostile tongue I cannot chew) shifts the emphasis of the poem from sexual and racial relations to the struggle for cultural hegemony. As the poem ends, the beat of drums calls the woman to rebellion. Unlike some of her North American counterparts, who view self-determination and racial and gender equality as an ongoing effort, for Morejón the Cuban Revolution accomplished many of its goals for equality. She writes as a Marxist in a Marxist society, assessing the history of black women from what was to her a position of political and social achievement.

A more personal portrayal of the black woman is found in the poem titled "Madre," a brief but beautiful poem of eighteen lines. The initial image is that of a woman from the African diaspora, a drifter. Reference to the sea serves as a reminder of the passage of slave ships across the Atlantic: "Mi madre no tuvo jardín / sino islas acantiladas / flotando, bajo el sol / en sus corales delicados" (My mother had no garden / but jagged islands / floating, under the sun / in their delicate corals). The first thirteen lines describe the poet's mother in terms of destitution and difference. A black woman, she lacked security, comfort, and privilege: "Ella no tuvo el aposento de marfil / ni la sala de mimbre / ni el vitral silencioso del trópico (She had no ivory chambre, / or wicked parlor / or the hushed stained-glass of the tropics). The last five lines of the poem affirm her worth as a mother and more importantly, her legacy as a woman. She is viewed as a provider of life and faith, as an example of strength and determination, and as a monument to the sacrifices of the past. She leaves behind her hands—"piedras preciosas" (precious stones)—to confront "los restos fríos del enemigo" (the cold remains of the enemy). Similar to "Mujer negra," which portrays women as participants in the construction of a national identity, "Madre" evokes a painful time of abandonment and neglect, of lives lived in orphanages where girls could not laugh or dream of a future, "y podía siquiera mirar el horizonte" (she could not even look at the horizon). In both of these poems, however, Morejón suggests that the strength of black women comes from the pain of their history and struggle to survive: "My mother had the handkerchief and the song / to cradle my body's deepest faith." Here Morejón discovers the legacy of black women in terms of the suffering they have endured. Lyrical expression through music has given them a voice that might otherwise have been repressed.

Subsequent to *Octubre imprescindible,* Morejón published four more collections during the 1980s: *Cuaderno de Granada* (1984; translated as *Grenada's Notebook,* 1984), *Piedra pulida* (Polished Stone, 1986), *Fundación de la imagen* (Foundation of the Image, 1988), and *Baladas para un sueño* (Ballads for a Dream, 1988), a series of seven poems decrying South African apartheid.

Morejón's attention to racial portrayal is not confined to women. Several poems in *Piedra pulida,* such as "Madrigal para cimarrones" and "Negro," are dedicated to the image of the Afro-Cuban male. Morejón speaks of the *cimarrones,* or runaway slaves, with love and awe, describing the strength and beauty of bodies that appear to be in concert with the hostility of the wild brush, the *manigua.* Their weapons serve as fertile ground for doves and native *Hutias,* and as the time for freedom approaches, these fearless men are reborn "como a dulces niños de una libertad ya conquistada" (as sweet boys from a liberty already conquered). By dedicating the poem to Cuban ethnographer and writer Miguel Barnet, who wrote the ethnographic novel *Biografía de un cimarrón* (1966; translated as *Autobiography of a Runaway Slave,* 1968), Morejón acknowledges the worthy addition to Afro-Cuban studies Barnet's book provided.

Like "Madrigal para cimarrones," the poem "Negro" provides a similar tribute to the black male past and present. There are echoes of Guillén in the presentation of black hair to discuss racial hatred and stereotyping. Again the image of the black body as a nesting ground for hummingbirds underscores the righteousness and beauty of the figure. The first part of the poem describes the man from the perspective of others, those who viewed him with fear and suspicion. There is a change in perspective in the last stanza as the poem adopts a plural voice to affirm the black man's legacy: "Nosotros amaremos por siempre / tus huellas y tu ánimo de bronce / porque has traído esa luz viva del pasado" (We will forever love / your steps and your strength of bronze / because you have brought the vibrant light of the past).

The reference to bronze connects the figure of this man to the nineteenth-century revolutionary patriot Maceo, known to all Cubans as the Titán de Bronce (Titan of Bronze), an allusion to his strength and mulatto skin. The use of the first-person plural confirms the intention of the poem as a tribute from the Cubans of the present to the cultural legacy left by Africans who brought their musical rhythms and ceremonial rituals with them ("palos de monte" may be a reference to the Afro-Cuban religion known as Palomonte, which is still practiced in the eastern part of Cuba). Racial and gender relations are explored in depth in the poems from the collections published in the 1980s. Although implicit in many poems, direct reference to Cuba's new society appears with decreasing frequency.

A rather unusual poem from this collection that is worthy of note is "Dama del unicornio" (Lady of the Unicorn). The title refers to an old painting of a woman, a "camafeo" (cameo) found by chance in a cold room (presumably in a museum) next to French tapestries, dusty and well worn by time and neglect. The discovery causes the poet to reflect on the incongruity of this image, "anacrónica fruta de lo imprevisto / a quien nadie compuso un madrigal" (anachronistic fruit of the unexpected / for whom no one composed a madrigal), conceived in another time and place. The viewer of the painting is a girl from the West Indies who scrutinizes the cameo's fantastic face in wonderment. A series of questions about the personal circumstances of this woman turns the figure into a source of speculation about the rendering of the lives of women in art. Interpreted in this manner, the painting becomes a lost document, a piece of history rescued from oblivion. As the girl contemplates the image, she tries to grasp her essence, to see beyond her fancy clothing–"la ves, la intentas comprender / en su polémica belleza" (you see her, you try to understand her / in her disputable beauty)–but she cannot find the right word to define so much meaningless ostentation. Though seemingly different in subject matter, this poem recalls "Amo a mi amo" in the tone of compassion with which Morejón writes about the forced submissiveness of women. This poem is an example of Morejón's gradual shift into a more profound and universal exploration of the condition of women. It is significant that the viewer is a young woman from somewhere in the Caribbean and that the subject of the painting represents an aberration, a kind of fantastic figure removed from the reality of contemporary women. Thus, the reader is led to reflect on the veracity of the representation of women in art, indeed, on the nature of art itself.

During the 1990s Morejón traveled frequently to the United States, where she came into contact with Cuban Americans. Through their eyes the poet came to

POESIA

Nancy Morejón

PIEDRA
PULIDA

*Paperback cover for Morejón's 1986 collection, which includes tributes to runaway
Cuban slaves of the colonial era (University of Memphis Library)*

an understanding of the fragmentation of identity that defines the experiences of Cuban exiles in the United States. Morejón's next book published in the decade of the 1990s is *Paisaje célebre,* which collects poems from the end of the 1980s and the early 1990s. Some of the poems from *Paisaje célebre* elaborate plastic images. Nautical motifs, solitude, and meditation on the Cuban diaspora are the more salient characteristics of *Paisaje célebre,* which West calls "more philosophical and rueful than her previous work, with a greater concern expressed about time and the nature of absence." The poem "Ante un espejo" (Before a Mirror), dedicated to the Cuban American Sonia Rivera Valdés, deals with the feeling of displacement felt by one who left Cuba as a child and cannot find a way to reconcile her divided identity: "y cuando ya estés vieja, / ante un espejo como el de Cenicienta / sonreirás algo triste / y en tus pupilas secas / habrá dos rocas fieles / y una esquina sonora de

tu ciudad" (and when you are an old woman / before a mirror, just like Cinderella's / you will smile half-sadly / and in your dry pupils / will be two faithful rocks / and a resounding corner of your city). The closing lines of the poem suggest the possibility of reconciliation at the end of life as the image in the mirror comes to terms with the memories that haunt her. The poem "Ana Mendieta" is dedicated to Cuban sculptor Ana Mendieta, who was exiled as a teenager and died by falling from her high-rise apartment in New York City. The poem depicts Ana as an object in flight, a multicolored kite that flees her adopted land in order to find peace in the Jaruco Mountains of Cuba. Ana's visit to her native Cuba is a kind of celestial rebirth, a spiritual journey that returns her to a sense of belonging. In both of these poems Morejón acknowledges the painful experience of Cuban exiles whose lives and identities forever changed because of the exodus of Cuban families after the revolution of 1959. While such experiences have been the subject of literary works by Cuban exiles living in the United States and Europe, it is significant that a Cuban should reflect on this subject.

In the early 1990s Morejón was appointed director of the magazine *Proposiciones* (Propositions), published by the Pablo Milanés Foundation, an independent cultural organization. The foundation ceased to function in 1995 when conflicts with the Ministry of Culture arose. The profound sense of disillusionment that Morejón experienced following the dismantling of the foundation is felt in her poetry. There is a shift away from her urban and familial world, away from the beloved city of her birth. The desire to escape to the countryside or to the sea and the introduction of a mythical geography set this collection apart from the previous ones. The title poem, "Paisaje célebre," is inspired by a painting of the Flemish painter Peter Breughel the Elder, *The Fall of Icarus* (circa 1555). In Breughel's work, Icarus has already fallen from the sky into the ocean; the figures in the painting seem oblivious to the wondrous act of a winged boy falling from the sky. Morejón, on the other hand, focuses her attention on Icarus's flight and portrays what seems like an impossible image: water encircled by fruit trees and a little man, alone, plowing over the water. The next stanza elaborates the image of the "hombrecillo" (little man) as a painter who, like Breughel, "pinta la soledad del alma / cercada por espléndidos labradores" (paints the solitude of the soul / encircled by splendid plowmen). The last line of the poem turns the reader's attention back to Icarus's flight: "Es el atardecer y necesito las alas de Icaro" (It is dusk and I need the wings of Icarus). The use of the word *cercada* (encircled) in reference to the soul clearly alludes to a feeling of entrapment, thus clarifying the desire to escape to the sea on the wings of Icarus. As evident in most poems from this collection, the predominant themes in Morejón's poetry from the 1980s and 1990s vary greatly from those in her best-known work. It is inaccurate to characterize these poems as new modes of expression, however. They are highly lyrical and polished creations, but the same attention to the musicality of the verse and the same commitment to aesthetics were already present in her earliest work.

Morejón's later books show a lessening of interest in social and political themes in her poetry. A new work, "El río de Martín Pérez" (The River of Martin Perez), was published in a book entirely handmade in Matanzas, Cuba, *El río de Martín Pérez y otros poemas* (The River of Martin Perez and Other Poems, 1996). *La Quinta de los Molinos* (The Windmill Manor, 2000) is the last of Morejón's collections containing poems written in the 1990s. An anthology of her work prepared by

Mario Benedetti, *Richard trajo su flauta y otros poemas* (Richard Brought His Flute and Other Poems) was printed in Spain in 1999; it comprises all of her most important work from the 1960s to the end of the 1990s.

La Quinta de los Molinos includes poems that along with those in *Paisaje célebre* represent a return to symbolic images. Beautiful and poignant, these poems reflect the difficult situation of Cuban intellectuals during what has been called "el Período Especial" (the special period) in Cuba, the period after the fall of the Soviet Union, which introduced major alterations in the quality of life of every Cuban. The poem "A la Quinta de los Molinos" (To the Windmill Manor) is a curious reference to an old cigar-making factory just outside Havana and to the colonial past: *quinta* means manor or plantation house, while in *molinos* (windmill) readers make an association to Don Quixote and to the primacy of fantasy and the imagination in literature. The first lines of the poem tell of a visit to the plantation where the poet finds a hare, perhaps desirous to escape to the Almendares River, which runs through the city of Havana and into the Caribbean Sea. In the second stanza the hare reappears, this time as a symbol of the poet's dreams and illusions: "sólo entonces me di cuenta / que su cuerpo había entrado, / por los aires, / al primer sueño de mi infancia" (only then did I realize / that its body had entered, / with the wind, / into the first dream of my childhood). The Quinta becomes a refuge and a place of meditation where the author seeks to find something lost long ago, the hare being a metaphor for the seductive power of the imagination.

The overall tone of anguish in "A la Quinta de los Molinos" also appears in several other poems from this collection. "Blusa colgada" (Hanging Blouse) exhibits the same sense of a pressing need for freedom. As the poet sees two ants running over one of her best blouses, her empathy with their frenzied journey is such that she does nothing to prevent it, allowing them to run free. The poem closes with a projection of her death, which she perceives as maybe distant or near, "para el caso es igual" (it is the same thing), meaning that death already calls upon her.

Nancy Morejón's poetry cannot be pigeonholed as feminist or even as Afro-Cuban or Afro-Caribbean, although all of these elements are present in her work. Nor can her expression be said to belong to Marxist Cuba exclusively. What can be said is that her poetry encompasses decades of great transition in Cuban society and literature and that it endures those changes. While her best-known works are those in which she explores race, gender, and national identity, her output in the last decades of the twentieth century and the beginning of the twenty-first century reveals a profound sense of discomfort and a need to situate her poetic voice within a mythical and metaphorical landscape. In her interview with Abudu, the poet herself, expressing her admiration for Edgar Allan Poe, mentions two elements that were important to Poe and that she considers critical to her own creativity: "the originality that flows from ecstasy as well as a unique sense of the beautiful." Nancy Morejón is an important author whose expression contributes much to the literature of social and political engagement yet maintains an unwavering adherence to aesthetics as the fundamental principle of poetry. In her acceptance speech for the Premio Nacional de Literatura de 2001, she summarized her aesthetics this way: "He buscado la belleza en todas partes y, al mismo tiempo, me he resistido a abandonar la tangible utopía que marca nuestras vidas y la época que nos ha tocado vivir" (I have searched for beauty in all places and, at the same time, I have refused to abandon the tangible utopia that brands our lives and the time in which we had to live).

Interviews:

Soledad Hernández, "Nancy Morejón: Hablando con la joven poesía cubana," *En Rojo,* 23–29 November 1979, p. 7;

Gabriel A. Abudu, "Nancy Morejón: An Interview," in *Singular Like a Bird: The Art of Nancy Morejón,* edited by Miriam DeCosta-Willis (Washington, D.C.: Howard University Press, 1999), pp. 37–42.

References:

Efraín Barradas, "La negritud hoy: Nota sobre la poesía de Nancy Morejón," *Areito,* 24 (April 1980): 33–39;

Catherine Davies, "Nancy Morejón," in *Encyclopedia of Latin American Literature,* edited by Verity Smith (Chicago: Fitzroy Dearborn, 1997), pp. 565–567;

Miriam DeCosta-Willis, ed., *Singular Like a Bird: The Art of Nancy Morejón* (Washington, D.C.: Howard University Press, 1999);

C. Rosegreen-Williams, "Re-writing the history of the Afro-Cuban Woman: Nancy Morejón's 'Mujer negra,'" *Afro-Hispanic Review,* 3 (September 1989): 7–13;

María Salgado, "La poesía tradicional y el compromiso ideológico en la creación femenina de la segunda promoción de la revolución cubana," in *La historia en la literatura iberoamericana: Memorias del XXVI Congreso del Instituto Internacional de Literatura Iberoamericana,* edited by Raquel Chang-Rodríguez and Gabriella de Beer (Hanover, N.H.: Ediciones del Norte, 1989);

Osvaldo Sánchez, "Herencia, miseria y profecía de la más joven poesía cubana," *Revista Iberoamericana,* 152–153 (July–December 1990): 1129–1142;

Gloria Feiman Waldman, "Affirmation and Resistance: Women Poets from the Caribbean," in *Contemporary Women Authors of Latin America: Introductory Essays,* edited by Doris Meyer and Margarite Fernández Olmos (Brooklyn, N.Y.: Brooklyn College Press, 1983), pp. 33–57;

Alan West, "Nancy Morejón: Poet of Cultural Crossroads," in *Tropics of History: Cuba Imagined* (Westport, Conn.: Bergin & Garvey, 1997), pp. 13–34.

Alvaro Mutis

(25 August 1923 –   )

Barbara P. Fulks
Davis and Elkins College

BOOKS: *La balanza,* by Mutis and Carlos Patiño Roselli (Bogotá: Trag, 1948);

Los elementos del desastre (Buenos Aires: Losada, 1953);

Diario de Lecumberri (Xalapa, Mexico: Universidad Veracruzana, 1960);

Los trabajos perdidos (Mexico City: ERA, 1965);

Summa de Maqroll el Gaviero: Poesía (1947–1970) (Barcelona: Barral, 1973);

La mansión de Araucaíma: Relato gótico de tierra caliente (Buenos Aires: Sudamericana, 1973);

Maqroll el Gaviero (Bogotá: Instituto Colombiano de Cultura, 1975);

Caravansary (Mexico City: Fondo de Cultura Económica, 1981);

Poesía y Prosa (Bogotá: Instituto Colombiano de Cultura, 1982);

La verdadera historia del flautista de Hammelin (Mexico City: Penélope, 1982);

Poemas (Mexico City: UNAM, 1982);

Los emisarios (Mexico City: Fondo de Cultura Económica, 1984);

Crónica regia; y, Alabanza del reino (Madrid: Cátedra, 1985);

Obra literaria, 2 volumes (Bogotá: Procultura, 1985);

Sesenta cuerpos (Medellín: Universidad de Antioquia, 1985);

Un homenaje y siete nocturnos (Mexico City: El Equilibrista, 1986);

La nieve del almirante (Madrid: Alianza, 1986);

Ilona llega con la lluvia (Bogotá: Oveja Negra, 1987);

La muerte del estratega: Narraciones, prosas y ensayos (Mexico City: Fondo de Cultura Económica, 1988);

La última escala del Tramp Steamer (Mexico City: El Equilibrista, 1988);

Un bel morir (Bogotá: Oveja Negra, 1989);

Amirbar (Madrid: Siruela, 1990);

Summa de Maqroll el Gaviero: Poesía (1948–1988) (Mexico City: Fondo de Cultura Económica, 1990);

El último rostro (Madrid: Siruela, 1990);

Abdul Bashur, soñador de navíos (Madrid: Siruela, 1991);

La mansión de Araucaíma y Cuadernos del Palacio Negro (Madrid: Siruela, 1992);

Antología, selected, with a prologue, by José Balza (Caracas: Monte Avila, 1992);

Obra poética (Bogotá: Arango, 1993);

Tríptico de mar y tierra (Bogotá: Norma, 1993);

Palabra en el tiempo (Bogotá: Alfaguara, 1997);

Contextos para Maqroll (Montblanc, Colombia: Instituto Colombiano de Cultura, 1997);

Reseña de los hospitales de ultramar y otros poemas, prologue by Octavio Paz (Xalapa, México: Universidad Veracruzana, 1997);

Summa de Maqroll el Gaviero: Poesía, 1948–1997, edited, with an introduction, by Carmen Ruiz Barrionuevo (Salamanca: Universidad de Salamanca, 1997);

De lecturas y algo del mundo (1943–1998), compiled, with a prologue and notes, by Santiago Mutis Durán (Bogotá: Planeta Colombiana, 1999).

Collection: *Empresas y tribulaciones de Maqroll el Gaviero* (Madrid: Siruela, 1993); translated by Edith Grossman as *The Adventures and Misadventures of Maqroll* (New York: New York Review of Books, 2002).

OTHER: Pablo Ortiz Monasterio, ed., *Historia natural de las cosas: 50 fotógrafos,* text by Mutis (Mexico City: Fondo de Cultura Económica, 1985);

Fábrida de santos, photographs by Tomás Casademunt, text by Mutis (Mexico City: Artes de México, 2000).

Colombian Alvaro Mutis is a prolific and world-renowned poet, novelist, and essayist whose work has been translated into English, French, Italian, German, Dutch, Portuguese, Swedish, Romanian, and Turkish. He has received several literary awards: Colombia's national prize for letters in 1974; the Mexican prizes Crítica de Los Abriles in 1985 and the Xavier Villarrutia award in 1988; France's Medicis Prize for the best book translated into French in 1989; Italy's Nonino Prize in 1990; the French Roger Caillois Prize in 1993; and Spain's Príncipe de Asturias de las Letras Prize and the Reina de Sofía Prize in poetry, both in 1997.

Alvaro Mutis (from La voz de Alvaro Mutis, *2001)*

The jury for the Spanish prizes stated that Mutis's prose and poetry are recognized worldwide as distinctively joining magic realism with the problems of contemporary humanity. Mutis, however, rejects the term "magic realism," a category he considers to have been created by European critics unfamiliar with the reality of the Latin American landscape and its inhabitants. In an interview in the 27 April 1997 edition of the Mexican newspaper *La Jornada Semanal* (The Weekly Journal) he described a worldview based on his belief that contemporary man leads an isolated and solitary existence, taunted by inventions destined to strip away the last vestiges of humanity and suffering the "brutal assault" of a communications technology that threatens to destroy the human voice, the basis of intimacy. Mutis's negative assessment of the present informs all his work and helps to explain his predilection for themes of death, destruction, and decay.

Mutis was born 25 August 1923 in Bogotá, Colombia. His father, Santiago Mutis Dávila, a specialist in international law, was a diplomat and a descendant of the Spanish scientist and priest Celestino Mutis, who arrived in Colombia at the end of the eighteenth century. In 1925 Mutis's father accepted a diplomatic post in Belgium and moved with his family to Brussels.

Alvaro began his schooling there, immersing himself in European culture under the tutelage of the Jesuits. When Alvaro was nine years old, his father died suddenly at the age of thirty-three. The family's future was now in the hands of Mutis's mother, Carolina Jaramillo. She was a strong and independent woman who reputedly paid little attention to social conventions. Some of the author's female characters display the same characteristics as his mother. After her husband's death, Carolina Jaramillo decided to return to Colombia with her family in order to manage the family's estates.

Mutis's maternal grandfather, an important figure in the creation of the short-lived independent Armenia, started the family's plantations in Colombia, and he had offices in Hamburg, Germany, to sell his products. He planted coffee and sugarcane and unsuccessfully searched for gold on his holdings. Mutis and his brother, Leopoldo, explored their grandfather's abandoned mine shafts as children when they returned from Europe to Colombia for vacations. Crossing the Atlantic in small ships, half cargo and half passenger, making various stops in the Caribbean, took around three weeks. Mutis has used these childhood experiences in his writing. The Coello farm, one of his maternal family's holdings, located in the confluence of the Coello and Cocora Rivers, was also influential in Alvaro's life. He and his brother were intimately familiar with the land. Years later, in the early 1950s, during the period in Colombia known as "la Violencia," the farm was taken from the family.

The young Alvaro's physical contact with the tropics, the land of coffee and bananas, of intense smells and colors and torrential rivers, gave him material for all his later work. The memories of Belgium, intimately connected to his father, and those of Coello were transformed in his poetic world into two lost paradises, and the contrast between Europe and America is one of the main themes of his work.

Mutis never completed his schooling, begun in Brussels in the Jesuit school of San Michel. He attended the Colegio Mayor de Nuestra Señora del Rosario in Colombia, where he was taught literature by the poet Eduardo Carranza. Mutis studied contemporary and classical Spanish literature as well as canonical Latin American poets such as Pablo Neruda, Vicente Huidobro, and César Vallejo. He did not, however, receive a high-school diploma, nor did he attend college. He stated that he had so much to read he could not waste time studying. In 1941, at the age of eighteen, he married Mireya Durán Solano, with whom he eventually had three children, and he began to work various jobs. At first he was not able to make a living writing, though he recognized his talent for letters. During this time Mutis directed a program on contemporary literature for the National Radio of Colombia. His friendships with the poet Jorge Zalamea, a previous director of the program, León de Greiff, and Aurelio Arturo influenced his desire to make literature his primary vocation. He expanded his reading to include French poetry and novels, Russian literature, and various works of history and adventure.

Some of his early work appeared in the journal *Vida* (Life), published by the Colombian Insurance Company, for which he was editor. During this time Mutis frequented various cafés in which two generations of poets met: Los Nuevos (The New Ones) admired the French writers André Malraux, Albert Camus, and Henri de Montherlant, while the poets of Piedra y Cielo (Rock and Sky) concentrated on the poets of the Spanish Generation of '27. Mutis preferred Los Nuevos, though he was never a member of the group. Nor did he belong to another group of writers, Mito (Myth), which published some of his poetry. Octavio Paz, the well-known Mexican writer, reviewed the work published by Mito and was responsible for Mutis's early recognition outside of Colombia.

From 1942 to 1948 Mutis continued his radio work, but now as a writer, news anchor, classical music commentator along with Otto de Greiff, and actor in literary programs written by Arturo Camacho Ramírez. During these years he also directed publicity for the Colombian Insurance Company, and he was head of public relations for LANSA, the national airline. These latter two jobs required constant travel, giving shape to the interminable displacement of the characters in his later novels.

Characteristic elements of Mutis's poetic style and tone are evident from his first collection of poems, *La balanza* (Balance, 1948). The tone is reflexive, depressive, even funereal, as in "Amén": "Que te acoja la muerte / con todos tus sueños intactos" (Let death receive you / with all your dreams intact). The settings for the poems are teluric, often riparian, and tropical, as, for example, in the prose poem "La creciente" (The Crescendo): "Al amanecer crece el río, retumban en el alba los enormes troncos que vienen del páramo. Sobre el lomo de las pardas aguas bajan naranjas maduras, terneros con la boca bestialmente abierta, techos pajizos, loros que chillan sacudidos bruscamente por los remolinos" (At daybreak the river rises, enormous trunks coming from the plains rumble in the dawn. Sliding down the brown water come ripe oranges, young cows with their mouths bestially open, thatched roofs, screaming parrots shaken sharply by the whirlpools). Mutis frequently uses the technique of enumeration, as well, as in "Miedo" (Fear):

> La mañana se llena de voces:
> Voces que vienen de los trenes
> de los buses de colegio
> de los tranvías de barriada
> de las tibias frazadas tendidas al sol
> de las goletas
> de los triciclos de los muñequeros de vírgenes infames
> del cuarto piso de los seminarios
> de los parques públicos
> de algunas piezas de pensión
> y de otras muchas moradas diurnas del miedo
>
> (The morning is filled with voices:
> Voices from the trains
> from the school buses
> from the neighborhood trolleys
> from the warm blankets hanging in the sun
> from the sailboats
> from the carts with infamous babydoll virgins
> from the fourth floor of the seminaries
> from the public parks
> from some hotel rooms
> and from many other daytime dwellings of fear).

Mutis's second collection of poems, *Los elementos del desastre* (Elements of the Disaster, 1953), includes some of his most representative verse. The first poem, "204," is an homage to Neruda. The title poem is replete with images of a world in decay, arrogant warriors marching to their death, insects in agony, crashing airplanes, sweet-smelling coffins. The protagonist Maqroll el Gaviero appears for the first time in this collection. In both his poetry and novels, Mutis uses Maqroll as an alter ego who, he says, reflects his own experiences and then transcribes them for him. Mutis chose the name Maqroll because it has no specific geographical, national, or regional connotation. The *q* without a *u* following suggests Arabic transcribed to Spanish, and thus the name has Mediterranean and Catalan resonances. A *gaviero* is a lookout on a ship, and this epithet fits Maqroll's itinerant lifestyle. Never described physically by Mutis, Maqroll is a wanderer, living on the margins of society and the law. In the prose poem "Oración de Maqroll" (Maqroll's Prayer), he offers up a prayer in which, among other petitions, he asks God to "haz que todos conciban mi cuerpo como una fuente inagotable de tu infamia" (make everyone conceive of my body as an inexhaustible fount of your infamy). Maqroll el Gaviero appears throughout Mutis's poems and is also the protagonist of his novels, which the author says are simply an expansion of his poetry. In "El húsar" (The Hussar), Mutis presents a character who comes from the West and meets his death in the tropics. This encounter of two different worlds, both in decay, becomes a paradigm in Mutis's poems.

In 1954 he married a second time, to María Luz Montané, with whom he had one daughter. He took a job as head of public relations with Esso (now Exxon), the multinational oil company. This job gave him the opportunity to provide financial support to many cultural projects in Colombia and to travel throughout the world. Perhaps influenced by the corrupt Colombian dictator General Gustavo Rojas Pinilla, however, Esso brought a judicial action against Mutis, accusing him of fraud, and in 1956 he was forced to flee to Mexico, where he was detained by Interpol and spent fifteen months in Lecumberri prison, an experience he recounts in *Diario de Lecumberri* (Lecumberri Diary, 1960).

In 1957, after Rojas Pinilla was deposed as dictator, Mutis was declared innocent and the case against him annulled. He remained in Mexico, befriended by Paz and the Spanish expatriate motion-picture director Luis Buñuel, and began working in television and movies. In 1958 he was hired by 20th Century-Fox and Columbia Pictures to sell movies made for North American television to Latin America. He also gave literary conferences at the University of Mexico during these years.

Mutis's next book after *Diario de Lecumberri* is *Los trabajos perdidos* (Lost Works, 1965), a collection of poems. These poems are more condensed than in his previous works, with fewer syllables per line and fewer lines per poem. The poet maintains his characteristic unsentimental tone and his thematic explorations of death and deterioration. "Un bel morir" (A Beautiful Death), expanded into a novella in 1989, is typical: "Cuando descienda la mano / habré muerto en mi alcoba / . . . Todo irá desvaneciéndose en el olvido" (When the hand descends / I will have died in my room / . . . Everything will be vanishing from memory).

In 1966 Mutis married his third wife, Carmen Miracle Feliú. In 1977 he began a weekly opinion series published in various Mexican newspapers. He also worked for Mexican television during this period, directing interviews with writers, and collaborated with Paz in the journals *Plural* (Plural) and *Vuelta* (Return). Mutis still resides in Mexico City.

With *Caravansary* (1981) Mutis expands his predilection for the narrative poem. A caravansary is a public building in the Middle East, used to shelter wayfarers and their beasts of burden. The spaces in these prose poems are characterized by Ernesto Volkening, in his introductory essay to Mutis's *Summa de Maqroll el Gaviero: Poesía, 1948–1988* (1990), as limitless, encompassing "endless plains, unknown places, dwellings in towns that no one has seen, scenes of great exploits, now only rumors, fables, half-voiced memories." The unifying theme in *Caravansary* is a meditation on death, evident in each poem. In "En los esteros" (In the Marshes), for example, Maqroll reflects on his life as superannuated vessels float down the river. Some of the passengers on the boats eat dead or dying animals that float by. Two passengers convulse and die after eating a river rat. Maqroll is accompanied by a malaria-infected woman. One day the boat's motor fails. Days later the boat is found with two bodies: the woman's is swollen and foul smelling, Maqroll's is "reseco como un montón de raíces castigadas por el sol. Sus ojos, muy abiertos, quedaron fijos en esa nada, inmediata y anónima, en donde hallan los muertos el sosiego que les fuera negado durante su errancia cuando vivos" (dry like a pile of roots punished by the sun. His eyes, wide open, remained fixed on that immediate and anonymous nothing where the dead find the serenity denied them during their wandering life). Once again the theme of decay and death in the tropics is evident in this prose poem.

Los emisarios (The Emissaries, 1984) begins with a quotation from the twelfth-century Sufi poet Al-Mutamar Ibn al Farsi: "Los Emisarios que tocan a tu puerta / tú mismo los llamaste y no lo sabes" (The emissaries that knock at your door / you yourself called them and you don't know it). The emissaries open doors to perplexing enigmas and death-like spaces. Once again the poems depict a world that creates its own destruction. "Funeral en Viana" (Funeral in Viana), for example, begins: "Hoy entierran en la iglesia de Santa María de Viana / a César, Duque de Valentinois. Preside el duelo / su cuñado Juan de Albret, Rey de Navarra. / En el estrecho ámbito de la iglesia / de altas naves de un gótico tardío, / se amontonan prelados y hombres de armas" (Today they are burying in Santa María de Viana church / César, Duke of Valentinois. Leading the mourning / his brother-in-law Juan de Albret, King of Navarre. / In the narrow space of the church / of the high naves of late gothic / gather prelates and men of arms). The poem goes on to describe the corpse of the young, noble warrior in intimate detail. He seems to have courted his own death in battle; precisely why, none of his retinue seems to know. His life was cut short, but he lived in the fullness of the knightly ideal of the Middle Ages.

Counterpoised to Maqroll's obsession with death and decay, the poems in *Los emisarios,* such as "Una calle de Córdoba" (A Street in Córdoba) and "Tríptico de la Alhambra" (Triptych of the Alhambra), also have historical themes often moderated by Maqroll in a voice that is traditional, theocratic, religious, and monarchical. These historical themes reflect Mutis's reactionary political posture. In a series of interviews with Eduardo García Aguilar included in his 1993 biography *Celebraciones y otros fantasmas: Una biografía intelectual de Alvaro Mutis* (Celebrations and Other Phantasms: An Intellectual Biography of Alvaro Mutis), Mutis claims that monarchies formerly provided civilization with a divinely inspired order, and he claims to have been a monarchist since childhood, even though he knows this form of rule is anachronistic. He states that Western, Christian civilization is the most extraordinary accomplishment of man on Earth, but it has been threatened by "el inmenso engaño de la democracia" (the immense deception of democracy) and the concomitant evils of liberal humanism and rationalism, all of which he attributes to the influence of the Protestant Reformation. The dreams of monarchy died, according to Mutis, with the decline of the Spanish Empire in the New World.

Indeed, Mutis is inspired by historical examples of hierarchically structured societies and empire-building personalities; he is intensely interested in the Byzantine Empire, the medieval Holy Roman Empire, Charles V, Philip II, and Napoleon Bonaparte. Spain's Golden Age, the historical period associated with the monarchs Charles V and Philip II, dominates the poems in the collections *Crónica regia; y, Alabanza del reino* (Royal Chronicle; and, Praise of the Reign, 1984) and *Un homenaje y siete nocturnos* (Homage and Seven Nocturnes, 1986).

In addition to the poems and prose poems included in various anthologies, Mutis has written several novellas: *La nieve del almirante* (The Snow of the Admiral, 1986), *Ilona llega con la lluvia* (Ilona Comes with the Rain, 1987), *La última escala del Tramp Steamer* (The Last Stop of the Tramp Steamer, 1988), *Un bel morir* (1989), and *Abdul Bashur, soñador de navíos* (Abdul Bashur, Dreamer of Ships, 1991). These works also feature Maqroll as a protagonist who wanders the globe, caught up in violent adventures in exotic places. They are collected in *Empresas y tribulaciones de Maqroll el Gaviero* (1993); the English-language versions, translated by Edith Grossman, are collected in *The Adventures and Misadventures of Maqroll* (2002).

In his prologue to *Reseña de los hospitales de ultramar y otros poemas* (Review of Overseas Hospitals and Other Poems, 1997) Paz writes that Alvaro Mutis's poetry and prose is characterized by a combination of "verbal splendor and the decomposition of matter," which, with its precise language of "vulgar horror," creates "the marvelous" through a "brusque descent into gratuitous and insignificant, though bewitching, images in the center of a familiar reality." Mutis's bleak vision reflects a world that does not correspond to the measure of his dreams, and he rejects modernity, albeit with an attitude of desperation rather than confrontation. Through his meticulous and recherché use of language, he creates a world brimming with sensual and funereal imagery, resurrects a heroic past invested with a wishful harmony derived from a divinely ordained hierarchical social and political order, and pictures a present in the throes of decay and death.

Letters:

Cartas de Alvaro Mutis a Elena Poniatowska (Mexico City: Alfaguara, 1998).

Interviews:

Fernando Quiroz, *El reino que estaba para mí: Conversaciones con Alvaro Mutis* (Barcelona: Norma, 1993);

"La Conspiración de los Zombies," *Jornada Semanal,* 27 April 1997 <http://www.jornada.unam.mx/1997/abr97/970427/sem-mutis.html>.

Biography:

Eduardo García Aguilar, *Celebraciones y otros fantasmas: Una biografía intelectual de Alvaro Mutis* (Bogotá: Tercer Mundo, 1993).

References:

Gastón Adolfo Alzate Cuervo, *Aspecto desesperanzado de la literatura: Sófocles, Hölderlin, Mutis* (Bogotá: Colcultura, 1993);

Dora Cajías de Villa Gómez, *Alvaro Mutis: La nueva geografía de la novela* (La Paz: UMSA, 1997);

Consuelo Hernández, *Alvaro Mutis: Una estética del deterioro* (Caracas: Monte Avila, 1995);

Hernando Motato, *Voces de la desesperanza* (Bucaramanga, Colombia: UIS, 1999);

Santiago Mutis Durán, ed., *Tras las rutas de Maqroll el Gaviero, 1988–1993: Visitaciones, entrevistas, estudios, notas críticas* (Bogotá: Instituto Colombiano de Cultura, 1993);

Belén del Rocío Moreno, *Cifras del azar: Una lectura psicoanalítica de la obra de Alvaro Mutis* (Bogotá: Planeta Colombiana, 1998);

Alberto Ruy Sánchez, *Cuatro escritores rituales: Rulfo, Mutis, Sarduy, García Ponce* (Toluca, Mexico: Instituto Mexiquense de Cultura, 1997).

Pablo Neruda

(12 July 1904 – 23 September 1973)

Eliana Rivero
University of Arizona

BOOKS: *Crepusculario* (Santiago: Claridad, 1923);

Veinte poemas de amor y una canción desesperada (Santiago: Nascimento, 1924); translated by W. S. Merwin as *Twenty Love Poems and a Song of Despair* (London: Cape, 1969; New York: Penguin, 1978);

Tentativa del hombre infinito (Santiago: Nascimento, 1926);

Anillos, by Neruda and Tomás Lago (Santiago: Nascimento, 1926);

El habitante y su esperanza (Santiago: Nascimento, 1926);

El hondero entusiasta (Santiago: Empresa Letras, 1933);

Residencia en la tierra: 1925–1931 (Santiago: Nascimento, 1933); enlarged as *Residencia en la tierra: 1925–1935,* 2 volumes (Madrid: Cruz & Raya, 1935); translated by Angel Flores in *Residence on Earth, and Other Poems* (Norfolk, Conn.: New Directions, 1946);

España en el corazón (Santiago: Ercilla, 1937); translated by Flores as *Spain in the Heart* in *Residence on Earth, and Other Poems;*

Las furias y las penas (Santiago: Nascimento, 1939);

Canto general de Chile: Fragmentos (Mexico City: Privately published, 1943);

Tercera residencia: 1935–1945 (Buenos Aires: Losada, 1947); translated by Donald Walsh in *Residence on Earth* (New York: New Directions, 1973);

Alturas de Macchu Picchu (Santiago: Librería Neira, 1947); translated by Nathaniel Tarn as *The Heights of Macchu Picchu* (London: Cape, 1966; New York: Farrar, Straus & Giroux, 1966);

Canto general (Mexico City: Talleres Gráficos de la Nación, 1950); excerpts translated by Ben Belitt as *Poems from the Canto General* (New York: Racolin, 1968);

Los versos del capitán, anonymous (Naples: L'Arte Tipografica, 1952); republished as Neruda (Buenos Aires: Losada, 1963); translated by Walsh as *The Captain's Verses* (New York: New Directions, 1972);

Las uvas y el viento (Santiago: Nascimento, 1954);

Pablo Neruda (photograph by Georges Saure)

Odas elementales (Buenos Aires: Losada, 1954); translated by Carlos Lozano as *Elementary Odes* (New York: Gaetano Massa, 1961);

Nuevas odas elementales (Buenos Aires: Losada, 1956);

Tercer libro de las odas (Buenos Aires: Losada, 1957);

Estravagario (Buenos Aires: Losada, 1958); translated by Alistair Reid as *Extravagaria* (London: Cape, 1972; New York: Farrar, Straus & Giroux, 1974);

Navegaciones y regresos (Buenos Aires: Losada, 1959);

Cien sonetos de amor (Santiago: Editorial Universitaria, 1959); translated by Stephen Tapscott as *One Hundred Love Sonnets* (Austin: University of Texas Press, 1986);

Canción de gesta (Havana: Casa de las Américas, 1960); translated, with an introduction, by Miguel Algarín as *Song of Protest* (New York: Morrow, 1976);

Las piedras de Chile (Buenos Aires: Losada, 1961); translated by Dennis Maloney as *The Stones of Chile* (Fredonia, N.Y.: White Pine, 1986);

Cantos ceremoniales (Buenos Aires: Losada, 1961); translated by Maria Jacketti as *Ceremonial Songs* (Pittsburgh: Latin American Literary Review Press, 1996);

Plenos poderes (Buenos Aires: Losada, 1962); translated by Reid as *Fully Empowered* (New York: Farrar, Straus & Giroux, 1975);

Memorial de Isla Negra, 5 volumes (Buenos Aires: Losada, 1964); translated by Reid as *Isla Negra: A Notebook* (New York: Farrar, Straus & Giroux, 1981);

Arte de pájaros (Santiago: Sociedad de Amigos del Arte Contemporáneo, 1966); translated by Jack Schmitt as *Art of Birds* (Austin: University of Texas Press, 1985);

Una casa en la arena (Barcelona: Lumen, 1966); translated by Maloney and Clark M. Zlotchew as *The House at Isla Negra: Prose Poems* (Fredonia, N.Y.: White Pine, 1988);

Fulgor y muerte de Joaquín Murieta: bandido chileno injusticiado en California el 23 de julio de 1853 (Santiago: Zig-Zag, 1967); translated by Belitt as *Splendor and Death of Joaquin Murieta* (New York: Farrar, Straus & Giroux, 1972; London: Alcove, 1973);

La barcarola (Buenos Aires: Losada, 1967);

Las manos del día (Buenos Aires: Losada, 1968);

Fin de mundo (Santiago: Sociedad de Arte Contemporáneo, 1969);

Aún (Santiago: Nascimento, 1969); translated by William O'Daly as *Still Another Day* (Port Townsend, Wash.: Copper Canyon, 1984);

Maremoto (Santiago: Sociedad de Arte Contemporáneo de Santiago, 1970); translated by Jacketti and Maloney as *Seaquake* (Fredonia, N.Y.: White Pine, 1990);

La espada encendida (Buenos Aires: Losada, 1970);

Las piedras del cielo (Buenos Aires: Losada, 1970); translated by James Nolan as *Stones of the Sky* (Port Townsend, Wash.: Copper Canyon, 1987);

Geografía infructuosa (Buenos Aires: Losada, 1972);

Incitación al nixonicidio y alabanza de la revolución chilena (Buenos Aires: Losada, 1973); translated by Teresa Anderson as *A Call for the Destruction of Nixon and Praise for the Chilean Revolution* (Cambridge, Mass.: West End, 1980);

La rosa separada (Buenos Aires: Losada, 1973); translated by O'Daly as *A Separate Rose* (Port Townsend, Wash.: Copper Canyon, 1985);

El mar y las campanas (Buenos Aires: Losada, 1973); translated by O'Daly as *The Sea and the Bells* (Port Townsend, Wash.: Copper Canyon, 1988);

Toward the Splendid City: Nobel Lecture (New York: Farrar, Straus & Giroux, 1974);

Jardín de invierno (Buenos Aires: Losada, 1974); translated by O'Daly as *Winter Garden* (Port Townsend, Wash.: Copper Canyon, 1986);

2000 (Buenos Aires: Losada, 1974); translated by Schaaf (Falls Church, Va.: Azul Editions, 1997);

El corazón amarillo (Buenos Aires: Losada, 1974); translated by O'Daly as *The Yellow Heart* (Port Townsend, Wash.: Copper Canyon, 1990);

Libro de las preguntas (Buenos Aires: Losada, 1974); translated by O'Daly as *The Book of Questions* (Port Townsend, Wash.: Copper Canyon, 1991);

Elegía (Buenos Aires: Losada, 1974); translated by Jack Hirschman as *Elegy* (San Francisco: David Books, 1983);

Defectos escogidos (Buenos Aires: Losada, 1974);

Confieso que he vivido (Barcelona: Seix Barral, 1974); translated by Hardie St. Martin as *Memoirs* (New York: Farrar, Straus & Giroux, 1977);

Para nacer he nacido, edited by Matilde Neruda and Miguel Otero Silva (Barcelona: Seix Barral, 1978); translated by Margaret Sayers Peden as *Passions and Impressions* (New York: Farrar, Straus & Giroux, 1982);

El río invisible, edited, with notes, by Jorge Edwards (Barcelona: Seix Barral, 1980);

Cuadernos de Temuco, 1919–1920, edited, with a prologue, by Victor Farías (Buenos Aires: Seix Barral, 1996);

Yo acuso: Discursos parlamentarios, edited by Leonidas Aguirre Silva (Bogota: Oveja Negra, 2002).

Collection: *Obras completas* (Buenos Aires: Losada, 1957; enlarged, 2 volumes, 1962; enlarged again, 1967; enlarged again, 3 volumes, 1973).

Editions in English: *A New Decade: Poems, 1958–1967,* edited, with an introduction, by Ben Belitt, translated by Belitt and Alastair Reid (New York: Grove, 1969);

Pablo Neruda: The Early Poems, translated by David Ossman and Carlos B. Hagen (New York: New Rivers, 1969);

New Poems (1968–1970), edited and translated, with an introduction, by Belitt (New York: Grove, 1972);

Five Decades: A Selection: Poems, 1925–1970, edited and translated by Belitt (New York: Grove, 1974);

Pablo Neruda: A Basic Anthology, selected, with an introduction, by Robert Pring-Mill (Oxford: Dolphin, 1975);

Late and Posthumous Poems, 1968–1974, edited and translated by Belitt (New York: Grove, 1988);

Selected Odes of Pablo Neruda, translated, with an introduction, by Margaret Sayers Peden (Berkeley: University of California Press, 1990);

Canto General, Fiftieth Anniversary Edition, translated by Jack Schmitt (Berkeley: University of California Press, 1991);

Odes to Common Things, selected by Ferris Cook, translated by Ken Krabbenhoft (Boston: Little, Brown, 1994).

PLAY PRODUCTIONS: *Romeo and Juliet,* adapted from William Shakespeare's play of that title, Santiago, Instituto de Teatro de la Universidad de Chile, 18 October 1964;

Fulgor y muerte de Joaquín Murieta, Santiago, Instituto de Teatro de la Universidad de Chile, 14 October 1967.

RECORDING: *Pablo Neruda Reading His Poetry,* Caedmon TC 1215, 1967.

Arguably the most widely read Latin American poet of all time, Pablo Neruda was awarded the Nobel Prize in literature in 1971. This honor came as the culmination of more than fifty years of writing poetry that moved readers the world over, for Neruda's verses of love, nature, and politics were heard across borders. In the Nobel citation the Swedish Academy praises him "for a poetry that with the action of an elemental force brings alive a continent's destiny and dreams." Both his lyrical voice and his committed, collective voice bespeak the passion and insightful observation that characterized his life and his works.

Born in Parral, a small town in southern central Chile, on 12 July 1904, Neftalí Ricardo Reyes Basoalto was the son of railroad engineer José del Carmen Reyes and elementary-school teacher Rosa Basoalto (who died of tuberculosis two months after the child came into the world). Reyes grew up surrounded by rainy forests and majestic mountains. When he was two years old, his father moved to Temuco and lived there throughout the boy's adolescence, in a wooden house with a small garden. He learned to read early and began to write timid verses, a point of contention with his father, who would not encourage his "daydreaming," and his schoolmates, who made fun of him. He grew up reading voraciously, as a lonely boy, in spite of the two siblings born of his father's second marriage, Laura and Rodolfo. At the age of sixteen Reyes was introduced to French poetry by the headmistress of Temuco's school for girls, Gabriela Mistral, a poet who in 1945 received the first Nobel Prize in literature awarded to a Latin American author.

His father's remarriage to Doña Trinidad Candia Marverde (whom Neruda fondly recalled in his autobiographical poetry as *la mamadre,* "the momother") was a blessing for Reyes. As a child he revered his stepmother, a sweet and silent woman of peasant stock who was close to the earth that he wrote of continually as a poet. The Reyes home was modest, but the boy had some privacy for his voracious reading. "En un minuto la noche y la lluvia cubren el mundo. Allí estoy solo y en mi cuaderno de aritmética escribo versos" (In one minute the night and the rain cover the world. I am there all alone and in my arithmetic notebook I write poems), he recalled in *Obras completas* (Complete Works, 1962). Throughout his whole life his childhood in southern Chile influenced his poetry, the geographical background taking on thematic importance. In his mature verses it became the substructure of his entire way of seeing and interpreting the world. Many years later Neruda recaptured his Temucan youth admirably in the first volume of his autobiographical verse memoir, *Memorial de Isla Negra* (1964; translated as *Isla Negra: A Notebook,* 1981), which he published on his sixtieth birthday. Some of the poems written during his formative years in Temuco are found in his first published book, *Crepusculario* (Twilights, 1923).

In 1918 Reyes had his first poem published in a Santiago magazine, which printed thirteen more of his compositions the next year. Two literary prizes followed, and then third place in the River Maule Floral Games poetry competition. In 1920 Reyes captured first prize for poetry in the spring festival in Temuco. Also that year he became a contributor to the literary journal *Selva Austral* (Southern Jungle) under the pen name Pablo Neruda, which he adopted in memory of the nineteenth-century Czechoslovak poet Jan Neruda. He began to dream about becoming a full-fledged poet and in 1921 left his frontier hometown and moved to Santiago, the capital, to train as a teacher of French. He never completed the study program. Soon after his arrival he won first prize in the poetry contest held by the Chilean University Student Federation with his poem "La canción de la fiesta" (The Festive Song). It is a *Modernista* piece, full of the rhythms and elegant images of early-twentieth-century Spanish American poetry and already displaying great dexterity in its handling of sonority and color. The young poet's head "estaba llena de libros, sueños y poemas zumbando como abejas" (was filled with books, dreams, and poems buzzing

Neruda and his first wife, María Antonieta (Maruka) Hagenaar, to whom he was married from 1930 to 1936
(photograph by Annemarie Heinrich)

around like bees), as he recalls in his *Confieso que he vivido* (I Confess That I Have Lived, 1974; translated as *Memoirs,* 1977). In 1923 he sold all of his possessions to finance the publication of *Crepusculario.* He published the volume under his pseudonym to avoid conflict with his family, who disapproved of his occupation. *Crepusculario* was the book that signaled his entry into the world of published poetry; he was between eighteen and nineteen when he wrote those verses.

Crepusculario includes some of the erotic poems for which the Chilean was known throughout his life, but mostly his themes here belong to nature, somewhat in

the vein of the French Symbolists such as Paul Verlaine. The section "Los crepúsculos de Maruri" (The Maruri Sunsets), particularly, exemplifies this thematic concern. Lines such as "La tarde sobre los tejados / cae / y cae . . . / Quién le dio para que viniera / alas de ave?" (The afternoon / falls / and falls / over the roofs . . . / Who gave it for this journey / the wings of a bird?), from the poem "La tarde sobre los tejados," convey the vague sadness about the impending demise of light, the approaching darkness, and its impact on the poet. The early love poetry of *Crepusculario* was not as accomplished and successful, however, as his *Veinte poemas de amor y una canción desesperada* (1924; translated as *Twenty Love Poems and a Song of Despair,* 1969). To date, the latter is the most published and reproduced collection of Latin American verse, having been translated into twenty-four languages. This book established Neruda's reputation as a poet of erotic and romantic love, opening his career to public acclaim.

It is difficult to overstate the impact of the publication of *Veinte poemas de amor y una canción desesperada.* The collection became one of the great success stories of its literary era in the Hispanic world. Over the years its style and themes dominated Spanish American poetic currents. By 1973, the last year for which statistics were available, more than two million copies of the Spanish text alone had been sold. The themes of these twenty-one compositions—powerful amorous poetry couched in earthy images—are the sensuous, desperate yearning of a man in love with the woman he sees disappearing from his life; the final "canción desesperada" of farewell; and the descriptions of a woman's body equated to the earth: passion, sensuality, ecstasy, descent into sorrow, and loneliness. *Veinte poemas de amor y una canción desesperada* is a work of exuberant and erotic love, an exaltation of woman and sensuality written from grief and the loneliness of melancholy.

Neruda has explained that there are basically two love stories in the book: the love that filled his adolescence in the provinces and the love he found later in the labyrinth of Santiago. In *Confieso que he vivido* the poet calls these women Marisol (literally, Mary Sun, or Sea and Sun) and Marisombra (Mary Shadow, or Sea and Shadow). These two images give rise to the earthy metaphors for the female body and soul that permeate the book, as in "Poema 19": "Niña morena y ágil, el sol que hace las frutas, / el que cuaja los trigos, el que tuerce las algas, / hizo tu cuerpo alegre, tus luminosos ojos / y tu boca que tiene la sonrisa del agua" (Nimble and bronze-skinned girl, the sun that makes fruits grow, / the sun that swells the wheat, the sun that plaits sea weeds, / this sun has built your merry body, your luminous eyes, / your mouth that curves with the water's smile). The exultation ends, however, in solitary grief in "Poema 20" and in "La Canción Desesperada" (The Song of Despair), with its images of shipwreck and desolation. The poet has found defeat in love: "Abandonado como los muelles en al alba. / Es la hora de partir" (Abandoned like the wharfs at dawn. / It is time to depart). The two women and the two moods of *Veinte poemas de amor y una canción desesperada* are captured in simple, even stark, language. Neruda had not yet taken the step that plunged him into the Surrealist world of images of *Residencia en la tierra: 1925–1935* (1935; translated as *Residence on Earth,* 1946), but intu-

itively he anticipated that gray landscape of doubt and nothingness on the horizon.

Between 1925 and 1927 Neruda became impatient with himself and with his work. In spite of the popularity of his first book, fortune was eluding him, and he was yet unknown outside of Chile. He made contact with the Ministry of Foreign Affairs, and in 1927 he got himself appointed as honorary consul of Chile to Rangoon, Burma. This appointment followed the standing Latin American tradition of honoring poets with diplomatic assignments. His knowledge of spoken English was sketchy and his consular experience nil. He was an adventurous, restless, twenty-three-year-old writer, a tall, somber young man with dark eyes and a taste for women, with a charismatic presence and little in the way of money or possessions.

During his long transoceanic journey to Rangoon, Neruda wrote reports and articles to newspapers in Chile and long letters to friends. These writings, as well as his poetry, continued when he arrived in the Orient. The East for him turned out to be a mixture of chaos, poverty, and fascinating perceptions of ancient cultures in contact with an oppressive colonial presence. Anguish and despair followed the poet, and he lived in almost abject poverty despite his appointment. Alcohol, poetry, and women were his escapes.

In Rangoon, a Burmese woman named Josie Bliss fell passionately in love with Neruda and followed him everywhere. In spite of his own attachment to her, the poet was disturbed and frightened by her extreme jealousy, and he left her behind when he was suddenly appointed Chilean consul in Ceylon (Sri Lanka) in 1928. On the boat he wrote his poem "Tango del viudo" (The Widower's Tango)—later to appear in the first volume of *Residencia de la tierra*—as a sad farewell to his jealous lover. Bliss surprised him by appearing on his doorstep in Colombo, Ceylon, however, and a second bitter farewell ensued some time later.

In 1929 Neruda attended a meeting of the Indian National Congress Party in Calcutta. The vast crowds only added to his developing feelings of alienation and loneliness. The Orient was for Neruda a composite of chaos, poverty, and oppression: a hell on earth. In this atmosphere he wrote the poems later collected in *Residencia en la tierra.* Published in 1933, it was the first of three volumes to carry that title. Most of its dark poems were written in Rangoon, Colombo, or aboard the ship that carried him home after his five-year stay in the Far East. The poems are filled with surrealistic images, illogical language, and the presence of material details, denoting his troubled state of being, both in the personal and social realms. He was poorly paid, constantly worrying about money, and suffering from depression. In Java he met María Antonieta (Maruka) Hagenaar,

Neruda and his longtime companion, Argentine painter Delia del Carril, circa 1936

marrying her on 6 December 1930 in a union that proved ill fated. Even his erotic poetry, for example, "Agua sexual" (Sexual Water), in *Residencia II,* of those years shows his problematic feelings and nihilistic worldview: "Y entonces hay este sonido: / Un ruido rojo de huesos, / un pegarse de carne, / y piernas amarillas como espigas juntándose. / Yo escucho entre el disparo de los besos, / escucho, sacudido entre respiraciones y sollozos" (And then I hear this sound: / a red noise of bones, / a sticking together of the flesh / and legs yellow as ears of wheat meeting. / I listen among the explosion of the kisses, / I listen, shaken between breathing and sobs). Some critics, upon reading his compositions of those years such as "Walking Around" and "Caballero solo" (Gentleman Alone), detect a nightmarish vision not unlike the one depicted by T. S. Eliot in his *The Waste Land* (1922). Much later, in *Confieso que he vivido,* the poet confirms that negative vision. Neruda, isolated and anguished, was forced into contemplating his own existential suffering and the sordid reality around him.

The *Residencia en la tierra* cycle comprises three books: *Residencia I,* covering the period from 1925 to 1931, and *Residencia II,* covering the period from 1931 to 1935, were published together in 1935; and *Tercera residencia: 1935–1945* (Third Residence: 1935–1945), published in 1947. While the three volumes have been published together as *Residencia en la tierra,* the first two

are primarily associated with the acute depression that the young poet suffered both in Chile and during, and immediately after, his devastating stay in the Far East. In a poetic manifesto that Neruda published in 1935, "Sobre una poesía sin pureza" (Toward an Impure Poetry), he affirms:

> Es muy conveniente, en ciertas horas del día o de la noche, observar profundamente los objetos en descanso: las ruedas que han recorrido largas, polvorientas distancias, soportando grandes cargas vegetales o minerales, los sacos de las carbonerías, los barriles, las cestas, los mangos y asas de los instrumentos del carpintero. De ellos se desprende el contacto del hombre y de la tierra como una lección para el torturado poeta lírico. Las superficies usadas, el gasto que las manos han infligido a las cosas, la atmósfera a menudo trágica y siempre patética de estos objetos, infunde una especie de atracción no despreciable hacia la realidad del mundo.

> (It is useful, at certain hours of the day and night, to look closely at the world of objects at rest: wheels that have crossed long, dusty spaces with their huge vegetal and mineral burdens, bags of coal from the coal bins, barrels, baskets, handles and hafts on a carpenter's tool chest. From them flow the contacts of man with the earth, like an object lesson for all troubled lyricists. The used surface of things, the wear that hands have given to things, the air, tragic at times, pathetic at others, of such things—all lend a curious attractiveness to reality).

Neruda is writing here as a true poet of matter, of nature, for whom nothing that exists in the external world is worthless. His vision of the world is anguished, however, dejected about the human condition. In this respect it can be called existentialist poetry; but since it combines words and images unexpectedly and gives voice to a flow of obscure imagery from the subconscious mind, it can also be called Surrealist. Loneliness easily overtakes Neruda when contemplating the immensity and empty spaces of nature, death, loss, and rejection.

In order to counteract and yet express these feelings, the poet uses the technique of enumeration, the construction of lists previously used by Walt Whitman, who revived this biblical rhetorical device. Neruda adds the modern element of chaos. He uses chaotic enumeration to combat loneliness and nihilistic tendencies and, at the same time, creates a faded, irrational world in his verses. One reads in one of his best-known poems of those years, "Walking Around": "Hay pájaros de color de azufre y horribles intestinos / colgando de las puertas de las casas que odio, / hay dentaduras olvidadas en una cafetera, / hay espejos / que debieran haber llorado de vergüenza y espanto, / hay paraguas en todas partes, y venenos, y ombligos" (There are sulphur-colored birds, and hideous intestines / hanging over the doors of houses that I hate, / and there are false teeth forgotten in a coffeepot, / there are mirrors / that ought to have wept from shame and terror, / there are umbrellas everywhere, and venoms, and umbilical cords). Like Pablo Picasso in his Cubist period, in *Residencia en la tierra* Neruda distorts human images and displaces objects; like the artist, the poet does not want to paint the world as attractive or beautiful but rather to give the reader an expression of his troubled and powerful vision.

There are, nevertheless, poems in *Residencia en la tierra* in which optimism prevails. In these poems—for example, "Entrada a la madera" (Entrance into Wood), "Estatuto del vino" (Statute of Wine), and "Apogeo del apio" (Triumph of Celery)—pure matter, isolated from the environment, is described. These poems are an exercise in exultant descriptions of the natural world and its elements, and in them Neruda delves into the world of pure matter, untainted by cosmic disharmony or urban decay. These poems anticipate his love for the pristine elements of life found later in his poetry.

During the years he wrote the poems in *Residencia en la tierra,* Neruda also discovered the people's cause in the Spanish Civil War. He was sent to Spain as Chilean consul in Barcelona in early 1934; his daughter and only child, Malva Marina, was born there in October, and shortly thereafter he was reunited with his friend, the great Spanish poet Federico García Lorca, whom he

had first met in Buenos Aires in 1933. At the end of 1934 Neruda was transferred to Madrid as consul and gathered in his house a veritable Who's Who of the Spanish literary and poetic circles of the time. He became close friends with two of the major poets of that generation, Rafael Alberti and Miguel Hernández, active members of the Spanish Communist Party.

Up until this time Neruda had been somewhat of a loner. Suddenly, in Spain he discovered solidarity, and he gave his time, energy, money, and poetic inspiration to the Spanish Republican cause. Together with the poet Manuel Altolaguirre, he founded a literary review called *Caballo verde para la poesía* (Green Horse for Poetry), a celebrated avant-garde journal for the arts, in 1935. When the Civil War broke out in 1936 and Lorca was shot to death by Francisco Franco's troops, Neruda took an active part in the defense of the Spanish Republic, under mortal attack by the Phalangist forces. Having moved to Paris, he edited the journal *Los poetas del mundo defienden al pueblo españoles* (Poets of the World Defend the Spanish People), and in 1937, with the Peruvian poet César Vallejo, he founded the Hispano-American Aid Group for Spain. In the same year Neruda published *España en el corazón* (Spain in My Heart), which includes some of his most powerful poetry, with images depicting the Fascist armies of Franco killing supporters of the Spanish Republic, above all his dear friend Lorca, as in "Explico algunas cosas" (I Am Explaining a Few Things): "Preguntaréis por qué su poesía / no nos habla del sueño, de las hojas, / de los grandes volcanes de su país natal? // Venid a ver la sangre por las calles, / venid a ver / la sangre por las calles, / venid a ver la sangre por las calles!" (And you will ask why doesn't his poetry / describe dreams and leaves / and the great volcanoes of his native land? // Come and see the blood in the streets, / come and see / the blood in the streets, / come and see the blood in the streets!).

In the same year, Neruda participated in a congress of writers gathered in Paris from around the Western world to support the Spanish cause: artists such as Ernest Hemingway, W. H. Auden, William Butler Yeats, Louis Aragon, and André Malraux expressed their solidarity. The writers even traveled to Madrid, in spite of the city being besieged and bombarded by Franco's forces. While in Madrid, Neruda met and fell in love with the Argentine painter Delia del Carril; they remained together until the early 1950s. The poet and his wife, Maruka Hagenaar, had separated in 1936; their daughter died in 1942 at the age of eight.

In *Confieso que he vivido* Neruda recounts his experience as a committed poet in war-torn Spain. He tells of solidarity, friendship, and hopes betrayed by histori-

Neruda in Paris in 1939, when he was serving as special consul supervising the immigration to Chile of refugees from the Spanish Civil War (Fundación Pablo Neruda)

cal events; and in the midst of this bloodshed Neruda found a public for his poetry. A decision was made during the war to reprint *España en el corazón,* and his friend Altolaguirre set up a printing press in an old monastery near Gerona to carry out the project. Paper was scarce, since the enemy lines were close and the city was in a state of siege, so pages for the book had to be improvised: a mixture of banners, old shirts, sheets, and bits and pieces of discarded paper were all mashed into pulp to make paper. "Supe que muchos habían preferido acarrear sacos con los ejemplares impresos antes que sus propios alimentos y ropas" (I learned that many of the Republican soldiers carried copies of the book in their sacks instead of their own food and clothing),

Neruda recalls in *Confieso que he vivido;* "Con los sacos al hombro emprendieron la larga marcha hacia Francia" (With those sacks over their shoulders they set out on the long march to France). Years later Neruda saw a copy of the book in the Library of Congress in Washington, D.C., exhibited in a glass case as one of the rare books of the twentieth century.

España en el corazón is an exceptional mixture of political and lyric poetry. It is powerful, among the finest political texts to come out of the Spanish Civil War. This contribution by Neruda to the Spanish people was much cherished. Years later, when Chile's democratically elected government was overthrown by a bloody coup, and the poet died within two weeks of that event in September 1973, Spanish poets published a volume in Spain titled *Chile en el corazón* (Chile in My Heart), dedicated to Neruda.

This period in Neruda's life marked his poetry forever, with his insistence on the materiality of images and his profound commitment to political causes. The same sentiment and imagery can be found in his great epic, *Canto general* (General Song, 1950; excerpts translated as *Poems from the Canto General*, 1968), which sings of the American continent from its beginnings to its contemporary political reality.

In 1937 Neruda returned to Chile, where he renewed his political activity, traveling throughout the country in 1938 and writing prolifically. During that year his father died in May and his stepmother in August. At this time Neruda began writing a long poem titled "Canto de Chile" (Song of Chile), which eventually became *Canto general*. In 1939 he was appointed as a special consul in Paris and given the task of supervising the migration to Chile of the defeated Spanish Republicans who had fled to France. In 1940 he returned to Chile but in the same year he left for Mexico to serve as Chile's consul general. Returning to Chile in 1943, he visited Cuzco and the ancient Inca fortress of Machu Picchu during a short trip to Peru. This experience proved highly significant in the evolution of his poetry.

Neruda was elected to the Senate two years later and joined the Communist Party. In 1945 he also received the National Prize in literature; that same year he began writing "Alturas de Macchu Picchu" (The Heights of Machu Picchu), the cornerstone of *Canto general*. When Chilean president Gabriel González Videla cracked down on his former Communist allies in 1947, Neruda published in the 27 November issue of *El Nacional* (Caracas, Venezuela) an uncollected document titled "Carta íntima para millones de hombres" (An Intimate Letter for Millions of Men), defying censorship in his country. Subsequently, he was arrested as a seditious politician. Chilean authorities declared communism illegal and expelled Neruda from the Senate, especially after his speech on the senate floor titled *Yo acuso* (I Accuse). He went into hiding, living underground for several months, and finally in 1949 fled the country and went into exile, carrying a thick manuscript with him. During those years he had written the poems of *Canto general*, first published in Mexico in 1950 (and also underground in Chile).

Canto general is the product of Neruda's unstinting commitment to social justice in Latin America and his choice of Marxist ideology as the way to achieve that goal. The book was first intended as a long poem to Chile, but while in Mexico, Neruda transformed it into an epic poem about the whole American continent, its nature, its people, and its historical destiny. It consists of approximately 231 poems brought together into fifteen sections and constitutes a pivotal part of Neruda's production. Shortly after its publication, *Canto general* was translated into ten languages. Many of the poems are undeniably political, and yet throughout the book runs a deep undercurrent of love for his native soil and for the continent, expressed in powerful yet delicate lyric verses.

One of the finest sections of *Canto general* is formed by "Alturas de Macchu Picchu," published separately in 1947 and later included in this vast work. Inspired by his 1943 visit to the Incan fortress and sanctuary nestled in the peaks of the Peruvian Andes, the poet speaks of the ancient city as "la cuna del relámpago y del hombre" (cradle of lightning and of man) and "madre de piedra" (mother of stone), and invokes *amor americano* (American love) for this primeval earth, symbol of origin for the American peoples. The poet wants to give voice to all forgotten workers and slaves in the Incan Empire: "Dadme la lucha, el hierro, los volcanes. // Apegadme los cuerpos como imanes. // Acudid a mis venas y a mi boca. // Hablad por mis palabras y mi sangre" (Give me the struggle, the iron, the volcanoes. // Cleave your bodies to mine like magnets. // Flow into my veins, into my mouth. // Speak through my words and through my blood).

Canto general is a poetic interpretation of continental history expressed in highly erotic love images. America is the bride and the woman raped by the pillage of European conquistadors, and later by multinational corporations such as United Fruit and Anaconda Mining. In this context *Canto general* exalts this pure female representation of America and its countries, as well as bitterly accuses her violators, as in "Ahora es Cuba" (Now It's Cuba) from the section "Los conquistadores" (The Conquistadors): "Cuba, mi amor, te amarraron al potro, / te cortaron la cara, / te apartaron las piernas de oro pálido / te rompieron el sexo de granada" (Cuba, my love, they tied you to the rack, / they cut your face with knives, / they spread open your legs of pale gold, / they broke open your pomegranate sex). At the same time, America is also the great mother, the feminine earth force configured into a large continent and into countries that were once inhabited by indigenous peoples and later invaded and conquered by Spaniards. As Neruda describes in "Amor América" (Love America) from the section "La lámpara en la tierra" (A Lamp on This Earth), in primeval times this huge landmass was in a virginal state; then she was desecrated and trampled upon by foreign powers: "Antes de la peluca y la casaca / fueron los ríos, ríos arteriales: / fueron las cordilleras, en cuya onda raída / cóndor o la nieve parecían inmóviles: / fue la humedad y la espesura, el trueno / sin nombre todavía, las pam-

Del Carril and Neruda visiting Chilean poet Gabriela Mistral, circa 1947 (Emilio Ellena and the Departmento de Fotografía y Microfilm, Universidad de Chile)

pas planetarias" (Before the wig and the frock-coat / were the rivers, arterial rivers: / were the mountains, in whose frayed wave / the condor or the snow seemed fixed: / there was humidity and thicket, thunder / still without name, the planetary plains).

Canto general, unified by a single vision, has been seen as inspired both by the Bible and by the poetic techniques of Whitman in *Leaves of Grass* (1855). Throughout its pages the figures of the men and women who populated and created Latin America and suffered injustice and death appear as heroes against a magnificent background of mountains, forests, oceans, and volcanoes. *Canto general* is a recognized masterpiece. In its pages the voices of the common people speak; their everyday lives are described; and their struggles are sung by a poet who embraces their lives and their stories. The heroes are the indigenous American populations and the common men and women; the villains are the invaders, the conquerors, the dictators, and the multinationals. In one of the best-known poems of the collection, "La United Fruit Co.," the poet utilizes an epic tone reminiscent of Genesis: "Cuando sonó la trompeta, estuvo / todo preparado en la tierra / y Jehová repartió el mundo / a Coca-Cola Inc., Anaconda, / Ford Motors, y otras entidades: / la Compañía Frutera Inc. / se reservó lo más jugoso, / la costa central de mi tierra, / la dulce cintura de América" (When the

trumpet sounded / everything was prepared on earth / and Jehovah divided the world / among Coca-Cola Inc., Anaconda, / Ford Motors, and other corporations: / For the United Fruit Company Inc. / the juiciest was reserved, / the central coast of my land / the sweet waist of America).

Nature imagery is powerful in *Canto general,* and one of the most recognized symbolic representations found in the book is the tree, which represents the forceful surge of natural currents against an order imposed from outside. Those who fought Spanish conquistadors, the Indian chieftains and rulers such as Cuahtémoc in Mexico, Caupolicán in Chile, and Tupac Amaru in Peru, are often compared to the forceful presence of native vegetation. Neruda writes of more than the common man and the natural wonders of South and Central America, however. In section 9, "Que despierte el leñador" (Let the Rail-splitter Awaken), the poet considers the United States and writes some of his most lyrical verses with an epic theme, honoring Abraham Lincoln. The last sections of *Canto general* are a paean to the seascapes of South America ("El gran océano" [The Great Ocean]) and an autobiographical long poem titled "Yo soy" (I Am).

The exile that had started in 1949 turned out to be longer than Neruda had anticipated. He traveled and lived in Europe for three years with a Chilean woman, Matilde Urrutia. She became his second wife in 1952.

Neruda's poetic style began to change. Out of these years came not only deeply felt political verses but also a collection of anonymously published love poetry, *Los versos del capitán* (1952; translated as *The Captain's Verses*, 1972). Neruda wanted to avoid hurting del Carril—hence his silent authorship. In *Los versos del capitán* the poet leaves behind the hermetic world of erotic love and idyllic nature imagery that characterizes *Veinte poemas de amor y una canción desesperada*. In poems such as "El amor del soldado" (The Soldier's Love), Neruda's passion for women and for the cause are fused: "Tienes que andar sobre las espinas / dejando gotitas de sangre. // Bésame de nuevo, querida. // Limpia ese fusil, camarada" (You have to walk over thorns / leaving little drops of blood. // Kiss me again, beloved. // Clean that rifle, comrade). The woman is represented as a combatant, and as such, will march through life with the poet; the lovers are united fighting for a cause.

During this time Neruda also wrote *Las uvas y el viento* (The Grapes and the Wind), a collection of poems published in 1954. In that work he recounts his travel during exile, under the influence of his political militancy and, in the second part, the clandestine love affair with Matilde. The poet writes joyfully of his socialist commitment, although the harsh denouncing tone of some of his compositions is softened by the presence of his beloved companion. From the late 1950s until his death, even though he touches on all the great themes he had already cultivated, his poetry is essentially personal. He did occasionally return to the stance of the public poet, however: in the book dedicated to the triumph of the Cuban Revolution, *Canción de gesta* (1960; translated as *Song of Protest,* 1976); in *Cantos ceremoniales* (1961; translated as *Ceremonial Songs,* 1996); in *La espada encendida* (The Flaming Sword, 1970) with its biblical overtones; and in the blatant diatribe *Incitación al nixonicidio y alabanza de la revolución chilena* (1973; translated as *A Call for the Destruction of Nixon and Praise for the Chilean Revolution,* 1980).

In 1952 the Chilean government withdrew the order to arrest leftist writers and political figures, and in that year Neruda returned to Chile and married Matilde Urrutia. The return to the land of his birth was the beginning of a new period in his poetic evolution. Neruda was received with great honors, purchased a house in Santiago that he would name "La Chascona" (after an affectionate name he gave Matilde), and although he continued to travel (he went to the Soviet Union in 1953 to receive the Lenin Peace Prize and the Stalin Peace Prize), he started to write his *Odas elementales* (1954; translated as *Elementary Odes,* 1961), a new departure in his exploration of the world around him. Never

had everyday objects, family life, and the essential substances of human existence been so elevated by poetry as in these deceptively simple verses.

At the University of Chile, Neruda gave five lectures in which he explained the origins and evolution of his poetry, and the trajectory that his verses had followed until then. In 1954 *Odas elementales* was published in Buenos Aires and received critical acclaim. In these poems Neruda returns to the basic elements of life, whether they be an onion, the smell of firewood, a child with a rabbit, a pair of blue socks, fish soup, a dictionary, or the atom. The poet abandons all artifice and rejoices in simplicity and purity, at the same time making an ideological statement: his materialistic view of life and politics. In a sense the odes could be said to have been written in a realist style that sing the praises of Earth, of human life and its most basic components.

Together Neruda's three books of odes—two more followed: *Nuevas odas elementales* (New Elementary Odes, 1956) and *Tercer libro de las odas* (The Third Book of Odes, 1957)—comprise more than 180 poems. Each poem celebrates being alive and enjoying the elements of ordinary life and examines objects as if they were under a microscope. In "Oda a la sal" (Ode to Salt), for example, he writes: "Polvo del mar, la lengua / de ti recibe un beso / de la noche marina: / el gusto funde en cada / sazonado manjar tu oceanía / y así la mínima, / la minúscula / ola del salero / nos enseña / no sólo su doméstica blancura, / sino el sabor central del infinito" (Dust of the sea, our tongue / receives a kiss / of the night sea from you: / taste recognizes / the huge ocean in each salty morsel, / and therefore the smallest, / the tiniest / wave of the shaker / brings home to us / not only your domestic whiteness / but the innermost flavor of infinity). This approach, it has been said, can be explained also by the fact that Neruda was an accomplished naturalist, specializing in marine life, and an avid collector of shells (a great part of his Nobel Prize cash award was spent on rare specimens). In "Oda a la alegría" (Ode to Joy) from *Odas elementales* the poet sings of natural objects as a man who is happy to be in this world: "porque aprendí luchando / que es mi deber terrestre / propagar la alegría. / Y cumplo mi destino con mi canto" (for I learned in my struggle / that it is my earthly duty / to spread joy / and I fulfill my destiny by singing).

A stylistic detail important to the odes is the typographical arrangement of the poems. In earlier collections Neruda had written in traditional Spanish meters or in long verses reminiscent of Whitman. In the odes he makes use of short verses, and there are many lines in his poems with only one word (for example, in "Oda a la lluvia marina" [Ode to Rain], from *Nuevas odas elementales,* seventeen lines are formed by one word, eigh-

Neruda in February 1949 (from the 1990 Madrid edition of Canto general*)*

vain man who expected, even demanded, praise from his critics; but he was also charming, good-humored, and a great conversationalist who enjoyed inviting people to his home and cooking for them. He collected many things, apart from shells: rare books, old bottles, knickknacks, postcards, and carved figureheads from ships. The royalties from his books had allowed him to build two new houses in which he often retreated from the world, one in Valparaiso, and the one that was his favorite during his last years, the wood and stone house in Isla Negra, facing the southern Pacific and its giant waves. The house on Isla Negra became a veritable museum, filled with all the objects he collected. During these years he wrote *Estravagario* (1958; translated as *Extravagaria,* 1972), *Cien sonetos de amor* (1959; translated as *One Hundred Love Sonnets,* 1986), and *La barcarola* (The Barcarole, 1967), as well as other texts of memoirs and travel prose.

Estravagario is a collection of diverse poems about life, on which the poet reflects—at times whimsically—with the maturity and serene gaze of a man who has seen much in the world. The opening poem sets the tone with its unconventional style and typography:

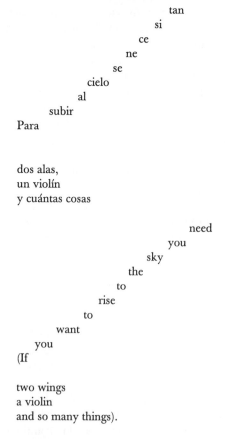

teen lines by two words, fifteen lines by three, and twelve lines by five or, rarely, six words). This simplified syntax contributes to the poetic effect of describing each object in detail, step by step. Neruda's poetics were now strongly based on clarity and simplicity and greatly contrast with his work previous to 1952. In addition, the imagery in the odes has become transparent in its meaning. The poems of *Residencia en la tierra* often include strange visions in which objects and abstract ideas are inextricably fused, and his earlier poems are often forged in long, flowing verses full of symbolic images. In the odes, however, and in the books that follow, Neruda has achieved his mature style, which is far from obscure. From the Spanish Civil War onward, his poetry becomes simpler and simpler.

In 1957 Losada published in Buenos Aires the first edition of his *Obras completas.* By this time, translations of Neruda's works had been published in virtually every well-known language, including Japanese and Persian. According to his close friends, Neruda was a

The act of reading this text requires an open, playful mind and a willingness to let go of preconceived notions about poetry. One can also see the influence of the vanguard poets, including the French and the Brazilians, in the creation of these lines that play not only with meaning but also with form.

In *Estravagario* three themes emerge that became an integral part of Neruda's contemplation of life during his later years: solitude, awareness of the passage of time, and consciousness of his own mortality. His home at Isla Negra, which served as a retreat from the world, appears often in the pages of the collection. Matilde, sand, seashells, ocean waves, the objects he has collected throughout his life, and driftwood and other objects floating in from the Pacific are all present in the poems. The material nature of reality and the human consciousness that observes the details of life, akin to the sentiments expressed in the odes, are well captured in the poem "Demasiados Nombres" (Too Many Names). The poet counts and recounts, in a manner reminiscent of his enumerations in *Residencia en la tierra,* although here objects have the luminosity imparted to them by a mind at peace, not struggling with pain and human misery: "Yo pienso confundir las cosas, / unirlas y recién nacerlas, / entreverarlas, desvestirlas, / hasta que la luz del mundo / tenga la unidad del océano, / una integridad generosa, / una fragancia crepitante" (I would like to mix and confuse things, / unite them, make them newborn, / mix them up and undress them / until all the world's light / has the oneness of the ocean, / its generous, vast wholeness, / its crackling, living fragrance).

Neruda published a slim volume of verse, *Navegaciones y regresos* (Voyages and Homecomings), in 1959. These poems were meant to be a continuation of the ode cycle, and in the prologue Neruda defines and defends his art: the poet is a worker, a craftsman. As in the other volumes of odes, this book mostly shows the Chilean as a joyful poet, immersed in the wonder of nature. The list of topics he treats range from the sublime to the mundane, as they had before: there are odes to an anchor, to the wings of the swallows that return in September, to his pet cat, to an elephant, to a chair, to fried potatoes. There is in the collection also a long political poem, "Oda a Lenin," written in celebration of the fortieth anniversary of the Russian Revolution. *Navegaciones y regresos* is the mark of Neruda's wish to continue writing in the manner of the elementary odes, although—since *Estravagario* had been published in the intervening years and had established a different quality of feeling in Neruda's poetic compositions—there is a tone to this volume that sets it apart from the other three books of similar poems.

Cien sonetos de amor, published also in 1959, continues in the vein of Neruda's paean to his beloved Matilde. Some critics have said that the poems in this collection remind them of a more polished version of

Veinte poemas de amor y una canción desesperada. The setting for these poems is the house at Isla Negra; there are only two figures in the book, the poet and Matilde. Everything around them is landscape or seascape, ocean spray, the smells of nature, the wind, the poet's memories. In sonnet XII, for example, Neruda instills in his language all the intense erotic expression that had served him well since his earlier books, and condenses images to convey his mature, fulfilled emotion: "amar es un viaje con agua y con estrellas" (love is a voyage with water and stars), he writes. "Amar es un combate de relàmpagos" (Love is a fight between two lightning flashes).

In the manner of a mystic poet, Neruda finds the intensity of his experience almost too much to describe in words, but he succeeds in conveying his passion as he had during his younger years. Nevertheless, it is not of Matilde alone that Neruda writes in these poems, but also the objects that surround them and make up their lives together. Their house, the beach, nature surrounding their space, the elements of night and day, are all part of the poetic world created in the book.

In 1960 *Canción de gesta* was published in Havana, fittingly, since its poems are a tribute to the Cuban Revolution and its heroes. In this work Neruda once more returns to his solidarity with the Communist cause. The poems retain some of the flavor once displayed in *Canto general,* but as a whole, revolutionary fervor succeeds over poetic prowess. *Canción de gesta* is more a product of Neruda's militancy than of his artistic genius, and most critics agree that the collection has more value as a political testimony than as poetry.

In 1961 two more collections of Neruda's poetry were published: *Las piedras de Chile* (translated as *The Stones of Chile,* 1986) and *Cantos ceremoniales.* In the preface to the former collection the poet explains: "Hace ya veinte años que dejé entre mis pensamientos este libro pedregal, nacido en las desamparadas costas y cordilleras de mi patria. . . . Deber de los poetas es cantar con sus pueblos y dar al hombre lo que es del hombre: sueño y amor, luz y noche, razón y desvarío. Pero no olvidemos las piedras! No olvidemos los tácitos castillos, los erizados, redondos regalos del planeta" (This flinty book, born in the wastelands along the coast and in the mountain ranges of my country, has lived for twenty years in my mind. . . . The poet must sing with his countrymen and give to mankind all that pertains to being a man: dreams and love, light and darkness, reason and vagary. But let us never forget the stones! We should never lose sight of these taciturn castles, the profile and bristling mass of our planet). Neruda's descriptions of rocks in the book are accompanied by photographs by Antonio Quintana. In recognizing the at times austere reality of the Chilean landscape, Neruda mixes sadness and hope. In "La gran mesa de piedra dura" (The Great Hard Rock Table), in which the whole of the country is seen as a bare stone surface, the people's poverty is recognized and lamented: "Nos sentamos junto a la mesa, / a la mesa fría del mundo, / y no nos trajo nadie nada, / todo se había terminado, / se lo habían comido todo // . . . todavía un niño espera, / él es la verdad de los sueños, / él es la esperanza terrestre" (We sat down all of us, together, around the table, / the cold table of our world, / and no one brought us anything, / everything had disappeared, / everything had been eaten already by others // . . . One child waits still, / the child who is the truth of every dream, / the child who is the hope of our earth).

Las piedras de Chile is both personal and public poetry. In it Neruda journeys up and down the steep slopes of his native mountains, and he interprets the landscape as it strikes his imagination. One of the distinctive traits of Neruda's volumes of poetry after 1950 and *Canto general* is also found here: the poetry is not just descriptive, it also features a narrative thread of history that weaves through it. In this work, personification and mythologizing of nature come to the fore, as they had in *Canto general*, with human qualities seen in the Chilean landscape as they had been seen before in the continental terrain.

Unlike the previous books, *Cantos ceremoniales* does not exhibit a clear thematic unity. The poems are divided into nine sections, with varied topics shared among them. Some portions recall the epic tone of *Canto general*, as, for instance, "La insepulta de Paita" (The Unburied Woman from Paita); the elegy devoted to Simón Bolívar's lover, Manuelita Sáenz; or "Cataclismo" (Cataclysm), about the devastating earthquake that shook southern Chile in 1960. There is also a long composition dedicated to the French-Uruguayan poet Isidore Lucien Ducasse, Comte de Lautreamont. Most critics agree that this is not one of Neruda's most memorable books, except perhaps for several poems. It seems, as Emir Rodriguez Monegal has put it, that "en casi todos ellos [los poemas] parece predominar la pompa de la materia poética sobre la espontaneidad creadora" (in almost all the poems the pomp of the poetic material) dominates over creative spontaneity.

Plenos poderes (translated as *Fully Empowered,* 1975) was published in 1962. In this book serenity prevails, as it had in other previous works. In the thirty-six poems included in the volume, there is a fullness of personal power, as is well expressed in "Deber del poeta" (The Poet's Obligations), in which Neruda defines what the poet must do, the duties he cannot escape. He must listen to "el lamento marino en mi conciencia" (the watery lament of consciousness), feel the hard rain, the blows of destiny, and gather it back in "una taza eterna" (a cup of eternity). In other words, the poet is obliged to pay attention and to record whatever others do not see or remember. Ultimately, the poet is the consciousness of mankind, who must try to preserve everything in a meaningful way so it can live eternally. Neruda happily accepts this awesome duty and writes in the ending poem, "Plenos poderes," that "y canto porque canto y porque canto" (I sing because I sing because I sing). In the poem "Oda para planchar" (In Praise of Ironing), Neruda links the poet's activity to an everyday act. Poetry is white, something that comes out of the water, covered with drops, and it becomes wrinkled when it dries, like laundry. Human hands must work it and restore it to its pristine state: "hay que extender la piel de este planeta, / hay que planchar el mar de su blancura / y van y van las manos, / se alisan las sagradas superficies / y así se hacen las cosas" (One has to spread out the skin of this planet, / one must iron the sea from its whiteness / and hands pass and pass, / the sacred surfaces are smoothed out / and that's how things are made).

The most ambitious book of this period is *Memorial de Isla Negra,* which comprises five volumes. It is autobiographical in nature and includes some of the most touching lyric poetry that Neruda ever wrote, about his childhood memories, his parents, his love life, his travels, his political ideas, and his aesthetic tastes. A series of autobiographical articles published in 1962 in a Brazilian journal, *O Cruzeiro Internacional,* gave origin to this poetry and later was the foundation for his posthumously published memoirs. In the five books that make up *Memorial de Isla Negra*–"Donde nace la lluvia" (Where the Rain Is Born), "La luna en el laberinto" (Moon in the Labyrinth), "El fuego cruel" (The Cruel Fire), "El cazador de raíces" (Hunting for Roots), and "Sonata crítica" (Critical Sonata)–one can find Neruda fully immersed in nostalgia and looking for self-knowledge.

In "Nacimiento" (Birth), the first poem in the collection, Neruda describes the house where he was born and the street where it stood. Both disappeared during an earthquake, and the adobe walls sank back into the dust. Neruda's mother died when he was a young child; the poet recalls a visit to her grave in the cemetery in Parral, where he cried out to her and received silence as the only answer: "y de allí se quedó sola, sin su hijo, / huraña y evasiva / entre las sombras. / Y de allí soy, de aquel / Parral de tierra temblorosa, / tierra cargada de uvas / que nacieron / desde mi madre muerta" (and there she remained alone, without her son, / elusive and evasive / among the shadows. / And that is where I come from, / a quake-ridden soil, from Parral, / a land abundant in grapes / springing up / from the dead body of my mother). This first book deals

A falsified Chilean document identifying Neruda as "Antonio Ruiz Lagorreta," which the poet used while a fugitive during the late 1940s (from Volodia Teitelboim, Neruda, *1984)*

with the poet's memories of childhood and adolescence; his discovery of nature, love, sex, and poetry; his first travels; and his own characteristic shyness.

"El niño perdido" (Little Boy Lost) is an equally moving poem, evoking the change brought on by time on Neruda's naive vision of the world and of himself. He tries to speak with the voice of the child he once was, even now in his present moment: "y de repente apareció en mi rostro / un rostro de extranjero / y era también yo mismo: / era yo que crecía, / eras tú que crecías, / era todo, / y cambiamos" (and suddenly appeared in my face / the face of a stranger, / and yet it was also my face. / It was I who was growing there / and you are growing with me / all of us one, / everything changing).

The second book, "La luna en el laberinto," continues the chronicle of Neruda's adolescence, and his first passionate love affairs, as well as his loneliness and anguish while living in the Far East. In "El fuego cruel,"

the third volume, poems about Neruda in Spain and the events of the Spanish Civil War are interspersed with poems reminiscing about his love affair with Josie Bliss in Rangoon and Colombo. In this book the topics become more varied and more political: war, commitments to leftist causes, and ideologies appear once more. For example, in "Los míos" (My People) Neruda recalls his verses from *España en el corazón* and points his finger at present-day killers in his native Chile who exploit natural resources and workers: "Yo dije: Ayer la sangre! / Vengan a ver la sangre de la guerra! / Pero aquí era otra cosa. / No sonaban los tiros, / no escuché por la noche / un río de soldados / pasar / desembocando / hacia la muerte. / Era otra cosa aquí, en las cordilleras / algo gris que mataba / humo, polvo de minas o cemento, / un ejército oscuro / caminando / en un día sin banderas" (I said: Yesterday the blood! / Come and see the blood of the war! / But here it was something else. / No guns sounded, / I didn't hear during the night / a river of soldiers / passing by, / flowing / toward death. / Here in the mountains it was something else, / something gray that killed, / smoke, dust from mines or cement, / a dark army / walking / in a day without banners).

Books 4 and 5 of *Memorial de Isla Negra,* while always focusing on Neruda's personal vision, are less directly autobiographical than the first three books, and there is no longer any attempt to describe life events or to follow a chronology. "El cazador de raíces" exhibits perhaps the finest poetic quality in all five volumes, and its subject matter is once again earth and nature, with an emphasis on the four elements of air, fire, earth, and water. In "Sonata crítica" the themes include Neruda's perception of art, literature in general, the role of the poet in the modern world, and the moral and metaphysical implications of living in a finite universe where hope and imperfection are constantly mingling.

In the poem "Arte magnética" (Magnetic Art), from the fifth book, Neruda returns to the question of what it means to be a poet. He affirms that it is only by immersing oneself fully into living that poetry can be born: "De tanto amar y andar salen los libros" (It is from endless loving and walking that books come forth). He ends by recounting how his life broke forth into poetry: "entre sangre y amor cavé mis versos, / en tierra dura establecí una rosa, / disputada entre el fuego y el rocío. / Por eso pude caminar cantando" (between blood and love I dug my verses, / in hard earth I established a rose, / fought over by fire and dew. / It is thus that I could walk along singing).

Memorial de Isla Negra is Neruda's most important work of the 1960s. Its autobiographical intent, however, should not let the reader forget that it is, above all, a poetic reconstruction of life. Neruda comes through in these poetic portraits with his intense human feelings, but he recognizes that the concrete events in his own life might not be consistently portrayed in his poetic memoirs. He acknowledges this fact in one of his prose accounts published in *O Cruzeiro Internacional* (January 1962) and posthumously in *Memoirs:* "Tal vez no viví en mí mismo; tal vez viví la vida de los otros. De cuanto he dejado escrito en estas páginas se desprenderán siempre—como en las arboledas de otoño y como en el tiempo de las viñas—las hojas amarillas que van a morir y las uvas que revivirán en el vino sagrado. Mi vida es una vida hecha de todas las vidas: las vidas del poeta." (Perhaps I have lived other people's lives. The pages of these memoirs of mine are like a forest in the fall, like vineyards in September, they give forth yellow leaves ready to die and ready to live again in the sacred wine. This is a life made out of all other lives, for a poet always has many lives).

In 1966 Neruda published two books. The first, *Arte de pájaros* (translated as *Art of Birds,* 1985), combines exquisite drawings of species native to Chile with poems dedicated to each specimen. A whimsical section of the large-sized volume includes "mythological" birds, such as "el pájaro yo" (the I bird) and "el pájaro ella" (the she bird), where colorful drawings portray birds of rare plumage with the photographed heads of Neruda and Matilde superimposed on the images; the same is done for friends of the couple. The second book published that year is *Una casa en la arena* (translated as *The House at Isla Negra: Prose Poems,* 1988), a volume in which Neruda mixed prose and poetry and illustrated with photographs of Isla Negra and his house. It includes, of course, the poet's personal life with Matilde in that environment, focusing first on nature and then on Neruda's personal involvement in the building of his home.

There is a similar vision in the love poems of *La barcarola* (the title refers to the song that gondoliers sing while steering lovers in their boats through the canals of Venice). The first section of the book is dedicated and addressed to Matilde, and all the compositions included therein were in fact first published in Neruda's autobiographical account of 1962. In this section, themes from the poet's earlier books come together again, as it gathers love poetry, nature poetry, poetry about Chile, and poems about the poet's own role and obligations. *La barcarola* is a complex book, in which many ingredients, many subjects, and many moods are combined. It is divided into multiple sections, with many of them titled simply "Sigue la barcarola" (The Barcarole Goes On). The most salient mood is that of introspection, and perhaps the most unifying motif is that of the constant rhythm of the verses. There are reminiscences of the poet's travels in Europe, and the year he spent in France with Matilde. The poem "Serenata de París" (Paris Serenade) recalls those cherished times: "Hermosa es la rue de la Huchette, / pequeña como una / granada / y opulenta en su pobre esplendor de vitrina harapienta: / allí entre los beatniks barbudos en este año del sesenta y / cinco / tú y yo transmigrados de estrella vivimos felices y sordos" (Beautiful is the Rue de la Huchette, tiny like a pomegranate, / and opulent in our poor splendor, just like a ragged showcase; / there, among the bearded beatniks in this year of sixty-five / you and I, transmigrants from a star, lived happy and oblivious).

Later in *La barcarola* Neruda devotes poems to the coastland of Chile, the plains of Patagonia crossed by horses, and his friend, the Chilean writer Rubén Azócar, who had died two years before. There are poems about the sound of bells in many places, the memory of turn-of-the-century Latin American poet Rubén Darío,

Neruda and Matilde Urrutia, who became his second wife in 1952

and many other historical figures. In the midst of these memories and associations, Neruda includes a narrative-dramatic poem, "Fulgor y muerte de Joaquín Murrieta" (Splendor and Death of Joaquin Murrieta). This long work gives a fictionalized account of the life and death of a Robin Hood–style bandit, identified by historians as a Mexican who helped the Spanish-speaking miners in California during the gold rush. Neruda, however, converts Murrieta into a Chilean folk hero. While it could be said that *La barcarola* is Neruda's most chaotic work, because of its multiple themes and the inclusion of a fledgling drama in its pages, it retains a lyric and romantic quality, and it richly reflects the personal experiences of the poet and his memories of art and people.

Between 1968 and 1973, in the five years before his death, Neruda published another series of works, comprising *Las manos del día* (The Hands of Day, 1968); *Fin de mundo* (World's End, 1969); *Aún* (1969; translated as *Still Another Day*, 1984); *La espada encendida; Las piedras del cielo* (1970; translated as *Stones of the Sky*, 1987); *Geografía infructuosa* (Barren Geography, 1972);

and *Incitación al nixonicidio y alabanza de la revolución chilena.* These years were what critics have called the "autumnal" period of Neruda's poetry. It was a period of enormous production for him, mainly of personal poetry. One volume had come after another in rapid succession since the early 1960s; despite his constant travels and public activities, the poet was no longer obliged to accept diplomatic work in order to live and could devote himself fully to writing. He spent more and more time at Isla Negra, and the peace he found there is reflected in a poetry that grew increasingly intimate and meditative as the years went on.

This serenity is one of the reasons Neruda turned his attention to autobiography, both in prose and in verse. Free from financial concerns, the poet concentrated on his own life, although always ready to comment on political events that aroused his interest. He traveled everywhere he was invited, always with Matilde at his side. Wherever they went, crowds gathered to hear the famous gravel voice, to hear Neruda lecturing and reading his poetry. His powerful presence and moving verses made him enormously popular. His career, which had integrated private and public concerns, had turned him into the people's poet. In 1962 a second edition of his complete works had been published. In 1964 his Spanish version of William Shakespeare's *Romeo and Juliet* (circa 1595–1596) was his first venture into the theater, produced in Santiago by the Instituto de Teatro de la Universidad de Chile (ITUCH, Theater Institute of the University of Chile), and performed on 18 October; later in 1964, it was published as a chapbook in Buenos Aires by Editorial Talía. This performance was followed by his second and last, the staging in October 1967 of his *Fulgor y muerte de Joaquín Murieta* (Splendor and Death of Joaquín Murrieta), also by ITUCH. In 1968 another edition of his complete works appeared.

His prolific writing at Isla Negra by no means meant that Neruda had abandoned active political participation, however, and in 1969 he was again deeply involved in Chilean politics, this time as the Communist Party's candidate for the presidency of Chile. Neruda later renounced his candidacy, however, in order to support his friend Salvador Allende when the latter became the sole candidate of all the leftist parties. The poet campaigned vigorously for Allende, and the leftist victory at the polls brought the poet hope for a new Chile in which social justice might at last abolish classism and poverty. In 1970 he was diagnosed with a serious form of cancer, and yet he agreed to represent the new government as Chile's ambassador to France.

Neruda was in France, working to renegotiate Chile's external debt, on 8 October 1971 when he received the news that he had been awarded the Nobel Prize. He traveled to Stockholm in December to receive it, and in his acceptance speech, *Toward the Splendid City* (published in 1974), he described his vision of a future for mankind, a paradise of everyday living, in which poets—the same as bakers—would play a significant role. Neruda returned to Chile in 1972, too ill to continue working as an ambassador. A huge rally was organized at the National Stadium to greet him.

The books Neruda published between 1968 and 1973, squeezed between the production of the mid 1960s and the later posthumous works, are, relatively speaking, not widely read or known. In part, this lack of attention might be the 1967 Losada edition of Neruda's *Obras completas* does not include all of these books. A fourth edition, published in 1973, does include them, but by this time the posthumous works were already appearing in print, overshadowing the previous books. According to some critics, it might also be true that Neruda's move toward mostly personal poetry in this period reduced his active reading public; he was no longer dealing with his principal themes of nature and history, but more with his own life and introspection.

Another consideration might be, perhaps, that Neruda was too prolific for his literary critics during this period. They concentrated on his five volumes of autobiographical verse, *Memorial de Isla Negra,* and on the prose memoirs *Confieso que he vivido*. It seems as if the poet, firing off a seemingly unending series of short books, left little time to absorb one before the next appeared.

Las manos del día, Fin de mundo, Aún, La espada encendida, Las piedras del cielo, Geografía infructuosa, and *Incitación al nixonicidio y alabanza de la revolución chilena* call for a careful reading, since some of these volumes do include representative verse of Neruda the lyric poet, except for the last one. *Incitación al nixonicidio y alabanza de la revolución chilena,* as the title implies, is a diatribe against the United States president that Neruda saw as a mortal enemy of the people of Chile. Nowhere else in his poetic work does Neruda express rage as he does on the pages of this book; this political pamphlet is full of furious broadsides, crafted in simple language with rhyme that is easy to understand and remember. Referring to the Vietnam War, his condemnation of Nixon is absolute; clearly, the death of this man who has become a menace to the world, says the poet, is the only solution. Unlike the passionate and lyrical poems of *España en el corazón* or the epic historical dimensions of *Canto general,* here Neruda directs his energy to denouncing a single man, for him the incarnation of treachery.

In a different manner, *Las manos del día* includes poignant verse about the role of the poet, full of imagery related to his writing, and expressing at times, in "El culpable" (The Guilty Ones), for example, his regret for not being a plain manual laborer: "Me declaro culpable de no haber / hecho, con estas manos que me dieron, / una escoba" (I declare myself guilty for not having / made, with these hands that they gave me, / a broom). The poems in this book are short and direct, but the tone remains one of introspection. Neruda is noting the passage of time and questioning whether his time on earth has been well spent. In "El golpe" (The Blow), speaking directly to the ink with which he has written his verses (he literally wrote all of his poems with green ink, on lined notebooks), he says: "Tal vez mejor hubiera / volcado en una copa / toda tu esencia, y haberla arrojado / en una sola página, manchándola / con una sola estrella verde / y que sólo esa mancha / hubiera sido todoh / lo que escribí a lo largo de mi vida, / sin alfabeto ni interpretaciones: un solo golpe oscuro / sin palabras" (Perhaps it would have been better / to have poured over into a cup / all your essence, and to have thrown it / on only one page, staining it / with one single green star / and that stain alone / would have been everything / that I wrote throughout my life: / without alphabet or interpretations / one single dark blow / without words).

Neruda's house at Isla Negra, his favorite location from the late 1950s until the end of his life (photograph by Milton Rogovin)

A year after the publication of *Las manos del día,* another book of his poetry, *Aún* (literally meaning "still" or "yet"), appeared. *Aún* is a single poem of 433 lines, written in the space of two days in July 1969. The dominant theme, personal like so many of the other works of this period, is the earth. Once again Neruda is seeking contact with nature and with his roots. A poem titled just "VI" states "Perdón si cuando quiero / contar mi vida / es tierra lo que cuento. / Ésta es la tierra. / Crece en tu sangre y creces. / Si se apaga en tu sangre / tú te apagas" (Forgive me if when I want / to tell my life / it's soil that I recount. / Such is the earth. / When it grows in your blood / you grow. / If it dies in your blood / you die). If this book anticipates, as some critics say, some of the poetry published posthumously in the dominant role it gives to nature, it equally signals the new positive role that silence plays in those later books: "Yo allí solo, buscando la razón de la tierra / sin hombres y sin alas, poderosa, / sola en su magnitud, como si hubiera / destruido una por una las vidas / para establecer su silencio" (And I was there all alone, looking for the reasons / of the earth's being, the earth without men / and without wings, yet all powerful, / alone in its majesty, as if it had / destroyed one by one every bit of life / in order to establish its silence).

In the same year as *Aún,* Neruda published still another, significantly different, book of poetry, *Fin de mundo.* Even though the purported theme of this collection of poems is to meditate on the state of global affairs, in the end the main topic remains the poet's own self. Neruda recognizes this in the poem "Siempre Yo" (Always I): "Yo que quería hablar del siglo / adentro de esta enredadera, / que es mi siempre libro naciente, / por todas partes me encontré / y se me escapaban los hechos" (I who wanted to speak of our century / within this twining, / within my book still being born, / everywhere I found myself / while events escaped me). Indeed, this book reflects events of the times—incessant wars, the horrors of Vietnam, the death of Che Guevara, the invasion of Prague by Soviet troops—but it is, nonetheless, a personally oriented book. Events are seen through the poet's own perspective, and he anguishes about the disappointments and unrealized dreams that have characterized the years during which he has lived. But the mood of *Fin de mundo* is more reflective than argumentative, and this quality makes the book more closely related to Neruda's personal poetry.

In all the books from 1968 onward Neruda apologizes, asking for forgiveness not only for the things he has done, but also primarily for the things he has not done. At times, there is a sense of despair in his poetry for not having been able to act more on behalf of human justice, as in *Las manos del día*. Nowhere does this despair take on such global proportions as in the poems of *Fin de mundo*. Neruda describes the twentieth century in the blackest terms: in "La ceniza" (Ash), he calls it "la edad de la ceniza" (the age of ash) and writes of "ceniza de niños quemados" (the ash of burned children) and "cenizas de ojos que lloraron" (the ash of eyes that cried); and in "Bomb," he writes: "en estos años nació / la usina total de la muerte / el núcleo desencadenado / y no nos bastó asesinar / a cien mil japoneses dormidos" (in these years was born / the complete factory of death, / the unchained atom, / and it wasn't enough for us to assassinate 100,000 sleeping Japanese). In *Fin de mundo* Neruda shows a subtle philosophical bent to his reflection on the state of world affairs that goes much beyond the political. There is a softer, gentler message about the human condition that in his purely political poetry. The collection also includes portraits of cities, countries, and well-known writers from Latin America, including Julio Cortázar, César Vallejo, and Gabriel García Márquez.

La espada encendida is one of Neruda's most unusual books. The title sets the work apart by referring to the Bible, specifically to Genesis in the Old Testament, and the sword with which an angel protected the entrance to the Garden of Eden after the Fall of Adam and Eve. This poem recounts a long and fantastic tale, the story of Rhodo and Rosía, survivors after the destruction of the world and its civilizations. Drawing strength from their love for each other, they sail out into the world in a new ark laden with escaping birds and beasts. As they draw clear of the land, they realize that the old god has died and that they are themselves the gods of the new age. They try to establish a dynasty to begin anew, only to be pursued by inner guilt and great explosions in the sky and in the center of the earth. The book ends on an optimistic note, however: through their love and through the presence of birds and animals around them, Rhodo and Rosía slowly learn that it is they who are in charge, not some unseen god, and the new world belongs to them. It might seem strange for a Marxist poet to use biblical themes and imagery, but the epic and mythological quality of Neruda's long narrative conveys a message about material hope in a world that is doomed to fail if it follows only the old order.

Also in 1970, Neruda published *Las piedras del cielo*, which Manuel Durán and Margery Safir have called a "sister book" to *Las piedras de Chile*. Here, the object of the poet's contemplation is not the giant boulders of Chilean geography, but rather small rocks and stones, as well as precious formations: in "Cuando se toca el topacio" (When You Touch the Topaz), he writes, "Cuando se toca el topacio / el topacio te toca: / despierta el fuego suave / como si el vino en la uva / despertara" (When you touch the topaz / the topaz touches you: / the smooth fire awakens /as if the wine in a grape / came to life). In this book the poet again questions the natural world, seeking out every secret that the silent minerals hold. At the same time, Neruda reflects on humankind: his thoughts on stones are also observations about the difference between the solid, silent life of rocks and that of human beings. His identification with the natural world—expressed, for example, in "Yo soy este desnudo mineral" (I Am This Naked Mineral)—is total in these poems: "piedra fui: piedra oscura / y fue violenta la separación, / una herida en mi ajeno nacimiento: quiero volver / a aquella certidumbre, / al descanso central" (I was stone: dark stone / and the separation was violent, / a wound in my alien birth: / I want to return / to that certitude, / to that central repose).

In 1972 *Geografía infructuosa* was published. This book was begun in Chile and finished in France, during the year before his death, when Neruda suffered from his terminal illness. The poems included in this collection are personal, referring to trips and surgeries and landscapes he will not see again, as well as to the hope that still lingers in his heart, and they reflect an impending sense of finality to his days on earth. In "El cobarde" (The Coward) there is a contrast between the observed regenerative powers of nature and the ebbing out of life: "voy sin vivir, ya mineralizado, / inmóvil esperando la agonía, / mientras florece el territorio azul / predestinado de la primavera" (I go along without living, already mineralized, / immobile, waiting for the agony, / while the blue hills flower / with the first fated signs of spring). *Geografía infructuosa* prefigures the major themes in the posthumous works: not only the awareness of oncoming death contrasted with the cycle of the seasons, but also solitude. In this book Neruda affirms that his solitude is a special territory, a geography in which being and oneness become fused and confused. Because of these themes, and also because of the period in which it was written and published, *Geografía infructuosa* constitutes a link between the works of the late 1950s through the early 1970s and the posthumous volumes. It closes the "autumnal" cycle of Neruda's poetry and anticipates the "winter" cycle: the eight books published after the poet's death. As Robert Pring-Mill

Neruda in 1963, reading at a political rally in Arauco, Chile (photograph by Selim Mohor)

notes, the fact that Neruda chose *Jardín de invierno* (1974; translated as *Winter Garden,* 1986) as the title of one of the major posthumous works shows that with *Geografía infructuosa* he was fully aware of the end of one cycle and the opening of another, the final cycle in his life, with the works that followed.

In the latter part of 1973 Neruda was bedridden, dying of cancer, yet working on his memoirs and the eight books of poetry he planned to publish on his seventieth birthday, 12 July 1974. He had written appeals to his friends in Europe, in the Americas, and in the socialist countries, begging them to come to the aid of Chile, desperately trying to prevent the coup d'état that everyone knew was imminent. On 23 September 1973, twelve days after the coup that left General Augusto Pinochet ruling his beloved country, Neruda died. His houses were vandalized and ransacked.

Even though Neruda had been ill for more than a year, his death came somewhat unexpectedly. "What brought about his sudden collapse," Pring-Mill wrote in the 3 October 1975 issue of *TLS: The Times Literary Sup-*

plement, "was the shock of the coup and of Allende's death. The President had been a close friend of the poet, and his end in the government palace hit Neruda as hard as Lorca's murder in Spain had hit him at the outbreak of the Spanish Civil War. His failing health gave way. His funeral, protected by the presence of foreign journalists, was the only time dissenting voices could be raised in Chile in defiance of the new regime."

Two of the eight posthumous books, *El mar y las campanas* (translated as *The Sea and the Bells,* 1988) and *La rosa separada* (translated as *A Separate Rose,* 1985), were published shortly after Neruda's death in 1973. Matilde Neruda had been allowed by the new government to leave Chile in November of that year, taking with her the manuscripts of the unpublished poems and the drafts of *Confieso que he vivido* to the house of Neruda's friend Miguel Otero Silva in Caracas. According to Losada, Neruda's publisher, the poet wanted the works to appear in the following sequence: *La rosa separada; Jardín de invierno; 2000* (1974; translated, 1997); *El corazón amarillo* (1974; translated as *The Yellow Heart,*

1990); *Libro de las preguntas* (1974; translated as *The Book of Questions,* 1991); *Elegía* (1974; translated as *Elegy,* 1983); *El mar y las campanas;* and *Defectos escogidos* (Selected Defects, 1974). This arrangement was not followed, and in 1973 *El mar y las campanas* was the first to appear in print.

The posthumous books are a body of work that Neruda himself did not shape into its final form. All of these poems were salvaged from the ransacking of the poet's homes after his death (La Chascona in Santiago, La Sebastiana in Valparaíso, and Isla Negra). The poet had nearly finished work on these books, but there is no way of knowing whether he would have published all the poems that were found, and in what order. The eight books vary in content, mood, and quality, and yet they can be seen as a group. For the most part they are all short compositions; there is not any hint at monumental poems of the type found and gathered in *Memorial de Isla Negra,* for example. The movement toward personal poetry reaches its culmination in these works.

Neruda wrote many of these compositions at a country retreat in France, where he had used some of the Nobel Prize money to buy a converted slate mill at Condé-sur-Iton, in Normandy. He and Matilde gave this country refuge the name of La Manquel (a word meaning "female condor" in the Mapuche language of the Indians of southern Chile). The great oak beams of the old mill by the stream recalled other timber in his Chilean houses, for example, in his beloved Isla Negra. At La Manquel, he completed *Geografía infructuosa* and *La rosa separada.*

These eight volumes often touch private realms of Neruda's life, an existence that he contemplates in solitude and silence. His great companion is, as always, nature. Some poems are metaphysical or even existential at times. The poet seeks to renew his bond with nature and to meditate on his own life, as well as on man's relationship to the natural forces that surround him and outlast him. There is also a unity of mood in several of the posthumous volumes. Neruda is almost always alone, a solitary figure, and books such as *Jardín de invierno, El mar y las campanas,* and *Elegía* are often characterized by nostalgic meditation. *El mar y las campanas* and *Jardín de invierno,* moreover, are clearly written by a man who is aware of his impending death. He feels no fear or regret, however. Instead, an acceptance of destiny and a calm and tranquil mood pervades most of this poetry.

In *El mar y las campanas,* the first of the posthumous books to appear in print, the reader finds many of the great themes concerning human existence that Neruda explores in his other final works. The poet is taking account of his own life and his own being. The book is a collection of intimate personal poetry, and the two elements of the title signify two aspects of Neruda's communion with nature that were always important to him: the sea, the primeval force that intrigued him and fascinated him since his youth, and which had always been physically and poetically present in his life; and the bells, which might also represent communication with the natural world, a call to remember life, and an upcoming death knell.

The bells and the sea are also seen here to share a rhythm that once more recalls the life-cycle symbolism ever present in Neruda's poetry; as the dying out of one wave brings on the next, so the echo created as one bell dies out serves to usher in the clear ring of the next. For the poet the association is a close one, as he indicates in "[Perdón si por mis ojos]" ([Forgive Me If Through My Eyes]): "que yo soy una parte / del invierno, /de la misma extensión que se repite / de campana en campana en tantas olas / y de un silencio como cabellera, / silencio de alga, canto sumergido" (that I am a part / of winter / of the flat expanse that is repeated / from bell to bell in endless waves, / a particle of silence like a woman's hair, / a silence of seaweeds, a submerged song).

La rosa separada grew out of a trip Neruda made to Easter Island in January 1971, as part of a team working on a television documentary for Channel 13, the cultural television channel of Chile. The poet had been long fascinated with the island, a Chilean territory, and its huge stone statues, and he had included several poems on the subject in his *Canto general,* in the penultimate section, "El gran océano." Again, absorption in nature prevails—for example, in the fifth poem of "La isla" (The Island): "Todas las islas del mar las hizo el viento. / Pero aquí, el coronado, el viento vivo, el / primero, / fundó su casa, cerró las alas, vivió: desde la mínima Rapa Nui repartió sus / dominios" (All the islands in the ocean were built by the wind. / But it is here that the High One, the living wind, the first wind, / established his home, folded his wings, dwelled: it is from this small Rapa Nui that he organized his empire). At the same time, the series of poems titled "Los hombres" (The Men), is about the people who populate or visit this singular place: "Somos torpes los transeúntes, nos atropellamos / de codos, / de pies, de pantalones, de maletas, / bajamos del tren, del jet, de la nave, bajamos / con arrugados trajes y sombreros funestos" (All of us who walk around are clumsy people. Our elbows get in the way, / our feet, our trousers, our suitcases, / we get off the train, the jet plane, the ship, we come down / with our wrinkled suits and our sinister hats). The treatment of the topic of human beings in apposition to Nature is similar in this collection to what Neruda had done in *Las piedras de Chile.* Moreover, in *La rosa separada*

Neruda in Stockholm to accept the 1971 Nobel Prize in literature

Neruda documents despair over the condition of modern man and his pitiful state.

Jardín de invierno focuses, more than any other work in this group, on the poet's consciousness of the cycles of life and death as they unfold in the natural world. In "El egoísta" (The Egoist), one reads: "Esta es la hora / de las hojas caídas, trituradas / sobre la tierra, cuando / de ser y de no ser vuelven al fondo / despojándose de oro y de verdura / hasta que son raíces otra vez / y otra vez, demoliéndose y naciendo, / suben a conocer la primavera" (This is the hour / of fallen leaves, / crumbled and crumpled / on the earth, when / to be and to not be return to the depths / leaving behind the gold and the greenery / until they are roots once again / and once again, torn down and being born, / they move up to know the springtime). In one of the most frequently quoted verses from the series, "Con Quevedo, en primavera" (With Quevedo, in springtime), the poet's wishes are stated in regard to his conception of immortality: a life in the earth, like the autumn leaves that return to the unending cycle of dissolution and regeneration: "dame por hoy el sueño de las hojas / nocturnas, la noche en que se encuentran / los muertos, los meta-

les, las raíces, / y tantas primaveras extinguidas / que despiertan en cada primavera" (give me for today the sleep of nocturnal / leaves, the night in which we come face to face / with the dead, the metals, the roots, / and so many extinguished springtimes / that awaken in each springtime). Notable in these two poems, which exemplify the poet's mood of these last collections, is the absence of sadness. Neither death nor the winter is portrayed as a negative or threatening force, but with the essential optimism of one who has lived and understands how the cycles of life unfold.

While still reflecting the stance of a man taking account before death, *2000* is significantly different from *Jardín de invierno*. In this collection Neruda leaves behind lyrical meditations and contemplates contemporary reality, constructing a series of poems that constitute a commentary on the state of the world, as he imagines it will be in the year 2000. *2000* is the slimmest of the last volumes, and the poetry included therein is not the most memorable left by the poet. Again, the primary thematic concern, as illustrated in "La tierra" (The Earth), is despair over the condition of modern man: "y cada día salió el pan a saludarnos / sin importarle la sangre y la muerte que / vestimos los hombres, / la maldita progenie que hace la luz del / mundo" (every day bread would come out to greet us / ignoring the blood and death that we men always wear, / we who are both the accursed race and the light of the world).

El corazón amarillo, also from the same year, offers poetry with a tone that is irreverent, playful, and even nonsensical at times. The themes are often social satire, with strange and amusing anecdotes to illustrate the absurdity of social customs. An example is the poem "Una situación insostenible" (An Untenable Situation), centered on the extravagant figures that make up the Ostrogodo family. Much of their conversation revolves around dead relatives, until one day something unusual happens: "Entonces en aquella casa / de oscuros patios y naranjos, / en el salón de piano negro, / en los pasillos sepulcrales, / se instalaron muchos difuntos / que se sintieron en su casa" (To that mansion of dark courtyards and orange trees, / to that drawing-room with its black piano, / to the tomb-like corridors, / many ghosts came to stay, / feeling perfectly at home). *El corazón amarillo* is not a substantial book, the poetry being often more pleasant than remarkable.

El libro de las preguntas, also from 1974, is perhaps the simplest and yet the most complex of the eight posthumous works. It is literally a book of questions: every verse ends with a question mark, and they are strung together without any necessary relationship between them. For example, in "Poema IV": "Cuántas iglesias tiene el cielo? / Por qué no ataca el tiburón / a las impávidas sirenas? Conversa el humo con las nubes? / Es verdad que las esperanzas / deben regarse con rocío?" (How many churches does Heaven hold? / Why don't the sharks attack / the serene mermaids? / Does the smoke talk to the clouds? / Is it true that hope must be watered with dew?) In each verse of these riddles, one is dealing with the unanswerable questions of life. Neruda, close to his death, provides the reader access into how he sees the world, the questions of his accumulated years of observing reality.

Elegía is Neruda's last look at Soviet Russia. He had already written extensively on the subject, beginning with his "Oda a Stalingrad" (Ode to Stalingrad) in *Tercera residencia.* In the latter work he contemplates the country that for forty years had represented the center of his political ideology and ideals. *Elegía* is a sentimental journey through the Soviet Union: imagining a final walk through Moscow, Neruda recalls poets such as Vladimir Mayakovsky, Aleksandr Sergeevich Pushkin, and Nazim Hikmet. Above all, one finds in the book revolutionary nostalgia, the remembrance of antifascist struggles with his comrades in art. In comparison with *Las uvas y el viento,* a book of joyous discovery of social-ist solidarity, *Elegía* contemplates and laments the passage of time for the same places that he wandered around twenty or thirty years earlier.

Defectos escogidos is the last posthumous collection to appear in print. It was planned as a collection of faults, both Neruda's own and those of other people. Most critics agree that the book as it was published was not the book that had been intended, however. Only twelve of its nineteen poems fit the theme, and none in the collection is particularly impressive. Most of the poems are not of great interest or importance for an understanding of Neruda's work, and there are printing errors (such as repetitions of lines from one poem to the other). Two poems, however, can be salvaged: "Otro castillo" (Another Castle) and "Orégano" (Oregano). The second one is a fine example of a composition in the style and theme of the elementary odes: "hasta que me encontré sobre un andén / o en un campo recién estrenado / una palabra: *orégano,* / palabra que me desenredó / como sacándome de un laberinto. / No quise aprender más palabra alguna" (until I found on a railroad track / or perhaps it was a newly sown field / a word: *oregano.* / This word made me unwind, / as if guiding me out of a labyrinth. . . . / I refused to learn any more words).

The eight volumes of posthumous works constitute almost a microcosm, recalling aspects of almost all Neruda's previous books: nature, love, politics, and an exploration of reality through the physical elements of life. In these collections the poetry reflects the poet's bent toward both the private and public realms, although in maturity, his tendency is to seek solitude. Neruda knew he was dying as he wrote them, and he turns in to himself and to nature. He approaches death with serenity, taking comfort in his own concept of immortality: the eternal cycle of dissolution and renovation that the earth offers to all, including humans. In "[Ahí está el mar? . . .]" ([Is That Where the Sea Is? . . .]) in *El mar y las campanas* he asks for silence for the final encounter: "y ahora, nada más, quiero estar solo / con el mar principal y la campana. / Quiero no hablar por una larga vez, / silencio, quiero aprender aún, / quiero saber si existo" (and now, nothing more, I want to be alone / with the primary sea and with the bells. / I want to not speak for a very long time, / silence, I want to learn still, / I want to know if I exist). In this sense, Pablo Neruda's poetry reveals a deeply rooted, material spirituality that only deepened at the end of his days.

Letters:

Cartas a Laura (Madrid: Ediciones Cultura Hispánica del Centro Iberoamericano de Cooperación, 1978).

Interviews:

Rita Guibert, "Pablo Neruda: The Art of Poetry XIV," *Paris Review,* 51 (Winter 1971): 149–175;

Margarita Aguirre, "Entrevista con Pablo Neruda," *Hispania,* 57, no. 2 (March 1974): 367–369.

References:

Marjorie Agosín, *Pablo Neruda,* translated by Lorraine Roses (Boston: Twayne, 1986);

Margarita Aguirre, *Las vidas de Pablo Neruda* (Buenos Aires: Grijalbo, 1973);

Jaime Alazraki, "Pablo Neruda, the Chronicler of All Things," *Books Abroad,* 46 (1976): 49–54;

Fernando Alegría, "Reminiscences and Critical Reflections," translated by Deborah S. Bundy, *Modern Poetry Studies,* special Neruda issue, 5, no. 1 (Spring 1974): 41–50;

Amado Alonso, "From Melancholy to Anguish," translated by Enrique Sacerio Garí, *Review '74,* special "Focus/Residence on Earth" issue (Spring 1974): 15–19;

Janine Aranda and Angela Kling, eds., *Der Dichter ist kein verlorener Stein: Über Pablo Neruda* (Darmstadt: Luchterhand, 1981);

René de Costa, *The Poetry of Pablo Neruda* (Cambridge, Mass.: Harvard University Press, 1979);

Manuel Durán and Margery Safir, *Earth Tones: The Poetry of Pablo Neruda* (Bloomington: Indiana University Press, 1981);

John Felstiner, "Neruda in Translation," *Yale Review,* 61 (1972): 226–251;

Felstiner, "Nobel Prize at Isla Negra," *New Republic* (25 December 1971): 29–30;

Hernán Loyola, "Itinerario de Pablo Neruda y esquema bibliográfico," *Anales de la Universidad de Chile,* special "Estudios sobre Pablo Neruda" issue, 157–160 (January–December 1971): 9–28;

Luis Monguió, "Kingdom of This Earth: The Poetry of Pablo Neruda," *Latin American Literary Review,* 1, no. 1 (Fall 1972): 13–24;

Eduardo Neale-Silva, "Neruda's Poetic Beginnings," *Modern Poetry Studies,* special Neruda issue, 5, no. 1 (Spring 1974): 15–22;

Robert Pring-Mill, "The Winter of Pablo Neruda," *TLS: The Times Literary Supplement,* 3 October 1975, pp. 1154–1156;

J. Frank Riess, *The Word and the Stone: Language and Imagery in Neruda's Canto general* (London: Oxford University Press, 1972);

Eliana Rivero, "Análisis de perspectivas y significación de *La rosa separada,*" *Revista Iberoamericana,* 42 (1976): 459–472;

Emir Rodríguez Monegal, *El viajero inmóvil: Introducción a Pablo Neruda* (Buenos Aires: Losada, 1966);

Enrico Mario Santí, "Fuentes para el conocimiento de Pablo Neruda, 1967–1974," in *Simposio Pablo Neruda: Actas,* edited by Isaac Jack Lévy and Juan Loveluck (Long Island City, N.Y.: Las Américas, 1975), pp. 355–382;

Alain Sicard, "Neruda, ou la question sans réponse," *Quinzaine Littéraire,* 129 (16 November 1971): 13–14;

Eliana Suárez Rivero, *El gran amor de Pablo Neruda: Estudio crítico de su poesía* (Madrid: Plaza Mayor, 1971);

Suárez Rivero, "Simbolismo temático y titular en *Las manos del día,*" *Mester,* 4, no. 2 (1974): 75–81.

Papers:

Almost all of Pablo Neruda's writings are held by the Fundación Pablo Neruda, Santiago.

Eunice Odio
(1922? – 23 March 1974)

Luis A. Jiménez
Florida Southern College

BOOKS: *Los elementos terrestres* (Guatemala City: El Libro de Guatemala, 1948);

Zona en territorio del alba: Poesía 1946–1948 (San Rafael, Mendoza, Argentina: Brígadas Líricas, 1953);

El tránsito de fuego (San Salvador: Ministerio de Cultura, 1957);

El rastro de la mariposa (Mexico City: Finisterre, ca. 1960–1969); translated by Catherine G. Bellver as *The Trace of the Butterfly* in *Five Women Writers of Costa Rica,* edited by Victoria Urbano (Beaumont, Tex.: Lamar University Press, 1978), pp. 33–43;

En defensa del castellano (Mexico City: Finisterre, 1972);

Antología: Rescate de un gran poeta, edited by Juan Liscano (Caracas: Monte Avila, 1975);

Eunice Odio: Obras Completas, 3 volumes, edited by Peggy von Mayer (San José: Editorial de la Universidad de Costa Rica, 1996);

Los trabajos de la cathedral (Mexico City: Espacio, n.d.).

Collections: *Territorio del alba y otros poemas,* edited by Italo López Vallecillos (San José: Editorial Universitaria Centroamericana, 1974);

La obra en prosa de Eunice Odio, edited, with an introduction, by Rima de Vallbona (San José: Editorial Costa Rica, 1980).

Although known mostly as a poet, Eunice Odio also wrote in the epistolary genre, in addition to short stories and critical essays on art and literature. Despite her solid poetic production, she has gained little public attention among the Costa Rican public and literary critics. Her poetry appears in many Costa Rican and Latin American anthologies and has been the subject of a limited number of critical articles in journals and newspapers, but few scholarly books or monographs on her work have ever been published. Alfonso Chase, a fellow Costa Rican critic, attributes this lack of critical interest to the fact that the poet openly disdained the mediocrity she perceived in her motherland and its people by calling them "Costarrisibles" (Laughable Costa Ricans). Though it may seem a contradiction, Chase also asserted that Odio "pertenece desde siempre a

Eunice Odio

nuestra cultura por derecho propio" (always has belonged to our culture by her own rights). He adds that her poetry, short stories, and essays are a valuable legacy to Costa Rican literary history, despite the fact that they remain mostly unknown and unread in the country's colleges and universities.

A descendant of Basque, Navarrian, and Catalonian ancestors, Eunice Odio was born in San José, Costa Rica, but the exact date of her birth is unclear;

some critics point to 1919 and others to 1922. She was an adventurous and inquisitive child who, at the age of four, showed her independence by starting to run away from home periodically to wander through the streets of the capital. According to Odio's letters to editor Juan Liscano, she learned to read after only two days in school. At the age of nine she was afflicted with chicken pox and measles and became so weak that she was sent to recuperate at her relatives' ranch deep in the jungle. There she discovered her lasting love for nature. In early adolescence the poet began to assert her rebellious nature in formal settings, an attitude that promoted quarrels with other intellectuals. These character traits are also reflected in her poetry, particularly in the capricious disposition of the verses. In Rima de Vallbona's opinion, Odio shows "una actitud de rebeldía profesional, sin restricciones a la Poesía, soledad total y hasta autodestrucción" (an attitude of professional rebelliousness, without restriction to Poetry, total solitude, even self-destruction).

At age eleven Odio lost her mother, but even more traumatic than this event was the poet's arranged marriage as an adolescent, a marriage that only lasted three years. In one of her letters to Liscano, Odio lamented: "Me casé o me casaron a la edad de dieciséis años" (I married or they married me at the age of sixteen). This incident appears to be behind her representation of traditional women in their roles as homemakers, a constant in her works. Some of her early poems began to appear in 1947 in the Costa Rican academic journal *Repertorio Americano* (American Repertoire), under the pseudonym Catalina Mariel. Several other short poems written between 1945 and 1949 were included in Rosario de Padilla's *Antología de poetas costarricenses* (Anthology of Costa Rican Poets, 1956) and later collected in *Obras Completas* (Completed Works, 1996). Unhappy with her personal and intellectual life in Costa Rica, however, she moved to Guatemala in 1947.

Odio's first book of poems, *Los elementos terrestres* (Terrestial Elements), was published in Guatemala in 1947, and it won the Premio Centroamericano "15 de septiembre" (Central American Prize "15th of September") in 1948. Miguel Angel Asturias, Guatemalan winner of the 1967 Nobel Prize in literature, was a member of the jury that year. Odio's success in Guatemala and the indifference she had faced in her own country moved her to become a Guatemalan citizen in 1948.

Los elementos terrestres, structurally divided into eight "cantos," is a song to love in which the poetic voice progresses from a dream and distant love in the first song, "Posesión en el sueño" (Possession in dreaming), and in the second one, "Ausencia de amor" (Absence of love), to the search for the beloved. The third poem, "Consumación" (Consummation), expresses the desire for an amorous encounter and the pleasure of fusing with the other. The fourth canto, "Canción del esposo amado" (Song to the Loved One), describes in poetic detail the physical love between the speaker and Adam, her lover. In the fifth canto, "Esterilidad" (Sterility), the speaking subject addresses the failures of the barren woman, her lack of permanence, and her subsequent feeling of solitude. In contrast, the sixth canto, "Creación" (Creation), expresses the fertility of life, the plenitude in the process of creation, and the exaltation of the fruitful woman. This canto adheres to a biblical concept of the world, its divine origin, and its cosmic fate. The seventh canto, "Germinación" (Germination), speaks of integration by means of universal love. The eighth and last, untitled, canto returns to the origin of things as a unifying theme. Based on the biblical stories of Creation and Eve's Fall, the speaker is finally reunited with Adam, the loved one. In the introduction to *Obras completas* Peggy von Mayer observed that *Los elementos terrestres* is the beginning of Odio's ascension "hacia más altas cumbres y completa la imagen de su poesía amorosa. Siempre hay un trasfondo metafísico, una integración profundamente ontológica, que trasciende la simple sensación erótica" (toward taller summits and completes the image of her love poetry. There is always a metaphysical background, an integration deeply ontological, that transcends the simple erotic sensation).

From 1948 to 1953, while still living in Guatemala, Odio wrote *Zona en territorio del alba* (Zone in the Territory of Dawn, 1953) to represent Central America in the series Brígadas Líricas (Lyrical Brigades), published in Mendoza, Argentina. This book of poems is grouped under two rubrics: "Canciones para cantarse bajo el sol" (Songs to Be Sung under the Sun) and "Tras un ángel que bajó a la mañana" (After an Angel Who Came Down in the Morning). The first rubric of the book consists of a series of lucid poems accented with child-like memories from Odio's youth. The main objective of this poetic exercise is to re-create the sounds of words and the feelings of happiness expressed in children's songs. The second rubric underscores the metaphysical depth that characterizes the text as a whole. The primary focus is on Jesus Christ, especially the eucharistic symbol of bread.

Also in 1948, the poet began writing an extensive allegorical poem, *El tránsito de fuego* (Path of Fire). Critics have considered this text her most important work. She completed it in 1954 before departing from Guatemala and published it in San Salvador in 1957. The text consists of 456 pages.

El tránsito de fuego is divided into four main sections: "Integración de los padres" (Integration of Parents), "Proyecto de mí mismo" (My Own Project), "Proyecto de los frutos" (Project of Fruits), and "La alegría de los creadores" (The Creator's Happiness).

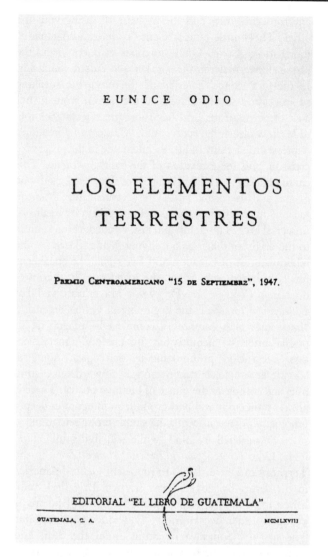

EUNICE ODIO

LOS ELEMENTOS
TERRESTRES

Premio Centroamericano "15 de Septiembre", 1947.

EDITORIAL "EL LIBRO DE GUATEMALA"

GUATEMALA, C. A.   MCMLXVIII

*Title page for Odio's first book, a song to love in eight
cantos published in 1948 (from Rima de Vallbone,
La obra en prosa de Eunice Odio, 1980)*

Each section is connected to the previous one through the recurrence of voices, themes, biblical myths, and mythological figures. Written in a dialogic form, the book was inspired by the prologue to the Gospel of St. John. The figure of Christ in Odio's text is not presented according to the Gospels, however, but rather as an autonomous and independent character linked to her own Christian esoteric belief. The protagonist, modeled after Odio's parents, is Ion. In the book, Ion is made synonymous with the Gospel through symbols representing water, light, and life. Elba D. Birmingham-Pokorny, in her essay "Busqueda y destierro: Un acercamiento a la escritura femenina de *Tránsito de fuego*" (Search and Banishment: An Approach to the Feminine Writing of *Path of Fire*) for the collection *La palabra innumerable: Eunice Odio ante la crítica* (The Innu-

merable Word: Eunice Odio in Front of the Critics, 2001), observed that in *El tránsito de fuego* Odio elaborates a discourse that portrays her identity and inner chaos. The poet's voice re-creates "el doloroso y solitario peregrinaje del hombre, del creador–de la humanidad–en búsqueda de sí mismo, de los otros, de Dios" (the painful and lonely pilgrimage of man, of the Creator–of humanity–in search of himself, others, God). Birmingham-Pokorny concluded that *El tránsito de fuego* is "un acto de fe en el poder mágico de las palabras" (an act of faith in the magic power of words).

Beginning immediately after Odio's arrival in Guatemala, she received many invitations to recite her poems. The Humanities Division of the Guatemalan Ministry of Aesthetic Education organized one of her first and most successful recitals, on 22 September 1947. She also began to publish in the journal *Cultura* (Culture) and to lecture on various topics in academic circles. Odio had moved to Guatemala to promote her poetic production and to widen her intellectual activities. In pursuit of this same goal she left Guatemala to travel through other Central American nations. In El Salvador she met Claudia Lars, with whom she established a friendship that lasted until Odio's death. Critics point out that these two women were the most innovative and universally appealing of female poets in Guatemala and El Salvador during the 1940s.

Odio's involvement with socialism started in Costa Rica and continued during her years in Guatemala. She became an ardent defender of leftist social and labor causes. In the late 1940s she became secretary for the Guatemalan Editorial Center of the Ministry of Public Education and a member of the Asociación Guatemalteca de Escritores y Artistas Revolucionarios (Guatemalan Association of Revolutionary Writers and Artists), or AGEAR, as well as of the writers of the SAKER-TI group, known as the "generación revolucionaria" (revolutionary generation), a group that edited several journals in which Odio often published. Her membership in SAKER-TI allowed her to communicate with the public and to broaden her reputation as an important Central American poetic voice.

What critics have called Odio's "aventura guatemalteca" (Guatemalan adventure) ended on 9 February 1954, when the poet moved to Mexico. Information about her stay in the Federal District as well as her stay in the United States the following year is scarce. The author's anti-American feelings, expressed while she was residing in New York, are widely known. She blamed the United States for a materialistic way of life that she considered disastrous from an ethical point of view. In contrast with this feeling, Odio loved New York, even though she called the city a "macho ciclópeo" (cyclopean macho). Despite the antagonistic attitude reflected in some of her poetry, she fuses the image of the Hudson River with a mythical vision of the Rio Grande of her childhood in Costa Rica. She also had visionary experiences while in New York, which are evident in her prose work. In an essay collected in *Obras completas,* Odio explains that she thought a great deal about "este extraño fenómeno de la curiosa transfiguración porque ha afectado mi vida entera en diversas formas" (this strange phenomenon of the curious transfiguration because it has affected my entire life in diverse ways).

Back in Mexico City in 1956, Odio met Fidel Castro. The poet's ideological change was evident when she published an article about the Cuban strongman. According to Mario A. Esquivel, some six years after meeting Castro, Odio called him a "viejo bailador de la danza soviética" (an old dancer of the Soviet dance). Esquivel adds in her defense that Odio had a passion for "la libertad, ya sea esta política, social o poética. Lo mismo ataca un Franco o un Somoza que a un Fidel Castro" (freedom, be it political, social or poetic. She attacks Franco or Somoza as well as Fidel Castro). After 1959 the poet broke away from some of her leftist ideals; as Liscano observed in the "Nota informativa" (Informative Note) to the 1975 *Antología: Rescate de un gran poeta* (Anthology: Rescue of a Great Poet), Odio "tenía una naturaleza apasionada, extrema, no desprovista de lucidez, tras el desencanto sufrido en la militancia ideológica" (had a passionate, extreme nature not exempt of lucidity, after the disenchantment she suffered in her ideological militancy).

Odio returned to Mexico City permanently in 1962 after another stay in New York. In Mexico she worked as a translator and journalist as a means of economic survival. During the subsequent years the writer's curiosity for mystery, paranormal experiences, the cabala, and the Rosicrucian Order was awakened. She claimed to be in the second "Grado Superior del Templo" (Superior Degree of the Temple). Odio's spiritual interests during these years are reflected in her literary production, for example in "Miguel Arcángel" (Michael the Archangel), a poem that was not published until 1966.

In 1962 Odio became a Mexican citizen. Her constant shifts in nationalities tended to cause confusion when she was introduced to an audience, as Esquivel noted: "en lugar de tener a Eunice Odio como costarricense se le solía presentar guatemalteca o . . . se le tenía por guatemalteca cuando ya era, por adopción, ciudadana mexicana" (instead of taking Eunice Odio for a Costa Rican she used to be introduced as Guatemalan or . . . she was taken for Guatemalan, when she already was, by naturalization, a Mexican citizen). Perhaps for this reason, many critics have called Odio

"ciudadana del mundo" (citizen of the world), as well as "apátrida" (countryless), a term that often appears in her poems. These epithets clearly depict the poet's wandering in and out of Costa Rica and her constant rejection of what she perceived as the provincial life in her land of origin.

Odio's life in Mexico soon became plagued by physical and spiritual vicissitudes, as well as by financial difficulties and alcohol addiction. In this respect, in a letter to Liscano of September 1975 included in *Antología,* Odio wrote that she could die unexpectedly because of "calvarios de crisis de salud física, que tanto aniquilan el cuerpo y la mente y el espíritu" (burdensome crises in physical health, that annihilate body, mind and spirit so much). Despite her ill health, Odio wrote two prose works during her final years in Mexico, *En defensa del castellano* (In Defense of the Castillian Language, 1972) and *El rastro de la mariposa* (translated by Catherine G. Bellver as *The Trace of the Butterfly* in *Five Women Writers of Costa Rica,* 1978).

Beginning in 1964 and until her death in 1974, Odio often collaborated in the prestigious Venezuelan journal *Zona Franca* (Free Zone). This collaboration led to an epistolary relationship with its editor, Liscano. Odio was found dead in her bathroom on 23 March 1974, some ten days after an apparent fall. Only a handful of friends attended the funeral in Mexico City. After her death Liscano published the letters she had written him in *Antología: Rescate de un gran poeta.*

Eunice Odio's poetic discourse has not yet been grasped by critics to its fullest extent. The poet herself foresaw this lack of recognition and acceptance by the public and critics at large. In a statement regarding lyric production in general, but which is equally applicable to her own poetic work, she underscored in a 1975 letter to Liscano that poetry and the poet are afflicted by a lack of identification. This allusion to her constant search for her true identity is a common thread in Odio's life and writings, and it is representative of the readers' and critics' misunderstandings of her works. This misunderstanding appears to be changing, however. In 2001 a collection of critical essays, *La palabra innumerable: Eunice Odio ante la crítica,* was published. This volume reveals the lyric dimension and literary significance of the poetry and prose of this Costa Rican author.

References:

Jorge Chen Sham and Rima de Vallbona, eds., *La palabra innumerable: Eunice Odio ante la crítica* (San José: Editorial de la Universidad de Costa Rica, 2001);

Mario A. Esquivel, *Eunice Odio en Guatemala* (San José: Instituto del Libro, 1983).

Olga Orozco
(17 March 1920 – 15 August 1999)

Constanza Gómez-Joines
Durham Technical Community College

BOOKS: *Desde lejos* (Buenos Aires: Losada, 1946);

Las muertes (Buenos Aires: Losada, 1951);

Los juegos peligrosos (Buenos Aires: Losada, 1962);

La oscuridad es otro sol (Buenos Aires: Losada, 1967);

Museo salvaje (Buenos Aires: Losada, 1974);

Cantos a Berenice (Buenos Aires: Sudamericana, 1977);

Mutaciones de la realidad (Buenos Aires: Sudamericana, 1979);

La noche a la deriva (Mexico City: Fondo de Cultura Económica, 1983);

En el revés del cielo (Buenos Aires: Sudamericana, 1987);

Con esta boca, en este mundo, selected, with an introduction, by Jacobo Sefamí (Mexico City: Universidad Autónoma Metropolitana, 1992);

También la luz es un abismo (Buenos Aires: Emecé, 1995).

Editions and Collections: *Las muertes. Los juegos peligrosos* (Buenos Aires: Losada, 1972);

Veintinueve poemas, introduction by Juan Liscano (Caracas: Monte Ávila, 1975);

Obra poética (Buenos Aires: Corregidor, 1979);

Antología (Buenos Aires: Centro Editor de América Latina, 1982);

Poesía: Antología, selected, with a prologue, by Telma Luzzani Bystrowicz (Buenos Aires: Centro Editor de América Latina, 1982);

Páginas de Olga Orozco seleccionadas por la autora, introduction by Cristina Piña (Buenos Aires: Celtia, 1984);

Antología poética (Madrid: Instituto de Cooperación Iberoamericana, 1985);

Olga Orozco: Antología poética (Buenos Aires: Fondo Nacional de las Artes, 1996);

Eclipses y fulgores: Antología (Barcelona: Lumen, 1998);

Talismanes: 27 poemas (Mexico City: Plaza & Janés, 1998).

Edition in English: *Engravings Torn from Insomnia: Selected Poems,* translated by Mary Crow (Rochester, N.Y.: BOA, 2002).

Olga Orozco is recognized as one of the greatest women poets in twentieth-century Spanish American

Olga Orozco

literature. She has written nine volumes of poetry, two works in prose, and one play. Her books have reached high sales numbers and have been read and studied extensively not only in Argentina, her place of birth, but in the United States and Europe as well. She has won many national and international literary prizes, the best-known of which are the Gran Premio de Honor de la Fundación Argentina para la Poesía (Great Honor Prize from the Argentine Poetry Foundation) in 1971; the Gran Premio del Fondo Nacional de las Artes (Great Prize from the National Arts Fund) in 1980; the Primer Premio de Poesía Esteban Echeverría (First Esteban Echeverría Poetry Prize) in 1981; the Primer Premio Nacional de Poesía (First National Poetry Prize) in 1988; the Gran Premio de Honor de la Sociedad Argentina de Escritores (Great Honor Prize from the Argentine Society of Writers) in 1989; the Premio Interamericano de Cultura "Gabriela Mistral" (Inter-American Cultural "Gabriela Mistral" Prize) and the Premio de Honor de la Academia Argentina de Letras (Argentine Liberal Arts Academy Honor Prize) in 1995; and the Premio Juan Rulfo (Juan Rulfo Prize) in 1998.

Concerning Orozco's life, scholars have had a difficult time collecting reliable biographical data. As Elba Torres de Peralta explains in *Spanish American Women Writers: A Bio-Bibliographical Source Book* (1990), "in countless interviews with the author, an attempt has been made to elucidate certain biographical details that would complement a comprehensive study of her texts. Her answers always allude to the fundamental motivation that constitutes the *numen* of her own vision of reality and of that space that contains the other. That *numen*, by its very nature, engenders a language that, without avoiding the questions, invariably represents the artistic efforts of the poet to reconstitute the 'neofantastic' world that she evokes through the word." Orozco repeatedly speaks of the spiritual force that motivates her writing, with answers that, like her poetry and fiction, re-create her own imaginative vision of the world while circumventing factual data and providing instead her own magical perception and experience of reality. As a result, biographical data is sketchy, and in many cases, specific temporal references are absent.

Olga Orozco was born in Toay, a small town in the province of La Pampa, Argentina, on 17 March 1920. Her father, Carmelo Gugliotta, was a Sicilian who arrived in Argentina in the 1900s, bought fields and woodlands in La Pampa, and set up a logging and sawmill operation. He married Olga's mother, Cecilia Orozco, a young woman from the nearby village of Santa Rosa, and together they had a son and three daughters. Orozco spent most of her childhood in Toay, in an affluent household with her parents, sisters, aunt, grandmother, and a brother who died in childhood. In interviews Orozco fondly remembers herself as a curious child with a heightened sensibility inspired by the landscapes of Toay; in a conversation coordi-

nated by Antonio Requeni and published in *Travesías: Conversaciones* (Journeys: Conversations, 1997), she describes her beloved native village as a place that looks "casi suizo por lo prolijo y lo bien delineado, pero cuando yo era chica era un lugar con rebeldes entrecruzamientos de ramajes, con montes, espacios desiertos, arenales misteriosos" (almost Swiss because of its meticulous and well-delineated appearance, but when I was a child it was a place where branches intertwined rebelliously, with hills, empty spaces, mysterious sand dunes). Her childhood experiences in Toay became much of her literary subject matter.

In 1928, at age eight, Orozco and her family moved to Bahía Blanca, where, at age ten, she wrote her first "organized" poem. Then, in 1936, her family moved to Buenos Aires, where she graduated from the teacher's school Normal Sarmiento in 1937 with a teaching degree. The following year she began her university studies, never to complete them, in the Faculty of Liberal Arts at the University of Buenos Aires. During this time she published her first poem in *Péñola* (Quill Pen), the student center magazine. In 1940 she became involved with the magazine *Canto* (Song), in which she published a few poems. Although only two issues of *Canto* were ever published, this magazine remains of utmost importance to Orozco's career, as it links her to the group of poets known as the "generación del cuarenta" (the generation of 1940). This group included Argentine intellectuals such as Daniel Devoto, Enrique Molina, Juan Rodolfo Wilcock, Julio Marsagot, and Miguel Ángel Gómez.

Although Orozco is said to form part of the generación del cuarenta, a denomination that defines her as a neo-Romantic poet, many critics argue that this categorization is only useful from a chronological standpoint, as it points to a group of Argentine writers writing at the same time and sharing the same social, political, literary, and historical context. Concerning her subject matter and style, however, Orozco resists categorization. Her poetry is highly original as it transforms immediate experience and reality into a magical and dream-like world of metaphysical inquiry. In her acceptance speech for the National Arts Fund Prize in 1980, reproduced in *Páginas de Olga Orozco seleccionadas por la autora* (Pages of Olga Orozco Selected by the Author, 1984), she explains: "el acto creador se convierte, en uno y otro caso, en arco tendido hacia el conocimiento, en ejercicio de transfiguración de lo inmediato" (the creative act becomes, time and time again, an arch laid out toward knowledge, an exercise in the transfiguration of the immediate). In the same speech she compares the role of the poet to that of an intermediary—an idea upheld by her symbolist predecessors—as she explains that the poet helps "las grandes

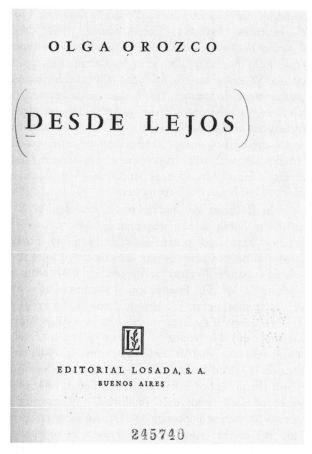

O L G A   O R O Z C O

(DESDE LEJOS)

EDITORIAL LOSADA, S. A.
BUENOS AIRES

245740

Title page for Orozco's first book (1946), a collection of poems that wistfully evoke people and places from her past (University of Kentucky Library)

catarsis, a mirar juntos el fondo de la noche, a vislumbrar la unidad en un mundo fragmentado por la separación y el aislamiento" (the great catharses, to look together into the depths of the night, to help discern the unity in a world fragmented by separation and isolation). Therefore, for Orozco, poetry is a means for self-exploration and understanding in an attempt to find a sense of unity and transcendence; her verses are detached from any sociopolitical context.

Shortly after her involvement with the magazine *Canto,* at age twenty Orozco married Gómez, the first of her two husbands; they never had any children. Like her, he was a poet of the generación del cuarenta and was a great source of inspiration for Orozco. In the years following her marriage, she worked for Radio Municipal (Municipal Radio) making commentaries on Argentine and Spanish classical theater. During this period of time, her friend Gonzalo Losada published her first book of poetry, *Desde lejos* (From Afar, 1946).

Desde lejos establishes Orozco's highly metaphorical style with poems that are nostalgic evocations and remembrances of times past. In "Quienes rondan la niebla" (Those Who Patrol the Fog) the speaker looks back to "los seres que fui" (the beings that I have been), an image that establishes the inherent multiplicity of the self. The speaker relives past experiences and intuitions, evoking dream-like and surrealistic landscapes suggestive of her beloved Pampa–a place of strong winds, sand dunes, foliage, meadows, plains, and hills. In some poems–"La abuela" (The Grandmother), "Para Emilio en su cielo" (For Emilio in His Heaven), and "Cuando alguien se nos muere" (When One of Us Dies)–she remembers deceased loved ones. In others, the speaker mourns familiar places that no longer exist; for example, in "'1889' (Una casa que fue)" ("1889" [A House That Once Was]) she exclaims: "Sólo quedan en pie las mudas escaleras que ascienden y descienden prolongando el corredor desierto, / los pálidos vestigios de los recintos desaparecidos / cuyas lápidas yacen al amparo piadoso de otros mundos" (Nothing remains but the silent stairs, up and down, extending the empty hall, / the bleached relics of vanished grounds / whose memorial stones lie under the solemn protection of other worlds). The poetic voice, filled with metaphysical anguish, reflects on the irreversible passage of time, described in "Flores para una estatua" (Flowers for a Statue) as the cause of that "triste decaer de las cosas terrestres" (the sad decay of earthly things). She is intensely aware of the transitoriness of life, described in "Quienes rondan la niebla" as "un resplandor de arena pasajera" (a splendor of passing sand). She refuses, however, to believe that human beings will dissolve into forgetfulness and oblivion; man will transcend, like her grandmother, who, in "La abuela," "nos mira ya desde la verdadera realidad de su rostro" (watches us from the true reality of her face).

After her contract as a commentator for Radio Municipal was over, the station offered her a job as a radio actress; she accepted and assumed the character of Mónica Videla. She held this job from 1947 to 1954 and simultaneously worked at another radio station, Radio Splendid. During this period of her life, Orozco published her second book, *Las muertes* (The Deaths, 1951). The poems in *Las muertes* intertextually evoke and re-create the deaths of many literary characters. The book is composed of seventeen poems, of which the first, with the same name as the collection, serves as the introduction. In this poem the poetic voice describes these dead characters as "los muertos sin flores" (the dead without flowers), that is, forgotten characters who "no nos legaron cartas, ni alianzas, ni retratos / . . . / Sus vidas se cumplieron sin honor en la tierra, / mas su destino fue fulmíneo como un tajo" (did not bequeath us letters, alliances, or portraits / . . . / Their lives were realized without honor on earth / and their destiny was fulminant like a slash). She sings the deaths of characters such as Gail Hightower, a figure in William Faulkner's *Light in August* (1932); Christoph Detlev Brigge, a character in Rainer Maria Rilke's *Aufzeichnungen des Malte Laurids Brigge* (1910; translated as *The Notebooks of Malte Laurids Brigge*, 1930); Maldoror, from the Comte de Lautréamont's *Les Chants de Maldoror* (The Songs of Maldoror, 1868–1869); Miss Havisham, from Charles Dickens's *Great Expectations* (1861); and Bartleby, from Herman Melville's tale "Bartleby, the Scrivener" (1853). The collection ends with a poem by the name of "Olga Orozco" in which the poet fictionalizes her own death. Throughout the volume the poetic voice points to an identification of humanity with these characters as she explains in the poem " . . . Lievens" that "Somos tantos en otros, que acaso es necesario desenterrar del fondo de cada corazón el semblante distinto" (We are so many in others, that it might be necessary to disinter from the depths of each heart the different double). These characters reach archetypal proportions as "sus muertes son los exasperados rostros de nuestra vida" (their deaths are the exasperated faces of our life), as Orozco writes in the first poem in the collection, "Las muertes" (The Deaths).

In 1962 Orozco published her third volume of poetry, *Los juegos peligrosos* (Dangerous Games). This volume is considered to be a milestone in her career and is described by Juan Liscano, in his introduction to *Veintinueve poemas* (Twenty-Nine Poems, 1975) as Orozco's richest book in dream materials, in memory, in anticipation, in symbols, in metaphors and images, in personal experience, in absences and nostalgias, in knowledge, and in opening to the otherworldly. In an oracular tone the speaker engages in an anguished questioning and exploration of that which lies beyond immediate reality in the hopes of unlocking the mystery of existence. In "La cartomancia" (Cartomancy) she resorts to tarot cards and astrology; in "Espejos a distancia" (Faraway Mirrors) she engages in a play of specular images; in "Repetición del sueño" (Repetition of the Dream) she plunges into dreams—a world of transformation; in "Para hacer tu talismán" (To Make Your Talisman) she provides a recipe for, and engages in, an esoteric ritual; in "Si me puedes mirar" (If You Can Look at Me) she communicates with the dead as she summons and questions her deceased mother; and in "Para destruir a la enemiga" (To Destroy the Enemy) she exorcizes the enemy, presumably death personified, by means of the act of naming. Throughout, questions such as "¿Quién soy? ¿Y dónde? ¿Y cuándo?" (Who am I? And where? And when?), as found in "Para ser otra" (To Be Another), attest to the speaker's quest for self-definition and understanding.

As in *Desde lejos,* the speaker of *Los juegos peligrosos* views the self as plural, dynamic, and irreducible; in "Sol en Piscis" (Sun in Pisces), a poem that explores Orozco's own astrological sign, the speaker describes herself as a collective entity encompassing the one "que ya fui" (that I have already been) and the one "que no he sido en éste y otros mundos" (that I have not been in this and other worlds). Furthermore, as in *Las muertes,* the speaker identifies herself with humanity as a whole; thus, in "Desdoblamiento en máscara de todos" (Unfolding into Every Person's Mask), she explains that "desde adentro de todos cada historia sucede en todas partes" (from inside all of us every story happens everywhere). For the speaker, this sense of identification between self and humanity is the result of mankind's shared condition and a history that began with man's creation and his Fall—the organizing metaphor of *Los juegos peligrosos.*

In "La caída" (The Fall) Orozco appropriates the story of Genesis and explores the biblical notion of man's dichotomous nature of body and soul—a constant in her work. The body, in the poem, is metaphorically represented as an "estatua de sal" (salt statue) and the soul is the "estatua del azul" (statue of the blue); the speaker mourns the loss of her celestial and prelapsarian condition: "Estatua del azul: yo no puedo volver. / Me exilaste de ti para que consumiera tu lado tenebroso" (Statue of the blue: I cannot return. / You exiled me from you so that I would consume your dark side). The speaker feels imprisoned and confined by her body, which is described as "la señal del exilio" (the sign of exile); in "Espejos a distancia" she describes the body as "Carne desconocida, / . . . / carne absorta, arrojada a la costa por el desdén del alma / Yo no entiendo esta piel con que me cubren para deshabitarme" (Unknown flesh / . . . / flesh engrossed in itself, hurled to the side by the soul's disdain / I don't understand this skin they cover me with in order to evict me). Carnal or earthly existence limits the access of the poetic voice to transcendental knowledge; it is the condition that results from man's creation and expulsion from the Garden of Eden.

Although the speaker of *Los juegos peligrosos* continually mourns her sense of isolation and fragmentation caused by man's fall from God, she feels, nevertheless, a sense of hope. For the speaker, as explained in "Desdoblamiento en máscara de todos," man is but a fragment of an all-encompassing unity: "Desde adentro de todos no hay más que una morada bajo un friso de máscaras" (From inside all of us there is nothing but a dwelling under a facade of masks). More specifically, all men are fragments of a mutilated and incomplete God:

Orozco (front) and her friend, the Argentine poet Alejandra Pizarnik, in Paris, 1962

"Cualquier hombre es la versión en sombras de un Gran Rey herido en su costado" (Any man is a shadow version of a Great King wounded in his side). God, however, will soon mend the fragments and reunite man's pieces, attaining the paradisiacal unity so much desired: "Es víspera de Dios. / Está uniendo en nosotros sus pedazos" (It is the day before God. / He is uniting his pieces in us); these verses conclude the volume and reflect the poet's faith in finding a sense of wholeness and transcendence.

In 1965, three years after the publication of *Los juegos peligrosos,* Orozco began to work as a journalist for the magazine *Claudia,* publishing under different pseudonyms. She held this job until 1974. During this time she published her first narrative work, *La oscuridad es otro sol* (Darkness Is Another Sun, 1967). In *Travesías* Orozco explains that this book surfaced as a result of therapy sessions conducted by her psychologist, Fernando Pagés Larraya. At his urging she began writing down dreams and random memories of her childhood and

youth. After reading these, Pagés Larraya suggested that if the material were ordered and revised she would have a book. Following his suggestion, Orozco wrote *La oscuridad es otro sol.* Told from the perspective of a young narrator named Lía, the narrative blurs the boundaries between fiction and reality as Orozco's vivid imagination transforms autobiographical anecdotes, creating a world where the supernatural is part of everyday reality.

Although no specific temporal reference is readily available, it may be deduced that some time after the publication of *La oscuridad es otro sol* Orozco met her second husband, the architect Valerio Peluffo, at the Argentine embassy in Paris. They spent twenty-five years together until his death in the 1990s. In *Travesías* she describes their marriage as a powerful and mystical union that transcended the boundaries of time and space. In the same published conversations Orozco reveals that she never felt the need to be a mother; furthermore, she explains that in her first marriage she did not have the stability needed to raise a child, and that in her second marriage she felt too old.

In 1974 Orozco published her next volume of poetry, *Museo salvaje* (Wild Museum). If *Los juegos peligrosos* explores the otherworldly, *Museo salvaje* explores the concrete as the speaker engages in an interrogation of her body as microcosm. In an interview by Jill S. Kuhnheim, translated in her book *Gender, Politics, and Poetry in Twentieth-Century Argentina* (1996), Orozco explains that all throughout her life she has had moments in which she has felt an overwhelming and sudden feeling of strangeness of her own body and its impossibility to contain, represent, and express her. She views the body as the phenomenon that makes life possible and limits it at the same time. She then explains that when she wrote *Museo salvaje* she was going through a more objective stage that enabled her to submerge herself to the depth of her tissues, viscera, and eyes, thus enabling her to give birth to the poems in the volume. Interestingly, in the same interview, Orozco explains that shortly after writing the poem about the eye, "En la rueda solar" (On the Solar Wheel), she went to the ophthalmologist and was diagnosed with high eye pressure; after writing the poem about the blood, "Corre sobre los muelles" (It Runs On the Piers) she was diagnosed with diabetes; and after writing the poem about the skeleton, "Mi fósil" (My Fossil) she found out that she had arthrosis.

Museo salvaje is composed of an introductory poem, "Génesis," and sixteen additional ones each dedicated to the body or to its different components: entrails, heart, head, hands, hair, eyes, sex organs, skin, ears, feet, nose, body tissues, skeleton, mouth, and blood. The first poem establishes the semantic content of the volume as it rewrites the biblical story of Genesis, culminating in mankind's creation: "y el alma descendió al barro luminoso para colmar la forma semejante a su imagen, / y la carne se alzó como una cifra exacta, / como la diferencia prometida entre el principio y el final" (and the soul descended into the luminous mud in order to fill the shape similar to its image, / and the flesh arose like an exact number / like the promised difference between the beginning and the end). These verses represent the moment in which the soul, severed from complete union with God, is thrust into mortality and carnal existence–a condition explored throughout the rest of the volume.

For the speaker, the body represents an obstacle, as it is the container that imprisons her soul and obstructs her connection with primordial unity and knowledge; as described in "Lamento de Jonás" (Jonas's Moan), it is a "guardián opaco que me transporta y me retiene / y me arroja consigo en una náusea desde los pies a la cabeza" (opaque sentinel that transports and retains me / and throws me into nausea from

head to toe). Images of enclosure, imprisonment, and separation from divine unity abound. In "Tierras en erosión" (Eroding Lands) her body tissues are witness to "esta noche de pájaro en clausura donde caigo sin fin, remolino hacia adentro" (this night like a caged bird in which I fall endlessly, inward swirl); in "Plumas para unas alas" (Feathers for Wings) she is but "un metro sesenta y cuatro de estatura sumergido en la piel / lo mismo que en un saco de obediencia y pavor. / Cautiva en esta piel" (one meter sixty-four in height submerged in the skin / just as a sack of obedience and dread. / Captive in this skin); in "Lugar de residencia" (Place of Residence) the heart is "como un pájaro en exilio, en la jaula del pecho" (like an exiled bird, in the cage of the chest); and in "El sello personal" (Personal Stamp) her feet are her "error de nacimiento, / mi condena visible a volver a caer una vez más" (birth error, / my visible sentence to fall once again). In "Animal que respira" (Animal That Breathes), however, the speaker is momentarily able to break free from the constraints of the body as she finds herself in symbiotic unity with the universe: "Aspirar y exhalar. Tal es la estratagema en esta mutual transfusión con todo el universo" (Inhaling and exhaling. Such is the stratagem in this mutual transfusion with the universe). These individual poems represent Orozco's attempt to understand and overcome the boundaries and limitations imposed by the body.

Orozco wrote her next volume, *Cantos a Berenice* (Songs to Berenice, 1977), after the death of her beloved cat, which she had for fifteen and a half years. The poems celebrate and portray Berenice as both a domestic animal and an otherworldly presence. In "Canto IV" the feline is described as the emissary of a remote zone; in "Canto V" she is the household goddess; and in "Canto XII," the interpreter of an impossible oracle. Furthermore, Berenice is the sacred embodiment of mythical and divine figures; for example, in "Canto V" she is the reincarnation of the Egyptian queen of Bubastis, while later in the same poem she becomes the embodiment of other Egyptian mythological figures such as Bastet and Bast. Throughout, the poet-speaker explores her relationship with this mythical being and establishes an irreducible identity with her. In "Canto X" the poet refers to the feline as "tú, mi otra yo misma en la horma hechizada de otra piel" (you, my other my self in the bewitched mold of another skin), once again establishing the inherent multiplicity of the self.

The last two cantos, XVI and XVII, are specifically dedicated to Berenice's death and include several allusions to the act of writing as an attempt to keep the cat and her memory of it alive. Thus, "Canto XVI" expresses her fear that her poems might not successfully inscribe the living image of her beloved feline: "Y qué cárcel tan pobre elegirías / si te quedaras ciega, ple-

*Paperback cover for Orozco's 1987 poetry collection, in which she displays a willingness
to accept limitations instead of engaging in a desperate outcry against them
(San Diego State University Library)*

gada entre los bordes mezquinos de este libro / como
una humilde flor, como un pálido signo que perdió su
sentido" (And what poor prison would you choose / if
you were left blind, and folded in the miserable edges of
this book / like a humble flower, like a pale sign that lost
its sense); she wonders if she may find Berenice in the
writings of other great authors: "¿No hay otro cielo allá
para buscarte? / ¿No hay acaso un lugar, una mágica
estampa iluminada, / en esas fundaciones de papel
transparente que erigieron los grandes, / . . . / Kipling,
Mallarmé, Carroll, Eliot o Baudelaire, / para alojar a
otras indescifrables criaturas como tú . . . ?" (Isn't there
another heaven in which to look for you? / Isn't there a
place, a magical illuminated image / in those foundations of transparent paper that the greats have founded
/ . . . / Kipling, Mallarmé, Carroll, Eliot or Baudelaire, /
in order to house other undecipherable creatures like
you . . . ?). Similarly, in "Canto XVII" the poet equates
her to the dead characters of her own book *Las muertes:*

"Tal vez seas ahora tan inmensa como todos mis muertos" (Perhaps you are now as great as all my dead
ones); she hopes that Berenice, like the literary characters in *Las muertes,* will live on, heroically, in the pages of
her book. These allusions to the act of writing itself and
to the power of literature increase in Orozco's later
books.

As she approached sixty years of age, Orozco
wrote *Mutaciones de la realidad* (Mutations of Reality,
1979) and initiated an exploration of her existential and
poetic trajectory. The emphasis of this book is on
self-examination as the poet looks to her own career,
one that she perceives as a disappointment and, in
many cases, a failure; the titles of many of the poems
reflect a sense of struggle and defeat: "Remo contra la
noche" (I Row Against the Night), "Rehenes de otro
mundo" (Hostages of Another World), "Los reflejos
infieles" (Unfaithful Reflections), "La imaginación abre
sus vertiginosas trampas" (Imagination Opens Its Ver-

tiginous Traps), and "Densos velos te cubren, Poesía" (Thick Veils Cover You, Poetry). The latter poem specifically alludes to the poetic act and considers the limitations of language and the failure of poetry as a means for finding transcendence and unity; the poem concludes: "¡Un puñado de polvo, mis vocablos!" (My words, a handful of dust!). Nowhere before this volume does Orozco express such a sense of futility and impossibility in reaching the prelapsarian unity she so much desires; as Cristina Piña explains in her introduction to *Páginas de Olga Orozco, Mutaciones de la realidad* is an inventory of failure and loss. Interspersed throughout, however, are hints of faith and optimism. For example, in one poem dedicated to a deceased poet and friend, Alejandra Pizarnik, the poetic voice exclaims: "en el fondo de todo hay un jardín. / Ahí está tu jardín" (In the end of everything there is a garden. / There is your garden).

Four years after the publication of *Mutaciones de la realidad,* Orozco published her next volume, *La noche a la deriva* (Night Adrift, 1983). This book reflects her life-long love for the visual arts; it is rich in visual imagery and includes poems dedicated to artists and paintings— "'Botines con lazos', de Vincent Van Gogh" ("Boots with Laces," by Vincent Van Gogh), and "Hieronymus Bosch en desusada compañía" (Hieronymus Bosch in Extraordinary Company)—as well as allusions to other painters, such as Ambrogio Lorenzetti and his painting, described as "El buen y el mal gobierno" (The Good and the Bad Government) in "Surgen de las paredes" (They Emerge out of the Walls).

Thematically, *La noche a la deriva* may be grouped together with Orozco's last two volumes, *En el revés del cielo* (On the Other Side of Heaven, 1987), and *Con esta boca, en este mundo* (With This Mouth, in This World, 1992), as all three evince a new and more mature posture. As in *Mutaciones de la realidad,* the poetic voice of the final three volumes engages in a retrospective exploration of her poetic trajectory. No longer, however, do the poems express a desperate outcry against limitations and struggles; instead, the poet appears to have come to terms with these limitations. For example, in "Para un balance" (To Reach a Balance), from *La noche a la deriva,* the speaker recapitulates her turbulent poetic career and optimistically concludes: "Tal vez haya ganado por la medida de la luz que te alumbra, / por la fuerza voraz con que me absorbe a veces un reino nunca visto y ya vivido, / por la señal de gracia incomparable que transforma en milagro cada posible pérdida" (Perhaps I have won because of the degree of light that enlightens you, / because of the voracious strength with which a kingdom never seen and already lived absorbs me, / because of the incomparable signal of grace that transforms each possible loss into a miracle). Similarly, "Con esta boca, en este mundo" (With This Mouth, in This World), a poem that begins the volume by the same name, recapitulates the speaker's poetic career: "He dicho ya lo amado y lo perdido, / trabé con cada sílaba los bienes y los males que más temí perder. / . . . / Hemos Ganado. Hemos perdido" (I have already said that which has been loved and lost, / I have fixed with each syllable the good and the evil that I was most scared to lose. / . . . / We have won. We have lost). The message is obvious: although it has been a trying and difficult voyage, the speaker has reached a sense of peaceful resignation. Along the same lines, in poems such as "Catecismo animal" (Animal Catechism), from *En el revés del cielo,* the speaker appears to come to terms with her body and the limitations it imposes. Although she still perceives it as an obstacle to transcendence, she goes so far as to defend it: "esta humilde morada donde el alma insondable se repliega" (this humble dwelling where my unfathomable soul retreats).

Another theme present in all three of her last volumes is Orozco's keen awareness of her imminent death: in "¿Lugar de residencia?" (Place of Residence?) the poetic voice exclaims: "despierto cada día sólo asida a mi muerte" (I wake up every day holding only to my death). As in her earlier works, images of sand and dust as representations of death abound. Strangely, her longing to transcend this world seems contradictory to her fear of death. In the interview in *Travesías* Orozco admits that she is afraid of death; when asked as to the reason she replies: "No me cabe la nada. No puedo pensar que después de la muerte hay nada. Debo de tener algún nudo de duda y entonces me veo presenciando mi propia nada en un relámpago, y eso es lo que me hace sentir terror" (I can't understand the concept of nothingness. I can't believe that nothingness is what happens after death. I must have some doubt and I therefore witness my own nothingness in a flash, and that is what makes me feel terrified). In the concluding poem of *La noche a la deriva,* "Cantata sombría" (Somber Cantata), the speaker rebelliously stands up to death, refusing to die. On two occasions the poetic voice exclaims: "me resisto a morir" (I resist to die); in the concluding line she questions "¿Y habrá estatuas de sal del otro lado?" (Will there be salt statues on the other side?), an interrogation that uses the familiar image of the salt statue and all that it represents—carnal and terrestrial existence—to indicate her desire to stay linked, in some way, to her earthly condition. She has learned to love the existence she consistently tries to escape.

In addition, all three volumes revisit themes found in her previous books: exile and separation from paradisiacal unity, the transitoriness of life, the passage of time, death, the inability of language to act as a means for transcendence, the multiplicity of the self, and metaphysical uncertainty in general. More specifically, there is a sense of the unrecoverable nature of people and times past. In the final volume Orozco dedicates a poem to the death of her beloved second husband, Peluffo, in which the speaker nostalgically exclaims: "Ah, si pudiera encontrar en las paredes blancas de la hora más cruel / esa larga fisura por donde te fuiste" (Oh, if I could only find in the white walls of time's most cruel hour / that fissure through which you left). Faced with the awareness of the fleetingness of life and with her own imminent death, the poet concludes her poetic trajectory with the request "Madre, madre, / vuelve a erigir la casa y bordemos la historia. Vuelve a contar mi vida" (Mother, mother, / build the house again and let's embroider the story. Recount my life again), in the hopes of reliving the fiction that is life and poetry.

In 1995 Orozco published *También la luz es un abismo* (Light Is Also an Abyss), her second and final narrative work. Written during the last decade of her life, this book serves as a sequel to *La oscuridad es otro sol;* like its predecessor, it blurs the boundaries between fiction and reality, recounting autobiographical anecdotes and experiences of her childhood from the point of view of the young narrator Lía.

On 15 August 1999 Olga Orozco died at age seventy-nine from circulatory problems after a two-month hospitalization. She was buried in a private cemetery in Pilar, Buenos Aires. In addition to nine volumes of poetry, two works in prose, and one play, she left behind fourteen other editions and collections that prove her literary success; she continues to be remembered as one of the greatest poets in Spanish American literature.

Interviews:

Jill S. Kuhnheim, "Interview in Buenos Aires, October 13, 1988," in her *Gender, Politics, and Poetry in Twentieth-Century Argentina* (Gainesville: University Press of Florida, 1996), pp. 161–173;

Antonio Requeni, *Travesías: Conversaciones* (Buenos Aires: Sudamericana, 1997);

Asunción Horno-Delgado, "Entrevista con Olga Orozco 'La poesía es un ejercicio de auto-humildad; ayuda a contemplar al otro, a acompañarlo,'" *Hispanic Poetry Review,* 1 (May 1999): 90–101.

References:

Stella Maris Colombo, *Metáfora y cosmovisión en la poesía de Olga Orozco* (Rosario, Argentina: Cuadernos Aletheia de Investigación y Ensayo, 1983);

Ana María Fagundo, "La poesía de Olga Orozco o la aproximación a lo indecible," in her *Literatura Femenina de España y las Américas* (Madrid: Fundamentos, 1995), pp. 209–219;

Jill S. Kuhnheim, "Cultural Affirmations: The Poetry of Olga Orozco and T. S. Eliot," *Confluencia: Revista Hispánica de Cultura y Literatura,* 5 (Fall 1989): 39–50;

Kuhnheim, "Unsettling Silence in the Poetry of Olga Orozco and Alejandra Pizarnik," *Monographic Review: Hispanic Women Poets,* 6 (1990): 258–273;

Elba Torres de Peralta, *La poética de Olga Orozco: Desdoblamiento de Dios en máscara de todos* (Madrid: Playor, 1987).

Nicanor Parra

(5 September 1914 –   )

Linda S. Maier
University of Alabama in Huntsville

BOOKS: *Cancionero sin nombre* (Santiago: Nascimento, 1937);

Poemas y antipoemas (Santiago: Nascimento, 1954)– includes *Manifiesto;* excerpts translated by Jorge Elliott as *Anti-poems* (San Francisco: City Lights Books, 1960);

La cueca larga (Santiago: Editorial Universitaria, 1958); enlarged as *La cueca larga y otros poemas,* edited by Margarita Aguirre and Juan Agustín Palazuelos (Buenos Aires: Editorial Universitaria de Buenos Aires, 1964);

Pablo Neruda y Nicanor Parra: Discursos, by Parra and Pablo Neruda (Santiago: Nascimento, 1962); translated, with an introduction, by Marlene Gottlieb as *Pablo Neruda and Nicanor Parra Face to Face: A Bilingual and Critical Edition of Their Speeches on the Occasion of Neruda's Appointment to the Faculty of the University of Chile* (Lewiston, Pa.: Edwin Mellen Press, 1997);

Versos de salón (Santiago: Nascimento, 1962);

Canciones rusas (Santiago: Editorial Universitaria, 1967);

Obra gruesa (Santiago: Editorial Universitaria, 1969);

Los profesores (New York: Antiediciones Villa Miseria, 1971);

Artefactos, illustrations by Guillermo Teieda (Santiago: Ediciones Nueva Universidad, 1972);

Emergency Poems, translated by Miller Williams (New York: New Directions, 1972);

Sermones y prédicas del Cristo de Elqui (Santiago: Universidad de Chile, 1977);

Nuevos sermones y prédicas del Cristo de Elqui (Valparaíso: Ganymedes, 1979);

El anti-Lázaro (Valparaíso: Gráfica Marginal, 1981);

Ecopoemas (Valparaíso: Gráfica Marginal, 1982);

Nicanor Parra (Valparaíso: Gráfica Marginal, 1982);

Poema y antipoema a Eduardo Frei (Santiago: América del Sur, 1982);

Chistes para desorientar a la poesía (Santiago: Galería Época, 1983);

Poesía política (Santiago: Bruguera, 1983);

Nicanor Parra

Coplas de Navidad (anti-villancico) (Santiago: Camaleón, 1983);

Hojas de Parra (Santiago: Ganymedes, 1985);

Fotopoemas, by Parra and Sergio Marras (Santago: Ornitorrinco, 1986);

Poemas para combatir la calvicie: Muestra de antipoesía, edited by Julio Ortega (Jalisco, Mexico: Universidad de Guadalahara, Fondo de Cultura Económica /

Mexico City: Consejo Nacional para la Cultura y las Artes, 1993);

Discursos de sobremesa (Concepción, Chile: Cuadernos Atenea, 1997).

Edition in English: *Poems and Antipoems,* edited by Miller Williams, translated by William Carlos Williams and others (New York: New Directions, 1967; London: Cape, 1968);

Sermons and Homilies of the Christ of Elqui, translated by Sandra Reyes (Columbia: University of Missouri Press, 1984);

Antipoems: New and Selected, edited by David Unger (New York: New Directions, 1985).

OTHER: *Poesía soviética rusa,* edited by Parra (Moscow: Progreso, 1965); republished as *Poesía rusa contemporánea* (Santiago: Ediciones Nueva Universidad, 1971).

SELECTED PERIODICAL PUBLICATIONS—
UNCOLLECTED: "Gato en el camino," *Revista Nueva,* no. 1 (1935);

"Ejercicios retóricos," *Extremo Sur,* no. 1 (December 1954): 4–6.

Based on his pursuit of literary renewal, Nicanor Parra is one of the most innovative poets of the Spanish language. He is considered the greatest living Chilean poet and—along with Vicente Huidobro, founder of the avant-garde school of Creationism; Gabriela Mistral, the first Spanish American author to be awarded the Nobel Prize in literature in 1945; and Pablo Neruda, also a Nobel laureate in 1971—one of the four most outstanding Chilean poets of the twentieth century. Like Mistral and Neruda, Parra has been considered a candidate for the Nobel Prize, though unlike them, he has not received this award. Parra has influenced his own and subsequent generations of Spanish American writers, and his work has been translated into all major languages, including English, notably by North American beatnik poets—such as Allen Ginsberg and Lawrence Ferlinghetti—with whose work his has been compared.

Parra's ambition to renovate poetic discourse has given rise to consistent evolution in his own work and culminated in his most significant contribution to Spanish American poetry, the concept of *antipoetry.* Although he has never offered a concrete definition of this term, Parra is a champion of accessible poetry and aims for direct communication with the masses through the use of colloquial language, humor, irony, and social criticism on themes of everyday life.

Parra's interest in ordinary speech patterns, wordplay, and traditional culture may be traced to his family background. One of nine children of Nicanor Parra and Clara Sandoval Navarrete, he was born on 5 September 1914 in San Fabián de Alico, near the city of Chillán, approximately two hundred miles south of the capital, Santiago; consequently, Parra is identified with the highland Andean region and national capital, while his compatriot Neruda is associated with the Pacific coastal region. Parra's family belonged to the provincial middle class; his father was an elementary-school teacher and musician, while his mother descended from a rural farming family and enjoyed singing folk songs. His sister, Violeta Parra, was a celebrated folksinger and craftsperson during the 1950s and 1960s, and her children—Nicanor Parra's niece and nephew, Ángel and Isabel Parra—are also involved in folk music and the preservation of Spanish American folk traditions. Because of his rather restless and bohemian character, Parra's father changed jobs frequently, forcing the family to move often; they lived mainly in the outskirts of Chillán and for short periods in Santiago, Lautaro, and Ancud.

Throughout his youth and early education Parra considered himself both a poet and a student of science. When he was eleven years old he embarked on the composition of an epic trilogy on the history of the Araucano Indians, Spaniards, and Chileans, a project he abandoned when he stopped writing poetry in early adolescence. In 1932 Parra went to Santiago, where he completed his final year of high school at the Internado Barros Arana (Barros Arana Boarding School). There he became acquainted with the school's leading intellectuals—Jorge Millas, Luis Oyarzún, and Carlos Pedraza—and resumed writing poetry. Parra's school friends, who later formed the nucleus of the group of prominent writers and artists of his generation, introduced him to current trends in Chilean, European, and North American culture and literature, including Surrealism. The following year Parra enrolled in the Instituto Pedagógico (Pedagogical Institute) at the University of Chile in Santiago, where he majored in mathematics and physics while training to become a teacher. As a university student Parra continued to associate with his boarding-school friends, and together, in 1935, they began publishing a literary magazine with a limited circulation, *Revista Nueva* (New Review). Parra contributed a short story, "Gato en el camino" (Cat in the Road), to the first issue and two years later published his first collection of poems, *Cancionero sin nombre* (Untitled Songs). In 1938 Parra graduated from college with a degree in mathematics and physics and spent the following six years teaching high school in Chillán.

In the year of Parra's college graduation, Chilean folklorist and poet Tomás Lago was commissioned by the Sociedad de Escritores de Chile (Society of Chilean Writers) to prepare an anthology, titled *Ocho nuevos poe-*

tas chilenos (Eight New Chilean Poets, 1939), of the eight most promising young poets in the country: Alberto Baeza Flores, Hernán Cañas, Óscar Castro, Omar Cerda, Jorge Millas, Luis Oyarzún, Victoriano Vicario, and Parra. Known as the Generation of 1938, these poets may be divided into two groups: the Grupo Mandrágora (Mandrágora Group), after its magazine titled *Mandrágora,* and the Internado (Boarding School) Group, which included Parra and his boarding-school friends Millas and Oyarzún. Their slogan was "Guerra a la metáfora, muerte a la imagen, viva el hecho concreto y otra vez: Claridad" (War on metaphor, death to imagery, long live concrete facts and again: clarity). These poets supported the Republican cause in the Spanish Civil War and empathized with Spanish poets who used popular themes and forms in their writing, namely, Rafael Alberti, Federico García Lorca, Miguel Hernández, and Antonio Machado. Like their Spanish counterparts, these poets were interested in folk ballads and poetry reflecting popular and traditional speech rhythms; they rejected metaphorical, avant-garde poetry and sought simplicity and accessibility in their own compositions. Their goals were further publicly manifested in 1942, when Lago published another anthology, *Tres poetas chilenos* (Three Chilean Poets), including texts by Castro, Vicario, and Parra, along with a prologue titled "Luz en la poesía" (Light in Poetry). In his preface Lago anticipated a return to simple forms and vernacular themes.

During the 1940s Parra continued his education in both science and literature while living abroad in the developed world. After six years of high-school teaching, he decided to pursue graduate study in physics at Brown University in Providence, Rhode Island, from 1943 to 1945, and later, from 1949 to 1951, he received a grant from the British Council to study cosmology at Oxford University. While in the United States and England, Parra became an admirer of North American and British writers who incorporated prosaic language and colloquial expressions in their poetic commentary on politics, manners, religion, and society. He was most influenced by his readings of British poets W. H. Auden, William Blake, C. Day Lewis, John Donne, T. S. Eliot, Louis McNeice, Ezra Pound, and Stephen Spender. While in the United States Parra read Walt Whitman in Spanish translation and, under his influence in 1943, wrote a series of twenty poems, "Ejercicios retóricos" (Rhetorical Exercises), which were published eleven years later in the Chilean magazine *Extremo Sur* (Extreme South). These poems reflect the author's transition toward antipoetry through his experimentation with free verse and use of a contemporary, urban setting. Parra further advanced his concept of antipoetry in 1948 through the publication in the

Paperback cover for Parra's first book, a 1937 collection modeled after the Spanish poet Federico García Lorca's 1928 Romancero gitano *(University of Arizona Library)*

Chilean magazine *Pro-Arte* of three poems—"La trampa" (The Trap), "La víbora" (The Viper), and "Los vicios del mundo moderno" (The Vices of the Modern World)—later included in his second book of poetry, *Poemas y antipoemas* (Poems and Antipoems, 1954).

When Parra returned to Chile from the United States in 1945, he joined the faculty at the University of Chile. In 1948 he was appointed the director of the school of engineering at the university, and four years later he was named professor of theoretical physics. In addition to teaching science and engineering, Parra was also invited to serve as visiting professor of Spanish American literature at Louisiana State University in Baton Rouge (1966–1967), and at New York University, Columbia University, and Yale University (1971). Parra has given poetry readings and lectures in many countries and conducts poetry workshops at his home institution. He is a member of the Academia Chilena de la Lengua (Chilean Academy of the Spanish Language) and has received many literary prizes, including a Guggenheim Fellowship (1972) and the Juan Rulfo Prize (1990). Parra has been married twice–to Ana

Troncoso and Inga Palmen—and has seven children. He presently resides in La Reina, a suburb of Santiago.

The model for Parra's *Cancionero sin nombre* was Spanish author García Lorca's *Romancero gitano* (Gypsy Ballads, 1928). García Lorca, murdered by Nationalist troops at the outset of the Spanish Civil War in 1936, was considered a martyr of the Republican cause as well as a literary genius. Composed in 1935–1936, the twenty-nine poems of *Cancionero sin nombre* are, like García Lorca's gypsy ballads, stylized versions of traditional, in this case Chilean, popular songs in ballad form (eight-syllable lines with assonant rhyme pattern) intended for oral recitation. Parra's early poems narrate stories on themes of love, children, and philosophical topics. He employs informal, colloquial language and popular speech and humor, features of his later antipoetry. Other techniques of Parra's first book of poetry include musical elements—for example, alliteration, assonance, refrain, and repetition; parallel structure of verses; rhetorical questions and exclamations; the use of personification and metaphor pertaining to nature and religion; and Surrealist and oneiric imagery. Although the book was awarded the Premio Municipal de Poesía (Municipal Poetry Prize) for 1938, it received, like much of Parra's work, mixed critical reviews. On the one hand, most critics immediately dismissed it, and Parra himself considers it a work of juvenilia. On the other, such respected writers as Lago and Mistral hailed Parra as a promising young poet; in fact, Lago considered Parra the leader of a movement toward more popular poetry, and Mistral stated, "Estamos ante un poeta cuya fama se extenderá internacionalmente" (We have before us a poet who will gain worldwide fame), as she was quoted in Margarita Aguirre and Juan Augustín Palazuelos's introduction to *La cueca larga y otras poemas* (The Long Dance and Other Poems, 1964).

Although Parra's next poetry collection did not appear until seventeen years later, in 1954, his gradual departure from poetic tradition is evident in the occasional poems composed during the 1940s and published in newspapers and magazines. Collectively, the texts of *Poemas y antipoemas* represent a seminal work in Spanish American verse. Parra's second book was awarded two literary prizes in 1954 and 1955–the Premio del Sindicato de Escritores de Chile (Writers' Union Prize) and the Premio Municipal de Poesía (Municipal Literary Prize), respectively. As the title implies, *Poemas y antipoemas* is a heterogeneous blend of poetic convention and innovation, and the three sections of the volume display the progressive shift from traditional poetic discourse to antipoetry. The poems in the first section conform to standard metric and rhyme patterns and retain neo-Romantic and post-*Modernista* traces. Similar to *Cancionero sin nombre,* many of these poems are ballads employing colloquial, spoken language and straightforward themes, such as love, nature, and nostalgia. Other poems are autobiographical and narrated in first person. Like the first group of poems, those in the second, transitional section follow conventional metric and rhyme patterns and include ballad forms. The satiric tone of these poems masks an intrinsic disillusion with daily life symptomatic of antipoetry, however.

The third section comprises the antipoems of the title and marks a radical break with previous poetic tradition, as Parra announces in the first poem of the group, "Advertencia al lector" (Warning to the Reader). As its title indicates, this antipoem is a warning that these texts may not be precisely what the reader anticipates after reading the preceding texts in the collection: "El autor no responde de las molestias que puedan ocasionar sus escritos / Aunque le pese / El lector tendrá que darse siempre por satisfecho" (The author will not answer for the annoyances which his writings may raise: / It may be hard on the reader / But he'll have to accept this from here on in). Drolly, Parra declares his revisionist aspirations: clarity, simplicity, and accessibility through the creation of a new poetic vocabulary and language. Furthermore, antipoetry reflects on social and existential issues.

Although Parra has consistently avoided formulation of any firm definition of antipoetry, certain basic notions of the concept may be derived from his work. The term *antipoet* was originally coined by Chilean poet Vicente Huidobro, founder of the avant-garde school of Creationism, in his poem in seven cantos, *Altazor* (1931; translated as *Altazor, or, A Voyage in a Parachute,* 1988). Parra, however, rejects Huidobro's exalted image of the poet as a god-like figure capable of creating his own poetic universe and instead views the antipoet as an ordinary individual who records common speech and experience. Whereas Huidobro is associated with French poetic tradition, Parra is more akin to British poetry yet opposes all previous poetic tradition—he is anti-Romantic, anti-*Modernista,* and anti-avant-garde—and proposes a sweeping reform of the genre. For all his iconoclasm, Parra's antipoetry coincides with a tradition of "impure" poetry in Spanish and Spanish American literature; first conceived by Pablo Neruda in 1935, "impure" poetry displays an anti-intellectual bent, employs colloquial language, and directly treats matters of real life, such as sociopolitical issues. Antipoetry contradicts the accepted notion of poetry as a discourse different from ordinary speech and intended only for an elite audience. Its primary objectives are twofold: to make poetry accessible to the general public and to disturb readers' complacency.

To accomplish these aims, antipoetry employs certain distinctive features. Rather than adhering to strict metric and rhyme forms, antipoetry tends to utilize free verse and prosaic language. Parra's work incorporates vocabulary not usually present in poetry as well as elements from everyday communication: namely, typical regional and Chilean expressions, slang words and street language, clichés and stock expressions, vulgarities, television and print advertisements, graffiti, newspaper and journalistic language, political slogans and speeches, and scientific language. Through the medium of explicit, conversational language, antipoetry strives to simplify poetic discourse and establish direct communication with a broad audience.

Humor and irony are other means to achieve this goal. Black humor calls attention to an underlying sense of anguish concerning the human condition. Parra's caustic wit attacks ideologies, institutions, structures, systems, and traditions designed to serve as a shield from the absurdity and chaos of human existence. His irreverence toward the pillars of society conveys a nonconformist, subversive attitude. Ambiguous and incongruous imagery as well as unusual and unexpected juxtapositions impart an ironic message in direct opposition to the surface meaning.

Given that the antipoet is an average person, the primary themes of antipoetry are commonplace issues related to the modern world and contemporary society with which all readers can identify. Parra enumerates some of these issues in "Los vicios del mundo moderno," published in *Poemas y antipoemas:* "Los vicios del mundo moderno: / El automóvil y el cine sonoro, / Las discriminaciones raciales, / El exterminio de los pieles rojas, / Los trucos de la alta banca, / La catástrofe de los ancianos, / El comercio clandestino de blancas realizado por sodomitas internacionales, / El auto-bombo y la gula" (The vices of the modern world: / The motor car and the movies, / Racial discrimination, / The extermination of the Indian, / The manipulations of high finance, / The catastrophe of the aged, / The clandestine white-slave trade carried on by international sodomites, / Self-advertisement and gluttony). A caricature of the tragic hero—in other words, an antihero—the antipoet inhabits a desolate and hostile world without hope of spiritual comprehension. The human race is simultaneously depicted as both responsible for and a victim of this decaying, dehumanized, and demoralized state of affairs. Any attempt at change is doomed to failure, however. The antipoetic worldview portrays life as a meaningless riddle with no solution.

Throughout his career Parra continued to cultivate and develop antipoetry as a work-in-progress. Parra, as quoted in Stephen M. Hart's *A Companion to Spanish-American Literature* (1999), has equated the anti-

poem to a mathematical theorem in which poetic language is reduced to its essence: "Maximum content, minimum of words. . . . Economy of language, no metaphors, no literary tropes." The long, complex verses of early antipoetry were eventually replaced by fragments, chaotic enumeration, and exaggerated repetition. Despite its spirit of constant evolution, the unswerving aim of antipoetry is the preservation of poetry as an accessible art form.

After the radical break with the past constituted by antipoetry, Parra's next book, *La cueca larga* (The Long Dance, 1958), the title of which refers to the national dance of Chile, at once represents an apparent return to the folkloric traditions of his first poetry collection as well as further development of poetry for the people. The four long poems that comprise this volume adhere to the traditional Spanish ballad form *(romance),* originally intended to be set to music or recited aloud, with eight-syllable lines and assonant rhyme in even-numbered verses. Parra demonstrates his ongoing experimentation with vernacular language and popular practices by incorporating local speech and humor of the Chilean lower classes as well as the classic figure of the Chilean cowboy *(huaso)* and cowboy patois. These poems are a literal celebration of wine, women, and song, and he writes in "Coplas del vino" ("Wine Ballad"): "El vino cuando se bebe / con inspiración sincera / sólo puede compararse / al beso de una doncella" (Drinking wine / with genuine inspiration / can only be compared / to kissing a young lady). *La cueca larga* was reprinted in an expanded version, *La cueca larga y otros poemas* (The Long Dance and Other Poems), in 1964.

Parra further refined his antipoetic technique in his next book, *Versos de salón* (Salon Verses, 1962), one of his most important poetry collections. As the title implies, Parra lampoons the conventions of poetic tradition and middle-class society. In a colloquial statement of poetic theory, the opening poem, "Cambios de nombre" (Name Changes), announces Parra's declaration of artistic independence and intention to revolutionize language: "A los amantes de las bellas letras / Hago llegar mis mejores deseos / Voy a cambiar de nombre a algunas cosas. / Mi posición es ésta: / El poeta no cumple su palabra / Si no cambia los nombres de las cosas" (To the lovers of belles lettres / I send my very best wishes / I am going to change the names of some things. / My position is this: / The poet isn't keeping his word / If he doesn't change the names of things). Again, as in his earlier "Advertencia al lector" of *Poemas y antipoemas,* Parra cautions the reader to be prepared for the turbulence of "La montaña rusa" (the roller coaster) represented by the shift from traditional poetry to antipoetry: "Durante medio siglo / La poesía fue / El paraíso del tonto solemne. / Hasta que vine yo / y me

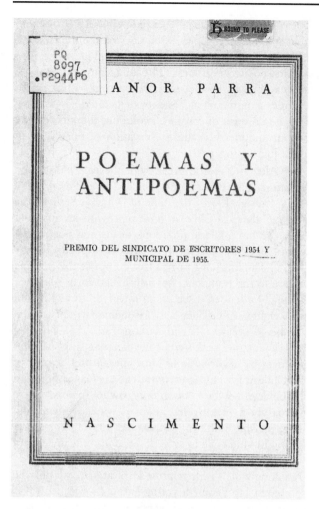

Ingerir una dosis de cognac
Distinguir una viola de un violín
Recibir en pijama a las visitas
Impedir la caída del cabello
Y tragar cantidades de saliva

(If you want to get to the heaven
Of the little bourgeois, you must go
By the road of Art for Art's sake
And swallow a lot of saliva:
The apprenticeship is almost interminable.
A list of what you must learn how to do:
Tie your necktie artistically
Slip your card to the right people
Polish shoes that are already shined
Consult the Venetian mirror
[Head-on and in profile]
Toss down a shot of brandy
Tell a viola from a violin
Receive guests in your pajamas
Keep your hair from falling
And swallow a lot of saliva).

Paperback cover for the second edition (1956) of the 1954 collection in which Parra makes a radical break with poetic tradition (George Washington University Library)

Here, however, Parra intermingles traditional hendecasyllabic (or eleven-syllable) lines with shorter, less complex verses than those in *Poemas y antipoemas* to produce a travesty of refinement. The previously long and intricate verses of antipoetry undergo fragmentation as Parra employs the techniques of chaotic enumeration and juxtaposition of unrelated images to reflect the incoherence and irrationality of the universe that he wants the reader to perceive firsthand. Furthermore, these poems depict existential insecurity, alienation, and despair in a tragicomic tone.

Owing to its provocative nature, antipoetry continued to elicit mixed critical reaction. On the one hand, *Versos de salón* was condemned in a 15 November 1964 review by Father Prudencio Salvatierra, a Capuchin priest, in the conservative newspaper *El Diario Ilustrado* (The Illustrated Daily): "¿Puede admitirse que se lance al público una obra como ésa, sin pies ni cabeza, que destila veneno y podredumbre, demencia y satanismo? . . . No puedo dar ejemplos de la antipoesía de esas páginas: es demasiado cínica y demencial. . . . Me han preguntado si este librito es inmoral. Yo diría que no; es demasiado sucio para ser inmoral. Un tarro de basura no es inmoral, por muchas vueltas que le demos para examinar su contenido" (Can a work like this, with neither head nor tail, that exudes poison and rottenness, madness and Satanism, be released to the public? . . . I cannot provide examples of antipoetry here: it is too cynical and demented. . . . They have asked me if this book is immoral. I would say not; it is too dirty to be immoral. A garbage can is not immoral, no matter how many times we walk around it trying to figure out what's inside). On the other hand, Neruda's opinion of

instalé con mi montaña rusa. / Suban, si les parece. / Claro que yo no respondo si bajan / Echando sangre por boca y narices" (For half a century / Poetry was the paradise / Of the solemn fool. / Until I came along / And built my roller coaster. / Go up, if you feel like it. / It's not my fault if you come down / Bleeding from your nose and mouth). He ridicules middle-class pretensions in "El pequeño burgués" (Litany of the Little Bourgeois) in a catalogue of mock precepts:

Él que quiera llegar al paraíso
Del pequeño burgués tiene que andar
El camino del arte por el arte
Y tragar cantidades de saliva:
El noviciado es casi interminable.
Lista de lo que tiene que saber:
Anudarse con arte la corbata
Deslizar la tarjeta de visita
Sacudirse por lujo los zapatos
Consultar el espejo veneciano
Estudiarse de frente y de perfil

antipoetry, as recounted on the dustjacket of *Versos de salon,* could not have been more different and complimentary: "Esta poesía es una delicia de oro matutino o un fruto consumado en las tinieblas" (This poetry is as delightful as the gilded tint of early morning or fruit ripened to perfection in the shadows).

In fact, the same year as the appearance of *Versos de salon,* Neruda and Parra coauthored the volume *Pablo Neruda y Nicanor Parra* (1962; translated as *Pablo Neruda and Nicanor Parra Face to Face: A Bilingual and Critical Edition of Their Speeches on the Occasion of Neruda's Appointment to the Faculty of the University of Chile,* 1997). The first half of the book transcribes Parra's welcome address to his fellow poet when he was made an honorary member of the Facultad de Filosofía y Educación (School of Philosophy and Education) at the University of Chile, while the second half records Neruda's acceptance speech. In his lecture Parra defends committed literature and praises Neruda for his activism on behalf of the masses.

Parra's indictment of polite society and literary propriety intensified the following year with the publication of a special edition of one of his most noted poems, *Manifiesto* (Manifesto, 1954), which restates many of the same points made in his 1962 speech. In this work, the title of which alludes to past literary pronouncements as well as Karl Marx and Friedrich Engels's *Communist Manifesto* (1848), Parra issues a public declaration of literary and sociopolitical beliefs. Juxtaposing past and present, this text denounces what poetry should not be and proclaims the proposition of poetic renovation: "Para nuestros mayores / La poesía fue un objeto de lujo / Pero para nosotros / Es un artículo de primera necesidad: / No podemos vivir sin poesía" (For our elders / Poetry was a luxury / But for us / It is an absolute necessity: / We cannot live without poetry). Parra insists on the ordinariness and indispensability of poetry and compares the poet, who shapes commonplace language into accessible form, to a bricklayer: "Nosotros sostenemos / Que el poeta no es un alquimista / El poeta es un hombre como todos / Un albañil que construye su muro: / Un constructor de puertas y ventanas. / Nosotros conversamos / En el lenguaje de todos los días / No creemos en signos cabalísticos" (We maintain / That the poet is not an alchemist / The poet is a man like everyone else / A bricklayer who builds his wall: / A builder of doors and windows. / We speak / In everyday language / We don't believe in cabalistic signs).

In contrast to Romantic and avant-garde notions of a poet's superiority, here the poet is an average human being: "Los poetas bajaron del Olimpo" (The poets have come down from Olympus). Parra condemns the contrived, hermetic style of past literature and extols clear, direct writing: "Nosotros repudiamos /

La poesía de gafas obscuras / La poesía de capa y espada / La poesía de sombrero alón. / Propiciamos en cambio / La poesía a ojo desnudo / La poesía a pecho descubierto / La poesía a cabeza desnuda" (We repudiate / Dark glasses poetry / Cloak and dagger poetry / Broad-brimmed hat poetry. / We propose instead / Naked eye poetry / Bared bosom poetry / Uncovered head poetry). Instead of trifling formal innovations, Parra advocates radical change and social commitment: "Contra la poesía de las nubes / Nosotros oponemos / La poesía de la tierra firme / —Cabeza fría, corazón caliente / Somos tierrafirmistas decididos / Contra la poesía de café / La poesía de la naturaleza / Contra la poesía de salón / La poesía de la plaza pública / La poesía de protesta social" (Instead of poetry in the clouds / We offer / Poetry on solid ground / —Cold head, warm heart / We are committed to the solid ground— / Instead of café poetry / The poetry of nature / Instead of salon poetry / The poetry of the public square / The poetry of social protest).

The same year Parra issued his poetic manifesto, he was invited for a six-month visit to the Soviet Union. Before returning to Chile he also traveled to the People's Republic of China. As a result of his experiences in the Soviet Union, Parra edited a volume of Russian poetry in Spanish translation–*Poesía soviética rusa* (Russian Soviet Poetry, 1965), which was republished in Santiago as *Poesía rusa contemporánea* (Contemporary Russian Poetry, 1971). In addition, during his 1963 stay and on his return to Chile the following year, Parra composed seventeen poems based on his impressions of the Soviet Union. These poems were first published in September 1966 in the magazine *Mundo Nuevo* (New World) and later as a separate book, *Canciones rusas* (Russian Songs, 1967). Unlike his previous antipoetry, these poems are lyrical, express deep personal feelings, and possess a melancholy, nostalgic tone. At the same time, Parra continues to write in a clear, transparent style free of imagery and experiments with typography and visual presentation. In this collection the Soviet Union appears as a symbol of hope and progress. For all his positive response to the Soviet Union and in spite of Parra's own literary proclamations on behalf of sociopolitical militancy as well as his contacts with socialism through his travels and editing projects, his writing has remained essentially nonideological yet subversive.

By the late 1960s Parra had laid the foundation for a volume of selected works, *Obra gruesa* (Basic Work, 1969), highlighting his bleak, antipoetic worldview. This collection includes all of his poetry published through 1969 with the exception of *Cancionero sin nombre.* It is divided into seven sections, the first four corresponding to each of Parra's books of poetry pub-

Paperback cover for Parra's 1962 collection, in which he lampoons both poetic conventions and middle-class society (William T. Young Library, University of Kentucky)

lished in the 1950s and 1960s, while the last three—"La camisa de fuerza" (Straightjacket), "Otros poemas" (Other Poems), and "Tres poemas" (Three Poems)—include texts that had not previously appeared as separate books. Typically, Parra makes fun of societal institutions and conventions in prosaic language and witty wordplay. In tribute to Parra's significant literary accomplishments to date, *Obra gruesa* was awarded Chile's Premio Nacional de Poesía (National Poetry Prize) in 1969.

In *Los profesores* (The Teachers, 1971), a long poem published in a limited edition in New York, Parra sustains his bitter social criticism in a parody of the academic world, with which, as a university professor himself, he is well acquainted. The poem alternates stanzas of typical pedantic questions with Parra's own sardonic reflections:

> Los profesores nos volvieron locos
> a preguntas que no venían al caso
> cómo se suman números complejos
> hay o no hay arañas en la luna
> cómo murió la familia del zar
> ¿es posible cantar con la boca cerrada?
> quién le pintó bigotes a la Gioconda
> . . . .
> Nadie dirá que nuestros maestros
> fueron unas enciclopedias rodantes
> exactamente todo lo contrario

> (Our teachers drove us nuts
> with their irrelevant questions:
> how do you add compound numbers
> are there or are there not spiders on the moon
> how did the family of the czar die
> can one sing with one's mouth shut
> who painted the mustache on the Mona Lisa
> . . . .
> No one can say that our teachers
> were walking encyclopedias
> quite the contrary).

Here, Parra underscores the senselessness of the entire educational system.

Throughout the years Parra's antipoetry became more and more truncated and austere, until it assumed new form in his *Artefactos* (Artifacts, 1972). Parra had begun to experiment with this poetic structure as early as 1967, and the artifact has been variously compared to a slogan, haiku, and graffiti for its verbal compression, minimalism, and fragmentation. For Parra, the artifact is language reduced to its essence and is the natural progression of antipoetry: "Los artefactos resultan de la explosión del antipoema. Se podría dar una definición al revés. Decir, por ejemplo, que el antipoema es un conglomerado de artefactos a punto de explotar" (Artifacts result from the explosion of an antipoem. It is possible to give a reverse definition. To say, for example, that an antipoem is a collection of artifacts about to explode). Published as a set of picture postcards with illustrations by artist Guillermo Teieda, *Artefactos* is both a literary and visual text, in the style of French avant-garde writer Guillaume Apollinaire's visual poetry, or calligrams. These poems are characterized by brevity (generally fewer than ten lines), detachment from poetic context, maximum verbal concentration, and incorporation of disparate styles of discourse (advertisements, popular sayings and expressions, newspaper headlines, and political slogans and speech, for example). The term *artifact* suggests an anthropological document or record of human social and cultural development. Consequently, in these poems Parra's critical eye is once again trained on societal defects. From his nonideological stance, he condemns all forms of monolithic government equally. For example, he insinuates the foibles of democracy in "U.S.A.": "Donde la libertad / es una estatua" (where liberty / is a statue). Likewise, he takes a dim view of Cuban socialism: "Si fuera justo Fidel / debiera creer en mí / tal como yo creo en él: / la historia me absolverá" (If Fidel were fair about it / he'd believe in me / just as I believe in him: / History will absolve me). In Parra's artifacts, linguistic condensation encompasses weighty ideas.

Parra's poetry of social criticism culminated in the publication of his *Emergency Poems* (1972). The medical terminology employed in the title and elsewhere in the collection points to the notion that the world and its society are now in a state of emergency or crisis. This book includes previously published texts, including "La camisa de fuerza," as well as several poems from the penultimate section of *Obra gruesa*, along with thirty-one new poems on social themes that mark the further expansion of Parra's thought and work. These texts examine contemporary social issues and display an even sharper, more irreverent tone than Parra's preceding poetry. For example, he confronts questions relating to poverty, hunger, and homelessness in a series of preposterous "Proposiciones" (Proposals) that reveal a sense of futility in the face of despair: "estoy triste no tengo qué comer / el mundo no se preocupa de mí / no deberían existir los mendigos / que vengo sosteniendo lo mismo / años de años / yo propongo que en vez de mariposas / en los jardines anden cangrejos / —creo que sería mucho mejor— / ¿imaginan un mundo sin mendigos?" (I'm sad I've got nothing to eat / nobody cares about me / there shouldn't be any beggars / I've been saying the same thing / for years / I propose that instead of butterflies / crabs should move in the gardens / —I think that would be a lot better— / can you imagine a world without beggars?). In "Tiempos modernos" (Modern Times) he contemplates pollution, militarism, and totalitarianism: "Atravesamos unos tiempos calamitosos / imposible hablar sin incurrir en delito de contradicción / imposible callar sin hacerse cómplice del Pentágono / Se sabe perfectamente que no hay alternativa posible / todos los caminos conducen a Cuba / pero el aire está sucio / y respirar es un acto fallido" (We're living through horrible times / it's impossible to say anything without contradicting yourself / impossible to hold your tongue without being a pawn of the Pentagon / Everyone knows there's no other possible choice / all roads lead to Cuba / but the air is filthy / and breathing is a waste of time).

During the late 1970s and early 1980s Parra, in a decisive moment in his poetic career, embraced not only social analysis but also a more prophetic, oracular style. Two volumes of poetry published at this time—*Sermones y prédicas del Cristo de Elqui* (Sermons and Homilies of the Christ of Elqui, 1977) and *Nuevos sermones y prédicas del Cristo de Elqui* (New Sermons and Homilies of the Christ of Elqui, 1979)—introduce this stage in the Chilean poet's career. In these works biblical references evoke commentary on contemporary sociopolitical reality and alarm for the future. The central persona and first-person narrator is folk legend Domingo Zárate Vega, a construction worker who left his job to become an itinerant preacher in the 1920s; he believed he was the reincarnation of Christ and was popularly known as the Christ of Elqui. Like most of Parra's poetic anti-

heroes, the Christ of Elqui is marginalized, poorly educated, and persecuted by mainstream society. His satirical observations and folk wisdom address a wide range of topics, including the Catholic Church and clergy, government, human rights abuses, and environmental violations. Parra's clever composition manages to present an absurd concept of human existence and provide veiled commentary on the Chilean military dictatorship of General Augusto Pinochet while evading censorship. In 1984 the English translation, *Sermons and Homilies of the Christ of Elqui*, received the first Richard Wilbur Prize for Poetry awarded by the American Literary Translators Association and the University of Missouri Press.

During the 1980s and 1990s, Parra published no fewer than ten books of poetry in which he continues to blend a prophetic tone with sociopolitical examination. Rather than rest on his laurels, Parra has persevered with his goal of poetic renovation through ongoing experimentation with new forms, and during the 1980s began writing in defense of the environment and treating ecological themes in his *ecopoemas* (ecopoems). In these poems Parra shows his solidarity with nature and the universe. For example, in an untitled poem from *Ecopoemas* (1982) he chides humanity for contaminating the earth: "El error consistió / en creer que la tierra era nuestra / cuando la verdad de las cosas / es que nosotros somos de la tierra" (The mistake we made was in thinking / that the earth belonged to us / when the fact of the matter is / we're the ones who belong to the earth). Furthermore, in another *ecopoema*, "Estimados alumnos" (Dear Students), from the same collection he wryly predicts the demise of human existence: "Buenas Noticias: / la tierra se recupera en un millón / de años / Somos nosotros los que desaparecemos" (Good News! / in a million years the earth / will be whole again / We'll be the ones long gone).

At this same time Parra also introduced his *chistes* (jokes) in which he exposes the Pinochet regime's political repression and censorship. As he writes in one of his untitled *chistes* from *Chistes para desorientar a la poesía* (Jokes For Disorienting Poetry, 1983): "Confío 100% en el lector / estoy convencido de que hasta los . . . / civiles / son capaces de leer entre líneas" (I trust the reading public 100% / I'm convinced that even . . . / civilians / can read between the lines). In another poem from the same collection he playfully jests about the serious matter of torture: "La tortura no tiene por qué ser / sangrienta / a un intelectual / por ejemplo, / basta con esconderle los anteojos" (Torture doesn't have to be / bloody / Take an intellectual / for example— / just hide his glasses). Another volume, *Hojas de Parra* (Pages of Parra, 1985), includes notable poems on the theme of death and innovatively incorporates others' texts in a new context without attribution so that the unwary reader might take them for Parra's own.

     Nicanor Parra is one of the most celebrated Spanish American poets of the twentieth century and is considered the greatest living poet in his native Chile. During a career that has stretched over more than six decades, Parra has not wavered from his quest for literary renovation. Although his most significant contribution to this reform effort is the concept of antipoetry, the consistent development of his work and ongoing experimentation throughout the years attest to his ceaseless striving for socially relevant, plainspoken poetry accessible to a broad audience.

Interviews:

Leonidas Morales T., *Conversaciones con Nicanor Parra* (Santiago: Editorial Universitaria, 1990);

Juan Andrés Piña, *Conversaciones con la poesía chilena: Nicanor Parra, Eduardo Anguita, Gonzalo Rojas, Enrique Lihn, Oscar Hahn, Raúl Zarita* (Santiago: Pehuén, 1990).

References:

Marjorie Agosin, "Contemporary Poetry of Chile," *Concerning Poetry,* 17 (Fall 1984): 43–53;

Agosin, "Pablo Neruda and Nicanor Parra: A Study of Similarities," *Poesis: A Journal of Criticism,* 6–7 (1984–1987): 51–60;

Margarita Aguirre and Juan Agustín Palazuelos, "Nicanor Parra, antipoeta," in Parra's *La cueca larga y otros poemas,* edited by Aguirre and Palazuelos (Buenos Aires: Editorial Universitaria de Buenos Aires, 1964), pp. 5–14;

Marlene Gottlieb, *No se termina nunca de nacer: La poesía de Nicanor Parra* (Madrid: Playor, 1977?);

Gottlieb, "Los parlamentos dramáticos de Nicanor Parra," *América Hispánica,* 5 (January–June 1991): 66–75;

Gottlieb, ed., *Nicanor Parra: Antes y después de Jesucristo: Antología de artículos críticos* (Princeton: Linden Lane, 1993);

Edith Grossman, *The Antipoetry of Nicanor Parra* (New York: New York University Press, 1975);

Sonja Karsen, "La poesía de Nicanor Parra," in *Actas del Sexto Congreso Internacional de Hispanistas, Celebrado en Toronto del 22 al 26 de agosto de 1977,* edited by Alan M. Gordon and Evelyn Rugg (Toronto: Department of Spanish and Portuguese, University of Toronto, 1980), pp. 411–414;

Leonidas Morales T., *La poesía de Nicanor Parra* (Santiago: Universidad Austral de Chile/Andrés Bello, 1970);

Julio Ortega, "Voces de Nicanor Parra," *Quimera: Revista de Literatura,* 108 (1991): 54–57.

Alejandra Pizarnik
(29 April 1936 – 25 September 1972)

Z. Nelly Martínez
McGill University

BOOKS: *La tierra más ajena* (Buenos Aires: Botella al mar, 1955);

La última inocencia (Buenos Aires: Ediciones Poesía, 1956);

Las aventuras perdidas (Buenos Aires: Altamar, 1958);

Arbol de Diana (Buenos Aires: Sur, 1962);

Los trabajos y las noches (Buenos Aires: Sudamericana, 1965);

Extracción de la piedra de locura (Buenos Aires: Sudamericana, 1968);

Nombres y figuras: Approximaciones (Barcelona: La esquina, 1969);

La condesa sangrienta (Buenos Aires: Aquarius, 1971); translated by Alberto Manguel as "The Bloody Countess" in *Other Fires: Short Fiction by Latin American Women,* edited by Manguel (Toronto: Vintage, 1992), pp. 70–87;

El infierno musical (Buenos Aires: Siglo XXI, 1971);

Los pequeños cantos (Caracas: Arbol de fuego, 1971);

Diario 1960–1961 (Rodanillo, Colombia: Museo Rayo, 1988).

Editions and Collections: *El deseo de la palabra* (Barcelona: Barral, Ocnos, 1975);

Entrevistas (Venezuela: Endymión, 1978);

Poemas, selected, with a prologue, by Alejandro Fontenia (Buenos Aires: Centro Editor de América Latina, Colección Capítulo, 1982);

Textos de Sombra y últimos poemas, edited by Olga Orozco and Ana Becciú (Buenos Aires: Sudamericana, 1982);

Alejandra Pizarnik/Semblanza, edited by Frank Graziano (México: Fondo de cultura económica, 1984);

Alejandra Pizarnik, edited by Cristina Piña (Buenos Aires: Centro Editor de América Latina, Colección Los grandes poetas, 1988);

Alejandra Pizarnik: Poesía completa, edited by Ana Becciú (Barcelona: Lumen, 2000);

Alejandra Pizarnik: *Poesía Completa,* edited by Ana Becciú (Barcelona: Lumen, 2000);

Obra completa, edited by Gustavo Zuluaga (Medellín, Colombia: Arbol de Diana, 2000);

Alejandra Pizarnik (photograph by Daniela Haman)

Alejandra Pizarnik: *Prosa completa,* edited by Ana Becciú (Barcelona: Lumen/Palabra en el Tiempo, 2002).

Editions in English: *Alejandra Pizarnik: A Profile,* edited by Frank Graziano, translated by Graziano, Maria Rosa Fort, and Suzanne Jill Levine (Durango, Colo.: Logbridge-Rhodes, 1987)–includes selections from "Journals" (1960–1968);

Exchanging Lives: Poetry and Translations, translated by Susan Bassnett (Leeds: Peepal Tree, 2002).

OTHER: Antonin Artaud, *Textos,* translated by Pizarnik and Antonio Lopez Crespo (Buenos Aires: Aquarius, 1971);

André Breton and Paul Eluard, *La inmaculada concepción,* translated by Pizarnik (Buenos Aires: Flor, 1972);

Marguerite Duras, *La vida tranquila,* translated by Pizarnik (Buenos Aires: Centro editor de America Latina, 1972).

Born in Buenos Aires on 29 April 1936 to Russian parents who had fled Europe and the Nazi Holocaust, Alejandra Pizarnik was destined for literary greatness as well as an early death. She died from an ostensibly self-administered overdose of barbiturates on 25 September 1972. A few words scribbled on a slate that same month, reiterating her desire to go nowhere "but to the bottom," sum up her lifelong aspiration as a human being and as a writer. The compulsion to head for the "bottom" or "abyss" points to her desire to surrender to nothingness in an ultimate experience of ecstasy and poetic fulfillment in which life and art would be fused, albeit at her own risk. "Ojalá pudiera vivir solamente en éxtasis, haciendo el cuerpo del poema con mi cuerpo" (If I could only live in nothing but ecstasy, making the body of the poem with my body), her poetic alter ego confides in *El infierno musical* (The Musical Hell, 1971), one of her pivotal works.

As attested by her poetry, death haunted her in the image of a female in many guises inhabiting a forbidden garden, some mysterious forest, a perilous riverbank, or the other side of the mirror: symbols of powerful unconscious drives forever dismantling her identity and unsettling her sense of a univocal self, while threatening to thrust her into the abyss of a definitive silence. The author sensed these menacing forces in language itself, a medium she experienced as essentially fluid and lacking in referential capability and thus as thwarting any attempt at self-expression; a medium wanting in the capacity to fix meaning, that is, to express it with precision, leaving no room for ambiguity. For the author, meaning endlessly receded into the horizon, as it were, just as her sense of self relentlessly altered under the impact of potent drives that appeared to encompass both language and the unconscious.

Thus, the experience of fluidity came to be the hallmark of her life, one that estranged her from her own self and language and forever defeated her dream of an improbable grounding center. Characteristically, she felt estranged even from her own name: "alejandra / debajo estoy yo / alejandra" (Alejandra / I am underneath / Alejandra), reads a poem, appropriately titled "Sólo un nombre" (Only a Name), included in the collection *La última inocencia* (The Last Innocence, 1956).

In fact, her sense of being a stranger or outsider marked every facet of her brief life. As the daughter of immigrant refugees and as a Jew, a woman, and a lesbian, she inhabited the margins of a paternalistic Christian society. As a person of superior intelligence as well as a certified schizophrenic, she also belonged on the periphery. It has already been suggested that she remained a stranger even to her own self as the experience of its dissolution in a symbolic game of shifting mirrors intensified. "Miedo de ser dos / camino del espejo" (Fear of being two / on the way to the mirror), she reflects in *Arbol de Diana* (Diana's Tree, 1962), "alguien en mí dormido / me come y me bebe" (someone asleep inside me / is eating and drinking my blood). In effect, underneath the conscious "I" of the speaking subject there lay in ambush a multifarious "other" that would feed off her or, to resort to one of her most cherished metaphors, would drink her blood. Whether symbolized by a mad queen or a young girl inhabiting the other shore, the other side of the mirror, a forbidden garden, or the forest, the terrifying "other" was the harbinger of death for the poet but also the source of her creativity. For Pizarnik, in effect, death was a cause of terror and fascination, as well as the springboard for a meditation on the ultimate meaning of life; it was also the allure to which she voluntarily surrendered in due course. To be sure, the facts of her life are so consubstantial with her poetic endeavors that a biographical reading of her work, one that would draw profusely on her journals, is unavoidable and, in fact, desirable. Worthy of note is that her father's death in 1966, six years before her own, proved to be a rite of passage for the author in relation to both her life and work. After his passing her life became less grounded as she was now obsessed by the fear of madness; her poetry also turned more violent. However potent, such violence also revealed Pizarnik's decisive insights into the nature of the poetic act as well as her awareness of the profound love attending the creative process.

Flora Alejandra Pizarnik grew up in a household in which Russian and Yiddish were spoken alongside Spanish, and where her mother and father, Rejzla Bromiker and Elias Pizarnik, struggled to inculcate in her and her sister, Myriam, a love for art and the humanities. Both parents were well versed in history and geography, and music was especially important to Elias, who played several instruments. Faithful to their roots, they also made sure that their offspring were instructed in the Jewish religion and traditions, and to that end they sent them to the Zalman Reizien Schule in Buenos Aires, an establishment led by progressive, free-thinking teachers of Eastern European stock. The couple could afford such niceties because, in a brief span, they had made a life for themselves and their family in an Argentina that was quite prosperous at the time.

Although somewhat idealized in later years, childhood was a conflicted period for Pizarnik, a stage of innocence betrayed by experience at an early age. Thus the image of a child-woman, evocative of an irretrievable childhood, haunts her poetry. The fact that she felt alienated from the members of her immediate family even as a child contributed to the perennial loneliness that plagued her life. While maintaining a love-hate relationship with her mother, who died in 1986, she faced a more daunting task in dealing with her father. Unyielding and exacting, Elias became a negative figure in Pizarnik's life. Only after his death in 1966 was she able to reconsider their relationship and gradually understand that, like herself, he had been an outsider all his life, and that, unlike her, he had been unable to reclaim a voice of his own. In a 1971 work, "Poema para el padre" (Poem for the Father), included in the collection *Textos de Sombra y últimos poemas* (Texts of Shadow and Last Poems, 1982) and reprinted in Ana Becciú's recent edition of the author's poetic works, she attempts to articulate that muted voice, to sing "the song they didn't let him sing except through his absent blue eyes." The blueness of his eyes, which added a new dimension to the symbolic use of that color in her work, points to a space of solace in an otherwise tormented journey.

Rather heavy and suffering from asthma and acne in her early years, she was compared unfavorably to her handsome sister, Myriam. She relied on drugs to control her weight, paving the way for what amounted to lifelong drug addiction. The fact that she stuttered, a handicap she eventually overcame, added to her woes during these formative years. If childhood was a conflicted stage in Pizarnik's life, however, adolescence was less so because of her successful attempts at self-assertion. Unconventional even in her daily attire and mannerisms, the author systematically challenged the bourgeois establishment. Her iconoclastic stance, which also translated into a deep awareness of the corrosive effects of language, manifested itself in the irreverent use of profanities and obscene jokes that turned her into the center of attention among her friends; they also challenged the image of the circumspect, well-spoken, and well-dressed young woman of the period, who aspired to wed, raise a family, and conform.

Capitalizing on her ability to manipulate the linguistic medium, she wrote masterful irreverent texts in later years, including "La bucanera de Pernambuco o Hilda, la polígrafa" (The Lady Buccaneer of Pernambuco or Hilda, the Polygraph), which is included in *Textos de Sombra y últimos poemas*. A tour de force, this work is brilliant in its use of puns, neologisms, and

ALEJANDRA PIZARNIK

ÁRBOL DE DIANA

S▼R

BUENOS AIRES

Title page for Pizarnik's 1962 collection of poems written in Paris, where she lived from 1959 to 1963 (Library of the University of Colorado at Boulder)

other forms of wordplay, all intended to break down clichés and disrupt conventional ways of thinking while deconstructing the absurd rules of society. It is also remarkable in its abundance of intertextual games vis-à-vis the works of such masters as her compatriot Jorge Luis Borges, whose art of allusion she pretends to replicate, and Lewis Carroll, whose nonsense games she embraces in this and other texts.

To sum up, then, if language was a medium that controlled her by undermining her sense of a stable self, it was also one she could control to some extent when she resorted to verbal humor to undermine canonized discourse. Language, however, performed another crucial role for Pizarnik as it served as a temporary refuge from her mad race toward the abyss of absolute silence.

In a way, her writing practices may be regarded as life-sustaining, a means to eschew a frightening, albeit enticing, nothingness. "Everything I say and do is to insure the continuity of my being, the existence of a language and thought of my own," she muses in her journal on 1 March 1961 and then adds, "but I inhabit fear, I am suspended from silence." In a similar vein, she confides in "Cold IV Hand Blue," published in *El infierno musical,* via her poetic alter ego: "Voy a ocultarme en el lenguaje / y por qué / tengo miedo" (I'll hide myself inside language / why / because I am afraid). Her survival appeared assured by her ability to engage in a poetic practice that conjured up nonrational forces but managed to protect her, at least temporarily, from a vertiginous fall into silence. In sum, her lived experience morphed into a linguistic exploration in which the desire to create and the need to survive coalesced. Pizarnik's revolutionary insights into the nature of language and its possibilities also fostered in the young woman a love of literature that led to her decision to become a writer herself.

The author's awareness of the fluidity of language and the impossibility of saying anything with precision because meaning never stabilizes, situates her within a generation of writers known as "the critical poets." Their artistic production throughout Latin America during a period spanning the 1960s through the 1980s proved as groundbreaking as that of the writers of the "Boom" in the 1960s and 1970s. Authors such as Octavio Paz, Borges, and Alberto Girri belonged to this illustrious group. Effectively echoing the post-structuralists' stance that regards language as a network of differences, the critical poets shared with Pizarnik the same distrust of its referential capability, the same frustration at its failure to fully express the self. With metapoetic concern, they wrote poems that were critical of their own construction, thus expressing their revolutionary awareness that meaning did not reside outside the poem but was created within it endlessly by the unceasing interplay of its linguistic components. "A critical poem," wrote Paz in *Pasado en claro* (1975), "is a poem that contains its own negation and . . . that makes of that negation the point of departure for the song." What is negated here is the possibility of a univocal meaning. What is affirmed, on the other hand, is the potential for a different kind of song—one in which meanings would proliferate and ambiguity would reign.

Starting early in her career, Pizarnik wrote poems that turned upon themselves to reflect on their own construction. In "Piedra fundamental" (Fundamental Stone), a crucial text in *El infierno musical,* the speaking subject expresses the frustration, endlessly reiterated throughout the poet's body of work, at the impossibility of verbalizing what she might have liked to verbalize.

"Creí que me había muerto, y que la muerte era decir un nombre sin cesar" (I thought that I had died, and that death meant to say a name incessantly), she observes in that piece and immediately adds, "No es esto, tal vez, lo que quiero decir. Este decir y decirse no es grato" (This is not, perhaps, what I am trying to say. This saying and saying oneself is not pleasant). Elsewhere in the same collection, the poetic voice alludes to the proclivity of language to produce meaning unceasingly when she remarks in "La palabra que sana" (The Words That Cure) that "Cada palabra dice lo que dice y además otra cosa" (each word says what it says and furthermore more and something else). The sense of being at a loss vis-à-vis the relentless proliferation of meaning, which is rendered even more dramatic by Pizarnik's experience of an ever-changing self, leads the poetic subject to affirm in the same text: "No puedo hablar con mi voz sino con mis voces" (I can't speak with my voice but only with my voices). In fact, the salient feature of her compositions is the continuous shifting of the poetic subject from one grammatical person to others, in what may aptly be described as a game of shifting mirrors. Eventually, the poet's experience with language led her to remark in her diary (25 July 1965) that, in the final analysis, "the principal thing in each of us is unsayable," a fact that would not prevent her, however, from investigating "by writing why the principal thing is unsayable."

Upon completion of her secondary studies, Pizarnik enrolled in the University of Buenos Aires and concentrated first on philosophy and later on literature and journalism. In these early days she also studied painting under the well-known Surrealist artist Juan B. Planas. Decisive to her development was the friendship she established with some of the best-known Latin American writers of the period. In addition to Borges, she came to know Julio Cortázar, Severo Sarduy, Paz, Mario Vargas Llosa, and Olga Orozco, her literary "mother." During these eventful years she began to familiarize herself with such great European authors as Stéphane Mallarmé; Isidore Lucien Ducasse, Comte de Lautreamont; Gérard de Nerval; Marcel Proust; Jean-Paul Sartre; James Joyce; André Gide; and Paul Claudel. In addition, she became well acquainted with André Breton and Paul Eluard and translated some of their works. It comes as no surprise that given her experience as a poet, which had placed her at the edge of rationality, she would readily embrace the Surrealists' project to access the unconscious and liberate its creative forces. The author also shared in their aspirations to embark on an experience that would transcend art and embrace life itself. In that she was also haunted by the idea of poetry as a self-sacrificing act, she exhibited affinity with the French "dark poets" such as Lautreamont.

Arguably, another factor impinging on her career was her coming of age as a writer during the period of cultural effervescence following the removal from office of Juan Domingo Perón. Although she did not openly share their leftist political orientation, she is considered a member of the Generation of '55, a constellation of poets born around 1930 who espoused Sartre's theory of *engagement*. Rather, her commitment was to the Surrealist experience, which she imbued with existentialist overtones. Pizarnik's acquaintance with the splendid European culture of the period generated her dream of journeying to Paris in search of a homeland, a dream made reality by a Guggenheim Fellowship in 1959.

During her four-year stay in Paris, the author wrote *Arbol de Diana,* an influential work that was prefaced by Paz and published in Buenos Aires in 1962. This collection was not, however, her first publication. Prior to her departure, three others had appeared in Buenos Aires: *La tierra más ajena* (The Strangest Land, 1955), *La última inocencia,* and *Las aventuras perdidas* (The Lost Adventures, 1958). Only her first publication bears her full name, Flora Alejandra Pizarnik. Throughout her life she published seven collections of poems, prose pieces with some of them exhibiting narrative dimensions, and expository prose. In addition, she left her journals, which were edited by Orozco and Becciú, another friend, shortly after her death.

The title of her first published work, *La tierra más ajena,* is suggestive of both the strangeness of the land that had rejected her parents and remained a mystery to her, and the strangeness of the metaphoric territory of her own experience where she felt fragmented and betrayed by language. Interestingly, Pizarnik used a quote from Arthur Rimbaud as an epigraph to this work, a poet she learned to appreciate increasingly in the course of her life. A brief piece she composed in the year of her death, which opens with the line "¿Quién es yo?" (Who Is I?), echoes the French poet's famous assertion "je est un autre" (I is an other) while alluding to her lifelong quest for an unambiguous sense of identity. This quest may have originated in infancy, a period when the child and the adult appear to have strangely coexisted in her life. "Recuerdo mi niñez / cuando yo era una anciana" (I remember my childhood when / I was an old woman), the poetic voice muses in "El despertar" (The Awakening), a poem from *Las aventuras perdidas* in which, by way of her poetic alter ego, the author takes stock of the first twenty years of her life. It is a life that began with an idyllic age of innocence soon to be betrayed by the awareness of death; followed by her emergence as a poet, that is, by her engagement in a creative process continually attended by the fear of fragmentation and death. As suggested in the title of one of her major works, she regarded this fear as the fuel igniting

Paperback cover for Pizarnik's 1968 poetry collection, which deals with the allure of death and the threat of madness (Ralph Brown Draughton Library, Auburn University)

her poetic practice and translating into a personal "musical hell." "El despertar" is articulated as an address to the Almighty in the guise of a passionate query as to what to do with her fear, rather than of a prayer for its appeasing. Noteworthy in Pizarnik's early collections are those texts, expressive of the poet's sense of a betrayed childhood, that show a child-woman engaging in absurd dialogues with Death and/or a mad Queen against a landscape reminiscent of Alice's Wonderland or the never-never land of fairy tales.

In these early collections the fear of death and fragmentation is compounded by the fear of loneliness at the realization of the futility involved in the pursuit of love. "Siniestro delirio amar a una sombra" (Sinister delirium to love a shadow), the poetic self laments in "Exilio" (Exile), a composition included in *Las aventuras perdidas.* A similar feeling is echoed in *Arbol de Diana* when the poetic voice laments, "sólo la sed / el silencio / ningún encuentro" (only thirst / silence / nothing encountered), thus revealing that the fear of nothingness and silence was also present within the realm of love. Whatever the nature of her fear, Pizarnik turned it into poetry, an expression of her personal hell.

Pizarnik's sojourn in Paris proved a watershed in her life, since it was marked by a broadening of her artistic horizons and a more daring attitude in the exploration of her sexuality and her search for love. At that early stage she was open to sexual encounters with members of both sexes, a stance that made her aware that love seldom materializes and that access to others is impossible. "How old the necessity to love," she wrote in her diary on 27 March 1961 and then lamented, "How impossible a friend's hand." She referred insistently in her diary to an unidentified G., a male lover who caused her to feel the pain of unrequited love. Interestingly, this reference is one of the few to love in her work in which the gender of the lover is specified. In the area of her professional life, Pizarnik fared much better while in Paris, as the Argentine colony welcomed her with open arms. Cortázar, among others, connected the young poet with several distinguished authors and knowledgeable people who encouraged her vocation. In addition, she met some of the European and French writers of the period such as Simone de Beauvoir, René Daumel, Henri Michaux, Italo Calvino, and Georges Bataille, whom she came to consider her literary "father." As well, she became acquainted with painters such as Joan Miró, Paul Klee, and Gustave Moreau. While in the French capital she embraced painting once again and participated in other cultural activities, including collaborations in well-known scholarly journals such as *Les Lettres Nouvelles* and *La Nouvelle Revue Française*. By dint of hard work while in Paris she managed to complete *Arbol de Diana,* the work that secured her prominence in the Argentine literary landscape of the time.

Despite the success of her Parisian life, she continued to struggle against her inner demons and the fear of being stalked by her cannibalistic "other." In effect, her sense of alienation from herself and her life was as disturbing as ever: "My life is missing. I am missing from my life," she wrote in her journal on 1 November 1960, and only a year later, on 5 January 1961, she reiterated her sense of despair when she reflected: "The horror of inhabiting myself, of being–how strange–my guest, my passenger, my place of exile." Her fear of being suspended, as it were, over the abyss did not deter her, however, from yielding to the familiar call to "descend to the last bottom," as she wrote on 11 November 1962, and surrender to a creative frenzy. At least once during her Parisian sojourn, she evoked her childhood in her journal and addressed her nostalgia for a paradise lost although, on this occasion, the sense of loss took on the dimension of rape, a metaphor that recurs in her work. "As a child I used to smile, I consented. My memory watches over the corpse of the one I was," she confides and immediately adds, "Voice of the raped woman rising into midnight."

Pizarnik's metaphoric reference to rape points to the forces, whether dictated by destiny or constructed by society, that violate the individual's integrity. These are the forces against which Pizarnik consistently rebelled, both as a social being and as a poet. At the same time, however, her poetic endeavors created a submissive state she would likewise occasionally challenge. "I would have preferred to sing the blues in any small bar full of smoke than to spend the nights of my life scratching into language like a madwoman," she wrote in her diary on 2 May 1962, thus expressing her hidden desire to have lived a normal life. A nocturnal singer, as she defines herself elsewhere because the night was her most creative period, the poet stubbornly searched for a grounding center to both her life and art. As it inevitably receded into the horizon, the center was forever absent. Undoubtedly, this sense of absence at the core of her existence and her art prevailed even under the splendor of her Parisian life. She returned to Buenos Aires in 1963. Over the next nine years, toward the end of her life, she published *Los trabajos y las noches* (Works and Nights, 1965), *Extracción de la piedra de locura* (Extraction of the Stone of Folly, 1968), *El infierno musical,* and *La condesa sangrienta* (The Bloody Countess, 1971).

Although Pizarnik's place as the most important voice of her generation had been ensured in Argentina by her trip to Paris and the publication of *Arbol de Diana,* her return to Buenos Aires was predictably anticlimactic. "Compared to my life here," she confessed in her diary on 21 July 1964, "life in Paris was magnificent." Her feverish cultural activities in the Argentine capital, as well as her association with well-known literati and other artists, failed to appease her internal demons or stave off her fear of death. Her ties to *Sur,* a most prestigious journal of international affairs, introduced her to the Buenos Aires artistic aristocracy. Not immune to fame or material gains, she understood the importance of connecting with the elite in her fields of endeavor. Among her new friends was Silvina Ocampo, sister of Victoria, the great lady of letters in Buenos Aires and founder of *Sur.* In addition to her literary work, she further pursued painting, which led to an exhibition in 1965 side by side with Manuel Mujica Láinez, a renowned figure in the art and literary worlds. Her ongoing attraction to such painters as the Swiss Klee or her compatriot Enrique Molina confirms her deep interest in Surrealism. In a rare note of tranquility, she wrote in her diary on 8 July 1964: "Surrealist painting makes me happy like nothing else in the world. Makes me happy and serene." Her collection of poems *Los trabajos y las noches* radically dispelled this illusion of serenity.

Death is present in this work with more poignancy than ever. So are the themes of an irretrievable childhood and unrequited love. Although *Los trabajos y*

El infierno musical

Alejandra Pizarnik

glo
nttuno
rgentina
htores
2

Paperback cover for Pizarnik's 1971 collection, in which she appears to take final stock of her life. She committed suicide the following year (University of Memphis Library).

las noches is the only collection including compositions in which the poetic voice addresses the beloved in amatory terms, it also reveals the poet's final disillusion with love and her decision "no sustentarme nunca de nuevo en el amor" (to never again support myself in love). She clearly preferred to transform her myriad amorous longings, as she did her fears, into poetry. However distressing and perilous an undertaking, poetry, "la palabra inocente" (the innocent word), as she defines it in this piece, is now her sole option. *Los trabajos y las noches* thus expresses Pizarnik's realization that poetry had become her sole option at a decisive period in her life–the period ushered in by her father's death in January 1966.

That same year the poet was awarded the coveted Primer Premio Nacional de Poesía (First National Poetry Prize), an honor that did nothing to mitigate the sense of desolation caused by her father's death. As the fact of death became more real to her and the fear of madness more intense, Pizarnik engaged in a poetic frenzy that resulted in the production of *Extracción de la piedra de locura*. Not everything was negative during the years that

followed her father's death, however. In 1968 she attempted to assert her independence from her family by moving into her own apartment. At about the same time she engaged in her first stable relationship, with a woman who possessed enough understanding to deal gently with her mood swings and drug addiction. Apart from the drugs prescribed by her psychiatrists to combat depression, the poet needed medication both to remain lucid while writing and to induce sleep.

The same year, she was awarded a second Guggenheim Fellowship and journeyed to Paris once again, a trip that turned out to be a mistake. In effect, the city she visited for the second time bore no resemblance to the Paris that had kept her in awe earlier on. Surrealists and "dark poets" were now relics of the past; her literary "father" himself, Bataille, had died; anti-Semitism was rampant in the French capital. Devastated by the experience, Pizarnik shortened her stay drastically and promptly returned home. A period of voluntary confinement ensued that resulted in her first suicide attempt and her institutionalization in 1970. After an extended stay at the mental hospital she was allowed weekend passes to visit family and friends. During one of those weekends, in September 1972, she attempted suicide again, successfully this time.

The previous year, 1971, had proved an extremely significant year for the author in that she met the woman who turned out to be the love of her life but who, as the recipient of an important award that took her to the United States, had to leave Pizarnik behind. It had also been a productive year that resulted in the publication of *El infierno musical* and *La condesa sangrienta*. Along with *Extracción de la piedra de locura,* these works may be interpreted as attempts to fulfill a need that took on especial poignancy during the last ten years of the poet's life. It was the need to create boundaries for her fragmented psyche and poetic production by writing "a single book in prose instead of poems and fragments. A book or a dwelling in which to take refuge," as she wrote in her diary on 28 September 1962. Boundaries eluded Pizarnik until the end, however. The musical hell proved deadly, although immensely illuminating, as she approached the end, as did the metaphoric attempt to extract the dreaded stone of folly.

A pivotal work in her brief career, *Extracción de la piedra de locura* reveals an intensification of the allure of death in the poet's life as well as a renewed awareness of the threat of madness. At the same time, it also discloses new dimensions in the array of feelings elicited by her poetic practice. For the first time in Pizarnik's entire production, the poetic subject, however briefly and tenuously, refers to the unfathomable "other" in rather positive terms as a place of love, and to the creative act itself in terms of a fiesta or celebration. Conceivably, at this point in her life the poet's creative practice generated novel insights into the nature of the poetic act and the role of language; the latter is experienced now as the medium to probe arcane secrets about life, love, death, and the joys of creativity, even as it gives a voice to the terrifying "other." Symbolized here by a girl "densa de música ancestral" (dense with ancestral music) wearing "su máscara de loba" (her mask of a wolf), who inhabits the poet and is transformed into a figure of death, this uncanny "other" urges the poetic subject to let herself fall into the abyss and risk madness and death, as she writes in "Fragmentos para dominar el silencio" (Fragments to Control Silence). Metaphorically lodged in the brain in the guise of a stone-like tumor, according to a medieval belief, madness appears here less as a curse than as a privilege. Rather than demanding its extraction, the poem subtly calls for its acceptance as the poetic subject ventures into the garden of death, which she also sees as a place of love as well as the place where she will surrender to the joyful, albeit painful, celebration of the birth of her "cuerpos poéticos" (poetic bodies).

Anticipating *El infierno musical,* a work in which she verbalizes her ardent desire to make "el cuerpo del poema con mi cuerpo" (the body of the poem with my body), Pizarnik describes her poetic act here in terms of childbirth and the poetic bodies as arising simultaneously from the womb and the throat. This translates into an ecstatic moment during which the poetic subject metaphorically regresses to a uterine stage and is herself reborn. Life and death thus coexist in a creative act that involves sexuality and the body in an essential way; it is also an act, however, that brings the poetic self to the edge of sanity and, once again, confronts her with absence and an unfathomable silence. "De pronto se deshizo: ningún nacimiento" (The whole thing fell apart suddenly: no birth), she laments, thus underlining the fact that the long-sought poem that would have provided her with boundaries and a grounding center had again eluded her. After surrendering to the fear and trembling as well as the joy attending the creative process and her own metaphoric rebirth, the poet's alter ego is once again left suspended over the abyss, uttering the same unanswerable questions that have continually haunted her: "Ebria de mí, de la música, de los poemas, por qué no dije del agujero de la ausencia" (Drunk on myself, on music, on poems, why didn't I mention the hole of absence?) she wonders. "Para qué este gran silencio?" (Why this great silence?) These unanswerable queries prefigure the questions posed at the end of *El infierno musical.*

Given the intimations of frenzied joy mixed with the pain and love attending her poetic experience, it is fair to argue that toward the end of her life Pizarnik may have come to terms with her poetic destiny, even as she laments the constant danger of insanity and abandons all hope of a grounding center and an ordinary life. Identifying with Antonin Artaud, an author she revered during her last years, she suggested as early as 18 August 1968 in her diary that they both shared an identical necessity, that of "a paroxysmal dissonance at the height of the most intolerable beauty . . . a necessity of convulsive and shaking life for lack of all possibility of immediate life." She qualified these words three days later when she wrote: "the importance of the August 15 fragment consists in that it names my wound." The apparent acceptance of this wound and hence of her destiny as a poet may be regarded as evidence of a transformed awareness on the poet's part, the awareness that life for her lay nowhere but within. In *El infierno musical,* a work in which she appears to take final stock of her life, she is moved to state categorically, by way of her poetic alter ego, "ya no soy más que un adentro" (I am nothing but an inside), an assertion in "Los de lo oculto" (Those of That Which Is Concealed) that prefigures the one in which she affirms, in "Los poseídos entre lilas" (The Possessed Among Lilas), "yo ya no existo" (I no longer exist) to the world.

El infierno musical includes a metaphor that encapsulates both the author's life and her work. Developed in the section "Piedra fundamental" (Fundamental Stone), the metaphor relates to a piano keyboard, a symbolic repository of the music to which Pizarnik had consistently aspired to gain access during her lifelong search for a homeland. By way of the poetic speaker, the author avows her lasting aspiration to penetrate the keys and thus enter the inside of the music in the hope of finding the much desired, albeit impossible, center. Characteristically, the poetic subject laments here in "Piedra fundamental" that "la música se movía, se apresuraba" (the music was moving, was hurrying) and that the center was nowhere to be found. If there is no center but only absence at the core of Pizarnik's experience, there is also a profound sense of solitude, born out of the realization that her poetry has not been intended to promote a dialogue but rather to affirm a double monologue, one, as she describes it in "Nombres y figuras" (Names and Figures), "entre yo y mi antro lujurioso, el tesoro de los piratas enterrado en mi primera persona del singular" (between myself and my luxurious cavern, the pirates' treasure buried in my first-person singular). This apparent indifference to others is soon dispelled, however, when the poetic self, speaking in "Los poseídos entre lilas," laments that her impotence vis-à-vis the forces enshrined in language and the inner self has also prevented her from singing on behalf of others. "Y no haber podido hablar por todos aquellos que olvidaron el canto" (And not having been able to speak for all those who forgot the song), grieves the poetic alter ego, perhaps also alluding to the fact that there was not much time left and that the end was near.

El infierno musical concludes with the vision of a woman looking out of a window and contemplating a city strewn with corpses and remains of all kinds—a projection of the poet's inner landscape. The questions with which Pizarnik closes this collection via the poetic subject, questions that are left unanswered, intimate the end. Pizarnik's last publication, La condesa sangrienta, is considered by many to be fraught with social implications as it appears to denounce the absolute power wielded by despotic rulers in her own country and the world over. In effect, after Perón's fall in 1955, the Argentine military establishment gradually strengthened its powers, a fact that inevitably led to the military takeover of 1976, four years after the author's death.

Pizarnik's life was shaped on the one hand by the Nazi Holocaust, which had remained indelibly embedded in her parents' minds, and on the other by the constant threat of military violence and despotism hanging over the Argentine people. Thus, many regard La condesa sangrienta, a work that focuses on the different kinds of torture inflicted upon innocent young women by a madwoman of noble birth, as a reflection of Argentine history at the time. Immediately after its publication the book became a classic among people, young and old, who condemn the abusive behavior of those who wield absolute power. The text constitutes a rewriting of Erzsébet Bathory: La Comtesse Sanglante (Erzsébet Bathory: The Bloody Countess, 1962), a work by the Surrealist French author Valentine Penrose. In this regard, La condesa sangrienta attests to Pizarnik's interest in exploring the dark side of human nature, the shadow. A character named Sombra (Shadow), who inhabits the proverbial forbidden garden or the riverside and stands as an alter ego of the author, recurs in her writings at the end of her life. In fact, this character figures prominently in the collection Textos de Sombra y últimos poemas, published posthumously by Orozco, her literary "mother" and another friend. La condesa sangrienta could also be considered an artistic, albeit extreme, rendering of the torture the author herself experienced by the disintegrating impact of unconscious drives, the realm of the shadow. This realm may be seen as replicated in the labyrinthine dungeon of the medieval castle in Csejthe, where Penrose's countess had set up her torture chambers at the time of the Hungarian Empire.

An historical personage from the Middle Ages, the notorious Bathory had relied on the strength of her spouse's illustrious family name to remain unpunished and thus all-powerful for six years while torturing hundreds of young women. In the tradition of vampirism, the countess believed she needed her victims' blood to ensure the preservation of her own youth and feed her dreams of immortality while satisfying her erotic desires. One of her methods of torture involved the Melancholy Mirror, a contraption that victimized the countess herself in a masochistic manner. As explained by the narrative voice, the lady would spend her day "delante de su gran espejo sombrío, el famoso espejo cuyo modelo había diseñado ella misma" (in front of her large dark mirror; a famous mirror she had designed herself). The reader is also informed that the mirror was an adequate emblem of the countess's experience of melancholia, an illness that implied the doubling of the self. Like Pizarnik in real life, who was obsessed by the doubling of her own self and its subsequent dissolution in a symbolic game of shifting mirrors, the countess was terrified by her reflections in the ominous surface. From her perspective, "nadie tiene más sed de tierra, de sangre y de sexualidad feroz que estas criaturas que habitan los fríos espejos" (no one has more thirst for earth, for blood, and for ferocious sexuality than the creatures who inhabit cold mirrors), a description that befitted her deepest inclinations and desires. The countess is fascinated with the dungeon in the castle, where she conducts her deadly rituals and loves the metaphoric "laberinto" (maze-shaped dungeon) of her own mind, "el lugar típico donde tenemos miedo; el viscoso, el inseguro espacio de la desprotección y del extraviarse" (the archetypal hell of our fears; the viscous, insecure space where we are unprotected and can get lost).

Alejandra Pizarnik's rendition of *La condesa sangrienta* is prefaced by a quotation from Sartre: "El criminal no hace la belleza: él mismo es la auténtica belleza" (The criminal does not make beauty; he himself is the authentic beauty). In stark contrast with the chosen preface, she closes her text with the heartfelt assertion that "la libertad absoluta de la criatura humana es horrible" (the absolute freedom of the human creature is horrible). Perhaps this assertion addresses the experience of absolute freedom she herself enjoyed, an experience that moved her to explore the space without boundaries of language and her unconscious and resulted in her own immolation.

Letters:

Correspondencia Pizarnik, edited by Ivonne Bordelois (Buenos Aires: Seix Barral, 1998);

From the Forbidden Garden: Letters from Alejandra Pizarnik to Antonio Beneyto, edited by Carlota Caulfield, translated by Caulfield and Angela McEwan (Lewisburg, Pa.: Bucknell University Press, 2003).

References:

Susan Bassnett, "Blood and Mirrors: Imagery of Violence in the Writings of Alejandra Pizarnik," in *Latin American Women's Writing: Feminist Readings in Theory and Crisis,* edited by Anny Brooksbank Jones and Catherine Davies (Oxford: Clarendon Press, 1996), pp. 127–147;

Bassnett, "Speaking with Many Voices: The Poems of Alejandra Pizarnik," in *Knives and Angels: Women Writers in Latin America,* edited by Bassnett (London: Zed, 1990), pp. 36–51;

Alicia Borinsky, "Alejandra Pizarnik: The Self and Its Impossible Landscapes," in *A Dream of Light and Shadow: Portraits of Latin American Women Writers,* edited by Marjorie Agosín (Albuquerque: University of New Mexico Press, 1995), pp. 291–302;

David William Foster, "Of Power and Virgins: Alejandra Pizarnik's *La condesa sangrienta,*" in his *Violence in Argentine Literature: Cultural Responses to Tyranny* (Columbia: University of Missouri Press, 1995), pp. 98–114;

Foster, "The Representation of the Body in the Poetry of Alejandra Pizarnik," in his *Sexual Textualities: Essays on Queer/ing Latin American Writing* (Austin: University of Texas Press, 1997), pp. 94–117;

Florinda F. Goldberg, *Alejandra Pizarnik: Este espacio que somos* (Gaithersburg, Md.: Ediciones Hispamérica, 1994);

Jill S. Kuhnheim, "The Struggle of Imagination: Alejandra Pizarnik and Olga Orozco," in her *Gender, Politics, and Poetry in Twentieth-Century Argentina* (Gainesville: University Press of Florida, 1996), pp. 64–89;

Cristina Piña, *Alejandra Pizarnik* (Buenos Aires: Planeta, 1991);

Thorpe Running, "Octavio Paz and the Magic of the Word" and "The Negative Poems of Alejandra Pizarnik," in *The Critical Poem: Borges, Paz, and Other Language-Centered Poets in Latin America* (London: Associated University Press, 1996), pp. 30–50, 87–104.

Papers:

Alejandra Pizarnik's papers are at Princeton University Library.

Pedro Prado
(8 October 1886 – 31 January 1952)

Heather L. Colburn
Northwestern University

BOOKS: *Flores de cardo* (Santiago: Imprenta Universitaria, 1908);

La casa abandonada: Parábolas y pequeños ensayos (Santiago: Imprenta Universitaria, 1912);

El llamado del mundo (Santiago: Imprenta Universitaria, 1913);

La Reina de Rapa Nui (Santiago: Imprenta Universitaria, 1914);

Los pájaros errantes: Poemas menores y breves divagaciones (Santiago: Imprenta Universitaria, 1915);

Los Diez: El claustro, La barca (Santiago: Imprenta Universitaria, 1915);

Ensayos sobre arquitectura y poesía (Santiago: Imprenta Universitaria, 1916);

Alsino (Santiago: Imprenta Universitaria, 1920);

Las copas (Buenos Aires: Glusberg, 1921);

Fragmentos de Karez-I-Roshan, by Prado and Antonio Castro Leal as Karez-I-Roshan (Santiago: Imprenta de Silva, 1922);

Un juez rural (Santiago: Nascimento, 1924; translated by Lesley Byrd Simpson as *A Country Judge* (Berkeley: University of California Press, 1968);

Androvar: Poema dramático (Santiago: Nascimento, 1925);

Camino de las horas (Santiago: Nascimento, 1934);

Otoño en las dunas (Santiago: Nascimento, 1940);

Esta bella ciudad envenenada (Santiago: Imprenta Universitaria, 1945);

No más que una rosa (Buenos Aires: Losada, 1946);

Antología: Las estancias del amor (Santiago: Editorial del Pacífico, 1949);

Viejos poemas inéditos (Santiago: Escuela Nacional de Artes Gráficas, 1949);

El llamado del mundo: Flores de cardo, Karez-I-Roshan, y textos inéditos, edited, with a prologue and notes, by René de Costa (Santiago: Editorial Universitaria, 1971).

Collections: *Poemas en prosa,* selected, with a prologue, by Antonio Castro Leal (Mexico City: México Moderno, 1923);

La roja torre de los diez, selected, with a prologue, by Enrique Espinosa (Santiago: Zig-Zag, 1961);

Pedro Prado (Archivo Fotografico, Universidad de Chile)

Pedro Prado: Antología, edited by Enrique Pascal G.-H. (Santiago: Editorial Nacional Gabriela Mistral, 1975).

OTHER: Manuel Magallanes Moure, *Sus mejores poemas,* edited by Prado (Santiago: Nascimento, 1926).

SELECTED PERIODICAL PUBLICATIONS– UNCOLLECTED:
POETRY
"Lemuria," *Atenea,* 1 (May 1924): 107–116.
FICTION
"Cuadro de estío–El inválido," *Independiente* (Santiago), first week of November 1905, p. 3;

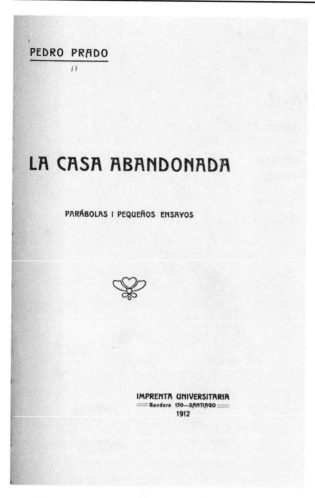

PEDRO PRADO

LA CASA ABANDONADA

PARÁBOLAS I PEQUEÑOS ENSAYOS

IMPRENTA UNIVERSITARIA
Bandera 130—SANTIAGO
1912

Title page for Prado's second book, in which he turns from free verse to the prose poem (Vanderbilt University Library)

"Cuando se es pobre," *Zig-Zag,* 2 (5 August 1906);

"La reina maga," *Zig-Zag,* 2 (23 December 1906);

"Prosas Bíblicas," *Nosotros,* 18 (March 1924): 369–372;

"El pueblo muerto," *Prensa* (Buenos Aires), 16 October 1925;

"La risa en el desierto," *Prensa* (Buenos Aires), 13 December 1925.

NONFICTION

"Gabriela Mistral, a los poetas de México," *Nación* (Santiago), 22 June 1922, p. 1;

"El arte obrero, la tradición y el porvenir de la arquitectura," *Nación* (Santiago), 2 July 1922, p. 7;

"Pablo Neruda y su libro Crepusculario," *Zig-Zag,* 9 (20 October 1923).

The 1949 recipient of Chile's National Prize in Literature, Pedro Prado played a foundational role in the artistic community of early-twentieth-century Santiago. Although lesser known than his compatriots Pablo Neruda, Gabriela Mistral, and Vicente Huidobro, Prado is credited with quietly laying the groundwork for a poetic revolution

in Chile that later had a marked effect on these more internationally recognized poets. Prado's work introduced both free verse and prose poetry to Chile, paving the way for more extreme formal and thematic experimentation by later poets.

Pedro Prado was born on 8 October 1886 to Absalón Prado and Laura Calvo Mackenna in Santiago, Chile. The son of a doctor and an aristocratic mother, Prado benefited from his family's economic and social standing throughout his life, never depending upon work for economic survival. When Prado was merely two years old, however, his mother died from complications of a second pregnancy, and thus his father became the primary caregiver. Despite the poet's young age at the time of his mother's death, her absence seems to have affected Prado a great deal throughout the remainder of his life. Although Absalón Prado was, by all accounts, a rather rigid and disciplined man, he and his son shared a close relationship, even sleeping in the same room, where they would chat every night. Prado studied humanities at the Instituto Nacional and, later, architecture in the School of Engineering at the Universidad de Chile.

In addition to architecture, Prado studied painting and edited *La Universidad,* a periodical that also published a few of his essays. Prado's official entry into the publishing world happened in 1905 when, using the pseudonym Álvaro J. Credo, he published a short story, "Cuadro de estío–El inválido" (A Summer Portrait–The Invalid) in a small Santiago newspaper, *El Independiente.* This initial publication was perhaps overshadowed by the death of his father in November of the same year. Prado continued writing, and on 5 August 1906 he published another short story, "Cuando se es pobre" (When One is Poor) in *Zig-Zag,* the same magazine that published Prado's "La reina maga" (The Wise Queen) as part of its annual Christmas competition in December of that year.

From his beginnings as a short-story writer, Prado turned to poetry and in 1908 published his first collection of poems, *Flores de cardo* (Thistle Flowers), a book written in free verse. *Flores de cardo* signals a shift away from *Modernista* poetic sensibilities toward a more diverse poetry. As the Chilean literary critics Julio Arriagada Augier and Hugo Goldsack note, the verses of this volume "enriquecen inesperadamente la temática usual, insinúan procedimientos más complejos de introspección, acuñan un mayor número de imágenes, . . . y sobre todo demuestran que la poesía puede y debe ser algo más que un confesionario de menudas tribulaciones sentimentales" (unexpectedly enrich the typical theme, suggest more complex methods of introspection, bring together a greater number of images, . . . and above all demonstrate that poetry can and should be something more than mere confession of trivial sentimental tribulations).

Paperback cover for Prado's 1915 collection, a series of essays about life and art that are not quite poetry but not quite prose (Duke University Library)

In 1910 Prado founded the *Revista Contemporánea* (Contemporary Journal), a journal dedicated to fomenting a serious intellectual climate in Chile. Although the magazine folded in 1911 with its fifth issue, *Revista Contemporánea* indicates the importance for Prado of considering intellectual aspects of artistic and literary production. In the same year as the magazine first appeared, Prado married Adriana Jaramillo Bruce, and their first child, a son named Pedro, was born. Moreover, in 1910 Prado became involved with the Congreso de Estudiantes (Student Congress) and journeyed to Buenos Aires as part of Chile's student delegation.

Prado's next major publication was *La casa abandonada: Parábolas y pequeños ensayos* (The Abandoned House: Parables and Small Essays) in 1912. In this collection he turns from free verse to the prose poem, a form that was debated at the time in Chile and elsewhere in terms of its poetic merit. Various critics point to *La casa abandonada* as Prado's best effort in his younger years, noting that this volume suggests the profundity in form and thought that characterize his later works. This innovative collection is followed by the return to free verse in *El llamado del mundo*

(The Beckoning World) in 1913. Of this small volume, the poem "Lázaro" stands out as one of the most lauded poems Prado was to write. In these verses, through the voice of the biblical Lazarus, Prado addresses the complex issue of death and resurrection in verses without formal meter and rhyme.

The following year Prado published his first novel, *La Reina de Rapa Nui* (The Queen of Rapa Nui, 1914), a rather short narrative of 150 pages. The narrative relates the encounter between "civilized" and "primitive" cultures on Easter Island (Rapa Nui in the language of the islanders). In the prologue Prado introduces an anonymous traveler/narrator as an older neighbor who left a manuscript that the younger man revised and titled "La reina de Rapa Nui." In the prologue, Prado's anonymous narrator comments on the problems of modern society, remarking that "Los pintores son los veraderos filósofos" (Painters are the true philosophers). Throughout the remainder of the novel, this conflict between mainland and ancient island cultures is manifested through the narrator's infatuation and love affair with the queen of Rapa Nui. This first novel treats a rather exotic fantasy with a simple literary

PEDRO PRADO

CAMINO DE
LAS HORAS

N A S C I M E N T O
SANTIAGO   1934   CHILE

Title page for Prado's collection of rigidly formal sonnets on such traditional themes as love, nostalgia, nature, and poetry (Vanderbilt University Library)

style, yet *La Reina de Rapa Nui* is a commentary on the universality of the human spirit with all its faults.

In 1915 Prado returned to poetry and published two collections—*Los pájaros errantes: Poemas menores y breves divagaciones* (The Wandering Birds: Minor Poems and Brief Wanderings) and *Los Diez: El claustro, La barca* (The Ten: The Cloister, The Boat). For many critics, *Los pájaros errantes* represents the culmination of Prado's prose poetry both in formal and thematic terms. Augier and Goldsack point to this collection as seminal in its utilization of antilyricism and antirationalism—two trends that were further developed by other poets, including Neruda and Huidobro. Moreover, Prado continues to employ natural images that are unquestionably from the Chilean landscape at the same time that he addresses what the critic Raúl Silva Castro, in *Pedro Prado* (1965), calls "el problema de los límites de la conciencia y el de la elección" (the problem of the limits of consciousness and choice). Throughout *Los pájaros errantes* Prado comments on this existential conflict between freedom and choice.

In contrast to the undeniable poetic nature of *Los pájaros errantes*, *Los Diez* is not quite poetry, yet not quite prose, either. As Silva Castro notes, *Los Diez* is more a series of parabolic essays about life and art, some even "sutiles poemas en prosa, en los cuales la forma es todo" (subtle prose poems in which form is everything), along with drawings by Prado himself. Again, there are disagreements among critics as to the merits of this volume, but its place in Chilean literature appears to be unquestionable, not only because of the combination of spiritual, aesthetic, and philosophical questions with a rather original literary style, but also because it introduced the artistic group by the same name, Los Diez.

Los Diez is a reference to a group of poets, painters, musicians, and literary critics, begun by Prado sometime in 1915, that was fundamental to the rise of the Generation of 1920. The actual number of members in Los Diez is disputed, but most agree that there were not ten members. Augier and Goldsack name nine initial members: Prado, Manuel Magallanes Moure, Ernesta A. Guzmán, Alberto Ried, Juan Francisco González, Alfonso Leng, Julio Bertrand, Armando Donoso, and Acario Cotapos. Silva Castro includes Alberto García Guerrero, Eduardo Barrios, and Augusto D'Halmar among the group's roster. According to Prado, Los Diez was not a formal sect or institution or society, but rather a group of artists, without an actual leader, united by their desire to foster and promote the arts. To this end, the group published the short-lived review *Los Diez* during 1916–1917. Despite the brief existence of the magazine, Los Diez published three short novels by Rafael Maluenda; another novel by Fernando Santiván; short stories by Federico Gana; an anthology of poetry and one of short stories; an issue dedicated to the Uruguayan writer and critic José Enrique Rodó; and the final number, dedicated wholly to Chilean music. In this way the group had a profound effect on Chilean literature, bringing to press art and literature that might not have seen light otherwise.

Amid the flurry of activity of Los Diez, Prado published a collection of essays, *Ensayos sobre arquitectura y poesía* (Essays on Architecture and Poetry, 1916), in which he considers various questions of the two subjects dear to his heart. Yet, several years passed before the publication of Prado's most internationally recognized work, the novel *Alsino* (1920). Subtitled a "*poema novelesco*" (novelized poem), *Alsino* is a rather fantastic tale about the eldest son of poor, alcoholic parents. The young boy constantly dreams of flying and, in his first unsuccessful attempt, falls to the ground and injures his back. Alsino's grandparents care for him during his paralysis, and eventually he is able to walk again, but is now a hunchback. The novel details the boy's journey across the Chilean landscape—his trials, tribulations, love, and eventual death. While critics are divided as to whether *Alsino* is a social allegory—commenting on the lack of social mobility in Chilean society or on the role of the poet in society—or simply a Chilean version of the Icarus myth, all agree that this novel remains Prado's best-known work. At the time of its release *Alsino* received a great deal of attention from the press and even appears to have laid groundwork for the mixing of reality and fantasy that came to characterize Latin American literature of the Boom.

In addition to being named director of the Museo de Bellas Artes (Museum of Fine Arts), in 1921 Prado published *Las copas* (The Goblets)—a collection of prose poems, several of which had been published in *Los Diez;* the next year another poetry collection, *Fragmentos de Karez-I-Roshan* (Fragments of Karez-I-Roshan), appeared. Since Rabindranath Tagore won the Nobel Prize in literature in 1913, the popularity of Eastern mysticism had made its way westward to the Americas from Europe. In response to what they considered to be a rather blind faith on the part of the Chilean reading public, Prado and the Mexican writer Antonio Castro Leal created a fictional literary figure, Karez-I-Roshan, and then set about creating a small volume of prose poems written by him. The book was complete with a photograph, a translator's note, and biography. The tome reportedly sold out in various bookstores and was welcomed with favorable reviews and praise from literary persons such as the *El Mercurio* critic Hernán Díaz Arrieta and even Gabriela Mistral. Finally, in 1922, Castro Leal confessed the truth behind the genesis of *Fragmentos de Karez-I-Roshan* in a letter to the editor of *El Mercurio.*

In 1924 Prado's last novel, *Un juez rural* (translated as *A Country Judge,* 1968), was published, as well as his political treatise, *Bases para un nuevo gobierno y un nuevo parlamento* (Bases for a New Government and a New Parliament). In contrast to *La reina de Rapa Nui* and *Alsino, Un juez rural* is more realist and less fantastic in content, and the role of Chile's landscape is not as prominent. Yet, Prado continues to imbue his narrative with poetic images in order to communicate profound philosophical musings and questions. *Un juez rural* relates the experience of an architect, Esteban Solaguren, who assumes the duties of a judgeship in the suburbs of Santiago and, during his brief tenure, comes to doubt both the decisions he has dealt and the possibility for justice to truly exist. This realization results in Solaguren's resignation from his post, as well as in his questioning of himself and of humanity at large. Ultimately, the former judge confronts his despair and inevitable death. Once again, Prado's maturity as a writer is evident in this novel—as in *Los pájaros errantes*—through the ways in which he combines *pensamiento* (thought) with *arte* (art). Under Prado's direction, Los Diez made a brief reappearance in the publishing world in 1924 with *Bases para un nuevo gobierno y un nuevo parlamento,* in which Prado makes suggestions for Chile's new constitution.

PEDRO PRADO

ESTA BELLA
CIUDAD
ENVENENADA

Santiago de Chile
1945

Title page for Prado's third collection of sonnets, in which he treats various forms of love: platonic, marital, and divine (Pollak Library, California State University at Fullerton)

Prado traveled to Bolivia in 1925 as a representative of his country in order to foment better artistic and intellectual relations between the two countries. In that same year, Prado also published *Androvar: Poema dramático* (Androvar: Dramatic Poem). More a play than a poem, *Androvar* tells the story of the teacher Androvar, his student Gadel, and Androvar's young wife, Elienai. The characters Jesus, Nun—a blind man whose sight is restored—and a few other minor personages round out the cast. *Androvar* explores the ideas of knowledge, freedom, and choice through its protagonist's desire to fuse his consciousness with that of Gadel and later Elienai so that the three can completely understand each other. The negative existential effects of the freedom to choose total knowledge are illustrated through both Gadel and Elienai's adulterous affair and Gadel's death at the end of the play, a death that both Elienai and Androvar also experience emotionally and psychologically since the three share one consciousness.

Several years passed before Prado published again. In 1927 the poet resumed his travel as a representative of Chile, this time to Bogotá, and he remained in Colombia

PEDRO PRADO

NO MÁS
QUE UNA ROSA

EDITORIAL LOSADA, S. A.
BUENOS AIRES

Paperback cover for Prado's 1946 sonnet collection, in which he uses the rose to symbolize love, death, and beauty (Vanderbilt University Library)

for eighteen months. In 1933 the poet's health began to decline, and the following year *Camino de las horas* (Path of the Hours) was published. This collection of sonnets signals a dramatic shift from Prado's free verse and prose poetry to one of the most traditional and rigid poetic forms. In contrast to the unified themes of *Androvar* and other previous works, the sonnets in *Camino de las horas* address love, nostalgia, nature, poetry, and other traditional themes.

In 1935 Prado again traveled throughout Latin America as part of a delegation, and he received the Premio Roma (Rome Prize), an award from the Italian Embassy in recognition for the poet's literary contributions. Despite another health setback, Prado also set out for the United States and Europe on his first trip outside the continent, as a correspondent for *El Mercurio*. The following year he returned to Chile, rather pessimistic after recognizing the inevitability of war in Europe. In 1940 he published *Otoño en las dunas* (Autumn in the Dunes), another collection of sonnets, the themes of which primarily deal with the poet's love for a woman other than his wife and the various questions and feelings that passion

awakens in him. In 1945 he was elected president of Chile's Sociedad de Escritores (Society of Writers), and in this same year another collection of sonnets, *Esta bella ciudad envenenada* (This Beautiful Poisonous City), was published. Again, the principal theme is love, in this case platonic love, his love for his wife, and even divine love.

The following year Prado published another volume of sonnets, *No más que una rosa* (Only a Rose), in which the flower assumes various roles as a symbol of love, death, beauty, and other abstractions. Three years later, in 1949, Prado was awarded the National Prize in Literature. In this same year he and Raúl Silva Castro compiled *Antología: Las estancias del amor* (Anthology: Stanzas of Love), a collection of sonnets from the poet's previous four books, as well as a few new poems. Also in 1949 he published his last volume, *Viejos poemas inéditos* (Old Unedited Poems), a small collection of older verse and prose poems, as well as the poet's acceptance speech for the National Prize. On 31 January 1952, Prado died at his seaside home at Viña del Mar of a cerebral hemorrhage.

Although Pedro Prado never completely rejected the Modernist aesthetic, he clearly paved the way for

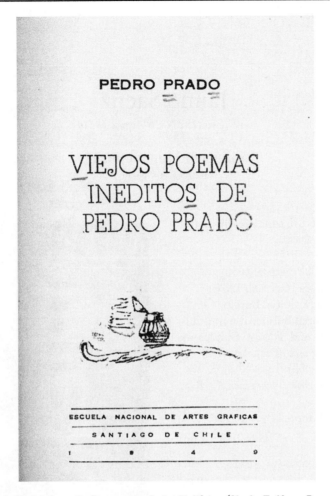

PEDRO PRADO

VIEJOS POEMAS
INEDITOS DE
PEDRO PRADO

ESCUELA NACIONAL DE ARTES GRAFICAS

SANTIAGO DE CHILE

1   9   4   9

Title page for Prado's last collection to appear during his lifetime (Charles E. Young Research Library, University of California, Los Angeles)

the literary avant-garde through his poetic innovations. Principal among these innovations was Prado's rejection of both meter and rhyme as necessary elements of poetry, clearly illustrated through his use of both free verse and prose poetry. His importance as a literary figure in early-twentieth-century Chile is also evident in the artistic group Los Diez. Although not the official leader of the group, Prado was one of the driving forces behind this artistic society, whose contributions include publishing various Chilean authors for the first time. Finally, Prado combined formal innovations with profound philosophical questions, resulting in a body of work that had a significant effect on younger writers such as Neruda, Mistral, and Huidobro.

Letters:

Cartas a Manuel Magallanes Moure (Santiago: Academia Chilena de la Lengua, 1986);

En batalla de sencillez: De Lucila a Gabriela: Cartas a Pedro Prado, 1915–1939, edited by Luis Vargas Saave-

dra, María Ester Martínez Sanz, and Regina Valdés Bowen (Santiago: Dolmen, 1993).

Bibliography:

Olga Blondet, "Bibliografía," in *Pedro Prado, 1886–1952: Vida y obra–Bibliografía–Antología,* edited by Raúl Silva Castro (New York: Hispanic Institute in the United States, 1959), pp. 85–89.

Biography:

Raúl Silva Castro, "Vida y obra," in *Pedro Prado, 1886–1952: Vida y obra–Bibliografía–Antología,* edited by Silva Castro (New York: Hispanic Institute in the United States, 1959), pp. 5–84.

References:

Julio Arriagada Augier and Hugo Goldsack, *Pedro Prado, un clásico de América* (Santiago: Nascimento, 1952);

John R. Kelly, *Pedro Prado* (New York: Twayne, 1974);

Raúl Silva Castro, *Pedro Prado* (Santiago: Andrés Bello, 1965).

Jaime Saenz

(8 October 1921– 16 August 1986)

Elizabeth Monasterios P.
University of Pittsburgh

See also the Saenz entry in *DLB 145: Modern Latin-American Fiction Writers, Second Series.*

BOOKS: *El escalpelo* (La Paz: El Progreso, 1955);

Muerte por el tacto (La Paz: Editora Nacional, 1957);

Aniversario de una visión (La Paz: Editorial Burillo, 1960);

Visitante profundo (La Paz: Editorial Burillo, 1964); translated by Kent Johnson and Forrest Gander as *Immanent Visitor: Selected Poems* (Berkeley: University of California Press, 2002);

El frío; Muerte por el tacto; Aniversario de una visión (La Paz: Editorial Burillo, 1967);

Recorrer esta distancia (La Paz: Editorial Burillo, 1973);

Obra poética (La Paz: Biblioteca del Sesquicentenario de la República, 1975);

Bruckner; y Las tinieblas (La Paz: Difusión, 1978);

Imágenes paceñas: Lugares y personas de la ciudad (La Paz: Difusión, 1979);

Felipe Delgado (La Paz: Difusión, 1979);

Al pasar un cometa: Poemas (1970–72) (La Paz: Altiplano, 1982);

La noche (La Paz: Talleres de Escuela de Artes Gráficas del Colegio Don Bosco, 1984);

Los cuartos (La Paz: Altiplano, 1985);

Vidas y muertes (La Paz: Huayna Potosí, 1986);

La piedra imán (La Paz: Huayna Potosí, 1989);

Los papeles de Narciso Lima Achá (La Paz: Instituto Boliviano de Cultura, 1991);

Obra inédita: Carta de amor, Santiago de Machaca, El señor Balboa (Cochabamba, Bolivia: Centro Simón I. Patiño, 1996);

Café y mosquitero: 1943, anonymous (La Paz: La Mariposa Mundial, 2000).

Edition: *Recorrer esta distancia, Bruckner, Las Tinieblas* (Santiago: Editorial Intemperie, 1996).

OTHER: Rolando Costa Arduz, *La otra mano,* prologue by Saenz (La Paz: Empresa Editora Novedades, 1967);

Blanca Wiethüchter, *Asistir al tiempo,* introduction by Saenz (La Paz: Imprentas Unidas, 1975);

Jaime Saenz

Guillermo Bedregal, *La Palidez,* prologue by Saenz (La Paz: Imprentas Unidas, 1975);

Rigoberto Paredes, *Mitos, supersticiones y supervivencias populares de Bolivia,* preface by Saenz (La Paz: Biblioteca del Sesquicentenario de la República, 1976);

Gustavo A. Otero, *Memorias de Gustavo Adolfo Otero,* prologue by Saenz (La Paz: Litografías e Imprentas Unidas, 1977);

Edgar Avila Echazú, *Antología Poética,* prologue by Saenz (La Paz, 1979);

Bedregal, *Ciudad desde la altura,* prologue by Saenz (La Paz: Imprenta y Librería Renovación, 1980);

Guido Orías, *Extranjero en estas cuatro dimensiones,* prologue by Saenz, *Hipótesis,* 17 (Fall 1983): 104–109.

SELECTED PERIODICAL PUBLICATIONS–
UNCOLLECTED: "La tensión," *Revista Nova* (September 1962);
"El Aparapita de La Paz," *Mundo Nuevo,* nos. 26–27 (August–September 1968): 4–8;
La Razón, 18 August 1991, pp. 1–5;
"Un obscuro y anonimo personaje," *Presencia Literaria,* 18 August 1996, pp. 8–9;
"Cuatro poemas para mi madre," *Geisha,* no. 6 (1998): 4–6;
"Micaela," *Mariposa Mundial,* no. 3 (September 2000): 74;
"Once poemas de 1944," *Ciencia y Cultura,* no. 7 (July 2000): 115–125.

Jaime Saenz is one of the consummate writers in contemporary Bolivian literature and has exercised more influence on the direction of this literature than any other single figure. Almost as important has been his impact on other disciplines such as philosophy, painting, literary criticism, historiography, and the analysis of contemporary cultural theory. Reticent to systems and deeply suspicious of conventional rationality, he belongs to a generation that, as he told Gonzalo López Muñoz in a 1965 interview published in *Presencia Literaria* (21 September 1986), "está frustrada. . . . Es una lástima, pero tantos valores han claudicado, se han rendido ante la pequeña tentación del vivir cómodo. Han dejado de ser lo que eran, han dejado de hacer lo que tenían que hacer" (is frustrated. . . . It's a pity, but so many talented people have succumbed to the temptations of an easy life. They have ceased to be what they were, they have left undone that which they had to do).

In the same interview Saenz stated that an artist must never lose contact with his reality, because it is only from that reality that he will be able to produce poetry. He added that from one's own reality emerges the other, the magic one, simultaneously satanic and divine. In this context it is easy to understand why Saenz embodies the image of a controversial writer; but controversies aside, his work has contributed to expanding the general understanding of artistic creation, and of what it is like to be both a marginal subject living in a marginal society and a poet observing, describing, and interrogating this marginality. This involvement with life and art makes Saenz a central figure in contemporary Bolivian art.

Saenz's work comprises many genres: verse, prose poems, narrative, drama, visual art, essay, articles, letters, and interviews, many of which remain uncollected. He is best known as a poet and narrator, particularly as

the creator of a poetic grammar deeply rooted in the Andean city of La Paz and steeped in alcohol, insanity, and death. Saenz attained international recognition during the late 1960s, when Aldo Pellegrini included him in his *Antología de la poesía viva latinoamericana* (Anthology of Latin American Literature, 1966). In 1974 his poetry reached an even wider audience when it appeared in Stefan Bacio's *Antología de la poesía latinoamericana, 1950–1970* (Anthology of Latin American Poetry, 1950–1970), accompanied by Bacio's assertion that Saenz's poetry is the most notable contribution of Bolivian literature to continental culture in the last half of the century. More recently his poetry and some of his narrative writings have been translated into English, Greek, German, and Italian. In Bolivia his work has been successfully adapted for video and theater. In the late 1980s Francisco Ormachea presented his video *Recorrer esta distancia* (winner of the Amalia Gallardo Prize), and Marcos Loayza produced *El olor de la vejez* (The Smell of Old Age), mainly a re-creation of Saenz's life. In 1998 David Mondaca produced and interpreted a dramatic monologue based on Saenz's work. This monologue, *No le digas* (Don't Tell Him), won the first prize at the Nacional Competition Peter Travesí at Cochabamba. In 2001 Mondaca produced a second monologue at the Santa Cruz International Theater Festival.

Jaime Saenz Guzmán was born on 8 October 1921 to Genaro and Graciela Guzmán Saenz in La Paz, a city that became an inexhaustible source of inspiration for his writing. He perceives La Paz as the site where ultimate marginality exists, a marginality he embodies in the figure of the *aparapita,* an Aymara word that means "el que carga" (the one who carries the load), which Saenz introduced into Bolivian literary language. Saenz describes the *aparapita* as an Aymara immigrant to the city, but also as someone who is possessed by an irrational thirst for knowledge, attempts to understand his new milieu, and, in many ways, gains possession of it.

At the time of Saenz's birth and throughout his childhood and adolescence, La Paz was a capital city experiencing the mixed blessings of modernity (railroad constructions, oil concessions to foreign companies, indigenous massacres, feminist uprisings, and increasing cultural activities), which brought liberalism, free trade, and racism to the foreground as the leading ideological trends. In this environment the young Saenz was fortunate enough to have as schoolteachers two important and well-known writers: Juan Capriles and Gregorio Taborga. The most inspiring literary figure he met came not from the classroom, however, but from work. At age ten, Saenz took a part-time job supervising the photo archives at the newspaper *La Razón* (Reason). There he met Franz Tamayo, the most influential, con-

Paperback cover for Saenz's 1964 collection of poems addressed to a mysterious visitor from an otherwordly realm (University of Southern California Library)

troversial, and enigmatic writer of that moment. In 1910 Tamayo had published a series of articles on education, later collected as *La creación de la pedagogía nacional* (The Creation of a National Pedagogy), in which he polemically vindicated Aymara heritage, stating the need to rebuild Bolivia on the basis of its indigenous majority. Three years after meeting Saenz, in the middle of the Chaco War (1932–1935), Tamayo won the presidential elections, but a military conspiracy against the former president, Daniel Salamanca, prevented him from taking office. Saenz, old enough to understand the implications of the war and the importance of Tamayo's thinking but still young enough not to have played any significant role in these events, was deeply marked by them. The problem of understanding Bolivia as a nation controlled by an unwanted indigenous majority forever stayed with him, becoming a constant in his work, especially in his *Felipe Delgado* (1979) and in the posthumously published *Los papeles de Narciso Lima Achá* (The Papers of Narciso Lima Achá, 1991), novels that take place in the 1930s.

Saenz's youthful admiration for Tamayo initiated a pattern of establishing links with older writers and artists. This tendency is evident in the intense relationships he cultivated with the writer and painter Arturo Borda; the vanguardist poet Hilda Mundy and her husband, the poet Antonio Ávila Jiménez; and Alberto Ufenast Vargas. The latter was without a doubt a major influence for young Saenz. In *Vidas y muertes* (Lives and Deaths, 1986), Saenz reveals that Ufenast was a Swiss immigrant who came to Bolivia around 1929 and married his aunt Esther (the "tía Esther" of his writings). In other writings Saenz attributes to Ufenast his spiritual formation, stating that he introduced him to German culture and to Johann Wolfgang von Goethe, Friedrich Nietzsche, Johannes Brahms, and Thomas Mann.

In *La piedra imán* (The Magnet Stone, 1989) Saenz describes his lonely childhood, explaining that his mother used to look at him sadly, because in her opinion he was reticent and elusive, not to mention shy; he did not like to play, laugh, or even cry; he never asked for anything, and he had no friends. These attitudes made his mother think that perhaps he was retarded or had some sort of birth defect, since he rarely left his room, hated school, and was scared of the sun. Only when hiding in corners and in darkness did he feel comfortable.

In 1938, at the age of seventeen, he took an unexpected yet decisive trip to Germany that changed the course of his life. He became part of a delegation of twenty-five young Bolivians invited by the government of Nazi Germany, apparently to be trained in military service. The Germans used this policy during the years that preceded World War II in an attempt to draw sympathizers to the cause of National Socialism. Later in Saenz's life the trip became a source of controversy, mainly because his warm reception of National Socialism led some to consider him a fascist. Saenz's enthusiasm lacked political engagement, however, and had little connection with his work. His excitement for Nazism could be compared to attitudes taken by other writers during the Nazi period, including, for instance, Martin Heidegger and Günter Grass, who in their early years sympathized with the Nazi cause. In Saenz's case, what remained of his German experience was a deep exposure to the teachings of Ufenast, who taught him to live at the limits of life, clamoring for change, for something new. Aside from this attitude, only occasional references to Germany are found in his work, with the exception of *Los papeles de Narciso Lima Achá*, in which one of the main characters is German. The portrayal of this German character proves, however, that Saenz, when dealing with German issues, was more interested in developing an intimacy with excessive and disturbing experiences than in re-creating the ideology

Paperback cover for Saenz's 1967 book, which combines new poems about the Andean cold with two earlier collections (Walter Royal Davis Library, University of North Carolina at Chapel Hill)

of National Socialism. This attitude places him closer to Nietzsche's claim in *Zur Genealogie der Moral* (1887; translated as *A Genealogy of Morals,* 1897) to question the worth of "our sinister European civilization."

Upon his return to Bolivia in 1939, Saenz resolved to dedicate himself to writing, but the economic demands of everyday life prevented him from doing so. For the next two years he became a public functionary, first at the Ministry of Defense and next at the Ministry of Revenue. He was nineteen years old when Ufenast died, leaving him in deep intellectual solitude, though he kept tenaciously writing what became his first book, *El escalpelo* (The Scalpel, 1955). Soon Saenz found a prolongation of Ufenast's presence and teachings in the monumental figure of his aunt, Esther, Ufenast's widow, who became a lifelong companion, surviving him by six years. Known simply as "la Tía," she is a constant presence in Saenz's works. Blanca Wiethüchter, in her *Memoria solicitada* (Solicited Memory, 1989), suggests that half of Saenz's

merits belong to his aunt. Although Aunt Esther permeates all of his work, it is in his tale *Los cuartos* (The Rooms, 1985) that he provides his ultimate fictional portrayal of her.

In 1942 Saenz was named head of the Press Division at the U.S. embassy, a job he kept until 1952. During these years as a journalist, McGraw-Hill of New York commissioned him to interview Emilio Villanueva, the dean of the Department of Architecture at the Universidad Mayor de San Andrés and also the creator of a provocative style in architecture that fused modern architectural concepts with Aymara aesthetics. The interview took place in 1951 and was followed by further meetings, some of which were hosted at the house of Ávila Jiménez, who had at that time lived at "La casa del poeta" (The Poet's House), a municipal property offered to well-known writers in recognition of their work. In these meetings Saenz and Villanueva discussed the exceptional qualities of Aymara dwellings, mainly made of adobe and built according to "a logic that remains largely beyond the comprehension of Western thought," as Saenz puts it in *Vidas y muertes*.

During these same years Saenz met Borda, who also had a great influence on him. Borda embodied the image of a true creator: for him, art was a space of reflection, freedom, and self-discovery. The first artistic community to which Saenz belonged comprised Borda, Ávila Jiménez, Mundy, and himself. Together they shaped an underground artistic avant-garde that articulated for the first time what had never before found expression in Bolivia: an Andean vanguard, openly marginal, rooted in the Aymara heritage and in the contemplation of the Illimani Mountain. Their unconventional lives, frequent bouts of drunkenness, rejection of any form of bourgeois behavior, and an antiestablishment stance kept them apart from other existing literary groups (mainly the second Gesta Bárbara, created in La Paz in 1944) and writers such as Oscar Cerruto, Díaz Villamil, or Guillermo Francovich. Their meetings were often held at Ávila Jiménez's home, where Saenz learned from his friends the mysteries of electricity, the mechanism of clocks, and the workings of many other sorts of devices. He even became an expert watchmaker and also had the time in 1944 to create *Cornamusa* (Bagpipes), an avant-garde literary review that only lasted one issue.

In 1943 he married Erika, a young woman who was visiting Bolivia with her German family. The marriage did not last long, but before it ended Erika gave birth to a boy who lived three days and, in 1947, to a girl, Jourlaine, who left Bolivia with her mother in 1948, once the marriage was over. A picture of an adult Jourlaine accompanied Saenz in his later life, moving with him from rented rooms to rented rooms, for he never owned a house.

Saenz's early years ended with two crucial events: the traumatic death of Borda, who died by mistakenly drinking muriatic acid at age seventy in 1953, and the 1952 Bolivian Revolution, a nationalist insurrection that ended the oligarchy of the tin industry, instituted universal suffrage, and carried out agrarian reform. The experience of this revolution never abandoned the poet, neither did the apocalyptic images of dead bodies piled high in the streets. As for "el Toqui Borda" (as his beloved friend was nicknamed), Saenz remembered him as an extraordinary man who lived and died painting the Illimani Mountain and as someone who prepared the way for socialism in Bolivia, given his role as founder of mining unions during the 1920s.

In 1954 Saenz started a new literary review, *Brújula* (Compass), which lasted three issues. His book *El escalpelo* was finally published in 1955. Mainly a collection of poetic prose, this book destroys the logical order of language and syntax and digs into those zones of

childhood rarely explored by Bolivian poetry: seclusion, illness, fascination with the human body, revelation of unveiled realities, and death. The book had an enthusiastic reception among friends, but the literary establishment showed little acceptance. In their opinion Saenz failed to satisfy the artistic canon. Unmoved by their rejection, Saenz continued to explore his own aesthetics.

Saenz's first collection of poetry, *Muerte por el tacto* (Death by Touch), was published in 1957 and dedicated to Ufenast. It introduces the poetic persona that Saenz explores in following books, an adult male depicted as an "ángel solitario y jubiloso" (solitary and jubilant angel) who "conspira contra la armoní" (conspires against harmony) and lives "mascando lo que no se sabe, pensando lo que no se sabe" (chewing the unknown and thinking the unknown). The following two books, *Aniversario de una visión* (Anniversary of a Vision) and *Visitante profundo* (translated as *Immanent Visitor: Selected Poems*, 2002), further develop the persona's journey through events in which he confronts unknown and yet jubilant presences that teach him how to perceive the other side of reality. So powerful are these presences that they compel the poetic persona to speak, to create a dialogue. In *Aniversario de una visión* he talks to a beloved vision:

–¡cómo me miras!,
de unos confines, de la infancia
y de los mares profundos de la juventud
. . . .
–y un gran llanto me sacude al deseo de
encontrarte,
y hablar contigo sobre la gratitud, sobre la
primavera y la alegría

(–how you look at me!,
from some margins, from infancy
and from the deep seas of youth
. . . .
–and a great weeping shakes me with the desire
to find you,
and to speak with you about gratitude, about
spring and happiness).

In *Visitante profundo* the speaker addresses a visitor, a traveler from beyond who fears the light and whose "lágrimas tan hermosas como las arañas" (tears are as beautiful as spiders). In the ensuing dialogue he expresses his wish to reach this visitor and his unattainable realm:

Ven; yo vivo de tu dibujo
y de tu perfumada melodía,
. . . .
te vi aparecer y no pude asirte, a turbadora distancia te llevaba el canto

y era mucha lejanía y poco tu aliento para alcan-
zar a tiempo un fulgor de mi corazón
. . . .
ven una vez; quiero cumplir mi deseo de adiós

(Come; I live from your portraiture
and from your perfumed melody,
. . . .
I saw you appear and I could not hold you, the song
carried you to a disturbing distance
and it was too much farness and little your breath to reach
on time a flash of my heart
. . . .
come once; I want to fulfill my desire for dissolution).

As the years passed, Saenz's contribution to the cultural life of La Paz became openly acknowledged. His
transition from a young to a mature writer and public figure was reinforced by his involvement in the cultural
scene. In 1965 he founded his third literary review, *Vertical*
(1965). That same year he met the philosopher Arturo
Orías Medina, who became a close friend and, after
Saenz's death, his legal proxy. By the end of the 1960s a
new, vigorous generation of artists and writers had
become Saenz's friends. Among these were the poets Jesús
Urzagasti and Blanca Wiethüchter, the painter Enrique
Arnal (who in 1967 sponsored Saenz's exhibition of drawings and skull collection), the composer Alberto Villal-
pando (with whom Saenz invented a musical instrument),
and the literary critic Luis Antezana. Together they
opened the way for a cultural revolution that changed the
direction of Bolivian contemporary art and literature. In
part, this achievement was possible because this group,
contrary to the previous one, was not stigmatized by the
shadow of marginality. Saenz, however, never renounced
his marginal position as one of the few writers with memory of the inner Aymara presence in Bolivia.

The last book of poems Saenz published in the
1960s is *El frío* (The Cold, 1967), which was published
along with *Muerto por el tacto* and *Aniversario de una visión*.
Here, the poetic persona of *Muerte por el tacto* encounters
el frío, perhaps the most obvious characteristic of
Andean life but also a powerful sign of proximity to
death. As in previous poems, the poetic persona
engages in a dialogue with the cold:

Tú, que siempre apareces en el invierno, año tras
año; tú, que te pierdes
y pasas por las calles, y sin quererlo me enseñas
a vivir y me ayudas a morir,
tú eres el frío, eres tú la ciudad, es tu presencia
una música con la virtud de escucharse tan sólo en
el olvido:
gracias a ti aprendí a decir adiós

(You, that always appear in winter, year after
year; you, that disappear

*Paperback cover for Saenz's 1982 collection, his only serious
attempt at love poetry (Wilson Library,
University of Minnesota)*

and go by the streets, and unwillingly, teach me
how to live and help me to die,
you are the cold, you are the city, it is your presence
a music with the virtue of being heard only in
oblivion:
thanks to you I learned to say goodbye).

In 1968, in the journal *Mundo Nuevo,* Saenz published "El *aparapita* de La Paz," an essay in which he
developed a poetic theory about the life and work of
this extremely marginal subject. Before Saenz, the existence of *aparapita* had been widely ignored by intellectuals, who considered them either as social parasites
opposed to any form of modern life or simply as alco-
holics. Contrary to this stereotypical opinion, Saenz
perceives the *aparapita* and his clothing (a patchwork of

La Paz - 1984

*Paperback cover for Saenz's long poem about death
(Marriott Library, University of Utah)*

different sizes, colors, and shapes) as an accurate representation of the city he inhabits, also made up of an infinite number of patches, sizes, colors, and shapes that betray its Aymara and colonial origins.

In 1970 Saenz accepted a professorship at the Universidad Mayor de San Andrés. Years later, at the same university, he established a creative writing workshop where a whole generation of Bolivian poets was trained, among them Marcia Mogro, Corina Barrero, Rubén Vargas, Carlos Mendizabal, Guillermo Bedregal, Leonardo García, and Elizabeth Johansen.

Hugo Banzer's dictatorship, which lasted from 1971 to 1978, and political turmoil prevented Saenz from regularly teaching his classes. When he did, not only the students who attended his lectures but also his colleagues attested to the rigor of his questions and the startling originality of his insights. Also during these years an informal group known as Talleres Krupp (Krupp Workshops) organized around him.

In 1973 Saenz published another extensive poem, *Recorrer esta distancia* (Traversing this Distance), consid-

ered by the critics as a major work that marks the poet's transition toward a second poetic phase. In this poem Saenz's poetic persona finally reaches a space where he can be and dwell with the other. To name this new space, Saenz coined a term that became an icon of his poetic grammar: *el estar* (the dwelling). This *estar* is found by means of contact with two constant poetic presences: the human body and a dark, subtle outfit of *ropaje* (clothes), which clearly refers to the *aparapita* clothing he had pointed out as the ultimate incarnation of the Aymara presence in the city:

> En el modo de mirar y de ser de este cuerpo—en
> el modo de ser del ropaje,
> en el modo de estar y no estar, oscuro y sutil del
> ropaje, encontré el secreto,
> encontré el estar

> (In the way of looking and being of this body—in
> the way of being of its clothes,
> in the way of being and not being, dark and subtle of the
> clothes, I found the secret,
> I found the dwelling).

In 1975 the National Committee of the Sesquicentennial of the Republic honored Saenz by publishing *Obra poética,* a collection of Saenz's work from *El escalpelo* through *Recorrer esta distancia* that includes a remarkable study by Wiethüchter.

During the course of the following years Saenz completed his poetic project. He first published *Bruckner; y Las tinieblas* (Bruckner; and The Darkness, 1978), a volume composed of two poems that continue the journey begun in *Muerte por el tacto.* Inspired by the Austrian composer Anton Bruckner, the first poem depicts how artistic creation takes shape and becomes possible. The second poem, *Las tinieblas,* is a beautiful poem in which the poetic persona first introduced in *Muerte por el tacto* finally dies. Although dead, his existence does not come to an end as he goes on thinking, living, and dismantling conventional rationality.

After *Bruckner; y Las tinieblas* Saenz returned to prose and fiction. *Imágenes paceñas: Lugares y personas de la ciudad* (Images from La Paz: City Places and Persons, 1979), a collection of short chronicles illustrated with photographs by Javier Molina, portrays the city's inner being, which emerges from sites still untouched by the machine of progress (Garita de Lima, Villa Victoria, Illampu Street, and El Calvario), as from those who inhabit them, such as *aparapitas,* women vendors, shoe shiners, and diviners. In 1979 Saenz also published *Felipe Delgado,* a novel he started in 1958. In this autobiographical novel, set in the 1930s, Felipe, the main character, undertakes a journey in many ways similar to the one carried out by the poetic persona of Saenz's poetry. This time, however, what moves the narrative and makes it so daring and powerful is the role played by alcohol, insanity, and death. Javier Sanjinés has suggested that what makes Felipe Delgado a fascinating character is precisely his closeness to these three elements, because they open bizarre and frightful ways of living. With this challenging narrative Saenz showed that the reality of Bolivia during the 1930s was best expressed through the cultural intrusions that had invaded and transformed the utopias of modernity.

Felipe Delgado was followed by a very intense body of prose, fiction, and poetry, but only three more volumes were published before his death: *Al pasar un cometa: Poemas (1970–72)* (On the Going Past of a Comet: Poems [1970–72], 1982), dedicated to his daughter, Jourlaine, and his only serious incursion into love poetry; *La noche* (The Night, 1984), another long poem that extends his own poetic journey after death; and *Los cuartos,* a tale written as a tribute to his aunt Esther, in which he explores a minimalist narrative.

By the time Saenz published *La noche,* his life had become precarious. He had been diagnosed with a serious pulmonary condition and with terminal malnutrition. The municipal government had awarded him the right to live in La casa del poeta, where he and Aunt Esther moved on 17 August 1983. Far from being a solution, however, this episode simply signaled the end. Wiethüchter remembers that Saenz entered the house to die. Though not immediately after his moving, Saenz did die in La casa del poeta on 16 August 1986, at sixty-four years of age.

Shortly after Jaime Saenz's death, two books were published: *La piedra imán* (1989), another autobiography, and *Vidas y muertes* (1986), a collection of biographies in which Saenz pays homage to his best friends, most admired artists, and favorite imaginary characters, including Borda, Julián Huanca, Ávila Jiménez, Ufenast, Feliciano Sirpa, Juan José Lillo, and Villanueva. Two other important narratives appeared in the 1990s: *Los papeles de Narciso Lima Achá* (The Papers of Narciso Lima Achá) in 1991, and *Obra inédita: Carta de amor, Santiago de Machaca, El señor Balboa* (Unpublished Work: Love Letter, Santiago de Machaca, Mr. Balboa) in 1996.

Interview:

Gonzalo López Muñoz, "Una entrevista con Jaime Saenz [1965]," *Presencia Literaria,* 21 September 1986, p. 1.

References:

Luis H. Antezana J., "Hacer y cuidar" and "Felipe Delgado de Jaime Saenz," in his *Ensayos y Lecturas* (La Paz: Altiplano, 1986), pp. 231–264, 333–382;

Antezana, "La poética del saco de aparapita," in *Sentidos Communes. Ensayos y Lecturas* (Cochabamba: FACES-CESU-UMSS, 1995), pp. 23–29;

Elías Blanco Mamani, *Jaime Saenz, el ángel solitario y jubiloso de la noche: Apuntes para una historia de vida* (La Paz: Gobierno Municipal de La Paz, 1998);

Blanco Mamani, "Poesía boliviana 1960–1980: Entre la realidada y el lenguaje," *Hipótesis,* 19 (1984): 313–327;

Leonardo García Pabón, *La Patria Intima: Alegorías nacionales en la literatura y el cine* (La Paz: Centro de Estudios Superiores Universitarios, UMSS y Plural Editores, 1998), pp. 213–248;

Pedro Lastra and Rigas Kappatos, "Poem VII from Anniversary of a Vision," in their *The Best 100 Love Poems of the Spanish Language, trads.* (Long Island City, N.Y.: Seaburn, 1998), pp. 206–207;

Eduardo Mitre, "Jaime Saenz: el espacio fúnebre," in *El árbol y la piedra: poetas contemporáneos de Bolivia* (Caracas: Monte Avila Editores, 1987), pp. 26–34;

La modernidad y sus hermenéuticas poéticas: poesía Boliviana del siglo XX (La Paz: Ediciones Signo, 1991);

Elizabeth Monasterios P., *Dilemas de la poesía latinoamericana de fin de siglo: José Emilio Pacheco y Jaime Saenz* (La Paz: Plural, 2001);

Oscar Rivera Rodas, "La poesía de Jaime Saenz," *Inti. Revista de Literatura Hispánica,* 18–19 (1984): 59–82;

Javier Sanjinés, "Marginalidad y grotesco en la moderna narrativa andina: El caso de Jaime Saenz," *Revista Unitas,* 9 (1993): 111–120;

Blanca Wiethüchter, "Estructuras de lo imaginario en la obra poética de Jaime Saenz," in Saenz's *Obra poética* (La Paz: Biblioteca del Sesquicentenario de la República, 1975), pp. 267–425;

Wiethüchter, *Memoria solicitada* (La Paz: Altiplano, 1989);

Wiethüchter and Alba María Paz Soldán, *Hacia una historia crítica de la literatura en Bolivia,* 2 volumes (La Paz: PIEB, 2002).

Pedro Shimose
(1940 –)

Joan Clifford
Duke University

BOOKS: *Triludio en el exilio* (La Paz: Signo, 1961);
Sardonia (La Paz: Universidad Mayor de San Andrés, 1967);
Poemas para un pueblo (La Paz: Difusión, 1968);
Quiero escribir, pero me sale espuma (Havana: Casa de las Américas, 1972);
Caducidad del fuego (Madrid: Cultura Hispánica, 1975);
El Coco se llama Drilo (La Paz: Difusión, 1976);
Reflexiones maquiavélicas (Madrid: Playor, 1980); translated by Michael Sisson as *Machiavellian Reflections* (Madrid: Verbum, 1992);
Bolero de Caballería (Madrid: Playor, 1985);
Riberalta y otros poemas (Santa Cruz de la Sierra: El País, 1996);
No te lo vas a creer (Santa Cruz de la Sierra, Bolivia: El País, 2000).
Collections: *Al pie de la letra* (Jaén: El Olivo, 1976);
Poemas, prologue by Teodosio Fernández (Madrid: Playor, 1988).

OTHER: Paulovich, *Apariencias,* illustrations by Shimose (La Paz: Difusión, 1967);
Antonio Paredes Candia, *Brujerías, tradiciones y leyendas,* illustrations by Shimose (La Paz: Difusión, 1969);
Diccionario de autores iberoamericanos, edited by Shimose (Madrid: Instituto de Cooperación Iberoamericana, 1982);
Oscar Cerruto, *Poesía,* includes notes, chronology, and bibliography by Shimose (Madrid: Ediciones Cultura Hispánica, Instituto de Cooperación Iberoamericano, 1985);
Historia de la literatura latinoamericana, edited by Shimose (Madrid: Playor, 1989);
Alvaro Mutis, edited by Shimose (Madrid: Instituto de Cooperación Iberoamérica, Ediciones de Cultura Hispánica, 1993);
Felipe Lázaro, *Entrevistas a Gastón Baquero,* prologue by Shimose (Madrid: Asociación Cultural Gastón Baquero/Betania, 1998);
Clara Díaz Pascual, *Desorden de lunas,* prologue by Shimose (Madrid: Betania, 1999);

Pedro Shimose (from the cover for Poemas para un pueblo, *1968; Delyte W. Morris Library, Southern Illinois University at Carbondale)*

Bolivia: Imagen y palabra, texts selected by Shimose (Barcelona: Bustamente, 2000).

SELECTED PERIODICAL PUBLICATIONS–UNCOLLECTED: "Panorama de la narrativa boliviana contemporánea," *Presencia literaria* (11 May 1975);
"Las lecciones de Nabokov," *Estafeta Literaria: Revista Quincenal de Libros, Artes y Espectáculos,* 620 (1977): 8–9.

Pedro Shimose Kawamura, born in Riberalta, Beni, Bolivia, in 1940, has established himself as a voice of the Bolivian people. Although best known for his poetry he is also a journalist, composer of popular music, art and cinema critic, fiction writer, and sketch artist. His literary creations have been recognized with both international and domestic prizes, the most prestigious of them, Cuba's Premio Internacional de Poesía de Casa de las Américas (International Poetry Prize of House of the Americas), was awarded in 1972. Shimose has distinguished himself within the Bolivian intellectual community and is a member of the Academy of Bolivian Language. In the 1950s Juan Quirós founded a literary group, Prisma (Prism), in which Shimose participated. His literary generation includes Octavio Campero Echazú, Jesús Urzagasti, and Oscar Rivera Rodas. Many critics note that other twentieth-century Latin American poets, such as César Vallejo, Nicolás Guillén, Pablo Neruda, Ernesto Cardenal, Octavio Paz, and Antonio Cisneros, have been influential in Shimose's writing. It is equally important to note, however, that as the son of Japanese immigrants, Shimose incorporates both Eastern and Western traits in his creative vision. The poet's treatment of social, political, and social themes specific to Bolivia expands to an exploration of the universal condition of modern man. Shimose manipulates language in terms of both content and its visual presentation, thus challenging the reader to experience his poems on various levels.

When he was nineteen years old Shimose moved from his hometown of Riberalta to La Paz. He began to study law, but after three years he decided that the only aspect of law that interested him concerned Indian rights and that "el abogado en Bolivia no es mâs que un instrumento de explotación de los débiles" (a lawyer in Bolivia is nothing more than an instrument of exploitation of the weak), as he is quoted in *Provocaciones* (Provocations, 1977). He thus abandoned his studies to become a full-time journalist. He contributed to such newspapers as the Democratic Christian publication *Presencia* (Presence) while also working as the director of the cultural newspaper *Reunión* (Reunion). At the age of twenty he won his first literary prize, the National Poetry Prize from the Confederación Universitaria Boliviana (Bolivian University Confederation). This initial recognition was followed by the first prize from Juegos Florales de Sucre in 1966 and the Premio de Cuento en la Alcaldía Municipal de la Paz (Short Story Prize in the Municipal Mayoralty of La Paz) in 1968. During these years Shimose became a professor of literature and the director of cultural extension at the Universidad Mayor de San Andrés de La Paz.

Shimose's first three works, *Triludio en el exilio* (Triludio in Exile, 1961), *Sardonia* (Sardinia, 1967), and *Poemas para un pueblo* (Poems for a People, 1968), respond to his life experiences, as he told Juan Manuel Rozas in 1972: "Mis libros corresponden, naturalmente, a mis vivencias. El primero corresponde a mi experiencia religiosa, si se puede llamar así; el segundo responde a una etapa de crisis; el tercero, podría decirse que es

un poemario con temática social" (My books correspond, naturally, to my life experiences. The first corresponds to my religious experience, if you can call it that; the second responds to a stage of crisis; the third, could be called a poetry collection with a social theme). *Triludio en el exilio* develops religious and human studies of Bolivian life. The poem "Moxitania," an indigenous name that designates Beni, the area of the country where he was born, is representative of his interest in the Bolivian experience; in it the poet speaks to a female entity that he loves, perhaps nature, while describing the regional flora and fauna. Shimose states in the interview with Rozas that Paul Claudel, Pierre-Jean Jouve, Emmanuel, and Saint-John Perse heavily influenced his writing in this collection of poetry.

Sardonia is the result of a period of crisis. Although the poet does not state what type of crisis, one may speculate that it is related to the ongoing political and social injustices in Bolivia as well as his trips to Europe, where he came in contact with several literary circles. Shimose admits that this second book—exhibiting characteristics from Surrealism, futurism, Dadaism, and absurdism—is influenced by the young European poets and by others such as Ezra Pound and Allen Ginsberg. These poems explore humanity's confrontation with a chaotic modern world, but they also include references to historical people and events from various times: Cleopatra, Jean-Paul Sartre, Maximilien-François-Marie-Isidore de Robespierre, Albert Einstein, César Vallejo, the Ku Klux Klan. The odd mixture of events and people deepens the impact of the violent and desperate modern themes Shimose elaborates. In "Carta a una estrella que vive en otra constelación" (Letter to a Star that Lives in Another Constellation) he shows how he manipulates the words on the page to represent his ideas on several levels. His condemnation of materialism takes on a political, a metaphorical, and a practical manifestation:

> Capitalismo popular,
> comunismo capitalista,
> cataclismo en el absurdo del absurdo,
> arce azucarero florecido en sintaxis,
> > sin taxis,
> > > ¡taxi!

> (Popular capitalism,
> capitalistic communism,
> cataclysm in the absurd of the absurd,
> flowered sugar maple in syntax,
> > without taxis
> > > ¡taxi!).

The reader must work with this text to absorb the diverse and multifaceted images of humanity in modern

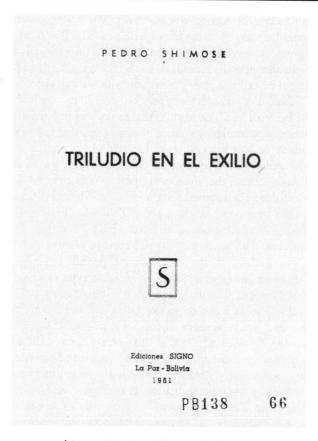

PEDRO SHIMOSE

TRILUDIO EN EL EXILIO

S

Ediciones SIGNO
La Paz - Bolivia
1961

PB138 66

*Title page for Shimose's first book of poems, about
what he considers the religious aspects of his life
(University of Georgia Library)*

preferíamos ser gringos, hablar francés y vestirnos a la
  inglesa,
pero ahora, aquí, entre vuelos de cóndores y águilas,
caminando las aguas de los lagos de Pátzcuaro y Titicaca,
me doy cuenta de que pertenezco a un continente de auroras,
tierra grande, tierra fresca, patria nuestra inmensurable,
y es legítimo mi orgullo cuando canto en Riberalta,
cuando sueño en Porto Alegre, cuando medito en La Habana,
cuando amo en Cartagena y cuando trabajo en Trujillo.
Voy con mi guajira huracanada,
con mi joropo de lluvias,
con mi malambo caliente,
voy con mi amor boliviano caminando el continente

(There was a time when being Latin American was painful.
They portrayed us with a broad-brimmed hat, a serape
  and two pistols.
There was a time when we ran away from being people of
  love and hope,
we preferred to be gringos, to speak French and to dress
  ourselves in the English style,
but now, here, between flights of condors and eagles,
walking the waters of the Pátzcuaro and Titicaca lakes,
I realize that I belong to a continent of dawns,
extensive land, fresh land, our immeasurable land,
and my pride is legitimate when I sing about Riberalta,
when I dream about Porto Alegre, when I meditate on
  Havana,
when I love in Cartagena and when I work in Trujillo.
I go with my silly violent wind,
with my rain dance,
with my hot *malambo*
I go with my Bolivian love walking the continent).

Other poems in this collection further explore violence
and social injustices in Bolivia. Eduardo Mitre suggests
that Shimose follows the secular "tradición romántica
basada en dos creencias: el poder subvertor de la palabra y la imagen del poeta como profeta conductor de
los pueblos" (secular romantic tradition based on two
beliefs: the subversive power of the word and the image
of the poet as motivating prophet of the people).

When President Hugo Banzer came to power in
August 1971, he instituted a period of violent repression, his fascist regime targeting many intellectuals.
Many writers, including Shimose, were forced into
exile. He moved to Madrid with his Spanish wife, Rosario Barroso, and two sons, Pedro Antonio and Pablo
Javier. Since November 1971 the poet has resided in the
Spanish capital, where he continues to write. He also
has worked for the Instituto de Cooperación
Iberoamericana (Institute of Ibero-American Cooperation) editing various publications, including *Diccionario
de autores iberoamericanos* (Dictionary of Ibero-American
Authors, 1982).

Shimose began to write *Quiero escribir, pero me sale
espuma* (I Want to Write, but Foam Comes out of Me,
1972) while still in Bolivia but finished it after relocating

society. The use of intertextuality, French and English
words, and innovative structures underlines Shimose's
awareness of the tensions of global ideologies on Bolivian society during the tumultuous 1960s.

Shimose's third book of poetry, *Poemas para un
pueblo,* is driven by descriptions of social injustices and
attention to the miserable conditions of the Bolivian
people. In this phase of his writing Shimose cites Neruda, but also other contemporary Bolivian poets such
as Oscar Cerruto, Franz Tamayo, Primo Castrillo,
Guillermo Viscarra Fabre, and Julio de la Vega as his
major influences. The latter five poets are Bolivian contemporaries of Shimose who also write revolutionary
poetry. The first poem in this collection, "Discurso
sobre América Latina" (Speech on Latin America), passionately relates the political and existential crisis in
Latin American identity. The third stanza reads:

Hubo un tiempo en que ser latinoamericano daba pena.
Nos presentaban con un sombrero alón, un sarape y dos
  pistolas.
Hubo un tiempo en que nos corríamos de ser el pueblo del
  amor y la esperanza,

to Madrid. When asked by Rozas if the book is similar to *Poemas para un pueblo,* Shimose denied it: "No, creo que no. El primero contempla Bolivia con los ojos; el segundo, con la inteligencia y el sentimiento desde el exilio" (No, I believe not. The first contemplates Bolivia with the eyes; the second, with the intelligence and feeling from exile). The profound examination of Bolivian life and its deplorable social conditions Shimose undertakes in this collection earned him the prestigious Premio Internacional de Poesía de Casa de las Américas in 1972. Some critics have described his poems as verbal collages, in part, because in addition to Spanish, they include phrases in Quechua and English. This fracturing of the Spanish language corresponds to his representation of themes discussing the conflict of national and international powers and their influence on the construction of Bolivian identity. Intertextual references to other works are present in this collection and continue to play an important role in his future writings.

Expanding on the theme of exile from the motherland, the poems in *Caducidad del fuego* (Lapse of Fire, 1975) show an evolution in Shimose's writing in both content and style. In this collection Shimose depicts how return from exile is complicated by historical, political, and existential causes. The attention he gives to word choice and typography increases the power of the condensed images included in this book. The poem "Irredento enigma" (Unrepentant Enigma) demonstrates the desperate search to find a new identity in exile:

Voy a ser nada
      sometido a tu fuerza. Voy
a terminar de ser
hueso roído en el exilio;
a estupidizarme en tu ardid,
      a consumirme,
      a oscurecerme
en el ludibrio de la noche.

Alma, dime qué soy

(I am going to be nothing
      forced to yield by your strength. I am going
to end up being
gnawed bone in exile;
by stupifying me in your ruse,
      by consuming me,
      by shadowing me
in the mockery of the night.

Soul, tell me what I am).

The themes of exile, the existential search, and love become intertwined in other poems in *Caducidad del fuego,* such as "Primavera, 6 a.m." (Springtime, 6 a.m.),

in which the lover is asked to provide an answer to the searching:

Ven, amor,
ilumina
mi sombra
cuando todo
sea
sombra.

Tú eres mi patria:
la inmensa y sola
ternura de la
tierra

(Come, love,
illuminate
my darkness
when everything
is
shadow.

You are my homeland:
the immense and only
tenderness of the
land).

Caducidad del fuego is the first book of poems in which Shimose treats love and erotic themes. The political and social themes found in previous works continue to evolve in this book, and yet the new dimension of seeking answers through love begins to have a greater role in Shimose's creative expression.

In 1975 Shimose was awarded the Segundo Premio Internacional Olivio (Second International Olivio Prize) for *Al pie de la letra* (Exactly to the Letter, 1976), an anthology of selected previously published poetry. The same year that the anthology was published, a collection of short stories, *El Coco se llama Drilo* (The Croco Is Named Dile) also appeared. *El Coco se llama Drilo* is the only collection of narrative fiction that Shimose has published to date. It includes scenes of contemporary society in which the colloquial dialogue creates an intimate atmosphere. The use of unconventional typography and intertextual games also are distinct characteristics of the collection. The short story "Pitágoras y el espíritu de geometría" (Pythagoras and the Spirit of Geometry) exemplifies these traits, beginning with the inclusion of an epigraph taken from Blaise Pascal. Shimose includes a discussion of a fictional text by an imagined author that provides a critique of Shimose's own story, since they use the same structures. The reader must work with the various layers of the text to decipher Shimose's definition of a short story.

Reflexiones maquiavélicas (1980; translated as *Machiavellian Reflections,* 1992) continues the themes found in

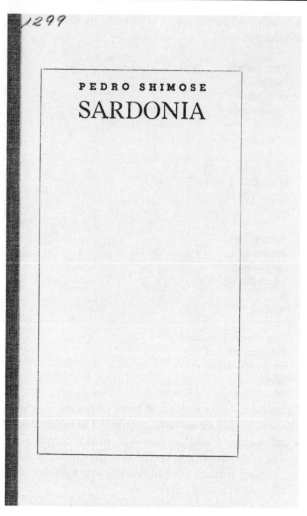

1299

PEDRO SHIMOSE
SARDONIA

*Paperback cover for Shimose's second book (1967), a collection
of poems that utilize historical figures from many eras and
multiple languages to illustrate the chaos of modern life
(Delyte W. Morris Library, Southern
Illinois University at Carbondale)*

Caducidad del fuego, but this publication, Mitre suggests, is based on "la sabiduría; una sabiduría, es cierto cargada de amargura y de escepticismo—de ahí su tono quedo, su austeridad verbal distante de todo lujo expresivo—, pero siempre purificados por la ironía y humor" (wisdom; a wisdom, certainly burdened with bitterness and with skepticism—from there the tone arrives, its verbal austerity distanced from all decorous expression—but always purified by the irony and humor). The majority of these poems are preceded by epigraphs from Niccolò Machiavelli, with which the poems establish ironical dialogues, while a few include direct references to the man and his political beliefs within the body of the poem. Although Shimose does portray the fallibility of man, María A. Salgado surmises that the skeptical conclusions about human nature in this book of poetry do not point toward "literatura de la desesper-

anza" (literature of despair) but that it rather "representa una original y pragmática lectura de las limitaciones de las Ideologías Políticas y de la Poesía (con mayúsculas) en el falible mundo extratextual" (represents an original and pragmatic reading of the limitations of the Political Ideologies and of Poetry [capitalized] in the fallible extra-textual world). Although man is condemned to be fallible, his humor, search for love, and continuing struggles in daily life define his humanity. Shimose's juxtaposition of his acceptance of the limitations of man with his attempt to express his inner self suggests that he finds meaning in everyday reality through his literary craft, a craft that has gained importance through the isolation and the disillusionment he has endured in his exile.

In 1984 Shimose returned to visit Bolivia. This experience helped to configure the poetry in *Bolero de Caballería* (Bolero of Chivalry or Military March, 1985), reintroducing a direct dialogue with his native land. Teodosio Fernández, in the prologue to the 1988 anthology *Poemas* (Poems), points out the differences, however, stating that in *Bolero de Caballería* "no hay lugar para la exaltación nativista de antaño: la patria es una experiencia íntima de extrañamiento ante una tierra natal que distancian los años de ausencia, y un dolor antiguo y profundo que llega desde los tiempos prehispánicos, ligado a la muerte y al silencio, renovado en quienes ahora sufren sin estridencias heroicas" (there is no place for the folkloric exaltation of years past; the country is an intimate experience of estrangement from a native land distanced by years of absence, and an ancient and profound pain comes from the pre-Hispanic past, connected to death and to silence, renewed in those that now suffer without heroic stridencies). Many poems describe the violent and unjust treatment of Bolivians by domestic and external political powers. The poem "Mural del tiempo" (Mural of Time) is representative in showing how this mistreatment has affected their identity:

> Ya no sé ni cómo ocurre que me acuerdo todavía
> de nosotros.
> Somos de aquí
> y de ninguna parte
>
> (I don't even know how it is that I remember it all,
> about us.
> We are from here
> And from nowhere).

Exterior conflicts have thrust the inner self into crisis; thus, the question of identity, individual and collective, appears in many of the poems in the collection.

Poemas includes the eight books of poetry Shimose had published by 1985. Fernández's prologue gives a concise overview of the poet's work. He observes that Shimose's poetry expresses the absurdities and the dehumanization apparent in modern civilization while developing a critical consciousness capable of irony, humor, and skepticism. He adds that Shimose uses as his main themes universal binary oppositions such as love and solitude, life and death, and liberty and oppression in order to develop his own voice, a voice that expresses modern social and political crises in his homeland and beyond.

In 1996 Shimose financed the publication of his book *Riberalta y otros poemas* (Riberalta and Other Poems). The reference to his hometown in the title of this collection indicates his strong connection to Bolivia. In 1999 Shimose received Bolivia's National Culture Award; it was presented to him by Hugo Banzer, the leader who had exiled him from the country thirty years before. Shimose called the award a democratic prize, thereby indicating that the gesture is an important part of the process of his reconciliation with the past. Although he continued to live in Spain, this recognition was a strong indication that Shimose was carrying on an active dialogue with the intellectual and cultural community in Bolivia.

His next publication, the poetry collection *No te lo vas a creer* (You Are Not Going to Believe It, 2000) is an exploration of love and isolation. It is divided into three uneven sections: the introduction, the body of the work, and the epilogue. The introduction consists of a single poem, "La musa visita al viejo poeta" (The Muse Visits the Old Poet); the main section, "Al dictado de la musa" (Dictated by the Muse), comprises thirty-six poems, all of which have one-word titles related to passion, love, the senses, and the body. There are references to traditionally romantic motifs such as gemstones, shipwrecks, the night, and music, but they are used to express feelings of passion, chaos, and the search for wholeness through the sexual union with another in contemporary settings. This book shows brief moments of pleasure intertwined with an unending search for an answer to or a way to escape aging, death, and solitude. The desire to join with another in order to escape from reality is clearly seen in the seventh stanza of "Sensaciones" (Sensations):

No hay mejor recompensa que la noche en tu cuerpo
ni estipendio más grato que tu abandono consentido.

Llévame a donde los sentimientos no se pudren.

Bórrame del mundo y su quebranto

(There is no better compensation than the night in your body
no more pleasing stipend than your consented abandon.

Carry me to where feelings will not spoil.

Erase me from the world and its pain).

Distribuidores: Editorial Librería "Difusión"

La Paz — Bolivia

1968

Paperback cover for Shimose's third book, a collection of poems that call attention to social injustice in Bolivia (Delyte W. Morris Library, Southern Illinois University at Carbondale)

Moving consecutively throughout the book, the reader notices that the content becomes more sexual, and the frequency of the speaker's abandonment by the lover increases as well. The contrast is explicit between the first poem, "Dulcinea," which promises an encounter with an "Amada, amante, amiga, compañera" (Loved, lover, friend, companion), and the failure of the relationship in the last poem, "Aldonza." In this last poem, Shimose appropriates characters from Miguel Cervantes's *Don Quixote* (1605, 1615) as a strategy that allows him to play with the language (dulcinear) and the concepts of fantasy and real life in order to portray his disillusionment:

Y yo te dulcineo en mi fracaso,
Y tú, sin compasión, me dulcineas:
pasas de largo sin hacerme caso

(And I sweeten you with my failure,
And you, without compassion, sweeten me:
you walk by without noticing me).

The last section of *No te lo vas a creer,* "Epílogo" (Epilogue), consists of a single poem, "La musa se va" (The Muse Is Leaving). It provides a possible explanation for the failure of the idealized union by suggesting that true identity is found in the mundane and sometimes unpleasant experiences of everyday life and that the passage of time will inevitably produce changes in individuals and relationships.

A reading of Pedro Shimose's poetic corpus establishes that he is an innovative writer conscious of contemporary themes and techniques. One stance that becomes a constant in his works and his life is his role as a witness of history, a role that has changed through time from a more limited national viewpoint to a broader, global approach. Shimose's exploration of the human condition ranges from his descriptions of Bolivian life to his studies of the common traits of modern man and of his own individual experience. His exploration of both internal and external realities is thorough and has undergone a major evolution. Dominated by his need to challenge the increasingly problematic political and social climates in Bolivia, his early poetry commonly utilizes references to regional flora and fauna as well as Bolivian colloquialisms. Upon leaving Bolivia in 1971 Shimose begins to reflect his immediate and different circumstances by addressing the plight of Everyman confronting solitude. Indeed, the exile experience has shaped his life and literary path. Shimose has made a home for himself in Spain, where he and his wife have raised their two sons and Spanish-born daughter, Ana Laicla and since have become grandparents; but his existential conflict remains, and the poet strives to find answers. The innovative evolution of his religious, social, political, erotic, and existential themes—carried out through his experimentation in typography and intertextuality—indicates that Shimose will successfully continue to adapt and modify his poetry to reflect new historical circumstances and personal experiences.

Interviews:

Juan Manuel Rozas, "Encuentro con Pedro Shimose, premio de poesía Casa de las Américas," *Ínsula: Revista Bibliográfica de Ciencias y Letras,* 306 (27 May 1972): 4–5;

Julián Pérez Alberto, "Entrevista con Pedro Shimose," *Alba de América: Revista Literaria,* 2, nos. 20–21 (July 1993): 497–501;

Geraldine Chaplin, actriz: Pedro Shimose, poeta (La Paz: Periodistas Asociados Televisión, Banco Boliviano Americano, 1993);

Debbie Lee, "Entrevista con Pedro Shimose," *PALARA,* 4 (Fall 2000): 84–89.

References:

Alfonso Gumucio Dagrón, *Provocaciones* (La Paz: Los Amigos del Libro, 1977, pp. 215–252;

Indice de la poesía Boliviana contemporánea, edited by Juan Quirós (La Paz: Librería Juventud, 1964);

Eduardo Mitre, "Pedro Shimose: Del fervor al escepticismo," in his *Poetas contemporáneos de Bolivia* (Caracas: Monte Avila, 1986), pp. 43–53;

María A. Salgado, "Una lectura maquiavélica de Pedro Shimose," *Revista hispánica moderna* (December 1995): 349–364.

José Asunción Silva

(27 November 1865 – 24 May 1896)

Alejandro Mejías-López
Indiana University

BOOKS: *Poesías* (Barcelona: Maucci, 1908; revised and enlarged, 1918; definitive edition, with notes by Baldomero Sanín Cano, Santiago: Cóndor, 1923);

Los mejores poemas (Mexico City: Cultura, 1917);

El libro de versos (Bogotá: Cromos, 1928);

De sobremesa: 1887–1896 (Bogotá: Cromos, 1925);

Prosas (Bogotá: Talleres de Ediciones Colombia, 1926);

Poesías completas (Buenos Aires: Sopena, 1941);

Nocturno (Bogotá: Talleres Editoriales del Ministerio de Educación Nacional, 1951);

Obra completa (Bogotá: Ministerio de Educación de la Revista Bolívar, 1955);

Obra completa, prologue by Miguel de Unamuno, notes by Baldomero Sanín Cano (Medellín: Bedout, 1968);

Antología de verso y prosa (Bogotá: Instituto Colombiano de Cultura, 1973);

Obra completa, edited by Eduardo Camacho Guizado (Miranda, Venezuela: Arte, 1977);

Intimidades (Bogotá: Instituto Caro y Cuervo, 1977);

Gotas amargas (Bogotá: Kelly, 1996);

Poesías: El libro de versos. Poesía dispersa. Poesías varias. Intimidades, edited, with an introduction and notes, by Rocío Oviedo y Pérez de Tudela (Madrid: Castalia, 1997).

Editions: *El libro de versos,* facsimile edition (Bogotá: Horizonte, 1945; enlarged, Bogotá: Prensas de la Biblioteca Nacional, 1946);

Poesías, edited, with notes, by Héctor H. Orjuela (Bogotá: Cosmos, 1973);

Obra completa, Critical Edition, edited by Orjuela (Nanterre, France: ALLCA XX, 1996).

José Asunción Silva published only a few poems and prose pieces in his lifetime, most of them in journals and newspapers. His collected works amount to no more than 130 poems, 11 prose pieces, and a novel. Yet, he is arguably the most renowned Colombian poet and, together with José Martí and Rubén Darío, one of the three most important voices of Latin American

José Asunción Silva (from Ricardo Cano Gaviria, José Asunción Silva, Una vida en clave de sombra, *1992; Thomas Cooper Library, University of South Carolina)*

Modernismo. In many ways, as Héctor H. Orjuela points out, Silva was the epitome of the modernist writer: torn between business and art to the point that the dilemma might have driven him to commit suicide. So little is known, however, not only about what made him kill himself so young but also about his private life that it has become a common practice among his biographers to quote José Juan Tablada's early remark: "Silva does not have a biography but a legend." From his birth date to his love life to his European trip to his premature death, conflicting accounts, rumors, and silence surround much of Silva's life. This confusion has also affected in different ways the editions and interpretations of his works and has made difficult the identification of works possibly published under still-unknown pseudonyms. In the 1990s, and in particular during the centenary of his death in 1996, there were significant new editions and a renewed interest in his life and works, although much work remains to be done. In any case, his relatively small poetic production stands out as one of the most innovative and influential of modern Hispanic poetry.

José Asunción Silva Gómez was born on 27 November 1865 in Bogotá, the first child of Ricardo Silva Frade and Vicenta Gómez Diago, an upper-middle-class family with ties to the political, economic, and literary elite of Colombia. The Silvas owned a ranch, Hatogrande, part of the estate of a distant relative and president of the country, Francisco de Paula Santander, which currently serves as summerhouse for Colombia's presidents. Ricardo Silva owned a business of imported luxury items and, as a fervent liberal, was sometimes involved in political activities. He was also a writer and participant in the literary group El mosaico (The Mosaic), the members of which included poets Rafael Pombo and Diego Fallon, as well as Jorge Isaacs, the author of the novel *María* (1867). The group gathered regularly at Silva's house, thus becoming an integral part of his son's intellectual upbringing.

Silva proved to be a talented child, skilled at drawing and able to read and write in Spanish when he was only two years old. By age four he could read and speak English and French, and he learned Italian and some rudimentary German not long after that. His education took place both at school, where he consistently obtained the highest grades, and at home. An avid reader who took advantage of his father's extensive library, he also participated in an astonishingly wide variety of cultural events and social gatherings with his father's friends, many of whom, such as Isaacs, Pombo, activist Helena Miralla, and scholar Rufino José Cuervo, became his mentors. Silva grew up in a highly refined and intellectual environment that marked his own personality and set him apart from most of his peers at school, who gave him nicknames such as "el niño bonito" (the pretty boy) and "José Presunción" (Presumptuous José).

Silva wrote his first known poem, "Primera comunión" (First Communion), when he was ten years old and, by the age of thirteen, his second one, "La crisálida" (The Chrysalis, 1884), which was eventually included in an anthology, edited by José Manuel Mar-

roquín and Ricardo Carrasquilla, with some of the best-known Hispanic poets of the time. The poem narrates the death of a little girl, whose soul leaves her body as a butterfly leaves her cocoon, leading the poet to ponder the afterlife. Death, arguably the most consistently recurring theme in his poetry, was not, however, a literary topos for Silva nor an excuse for philosophical musings; on the contrary, it had a concrete presence in Silva's life from the beginning. Hatogrande, where he spent part of every year, had been the scene of two violent deaths that haunted his family for years: first, the brutal and never-resolved murder of his grandfather in the presence of the grandfather's brother Antonio María; and soon after, the suicide for no apparent reason of Guillermo Silva, Ricardo's business partner and best friend. Moreover, three of Silva's siblings, Guillermo, Alfonso, and Inés, had died by the time he was twelve.

Among the many poets he read in his early years, Gustavo Adolfo Bécquer, who always remained an important model for him, Edgar Allan Poe, Victor Hugo, and, later on, José Martí and Manuel Gutiérrez Nájera proved to be the most influential in his work. Translating poetry from English, French, and Italian into Spanish was an integral part of his development as a poet, and his translations were some of the first works he published. In Bogotá, Silva soon gained the reputation of being a child prodigy.

The year 1880 marked a turning point in Silva's life as well as in the political history of Colombia. Rafael Núñez, whom Silva's family supported, became president, and his administration implemented a controversial program known as the Regeneración (Regeneration). President Núñez remained in control of Colombian politics for fourteen years, and his policies ultimately had an indirect impact on the Silvas' economic downfall. That same year, Silva ended his formal education and had the choice of either traveling through Europe with the school or pursuing studies in either philosophy or law in Bogotá. Concerned, however, about the fragile health of his father, who suffered from chronic typhitis, an incurable disease at the time, Silva opted for staying home to help. From then on Silva's life was divided between commerce and his artistic vocation. This tension is an integral part of his work, which in many ways is a reaction against everything brought about by modernization, capitalism, and middle-class values.

Between 1880 and 1884 Silva began writing a series of original poems and translations from French and Italian that make up his first known poetry collection, *Intimidades* (Intimate Thoughts), a work that remained unpublished until 1977. Many of his later themes—death, love, time and memory, and the tension

Silva's parents, Ricardo Silva Frade and Vicenta Gómez Diago de Silva
(Casa Silva, Bogotá)

between ideals and reality—are present in this early collection. Three love poems in this book are dedicated to an unidentified male poet, "A de W," which, aside from rumors or legends, is the most that is known about Silva's love interests, male or female.

In 1883 Silva's father, worried about the state of his health and in preparation for a trip to France that kept him away from the store for some time, petitioned the court that his son be considered emancipated and of legal age to conduct business at eighteen rather than twenty-one. This request was granted in December, and the business became "Ricardo Silva and Son," the name it kept until its end.

At the request of editors who knew of his growing reputation as a poet and who had heard his poems at literary gatherings, Silva began reluctantly submitting some of his compositions for publication. Following the translations of two French poems, he published his own "Nota perdida VI" (Lost Note VI, 1884), the first example of a satirical tone that characterizes some of his later poetry, and "La crisálida." After two prolific years, in which he wrote approximately forty of the fifty-nine poems that compose *Intimidades,* his literary activity slowed in 1884 because of newly acquired responsibilities. While his father was away in Europe, Silva had to take care of business and family, at a time when the country went into a severe economic crisis worsened by uprisings against the second administration of Núñez.

That year Silva also found himself indirectly involved in a scandal. Writer José María Vargas Vila publicly accused his boss, Tomás Escobar, a priest and the director of the school where Silva had last studied and a family friend, of having sexual relations with his pupils. As a former student of Escobar's, Silva signed a letter in defense of the priest with a group of his fellow students and had it published in several newspapers. Shortly thereafter, however, one of the signers publicly retracted, alleging that his peers had pressured him into signing. Public accusations continued for some time until Escobar's formal prosecution. He was found not guilty the following year, however, and continued to frequent the company of the Silvas.

Upon his return from Europe, his father notified Silva that his great-uncle Antonio María, who resided in France, had invited him to visit in order to meet him before he died. Silva departed on 25 October 1884, arriving in Paris early in December, only to find that his uncle's death had occurred before he had even set sail from Colombia. Silva stayed in Europe, however, and used the trip in part to deal with business matters. He also soon established contact with the group of Colombian intellectuals residing in France, particularly his friend Juan Evangelista Manrique, the brothers Cuervo, and José María Torres Caicedo, who introduced him to the literary and artistic circles of the French capital. There Silva met Paul Bourget, Guy de Maupassant, Gustave Moreau, Carolus Durán, and Stéphane Mallarmé, who gave him signed reproductions of several of Moreau's drawings and a copy of Joris-Karl Huysmans's *A rebours* (1884; translated as *Against the Grain,* 1922), the main model for Silva's own later novel, *De sobremesa: 1887–1896* (After Dinner: 1887–1896, 1925).

In March 1885 Silva traveled to Madrid and Seville, returning to Paris in May, where he witnessed the state funerals for Hugo. In July his poem "Realidad" (Reality), a translation of Hugo's "Les Complications du Ideal" (Complications of the Ideal, 1865), was published in Bogotá. Increasingly interested in medicine and psychology, topics that soon after began to appear in many of his works, that summer Silva attended the lectures given by J. M. Charcot at the Salpêtriére. In August he left for London, where he spent more than a month dividing his time between commercial assignments for his father and exploring the social, political, and artistic life of the city, especially the works of the Pre-Raphaelites. Back on the Continent, Silva traveled in Switzerland and possibly Belgium, Holland, and Italy. In Brienz, Switzerland, he wrote the sonnet "A un pesimista" (To a Pessimist, 1886). When he returned to Paris, Silva learned that the civil war in Colombia had finally ended, though not the long economic crisis that continued to affect the family business.

During his stay in Europe, Silva read avidly and bought as many books as he could afford. They left an indelible imprint on the young poet's mind and work: works by Charles Baudelaire, Mallarmé, the symbolists, the Parnasianists, the Pre-Raphaelites, and Maria Bashkirtseff in poetry and the plastic arts; Honoré de Balzac, Gustave Flaubert, Emile Zola, de Maupassant, and Huysmans in prose; Paul Bourget in psychology; and Arthur Schopenhauer and Friedrich Nietzsche in philosophy. His travels to and through Europe were indeed a defining moment in his poetic career, so much so that in the last days of his life, Silva was still reliving them through the hero of *De sobremesa.*

Silva embarked for Colombia in November 1885. In a stopover in New York City he had the chance to meet Martí, who gave him a signed copy of his recently published *Ismaelillo* (Little Ishmael, 1882). In December, as he was arriving, Colombia changed its official name from the United States of Colombia to the Republic of Colombia, and President Núñez was elected for his third, and longest, administration. At home his family greeted him with disastrous news: a robbery at the store a few days earlier had put the already troubled business in a dire financial situation. The inheritance from his great-uncle Antonio María, which his father finally received in January, saved them from insolvency. Gone to Europe to replenish the store, his father left Silva once again in charge of things at home.

Silva's year in Europe had increased his persistent sense of estrangement from the social environment in Bogotá, where he was perceived by many as arrogant, aloof, and refined to the point of what was seen as effeminacy, a perception that many thought confirmed by his alleged celibacy. As in his school days, he was tauntingly nicknamed, now called "el casto José" (chaste Joseph) and "José Pendolphi." Silva, nonetheless, joined the literary meetings hosted by his schoolmate and fellow writer José Rivas Groot, a gathering of young writers who were putting together an anthology of recent Colombian poetry. His friend Antonio José Restrepo published his poem "A un pesimista" in the journal *La siesta* in April 1886, and that same month the anthology *La lira nueva* (The New Lyre, 1886) was published. It included eight of his poems: "Estrofas" (Strophes), "La voz de marcha" (The Marching Voice), "Estrellas fijas" (Fixed Stars), "El recluta" (The Soldier), "Resurrecciones" (Resurrections), "Obra Humana" (Human Work), "La calavera" (The Skull), and "A Diego Fallon" (To Diego Fallon). It is the largest sample of Silva's poetry published in his lifetime and meant the consolidation of his recognition as a poet in Colombia. Furthermore, it is mainly, though not solely, because of his presence in *La lira nueva* that most critics identify this anthology as the beginning of *Modernismo* in that country. That same year, two of his early poems, "La crisálida" and his translation of Pierre Jean de Béranger's "Las golondrinas" (The Swallows), came out in another anthology, *Parnaso Colombiano* (Colombian Parnassus), edited by Julio Añez.

Thus, Silva became, in spite of his relatively small number of published poems, an increasingly important figure in the Colombian literary milieu. He met writer Baldomero Sanín Cano, who became one of his most intimate friends, and socialized frequently with the artist Alberto Urdaneta, in whose honor he wrote "Taller moderno" (Modern Workshop, 1887). Between 1886 and 1890 Silva published a variety of works connected to several literary debates: the poem "Futuro" (Future, 1886); the essay "Crítica Ligera" (Light Criticism, 1888); a prologue to Federico Rivas Frade's poem *Bienaventurados los que lloran* (Blessed Are Those Who Cry, 1889); and the parable "Protesta de la Musa" (The Muse's Protest, 1891). This last piece is a perfect example of *Modernista* poetic prose in its form and in its reflections on art and the artist. Through the character of the Muse, Silva voices his own belief in the sacredness of art and its fundamentally aesthetic nature but also in the responsibility of the artist to make it a tool of social justice and redemption for humankind:

> la misión del poeta es besar las heridas y besar a los infelices en la frente, y dulcificar la vida con sus cantos, y abriles, a los que yerran, abrirles amplias, las puertas de la Virtud y del Amor . . . ; yo canto las luchas de los pueblos, las caídas de los tiranos, las grandezas de los hombres libres . . . , pero no conozco los insultos ni el odio

> (the mission of the poet is to kiss wounds and to kiss the forehead of the unhappy, and to sweeten life with his songs, and to open wide the doors of Virtue and Love to those who blunder . . . ; I sing the struggle of the people, the downfall of tyrants, the greatness of free men . . . , but I know not of insults nor hatred).

Most critics suspect that Silva published much more during these and future years under a variety of pseudonyms, but the list of works attributed to him with certainty remains short. In addition to writing, Silva also kept alive his other passion: painting. One of his works, a reproduction of Samuel Edmund Waller's *The Duel,* was part of the Primera Exposición Nacional de Bellas Artes (First National Exhibit of Fine Arts) in Bogotá in 1886. His interest in painting and drawing, which began in childhood, became a recurrent element in his poetry and a central theme in much of his prose.

In June 1887 Silva's father died, leaving his business in a precarious situation. A large number of creditors, low sales, and an economic crisis that had affected Colombia for more than three years had left the store on the verge of bankruptcy. Silva, nonetheless, managed to save it and keep it going for a few more years. His literary work became a not-always-reachable oasis in the midst of his commercial activities, as he told his friend Cuervo in a 10 April 1889 letter: "A mí mismo me da risa cuando, cogido por alguien y obligado, paso de las liquidaciones de facturas, la venta diaria y los cálculos de intereses, a descansar un minuto en las cosas del arte, como en un lugar más alto, donde hay aire más puro y se respira mejor . . ." (Even I find it funny when, caught and forced by someone, I go from paying bills, daily sales, and interest calculations to resting for a minute in artistic affairs, as if in a higher place where the air is purer and breathing easier . . .). In 1889 he gave the manuscript of his first book of poems, *Intimidades,* to Paquita Martín, a friend of his sister and confidante Elvira, while he slowly worked on two new collections, *Gotas amargas* (Bitter Drops, 1918) and *El libro de versos* (Book of Verses, 1928).

On 11 January 1891, when he had hardly recovered from the loss of his father, his sister Elvira died. A

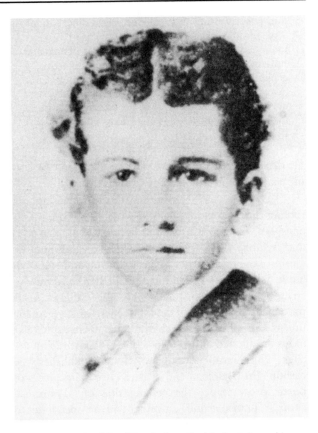

Silva, age nine (from Ricardo Cano Gaviria, José Asunción Silva, Una vida en clave de sombra, *1992; Thomas Cooper Library, University of South Carolina)*

severe case of pneumonia, initially misdiagnosed and mistreated as typhoid fever, caused her death in a matter of six days. With Elvira, he not only lost a beloved family member, the fourth of a family of seven in his lifetime, but also one of his closest and dearest friends. Elvira's death produced a commotion in Bogotá, triggering an outpouring of grief expressed in articles and literary pieces dedicated to her memory, the best-known of which was a poem by Jorge Isaacs. That same year Silva's business finally failed, obliging him to deal with grief and creditors at the same time. In an 1891 letter to Guillermo Uribe, one of the creditors, he describes his physical and emotional state during those days:

> El día 6 de enero cayó mi hermana enferma gravemente, no volví a salir de mi casa hasta el día 11 en que la llevé al cementerio. Enseguida, moribundo de dolor y de sufrimiento, caí a cama, no pude moverme en muchos días, vencido de dolor, no podía coordinar dos ideas, no podía pensar. . . . los músculos no me sostenían, tenía el alma destrozada; yo comprendía que usted estaba urgido por su dinero, pero no podía devolvérselo en ese momento. No podía pensar sino en que Elvira estaba muerta

(On January 6 my sister fell severely ill and I didn't leave the house again until January 11 when I took her to the cemetery. I had to stay in bed, dying of pain and suffering; I could not coordinate two thoughts, I couldn't think. . . . my muscles would not support me, my soul was torn apart; I could understand that you needed your money back, but I could not pay you at that time. I could not think anything other than that Elvira was dead).

He declared bankruptcy, thus beginning a long process of repaying debts that took more than two years.

The year after his sister's death, Silva's grandmother died, prompting him to write "Los maderos de San Juan" (The Wood of Saint John's, 1892), a circular and self-referential poem, in which a grandmother glimpses the future woes of her grandson and he, as an adult, is inspired by the memory of her sufferings to write her a poem after her death. *Modernista* in form, particularly in the use of the fourteen-syllable verse, the unusual strophes, and its rhythm, this poem stands out in his production for the disposition of the words on the page, which recalls a calligram. He also published "Al carbón" (In Charcoal) and "Pastel," two short pieces of poetic prose under the general title of "Transposiciones" (Transpositions), together with an open letter to his friend Doña Rosa Ponce de Portocarrero that served as a prologue. Both pieces are classic examples of Silva's interest in blending literature and the plastic arts.

In sharp contrast to his personal and economic distress—he ended up forced to sell his own library in order to finish paying his debts—the remaining three years of Silva's life were intensely productive and increasingly successful in the literary arena. The year 1894, in particular, was arguably the most important of his literary career, owing to the publication of his two best-known poems: "Sinfonía color de fresas con leche" (Symphony in the Color of Strawberries and Milk) and "Nocturno" (Nocturne), later called "Una noche" (A Night) and then "Nocturno III." He wrote the first one under the pseudonym of Benjamín Bibelot Ramírez and dedicated it to "los colibríes decadentes" (the decadent hummingbirds). It is a series of seven sextets filled with all the clichés of a certain type of *Modernista* poetry, exotic and grandiloquent, commonly associated with Darío, the foremost representative of the movement. Silva, however, did not direct this magnificent and hilarious parody against the Nicaraguan poet, whom he in fact admired, but against the profusion of bad imitators that Darío's original style had generated. It became an immediate success and was reprinted in magazines and journals all over Latin America.

"Nocturno," unanimously considered Silva's masterpiece, stands in contrast to "Sinfonía color de fresas con leche" as a highly innovative and emotionally powerful poem about love and death. Divided into two parts, the poem speaks of two different nights, one in the past and the other in the present, separated by the death of the beloved. Its originality, as critics Eduardo Camacho Guizado and Betty Tyree Osiek have pointed out, resides largely in its formal structure, since it builds on a tension between rhythmic patterns and metric irregularity. According to Camacho Guizado, Silva in this poem breaks for the first time in Hispanic poetry from the classical metrical norms, traditionally based on syllables and not on feet, thus establishing a model for the later experimentations of Darío. The alliteration and repetition of certain verses and images further emphasizes the almost funereal rhythm of the poem:

> Una noche
> Una noche toda llena de perfumes, de murmullos y de
>   música de alas,
> Una noche
> En que ardían en la sombra nupcial y húmeda, las luciér-
>   nagas fantásticas,
> A mi lado, lentamente, contra mí ceñida, toda,
>   Muda y pálida
> Como si un presentimiento de amarguras infinitas,
> Hasta el fondo más secreto de tus fibras te agitara,
> Por la senda que atraviesa la llanura florecida
>   Caminabas,
>   Y la luna llena
> Por los cielos azulosos, infinitos y profundos esparcía su
>   luz blanca,
>   Y tu sombra
>   Fina y lánguida,
>   Y mi sombra
> Por los rayos de la luna proyectada
> Sobre las arenas tristes
> De la senda se juntaban
>   Y eran una
>   Y eran una
> Y eran una sola sombra larga!
> Y eran una sola sombra larga!
> Y eran una sola sombra larga!
>
> (One night
> One night filled with perfumes, with whispers, and with
>   the music of wings
>   One night
> In which fantastic fireflies glowed in the nuptial and humid
>   shadows,
> Gently, your body pressed against mine,
>   silent and pale,
> As if the foreshadowing of infinite sorrows
> Troubled you in your deepest and most secret self,
> Through the path crossing the blooming plains
>   You were walking
>   And the full moon
> Spread its white light over the infinite and deep blue sky
>   And your shadow,
>   Languid and fine,

And my shadow,
Projected by the moonlight
Over the sad sands
Of the path were merging
　And they were one
　And they were one
And they were one long lone shadow!
And they were one long lone shadow!
And they were one long lone shadow!).

The formal tension of the poem also translates into its content. There is not a direct commentary on death in the poem, yet the sense of loss permeates every line, as does the unsolvable separation between the realm of life and the mysteries of death. Furthermore, the poem only obliquely mentions love, yet love is at its core.

Its irreducibly contradictory nature seems to have seeped into its critical reception as well. Virtually every critic has read it as a poem about Silva and his sister Elvira, but they have interpreted it two quite different ways. After the first edition of *Poesías* (Poems) in 1908, some understood the "Nocturno" to be a love poem and speculated about a possible incestuous relationship between brother and sister. Nothing, however, in the poem indicates any connection to Elvira other than the fact that both she and the woman in "Nocturno" died. The vast majority of critics strongly reject the incest interpretation as immoral and groundless and–evidently overlooking the words "sombra nupcial" (nuptial shadow) in the fourth verse–think that the poem is about chaste fraternal love. Whatever the case, "Nocturno" soon developed a cult of admirers in *Modernista* circles, entering the canon as one of the most emblematic pieces of the period. Moreover, this poem is one of the most anthologized poems in Hispanic literature.

A much-needed break from Silva's economic and personal misery in Bogotá came about with his appointment as secretary of the Colombian diplomatic delegation in Caracas. On the way he stopped for a few days in Cartagena, where, in addition to publishing "Nocturno," he had the chance to meet several times with President Núñez himself. In Venezuela he soon was acquainted with the literary and artistic circles, particularly with Pedro César Dominici, Pedro Emilio Coll, and the staff at the renowned journal *El cojo ilustrado.* Living in Caracas, however, did not save him from the same social prejudices as in Bogotá, responsible this time for the nickname "la casta Susana" (chaste Susan). Prejudice aside, Silva worked intensely on his two projected poetry collections, *El libro de versos* and *Gotas amargas,* as well as on his novel, *De sobremesa,* and a series of short stories that he planned to group under the title of "Cuentos negros" (Dark Tales). His two short pieces "Al carbon" and "Pastel" were reprinted in the Mexican journal *Revista Azul,* one of the most important vehicles

Silva's sister Elvira, whose death in 1891 is reflected in "Nocturno," the poem generally considered his masterpiece (Casa Silva, Bogotá)

of the *Modernista* movement. In September, President Núñez died in Colombia, and Silva published "Doctor Rafael Núñez" (1894), an article eulogizing him as both a public and a literary figure.

The following January, Silva was struck by misfortune yet again. The ship *Amérique,* in which he was returning home on vacation, shipwrecked off the coast of Colombia, and he lost all his manuscripts to the sea. Thereafter, Silva spent most of his time rewriting his works from scratch, particularly his novel, in which he had placed much hope. To make matters worse, another civil war had begun in Colombia, making it impossible for him to obtain from the president another appointment as ambassador in Venezuela or consul in Europe, the main reason for his ill-fated trip home. Silva returned to Caracas, where he worked for another two months until, without prior notice, he left again for Bogotá, this time indefinitely. Three more of his poems were published that year: "Paisaje Tropical" (Tropical Landscape), "Crepúsculo" (Twilight), and "Sus dos mesas" (Her Two Tables), an interesting poem in its critique of the limitations suffered by women after marriage.

In a reception offered by the Venezuelan ambassador on 28 October 1895, Silva performed a public reading of his "Al pie de la estatua" (At the Feet of the

Paperback cover for Silva's first book (1908), which includes "Nocturno" (from Juan Gustavo Cobo-Borda, José Asunción Silva, Bogotano Universal, *1988)*

Statue), a long poem with epic undertones that celebrates the character and the deeds of Simón Bolívar and laments the Latin American history of war and violence after independence. The importance of public readings for the diffusion of Silva's works cannot be underestimated, since it was a vehicle for the circulation of his poetry, as his friend Sanín Cano was quoted in Fernando Charry Lara's *José Asunción Silva, vida y creación* (1985): "Sin ser publicadas, muchas de esas poesías adquirieron carta de naturaleza en los salones donde había preocupaciones literarias. Llegaron a ser propiedad del público sin salir a la prensa, cuando amigos y admiradores las recibieron en la memoria, y por una especie de tradición anticipada las distribuyeron a

los cuatro vientos" (Without being published, many of those poems acquired currency in the literary salons. They became public property without coming out in print, when friends and admirers memorized them and by a sort of anticipated tradition propagated them all around).

Silva's last act of entrepreneurship was the creation of a tile factory, but it also failed, putting him in debt once again. He spent his last days finishing the rewrite of his novel *De sobremesa,* which although completed by the time of his death, was not published until three decades later. On 23 May 1896 Silva organized a dinner party at his home and performed his last public reading, of his poem "Don Juan de Covadonga." This poem tells the story of Don Juan, a libertine who, regretting his lifestyle, leaves his worldly life and takes refuge at the monastery where his brother Hernando is a prior, only to find that his brother spends his days fighting his own longing for Don Juan's lifestyle. The seemingly unresolvable tension between flesh and spirit, desire and nirvana, a recurring one in Silva's poetry, is also one of the organizing principles of the novel he had just finished, and ultimately a constant in his own life. That night, after the party was over and the last guest had departed, Silva killed himself with a gunshot through his heart. He was thirty years old.

Silva had left a complete manuscript of his major poetry collection, *El libro de versos,* as well as a complete version of *De sobremesa.* Although the former was included in the early editions of his collected poetry, it was not published by itself as a book until almost three decades later, in 1923. *El libro de versos* is a formally innovative collection of poems dominated thematically by a preoccupation with irreducible tensions: between life and death, the present and the past, reality and dreams and desires. According to Camacho Guizado, a longing for transcendence is the theme that permeates Silva's poetry; in a similar vein, Alfredo A. Roggiano has characterized Silva's poetics as an obsession with the impossible.

José Asunción Silva's other collection of poetry, *Gotas amargas,* not published by itself in book form until 1996, survived as the result of the compilation and editorial efforts of Silva's friends after his death. Largely ignored because of both its satirical, irreverent, and sexual content as well as its seemingly prosaic language, *Gotas amargas* only began receiving the critical attention it deserves in the 1990s. Some critics consider it to be a key precedent to the exploration of colloquial language in poetry that has become one of the most important Latin American poetic traditions of the twentieth century, with such examples as Pablo Neruda's *Odas elementales* (1954; translated as *Elementary Odes,* 1961) and Nicanor Parra's *antipoesía* (antipoetry). *El libro de versos* and *Gotas amargas* stand in sharp contrast to each other and, thus, are the best testimony to a poet who was caught in, and obsessed with, insoluble contradictions in both his art and his life.

Letters:
Cartas: 1881–1896, edited, with notes, by Fernando Vallejo (Bogotá: Casa Silva, 1996).

Biographies:
Ricardo Cano Gaviria, *José Asunción Silva, Una vida en clave de sombra* (Caracas: Monte Ávila, 1992);

Enrique Santos Molano, *El corazón del poeta* (Bogotá: Nuevo Rumbo, 1992);

Fernando Vallejo, *Chapolas negras* (Bogotá: Santillana, 1995).

References:
Eduardo Camacho Guizado, *La poesía de José Asunción Silva* (Bogotá: Universidad de los Andes & Editorial Revista Colombiana, 1968);

Fernando Charry Lara, ed., *José Asunción Silva, vida y creación* (Bogotá: Procultura, 1985);

Juan Gustavo Cobo-Borda, *José Asunción Silva, Bogotano Universal* (Bogotá: Villegas, 1988);

Cobo-Borda, "El primer José Asunción Silva: *Intimidades, 1880–1884,*" in Silva's *Obra completa,* Critical Edition, edited by Héctor H. Orjuela (Nanterre, France: ALLCA XX, 1996), pp. 513–532;

Gustavo Mejía, "José Asunción Silva: Sus textos, su crítica," in Silva's *Obra completa,* Critical Edition, pp. 471–500;

Orjuela, "José Asunción Silva: Conflicto y transgresión de un intelectual modernista," in Silva's *Obra completa,* Critical Edition, pp. 422–442;

Betty Tyree Osiek, *José Asunción Silva* (Boston: Twayne, 1978);

Alfredo A. Roggiano, "Poética y estilo de José Asunción Silva," in Silva's *Obra completa,* Critical Edition, pp. 567–574.

Alfonsina Storni

(29 May 1892 – 25 October 1938)

Gwen Kirkpatrick
University of California, Berkeley

BOOKS: *La inquietud del rosal* (Buenos Aires: La Facultad, 1916);

El dulce daño (Buenos Aires: Sociedad Cooperativa Editorial Limitada, 1918);

Irremediablemente . . . (Buenos Aires: Sociedad Cooperativa Editorial Limitada, 1919);

Languidez (Buenos Aires: Sociedad Cooperativa Editorial Limitada, 1920);

Las mejores poesías de los mejores poetas: Alfonsina Storni (Barcelona: Cervantes, 1923);

Ocre (Buenos Aires: BABEL, 1925);

Poemas de Gabriela Mistral, Juana de Ibarbourou, Delmira Agustini, Alfonsina Storni (Bogotá: Ediciones Colombia, 1925);

Poemas de amor (Buenos Aires: Nosotros, 1926);

El amo del mundo: Comedia en tres actos (Buenos Aires, 1927);

Dos farsas pirotécnicas (Buenos Aires: Cooperativa Editorial "Buenos Aires," 1932);

Mundo de siete pozos (Buenos Aires: Tor, 1934);

Antologia poética (Buenos Aires: Espasa-Calpe, 1938);

Mascarilla y trébol: Círculos imantados (Buenos Aires: El Ateneo, 1938);

Antología poética, prologue by Storni (Buenos Aires & Mexico City: Espasa-Calpe Argentina, 1940);

Obra poética (Buenos Aires: Roggero-Ronal, 1946);

Teatro infantil (Buenos Aires: Roggero, 1950);

Los mejores versos (Buenos Aires: Nuestra América, 1958);

Cinco cartas; y, Una golondrina (Buenos Aires: Instituto de Amigos del Libro Argentino, 1959);

Alfonsina Storni: Antología, edited by María de Villariño (Buenos Aires: Ministerio de Educación y Justicia, Dirección General de Cultura, 1961);

Poesías, prologue by Alejandro Alfonso Storni (Buenos Aires: Universitaria de Buenos Aires, 1961);

Obra poética completa (Buenos Aires: Sociedad Editora Latino Americana, 1961);

Alfonsina Storni, Edición Conmemorativa, edited by Carlos A. Andreola (Buenos Aires: Nobis, 1963);

Alfonsina Storni

Poesías sueltas (Buenos Aires: Sociedad Editora Latino Americana, 1964);

Teatro infantil (Buenos Aires: Librería Huemul, 1973);

Obras completas (Buenos Aires: Sociedad Editora Latino Americana, 1976);

Antología mayor: Alfonsina Storni, introduction by Jorge Rodríguez Padrón (Madrid: Hiperión, 1994);

Poesías completas (Buenos Aires: Sociedad Editora Latino Americana, 1996);

"Si quieres besarme—besa": Selección de sus más bellas poeías (Buenos Aires: Planeta Argentina, 1996);

Poemas (Buenos Aires: El Francotirador, 1996);

"Quisiera esta tarde—": Poemas de amor (Rosario, Argentina: Ameghino, 1997).

Editions in English: *Alfonsina Storni: Argentina's Feminist Poet,* edited and translated by Florence Williams Talamantes (Los Cerrillos, N.Mex.: San Marcos Press, 1975);

Selected Poems, translated by Dorothy Scott Loos (Brattleboro, Vt.: Amana, 1986);

Selected Poems, edited by Marion Freeman, translated by Freeman, Mary Crow, Jim Normington, and Kay Short (Fredonia, N.Y.: White Pine, 1987);

Nosotras-y la piel, edited by Mariela Méndez, Graciela Queirolo, and Alicia Salomone (Buenos Aires: Alfaguava, 1998).

OTHER: "Six Poems," in *Women's Writing in Latin America: An Anthology,* edited by Sara Castro-Klarén, Sylvia Molloy, and Beatriz Sarlo (Boulder, Colo.: Westview Press, 1991), pp. 143–147;

"An Old Story," "Letter to the Eternal Father," "Against Charity," "The Immigrant Girl," and "Women and Love," in *Rereading the Spanish American Essay: Translations of Nineteenth and Twentieth Century Women's Essays,* edited by Doris Meyer, translated by Patricia Steiner (Austin: University of Texas Press, 1995), pp. 99–118.

SELECTED PERIODICAL PUBLICATIONS–
UNCOLLECTED: "De la vida," *Fray Mocho,* 1, no. 23 (4 October 1912): n.p.;

"El amo del mundo," *Bambalinas,* 9, no. 470 (6 April 1927): 1–39;

"Entretelones de un estreno," *Nosotros,* 21, no. 215 (April 1927): 48–55;

"Autodemolición," *Repertorio Americano,* 11, no. 21 (7 June 1930): 329, 331;

"Alrededor de la muerte de Lugones," *Nosotros,* second series 3, nos. 26–28 (May–June 1939): 218–221.

Alfonsina Storni is one of Latin America's most widely read poets. She gained early fame through the publication of her first books of poetry, partly through their explicitly confessional nature and accessible style, but also because of her independent, and even defiant, posture regarding the status of women. Her dramatic suicide in 1938 added to her almost legendary status as a writer and public figure, and in subsequent decades both her poetry and her personal story have acquired almost mythic status. "Alfonsina" is the title of a popular song based on her life and death, and her personal history, poetry, theatrical works, journalism, and other writings have inspired documentaries, biographies, and academic studies. Poetry recitals, popular throughout a great deal of the century, did not fail to include verses by Storni. Although primarily a lyric poet, she captured as well in her writings a colloquial vein and often revealed a quick turn of humor.

With a resurgence of feminist activity in the last decades of the twentieth century, Storni's writings have been the object of renewed interest because of her explicit emphasis on the condition of women under patriarchy. As Beatriz Sarlo has stated, "En su poesía se invierten los roles sexuales tradicionales y se rompe con un registro de imágenes atribuidas a la mujer" (In her poetry traditional sex roles are inverted and there is a break with the register of images attributed to women). Her best-known poems, "Tú me quieres blanca" (You Want Me White) and "Hombre pequeñito" (Little Man), can be read as insolent responses to the demands placed on women by a male-dominated society. Storni, along with the Uruguayan poet Delmira Agustini, are the two major figures in changing the nature of female eroticism in poetry in Spanish. Her stance created immense negative reaction and criticism as well as popular readership. Her own modest social-class condition and status as single mother added to many of the prejudices against her. Much of her poetry is autobiographical and reflects her independent and often defiant stance, as, for example, in her first collection, *La inquietud del rosal* (The Restlessness of the Rosebush, 1916): "Yo soy como la loba. Ando sola y me río / del rebaño. El sustento me lo gano y es mío / donde quiera que sea . . ." (I am like the she-wolf. I travel alone and laugh / at the pack. I earn my own living and it is mine / wherever I want).

Born in Sala Capriasca in the Swiss canton of Ticino on 29 May 1892, she immigrated at four years of age to the provinces of Argentina, first in San Juan, then in Rosario in the province of Santa Fe, finally settling in Buenos Aires in 1912. In many ways her personal history is paradigmatic of a new class of literary and professional women who emerged from modest beginnings and gained access to opportunities through the public-education system. Along with her studies, throughout childhood and adolescence she worked in the family café and then as a seamstress along with her mother and older sister. At her father's death in 1906 she began to work in a hat factory in Rosario as well to help make ends meet in the family. Early on she demonstrated her ability to engage in multiple activities while at the same time developing her literary and theatrical interests. At fifteen she joined a traveling theater company and spent three years with them. In 1909 she entered a two-year teacher-training program as *maestra rural* (rural teacher), through the Escuela Normal Mixta de Maestros rurales (Co-Ed Normal School for Rural Teachers) in Coronda, ending her formal education in 1911 at nineteen years of

*Paperback cover for Storni's first book of autobiographical poems
written while she worked at factory and office jobs in Buenos
Aires (from Josefina Delgado,* Alfonsina Storni:
Una biografía esencial, *2001)*

age. She then took a teaching job at an elementary school in Rosario. Even earlier, however, Storni had begun her literary career. Previous to her normal-school training she had joined a theater company in Rosario and had also begun to publish in the magazine *Monos y Monadas* (Monkeys and Monkey Business) and *Mundo Rosarino* (World of Rosario). Throughout most of her adult life Storni continued to combine teaching positions and an active writing career in multiple genres. As Rachel Phillips describes in her 1975 study of Storni's life and works, her career defied many of the expectations created by her background: "one is forced to postulate a dismal intellectual background for Storni in her formative years. The evidence points to an extremely limited education in the provinces of Argentina, which was brought to an early end by the need for Alfonsina to help support her family." Yet, despite the limitations of her intellectual background, she managed to achieve some of the dreams of immigration by forging a writing career that has made her one of Latin America's best-known poets.

Storni's life took a dramatic turn after her first year of full-time teaching. She made the move to Buenos Aires when she was expecting a child and, as an unmarried woman, needed to escape the reduced social and professional circles of the provinces where her condition as unmarried mother would make a teaching position impossible. Her son, Alejandro Alfonso Storni, was born in 1912. In Buenos Aires she worked at office and factory jobs for three years while writing *La inquietud del rosal*. Despite the financial hardships of these early years, Storni moved quickly to insert herself into the writing world, and as early as 1913 began to publish in the popular magazine *Caras y Caretas* (Faces and Masks). By 1916, the year she published her first book of poetry, she also contributed essays to magazines such as *La Nota* (The Note), *El Hogar* (Home), *Mundo Argentino* (Argentine World), and *Nosotros* (Us). During this first period her writing is remarkable, both in poetry and in journalism. Her direct style and frank manner of addressing age-old questions of women's lives—love, maternity, independence, and dependence, as well as her acute observations on urban life and increasing modernization, make this early writing truly notable. Although she later dismissed some of her early poetry as naive and sentimental, it forms the basis of her widest readership. After her first book, she published *El dulce daño* (Sweet Hurt, 1918), *Irremediablemente . . .* (Irremediably . . . , 1919), *Languidez* (Languor, 1920), *Ocre* (Ocher, 1925), *Poemas de amor* (Love Poems, 1926), *Mundo de siete pozos* (World of Seven Wells, 1934), and *Mascarilla y trébol: Círculos imantados* (Mask and Clover, 1938). Later anthologies have included many poems published individually and not collected in previous volumes.

In many ways Storni's career paralleled that of a new generation of women who entered the middle class and professional sphere through teacher-training opportunities. During the same period the Chilean poet Gabriela Mistral achieved wide recognition following a similar path: the normal schools of the provinces, early publications in provincial newspapers, and later a career combining teaching and writing. It should be noted, however, that Mistral lived most of her adult life outside of Chile, while Storni remained in Argentina. Like women in many parts of the world in the early decades of the twentieth century, her migration to an urban center, need to find paid employment, and physical separation from her family brought about personal, economic, and social changes that marked modern life throughout the century. Especially in Argentina, as in the United States, the burgeoning middle class were, like Storni, often of immigrant backgrounds, and the rapidly expanding service sector, from working-class to more middle-class groups such as teachers and journalists, made room for women to enter the workforce outside the home. Storni's journalistic article "The Perfect Typist" for *La Nación* (The Nation, 9 May 1920) ironically sketches the "recipe" for molding a new class of women service workers: "Select a young woman from eighteen to twenty-one years old who lives in an apartment building in any distant neighborhood. Discreetly paint her eyes. Bleach her hair. File her nails. Tailor her a fashionable little suit, quite short. Flatten her stomach. . . . Put a bird inside her head (preferably a blue one). Send her to a commercial academy for two or three months. (Up to five pesos a month.) Then keep her waiting on commercial ads for one, two, or three years. Hire her for very little." This sketch highlights the dream-building process used in the recruitment of women for office work and ironizes the precarious realities of this new working sector.

Buenos Aires after World War I was a prosperous and expanding metropolis, fueled by agricultural exports and massive European immigration. Because of the success of the public-school system, literacy rates were high, with more than 65 percent of the Buenos Aires population considered functionally literate in 1914, a strikingly strong figure when compared with almost any other nation. Storni often wrote about the changes wrought by increased urbanization and the quickening pace of life, as in the early poem "Cuadros y ángulos" (Squares and Angles) from *El dulce daño:*

> Casas enfiladas, casas enfiladas
> Casas enfiladas
> Cuadrados, cuadrados, cuadrados.
> Casas enfiladas.
> Las gentes ya tienen el alma cuadrada,
> Ideas en fila
> Y ángulo en la espalda.
> Yo misma he vertido ayer una lagrima,
> Dios mío, cuadrada
>
> (Houses in a row, houses in a row,
> Houses in a row.
> Squared, squared, squared.
> Houses in a row.
> People now have their souls squared,
> ideas in a row,
> angle in their back.
> Yesterday I myself,
> oh Lord, shed a squared tear).

As in much of the industrializing world, citizens of Buenos Aires found themselves in a scene of rapid change, new technologies, and altered rhythms of life.

In this matrix of rapidly rising economy and mobile social status, Storni found a receptive public for her themes of modern womanhood and lyric questionings. Her readership was largely middlebrow, and she did not enter into avant-garde formal experimentation

until late in her career. Many of her readers were women, introduced to her work through publications specifically designed for female audiences. A strong women's movement in Argentina in the early decades of the twentieth century had lobbied for changes in women's status, particularly in the areas of health and labor legislation. The struggle for female suffrage was also prominent, and Storni added her voice both in public meetings and in journalistic articles, but she did not live to see Argentina give women the right to vote in midcentury. Storni particularly championed women's civil rights, especially those of single mothers and illegitimate children, as in her article "Women's Civil Rights" (*La Nota,* 22 August 1919).

Despite her concern for women's issues and social justice, Storni does not center her writings on specific political issues or movements. The social structures she most often examines in her poetry, dramatic works, and journalism are those created by familial and gender roles, and she often views institutions outside this area, such as government and religion, from the perspective of family and gender structures. Storni's journalistic essays and social commentary, although not the most important part of her career, offer an invaluable perspective on her time and place and as well on her own development. Early after her arrival in Buenos Aires she began to contribute to journals and newspapers. Some of the first essays are striking in their serious approach to radical social reform. As an inheritor of a vigorous feminist movement in Latin America, Storni used the "women's page" of major daily newspapers and magazines to set forth her own version of feminism. In many respects her efforts exemplified the rise and decline of women's activism during her lifetime. More traditional than many of her feminist friends, she nonetheless championed many feminist concerns of her day. On a more personal level, her sense of social urgency waned as she received wider critical acclaim and felt greater social acceptance.

By 1920 she began to work as a regular contributor to *La Nación,* one of the two major newspapers of the period. These articles concern almost all areas of women's experience: working women and their occupations, the relationship of women to national and cultural tradition, the role of the church, single mothers, female poverty, migration to the city, and fashion. Many of her contributions for *La Nación* were published under the pseudonym "Tao Lao." With some striking exceptions, most of her columns responded to the demands of the commercial press. The form of the sketch, which she often used, makes few claims to permanence. These pieces are often impressionistic observations with highly personalized judgments. In a kind of urban adaptation of the travelogue, they record vignettes of daily life in Buenos Aires–the subway crowds, shoppers, female "types"–in a chatty tone with frequent asides to the reader. They gain their appeal by mixing trite feminine stereotypes with issues of basic economic and social concern to women.

Storni's lasting fame is as a poet. Much of her poetry reads like an inventory of the concerns of women, particularly nonconformist women, with its anger at male expectations, the seeming impossibility of equality in love, and the dissatisfaction at the traditional roles imposed on women. It is as if the female voice in her poetry speaks from (and against) the vision of the woman embodied in a male discourse. The earth, the sea, the female body, and love are seen in terms of passion, despair, and yearning for fulfillment on an ideal plane. One of her most enduring types of poems is the pattern of a female self addressing a male "tú" (you), often by a series of rhetorical questions. This pattern, often verging on stereotype, engages a wide variety of readers in echoing many of the joys and frustrations of erotic love and sentimental attachments within family and social structures. Undoubtedly the most celebrated poem of this nature is "Tú me quieres blanca," from *El dulce daño,* in which a woman insolently responds to male demands for female purity. The poem opens with a series of declarations on the man's expectations of the woman: "Tú me quieres alba, / Me quieres de espumas, / Me quieres de nácar. / Que sea azucena / Sobre todas, casta. / De perfume tenue. / Corola cerrada" (You want me to be dawn's light, / Like foam, / Like mother of pearl. / You want me to be a lily, / Above all, pure. / Of faint perfume. / A closed corolla). To this list of demands, she contrasts a vivid portrait of a worldly, multicolored "you": "Tú que en los jardines / Negros del engaño / Vestido de rojo / Corriste al estrago" (You who in the black gardens / of deceit, / dressed in red, / ran to destruction). The response is insolent and cutting. She presents another series of demands, in which the man must accomplish a series of acts of purification: "Huye hacia los bosques; / Vete a la Montaña; / Límpiate la boca; / Vive en las cabañas; // Bebe de las rocas; / Duerme sobre escarcha; / Renueva tejidos / Con salitre y agua" (Flee to the forest; / Go to the Mountain; / Wash out your mouth; / Live in the cabins; // Drink from the rocks; / sleep on the frost; / renew your tissues / With saltpeter and water). Then, and only then, after the series of purifications is completed, can he make demands of purity: "Entonces, buen hombre, / Preténdeme blanca, / Preténdeme nívea, / Preténdeme casta" (Then, good man, / Expect me to be white, / Expect me to be like snow, / Expect me to be chaste).

Another poem, "Hombre pequeñito" from *Irremediablemente . . .* , is even more explicit in its rejection of male-imposed limits. It takes the classic image of the

bird in a cage and fashions a sarcastic response from the little bird itself:

> Hombre pequeñito, hombre pequeñito,
> Suelta a tu canario que quiere volar . . .
>
> Estuve en tu jaula, hombre pequeñito,
> Hombre pequeñito qué jaula me das.
> Digo pequeñito porque no me entiendes,
> Ni me entenderás.
>
> Tampoco te entiendo, pero mientras tanto
> Ábreme la jaula, que quiero escapar;
> Hombre pequeñito, te ame media hora,
> No me pidas más
>
> (Little man, little man,
> Let your little canary go, it wants to fly . . .
>
> I was in your cage, little man,
> Little man what a cage you have given me.
> I say "little" because you don't understand me,
> and you'll never understand me.
>
> I don't understand you either,
> But meanwhile, open the cage, I want to get out.
> Little man, I love you for half an hour,
> Don't ask me for more).

It would be difficult to ask for a clearer manifesto of female liberty, but even more unsettling for Storni's contemporary readers was the assertion of a woman's right to love and to leave–"te amé media hora, / No me pidas más"–a reversal of the traditional male/female dynamic.

Obviously, such explicitly and sometimes sarcastic poetic assertions by Storni concerning relations between men and women did not earn her widespread approval. Her defiant posture in poetry, her status as an unwed mother, her middlebrow audience, and her modest class background prevented her from circulating in the most highly regarded circles. Nonetheless, she was rewarded for her literary fame with a series of teaching positions in public schools to which she devoted enormous energy. Her constant exposure through periodical publications–articles, short stories, chronicles–as well as speaking engagements added to her popularity, if not to real financial security.

Until the publication of her last two volumes of poetry, however, the personal feminine stance, expressed in traditional forms of poetry, marks her trajectory. In *Irremediablemente . . .* two somber poems are reflections on the legacy of women throughout time. "Peso ancestral" (Ancestral Weight) speaks to the tradition of silence and repressed emotion throughout the centuries:

Storni reading her poems to an audience of women in July 1925, shortly after the publication of Ocre

Tú me dijiste: no lloró mi padre;
Tú me dijiste: no lloró mi abuelo;
No han llorado los hombres de mi raza,
Eran de acero.

Así diciendo te broto una lágrima
Y me cayó en la boca . . . más veneno
Yo no he bebido nunca en otro vaso
Así pequeño

(You told me: my father didn't cry;
You told me: my grandfather didn't cry;
The men of my race didn't cry,
They were of steel.

And saying this a tear fell from you
And landed on my mouth . . . I have never drunk
Such venom from any other glass
So small).

This poem, with its terse force and deep sorrow, is a fine example of Storni's ability to transmit strong emotion in a few swift strokes.

The sonnet "Bien pudiera ser" (It could well be) follows in the same vein and evokes the depths of sub-merged pain throughout generations: "Pudiera ser que todo lo que en verso he sentido / No fuera mas que aquello que nunca pudo ser, / No fuera mas que algo vedado y reprimido / De familia en familia, de mujer en mujer" (It might be that all that I have felt in poetry / Were no more than something that could never be. / It might not be more than something forbidden and repressed, / From family to family, from woman to woman). As in the previous poem, abstract or emotional issues are rendered in unmistakably corporal form, so that the pain is visceral as well as spiritual: "Y todo esto mordiente, vencido, mutilado, / todo esto que se hallaba en su alma encerrado, / pienso que, sin quererlo, lo he libertado yo" (And all this gnawing, conquered, mutilated matter, / all this found locked in her soul, / without meaning to, I think I have liberated it).

Although more-contemporary anthologies have featured poems that show Storni's nonconformist stance, a great deal of her poetry is dedicated to love and its joys and pains. An ironic note arises even in the most doleful poems, however, as in "Indolencia" (Indolence) from the volume *Ocre:*

–¿Salomé rediviva?–Son más pobres mis gestos.
Ya para cosas trágicas malos tiempos son estos.
Yo soy la que incompleta vive siempre su vida.

Pues no pierde su línea por una fiesta griega
Y al acaso indeciso, ondulante, se pliega
Con los ojos lejanos y el alma distraída

(–Salome revived?–My gestures are poorer than hers.
For tragic things these times now are bad.
I am the one who incompletely always lives her life.

So don't lose your figure for a Greek party
And for the indecisive, undulating maybe, fold over
With distant eyes and distracted soul).

The volume *Ocre* shows signs of what is to come in Storni's poetry, although the volume remains largely faithful to the traditions of rhyme and meter. The poem "Versos a la tristeza de Buenos Aires" (Verses to the Sadness of Buenos Aires) presages a series of reflective cityscapes in her later works, and her self-reflexive stance moves from contemplative sorrow, as in "De mi padre se cuenta" (Of My Father It Is Said), to light ironies in "Epitafio para mi tumba" (Epitaph for My Tomb). The volume also includes a kind of light-hearted *art poétique* in "La palabra" (The Word): "Naturaleza: gracias por este don supremo / Del verso, que me diste; / Yo soy la mujer triste / A quien Caronte ya mostró su remo. // ¿Que fuera de mi vida sin la dulce palabra? / Como el óxido labra / Sus arabescos ocres, / Yo me grabe en los hombres, sublimes o mediocres" (Nature: thanks for this supreme gift / Of verse that you gave me; / I am the sad woman / To whom Charon already has shown his oar. // What would my life be without the sweet word? / Just as acid traces / its ochre arabesques, / I engraved myself on men, sublime or mediocre).

After *Ocre* and *Poemas de amor,* Storni did not publish another major book of poetry until *Mascarilla y trébol,* in which there is a definite change of thematics and of form. In the intervening years Storni dedicated much of her writing to the theater. As Phillips has pointed out, "It is one of the anomalies of Storni's life that while much of her poetry draws for its themes upon the private regions of her spiritual existence, her outward life was for years connected with that least private of spheres, the theater." Since she had joined a theater company at age fifteen, she had been involved in the theater and worked three years as a traveling actress before entering teacher-training school. Since 1919 she had worked as a teacher of literature and drama, and in 1921 she earned a post as teacher of drama at the Teatro Infantil Municipal Labarden (Labarden Municipal Children's Theater). The plays she wrote for children during those years were published in

1950. Her first major drama (not a children's play), *El amo del mundo* (The Master of the World), was performed in 1927 in Buenos Aires and met with little success. Originally titled "Dos mujeres" (Two Women), the play tells the story primarily of a confrontation between two women and a man, Claudio, and his refusal to accept an unmarried mother as his wife. With obvious parallels to the life of Storni herself, the plot was developed without the canny humor and irony often present in her poetry. The main character, Márgara, must struggle against social prejudice, misunderstanding, and ultimately rejection. As Josefina Delgado recounts the experience in her biography of Storni, the entire production was taken largely out of her hands and distorted, leaving her frustrated and angry. She was deeply hurt by the mainly negative reaction of the critics, especially since the play had been so revealing of her own life. Her next major plays, *Dos farsas pirotécnicas* (Two Pyrotechnic Farces), published in 1932, were inspired by a trip she made to Spain in 1930, where she was exposed to the theater of Ramón del Valle-Inclán. They marked a new kind of experimental dramaturgy for Buenos Aires. The first farce, "Cimbelina en 1900 y pico" (Cymbeline in 1900 or So), is based on William Shakespeare's play *Cymbeline* (1609) and is composed of six short acts, a prologue, and an epilogue. As in Luigi Pirandello's *Sei personaggi in cerca d'autore* (1921; translated as *Six Characters in Search of an Author,* 1922), the characters comment on the nature of their own creation and on the intentions of the author. The second, "Polyxena y la cocinerita" (Polixena and the Little Cook), is based on Euripedes' play *Hecuba* (circa 424 B.C.) and reduces the tragedy to farce. Polyxena, Hecuba's daughter, in the original play is sacrificed on Achilles' tomb, unleashing a spiral of revenge by her mother. In Storni's version the daughter becomes a kitchen maid, and although the theme is human cruelty, the kitchen setting, contemporary details, quick shifts of humor, and self-reflexiveness convert it to farce.

The publication in 1934 of *Mundo de siete pozos* marks a significant change in Storni's poetry. On the formal level she largely leaves behind meter and rhyme and develops another style based on often idiosyncratic rhythms. Changed too are the topics she treats. The world viewed here is primarily the universe of the body, and the close-up visual focus, along with the altered rhythms, distance this poetry from the autobiographical vein of her earlier poetry. With the changes in perspective of time and distance, like those of cinema and photography, these poems decentralize the bodily focus, opening up unsettling vistas toward a mysterious understanding. A section of the book, "El mundo de siete puertas" (the world of seven doors), examines the head and parts of the body framed in landscape terms, as in the description of the ear:

pozos de sonidos,
caracoles de nácar donde resuena
la palabra expresada
y la no expresa;
tubos colocados a derecha e izquierda
para que el mar no calle nunca,
y el ala mecánica de los mundos
rumorosa sea

(wells full of sounds,
mother-of-pearl spiral shells where resounds
the uttered
and unuttered word;
tubes arranged to the right and to the left
to keep the sea from ever turning silent,
to keep the mechanical wing of the worlds
full of sound).

The microscopic focus of much of *Mundo de siete pozos* and *Mascarilla y trébol* gives rein to a more unsettling, less conventionally poetic framing of the body, landscape, and cityscapes. The series of cityscapes in *Mascarilla y trébol*–"Río de la Plata en Negro y Ocre" (River Plate in Black and Ocher), "Río de la Plata en gris aureo" (River Plate in Golden Gray), and "Río de la Plata en arena pálido" (River Plate in Pale Sand)–disclose the underside of a city whose cavernous mouth opens to receive and discharge its wares. The devouring mouth, while metonymically referring back to the moon, is detached from a personal expression:

La niebla había comido su horizonte
y sus altas columnas agrisadas
se echaban hacia el mar y parapetos
eran sobre la atlántica marea.

Se estaba anclado allí, ferruginoso,
viendo venir sus padres desde el norte;
dos pumas verdes que por monte y piedra
saltaban desde el trópico a roerlo

(The fog had devoured its horizon
and its tall, grayish pillars
cast themselves into the sea and were ramparts
over the Atlantic tide.

It remained anchored there, rusty,
seeing its forefathers come from the north;
two green panthers that jumped from the tropics
through the hills and rocks to gnaw at it).

Storni's break with traditional forms and the less subjective tone in her last two volumes respond in part to her incorporation of vanguardist techniques that had marked the poetry of the 1920s, in Argentina especially with the *ultraísta* movement led by Jorge Luis Borges.

MASCARILLA Y TREBOL

– CIRCULOS IMANTADOS –

ALFONSINA STORNI
1   9   3   8

Paperback cover for her final collection published during Storni's lifetime. In it and its predecessor, Mundo de siete pozos *(1934), she makes a decisive break with traditional poetic forms (from Josefina Delgado,* Alfonsina Storni: Una biografia esencial, *2001).*

Her innovations are not merely a late response to literary movements, however. By moving away from the topics of love and eroticism and by incorporating elements outside the personal sphere, particularly with the emphasis on landscapes and cityscapes, Storni forges a new independence in her writing. Her ironies, concise and cutting, are conveyed in shortened phrases, interrupting the flow of what start out to be rapturous love poems. In the introduction to *Mascarilla y trébol* Storni describes the development process of "estos anitsonetos de postura literaria" (these antisonnets of literary posture), stressing the spontaneous nature of their creation and the exaltation of "aquel micromundo" (that microworld) formed by the close-up focus, and attributes the change to fundamental psychic changes she has undergone in the previous few years. The innovations clearly show her awareness of contemporary poetic currents but also represent a personal and literary maturity.

In 1935, a year after the publication of *Mundo de siete pozos,* Storni was diagnosed with breast cancer and underwent surgery to have one breast removed. The next few years were marked by her struggle with cancer, part of which emerges in her poetry as a confrontation with the physicality of the world, a distancing from a personal focus. The illness and decline of the writer Horacio Quiroga, for whom Storni had felt great passion and friendship, was a serious blow. Despite his fame as a writer, when Quiroga committed suicide in 1937, he was in such reduced economic circumstances that there were not enough funds for his burial. As she became increasingly aware of her own decline because of her cancer, Storni struggled to finish her most important works. Late in 1937 she turned in the manuscript of her last book and in 1938 prepared an anthology of her poetry.

One of the most important public events of her life occurred in 1938. She and Mistral were invited to Montevideo to participate in a program with the Uruguayan poet Juana de Ibarbourou. The meeting gathered the three most prominent women poets of Latin America of the time, and from the speeches the three gave it is clear that they and their audience were aware of the significance of the event. Storni praised her fellow writers and stated her admiration for the heroism of earlier women writers, often erased in their own time. In late October of the same year, she made a trip to the seaside city of Mar del Plata. On 25 October 1938, the day of her suicide, she mailed to the major newspaper a farewell poem to her friends and readers, "Voy a dormir" (I Am Going to Sleep), to be published along with the news of her suicide. She then walked into the sea. This last dramatic and mournful gesture has undoubtedly contributed to the legend of Storni.

The major literary journal *Nosotros,* to which Storni had contributed from 1918 until her death, published shortly after her death a series of tributes to her and evaluations of her work. Even in this collection, one can see mixed appraisals of Storni and her work. Her personal image as defiant, unconventional, and often reckless in her opinions and actions, given the norms for women of the day, complicated the reception of her writings. During her life Storni had often received harsh criticism from writers, such as Borges, and literary critics. Their literary evaluations are often tinged, however, with their disapproval of her person. "Aesthetic impurity" and "resentment," the kind of terms typically employed to describe her writings, reveal not so much a literary evaluation as a personal judgment.

Alfonsina Storni was not just an immigrant to Argentina but was also a foreign immigrant to the Argentine world of letters. Her gender, social class, reduced education, single motherhood, and professional ambition did not fit the most prestigious literary circles. She did make her place in other literary spheres, however, and became the first woman to attend certain reunions of writers and artists and to be appointed as a judge for literary contests, eventually gaining considerable official recognition from her peers. Throughout her career she was widely read, with a readership expanded by the publication of her constant contributions, both of poems and social commentary, to the major newspapers and journals of her day and by her participation in public performances. Storni has become a legend, not just in Argentina but also in the Spanish-speaking world. Although she later rejected part of her early poetry, which is most explicit in its personal despair with love and defiance of social hypocrisy, these poems are most closely associated with that legend. She was truly a pathfinder for women in literature. Many of the topics she dealt with that were so heatedly rejected by her contemporary critics have found legitimacy through several generations of writers and readers.

Biography:

Josefina Delgado, *Alfonsina Storni: Una biografía esencial* (Buenos Aires: Planeta, 1990; corrected and enlarged, 2001).

References:

Tamara Kamenszain, "La soltera como madre postuma (AS)," in her *Historias de amor y otros ensayos sobre poesía* (Buenos Aires: Paidós, 2000), pp. 31–44;

Gwen Kirkpatrick, "Alfonsina Storni as 'Tao Lao': Journalism's Roving Eye and Poetry's Confessional Eye," in *Reinterpreting the Spanish American Essay: Women Writers of the Nineteenth and Twentieth Centuries,* edited by Doris Meyer (Austin: University of Texas Press, 1995), pp. 135–147;

Rachel Phillips, *Alfonsina Storni: From Poetess to Poet* (London: Tamesis, 1975);

Beatriz Sarlo, *Una modernidad periférica: Buenos Aires, 1920 y 1930* (Buenos Aires: Ediciones Nueva Visión, 1999);

Mark I. Soto-Smith, *El arte de Alfonsina Storni* (Bogotá: Tercer Mundo, 1986).

Jorge Teillier
(24 June 1935 – 29 April 1996)

Lisa Nalbone
University of Central Florida

BOOKS: *Para ángeles y gorriones* (Santiago: Puelche, 1956);

El cielo cae con hojas (Santiago: Alerce, 1958);

El árbol de la memoria (Poemas del país de Nunca Jamás) (Santiago: Arancibia, 1963);

Actualidad de Vicente Huidobro (Bogotá: Espiral, 1964);

Los trenes de la noche y otros poemas (Santiago: Universitaria, 1964);

Poemas secretos (Santiago: Universitaria, 1966);

Crónicas del forastero (Santiago: Arancibia, 1968);

Muertes y maravillas (Santiago: Universitaria, 1971);

Los trenes que no has de beber: Fragmentos de poemas (San Salvador: El Laberinto, 1977);

Para un pueblo fantasma (Valparaiso, Chile: Ediciones Universitarias de Valparaíso, 1978);

Cartas para reinas de otras primaveras (Chile: Manieristas, 1985);

El molino y la higuera (Santiago: Azafrán, 1993);

La isla del tesoro (Santiago: Dolmen, 1996);

Hotel Nube (Concepción, Chile: LAR, 1996);

En el mundo corazón del bosque (Santiago: Fondo de Cultura Económica, 1997);

Por un tiempo de arraigo, edited by Jaime Quezada (Santiago: LOM, 1998);

Prosas (Santiago: Sudamericana Chilena, 1999).

Editions and Collections: *Crónicas del forastero,* prologue by Jaime Valdivieso (Buenos Aires: Colihue, 1999);

El árbol de la memoria y otros poemas, edited by Pedro Lastra (Santiago: LOM, 2000).

Editions in English: *From the Country of Nevermore: Selected Poems,* translated, with an introduction, by Mary Crow (Middletown, Conn.: Wesleyan University Press, 1990);

In Order to Talk with the Dead: Selected Poems, translated, with an introduction, by Carolyne Wright (Austin: University of Texas Press, 1993).

OTHER: *Poesía universal traducida por poetas chilenos: Antología,* edited by Teillier (Santiago: Universitaria, 1996).

Jorge Teillier (photograph by Patricia García Villarroel)

Jorge Teillier ranks among the prominent twentieth-century poets of Chile. The majority of his work focuses on a wide gamut of scenes that portray life in the Chilean countryside within a highly personalized frame that captures its subtle nuances, yet at times appears temporally detached. The grandson of French settlers in Chile, Teillier always acknowledged his French background while at the same time nurturing his Chilean roots. The influence of his childhood in his hometown of Lautauro emanates

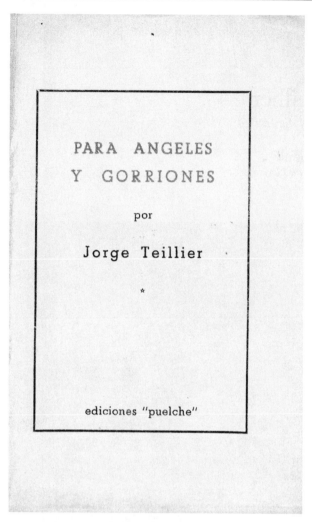

Paperback cover for Teillier's first book (1956), a collection of poems that evoke a contemplative attitude (University Library, University of California, Davis)

addition, he has edited literary magazines and translated poems from French into Spanish.

Teillier was born in Lautauro, in the province of Cautín in the south of Chile, on 24 June 1935, the eldest of six siblings. He entered school at the age of four, at which time he could already read and write, a skill he acquired in part because of his retreat into solitude upon the death of his sister. Teillier began writing verses at the age of twelve, when he was reading the fiction of foreign writers such as Jules Verne and Robert Louis Stevenson. The influence of these works is easily identifiable in his poetry. Other foreign literary influences are Paul Verlaine, Charles Baudelaire, and Stéphane Mallarmé, as well as the *Modernisto* and symbolist writers Rubén Darío, Antonio Machado, and Federico García Lorca. Additionally, Teillier admired the work of his fellow Chileans Pablo de Rokha, Rosamel del Valle, Teófilo Cid, Vicente Huidobro, and, in particular, Pablo Neruda. Teillier published his first book of poetry, which he considered perhaps his finest, *Para ángeles y gorriones* (For Angels and Sparrows) in 1956, when he was twenty-one years old.

After studying history at the University of Chile and teaching for one year, Teillier became editor of the *Bulletín,* the literary journal of the university. In Carlos Olivárez's *Conversaciones con Jorge Teillier* (Conversations with Jorge Teillier, 1993), the poet states that he was programmed to study history by his teachers, who instilled in him a love for the history of Chile. This love is reflected in the content of his poetry, which incorporates many historical references in terms of both geography and events. Additionally, his areas of interest in his formative years consisted of the history of Mexico, particularly the Mexican Revolution and the revolutionary leader Emiliano Zapata, and also the poetry of Mexico and Peru, which he deemed fundamental pillars of Latin American literature.

Teillier belongs to the group of poets classified as the Generation of the 1950s, which also includes Miguel Arteche, Efraín Barquero, David Rosenmann Taub, Alberto Rubio, Armando Uribe Arce, and Enrique Lihn. These writers broke from the poetry of the so-called Second Vanguard, with its propensity toward Surrealist imagery and social statement. The Generation of the 1950s built upon the initial criticism of the second vanguard begun by the Generation of '38.

Teillier's early works reflect a proximity to nature, specifically the natural environment of southern Chile. During these developmental years, according to Mary Crow in her introduction to the English-language collection of Teillier's poetry *From the Country of Nevermore: Selected Poems* (1990), although Teillier admired the poetry of Neruda, he preferred to focus his writings on the "psyche of politics or on the poor" instead of on

throughout his poetry; critics have pointed out that he is a writer who captures the mythical space of his homeland. The southern region of Chile, where Lautauro is located, is associated with the cultural influence of the indigeneous Mapuches as well as with the rough terrain of thick forests and heavy rainfall, a lugubrious combination that allows the poet to teeter between optimistic and pessimistic modes of thought in his poetry. Lautauro was founded in 1882 by the "Expedición Recabarren" (Recabarren Expedition), and Teillier's poetry reflects an acute awareness of the past and legacy of the area. Despite his emphasis on his homeland, however, the universal quality of his poetry has led to the translation of his works into French, Italian, Swedish, Czechoslovakian, Russian, Rumanian, Polish, and English. Although primarily a poet, Teillier has also edited an anthology of poetry from around the world and written many articles, short stories, and critical essays. In

Teillier and his son, Sebastian Teillier Arredondo, August 1989 (photograph by Patricia García Villarroel)

political poems, as the Nobel laureate did. Thus, the political focus on reform and social renovation of other poets shifts to a focus on what Teresa R. Stojkov calls "the underlying metaphysical journey that is a precondition of the poet's return home." An additional aspect of his work is that it at times alludes to his nostalgia for memorabilia from the United States of the 1920s and 1930s, an interest in line with this penchant for looking for inspiration in the commonality of elements of the past. A self-proclaimed pessimist, Teillier finds value in seeking to re-create the past, both nostalgic and melancholic, and reaching toward one's formative years of infancy, crafting meaning from memory. This approach renders the present unimportant and, even more so, the future. Carolyne Wright, in her introduction to *In Order to Talk with the Dead: Selected Poems* (1993), attests to the idiosyncrasies of the past in his poetry: "Teillier believes in the capacity of beloved objects to retain a certain power and presence by virtue of human contact,

and the value which people have invested in them: they become mediums of communion with this now lost, hermetic, almost magical order of life in the past."

When commenting on *Para ángeles y gorriones,* Jaime Valdivieso, in his 1999 edition of *Crónicas del forastero* (Chronicles of the Outsider, 1968), states that the poems evoke a contemplative attitude that points to the poet's evasive spirit, which dreams of the present becoming the past. Additionally, Jaime Quezada, in his introduction to the posthumously published Teillier collection *Por un tiempo de arraigo* (During a Time of Taking Root, 1998), comments on several predominant themes in Teillier's poetry, including reference to the *frontera* (border) territory of Chile, and places the concept of the town as a mythical center; the evocation of childhood memories and of paradise lost, which complements the nostalgia present in his poetry; the aspect of conjuring and re-creating myths; and an appreciation of time and history. These prominent themes are found

*Paperback cover for the 1998 posthumously published volume
of Teillier's previously uncollected poems from the 1960s
(Howard-Tilton Memorial Library,
Tulane University)*

Sarmiento further comments on Teillier's literary contributions, stating that "el ciclo que se cierra en esta obra es el ciclo mítico de la invasión y caída del paraíso" (the cycle that closes out this work is the mythical cycle of the invasion and fall from paradise). Parallel to this interpretation are Wright's comments regarding the appearance of a political thread in various poems that appear after 1968 and throughout the regime of Augusto Pinochet, which expresses opposition to certain aspects of the living conditions in Chile. According to Gómez, the dichotomy between national past and present is also found, for example, in *Por un tiempo de arraigo*. Although it was not published until 1998, the collection includes previously unpublished poems or poems in their original version that were written primarily in the 1960s.

Teillier's collections represent poems written in isolation, other than *Muertes y maravillas,* perhaps his most comprehensive or representative work. The collection is an anthology comprising an extensive prologue written by the poet and eight sections: "Poems," written between 1953 and 1970 and "dedicated to the Inhabitants of the Country of Nevermore"; "Book of Homage," including poems dedicated to Lewis Carroll, Stevenson, Cid, and Teillier's father; "Things Seen," thirty-eight enumerated stanzas that include references to such objects as snow, trees, dogs, a fly, a glass of beer, and train whistles; "The Trains of the Night," a poem comprising thirty-one stanzas divided into sixteen numbered sections; "Crónicas del forastero," a partial publication of the 1968 collection of the same title; "Thirty Years Later," a chronicle of historic events coupled with the poet's own observations and comments; "Farewell"; and a final section, "Approaches to the Poetry of Jorge Teillier," written by Alfonso Calderón. Both the prologue and the final section by Calderón have served extensively as biographic and bibliographic sources in the study of Teillier's work.

Another of Teillier's collections, *La isla del tesoro* (Treasure Island), was first published in 1982; however, the corrected second edition, which also includes additional poems, is considered the definitive edition of this title. Among the subjects of these poems are outlaws, drunks, pirates, and hallucinating travelers. These characters convey a sense of marginalization in society, a thematic trend found in much of Teillier's work.

Valdivieso has written about Teillier that "su mundo se perfila insólita y tenazmente definitivo" (his world is unusually and tenaciously outlined), a quality that is found in his work from his first publication, setting him apart from other Chilean poets with multiple themes and styles such as Neruda, Huidobro, and Gabriela Mistral. The core themes and styles in his initial publication resonate in subsequent texts. Valdivieso

within simple lyricism that reflects an ethnocultural awareness. While somewhat similar in his interpretation, Christián Gómez O. highlights the themes of the village as a mythical space, infancy as a golden age, and the backdrop of the *frontera* atmosphere. Some of Teillier's poems echo the style of Edgar Allan Poe, especially those in his collection *El árbol de la memoria (Poemas del páis de Nunca Jamás)* (The Tree of Memory: Poems from the Land of Nevermore, 1963).

Furthermore, Teillier emphasizes in his poetry the importance of the creation of myth, of a time and space that transcends the ordinariness of the everyday, through the use of ordinary vocabulary, according to his prologue to *Muertes y maravillas* (Deaths and Wonders, 1971). In this light, the language of his poems is characterized by straightforward expressions and traditional imagery. By his own account Teillier illustrates the details of daily living rather than abstract notions.

Óscar Sarmiento divides Teillier's poetry into two stages, the first symbolized by paradise and the second symbolized by apocalypse, so that in the second stage the previous themes of encounter and communion are replaced with loss and excommunication.

also affirms that Teillier demonstrates openness and tolerance for humanity and for literature. This quality has allowed him to read a broad spectrum of authors, and as a result his works, especially the later collections such as *Cartas para reinas de otras primaveras* (Letters to Queens of Other Springs, 1985) and *El molino y la higuera* (The Mill and the Fig Tree, 1993), include a wide range of poetic subjects.

Teillier's poetry is characterized by a series of polarities, which Eduardo Llanos Melussa enumerates: "marginación y participación profundas, retraimiento y cálida proximidad, introspección y diálogo, paisaje e interioridad, conciencia viva del aquí-ahora y eterno retorno al País de Nunca Jamás, resignación y alegría, aceptación del propio sino y evasión nostálgica hacia un pasado o un trasmundo mítico" (profound marginalization and participation, withdrawal and warm proximity, introspection and dialogue, landscape and the interior, an awareness of the here and now and eternal return to the Land of Nevermore, resignation and joy, acceptance of destiny itself and nostalgic evasion toward a mythical past or mythical world). In *En el mundo corazón del bosque* (In the World of the Forest's Heart, 1997), one of Teillier's last collections, published the year after the poet's death, he expresses the personalized, lingering proximity to nature in the last poem of the collection: "Si alguna vez / mi voz deja de escucharse / piensen que el bosque habla por mí / con su lenguaje de raíces" (If sometime / my voice is no longer heard / think that the forest speaks for me / with its language of roots). The interplay between the importance of legacy and the role of nature, as well as the simplicity of expression, that have both appeared throughout the poet's lifetime of work emanates in this message in Teillier's own voice.

Many of Teillier's poems take place in the southern countryside of Chile, during rainy days, capturing beliefs and superstitions, evoking the sound of trains, or talking about death, as Crow observes. The corpus of his poetic creation, she describes, stops short of sentimentality through use "of simple, matter-of-fact conclusions and exclusion of self-pity."

Teillier's lyricism, according to Calderón, marks the combination of a visible yet dream-like landscape, a return to a paradisiacal as well as shadowed past. Calderón also comments on Teillier's literary contributions, which include the creation of a new mythical poetics, an emotive nucleus of language, the discovery of a subjective metarealism, and the development of a rich literary tradition. It is important to note that Teillier reveals in the Olivárez interview that he does not like to be considered solely a *poeta lárico* (homeland poet), a phrase that frequently appears in discussions of his poetry, because he believes it does not accurately describe the scope of his work.

Teillier won various prizes throughout his career, including the Municipal Prize in poetry in 1961; the CRAV in 1968; first place in the Gabriela Mistral Literary Games; the Alerce Prize of the Society of Writers of Chile; the Eduardo Anguita Prize of the University Press; the National Council of Books and Reading award for the best book of poetry; and first prizes in the Floral Games of the magazine *Paula* and those of the 150th Commemoration of the National Flag. He was the director of the Santiago journal of poetry *Orfeo* and was also involved with regional publications such as *Tricle,* published by the Austral University of Chile in Valdivia, *Arúspice,* and *Teibada.*

Jorge Teillier died on 29 April 1996 in Santiago. His manner of capturing the lore of the Chilean countryside in a mythical and nostalgic fashion attests to his admiration for his homeland during times when the author himself perceives a distancing of the self that is minimized through the reality of his poetic subjects. Teillier's poetry reflects an awareness of identity through the approximation of *origen,* examined while considering the relevance of the past. In this manner Teillier receives recognition for highlighting the Chilean landscape in a distinct mythical backdrop while underscoring the height of sentiment he experiences upon depicting a robust past entwined with the uncertain present.

Interview:

Carlos Olivárez, *Conversaciones con Jorge Teillier* (Santiago: Los Andes, 1993).

References:

Alfonso Calderón, "Aproxmiaciones a la poesía de Jorge Teillier," *Anales de la Universidad de Chile,* 135 (1965): 153, 155;

Christián Gómez O., "El poeta, la palabra, el mundo," *Revista Chilena de Literatura,* 55 (November 1999): 135;

Eduardo Llanos Melussa, "Jorge Teillier, poeta fronterizo," *Casa de las Américas,* 33 (April–June 1993): 114;

Óscar Sarmiento, "La desconstrucción del autor: Enrique Lihn y Jorge Teillier," *Revista Chilena de Literatura,* 42 (August 1993): 242–243;

Teresa R. Stojkov, "Jorge Teillier: The Vocation of a Poet," *World Literature Today,* 70 (Spring 1996): 311–315.

Salomé Ureña de Henríquez

(21 October 1850 – 6 March 1897)

Enid Valle
Kalamazoo College

BOOKS: *Poesías de Salomé Ureña de Henríquez coleccionadas por la Sociedad literaria "Amigos del país"* (Santo Domingo: García, 1880);

Poesías, edited, with a prologue, by Pedro Henríquez Ureña (Madrid: "Europa," 1920);

Poesías completas, prologue by Joaquín Balaguer (Trujillo, Dominican Republic: Impresora Dominicana, 1950; revised edition, Santo Domingo: Bellas Artes y Cultos, 1975; revised again, Santo Domingo: ONAP, 1985);

Poesías completas, prologue and notes by Diógenes Céspedes (Santo Domingo: Ediciones de la Fundación Corripio, 1989).

Edition: *Poesías completas,* Edición especial de la XXIV Feria Nacional del Libro "Salomé Ureña de Henríquez" (Santo Domingo: Comisión Permanente de la Feria Nacional del Libro, 1997).

Salomé Ureña de Henríquez has been called the first great poet of the Dominican Republic. Her name appears next to those of José Joaquín Pérez and Gastón Deligne, the other two Dominican poets who, together with her, are the most prominent figures of their generation. Some literary critics also place her name next to those of other Spanish American poets such as Ecuadoran José Joaquín Olmedo and Cubans José María Heredia and Gertrudis Gómez de Avellaneda. Her poetic works, close to sixty compositions, include the epic and the lyric, in a variety of meters and themes. Among the poems for which she is best known are "La gloria del progreso" (The Glory of Progress, 1873), "Ruinas" (Ruins, 1876), "La fe en el porvenir" (Faith in the Future, 1878), "Anacaona" (1880), and "Sombras" (Shadows, 1881). Besides her literary work, Ureña de Henríquez is also known for her pioneer work as founder, in 1881, of the first higher-education institution for women, the Instituto de Señoritas (Institute for Young Women), in the Dominican Republic. The life and poetic works of Ureña de Henríquez are marked, on the one hand, by the family environment in which

Salomé Ureña de Henríquez

she lived and, on the other hand, by the political events of her country.

Salomé Ureña Díaz was born 21 October 1850 in Santo Domingo, capital of the Dominican Republic, to Nicolás Ureña de Mendoza and Gregoria Díaz y León. Political and cultural interests constituted the prevailing milieu in which she grew up. Her father was a lawyer, a teacher, a journalist who founded the newspaper *El Progreso* (Progress) in 1853, and a poet who, during his time, was considered to be a good one. Since childhood Salomé showed a liking for studying: she received a primary education, and, later on, her father guided her studies in subjects such as literature, arithmetic, and botany. She studied the classics from Spain as well as French and English literature.

During her childhood and adolescence, because of the conflicts between Haiti and the Dominican Republic that eventually gave rise to civil strife, political life was turbulent. In colonial times Spain had seized the eastern half of Hispaniola–the island shared by Haiti and the Dominican Republic–where it established Santo Domingo. In 1697 Spain handed over to France the western part of the island, and in 1795 the Spanish Crown gave up the whole island to the French. After failed attempts at separation from Haiti, under whose domination Santo Domingo had been for two decades, in 1844 Santo Domingo seceded, and the Dominican Republic was proclaimed. Since frontier conflicts continued, however, the Dominican government reincorporated the new republic to Spain in 1861. That event, in its turn, sowed discord among the inhabitants and brought about the Guerra de Restauración (War of Restoration), which culminated in the Spaniards abandoning the eastern half of the island in 1865. By that time Ureña began to write poetry.

Traditionally, literary critics divide Ureña de Henríquez's works by themes and by the rate of her poetic output. Her most productive period, during which the homeland and progress are the predominant themes, lasted from 1872 to 1880. From 1881 until her death in 1897, the poet wrote fewer poems, many of them about family and love. That division, according to Sherazada Vicioso in *Salomé Ureña de Henríquez (1850–1897): A cien años de un magisterio* (Salomé Ureña de Henríquez's Teachings [1850–1897]: A Century Later, 1997), had been suggested by the poet's husband, Francisco Henríquez y Carvajal, in a letter he wrote to his son, the writer and critic Pedro Henríquez Ureña. Joaquín Balaguer, in his 1950 prologue to Ureña de Henríquez's poetic works, places his attention on aspects of her work such as metrics, rhyme, lexicon, and literary influences. Diógenes Céspedes, in his prologue to the 1989 edition of Ureña's *Poesías completas,* explores the influence of positivism on her works. Other critics study her compositions in light of her political and pedagogical ideas and take into consideration the fact that the poet, as a writer and a woman, lived under societal restrictions.

Ureña de Henríquez's first published poems, at the age of seventeen, appeared in 1867 under the pseudonym of "Herminia." From the moment she started publishing, her poems were well received, even though at the beginning there was suspicion that they belonged to her father. In 1874 Ureña de Henríquez abandoned her pseudonym and, under her real name, continued to publish in Dominican newspapers and, later, in foreign ones. In the anthology *Lira de Quisqueya*

(Lyre of Quisqueya, 1874), edited by José Castellanos, considered to be the first anthology of Dominican poets, some of her already known compositions are collected for the first time.

Between the years of 1870 and 1880 Ureña de Henríquez wrote more than thirty poems: about the homeland; about the need and hope for progress; about friends and acquaintances dead or exiled because of political circumstances; about her sentimental life. The patriotic poems, which make evident her political inclinations as well as her preoccupation with the destiny of her country, brought her immediate fame. This circumstance is partially explained by the fact that, after the end of the Guerra de Restauración in 1865, in the span of three years the country had five presidents, and instability was part of everyday life. Buenaventura Báez's rise to power, culminating in his fourth term as president, opened the way to political rivalries and many exiles. His three previous administrations had already coincided with Ureña de Henríquez's childhood and adolescence.

The poetic works of Ureña de Henríquez show both her concern for the development of her country and its possibilities of achieving progress and her unfailing love for her homeland. In 1873 she wrote "La gloria del progreso" (The Glory of Progress). Written in seven- and eleven-syllable lines, the poem warns about the insufficiency of liberty and valor and calls for a fight for progress; for the poet, progress is the illuminating light that provides movement and life. The many labors performed by citizens, whether they are artisans, architects, or workers, contribute to knowledge; thus, the abandonment of violence and the subsequent dedication to the acquisition of knowledge can only lead to calmness and peace. The poem ends with a call to the youth on whom the progress and future of the country depend. Topics such as progress, the calling to responsibility of the younger generation, and the lamentation about violence appear in other poems of 1874, such as "A los dominicanos" (To the Dominicans) and "A la Patria" (To the Homeland). Some critics have seen in Ureña de Henríquez's use of the topic of progress a direct influence of the positivist philosophy espoused by Eugenio María de Hostos (1839–1903), a Puerto Rican educational reformer and prolific essayist, even though he did not arrive in the Dominican Republic until 1875. Hostos believed that reason and progress were major objectives that could be achieved through an education that sharpened critical thinking.

In keeping with her concern for progress, the poet meditates upon the past, present, and future of the homeland. In the poem "Ruinas" (Ruins, 1876), considered by Balaguer to be one of her true masterpieces, the contemplation of the ruins of Santo Domingo prompts the poet to ask about "la bella historia de otra edad luciente" (the beautiful history of a former luminous age) and thus to request that the country stand up and fight to recuperate its hopes. According to Ester Gimbernat González in her essay "Salomé Ureña, patriota y letrada" (Salomé Ureña, Patriot and Woman of Letters, 1999), the poem puts forth an enterprise to be carried into the future.

"La fe en el porvenir" (Faith in the Future, 1878) calls for allowing the younger generation to act—"¡Ah, no la detengáis! / . . . / Dejadla proseguir" (Ah, don't stop her! / . . . / Let her proceed)—asserting that impatience, ardor, ambition, boldness, and admiration are the inherent qualities of youth. Both the present and the future are in the hands of youth, as the last two lines of the poem declare: "tuya es la lucha del presente aciago, / tuya será del porvenir la gloria" (yours is the struggle of the ill-fated present / yours will be the future's glory). Another two poems, written that same year, "A Quisqueya" (To Quisqueya) and "A mi Patria" (To My Homeland), reiterate the concern and love for the poet's country and the conviction that in endeavors such as arts and sciences resides the possibility of peace and freedom.

In 1878, already well known and respected for her poetic works, Ureña de Henríquez received a public recognition. The Sociedad de Amigos del País (Society of Friends of the Country), a group that promoted interest in social issues and fostered cultural activities through weekly meetings, poetry readings, and lectures, awarded her a medal, financed through public subscription. Such a public act confirmed her as the national poet.

As important as her patriotic poems, are Ureña de Henríquez's sentimental or intimate ones, even though Balaguer considers them to be of inferior quality. Melancholy, love, and yearning are the themes at the center of those works and are best exemplified in the passionate verses of "Quejas" (Complaints) and "Amor y anhelo" (Love and Longing) from 1879. In "Quejas" the poet laments the absence of a loved one, while "Amor y anhelo" expresses love and desire for someone. Vicioso points out that the latter poem has sexual connotations, which perhaps accounts for the fact that this poem is left out of the poetry collection of 1920 edited by the poet's second son, Pedro Henríquez Ureña. More-recent literary criticism concurs that the personal side of Ureña de Henríquez can best be found in her sentimental poetry.

Ureña de Henríquez's longest work, "Anacaona," is an epic poem from 1880. The name "Anacaona" refers to an Indian queen who ruled Hispaniola in 1500 and who was hanged by the Spaniards for attempting a rebellion against Spain. Céspedes observes that the

poem amounts to a search, in those troubled and uncertain years, for a Dominican identity, while René Izquierdo, in his 1993 essay "El feminismo en la obra de Salomé Ureña" (Feminism in the Works of Salomé Ureña), sees in it a display of archetypal figures.

Major changes took place in the life of Ureña de Henríquez in 1880: marriage, establishment of the Escuela Normal (Normal School), a shift in politics, and publication of her poetry in one volume. She married Francisco Henríquez y Carvajal, who was also interested in politics and in the new pedagogical ideas brought by Hostos to the Dominican Republic. Hostos advocated the political independence of the Spanish-speaking Antilles and promoted the idea of progress as rooted in rational and lay education. In Santo Domingo that same year, he founded the Escuela Normal to train teachers, an event that motivated Henríquez y Carvajal to join him as a teacher and prompted Salomé to create the following year the Instituto de Señoritas. At the same time, the political situation became hopeful, as the administration of the new president, Archbishop Fernando Arturo de Meriño, was full of promise. Ureña de Henríquez's poem "Luz" (Light, 1880) seems to coincide with that new expectation since, among the patriotic poems, it is one of the most optimistic ones: in it the poet compares her past feelings of sadness to the present moment, which brings peace and hope. That same year the Sociedad de Amigos del País published Ureña de Henríquez's first book of poetry, *Poesías de Salomé Ureña de Henríquez coleccionadas por la Sociedad literaria "Amigos del país"* (Poems of Salomé Ureña de Henríquez Collected for the Literary Society of "Friends of the Country"), which comprises thirty-three poems, "Anacaona," and a prologue by Archbishop Meriño.

From 1881 on, Ureña de Henríquez's poetic output diminished. To explain why she did not write as much as before, critics assert reasons such as hopelessness about the political situation and her dedication to the Instituto and to raising a family. "Sombras" (Shadows, 1881), considered by Balaguer to be another one of her masterpieces and "una de las composiciones más limpiamente versificadas" (one of the most cleanly versified compositions), centers on fatigue and lack of strength because of the absence of a positive and progressive light: "el alma siente / morir la fe que al porvenir aguarda" (the soul feels the death / of the faith that awaits the future). Since uncertainty has taken hold, the poet asks the "melancólicos genios de mi suerte" (melancholic muses of my fate) to bring back her hope and enthusiasm. According to Silveria R. de Rodríguez Demorizi in *Salomé Ureña de Henríquez* (1944), the origin of "Sombras" can be found in the poet's despair as she realized the new government's failure to bring peace to the country. In 1881 Meriño's administration approved a decree, known as the San Fernando decree, against any citizen who was known to possess arms. Enforcement of the decree led to many civilian deaths.

Ureña de Henríquez wrote eight more poems between 1881 and 1887. During those years she devoted her efforts to the Instituto de Señoritas, which she directed for more than a decade. Although the project was partially funded by the government, funds were not always readily available to carry on the institute's mission of training teachers, a situation that placed a strain on the Henríquez Ureña family's resources as well as the director's energies. Additionally, by 1884 the poet had given birth to three sons, Fran, Pedro, and Max.

With the exception of "Sombras" and "Mi ofrenda a la patria" (My Offering to the Homeland, 1887), the poems she wrote during those years tend to be classified by critics as intimate, sentimental, or "domestic" ones. Céspedes details the difficulties a woman poet had to face in those times, in order to express her innermost feelings. "En el nacimiento de mi primogénito" (Upon the Birth of My Firstborn, 1882), extols parenthood and its responsibilities; "En horas de angustia" (Agonizing Hours, 1884) traces step-by-step a child's sickness, diagnosis, and recovery and records each one of the mother's emotions; "¿Qué es patria?" (What Is a Homeland?, 1887) attempts to answer, to a three-year-old, the titular question. Vicioso contends that within the nonpatriotic poems Ureña is able to escape, as a woman, from her own limitations and from social restrictions. Yet, Catharina Vallejo, in her essay "Trascendencia poética del binarismo de lo público y lo doméstico en la obra de Salomé Ureña de Henríquez" (1998), perceives a poetic voice in "En el nacimiento de mi primogénito" that chooses to put aside her own identity and instead places her attention, on such a special occasion, on either the husband or the son.

When the Instituto de Señoritas had its first commencement in 1887, instead of delivering a speech, Ureña de Henríquez read her poem "Mi ofrenda a la patria." In it the poet explains her relative lack of poetic output, asserts her belief in education as a tool to effect changes, and states the need to educate women. She presents a forceful, positive image of women as seed bearers of virtue and science. The work, generally included among the patriotic poems, has become the object of attention for its call to a more just and equal society and for its apparent feminist point of view.

In the subsequent four years the poet carried on by herself the family responsibilities and the directorship of the Instituto. Her husband, who had accepted a government scholarship to study medicine in France, was absent from her life from 1887 until 1891. "Tristezas" (Sorrows, 1888), "Angustias" (Agonies, 1888), and

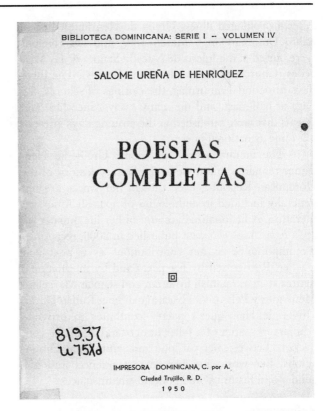

BIBLIOTECA DOMINICANA: SERIE I -- VOLUMEN IV

SALOME UREÑA DE HENRIQUEZ

POESIAS COMPLETAS

819.37
u75Xd

IMPRESORA DOMINICANA, C. por A.
Ciudad Trujillo, R. D.
1950

Paperback cover for the first of several editions of Ureña de Henríquez's poetic works (Howard-Tilton Memorial Library, Tulane University)

"Adelante" (Carry On, 1889), all dedicated to her husband, reveal the anxiety and distress the poet experienced during those years. The last stanza of "Angustias" aptly summarizes the poet's feelings regarding her husband's absence: "¡Acaba, llega! ¡Que el hogar sin calma / es de mis penas íntimas remedio; / que tiemblo por los hijos de mi alma; / que la vida sin ti me causa miedo!" (Get done, return! The home without peace / mirrors my intimate sorrows; / I tremble for my dear children; / life without you frightens me!).

Owing to financial reasons and Ureña de Henríquez's poor health, the Instituto was closed in 1893. The following year, after giving birth to her daughter, Camila, the poet's health suffered to the point where she found herself close to death, an experience she describes in the poem "Umbra" (Shadows), which she dedicated to her husband. Later that year, as her health improved, she composed "Resurrexit" (He/She/It Has Risen).

During the remaining years of her life, devoted to her children and to long periods of rest, Ureña de Henríquez finished her poem "Mi Pedro" (My Pedro, 1896), which she had begun in 1890. In 1896 former students of the Instituto reestablished the school, and soon after it was renamed Instituto Salomé Ureña.

After a prolonged illness Ureña de Henríquez died in Santo Domingo on 6 March 1897, and her remains were buried at the Iglesia de Nuestra Señora de las Mercedes (Church of Our Lady of the Graces). The three days of national mourning, the closings of schools, the flags at half-mast, and the many essays, speeches, and poems that were published in the ensuing days attest to her fame as national poet.

The literary works of Salomé Ureña de Henríquez remain a milestone to the literary history of the Dominican Republic, even though her works are not generally included in anthologies of Spanish American literature. A fictionalized account of her life, Julia Alvarez's *In the Name of Salomé,* published in 2000, recaptures the importance of her contributions as a poet and teacher. Recognized by her peers and by international figures such as Spanish historian and scholar Marcelino Menéndez y Pelayo and Nicaraguan poet Rubén Darío, Ureña de Henríquez's poetry continues to provoke scholars in search of a fuller understanding of the connections between her patriotic and sentimental compositions, her work and her correspondence, and her gender and historical and political circumstances.

References:

José Alcántara Almánzar, "Salomé Ureña," in his *Estudios de poesía dominicana* (Santo Domingo: Alfa y Omega, 1979), pp. 51–71;

Ester Gimbernat González, "Salomé Ureña, patriota y letrada," in *La voz de la mujer en la literatura hispanoamericana fin-de-siglo,* edited by Luis A. Jiménez (San José: Universidad de Costa Rica, 1999), pp. 101–113;

René Izquierdo, "El feminismo en la obra de Salomé Ureña," *Revista Interamericana de Bibliografía,* 43 (1993): 611–631;

Marcelino Menéndez y Pelayo, "La poesía en Santo Domingo," in *Homenaje a Menéndez y Pelayo,* Publicaciones Universidad de Santo Domingo, no. 109 (Trujillo, Dominican Republic: Pol, 1957), pp. 13–58;

María del Carmen Prosdocimi de Rivera, "Reeditan 'Poesías Completas' de Salomé Ureña de Henríquez," in her *Presencias* (Santo Domingo: Colección Banreservas, 1999), pp. 409–412;

Silveria R. de Rodríguez Demorizi, *Salomé Ureña de Henríquez* (Buenos Aires: López, 1944);

Emilio Rodríguez Demorizi, *Salomé Ureña y el Instituto de Señoritas: Para la historia de la espiritualidad dominicana* (Trujillo, Dominican Republic: Impresora Dominicana, 1960);

Catharina Vallejo, "Trascendencia poética del binarismo de lo público y lo doméstico en la obra de Salomé Ureña de Henríquez," in *Poéticas de escritoras hispanoamericanas al alba del próximo milenio,* edited by Lady Rojas-Trampe and Vallejo (Miami: Ediciones Universal, 1998), pp. 35–48;

Sherazada Vicioso, *Salomé Ureña de Henríquez (1850–1897): A cien años de un magisterio* (Santo Domingo: Editora de Colores, 1997).

Cintio Vitier

(25 September 1921 –)

Violeta Padrón
Wake Forest University

BOOKS: *Poemas (1937–1938)* (Havana, 1938);
Luz ya sueño (Havana, 1938);
Sedienta cita (Havana: Ucar, García, 1943);
Extrañeza de estar (Havana: Ucar, García, 1944);
De mi provincia (Havana: Orígenes, 1945);
Capricho y homenaje (Havana: Ucar, García, 1947);
El hogar y el olvido (Havana: Orígenes, 1949);
Sustancia (Havana, 1950);
Conjeturas (Havana: Ucar, García, 1951);
Vísperas, 1938–1953 (Havana: Orígenes, 1953);
Canto llano (Havana: Orígenes, 1956);
La luz del imposible (Havana, 1957);
Lo cubano en la poesía (Santa Clara, Cuba: Universidad Central de Las Villag, Departamento de Relaciones Culturales, 1958);
Estudios críticos, by Vitier and Fina García Marruz (Havana: Biblioteca Nacional José Martí, 1964);
Testimonios, 1953–1968 (Havana: UNEAC, 1968);
Temas martianos, by Vitier and García Marruz (Havana: Biblioteca Nacional José Martí, 1969);
Poetas cubanos del siglo XIX: Semblanzas (Havana: UNEAC, 1969);
Crítica sucesiva (Havana: UNEAC, 1971);
Poética (Madrid: Joaquín Giménez Arnau, 1973);
Ese sol del mundo moral: Para una historia de la eticidad cubana (Mexico City: Siglo XXI, 1975);
De Peña Pobre: Memoria y novela (Mexico City: Siglo XXI, 1978);
La fecha al pie (Havana: UNEAC, 1981);
Temas martianos: Segunda serie (Havana: Letras Cubanas, 1982);
Los papeles de Jacinto Finalé (Havana: Letras Cubanas, 1984);
Rajando la leña está (Havana: Letras Cubanas, 1986);
Rescate de Zenea (Havana: UNEAC, 1987);
Hojas perdidizas (Mexico City: Equilibrista, 1988);
Crítica cubana (Havana: Letras Cubanas, 1988);
Palabras a la aridez (Buenos Aires: Ultimo Reino, 1989);
Poemas de mayo y junio: 1988 (Valencia, Spain: Pre-Textos, 1990);
Cuentos soñados (Havana: UNEAC, 1992);

Cintio Vitier (from the paperback cover for Nupcias, *1993; Howard-Tilton Memorial Library, Tulane University)*

Versos de la nueva casa, 1991–1992 (Caracas, Venezuela: Pomaire, 1993);
Nupcias (Havana: Letras Cubanas, 1993);
Antología poética, selected, with a prologue, by Enrique Saínz (Havana: Letras Cubanas, 1993);

Paperback cover for Vitier's anthology of poems by
members of the Orígenes group (Howard-Tilton
Memorial Library, Tulane University)

Prosas Leves (Havana: Letras Cubanas, 1993);

Dama pobreza (Bogotá: Gradiva, 1994);

Para llegar a Orígenes: Revista de arte y literatura (Havana: Letras Cubanas, 1994);

Lecciones cubanas (Havana: Pueblo y Educación, 1996);

Poesía (Havana: Ediciones Unión, UNEAC, 1997);

Resistencia y libertad (Havana: Ediciones Unión, UNEAC, 1999);

Poesía escogida, by Vitier and García Marruz (Bogotá: Norma, 2000).

Collection: *Antología poética* (Havana: Letras Cubanas, 1981).

OTHER: *Diez poetas cubanos: 1937–1947,* edited by Vitier (Havana: Orígenes, 1948);

Cincuenta años de poesía cubana (1900–1952): Ordinación, antología y notas, edited by Vitier (Havana: Dirección de Cultura, Ministerio de Educación, 1952);

Las mejores poesías cubanas: Antología, edited by Vitier (Lima: Organización Continental de los Festivales del Libro, 1959);

Los grandes románticos cubanos: Antología, edited by Vitier (Havana: Organización Continental de los Festivales del Libro, 1960);

Los poetas románticos cubanos: Antología, edited by Vitier (Havana: Consejo Nacional de Cultura, 1962);

La critica literaria y estetica en el siglo XIX cubano, selected, with a prologue, by Vitier (Havana: Biblioteca Nacional José Martí, Departamento Colección Cubana, 1968);

Flor oculta de poesía cubana (Siglos XVIII y XIX), selected by Vitier and Fina García Marruz (Havana: Arte y Literatura, 1978);

Juan Ramón Jiménez en Cuba, compiled, with prologue and notes, by Vitier (Havana: Arte y Literatura, 1981);

La literatura en el Papel Periódico de La Habana, 1790–1805, edited by Vitier and García Marruz (Havana: Letras Cubanas, 1990);

Poesía y poética del grupo Orígenes, edited by Vitier (Caracas: Ayacucho, 1994).

In the prologue to his *Ese sol del mundo moral: Para una historia de la eticidad cubana* (That Sun from the Moral World: Toward a History of Cuban Ethics, 1975) Cintio Vitier defines himself as an "aspirante vitalicio a poeta y a cristiano" (a lifelong candidate to becoming a poet and a Christian). A Catholic intellectual, he has devoted his life to poetry, as exemplified by his many titles, prizes, and other literary distinctions, such as the 1989 Cuban National Poetry Prize. In his long career as poet and literary critic Vitier has published many volumes of poetry, essays, and novels and has written and edited some pivotal works on Cuban literature, including his 1948 anthology of the Orígenes poets, *Diez poetas cubanos: 1937–1947* (Ten Cuban Poets: 1937–1947), and *Lo cubano en la poesía* (Cubanness in Poetry, 1958), a study key to understanding both Cuban poetry and the Cuban character; many of these works have been translated into several languages.

The son of the essayist, educator, and literary critic Medardo Vitier and María Cristina Bolaños, Cintio Vitier was born in Key West, Florida, on 25 September 1921. The family soon moved back to the Cuban province of Matanzas, where Vitier grew up and attended a private school founded by his father. From an early age he showed an interest in literature and read incessantly. The author himself acknowledges the important role played in his education by his father's library, which among its many cherished volumes held collections of Cuban and Spanish American masters, classical Spanish works, and some books in English.

When Vitier was fifteen, his father was named secretary of education in the administration of President Carlos Mendieta, and the family moved to

Havana. Though his father soon resigned from this position, they remained in the capital, where Vitier first attended the private school La Luz (The Light) and then a public secondary institution. While at school Vitier began to devote himself to poetry. His youthful efforts were collected in the 1938 book *Poemas (1937–1938)* (Poems [1937–1938]). Some of these texts were also included in *Luz ya sueño* (Light Already a Dream, 1938), Vitier's second, and one of his better-known, books of poems. During the 1930s Vitier met fellow poet Eliseo Diego, who became his lifelong friend. In 1936 both friends founded the journal *Luz* (Light), in which Vitier published some of the poems he later collected in *Luz ya sueño*. Vitier also met the Spanish poet Juan Ramón Jiménez, who lived in Cuba from 1936 until 1939 after exiling himself from Spain at the outbreak of the civil war. Vitier's encounter with Jiménez proved crucial in his career. The Spaniard influenced his early verses, a debt that Vitier has always acknowledged. Jiménez not only wrote the prologue to *Luz ya sueño* but he also assisted with the revision and selection of poems for that book. Despite Jiménez's involvement, however, *Luz ya sueño* is prominently marked by Vitier's characteristic style. This book emphasizes his metaphysical inquiries into the unknown in a peculiar style that Enrique Saínz defines as "a metaphysics of the concrete," a theme Vitier continues to develop in subsequent books. Other themes presented in this book are knowledge and the "alienation of being," as García Marruz characterized it.

After completing his secondary education, Vitier attended the law school at the University of Havana and received his doctorate in law in 1947, although he has never practiced this profession. Instead, he has taught at the Escuela Normal (Teacher's College) in Havana and at the Central University of Las Villas, a school his father helped to found. During these years Vitier married the poet Fina García Marruz and became the father of two children, one of whom, Jose María, is an accomplished musician.

The 1940s were crucial years in Vitier's professional career. He continued to write and publish poetry consistently, but he also joined the Orígenes (Origins) group, writers who published the journal of that title from 1944 to 1956. *Orígenes* was founded by José Lezama Lima and became a forum for a new style of poetry that became a cultural movement. The name *Orígenes* alludes to the poets' concept of the importance of constant rebirth in poetry and culture. Other poets of the Orígenes group are Gastón Baquero, García Marruz, Eliseo Diego, Octavio Smith, and Lorenzo García Vega. Vitier has written extensively on the movement and its members, who are also known as the Third Republican Generation. They are characterized

CINTIO VITIER

CANTO LLANO

ORÍGENES

LA HABANA

1956

Paperback cover for Vitier's collection of fifty short poems inspired by the Bible and the writings of Thomas Aquinas (Doe Library, University of California, Berkeley)

by a profound interest in lyrical expression rather than in social concerns. Their aloofness from their social context is related to their search for Cuban identity, together with metaphysical and universal pursuits.

Vitier's multifaceted poetry deals with a variety of topics ranging from time in its existential dimension to the nature of poetry, daily events in their poetic manifestations, and Cuban identity. His first books reflect on memory and the role of language in the creative process. This stage of his poetry is regarded as highly lyri-

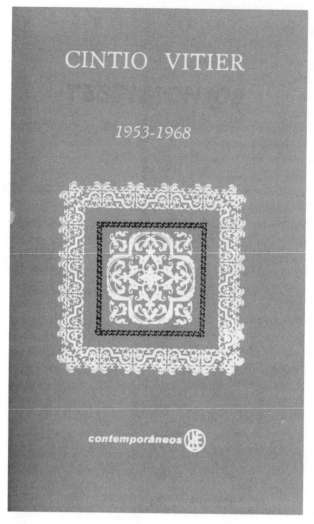

Paperback cover for Vitier's 1968 collection, Testimonios, 1953–1968, *which shows a new engagement with social concerns (Homer Babbidge Library, University of Connecticut)*

cal and hermetic; Vitier himself has referred to it as his "conciencia de la poesía" (conscience of poetry). Philip Ward, writing in *The Oxford Companion to Spanish Literature,* describes this type of poetry as erudite and deems that this stage includes all the poet's production prior to *Canto llano* (Plain Song, 1956), which Ward considers one of his best books. Among other early books are *Sedienta cita* (Thirsty Date, 1943), influenced by the Peruvian poet César Vallejo, which shows greater complexity than *Luz ya sueño; Extrañeza de estar* (Strangeness of Being, 1944), another rather complex work in which the poet reflects on the "strangeness of existence"; *De mi provincia* (From My Province, 1945), written in blank verse, which depicts memories from his childhood in the province of Matanzas; and *Capricho y homenaje* (Whim and Homage, 1947), an experiment in a form that further ponders the topic of existence.

In 1948 Vitier published *Diez poetas cubanos: 1937–1947.* During the following years, prior to the publication of *Canto llano* in 1956, he also published *Vísperas, 1938–1953* (Vespers, 1938–1953, 1953), a selection of his poetry that, according to Saínz, established "una distancia íntima entre el poeta y el mundo, entre la percepción y el intelecto" (an intimate distance between the poet and the world, between perception and intellect). Another important book of this early period is *El hogar y el olvido* (Home and Forgetfulness, 1949), in which, according to Enildo García in the *Dictionary of Twentieth-Century Cuban Literature* (1990), "the poet sets out to discover the light of the kingdom of the spirit and through a journey of faith, attempts to reach the 'hogar imposible del alma' (the impossible home of the soul)." *Sustancia* (Substance, 1950) and *Conjeturas* (Conjectures, 1951) also share the central topic that concerned Vitier

POESIA

NUPCIAS

Cintio Vitier

LETRAS CUBANAS

*Paperback cover for the fourth compilation (1993) of Vitier's poems (Howard-Tilton
Memorial Library, Tulane University)*

during his early years, the existential problem of the absolute; for García, *Conjeturas* deals with "the impossibility of grasping the absolute as such."

The last book of this first period dealing with the "conciencia de la poesía" is *Canto llano,* a book essential for understanding Vitier's poetic production. It consists of fifty short poems influenced by the Psalms, the New Testament, and the writings of Thomas Aquinas. For Max Henríquez Ureña, *Canto llano* shows deep reflection and a special concern for metric form since the poet, who had stopped using fixed meters in previous books, returns to this type of verse.

In 1958 Vitier published *Lo cubano en la poesía,* his best-known and most influential book of literary criticism. It developed from a series of conferences that he gave at the Lyceum of Havana between October and December 1957. In his essay "Reconstructing Cubanness: Changing Discourses of National Identity on the Island and in the Diaspora during the Twentieth Century" (2000), Jorge Duany describes the book as "an insightful though idiosyncratic interpretation of the evolution of a sense of Cubanness through the major poetic texts written on the island and sometimes in the diaspora from Spanish colonial times to 1950s." In the essays in *Lo cubano en la poesía* Vitier studies Cuban poets such as José María de Heredia, José Martí, Julián del Casal, Nicolás Guillén, and Lezama Lima. He concludes that *lo cubano* (Cubanness) is a rather elusive term since it is not "a mobile and preestablished essence." Vitier, in an attempt to better understand Cubanness and how it is expressed through poetry, identifies some common themes in Cuban literature that help define the essence of its people's lyrical manifestations. The notion of *lejanía* (the evocation of the island from afar, usually from exile), present in this work, has become a key term in analyzing Cuban poetry.

After the Cuban Revolution in 1959, Vitier's poetry changed and became more involved with political events, as both the poet and his wife chose to live and write within the confines of Fidel Castro's Cuba. His poems show a departure from previous lyrical concerns to embrace the political and social moment in which the Cuban revolutionaries took power. Some critics, such as Ward, regard the poetry written soon after 1959 as of lesser quality than his previous poetic production. The 1968 collection *Testimonios, 1953–1968* (Testimonies, 1953–1968), however, displays fine examples of committed poetry. In this compilation, as Saínz points out, the poet includes some of the topics present in his previous works but in a different type of discourse, more mature and in consonance with his new social concerns. *Testimonios, 1953–1968,* as John Garganigo comments, displays an intense interest in social problems as the poet tries to respond to the new historical moment he experiences.

Since 1962 Vitier has also worked at the José Martí National Library and has devoted a great deal of his research to the Cuban poet and leader of Cuban independence Martí. One of the products of this research has been the critical edition of Martí's works that he directed at the Center for Martí Studies, where he is an honorary president. He continued to write during these years, and in 1978 he published *De Peña Pobre: Memoria y novela* (From Peña Pobre: Memoirs and Novel), the story of three generations of a Cuban family. In this autobiographical novel the author also outlines the beginnings and development of the Orígenes group. Vitier has published two more novels, *Los papeles de Jacinto Finalé* (Jacinto Finalé's Papers, 1984) and *Rajando la leña está* (Chopping Wood, 1986), that, along with *De Peña Pobre,* form a trilogy. *Los papeles de Jacinto Finalé* tells the story of a deceased character that has a deep influence in the people who survive him, while *Rajando la leña está* pays homage to Cuban music. Both deal with the period in Cuban history that extends from 1959 to the date of publication in the 1980s. *La fecha al pie* (Date at the Bottom of the Page), published in 1981, represents a new way of understanding the relationship between poetry and reality.

Vitier's books published in the late 1980s and early 1990s are *Hojas perdidizas* (Stray Leaves, 1988), *Poemas de mayo y junio: 1988* (Poems of May and June: 1988, 1990), *Versos de la nueva casa, 1991–1992* (Verses of the New House, 1991–1992, 1993), and *Dama pobreza* (Lady Poverty, 1994). These works evoke lifetime memories in a somewhat autobiographical account. Also in 1993 Vitier published *Nupcias* (Nuptials), the fourth compilation of his poems. Saínz characterizes *Nupcias* as a testimonial text that also shows significant lyrical warmth. He considers the poems in this book representative of a direct kind of poetry in which metaphors are visible and rooted in reality.

Although Vitier has resided in Havana since the Cuban Revolution, he traveled and lectured abroad in Latin America and Europe in the 1980s and 1990s. Most recently he and his wife served in the resident poet program of the Residencia de Estudiantes in Madrid, a project that brings Latin American authors to the institution. In 1999 Vitier's more than fifty years of dedication to Cuban letters were publicly recognized with the award of an honorary doctorate from the Universidad Central de las Villas.

As the author of an impressive collection of works, it can be said that Cintio Vitier's poetry, from the more obscure and lyrical poems of his first books to his politically committed texts after 1959, is one of Cuba's finest lyrical expressions. His critical works and essays as well as his interest in José Martí have also contributed to making him one of his country's most influential and respected contemporary scholars.

References:

Jorge Duany, "Reconstructing Cubanness: Changing Discourses of National Identity on the Island and in the Diaspora during the Twentieth Century," in *Cuba, the Elusive Nation: Interpretations of National Identity,* edited by Damián J. Fernández and Madeline Cámara Betancourt (Gainesville: University Press of Florida, 2000), pp. 24–25;

John Garganigo, "Cintio Vitier de la conciencia de la poesía a la poesía de la conciencia," *Revista de Estudios Hispánicos,* 14, no. 1 (1980): 93–100;

Max Henríquez Ureña, *Panorama histórico de la literatura cubana* (New York: Las Americas, 1963), p. 440.

Adela Zamudio
(Soledad)
(11 October 1854 – 2 June 1928)

María Tenorio and Fernando Unzueta
Ohio State University

BOOKS: *El misionero: Poema relijioso* (Cochabamba, Bolivia: Imprenta de El Heraldo, 1879);

Ensayos poéticos de Adela Zamudio (boliviana) (Buenos Aires: Peuser, 1887);

Violeta o la princesa azul (Cochabamba, Bolivia, 1890);

El castillo negro (Cochabamba, Bolivia, 1906);

Ráfagas (Paris: Ollendorff, 1913);

Íntimas (La Paz: Velarde, 1913; revised edition, edited, with an introduction and chronology, by Leonardo García Pabón, La Paz: Plural, 1999);

Novelas cortas (La Paz: Editorial La Paz, 1943);

Cuentos breves (La Paz: Editorial La Paz, 1943);

Peregrinando: Poesías (La Paz: Editorial La Paz, 1943); revised and enlarged as *Poesías,* edited, with an introduction, by Eduardo Ocampo Moscoso (Cochabamba, Bolivia: Imprebol, 1993).

Adela Zamudio is Bolivia's most widely acclaimed female intellectual and a founding figure of its feminist movement. She dedicated herself to writing and teaching and vigorously defended the causes of the Bolivian Liberal Party in public forums. In addition to essays, she wrote a novel, short stories, light dramatic works, and poetry. She is arguably the country's best-known poet, both the pinnacle of its belated Romanticism and, in a personal way, a bearer of some of the changes that transformed the literary field around 1900.

Adela Zamudio was born 11 October 1854 in Cochabamba, where she later settled after living in the small towns of Corocoro, Corani, and Viloma. Her father, Adolfo Zamudio, was an Argentinean émigré and engineer, and her mother, Modesta Ribero, a member of a wealthy mining family from La Paz. The country was undergoing a series of political upheavals, often marked by violent changes in government. Adela grew up in a privileged social environment and enjoyed the fruits of a largely European culture, in contrast with that of an illiterate and Quechua-speaking majority. She

Adela Zamudio (from Ráfagas, *1913; Dartmouth College Library)*

attended a religious elementary school but was largely self-taught after that.

Most of Zamudio's works appeared first in newspapers. Accordingly, Augusto Guzmán, in his *Adela Zamudio: Biografía de una mujer ilustre* (Adela Zamudio: Biography of an Illustrious Woman, 1955), has noted the difficulties in reconstructing an exact chronology for their publication, particularly before 1877, when the newly founded periodical in Cochabamba, *El Heraldo* (The Herald), started printing many of her texts. That same year, some of her other poems were published in *La Revista de Cochabamba* (The Cochabamba Journal)

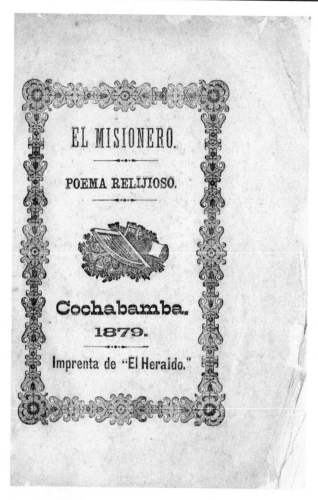

*Paperback cover for Zamudio's first book, a long poem about a Franciscan missionary
who is killed by a primitive tribe (Cornell University Library)*

and *El Album Literario* (The Literary Album) of Sucre. In this sense Zamudio continued the recently established tradition of Bolivian women authors, such as María Josefa Mujía and Mercedes Belzu de Dorado, to publish in public papers. Zamudio signed her early compositions as "Soledad" (Solitude). This "sugestivo pseudónimo" (suggestive pen name), as José Macedonio Urquidi indicates, echoes the title and the protagonist's name of Bartolomé Mitre's sentimental novel, published in *La Epoca* (The Epoch) of La Paz in 1847. Mitre, an Argentinean émigré like Zamudio's father, was a friend of her mother. Besides this biographical connection, solitude is a central theme in her writings. In 1879 Zamudio's fifteen-year-old cousin, Daría Ribero, died, and she wrote a poem for her. Leonardo García Pabón observes in the chronology of his 1999 edition of *Íntimas* (Intimacies; originally published in 1913) that Zamudio outlived all of her family members. Thus, frequent confrontations with death marked her life. García Pabón also records that around 1873 Zamudio held and even-

tually broke an engagement with Jesús Blanco, her cousin. This is the only romantic relationship attributed to her.

The press owned by *El Heraldo* published Zamudio's long religious poem, *El misionero* (The Missionary), in 1879. The poem celebrates an untamed and lush natural environment, but, most of all, it is an elegy about a Franciscan's apostolic deeds among savages who are preparing to sacrifice him. The last section of the poem, "La tumba en el bosque" (The Tomb in the Woods), details the existence of a cross on the tomb where the missionary rests and praises him as a "Bendito mártir de la fé cristiana" (Blessed martyr of the Christian faith). While "otras tribus bárbaras, crueles" (other barbarous, cruel tribes) may have killed him, those he converted and who loved him buried him in a Christian manner, making his martyrdom worthwhile.

In 1887 Adolfo Zamudio traveled to Buenos Aires carrying his daughter's manuscript and had it published as *Ensayos poéticos de Adela Zamudio (boliviana)*

(Poetic Essays by Adela Zamudio [Bolivian], 1887). For the first time Zamudio signed her poems with her name rather than with the pseudonym Soledad, a practice that continued from then on. In a generous prologue, the Spanish writer Juan José García Velloso highlights the range and depth of the compositions, as well as their "idealismo romántico" (Romantic idealism). Most of Zamudio's early poems were collected in her first poetry book, although some, such as "A mi madre" (To My Mother), which was written in 1876 according to Guzmán, only appeared after her death, in *Peregrinando: Poesías* (Pilgrimages: Poems, 1943). She also dedicated two poems to her younger sister, Amalia.

This collection of twenty poems includes three of the five songs of *El misionero*. The opening line of the first song reads, "¡Cuán hermoso es el suelo de Bolivia!" (How beautiful is the soil of Bolivia!), and the detailed descriptions of the country's lowlands make it easy to locate geographically; but "Otoño" (Autumn) and "Primavera" (Spring) feature only some conventional mentions of the cyclical changes in nature. The rest of the poems eschew the descriptiveness common to Romantic poetry. Some poems reproduce conventional religious themes. Increasingly, however, godly love is called on to fill in for human loss, including the loss of life and of human love. The tensions between a person's solitude and religious consolation increase in "M.L. (Suicida)" (M.L. [Suicide]), later anthologized as "A un suicida" (To a Suicide). In this poem, as Angela Renee Felix argues, Zamudio questions the religious dogmatism of society and its easy condemnation of a person who commits suicide. Whereas the poem ultimately accepts divine will, it also respects the pain of suicidal impulses, prays for the person who suffered them, and depicts him as a "renegado," (renegade), dangerously resembling a poet. Besides thematizing loss and death, several other poems of *Ensayos poéticos* also deploy a pessimistic tone. Confronted with cyclical and unavoidable change, in "Primavera," "Otoño" (subtitled "Melancolía," Melancholy), and "Ayer y hoy" (Yesterday and Today) Zamudio responds with contemplative sadness to the loss of youth and the passing of time. Only "La violeta" (The Violet) opens up a possibility for hopeful renovation.

Another series of poems, including "Baile de máscaras" (Mask Dance) and "Progreso" (Progress), includes critiques of the social mores of the period. In particular, they question how the languages, discourses, and behaviors of society help distort reality and human emotions and contribute to the subordination of women. As García Pabón contends in "Máscaras, cartas y escritura femenina: Sobre la obra de Adela Zamudio (1854–1928)" (Masks, Letters, and Feminine Writing: On the Works of Adela Zamudio [1854–1928], 1993),

Zamudio poses the role of the poet as that of a social critic that may be able to undermine social masks and distortions. "A la poetisa María Josefa Mujía (Ciega)" (To the [Blind] Poet María Josefa Mujía) and "Peregrinando" (Pilgrimages) reflect on the role of poets in an increasingly alienating world. While the first composition captures and voices the sufferings of humanity, "Peregrinando" denounces the world as an inhospitable place for poetry and its ideals. Oscar Rivera-Rodas, in his *La poesía hispanoamericana del siglo XIX (Del romanticismo al modernismo)* (Hispanic American Poetry of the Nineteenth Century [From Romanticism to Modernism], 1988), detects a total lack of compatibility between the poet and society in Zamudio's conception of poetry, an attitude he finds characteristic of the transition between Romanticism and *Modernismo*.

A year after the publication of her *Ensayos poéticos,* in 1888, La Paz's Literary Circle named Zamudio a "socia de honor" (honorary member) along with the Argentine Manuela Gorriti de Belzu. As Eduardo Ocampo Moscoso points out, she had acquired her own poetic personality, and the most important literary figures of the country appreciated her work. The following years she took up painting, and in 1896 she published *El alegre carnaval* (The Happy Carnival), a humorist newspaper. After the ascent of the Liberal Party to power, Zamudio accepted a teaching position at the San Alberto School at the age of forty-five. This position was the official beginning of her long dedication to pedagogy. Her playful dramatic works, *Violeta o la princesa azul* (Violet or the Blue Princess, 1890), a "juguete dramático" (dramatic toy), and *El castillo negro* (The Black Castle, 1906), both written in verse, are examples of her preoccupation with children's education. From 1901 to 1905 Zamudio taught drawing and painting to young women at an academy she founded, and in 1905 she became principal of the newly established Escuela Fiscal de Señoritas (Public School for Young Women).

With the new century Zamudio turned increasingly toward prose writing. In 1901 she published her first short stories, and she continued to do so for the following decades. Her collected narratives appeared posthumously in two volumes, *Cuentos breves* (Brief Stories, 1943) and *Novelas cortas* (Short Novels, 1943), an unnecessary and arbitrary separation, according to Guzmán. Many of her approximately two dozen stories are based in actual local events or anecdotes. Their language is sober and descriptions realistic, and they highlight the virtues, foibles, and contradictions of the characters.

Zamudio continued to write and publish: her 1903 poem "¿Quo vadis?" (Who's There?), first published in the newspaper *El Comercio,* raised some controversy. The poem criticizes the riches of the Catholic

ADELA ZAMUDIO

RÁFAGAS

(POESIAS)

PARÍS
Sociedad de Ediciones Literarias y Artísticas
LIBRERÍA PAUL OLLENDORFF
50, CHAUSSÉE D'ANTIN, 50

*Title page for Zamudio's 1913 collection, in which she evinces
a post-Romantic and anti-*Modernista *approach
(Dartmouth College Library)*

Church and the historical excesses of the Inquisition and was perceived as an antireligious text by conservative Catholics. Nevertheless, like much of the author's poetry, it is really a denunciation of the horrors of the modern world, such as violence and the threat of war, political injustice, and social inequality, horrors that become more significant when seen in light of Christ's teachings and Passion.

Conservative Catholics felt threatened by many Liberal reforms, including nonreligious public education, with which Zamudio associated. In 1913, an upper-class association of Catholic women petitioned the Bolivian congress to reinstate religious education in order to avoid raising "una generación de criminales" (a generation of criminals). They withdrew about fifty of their daughters from Zamudio's school in order to transfer them to a newly established school for young women directed by the Italian priest Francisco Pierini. The Catholic women organized a children's cultural event to raise funds for the Clase Superior, a school that centered on the teaching of morality. The event, however, included the representation by children of operettas of doubtful morality, a contradiction Zamudio was

quick to point out in her article "Reflexiones" (Reflections), published on 23 September 1913 in *El Heraldo* ten days after the performance. Pierini, in turn, published several articles attacking the poet in a rather inept defense of the fund-raiser, to which Zamudio replied with a "Carta abierta" (Open Letter) to Pierini. Both "Reflexiones" and the "Carta abierta" were reprinted in *Poesías* (Poems, 1993), a revised edition of *Peregrinado*. This "polémica" (public controversy) showed Zamudio's sharp intellect and principled defense of an ethical public education without religious interference. She would not cede the high moral ground to conservatives, Catholic or not. It also made clear the enthusiastic support she had among the mostly male intellectuals in Bolivia.

Her epistolary novel, *Íntimas,* on the other hand, did not receive similar endorsement from the same intellectuals. Ocampo Moscoso quotes two of her friends and admirers of her poetry, Demetrio Canelas and Claudio Peñaranda, expressing serious qualms about the novel. Zamudio's response to Peñaranda, included in García Pabón's edition, elucidates the gender connotations of her novel, which concentrates on women's feelings, and the reactions it elicited. She describes *Íntimas* as a "cuentecito para mujeres, inspirado en confidencias de almas femeninas, tímidas y delicadas" (little story for women, inspired in the confidences of feminine souls, shy and delicate). García Pabón argues in "Máscaras, cartas y escritura femenina" that Zamudio's radical defense of literary texts written by women and intended for women was particularly threatening to male critics vested in the association between national novels and a patriarchal state.

Although Zamudio intended to title her second poetry book "Peregrinando," it was published as *Ráfagas* (Wind Gusts, 1913) in Paris. The book comprises twenty-three poems, seven of which had already appeared in *Ensayos poéticos,* and most of the others had been published in newspapers in the previous twenty-five years. According to Guzmán, the author took both a post-Romantic and anti-*Modernista* stance with this book and consolidated her position as Bolivia's most celebrated pre-*Modernista* poet. The range of poems included in the collection defies even this broad evaluation. Several are more avowedly Romantic than those from the earlier *Ensayos poéticos,* playing melancholic and nostalgic notes or using nature to reflect or to express the poet's subjectivity. "A un árbol" (To a Tree), however, describes nature as a means for social commentary. Another poem from the collection, "Tristeza" (Sadness), subtitled "Canción" (Song), was set to music and became quite popular.

Ráfagas also includes two long narrative poems. "¡Solo en el mundo!" (Alone in the World!) describes the grief of a maiden whose secret love dies in a battle of the Pacific War. In "Loca de hierro" (Iron Madwoman) the misdeeds of a friend drive a female character to "enloquecí" (madness) and silence; yet, she is able to care for the people who need her. "Poeta" (Poet) expands on the antagonism between the poet and the environment discussed in "Peregrinando." A stranger to worldly endeavors, the poet's role is clearly defined: "De las grandezas de la edad presente / Muestra la falsedad y la miseria" (Show the falseness and misery / Of the great things of the present age). "Fin de siglo" (End of the Century) articulates a similarly modern sensibility by providing a strong critique of humanity's progress: while "el mundo se desquicia" (the world unhinges), science can only offer "El horrible consuelo de la nada" (the horrible consolation of nothingness).

In some poems Zamudio confronts gender inequalities and the subordination of women directly. In "Progreso" (Progress), new times and male discourses about the "educación moral de las mujeres" (moral education of women) have eclipsed romantic love and turned marriage into a necessary but unfulfilling social arrangement for women. "Nacer hombre" (Born a Man), a satire with close parallels to the seventeenth-century Mexican nun Sor Juana Inés de la Cruz's "Hombres necios" (Foolish Men, circa 1690), is probably Zamudio's most critically praised poem, particularly in more-recent years. In the poem she criticizes society's unfair naturalization of male superiority and women's lack of a basic political right: "Una mujer superior / en elecciones no vota, / y vota el pillo peor; / (Permitidme que me asombre) / con sólo saber firmar / puede votar un idiota / porque es hombre" (A superior women / does not vote in elections, / but the worst male crook votes; / [Excuse my amazement] / an idiot can vote / by only knowing how to sign / because he is a man).

In 1915 La Paz's prestigious Circle of Fine Arts, the renamed cultural organization that had made Zamudio an honorary member, designated her as the Mantenedora de los Juegos Florales (Keeper of the Poetic Games). Zamudio's reception in La Paz was worthy of such a "distinguished writer"–according to a daily newspaper Guzmán quotes, "una verdadera apoteosis al talento con que brilla en la literatura nacional" (a true apotheosis to the talent with which she shines in the field of national literature).

Her speech for the occasion is reproduced in *Poesías* as "Discurso de Adela Zamudio, mantenedora de los Juegos Florales." It is an eloquent praise of poetry, one that serves to justify her own varied writings. Starting from a conventional Romantic attitude, she claims a poet is an "obrero del pensamiento" (thought worker) and poetry "la manifestación más elevada y más

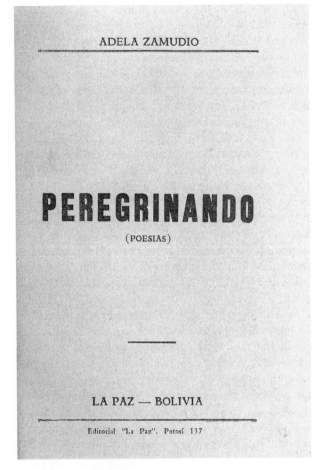

ADELA ZAMUDIO

PEREGRINANDO

(POESIAS)

LA PAZ — BOLIVIA

Editorial "La Paz", Potosí 137

Paperback cover for the 1943 posthumously published collection of poetry from throughout Zamudio's career (Anderson Library, University of Minnesota)

sintética de la cultura de un pueblo" (the highest and most synthetic manifestation of a nation's culture). The poet, in sum, is the "genio" (genius) or "la brillante floración de un pueblo" (the brilliant flower of a people). Approaching many *Modernista* manifestos, she then argues that poetry has a "enemigo formidable" (formidable enemy) in "positivismo" (positivism), dominant in science and "vida práctica" (practical life) but also encroaching in the literary arena. Thus, she calls for poetry, the "lírica expresión del entusiasmo ante la belleza" (lyric expression of the enthusiasm before beauty), to preserve the "divino ideal" (divine ideal). Finally, in the midst of World War I, she predicts that the "imaginación creativa" (creative imagination) and poetry, defined using avant-garde phrasing as a "blanca visión indestructible" (white indestructible vision), will survive all changes and catastrophes.

In 1920, during its last year in power, the Liberal government established a women's high school in Cochabamba and named Zamudio as its principal. In

1922 she published an essay titled "La misión de la mujer" (Women's Mission) in the journal *Arte y Trabajo* (Art and Work). García Pabón observes that this essay summarizes Zamudio's feminist thought, the ideas she embodied throughout her life. In 1925 she went into involuntary retirement after twenty-five years of service as a teacher. A year later, in a unique event in the history of the country, the president of the republic, Hernando Siles, gave her an honorary crown in recognition of her long and brilliant literary career and for her role as a "pensadora" (thinker). She died on 2 June 1928. The words she wrote in "Mi epitafio" (My Epitaph) are engraved on her tombstone: "Vuelvo a morar en ignorada estrella / Libre ya del suplicio de la vida, / Allá os espero; hasta seguir mi huella / Lloradme ausente, pero no perdida" (I take flight to inhabit an unknown star / Free finally from the suffering of life, / There I wait for you. Until you follow my path / Cry me absent, but not lost).

The formal, presidential, recognition at the end of the poet's life represents well her reputation and standing in Bolivian letters. "Soledad" published in many genres and excelled in all. Her short stories explore society's costumes and idiosyncrasies, her novel *Íntimas* opens a new, feminine, literary space, and her poems are both the crowning jewel of Bolivian Romanticism and introduce some of the most significant literary innovations of the period. Adela Zamudio's poetry addresses women's and religious issues in unconventional ways; it provides incisive social critiques and questions the ambiguities and artificiality of modern times.

Biography:
Augusto Guzmán, *Adela Zamudio: Biografía de una mujer ilustre* (La Paz: Juventud, 1955).

References:
Dora Cajías de Villa Gomez, *Adela Zamudio: Transgresora de su tiempo* (La Paz: Ministerio de Desarrollo Humano, 1997);

Leonardo García Pabón, "Máscaras, cartas y escritura femenina: Sobre la obra de Adela Zamudio (1854–1928)," *Romance Languages Annual,* 5 (1993): 401–407;

José Macedonio Urquidi, "Adela Zamudio," in *Bolivianas ilustres: Estudios biográficos y críticos. La cultura femenina en nuestra evolución republicana* (La Paz: Escuela Tipográfica Salesiana, 1918), pp. 112–157;

Eduardo Ocampo Moscoso, *Adela Zamudio* (La Paz: Biblioteca Popular Boliviana de Ultima Hora, 1981);

Oscar Rivera-Rodas, *La poesía hispanoamericana del siglo XIX (Del romanticismo al modernismo)* (Madrid: Alhambra, 1988), pp. 198–202.

Books for Further Reading

Acosta, Oscar, ed. *Poesía hondureña de hoy: Antología.* Tegucigalpa: Nuevo Continente, 1971.

Albizúrez Palma, Francisco. *Poesía centroamericana Postmodernista y de Vanguardia.* Guatemala City: Editorial Universitaria, 1994.

Alegría, Claribel, and Darwin J. Flakoll, eds. *On the Front Line: Guerrilla Poems of El Salvador.* New York: Curbstone, 1989.

Álvarez González, Aurora, and Rosario Armendáriz Agorreta. *Panorama de la Literatura Paraguaya.* Asunción: Loyola, 1967.

Antología de la poesía moderna. Mexico City: Universidad Autónoma de México, 1971.

Ara, Guillermo. *Suma de poesía argentina (1538–1968): Crítica y antología.* Buenos Aires: Kapelusz, 1970.

Aray, Edmundo. *Poesía de Cuba: Antología viva.* Caracas: Universidad de Carabobo, Ediciones de la Dirección de Cultura, 1976.

Arce de Vázquez, Margot, and others. *Lecturas Puertorriqueñas: Poesía.* Sharon, Conn.: Troutman, 1968.

Arellano, Jorge Eduardo, ed. *Antología general de la poesía nicaragüense.* Managua: Distribuidora Cultural, 1984.

Armani, Horacio, ed. *Antología esencial de poesía argentina: 1900–1980.* Buenos Aires: Aguilar, 1981.

Arráiz Lucca, Rafael, ed. *Veinte poetas venezolanos del siglo XX: Antología.* Caracas: Fondo Editorial 60 Años, 1998.

Arteche, Miguel, ed. *Antología personal de la poesía chilena contemporánea.* Santiago: Zig-Zag, 1985.

Arza, María, and Ximena Adriasola. *La mujer en la poesía chilena: 1784–1961.* Santiago: Nascimento, 1963.

Ballagas, Emilio. *Mapa de la poesía negrista americana.* Buenos Aires: Pleamar, 1946.

Ballagas, ed. *Lira negra: Selecciones afroamericanas y españolas.* Madrid: Aguilar, 1962.

Barjalía, Juan Jacobo. *La poesía de Vanguardia de Huidobro a Vallejo.* Buenos Aires, 1965.

Barriga López, Leonardo, ed. *Crítica y antología de la poesía colombiana.* Bogotá: Secretaría Ejecutiva Permanente del Convenio "Andrés Bello," 1981.

Beckett, Samuel, trans. *The Bread of Days: Eleven Mexican Poets.* Covelo, Cal.: Yolla Bolly, 1994.

Bedregal, Yolanda, ed. *Antología de la poesía boliviana.* La Paz & Cochabamba: Los Amigos del Libro, 1977.

Bellini, Giuseppe. *Historia de la literatura hispanoamericana.* Madrid: Castalia, 1985.

Bellini. *La poesía modernista*. Milan: La Goliardica, 1961.

Benavides, Rafael Courtoesie, and Sylvia Lago, eds. *Antología plural de la poesía uruguaya del siglo XX*. Montevideo: Planeta, 1996.

Benedetti, Mario. *Los poetas comunicantes*. Montevideo: Marcha, 1972.

Blanco, José Joaquín, ed. *Crónica de la poesía mexicana*. Culiacán, Mexico: Universidad Autónoma de Sinaloa, 1979.

Britos Serrat, Alberto, ed. *Antología de poetas negros uruguayos*. Montevideo: Mundo Afro, 1990.

Brotherston, Gordon. *Latin American Poetry: Origins and Presence*. Cambridge: Cambridge University Press, 1975.

Câlinescu, Matei. *Faces of Modernity: Avant-garde, Decadence, Kitsch*. Bloomington: University of Indiana Press, 1977.

Cardenal, Ernesto, ed. *Poesía cubana de la Revolución*. Mexico City: Extemporáneos, 1976.

Cardenal, ed. *Poesía nueva de Nicaragua*. Buenos Aires: Carlos Lohlé, 1974.

Carrera Andrade, Jorge. *Reflections on Spanish-American Poetry*. Albany: State University of New York, 1973.

Castillo, Homero, ed. *Estudios críticos sobre el Modernismo*. Madrid: Gredos, 1968.

Castro Leal, Antonio, ed. *La poesía mexicana moderna*. Mexico City: Academia Mexicana de la Lengua, 1953.

Cea, José Roberto, ed. *Antología general de la poesía en El Salvador*. San Salvador: Editorial Universitaria de El Salvador, 1971.

Ceide Echeverría, Gloria. *El haikai en la lírica mexicana*. Mexico City: Andrea, 1967.

Cevallos Mesones, León. *Los Nuevos: Cisneros, Henderson, Hinostroza, Lauer, Martos, Ortega*. Lima: Editorial Universitaria, 1967.

Charry Lara, Fernando. *Poesía y poetas colombianos*. Bogotá: Procultura, 1985.

Charry Lara and Rogelio Echavarría, comps. *Antología de la poesía colombiana*. 2 volumes. Bogotá: Presidencia de la República, 1996.

Chávez, Fermín. *Poesía rioplatense en estilo gaucho*. Buenos Aires: Culturales Argentinas, 1962.

Chirinos Arrieta, Eduardo. *El techo de la Ballena: Aproximaciones a la poesía peruana e Hispanoamericana contemporánea*. Lima: Pontificia Universidad Católica del Perú, 1991.

Cobo Borda, J. G. *Historia portátil de la poesía colombiana (1880–1995)*. Bogotá: Tercer Mundo, 1995.

Cobo Borda. *Poesía colombiana (1880–1980)*. Medellín: Universidad de Antioquia, 1987.

Coester, Alfred, ed. *An Anthology of the Modernist Movement in Spanish America*. New York: Gordian, 1970.

Collazos, Óscar. *Recopilación de textos sobre los vanguardistas hispanoamericanos*. Havana: Casa de las Américas, 1970.

Corvalán, Octavio. *Modernismo y Vanguardia*. New York: Las Américas, 1967.

Corvalán. *El Postmodernismo*. New York: Las Américas, 1961.

Crogliano, María Eugenia, ed. *Antología de la poesía argentina: Siglos XIX y XX*. Buenos Aires: Kapelusz, 1975.

Cuesta, Jorge, ed. *Antología de la poesía mexicana moderna*. Mexico City: Fondo de Cultura Económica, 1998.

Dauster, Frank N. *Ensayos sobre poesía mexicana: Asedio a los contemporáneos*. Mexico City: Andrea, 1963.

Debicki, Andrew O. *Poetas hispanoamericanos contemporáneos: Punta de vista, perspectiva, experiencia*. Madrid: Gredos, 1976.

Díez Echarri, Emiliano, and José María Roca Franquesa. *Historia de la literatura española e hispanoamericana*. Madrid: Aguilar, 1968.

Duverrán, Carlos Rafael, ed. *Poesía contemporánea de Costa Rica: Antología*. San José: Editorial Costa Rica, 1973.

Echevarría, Eduardo González, and Enrique Pupo-Walker, eds. *The Cambridge History of Latin American Literature*, volume 2: *The Twentieth Century*. Cambridge & New York: Cambridge University Press, 1995.

Escalona-Escalona, José Antonio. *Antología general de la poesía venezolana*. Madrid: Edime, 1966.

Escobar Galindo, David, ed. *Índice antológico de la poesía salvadoreña*. San Salvador: UCA, 1987.

Fernández, Teodosio. *La poesía hispanoamericana: Hasta final del Modernismo*. Madrid: Taurus, 1989.

Fernández. *La poesía hispanoamericana en el siglo XX: Poesía negra, vanguardia, surrealismo, creacionismo*. Madrid: Taurus, 1987.

Ferro, Helen. *Antología comentada de la poesía hispanoamericana: Tendancias, temas, evolución*. New York: Las Américas, 1965.

Ferro. *Del Modernismo al compromiso político: Antología temática de la poesía hispanoamericana*. Buenos Aires: Cuarto Poder, 1975.

Fierro, Enrique. *Antología de la poesía rebelde hispanoamericana*. Montevideo: Banda Oriental, 1976.

Flores, Ángel, ed. *Spanish American Authors: The Twentieth Century*. New York: Wilson, 1992.

Flores and Kate Flores, eds. *Poesía feminista del mundo hispánico: Desde la edad media hasta la actual*. Mexico City: Siglo Veintiuno, 1984.

Forster, Merlin H. *Los Contemporáneos: 1920–1932*. Mexico City: Andrea, 1964.

Forster. *Historia de la poesía hispanoamericana*. Clear Creek, Ind.: American Hispanist, 1981.

Franco Openheimer, Félix, ed. *Poesía hispanoamericana*. Mexico City: Orin, 1958.

Galemire, Julia. *17 poetas uruguayos de hoy*. Canelones, Uruguay: C. Marchesi, 1996.

García Prada, Carlos. *Estudios hispanoamericanos*. Mexico City: El Colegio de México, 1945.

García Saucedo, Jaime, ed. *Poetas jóvenes de Panamá: 1969–1982*. Mexico City: Signos, 1982.

Giménez Pastor, Marta, ed. *Selección poética femenina: 1940–1960*. Buenos Aires: Culturales Argentinas, 1965.

Girgado, Luís Alonso, ed. *Antología de la poesía hispanoamericana del siglo XX*. Madrid: Alhambra Longman, 1995.

González, Mike, and David Treece. *The Gathering of Voices: The Twentieth Century Poetry of Latin America*. New York & London: Verso, 1992.

González Vigil, Ricardo, ed. *Poesía peruana siglo XX*. Lima: COPÉ, 1999.

Guibert, Rita. *Seven Voices: Seven Latin American Writers Talk to Rita Guibert*. New York: Knopf, 1973.

Gullón, Ricardo. *Direcciones del Modernismo*. Madrid: Gredos, 1964.

Gutiérrez, Ernesto, and José Reyes Monterrey. *Poesía nicaragüense post-dariana*. Managua: Universidad Autónoma de Nicaragua, 1967.

Gutiérrez, Franklin, ed. *Antología histórica de la poesía dominicana del siglo XX: Movimientos, grupos, tendencias, manifiestos y enunciados*. New York: Alcance, 1995.

Hahn, Óscar. *Antología virtual*. Santiago: Fondo de Cultura Económica, 1996.

Henríquez Ureña, Max. *Breve historia del Modernismo*. Mexico City: Fondo de Cultura Económica, 1954.

Hoz, Leon de la, ed. *La poesía de las dos orillas: Cuba (1959–1993): Antología*. Madrid: Libertarias/Prodhufi, 1994.

Índice de la poesía contemporánea en Colombia desde Silva hasta nuestros días. Bogotá: Librería Suramérica, 1946.

Jaramillo Levy, Enrique, ed. *Poesía panameña contemporánea: 1929–1979*. Mexico City: Liberta-Sumaria, 1980.

Jiménez, José Olivio. *Antología de la poesía hispanoamericana contemporánea: 1914–1970*. Madrid: Alianza, 1971.

Jiménez, Juan Ramón. *La poesía cubana en 1936*. Havana: Institución Hispanoamericana de Cultura, 1937.

Jiménez, Mayra, ed. *Poesía de las fuerzas armadas: Talleres de poesía*. Managua: Ministerio de Cultura, 1985.

Jrade, Cathy Login. *Modernismo, Modernity, and the Development of Spanish American Literature*. Austin: University of Texas Press, 1998.

Jrade. *Rubén Darío and the Romantic Search for Unity*. Austin: University of Texas Press, 1983.

Kirkpatrick, Gwen. *The Dissonant Legacy of Modernismo: Lugones, Herreray y Reissig, and the Voices of Modern Spanish American Poetry*. Berkeley: University of California Press, 1989.

Kuhnheim, Jill S. *Gender, Politics, and Poetry in Twentieth-Century Argentina*. Gainesville: University Presses of Florida, 1996.

Lázaro, Felipe, ed. *Poetas cubanos en España: Antología*. Madrid: Betania, 1988.

Legaspi de Arismendi, Alcira. *Muestra de poesía uruguaya*. Montevideo: Monte Sexto, 1987.

León, Luis, ed. *Poetas parnasianos y modernistas: Antología*. Caracas: Dirección de Cultura, 1946.

Lezama Lima, José, ed. *Antología de la poesía cubana*. Havana: Consejo Nacional de Cultura, 1965.

El límite volcado: Antología de la Generación de Poetas de los Ochenta. San Juan: Isla Negra, 2000.

López Lemus, Virgilio, ed. *Poetas de la Isla: Panorama de la poesía cubana contemporánea*. Seville: El Unicornio Núm. 3, 1995.

Luna, Violeta. *La lírica ecuatoriana actual: Guía de análisis literario.* Guayaquil: Casa de la Cultura Ecuatoriana, 1973.

Luna Mejía, Manuel, ed. *Índice general de la poesía hondureña: Antología.* Mexico City: Latinoamericana, 1961.

Madrigal, Luis Iñigo, ed. *Historia de la literatura hispanoamericana,* volume 2: *Del Neoclasicismo al Modernismo.* Madrid: Cátedra, 1997.

Marcos, Juan Manuel. *El ciclo romántico modernista en el Paraguay.* Asunción: Criterio, 1977.

Márquez, Robert, ed. *Latin American Revolutionary Poetry.* New York: Monthly Review Press, 1974.

Martínez O., Arístides. *Panamá: Poesía escogida.* San José, Costa Rica: EDUCA, 1998.

Marting, Diane E., ed. *Spanish American Women Writers: A Bio-bibliographical Guide.* Westport, Conn.: Greenwood Press, 1990.

Marting, ed. *Women Writers of Spanish America: An Annotated Bio-Bibliographical Guide.* Westport, Conn.: Greenwood Press, 1987.

Maub, José Carlos. *Antología de la poesía femenina argentina.* Buenos Aires: Ferrari, 1930.

Medina Vidal, Jorge. *Visión de la poesía uruguaya en el siglo XX.* Montevideo: Diaco, 1969.

Méndez de la Vega, Luz. *Poetisas desmitificadoras guatemaltecas.* Guatemala City: Tipografía Nacional, 1984.

Milán, Eduardo. *Una cierta Mirada: Crónica de poesía.* Mexico City: Universidad Autónoma Metropolitana, 1989.

Miró, Rodrigo. *Índice de la poesía panameña contemporánea.* Santiago: Ercilla, 1941.

Mojica Llanos, Carlos Alberto. *Colombia y sus mayores poetas.* Tunja, Colombia: Deptal, 1968.

Molina, Alfonso. *Antología de la poesía revolucionaria del Perú.* Lima: América Latina, 1966.

Monge, Carlos Francisco, ed. *Costa Rica: Poesía escogida.* San José: EDUCA, 1998.

Monsivais, Carlos. *La poesía mexicana del siglo XX: Antología.* Mexico City: Empresas Editoriales, 1966.

Montes Brunet, Hugo. *La lírica chilena de hoy.* Santiago: Zig-Zag, 1967.

Montes Huidobro, Matías, and Yara González. *Bibliografía crítica de la poesía cubana.* Madrid: Plaza Mayor, 1972.

Morales, Jorge Luis. *Poesía afro-antillana y negrista: Puerto Rico, República Dominicana, Cuba.* Río Piedras: Universidad de Puerto Rico, 1981.

Morales Santos, Francisco, ed. *Nueva poesía guatemalteca.* Caracas: Monte Ávila, 1990.

La mujer y la poesía en Panamá. Panama City: INAC, 1977.

Muschietti, Delfina, ed. *Poesía argentina del siglo XX: Antología.* Buenos Aires: Colihue, 1982.

Nómez, Naín. *Antología crítica de la poesía chilena.* Santiago: LOM, 1996.

Nómez. *Poesía chilena contemporánea: Breve antología crítica.* Santiago: Andrés Bello, 1992.

O'Hara, Edgar. *Poesía joven del Perú.* [Lima]: Punto de Partida, 1982.

Onís, Federico de, ed. *Antología de la poesía española e hispanoamericana 1888–1932.* New York: Las Américas, 1961.

Orjuela, Héctor H. *Bibliografía de la poesía colombiana.* Bogotá: Instituto Caro y Cuervo, 1971.

Ortega, Julio, ed. *Antología de la poesía hispanoamericana actual.* Mexico City: Siglo Veintiuno, 1987.

Oviedo, José Miguel. *Antología de la poesía cubana.* Lima: Paradiso, 1968.

Paggoli, Renato. *The Theory of the Avant-Garde.* Cambridge, Mass.: Harvard University Press, 1968.

Paredes-Candia, Antonio. *Panorama de la poesía boliviana.* La Paz: ISLA, 1981.

Pearanda Barrientos, Ángel. *Nuestra historia en la poesía.* La Paz: Gisbert, 1975.

Pedemonte, Hugo Emilio. *Poetas uruguayos contemporáneos.* Milan: Cisalpino, 1965.

Pereda Valdés, Ildefonso. *Lo negro y lo mulato en la poesía cubana: Exilio 1959–1971.* Madrid: Playor, 1973.

Pérez, Darío Espina. *107 poetas cubanos del exilio.* San José, Costa Rica: LIL, 1988.

Pérez Pazmiño, Ismael, ed. *Poesía ecuatoriana del siglo XX.* Quito: Casa de la Cultura Ecuatoriana, 1976.

Perrone, Alberto M. *La poesía argentina.* Buenos Aires: Centro Editor de America Latina, 1979.

Pesántez Rodas, Rodrigo. *Modernismo y posmodernismo en la poesía ecuatoriana.* Azogues: Casa de la Cultura Ecuatoriana, 1995.

Phillips, Allen W. *Cinco estudios sobre literatura mexicana moderna.* Mexico City: Secretaría de Educación Pública, 1974.

Pla, Josefina. *Antología de poesía paraguaya.* Madrid: Imprenta Nacional del Boletín Oficial del Estado, 1966.

Puebla, Manuel de la, ed. *Poesía joven en Puerto Rico.* Río Piedras, Puerto Rico: Mairena, 1981.

Puebla, ed. *Poesía militante puertorriqueña.* San Juan: Instituto de Cultura Puertorriqueña, 1979.

Rama, Ángel. *Los poetas modernistas en el mercado económico.* Montevideo: Universidad de la República, 1967.

Rama. *Rubén Darío y el modernismo: Circunstancia socio-económica de un arte americano.* Caracas: Ediciones de la Biblioteca de la Universidad Central de Venezuela, 1970.

Ramos García, Luis A., and Edgar O'Hara. *The Newest Peruvian Poetry in Translation.* Austin: Texas Studia Hispanica, 1979.

Rela, Walter. *Poesía uruguaya siglo XX: Antología.* Montevideo: Alfar, 1994.

Resnick, Seymour. *Spanish American Poetry: A Bilingual Selection.* New York: Harvey House, 1964.

Rivera-Rodas, Óscar. *Cinco momentos de la lírica hispanoamericana: Historia literaria de un género.* La Paz: Instituto Boliviano de Cultura, 1978.

Rivera-Rodas. *La poesía hispanoamericana en el siglo XIX: Del Romanticismo al Modernismo.* Madrid: Alhambra, 1988.

Rodríguez, Alfonso García, and Ángel García Aller, eds. *Antología de poetas hispanoamericanos contemporáneos.* Palencia, Spain: Nebrija, 1999.

Rodríguez, María Luisa. *Poesía revolucionaria guatemalteca.* Madrid: Zero, 1969.

Rodríguez-Alcalá, Hugo. *Poetas y prosistas paraguayos y otros ensayos breves.* Asunción: Don Bosco, 1988.

Rodríguez Castelo, Hernán, ed. *Lírica ecuatoriana contemporánea,* volume 1. Quito: Círculo de Lectores, 1979.

Rosa-Nieves, Cesáreo. *Aguinaldo lírico de la poesía puertorriqueña,* revised edition. 3 volumes. Río Piedras, Puerto Rico: Edil, 1971.

Rowe, William. *Poets of Contemporary Latin America: History and the Inner Life.* Oxford & New York: Oxford University Press, 2000.

Rueda, Manuel, ed. *Dos siglos de literatura dominicana: Siglos XIX–XX,* volume 2: *Poesía.* Santo Domingo: Colección Sesquicentenario de la Independencia Nacional, 1996.

Ruiz Martínez, Luís Honorio. *La renovación poética en el Ecuador.* Ibarra, Ecuador: Imprenta Municipal, 1969.

Russotto, Márgara. *Bárbaras e ilustradas: Las máscaras del género en la periferia moderna.* Caracas: Fondo Editorial Tropykos, 1997.

Salas, Alejandro. *Antología comentada de la poesía venezolana.* Caracas: Alfadil, 1989.

Sánchez Quell, Hipólito. *Triángulo de la poesía rioplatense.* Buenos Aires: Americalee, 1953.

Santana, Francisco. *Evolución de la poesía chilena.* Santiago: Nascimento, 1976.

Saz, Agustín del. *Antología general de la poesía mexicana: Siglos XVI–XX.* Barcelona: Bruguera, 1972.

Saz. *Antología general de la poesía panameña: Siglos XIX y XX.* Barcelona: Bruguera, 1974.

Schulman, Ivan A. *Génesis del Modernismo: Martí, Nájera, Silva, Casal.* Mexico City: El Colegio de México, 1966.

Schulman. *El Modernismo hispanoamericano.* Buenos Aires: CEAL, 1969.

Serrato, José Eduardo. *10 poetas jóvenes de México.* Mexico City: Alpe, 1996.

Silva-Santisteban, Ricardo. *Antología general de la poesía peruana.* Lima: Biblioteca Nacional del Perú, 1994.

Sosa, Roberto. *Honduras: Poesía escogida.* San José: EDUCA, 1998.

Stimson, Frederick S. *The New Schools of Spanish American Poetry.* Valencia, Spain: Estudios de Hispanófila, 1970.

Stone, Alice Blackwell. *Some Spanish American Poets.* New York: Biblio & Tarunen, 1968.

Suárez Miraval, Manuel. *Poesía indigenista.* Lima, 1959.

Tello, Jaime. *Contemporary Venezuelan Poetry: An Anthology.* Caracas: PEN International, 1983.

Torres, Eddy. *Poesía de autores colombianos.* Bogotá: Caja Agraria, 1975.

Tous, Adriana. *La poesía de Nicolás Guillén.* New York: Video Arch, 1996.

Valdés, Héctor, ed. *Poetisas mexicanas: Siglo XX*. Mexico City: Universidad Autónoma de México, 1976.

Valle-Castillo, Julio. *Nicaragua: Poesía escogida*. San José: EDUCA, 1998.

Vallejos, Roque. *Antología crítica de la poesía uruguaya contemporánea*. Asunción: Don Bosco, 1968.

Vatte-Castillo, Julio. *Nicaragua: Poesía escogida*. San José: EDUCA, 1998.

Vescarra Fabre, Guillermo. *Poetas nuevos de Bolivia*. La Paz: Trabajo, 1941.

Villegas, Juan. *Interpretación de textos poéticos chilenos*. Santiago: Nascimento, 1977.

Vitier, Cintio. *Lo cubano en la poesía*. Havana: Relaciones Culturales, 1958.

Wey, Walter. *La poesía paraguaya*. Montevideo: Alfar, 1951.

Yurkiévich, Saúl. *Fundadores de la nueva poesía latinoamericana: Huidobro/Vallejo/Borges/Neruda/Paz*. Barcelona: Seix Barral, 1971.

Contributors

Álvaro A. Ayo . . . . *University of Tennessee, Knoxville*

Daniel Balderston . . . . *University of Iowa*

Aída Beaupied . . . . *Pennsylvania State University*

Ruth Lorraine Budd . . . . *Longwood University*

Barbara Clark . . . . *Averett University*

Joan Clifford . . . . *Duke University*

Heather L. Colburn . . . . *Northwestern University*

Luis Correa-Díaz . . . . *University of Georgia*

Santiago Daydí-Tolson . . . . *University of Texas at San Antonio*

Maria Elva Echenique . . . . *University of Portland*

Keith Ellis . . . . *University of Toronto*

Barbara P. Fulks . . . . *Davis and Elkins College*

Ana Garcia Chíchester . . . . *Mary Washington College*

Leonardo García Pabón . . . . *University of Oregon*

Cedomil Goic . . . . *Pontificia Universidad Católica de Chile*

Constanza Gómez-Joines . . . . *Durham Technical Community College*

Juan Carlos González Espitia . . . . *University of North Carolina at Chapel Hill*

Jana F. Gutiérrez . . . . *Auburn University*

Luis A. Jiménez . . . . *Florida Southern College*

Gwen Kirkpatrick . . . . *University of California, Berkeley*

Rafael Lara-Martínez . . . . *New Mexico Tech*

Linda S. Maier . . . . *University of Alabama in Huntsville*

Delmarie Martínez . . . . *Barry University*

Z. Nelly Martínez . . . . *McGill University*

Alejandro Mejías-López . . . . *Indiana University*

Elizabeth Monasterios P. . . . . *University of Pittsburgh*

Oscar Montero . . . . *Lehman College and The Graduate School and University Center, The City University of New York*

Lisa Nalbone . . . . *University of Central Florida*

Violeta Padrón . . . . *Wake Forest University*

Mari Pino del Rosario . . . . *Greensboro College*

Eliana Rivero . . . . *University of Arizona*

Ana Patricia Rodríguez . . . . *University of Maryland, College Park*

Josefa Salmón . . . . *Loyola University*

Michele Morland Shaul . . . . *Queens College*

Lee Skinner . . . . *University of Kansas*

Emily E. Stern . . . . *University of North Carolina at Chapel Hill*

María Tenorio . . . . *Ohio State University*

Elizabeth Ely Tolman . . . . *University of North Carolina at Chapel Hill*

Fernando Unzueta . . . . *Ohio State University*

Enid Valle . . . . *Kalamazoo College*

Sarah Mead Wyman . . . . *University of North Carolina at Chapel Hill*

Cumulative Index

Dictionary of Literary Biography, Volumes 1-283
Dictionary of Literary Biography Yearbook, 1980-2002
Dictionary of Literary Biography Documentary Series, Volumes 1-19
Concise Dictionary of American Literary Biography, Volumes 1-7
Concise Dictionary of British Literary Biography, Volumes 1-8
Concise Dictionary of World Literary Biography, Volumes 1-4

Cumulative Index

DLB before number: *Dictionary of Literary Biography,* Volumes 1-283
Y before number: *Dictionary of Literary Biography Yearbook,* 1980-2002
DS before number: *Dictionary of Literary Biography Documentary Series,* Volumes 1-19
CDALB before number: *Concise Dictionary of American Literary Biography,* Volumes 1-7
CDBLB before number: *Concise Dictionary of British Literary Biography,* Volumes 1-8
CDWLB before number: *Concise Dictionary of World Literary Biography,* Volumes 1-4

B

F

Cumulative Index

N

Q

R

T

ISBN 0-7876-6820-6

90000